MW01127158

Microsoft®
Windows NT®
Server
Networking Guide

Microsoft Press

PUBLISHED BY
Microsoft Press
A Division of Microsoft Corporation
One Microsoft Way
Redmond, Washington 98052-6399

Library of Congress Cataloging-in-Publication Data
Microsoft Windows NT Server resource kit :   for Windows NT Server
    version 4.0 / Microsoft Corporation.
        p.   cm.
    Includes index.
    ISBN 1-57231-344-7
    1. Microsoft Windows NT.   2. Client/server computing.
 I. Microsoft Corporation.
 QA76.76.W56M5317   1996
 005.7'1369--dc20   96-33396
                                                           CIP

Printed and bound in the United States of America.

8 9   WCWC   2 1 0 9 8

Distributed to the book trade in Canada by Macmillan of Canada, a division of Canada Publishing Corporation.

A CIP catalogue record for this book is available from the British Library.

Microsoft Press books are available through booksellers and distributors worldwide. For further information about international editions, contact your local Microsoft Corporation office. Or contact Microsoft Press International directly at fax (206) 936-7329.

Part Number: 097-0001650 (Networking Guide)

Acquisitions Editor: Casey Doyle
Project Editor: Stuart J. Stuple

This book is dedicated to creating self-sufficient network administrators!

Contributors to this book include the following:

Technical Editors

Patricia Solon, Sharon Tighe

Copy Editor

J. Elise Ellinghausen

Proofreader

Kimberly O'Neal

Managing Editor

Sonia Marie Moore

Technical Writers

Janet Anderson, Marc Genty, Jeff Howard, Jan Jolan James, Chris Kagen, Richard Lerz, Peter Lovejoy, Laura Sheppard, Maureen Sullivan

Writing Manager

Peggy Etchevers

Production Lead

Nikole Faith

Production Team

Cathy Pfarr, Keri Segna, Jeff Weaver, Todd White

Indexers

Jane Dow, Ronnie Maier, Barbara Sherman

Production Manager

Karye Cattrell

Lead Graphic Designer

Chris Blanton

Design Support Team

Johnni Cutler, Amy Iffland, Casey McGahan, Wendy Salvatori, Gabriel Varela, Sue Wyble, Jan Yeager

Software Program Managers

Louis Kahn, Ryan Marshall

Software Developer

Martin Holladay

Software Tester

Cliff Hudson

Technical Marketing Liaison

Ty Carlson

Technical Consultants

Pradeep Bahl, John Ballard, Denise Y. Deng, Michele Freed, James Gilroy, Cory Hendrix, John Jacobs, Ian Jose, Bin Li, David S. Loudon, Dave Macdonald, Mike Massa, Dan Perry, Rodger Seabourne, Munil Shah, and numerous other hardworking Windows NT Developers, Program Managers, and Product Support Specialists

Product Support Liaisons

Roger Bruist, Todd Hafer

And special thanks to the following people and companies for contributing to the success of the Windows NT Server Resource Kit interoperability lab:

John Allen, Hal Antonson, Howard Bishansky, Bruce Burns, Gregory DeJarnette, Sudheer Dhulipalla, Paul Donnely, Ken Evans, Alex Foskett, Paul Goode, Elise Hammond, Bob Hyman, Doreen Kindred, Richard Lerz, Georgia Marra, Giuseppe Mascarella, Mark Roy, Serge Sozonoff, Prashanth Viswanath, Sam White, Vaughn Winslow, American Power Conversion Corporation (APC); Bay Networks, Inc.; Crystal Computer Services, Inc.; Digital Equipment Corporation; Eicon Technology; Hummingbird Communications, LTD; Intergraph Corporation; Lantronix Corporation; Octopus Technologies, Inc.; Walker Richer & Quinn, Inc.; Wall Data, Inc.

Contents

Figures and Tables

Tables

Introduction

Welcome to the *Microsoft® Windows NT® Server Resource Kit: Windows NT Server Networking Guide*.

The *Microsoft Windows NT Server Resource Kit* for version 4.0 consists of three new volumes and a single compact disc (CD) containing programs for both Windows NT Workstation and Windows NT Server. An online version of the new, comprehensive *Windows NT Workstation Resource Guide* is also available on the CD. Update books for the *Windows NT Server Resource Kit* will be released on a semi-annual basis. They will contain new information and major revisions of existing topics.

The *Windows NT Server Networking Guide* presents detailed information that is specific mainly to using Windows NT Server on or with a network, plus topics that are either new for version 4.0 or reflect issues that our Product Support people consider timely and important. This information is intended to be an in-depth, technical supplement to the printed and online documentation included as part of the Windows NT Server version 4.0 product. It does not replace that information as the source for learning how to use the product features and programs.

This introduction includes the following types of information you can use to get started.

- The first section outlines the contents of this book, so that you can quickly find pertinent technical details.

- The second section introduces the *Windows NT Server Resource Kit* CD.

- The third section describes the support policy for the *Windows NT Server Resource Kit*.

About the Windows NT Server Networking Guide

This book includes the following chapters.

Part I, About Windows NT Server Networking

Chapter 1, "Windows NT Networking Architecture," describes the layered networking architecture built into Windows NT, and how it fits into the Open Systems Interconnect (OSI) model. It also describes the Windows NT transfer protocols, distributed processing, the distributed component object model (DCOM), network resource access, workstation and server services, services for Macintosh, and the Remote Access Service (RAS).

Chapter 2, "Network Security and Domain Planning," describes the security model built into Windows NT. It also introduces the security architecture and how the features work over the network domain structure to provide a secure network. The chapter concludes with extensive and detailed advice for planning a domain structure (including a description of the Microsoft corporate domain model), and a section on troubleshooting security problems.

Chapter 3, "Windows NT Browser Service," describes the browser service built into Windows NT. It presents the different types of browser computers, and tells how Windows NT ensures that the browse list (the visual display of all available network devices) is always accessible. The chapter also describes how to select computers to be browsers and how browsing across a wide area network (WAN) is handled.

Part II, Network Interoperability

Chapter 4, "Terra Flora: A Fictitious Case Study," introduces Terra Flora corporation, a fictitious international floral company, and gives background information about the corporation. This corporation will be used to illustrate the ability of heterogeneous networks to operate together using Windows NT Server. The networking model that Terra Flora Corporation will implement, as shown in the network diagram on the inside back cover of this book, contains four levels of server services and provides a brief introduction to the levels and services offered at each level.

Chapter 5, "Network Services: Enterprise Level," presents various decisions Terra Flora had to make about its network and explains the procedures for implementing and configuring those choices. These issues include their network protocol standard, addressing, logons, centralized services, backups, and connecting to the Internet and remote access.

Part III, TCP/IP

Chapter 6, "TCP/IP Implementation Details," provides additional detail about the architecture of Transmission Control Protocol/Internet Protocol (TCP/IP), including information about TCP/IP advanced configuration options and descriptions of the client/server services that make it easier to administer TCP/IP networks.

Chapter 7, "Managing Microsoft DHCP Servers," describes the client/server architecture of the Dynamic Host Configuration Protocol (DHCP) and planning for DHCP server installation, managing the DHCP database, and troubleshooting DHCP service problems.

Chapter 8, "Managing Microsoft WINS Servers," describes the architecture of the Windows Internet Name Service (WINS)—an RFC-compliant NetBIOS name server for TCP/IP networks, and discusses planning for WINS server implementation.

Chapter 9, "Managing Microsoft DNS Servers," describes the Domain Name System and Microsoft DNS Server, and includes information on the implementation of domain, zone, and Microsoft DNS server and client concepts; planning issues for DNS, WINS, and Internet security; and using DNS Manager to configure and manage Microsoft DNS Server.

Chapter 10, "Using LMHOSTS Files," provides information about the LMHOSTS file that contains static mappings of "friendly" NetBIOS computer names to IP addresses to enable computers to locate resources on the Internet or on routed TCP/IP intranets.

Chapter 11, "Using SNMP for Network Management," describes the Simple Network Management Protocol (SNMP) of the TCP/IP protocol suite and its implementation under Windows NT.

Chapter 12, "Troubleshooting Tools and Strategies," presents information about the TCP/IP programs that are used specifically for connectivity troubleshooting on TCP/IP-based intranets.

Part IV, Using Windows NT Server Networking

Chapter 13, "Using NetBEUI with Windows NT," describes the implementation of the NetBEUI transport under Windows NT for administrators and support personnel who support legacy networks (LANS) using the NetBEUI protocol.

Chapter 14, "Using DLC with Windows NT," provides information about the Data Link Control (DLC) protocol under Windows NT, which provides connectivity to IBM mainframes and to LAN printers attached directly to the network.

Chapter 15, "Remoteboot," explains how a computer running Windows NT Server can start client computers (MS-DOS®, Microsoft Windows® 3.1, and Microsoft Windows 95) over the network.

Chapter 16, "Microsoft Network Client Version 3.0 for MS-DOS," describes how to install, use, and troubleshoot Microsoft Network Client version 3.0 for MS-DOS. Network Client is software that you install on a computer running the MS-DOS operating system so that the computer can use resources on a network.

Part V, Appendixes

Appendix A, "TCP/IP Utilities Reference," provides a listing and description of the TCP/IP programs and commands that are supported by Windows NT for intranet and Internet troubleshooting and connectivity.

Appendix B, "Port Reference for Microsoft TCP/IP," describes the well-known and registered port assignments that are supported by Microsoft TCP/IP for Windows NT.

Appendix C, "MIB Object Types for Windows NT," provides listings of the SNMP managed-objects implemented in Windows NT.

Appendix D, "Windows Sockets," is primarily for the developer. This appendix provides information about using Windows Sockets and developing Windows Sockets programs for Windows NT.

Appendix E, "RAS Reference," provides an overview of the most important modem compatibility standards and how they work within the Remote Access Service (RAS). This appendix also presents a series of quick-reference charts to give you a high-level perspective on how RAS works during a call to a Windows NT RAS server, and reference tables for RAS server and client computers that detail the different versions of RAS and the features they support.

Appendix F, "Routers and Switches," provides an overview of routing and switching technologies, descriptions of the routing and switching equipment selected and installed at Terra Flora, and the technical and business reasons for those choices.

Appendix G, "NetBIOS Names," lists the 16th character of a NetBIOS computer name that uniquely identifies the networking client service, such as workstation or browser. The 16th character is recognized and used in WINS and LMHOSTS name resolution services.

Index to this Windows NT Server Networking Guide.

Resource Kit Compact Disc

The *Windows NT Server Resource Kit* CD includes a wide variety of tools and programs to help you work more efficiently with both Windows NT Workstation and Windows NT Server. You can read about some of the enhancements made to the existing tools and programs as well as new ones that have been added for this version 4.0 release in the Introduction to the *Windows NT Server Resource Guide.*

The CD that accompanies the *Windows NT Server Resource Kit* contains programs that apply to information in the *Windows NT Workstation Resource Guide,* the *Windows NT Server Resource Guide,* the *Windows NT Server Networking Guide*, and the *Windows NT Server Internet Guide.* This new CD replaces all previous ones. It includes a collection of information resources, tools, and programs that can make networking and working with the Windows NT platform even easier.

Note The programs on this CD are designed and tested for the U.S. version of Windows NT version 4.0. Use of these programs on any other version of Windows NT can cause unpredictable results.

A large Help file with explanations of and user actions for the majority of the messages included in Windows NT version 4.0, and a large Help file of Performance Counter Definitions are just two of the major items included on the *Windows NT Server Resource Kit* CD. Updates to these files and others will be provided, when available, on the Microsoft Internet web site for the Windows NT Resource Kits. See the Rktools.hlp file for the exact site address, as well as the addresses of other Microsoft information sites.

After installing the *Windows NT Server Resource Kit*, please refer first to the following three files:

- The Readme.wri file, which contains a complete list of all the tools and programs on the *Windows NT Server Resource Kit* CD and additional setup instructions for some of them.

- Either the Rkdocw.hlp file (for Windows NT Workstation) or the Rkdocs.hlp file (for Windows NT Server), which provides a single entry point for all of the major components of the Resource Kit's online documentation.

- The Rktools.hlp file, which provides an overview of the Resource Kit tools and programs and basic instructions on how to use many of them, along with links to additional documentation and, in some cases, to the actual program files.

The most current corrections to those tools and programs and their documentation, as well as the POSIX and Perl source code files, are available on the Internet at the following Microsoft FTP site:

ftp://ftp.microsoft.com/bussys/winnt/winnt-public/reskit/nt40/

Resource Kit Support Policy

The SOFTWARE supplied in the *Windows NT Server Resource Kit* is not officially supported. Microsoft does not guarantee the performance of the *Windows NT Server Resource Kit* tools, response times for answering questions, or bug fixes to the tools. However, we do provide a way for customers who purchase the *Windows NT Server Resource Kit* to report bugs and receive possible fixes for their issues. You can do this either by sending Internet mail to RKINPUT@MICROSOFT.COM or by referring to one of the options listed in the *Start Here* book, which is included with your Windows NT Server product. This mail address is only for issues related to *Windows NT Server Resource Kit*.

PART I

About Windows NT Server
Networking

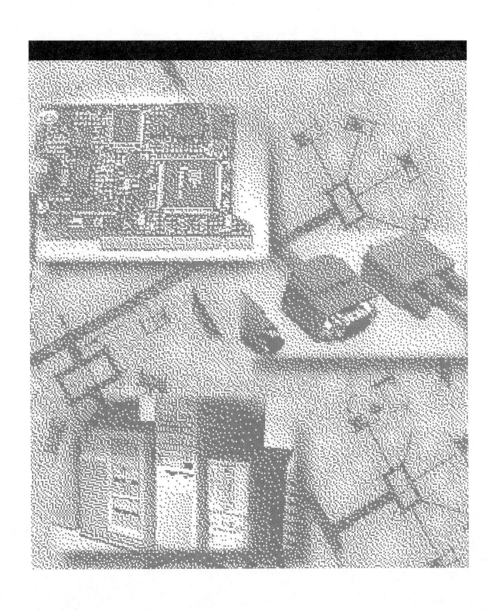

C H A P T E R   1

Windows NT Networking Architecture

The Microsoft Windows NT operating system was designed and built with fully integrated networking capabilities. These networking capabilities differentiate Windows NT from other operating systems, such as MS-DOS, OS/2, and UNIX, in which network capabilities are installed separately from the core operating system.

This chapter introduces the Windows NT networking architecture. It provides you with descriptions of the following topics.

- The design goals and rationale for the Windows NT operating system.

- The basic components of the Windows NT operating system architecture.

- The basics of networking architecture in general. This includes a detailed description of the model on which Windows NT was designed, as well as the industry standards and specifications.

- The Windows NT vertical layers and the interfaces for communication between layers.

- The Windows NT network protocols, which enable layers on two different computers to communicate with each other.

- Distributed processing of applications across the network and the mechanisms Windows NT uses to create connections between servers and workstations.

- The mechanisms for sharing resources across the network, including Multiple Universal Naming Convention Provider (MUP) and Multi-Provider Router (MPR).

- The workstation and server services.

- How binding options work, enabling communications between network layers.

- How Remote Access Service (RAS) works to connect remote or mobile clients to corporate networks.

- How Services for Macintosh are built into Windows NT, allowing Apple Macintosh clients to connect to a Windows NT Server as if it were any other AppleShare server.

Windows NT Operating System Design and Basics

Two primary forces shaped the design of the Windows NT operating system: market requirements and prudent, vigorous design.

Microsoft customers around the world provided the market requirements. Customers wanted the following features.

- Portability across families of processors, such as the Intel x86 line
- Portability across different processor architectures, such as complex instruction set computing (CISC), such as the Intel x86 processors, and reduced instruction set computing (RISC), such as MIPS, DEC, and PowerPC
- Transparent support for single-processor and multiprocessor computers
- Support for distributed computing
- Built-in networking
- Industry standards compliance, such as POSIX
- Certifiable security, such as C2, Functional C2, and E3

Leading-edge thinkers in operating system theory and design developed the design goals, complementing the market requirements. The following features have been built into the Windows NT design.

- *Extensibility*, or modularity of Windows NT. The modular design allows Microsoft to add new modules to all levels of the operating system without compromising its existing stability.
- *Portability*, or the ability of Windows NT to run on both CISC and RISC processors.
- *Scalability*, or the ability to take full advantage of symmetric multiprocessing hardware.
- *Reliability and robustness*, which means that the architecture protects the operating system and its applications from damage. Applications run in their own processes and cannot read or write outside of their own address space. The operating system, in the kernel, is isolated from applications, which interact with the kernel using only well-defined user-mode application programming interfaces (APIs).

- *Performance*, or speed of activity. By running its high-performance subsystems in kernel mode where they interact with the hardware and with each other without thread and process transitions, Windows NT 4.0 improves performance, particularly for graphics-intensive applications, such as Microsoft PowerPoint®, by as much as 20 percent.

- *Compatibility*, which means that Windows NT 4.0 continues to support MS-DOS, OS/2, Windows 3.x, and POSIX applications, as well as the FAT file system and a wide variety of devices and networks.

Windows NT continues to blend together real-world experience in operating systems with some of the best ideas from the computing industry and academia on operating system theory.

Open Systems and Industry Standards

Open Systems are systems designed to incorporate all devices regardless of manufacturer and accept third party add-on hardware or software products. Industry standards fall into two categories: *de jure* and *de facto*.

De jure standards have been created by standards bodies, such as the American National Standards Institute (ANSI), the Institute of Electrical and Electronic Engineers (IEEE), and the International Standards Organization (ISO). For example, the ANSI American Standard Code for Information Interchange (ASCII) character encoding standard, the IEEE Portable Operating System Interface for UNIX (POSIX) standard, and the ISO Open System Interconnection (OSI) reference model for computer networks are all *de jure* standards.

De facto standards have been widely adopted by industry but are not endorsed by any of the standards bodies. An example of a *de facto* standard is the Transmission Control Protocol/Internet Protocol (TCP/IP) network communications protocol. *De facto* standards exist either to fill gaps left by the implementation specifications of the de jure standards or because no standard currently exists for the particular area.

Open systems based solely on *de jure* industry standards do not yet exist and probably never will because of the very different natures of the computer industry and the academic-standards process. The speed with which the technology changes is staggering, and the formal standards process can't keep pace with it. Various composites of system standards exist because the market demands that solutions be implemented immediately. In today's open systems, both *de facto* and *de jure* standards are combined to create interoperable systems. It is the strategic combination of both types of standards that enables open systems to keep pace with rapidly changing technology.

One key element of this middle-of-the-road approach is the use of strategically placed layers of software, to allow the adjoining upper and lower layers of software within the operating system to provide different functions that work together. These software layers provide a standardized set APIs to the software layers above and below themselves. A good example is the Network Device Interface Specification (NDIS), which was jointly developed by Microsoft and 3Com in 1989. Another example is the Desktop Management Interface (DMI) created by the Desktop Management Task Force (DMTF), an industry organization with more than 300 vendor members, including Microsoft, Intel, IBM, and Novell.

The benefit of this architecture is that it allows software modules above and below the layer to be substituted for software modules developed using the same standards. This means you can start out with a module that implements a *de facto* standard and later supplement or replace it with one that implements a *de jure* standard. In effect, you end up with the best of both worlds—open systems and industry standards.

Client/Server Computing

The Windows NT operating system is designed for client/server computing. Client/server computing generally means connecting a single-user, general-purpose workstation (client) to multiuser, general-purpose servers, with the processing load shared between both. The client requests services, and the server responds by providing the services.

The Windows NT operating system also extends the client/server model to individual computers. For example, the user runs applications, which are clients that request services from the protected subsystems, which are servers. The idea is to divide the operating system into several discrete processes, each of which implements a set of cohesive services, such as process-creation or memory-allocation. These processes communicate with their clients, with each other, and with the kernel component of the server by passing well-defined messages back and forth.

The client/server approach results in a modular operating system. The servers are small and self-contained. Because each runs in its own protected, user-mode process, a server can fail without taking down the rest of the operating system. The self-contained nature of the operating-system components also makes it possible to distribute them across multiple processors on a single computer (symmetric multiprocessing) or even across multiple computers on a network (distributed computing).

Object-Based Computing

Software *objects* are a combination of computer instructions and data that models the behavior of things, real or imagined, in the world. Objects are composed of the following elements.

- Attributes, in the form of program variables, which collectively define the object's state
- Behavior, in the form of code modules or methods that can modify those attributes
- An identity that distinguishes one object from all others

Objects interact with each other by passing messages back and forth. The sending object is known as the *client* and the receiving object is known as the *server*. The client requests, and the server responds. In the course of conversation, the client and server roles often alternate between objects. Windows NT is not an object-oriented system in the strictest sense, but it does use objects to represent internal system resources.

Windows NT uses an object metaphor that is pervasive throughout the architecture of the system. When viewed using Windows NT, all of the following appear as ordinary objects.

- Devices, such as printers, tape drives, keyboards, and terminal screens
- Processes and threads
- Shared memory segments
- Access rights

Multitasking and Multiprocessing

Multitasking and multiprocessing are closely related terms that are easily confused. *Multitasking* is an operating-system technique for sharing a single processor among multiple threads of execution. *Multiprocessing* refers to computers with more than one processor. A multiprocessing computer can execute multiple threads simultaneously, one thread for each processor in the computer. A multitasking operating system only appears to execute multiple threads at the same time; a multiprocessing operating system actually does so.

Multiprocessing operating systems can be either asymmetric or symmetric. The main difference is in how the processors operate. In asymmetric multiprocessing (ASMP), the operating system typically sets aside one or more processors for its exclusive use. The remainder of the processors run user applications. In symmetric multiprocessing (SMP), any processor can run any type of thread. The processors communicate with each other through shared memory. The Windows NT operating system is an SMP system.

SMP systems provide better load-balancing and fault tolerance. Because the operating system threads can run on any processor, the chance of hitting a CPU bottleneck is greatly reduced. A processor failure in the SMP model will only reduce the computing capacity of the system. In the ASMP model, if the processor that fails is an operating system processor, the whole computer can go down.

SMP systems are inherently more complex than ASMP systems. A tremendous amount of coordination must take place within the operating system to keep everything synchronized. For this reason, SMP systems are usually designed and written from the ground up.

Kernel and User Mode

In modern operating systems, applications are kept separate from the operating system itself. The operating-system code runs in a privileged processor mode known as the *kernel*, and has access to system data and hardware. Applications run in a nonprivileged processor mode known as *user mode*, and have limited access to system data and hardware through a set of tightly controlled APIs.

One of the design goals of the Windows NT operating system was to keep the base operating system as small and efficient as possible. This was accomplished by allowing only those functions that could not reasonably be performed elsewhere to remain in the base operating system. The functionality that was pushed out of the kernel ended up in a set of nonprivileged servers known as the *protected subsystems*. The protected subsystems provide the traditional, operating-system support to applications through a feature-rich set of APIs.

This design results in a very stable base operating system. Enhancements occur at the protected subsystem level. New protected subsystems can even be added without modification to either the base operating system or the other existing protected subsystems.

Executive

The executive is the kernel-mode portion of the Windows NT operating system and, except for a user interface, is a complete operating system unto itself. The executive is never modified or recompiled by the system administrator.

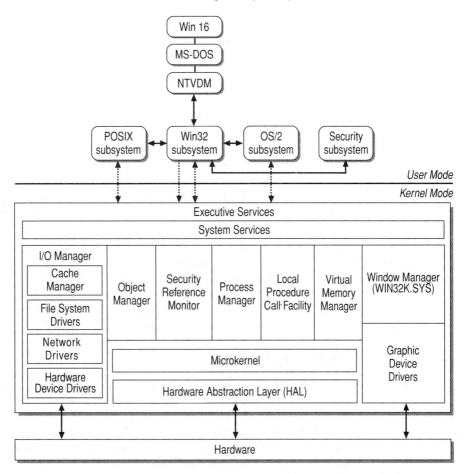

Figure 1.1   Windows NT operating system architecture

The executive is actually a family of software components that provide basic operating-system services to the protected subsystems and to each other. The executive components are listed below.

- I/O Manager
- Object Manager
- Security Reference Monitor
- Process Manager
- Local Procedure Call Facility
- Virtual Memory Manager
- Window Manager
- Graphics Device Interface
- Graphics Device Drivers

The executive components are completely independent of one another and communicate through carefully controlled interfaces. This modular design allows existing executive components to be removed and replaced with ones that implement new technologies or features. As long as the integrity of the existing interface is maintained, the operating system runs as before. The top layer of the executive is called the *System Services,* which are the interfaces between user-mode protected subsystems and kernel mode. For details on the executive and its components, see Chapter 1, "Windows NT Architecture," in the Microsoft Windows NT Workstation 4.0 *Online Resource Guide*.

Protected Subsystems

The protected subsystems are user-mode servers that are started when Windows NT is started. There are two types of protected subsystems: integral and environment. An *integral subsystem* is a server that performs an important operating system function, such as security. An *environment subsystem* is a server that provides support to applications written for or native to different operating system environments, such as OS/2.

Windows NT currently ships with three environment subsystems: the Win32® subsystem, the POSIX subsystem, and the OS/2 subsystem.

The Win32 (or 32-bit Windows) subsystem is the native subsystem of Windows NT. It provides the most capabilities and efficiencies to its applications and is the subsystem of choice for new software development. The POSIX and OS/2 subsystems provide compatibility environments for their respective applications and are not as feature-rich as the Win32 subsystem.

Basic Concepts of Network Architecture

Networking software must perform a wide range of functions to enable communications among computers. Some of these functions are listed below.

- Device and I/O redirection
- Process address registration
- Interprocess connection
- Password encryption and decryption
- Message segmentation and desegmentation
- Frame routing between networks
- Frame delimiting and media-access arbitration
- Pulse encoding of bits

To reduce the design complexity of a network, these functions are organized into groups, which are then allocated to a series of layers. The purpose of each layer is to offer services to the other layers, shielding the layers from the details of how the offered services are actually implemented. The services provided by a particular layer are a product of the network functions allocated to that layer and are usually built upon services offered by other layers. The design of the set of layers and of how they function with each other constitutes a *network architecture*.

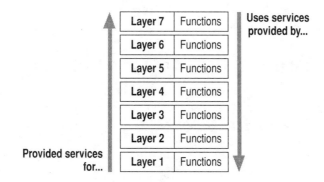

Figure 1.2   Layered design of network services

Communication Between Layers

Communication between layers within a computer is handled differently from communication between two computers. The layers within a computer communicate with each other using vertical interfaces. The layers on different computers communicate with their counterparts using protocols.

Peer Relationships—Protocols

Peer-to-peer communications are performed using protocols. For example, layer 4 on one computer carries on a conversation with layer 4 on another computer. The rules and conventions used in this conversation are collectively known as the layer-4 protocol. The communication between the layers is considered peer-to-peer communication. Functions performed in layer 4 of one computer are communicated to layer 4 of another computer.

Vertical Relationships—Interfaces

Each layer ultimately communicates with its peer on the other computer. However, no data passes directly from layer 4 on one computer to layer 4 on another. Instead, each layer passes data and control information to the layer immediately below it, until the lowest layer is reached and the data is transmitted onto the network media. The receiving computer then passes the data and control information from layer to layer until it reaches its own layer 4.

There is a well-defined interface between each pair of layers. The interface defines which services the lower layer offers to the upper one and how those services will be accessed.

Transmitting and Receiving Data Across a Network

When two computers transmit data over the network, one is a transmitting or sending computer and one is a receiving computer. Data is passed in *frames*, which are messages broken into smaller units with transport headers attached. To understand how frames are transferred through a network, we need to look at both ends of the transfer process: transmitting and receiving.

Transmitting

Data frames are formed whenever the sending computer initiates a request for communication. Frame formation begins at the highest layer and continues down through each successive layer. The protocol at each layer adds control information (in the form of headers and trailers) to the data that was passed down from the layer above. The frame is then passed to the layer below according to the definition of the interface. Eventually, the data passes through all layers of the protocol stack and is transmitted onto the network media.

Receiving

At the receiving end, the frame is passed from the lower layers to the higher layers in accordance with the definition of the interfaces. The protocol at each layer interprets only the information contained in the headers and trailers that were placed there by its peer on the transmitting end. The protocol considers the rest of the frame to be the data unit, which it is responsible for delivering to the layer above it.

The Open Systems Interconnect Model

In the early years of networking, sending and receiving data across a network was confusing because large companies, such as IBM, Honeywell, and Digital Equipment Corporation had individual standards for connecting computers. The transmit and receive processes had to "talk" to the same protocols to communicate. It was unlikely that applications operating on different equipment from different vendors would be able to communicate. Vendors, users, and standards bodies needed to agree upon and implement a standard architecture that would allow computer systems to exchange information even though they were using software and equipment from different vendors.

In 1978, the International Standards Organization (ISO) introduced a model for Open Systems Interconnect (OSI) as a first step toward international standardization of the various protocols required for network communication. This ISO OSI model incorporates the following qualities.

- It is designed to establish data-communications standards that promote multivendor interoperability.

- It consists of seven layers, with a specific set of network functions allocated to each layer and guidelines for implementation of the interfaces between layers.

- It specifies the set of protocols and interfaces to implement at each layer.

OSI Layers

Each layer of the OSI model exists as an independent module. In theory, you can substitute one protocol for another at any given layer without affecting the operation of layers above or below, although you probably wouldn't want to do so.

The principles used to create the seven-layer model are listed below.

- A layer should be created only when a different level of abstraction is required.
- Each layer should perform a well-defined function.
- The function of each layer should be chosen with the goal of defining internationally standardized protocols.
- The layer boundaries should be chosen to minimize the information flow across the interfaces.
- The number of layers should be large enough to enable distinct functions to be separated, but few enough to keep the architecture from becoming unwieldy.

The following diagram shows the numbering of the layers, beginning with the physical layer, which is closest to the network media.

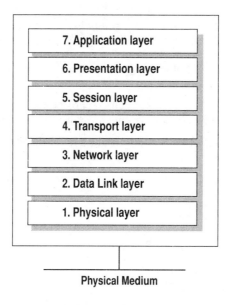

Figure 1.3   Layers of the OSI model

Physical Layer

The physical layer is the lowest layer of the OSI model. This layer controls the way unstructured, raw, bit-stream data is sent and received over a physical medium. This layer describes the electrical or optical, mechanical, and functional interfaces to the physical network medium. The physical layer carries the signals for all of the higher layers.

Data-encoding modifies the simple, digital-signal pattern (1s and 0s) used by the computer to better accommodate the characteristics of the physical medium and to assist in bit and frame synchronization.

Data encoding resolves the following issues.

- Which signal pattern represents a binary 1
- How the receiving station recognizes when a "bit-time" starts
- How the receiving station delimits a frame

Physical medium attachment resolves the following issues.

- Whether an external transceiver will be used to connect to the medium
- How many pins the connectors have and what each pin is used for

The transmission technique determines whether the encoded bits will be transmitted by means of baseband (digital signaling or broadband (analog) signaling.

Physical-medium transmission determines whether it is appropriate to transmit bits as electrical or optical signals, based on the following criteria.

- Which physical-medium options can be used
- How many volts should be used to represent a given signal state in the specific physical medium

Data-link Layer

The data-link layer provides error-free transfer of data frames from one computer to another over the physical layer. The layers above this layer can assume virtually error-free transmission over the network.

The data-link layer provides the following functions.

- Establishing and terminating alogical link (virtual-circuit connection) between two computers identified by their unique network interface card (NIC) addresses
- Controlling frame flow by instructing the transmitting computer not to transmit frame buffers
- Sequentially transmitting and receiving frames

- Providing and expecting frame-acknowledgment, and detecting and recovering from errors that occur in the physical layer by retransmitting non-acknowledged frames and handling duplicate frame receipts

- Managing media access to determine when the computer is permitted to use the physical medium

- Delimiting frames to create and recognize frame boundaries

- Error-checking frames to confirm the integrity of the received frame

- Inspecting the destination address of each received frame and determining if the frame should be directed to the layer above

Network Layer

The network layer controls the operation of the subnet. It determines which physical path the data takes, based on the network conditions, the priority of service, and other factors.

The network layer provides the following functions.

- Transferring the frame to a router if the network address of the destination does not indicate the network to which the station is attached

- Controlling subnet traffic to allow an intermediate system to instruct a sending station not to transmit its frame when the router's buffer fills up. If the router is busy, the network layer can instruct the sending station to use an alternate router

- Allowing the router to fragment a frame when a downstream router's maximum transmission unit (MTU) size is less than the frame size. The frame fragments will be reassembled by the destination station

- Resolving the logical computer address (at the network layer) with the physical network-interface-card (NIC) address (at the data-link layer), if necessary

- Keeping an accounting record of frames forwarded by subnet intermediate system to produce billing information

The network layer at the transmitting computer must build its header in such a way that the network layers residing in the subnet's intermediate systems can recognize the header and use it to route the data to the destination address.

This layer eliminates the need for higher layers to know anything about the data transmission or intermediate switching technologies used to connect systems. The network layer is responsible for establishing, maintaining, and terminating the connection to one or to several intermediate systems in the communication subnet.

In the network layer and the layers below it, the peer protocols are between each computer and its immediate neighbor, which is often not the ultimate destination computer. The source and destination computers may be separated by many intermediate systems.

Transport Layer

The transport layer makes sure that messages are delivered in the order in which they were sent and that there is no loss or duplication. It removes the concern from the higher layer protocols about data transfer between the higher layer and its peers.

The size and complexity of a transport protocol depend on the type of service it can get from the network layer or data link layer. For a reliable network layer or data-link layer with virtual-circuit capability, such as NetBEUI's LLC layer, a minimal transport layer is required. If the network layer or data-link layer is unreliable or supports only datagrams (as TCP/IP's IP layer and NWLink's IPX layer do), the transport layer should include frame sequencing and acknowledgment, and associated error-detection and recovery.

Functions of the transport layer include the following tasks.

- Accepting messages from the layer above and, if necessary, splitting them into frames
- Providing reliable, end-to-end message delivery with acknowledgments
- Instructing the transmitting computer not to transmit when no receive buffers are available
- Multiplexing several process-to-process message streams or sessions onto one logical link and keeping track of which messages belong to which sessions

The transport layer can accept large messages, but there are strict size limits imposed by the layers at the network level and lower. Consequently, the transport layer must break up the messages into smaller units, called *frames,* and attach a header to each frame.

If the lower layers do not maintain sequence, the transport header (TH) must contain sequence information, which enables the transport layer on the receiving end to present data in the correct sequence to the next higher layer.

Unlike the lower subnet layers, whose protocols are between immediately adjacent nodes or computers, the transport layer and the layers above it are true source-to-destination layers. They are not concerned with the details of the underlying communications facility. Software for layers on the source computer at the transport level and above carries on a conversation with similar software on the destination computer, using message headers and control messages.

Session Layer

The session layer establishes a communications session between processes running on different computers, and can support message-mode data transfer.

Functions of the session layer include:

- Allowing application processes to register unique process addresses, such as NetBIOS names. It provides the means by which these process addresses can be resolved to the network-layer or data-link-layer NIC addresses, if necessary.

- Establishing, monitoring, and terminating a virtual-circuit session between two processes identified by their unique process addresses. A virtual-circuit session is a direct link that seems to exist between the sender and receiver: In reality, the connection is established through circuits.

- Delimiting messages, to add header information that indicates where a message starts and ends. The receiving session layer can then refrain from indicating any message data to the overlying application until the entire message has been received.

- Informing the receiving application when buffer space is insufficient for the entire message and that the message is incomplete (called *message synchronization*). The receiving session layer may also use a control frame to inform the sending session layer how many bytes of the message have been successfully received. The sending session layer can then resume sending data at the byte following the last byte acknowledged as received. When the application subsequently provides another buffer, the session layer can place the remainder of the message in that buffer and indicate to the application that the entire message has been received.

- Performing other support functions that allow processes to communicate over the network, such as user authentication and resource-access security.

Presentation Layer

The presentation layer serves as the data translator for the network. This layer on the sending computer translates data from the format sent by the application layer into a common format. At the receiving computer, the presentation layer translates the common format to a format known to the application layer.

The presentation layer provides the following functions.

- Character-code translation, such as from ASCII to EBCDIC
- Data conversion, such as bit order, CR-to-CR/LF, and integer-to-floating point
- Data compression, which reduces the number of bits that need to be transmitted
- Data encryption, which renders data unreadable until it has been unencrypted, for security purposes. An example is password encryption

Application Layer

The application layer serves as the window for users and application processes to access network services. The application layer provides the following functions.

- Resource sharing and device redirection
- Remote file access
- Remote printer access
- Interprocess communication support
- Remote procedure call support
- Network management
- Directory services
- Electronic messaging, including e-mail messaging
- Simulation of virtual terminals

Data Flow in the OSI Model

The OSI model presents a standard data flow architecture, with protocols specified in such a way that layer *n* at the destination computer receives exactly the same object as was sent by layer *n* at the source computer.

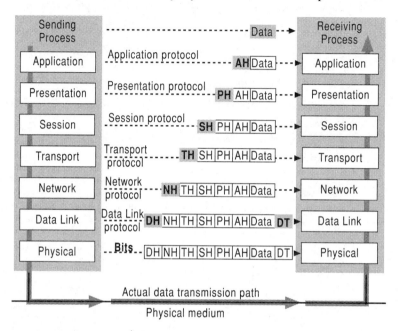

Figure 1.4 OSI model data flow

The sending process passes data to the application layer, which attaches an application header (AH) and then passes the frame to the presentation layer.

The presentation layer can transform data in various ways, if necessary, such as by translating it and adding a header. It then gives the result to the session layer. The presentation layer is not "aware" of which portion (if any) of the data received from the application layer is AH and which portion is actually user data, because that information is irrelevant to the presentation layer's role.

The process is repeated from layer to layer until the frame reaches the data-link layer. There, in addition to a header, a data trailer (DT) is added to aid in frame synchronization. The frame is then passed down to the physical layer, where it is actually transmitted to the receiving computer.

On the receiving computer, the various headers and the DT are stripped off one by one as the frame ascends the layers and finally reaches the receiving process.

Although the actual data transmission is vertical, each layer is programmed as if the transmission were horizontal. For example, when a sending transport layer gets a message from the session layer, it attaches a transport header (TH) and sends it to the receiving transport layer. The fact that the message actually passes to the network layer on its own machine is unimportant.

Vertical Interface Terminology in the OSI Model

In addition to defining the ideal seven-layer architecture and the network functions allocated to each layer, the OSI model also defines a standard set of rules and associated terms that govern the interfaces between layers.

The active protocol elements in each layer are called *entities*, which are typically implemented by means of a software process. For example, the TCP/IP protocol suite contains two entities within its transport layer: Transmission Control Protocol (TCP) and User Datagram Protocol (UDP). Entities in the same layer on different computers are called *peer entities*.

The layer directly below layer-*n* entities implements services that will be used by layer *n*.

For data transfer services, OSI defines the terminology for the discrete data components passed across the interface and between peer entities, as described in the following example.

- The layer-*n* entity passes an *interface data unit* (IDU) to the layer-*n–1* entity.
- The IDU consists of a *protocol data unit* (PDU) and some *interface control information* (ICI).
- The PDU is the data that the layer-*n* entity wishes to pass across the network to its peer entity. It consists of the layer-*n* header and the data that layer *n* received from layer *n+1*.
- The layer-*n* PDU becomes the layer *n–1* service data unit (SDU), because it is the data unit that will be serviced by layer *n*.
- The ICI is made up of control information, such as the length of the SDU, and the addressing information that the layer below needs to do its job.
- When layer *n–1* receives the layer-*n* IDU, it strips off and "considers" the ICI, adds the header information for its peer entity across the network, adds ICI for the layer below, and passes the resulting IDU to the layer *n–2* entity.

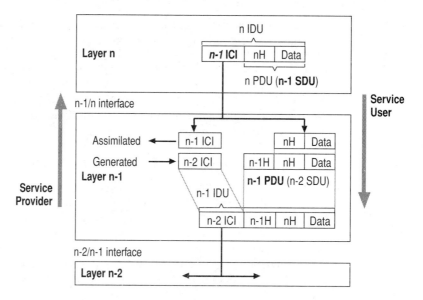

Figure 1.5   Vertical interface entities

Problems can occur in the data-flow path between two network stations. These problems can include errant, restricted, or even halted communication. Vertical and peer-trace utilities can be developed by third-party vendors to trace network communication errors.

Vertical Interface Trace Utilities

Layer entities within a computer can call layer entities above and below them by means of established interface-call mechanisms (such as an interrupt in MS-DOS or, in Windows NT, an API-function call or IRP submission)and then pass a defined IDU structure. These call mechanisms provide the means to write a trace utility, which can do the following items.

- Capture the interface-call-mechanism entry point, saving the original entry point.

- Gain control when the entry point is called.

- Examine the structure being passed, "snapshot" all or part of the IDU structure, and then write the snapshot to a buffer or log file.

- Pass control to the original entry point.

If the data-flow problem is due to a layer entity's passing incorrect or incorrectly formatted ICI information, an examination of the log generated by the interface trace utility should reveal the cause of the problem. Vertical-interface trace utilities that can be used to troubleshoot networking include the NBTRAP (NetBIOS interface trace) utility for MS-DOS and the TDITRACE (Transport Driver Interface interface trace) utility for Windows NT, among others.

Peer-protocol Trace Utilities

A specially configured computer can connect to the physical medium to receive
and examine all frames sent to and from specified network addresses. The user
can set the computer software to display frame-header information at any
functional layer. The user can then view peer-protocol conversations between
selected computers. If the data-flow problem is due to an error in the peer
protocol, the user can detect it by examining the trace. Peer-protocol trace utilities
include Sniffer from Network General and Microsoft Network Monitor, among
others.

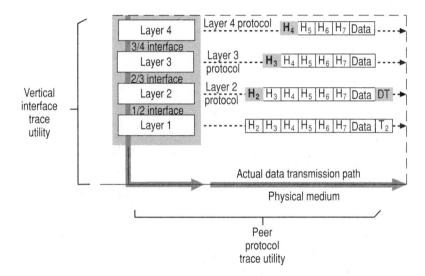

Figure 1.6   Troubleshooting, using a Data Flow Trace

IEEE Standard 802 for Low-level Protocols

Recognizing a need for standards in the local area network (LAN) market, the IEEE undertook Project 802. Named for the year (1980) and month (February) of its inception, Project 802 defines a family of low-level protocol standards at the physical and data-link layers of the OSI model.

Under the terms of IEEE 802, the OSI data-link layer is further divided into two sublayers: Logical Link Control (LLC) and Media Access Control (MAC).

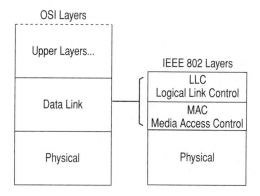

Figure 1.7   Comparison of IEEE layers and the OSI model

Data-link-layer functions allocated to the LLC sublayer include the following.

- Establishing and terminating links
- Controlling frame traffic
- Sequencing frames
- Acknowledging frames

Data-link-layer functions allocated to the MAC sublayer include the following items.

- Managing media access
- Delimiting frames
- Checking frame errors
- Recognizing frame addresses

Project 802 specifications include the following categories.

- 802.1 Overview of project 802, including higher layers and internetworking
- 802.2 Logical Link Control (LLC)
- 802.3 Carrier Sense Multiple Access with Collision Detect (CSMA/CD)
- 802.4 Token Bus
- 802.5 Token Ring
- 802.6 Metropolitan Area Network
- 802.7 Broadband Technology Advisory Group
- 802.8 Optical Fiber Technology Advisory Group
- 802.9 Voice/Data Integration on LANs
- 802.10 Standard for Interoperable LAN Security

The low-level protocol specifications 802.3 CSMA/CD, 802.4 Token Bus, and 802.5 Token Ring differ at the physical layer and MAC sublayer, but are compatible at the LLC sublayer.

The 802 standards have been adopted by the following standards bodies.

- ANSI, as American National Standards
- National Bureau of Standards (NBS), as government standards
- ISO, as international standards (known as ISO 8802)

ANSI FDDI Specification

Closely related to the IEEE 802 standards is a more recently developed low-level protocol standard, Fiber Distributed Data Interchange (FDDI). FDDI was developed by ANSI and is based on the use of fiber-optic cable.

FDDI differs from the IEEE 802 standards at the physical layer and MAC sublayer, but is compatible with the IEEE standards at the LLC sublayer.

Data-transfer Services

Protocol entities within a network architecture provide various types of data-transfer services from a layer to the layers above it. The most prevalent data-transfer services are called *reliable connection* and *unreliable connectionless*.

A *connection service* requires a virtual circuit or connection to be established from the source computer to a single destination computer before any data transfer can take place. A connection acts like a tube: The sender pushes objects in at one end, and the receiver takes them out at the other end, in proper sequence. Because sequencing is provided, a message that is larger than the maximum transmit-frame size can be broken down into multiple frames, sent across the network, and re-sequenced at the receiving computer.

A *connectionless service* requires no initial connection and offers no guarantee that the data units will arrive in sequence. No connection is required, so messages can be sent to one or multiple destination stations. No sequencing is provided, so messages can be sent only in single-frame size.

A *reliable service* never loses data because the receiver acknowledges receipt of all data sent. If the sender doesn't receive acknowledgment, it re-sends.

With an *unreliable service*, no acknowledgments are sent, so there is no guarantee that data sent was ever received.

Microsoft network products require that the underlying network drivers provide both reliable-connection and unreliable-connectionless data-transfer services.

Microsoft network products use unreliable-connectionless data transfer only when there is a need to send data simultaneously to many stations. Often, unreliable-connectionless data transfer is used to locate the name of a computer. Once the computer name is received, reliable-connection data transfer is used to connect to the computer and complete the desired transaction. For example, an unreliable-connectionless data transfer may be sent to all computers in a domain (such as **net send /d:***<domain name>* **"hello"**) to find the name of a server that provides a particular service.

Data-transfer Modes

Different protocol entities offer different modes by which data can be transferred across the network from one process to another. As indicated in Table 1.1, some protocols, such as the NetBEUI NBFP, support more than one data-transfer mode.

Table 1.1   Data-transfer Mode Definitions and Protocols

Data-transfer mode	Mode type	Definition	Protocol
Reliable connection	Message mode	Message delimination and synchronization	NetBEUI NBFP, TCP/IP NetBT, NWLink NBIPX
	Byte-stream mode	Byte granular data sequencing and acknowledgment	TCP/IP TCP
	Packetstream mode	Packet granular data sequencing and acknowledgment	NetBEUI, LLC, MSDLC, NWLink SPX
Unreliable connectionless	Datagram mode		NetBEUI NBFP and LLC;MSDLC, TCP/IP UDP and IP; NWLink IPX

The following sections discuss the attributes of various data-transfer modes.

Reliable Connection Message Mode

When the sending client submits a larger-than-packet-size message to be sent, the sending protocol entity breaks the message into frame-sized segments. These include message-delimiter information in the protocol header, which identifies where the client submitted message starts and ends. This process allows the receiving-protocol driver to receive the entire client message before indicating the data to the receiving client.

If the receiving-client buffer fills up before the receiving-station protocol entity has received the entire message, it will still provide the partial message to the receiving client. It will also indicate that the data provided is a partial message and that the receiving client must supply another buffer to receive the remaining portion of the message.

When the receiving-protocol entity has received the entire message, it returns a message to the sending-protocol entity, acknowledging receipt of the entire message.

Reliable Connection Byte-stream Mode

When the sending client submits a larger-than-packet-size message, the sending-protocol-driver entity breaks the message into segments but does not include message-delimiter information in the protocol header. The receiving-station-protocol entity provides the data to the receiving client when the receiving client provides the buffers to receive it, without any regard to the original message size.

When the receiving-protocol entity provides the data to the receiving client, it returns a byte acknowledgment to the sending-protocol entity, acknowledging receipt of all data up to a specified byte. The sending client can then begin sending the message at the last byte acknowledged.

Reliable Connection Packetstream Mode

In this mode, the sending client can submit only packet-size messages. The receiving protocol provides the packet-by-packet data in sequence to the receiving client.

While the receiving protocol entity provides a frame of data to the receiving client, it returns a message to the sending protocol entity, acknowledging receipt of all packets up to the specified packet number.

Note The Windows Sockets emulator emulates message-mode data transfer over the NWLink SPX packet stream. The Sockets emulator component will break large messages into packets and place message delimiters in the packet stream. The receiving Sockets emulator will not provide the received data to the receiving Sockets client until the entire message has been received.

Unreliable Connectionless Datagram Mode

The sending client can submit only packet-size messages to be sent. If the data unit received is larger than the receiving client's next receive buffer, then as much of the received data unit as will fit is placed in the receiving client's buffer and provided to the client. The portion of the received data unit that could not fit in the client buffer is simply lost; no associated error is returned to the receiving client. If the data unit received is smaller than the client buffer, the protocol entity will place the received data unit in the client buffer and immediately provide the message, without waiting for more data to be received.

No acknowledgment is returned to the sending-protocol entity.

The following diagram illustrates the data transfer process: 'S' (on the right side of the diagram) indicates a SUCCESS return status code on the receive. 'E' indicates an error status on the receive: ERROR_MORE_DATA on message mode data transfer.

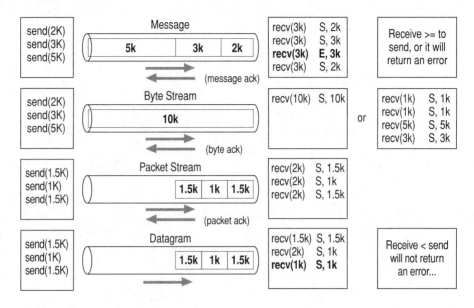

Figure 1.8   Data-transfer modes

The Windows NT Layered Network Architecture

A significant difference between the Windows NT operating system and other operating systems is that the networking capabilities were built into the system from the ground up. With MS-DOS, Windows 3.*x*, and OS/2, networking was added to the operating system.

By providing both client and server capabilities, a computer running Windows NT Server or Windows NT Workstation can be either a client or server in either a distributed-application environment or a peer-to-peer networking environment.

The following illustration shows the specific way Windows NT implements the OSI model.

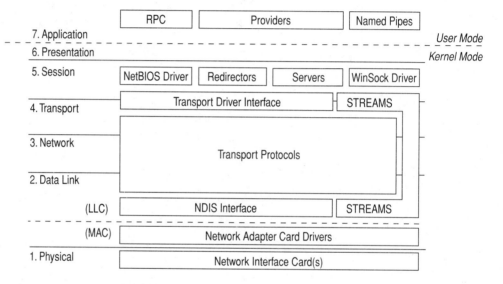

Figure 1.9   Windows NT layered network architecture

To understand the Windows NT operating system capabilities, it is important to understand the network architecture. The networking architecture with its layered organization provides expandability by allowing other functions and services to be added.

The rest of the chapter is devoted to an explanation of the concepts and features of the Windows NT layered networking architecture, including the following topics.

- Boundary layers
- Network protocols
- Streams
- Distributed processing
- Distributed component object model
- Network resource access
- Workstation service
- Server service
- Binding options
- Remote Access Service
- Services for Macintosh

Boundary Layers

A *boundary* is the unified interface between the functional layers in the Windows NT network architecture model. Creating boundaries as breakpoints in the network layers helps open the system to outside development, making it easier for outside vendors to develop network drivers and services. Because the functionality that must be implemented between the layers is well defined, developers need to program only between the boundary layers instead of going from the top to the bottom. Boundary layers also enable software developed above and below a level to be integrated without rewriting.

There are two significant boundary layers in the Windows NT operating system network architecture: the Network Driver Interface Specification (NDIS) 3.0 boundary layer and TDI boundary layer.

The NDIS 3.0 boundary layer provides the interface to the NDIS wrapper and device drivers.

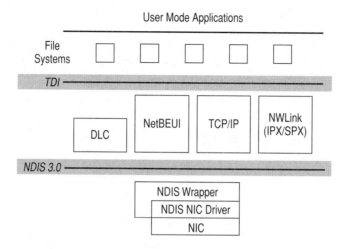

Figure 1.10   Windows NT boundary layers

Transport Driver Interface

TDI is a common interface for a driver (such as the Windows NT redirector and server) to communicate with the various network transports. This allows redirectors and servers to remain independent of transports. Unlike NDIS, there is no driver for TDI; it is simply a standard for passing messages between two layers in the network architecture.

Network Driver Interface Specification 3.0

In 1989, Microsoft and 3Com jointly developed a specification defining an interface for communication between the MAC sublayer and protocol drivers higher in the OSI model. Network Driver Interface Specification (NDIS) is a standard that allows multiple network adapters and multiple protocols to coexist. NDIS permits the high-level protocol components to be independent of the network interface card by providing a standard interface. The network interface card driver is at the bottom of the network architecture. Because the Windows NT network architecture supports NDIS 3.0, it requires that network adapter-card drivers be written to the NDIS 3.0 specification. NDIS 3.0 allows an unlimited number of network adapter cards in a computer and an unlimited number of protocols that can be bound to a single adapter card.

In Windows NT, NDIS has been implemented in a module called Ndis.sys, which is referred to as the NDIS wrapper.

The NDIS wrapper is a small piece of code surrounding all of the NDIS device drivers. The wrapper provides a uniform interface between protocol drivers and NDIS device drivers, and contains supporting routines that making it easier to develop an NDIS driver.

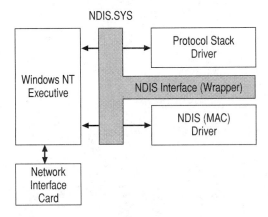

Figure 1.11   NDIS Wrapper

Previous implementations of NDIS required a protocol manager (PROTMAN) to control access to the network adapter. The primary function of PROTMAN was to control the settings on the network adapter and the bindings to specific protocol stacks. The Windows NT operating system networking architecture does not need a PROTMAN module because adapter settings and bindings are stored in the registry and configured using Control Panel.

Because the NDIS wrapper controls the way protocols communicate with the network adapter card, the protocols communicate with the NDIS wrapper rather than with the network adapter card itself. This is an example of the modularity of the layered model. The network adapter card is independent from the protocols; therefore, a change in protocols does not require changing settings for the network adapter card.

Network Protocols

The Windows NT operating system ships with four network protocols:

- Data Link Control (DLC)
- NetBEUI
- TCP/IP
- NWLink (IPX/SPX)

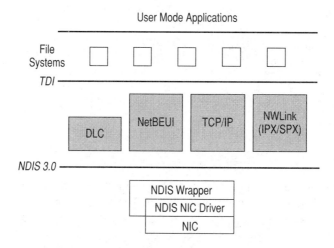

Figure 1.12   Windows NT network protocols

Data Link Control

Unlike the other protocols, the Data Link Control (DLC) protocol is not designed to be a primary protocol for network use between personal computers. DLC provides applications with direct access to the data-link layer but is not used by the Windows NT operating system redirector. Since the redirector cannot use DLC, this protocol is not used for normal-session communication between computers running Windows NT Server or Windows NT Workstation.

The DLC protocol is primarily used for two tasks.

- Accessing IBM mainframes, which usually run 3270 applications.
- Printing to Hewlett-Packard printers connected directly to the network.

Network-attached printers, such as the HP III, use the DLC protocol because the received frames are easy to take apart and because DLC functionality can easily be coded into read-only memory (ROM).

DLC needs to be installed only on those network machines that perform these two tasks, such as a print server sending data to a network HP printer. Client computers sending print jobs to the network printer do not need the DLC protocol; only the print server communicating directly with the printer needs the DLC protocol installed.

The registry location for the DLC parameters is:

HKEY_LOCAL_MACHINE\System\CurrentControlSet\Services\DLC

The registry entry for the DLC driver indicates that it is loaded after the kernel has been started (Start 0x1), and it is dependent on having an NDIS group service available. Its linkage shows that it is bound to the network adapter by the appropriate NDIS device driver.

NetBIOS Extended User Interface

IBM introduced NetBIOS Extended User Interface (NetBEUI) in 1985. NetBEUI was developed for small departmental LANs of 20 to 200 computers. It was assumed that these LANs would be connected by gateways to other LAN segments and mainframes.

NetBEUI version 3.0 is included with Windows NT Server and Windows NT Workstation. It features the following advantages.

- Provides a fast protocol on small LANs
- Breaks the 254-session barrier of previous versions of NetBEUI
- Provides much better performance over slow links than previous versions of NetBEUI
- Is completely self-tuning and has good error protection
- Uses a small amount of memory
- Does not require configuring

NetBEUI has two disadvantages.

- NetBEUI is not routable.
- NetBEUI performance across WANs is poor.

The registry location for the NetBEUI parameters is:

HKEY_LOCAL_MACHINE\System\CurrentControlSet\Services\NBF

The NetBEUI registry entry looks like the DLC entry. Like the DLC driver, NetBEUI is dependent on having an available NDIS group service. Also, under the linkage key, NetBEUI is bound to the network adapter entry by way of the NDIS device driver entry.

Strictly speaking, NetBEUI 3.0 is not truly NetBEUI because it is not inherently extending the NetBIOS interface. Instead, its upper-level interface conforms to the TDI. However, NetBEUI 3.0 still uses the NetBIOS Frame Format (NBF) protocol and is completely compatible and interoperable with previous versions of NetBEUI.

Network applications speaking directly to the NetBEUI 3.0 protocol driver now must use TDI commands instead of NetBIOS commands. This is a departure from earlier implementations of NetBEUI on MS-DOS and OS/2, which provided the programming interface as part of the transport's device driver. There is nothing wrong with this, but in the Windows NT operating system implementation, the programming interface (NetBIOS) has been separated from the protocol (NetBEUI) to increase flexibility in the layered architecture. Two points summarize the difference between these two.

- NetBEUI is a protocol.
- NetBIOS is a programming interface.

Transmission Control Protocol/Internet Protocol

TCP/IP is an industry-standard suite of protocols designed for WANs. It was developed in 1969, resulting from a Defense Advanced Research Projects Agency (DARPA) research project on network interconnection.

DARPA developed TCP/IP to connect its research networks. This combination of networks continued to grow and now includes many government agencies, universities, and corporations. This global WAN is called the *Internet.*

The Windows NT TCP/IP allows users to connect to the Internet and to any machine running TCP/IP and providing TCP/IP services.

Some of the advantages of TCP/IP protocol are that it provides the following functions.

- Providing connectivity across operating systems and hardware platforms
- Providing access to the Internet
- Providing a routable protocol
- Supporting Simple Network Management Protocol (SNMP)
- Supporting Dynamic Host Configuration Protocol (DHCP), which provides dynamic IP-address assignments
- Supporting Windows Internet Name Service (WINS), which provides a dynamic database of IP address-to-NetBIOS name-resolution mappings

The registry location for TCP/IP parameters is:

HKEY_LOCAL_MACHINE\System\CurrentControlSet\Services\Tcpip

NWLink (IPX/SPX)

NWLink is an IPX/SPX-compatible protocol for the Windows NT network architecture. It can be used to establish connections between computers running Windows NT Server or Windows NT Workstation and MS-DOS, OS/2, and Microsoft Windows through a variety of communication mechanisms.

NWLink is simply a protocol. By itself, it does not allow a computer running Windows NT Server or Windows NT Workstation to access files or printers shared on a NetWare server, or to act as a file or print server to a NetWare client. To access files or printers on a NetWare server, a redirector must be used, such as the Client Service for NetWare (CSNW) on Windows NT Workstation or the Gateway Service for NetWare (GSNW) on Windows NT Server.

NWLink is useful if there are NetWare client/server applications running that use Sockets or NetBIOS over the IPX/SPX protocol. The client portion can be run on a Windows NT Server or Windows NT Workstation system to access the server portion on a NetWare server, and vice versa.

NWNBLink contains Microsoft enhancements to Novell NetBIOS. The NWNBLink component is used to format NetBIOS-level requests and pass them to the NWLink component for transmission on the network.

The registry location for NWLink parameters is:

HKEY_LOCAL_MACHINE\System\CurrentControlSet\Services\NWLINK

Streams

Streams are multiple data channels that allow broader bandwidth for data transfer. There are two reasons for writing a protocol to use the Streams device driver.

- Streams makes it easier to port existing protocols to the Windows NT operating system.

- Streams encourages protocols to be organized in a modular, stackable style, thus moving closer to the original vision of the OSI model.

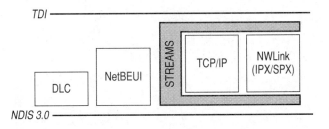

Figure 1.13   Windows NT 3.1 Streams

In Windows NT version 3.1, both TCP/IP and NWLink were surrounded by a Streams device driver. Calls to the TCP/IP or NWLink protocol first passed through the upper layer of the Streams device driver, and then to the NDIS device driver by way of the lower layer of the Streams device driver. The streams device driver exposes the TDI interface at its top and the NDIS interface at the bottom. Streams is a significant departure from the way protocols were developed for MS-DOS and OS/2.

Streams has one great disadvantage: overhead. The protocol requires more instructions to pass a request from the TDI through Streams than if Streams were not used. This is why TCP/IP and NWLink do not use Streams in Windows NT version 3.5 or later.

Distributed Processing

A powerful computer can share its processing power, executing tasks on behalf of other computers. Applications that split processing between networked computers are called *distributed applications*. A client/server application is a distributed application in which processing is divided between a workstation (the client) and a more powerful server. The client portion is sometimes referred to as the front end and the server portion is sometimes referred to as the back end.

The client portion of a client/server application usually consists of just the user interface to the application. It runs on the client workstation and takes a low-to-average amount of processing power. Typically, processing done by the client portion requires a large network bandwidth. For example, the client portion would handle screen graphics, mouse movements, and keystrokes.

The server portion of a client/server application often requires large amounts of data storage, computing power, and specialized hardware. It performs operations that include database lookups, updates, and mainframe data access.

The goal of distributed processing is to move the actual application processing from the client system to a server system with the power to run large applications. During execution, the client portion formats requests and sends them to the server for processing. The server executes the request.

Distributed Component Object Model

In addition to supporting component object model (COM) for interprocess communication on a local computer, Windows NT Server now supports distributed component object model (DCOM). DCOM (or Networked OLE) is a system of software objects designed to be reusable and replaceable. The objects support sets of related functions, such as sorting, random-number generation, and database searches. Each set of functions is called an *interface*, and each DCOM object can have multiple interfaces. When applications access an object, they receive an indirect pointer to the interface functions. From then on, the calling application doesn't need to know where the object is or how it does its job.

DCOM allows you to efficiently distribute processes across multiple computers so that the client and server components of an application can be placed in optimal locations on the network. Processing occurs transparently to the user. Thus, the user can access and share information without needing to know where the application components are located. If the client and server components of an application are located on the same computer, DCOM can be used to transfer information between processes. DCOM is platform independent and supports any 32-bit application that is DCOM-aware.

Note Before you can use an application with DCOM, you must use DCOM Configuration to set the application's properties.

Advantages of Using DCOM

DCOM is the preferred method for developers to use in writing client/server applications for Windows NT.

With DCOM, interfaces can be added or upgraded without deleting the old ones, so applications aren't forced to upgrade each time the object changes. Functions are implemented as dynamic-link libraries, so changes in the functions, including new interfaces or the way the function works, can be made without recompiling the applications that call them.

Windows NT 4.0 supports DCOM by making the implementation of application pointers transparent to the application and the object. Only the operating system needs to know if the function called is handled in the same process or across the network. This frees the application from concerns with local or remote procedure calls. Administrators can choose to run DCOM applications on local or remote computers, and can change the configuration for efficient load balancing.

For example, suppose your company's payroll department uses an application with DCOM to print paychecks. When a payroll employee runs a DCOM-enabled client application on a desktop, the application starts a business-rules server. Then, the server application connects to a database server and retrieves employee records, such as salary information. The business-rules server then transforms the payroll information into the final output and returns it to the client to print.

Your application may support its own set of DCOM features. For more information about configuring your application to use DCOM, see your application's documentation.

DCOM builds upon remote procedure call (RPC) technology by providing a more scalable, easier-to-use mechanism for integrating distributed applications on a network. A distributed application consists of multiple processes that cooperate to accomplish a single task. Unlike other interprocess communication (IPC) mechanisms, DCOM gives you a high degree of control over security features, such as permissions and domain authentication. It can also be used to launch applications on other computers or to integrate web-browser applications that run on the ActiveX™ platform.

Microsoft Visual Basic®, Enterprise Edition customers who are currently using Remote Automation can easily migrate their existing applications to use DCOM. For more information, see your Visual Basic documentation or visit the Visual Basic web site at www.microsoft.com/vbasic.

Setting Security on DCOM Applications

The Windows NT 4.0 security model is easily extended to DCOM objects. Administrators set permissions on DCOM applications and can vary those permissions for local and remote execution.

Once a DCOM-enabled application is installed, you can use DCOM Configuration (in Control Panel) for the following purposes.

- To disable DCOM so that it can't be used for the computer or the application.
- To set the location of the application.
- To set permissions on the server application by specifying which user accounts can or cannot access or start it. You can grant permissions that apply to all applications installed on the computer or to only a particular application.
- To set the user account (or identity) that will be used to run the server application. The client application uses this account to start processes and access resources on other computers in the domain. If the server application is installed as a service, you can run the application using the built-in System account or a Windows NT Server service account that you have created.
- To control the level of security (for example, packet encryption) for connections between applications.

The computers running the client application and the server application must both be configured for DCOM. On the computer running as a client, you must specify the location of the server application that will be accessed or started. For the computer running the server application, you must specify the user account that will have permission to access or start the application, and the user account that will be used to run the application.

Interprocess Communication Mechanisms for Distributed Processing

The connection between the client and server portions of distributed applications must allow data to flow in both directions. There are a number of ways to establish this connection. The Windows NT operating system provides seven different Interprocess Communication (IPC) mechanisms.

- Named Pipes
- Mailslots
- NetBIOS
- Windows Sockets
- Remote Procedure Calls (RPCs)
- Network Dynamic Data Exchange (NetDDE)
- Server Message Blocks (SMBs)
- Distributed Component Object Model (DCOM)

Named Pipes and Mailslots

A pipe is a portion of memory that can be used by one process to pass information to another. A pipe connects two processes so that the output of one can be used as input to the other.

Named pipes and mailslots are actually written as file system drivers, so implementation of named pipes and mailslots differs from implementation of other IPC mechanisms. There are entries in the registry for NPFS (Named Pipe File System) and MSFS (Mailslot File System). As file systems, they share common functionality, such as security, with the other file systems. Local processes can also use named pipes and mailslots. As with all of the file systems, remote access to named pipes and mailslots is accomplished through the redirector.

Named pipes provide connection-oriented messaging. Named pipes are based on OS/2 API calls, which have been ported into the Win32 base API set. Additional asynchronous support has been added to named pipes to make support of client/server applications easier.

In addition to the APIs ported from OS/2, the Windows NT operating system provides special APIs that increase security for named pipes. Using a feature called *impersonation,* the server can change its security identity to that of the client at the other end of the message. A server typically has more permissions to access databases on the server than the client requesting services has. When the request is delivered to the server through a named pipe, the server changes its security identity to the security identity of the client. This limits the server to only those permissions granted to the client rather than its own permissions, thus increasing the security of named pipes.

The mailslot implementation in the Windows NT operating system is a subset of the Microsoft OS/2 LAN Manager implementation. The Windows NT operating system implements only second-class mailslots, not first-class mailslots. Second-class mailslots provide connectionless messaging for broadcast messages. Delivery of the message is not guaranteed, although the delivery rate on most networks is quite high. Connectionless messaging is most useful for identifying other computers or services on a network, such as the Computer Browser service offered in the Windows NT operating system.

For a description of connectionless messaging, see "Data Transfer Modes," earlier in this chapter.

NetBIOS

NetBIOS is a standard programming interface in the personal-computing environment for developing client/server applications. NetBIOS has been used as an IPC mechanism since the introduction of the interface in the early 1980s.

A NetBIOS client/server application can communicate over various protocols:

- NetBEUI Frame protocol (NBF).
- NWLink NetBIOS (NWNBLink).
- NetBIOS over TCP/IP (NetBT). NetBT provides RFC 1001/1002 NetBIOS support for the TCP/IP protocol stack.

From a programming perspective, higher-level IPC mechanisms, such as named pipes and RPC, have superior flexibility and portability.

NetBIOS uses the following components.

- Netapi32.dll, which shares the address space of the NetBIOS user-mode application. (However, Netapi32.dll is used for more than NetBIOS requests.)
- NetBIOS emulator, which provides the NetBIOS mapping layer between NetBIOS applications and the TDI-compliant protocols.

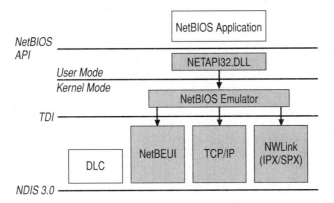

Figure 1.14   NetBIOS programming interface

MS-DOS and NetBIOS applications are hard-coded to use a specific LANA number for communicating on the network. You can assign a LANA number to each network route. The network route consists of the protocol driver and the network adapter that will be used for NetBIOS commands sent to its assigned LANA number.

▶ **To assign a LANA number to a network route**

1. Click **Start,** point to **Settings,** and click **Control Panel**.

2. Double-click **Network**.

3. Click the **Services** tab.

4. Click **NetBIOS Interface,** and then click **Properties**.

   The **NetBIOS Configuration** dialog box appears.

5. Click the number you want under **Lana Number,** and then click **Edit.**

6. Type a new number, and click **OK.**

Windows Sockets

The Windows Sockets API provides a standard interface to protocols with different addressing schemes. The Sockets interface was developed at the University of California, Berkeley, in the early 1980s. The Windows Sockets API was developed to migrate the Sockets interface into the Windows and Windows NT environments. Windows Sockets was also developed to help standardize an API for all operating system platforms. Windows Sockets is supported on the following protocols.

- TCP/IP
- NWLink (IPX/SPX)

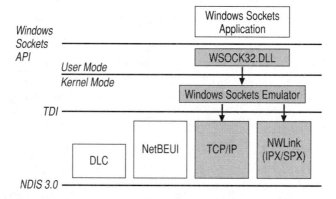

Figure 1.15   Windows Sockets programming interface

Windows Sockets consists of the following items.

- Wsock32.dll, which shares the address space of the Windows Sockets user-mode application.
- Windows Sockets emulator,which provides the Windows Sockets mapping layer between the Windows Sockets applications and the TDI-compliant protocols.

Remote Procedure Call

Much of the original work on Remote Procedure Call (RPC) was initiated at Sun Microsystems. This work has been carried forward by the Open Software Foundation (OSF) as part of their Distributed Computing Environment (DCE). The Microsoft RPC implementation is compatible with the OSF/DCE standard RPC.

It is important to note that it is *compatible* but not *compliant*. In this situation, compliance implies that you started with the OSF source code and worked forward. For a number of reasons, Microsoft developed RPC from the ground up.

The RPC mechanism is completely compatible with other DCE-based RPC systems, such as the ones for HP and IBM/AIX systems, and will interoperate with them.

The Microsoft RPC mechanism is unique in that it uses the other IPC mechanisms to establish communications between the client and the server. RPC can use the following to communicate with remote systems:

- Named pipes
- NetBIOS
- Windows Sockets

If the client and server portions of the application are on the same machine, local procedure calls (LPCs) can be used to transfer information between processes. This makes RPC the most flexible and portable of the IPC choices available.

RPC is based on the concepts used for creating structured programs, which can be viewed as having a "backbone" to which a series of "ribs" can be attached. The backbone is the mainstream logic of the program, which should rarely change. The ribs are the procedures that the backbone calls on to do work or perform functions. In traditional programs, these ribs were statically linked to the backbone and stored in the same executable.

Windows and OS/2 use data-link libraries (DLLs). With DLLs, the procedure code and the backbone code are in different pieces. This enables the DLL to be modified or updated without changing or redistributing the backbone portion.

RPC takes the concept one step further and places the backbone and the ribs on different computers. This raises many issues, such as data formatting, integer-byte ordering, locating which server contains the function, and determining which communication mechanism to use.

RPC is the developer's preferred method for writing client/server applications for Windows NT. The components necessary to use a remote procedure call are the following items.

- Remote Procedure Stub (Proc Stub), which packages remote procedure calls to be sent to the server by means of the RPC run time.
- RPC Run Time (RPC RT), which is responsible for communications between the local and remote computer, including the passing of parameters.
- Application Stub (APP Stub), which accepts RPC requests from RPC RT, unwraps the package, and makes the appropriate call to the remote procedure.
- Remote Procedure, which is the actual procedure that is called by the network.

Client applications are developed with a specially compiled "stub" library. The client application "thinks" it will call its own subroutines. In reality, these stubs will transfer the data and the function to the RPC RT module. This module will be responsible for finding the server that can satisfy the RPC command. Once found, the function and data will be sent to the server, where they are picked up by the RPC RT component on the server. The server piece then loads the library needed for the function, builds the appropriate data structure, and calls the function.

The function interprets the call as coming from the client application. When the function is completed, any return values will be collected, formatted, and sent back to the client through the RPC RT. When the function returns to the client application, it will have the appropriate returned data or an indication that the function failed.

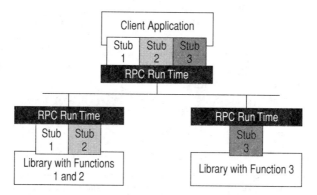

Figure 1.16   How RPC calls operate

Network Dynamic Data Exchange

Network Dynamic Data Exchange (NetDDE) is an extension of the Dynamic Data Exchange (DDE) protocol that has been in use since Windows version 2.x. NetDDE enables users to use DDE over a NetBIOS-compatible network. To understand NetDDE, you need to know something about DDE.

DDE is a protocol that allows applications to exchange data. To perform such an exchange, the two participating applications must first engage in a DDE conversation. The application that initiates the DDE conversation is the DDE client application, and the application that responds to the client request is the DDE server application.

A single application can be simultaneously engaged in multiple DDE conversations, acting as the DDE client application in some DDE conversations and as the DDE server application in others. This allows a user to set up a DDE link between applications and have one of the applications automatically update another.

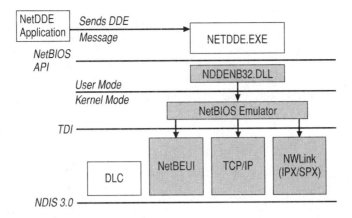

Figure 1.17   NetDDE

NetDDE extends all of the DDE capabilities so that they can be used across the network, using the NetBIOS emulator. This enables applications on two or more workstations to dynamically share information. NetDDE is not a special form of DDE but rather a service that examines the information contained in a DDE conversation and looks for a special application name. Implementing NetDDE in this manner allows any DDE application to take advantage of NetDDE without modification.

The NetDDE service examines DDE requests, looking for the use of a special application name reserved by NetDDE, which is preceded by the name of the remote system. The reserved application name is NDDE$; therefore, NetDDE is looking for DDE requests that use an application name in the following form: \\<*servername*>\ndde$.

Before a user can connect to a printer or directory from a remote location, the printer or directory must be shared. Similarly, a NetDDE share must be created on a computer before an application on that computer can use NetDDE to communicate with the application on another computer. NetDDE-aware applications, such as Chat, automatically create a NetDDE share for themselves during installation. For other applications, a NetDDE share can be created with ClipBook Viewer, and data can then be exchanged through the ClipBoard. In addition, Windows NT includes the DDE Share utility (Ddeshare.exe), which can be used to set up a NetDDE share so that applications can directly exchange data.

NetDDE shares are defined in the registry. They are accessed by communicating with the Network DDE Service Data Manager (DSDM), which is the Windows NT operating system service that supports the rest of NetDDE.

Because NetDDE is simply an extension of DDE, the same APIs used to establish a DDE conversation are used to establish NetDDE conversations.

In Windows NT 3.1, the NetDDE services automatically load at system startup. In Windows NT 3.5 and later, the default startup type for NetDDE is manual, which improves startup time. The startup type for the NetDDE services can be configured through Control Panel.

Server Message Blocks

The Server Message Blocks (SMB) protocol, developed jointly by Microsoft, Intel, and IBM, defines a series of commands used to pass information between networked computers. The redirector packages network-control-block (NCB) requests meant for remote computers in a SMB structure. SMBs can be sent over the network to remote devices. The redirector also uses SMBs to make requests to the protocol stack of the local computer, such as "Create a session with the file server."

SMB uses four message types, which are listed below.

- Session control messages, which consist of commands that start and end a redirector connection to a shared resource at the server.
- File messages, which are used by the redirector to gain access to files at the server.
- Printer messages, which are used by the redirector to send data to a print queue at a server and to get status information about the print queue.
- Message messages, which allow an application to exchange messages with another workstation.

The provider DLL listens for SMB messages destined for it and removes the data portion of the SMB request so that it can be processed by a local device.

SMBs provide interoperability between different versions of the Microsoft family of networking products and other networks that use SMBs, including those on the following list.

- MS® OS/2 LAN Manager
- Microsoft Windows for Workgroups
- IBM LAN Server
- MS-DOS LAN Manager
- DEC PATHWORKS
- Microsoft LAN Manager for UNIX
- 3Com 3+Open
- MS-Net

Network Resource Access

Applications reside above the redirector and server services in user mode. Like all other layers in the Windows NT networking architecture, there is a unified interface for accessing network resources, which is independent of any redirectors installed on the system. Access to resources is provided through one of two components: the Multiple Universal Naming Convention Provider (MUP) and the Multi-Provider Router (MPR).

Multiple Universal Naming Convention Provider

When applications make I/O calls containing Universal Naming Code (UNC) names, these requests are passed to the Multiple Universal Naming Convention Provider (MUP). MUP selects the appropriate UNC provider (redirector) to handle the I/O request.

Universal Naming Convention Names

UNC is a naming convention for describing network servers and the share points on those servers. UNC names start with two backslashes followed by the server name. All other fields in the name are separated by a single backslash. A typical UNC name would appear as: \\server\share\subdirectory\filename.

Not all of the components of the UNC name need to be present with each command; only the share component is required. For example, the command **dir***servername**sharename* can be used to obtain a directory listing of the root of the specified share.

Why MUP?

One of the design goals of the Windows NT networking environment is to provide a platform upon which others can build. MUP is a vital part of allowing multiple redirectors to coexist in the computer. MUP frees applications from maintaining their own UNC-provider listings.

How MUP Works

MUP is actually a driver, unlike the TDI interface, which merely defines the way a component on one layer communicates with a component on another layer. MUP also has defined paths to UNC providers (redirectors).

I/O requests from applications that contain UNC names are received by the I/O Manager, which in turn passes the requests to MUP. If MUP has not seen the UNC name during the previous 15 minutes, MUP will send the name to each of the UNC providers registered with it. MUP is a prerequisite of the Workstation service.

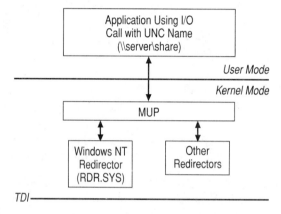

Figure 1.18   Multiple Universal Naming Convention Provider

When a request containing a UNC name is received by MUP, it checks with each redirector to find out which one can process the request. MUP looks for the redirector with the highest registered-priority response that claims it can establish a connection to the UNC. This connection remains as long as there is activity. If there has been no request for 15 minutes on the UNC name, then MUP once again negotiates to find an appropriate redirector.

Multi-provider Router

Not all programs use UNC names in their I/O requests. Some applications use WNet APIs, which are the Win32 network APIs. The Multi-Provider Router (MPR) was created to support these applications.

MPR is similar to MUP. MPR receives WNet commands, determines the appropriate redirector, and passes the command to that redirector. Because different network vendors use different interfaces for communicating with their redirector, there is a series of provider DLLs between MPR and the redirectors. The provider DLLs expose a standard interface so that MPR can communicate with them. The DLLs "know" how to take the request from MPR and communicate it to their corresponding redirector.

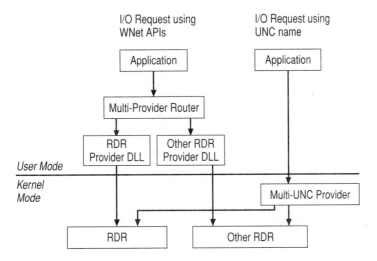

Figure 1.19   Multi-provider Router

The provider DLLs are supplied by the network-redirector vendor and should automatically be installed when the redirector is installed.

The Workstation Service

All user-mode requests go through the Workstation service. This service consists of two components.

- The user-mode interface, which resides in Lmsvcs.exe in Windows NT 3.1 and Services.exe in Windows NT 3.5 and later.
- The redirector (Rdr.sys), which is a file-system driver that interacts with the lower-level network drivers by means of the TDI interface.

The Workstation service receives the user request, and passes it to the kernel-mode redirector.

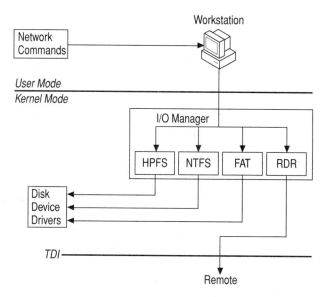

Figure 1.20   Workstation Service

Windows NT Redirector

The redirector (RDR) is a component that resides above TDI and through which one computer gains access to another computer. The Windows NT operating system redirector allows connection to Windows for Workgroups, LAN Manager, LAN Server, and other MS-Net-based servers. The redirector communicates to the protocols by means of the TDI interface.

The redirector is implemented as a Windows NT file system driver. Implementing a redirector as a file system has several benefits, which are listed below.

- It allows applications to call a single API (the Windows NT I/O API) to access files on local and remote computers. From the I/O Manager perspective, there is no difference between accessing files stored on a remote computer on the network and accessing those stored locally on a hard disk.

- It runs in kernel mode and can directly call other drivers and other kernel-mode components, such as Cache Manager. This improves the performance of the redirector.

- It can be dynamically loaded and unloaded, like any other file-system driver.

- It can easily coexist with other redirectors.

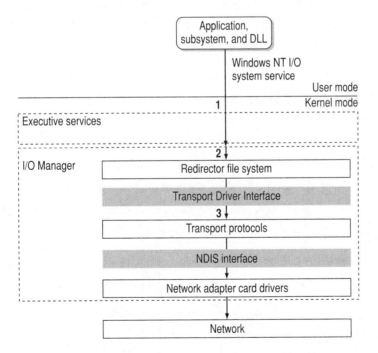

Figure 1.21   Windows NT redirector

Interoperating with Other Networks

Besides allowing connections to LAN Manager, LAN Server, and MS-Net servers, the Windows NT redirector can coexist with redirectors for other networks, such as Novell NetWare and Banyan VINES.

While Windows NT includes integrated networking, its open design provides transparent access to other networks. For example, a computer running Windows NT Server can concurrently access files stored on Windows NT and NetWare servers.

Providers and the Provider-interface Layer

For each additional type of network, such as NetWare or VINES, you must install a component called a *provider*. The provider is the component that allows a computer running Windows NT Server or Windows NT Workstation to communicate with the network. The Windows NT operating system includes two providers; Client Services for NetWare and Gateway Services for NetWare.

Client Services for NetWare is included with Windows NT Workstation and allows a computer running Windows NT Workstation to connect as a client to the NetWare network. The Gateway service, included with Windows NT Server, allows a computer running Windows NT Server to connect as a client to the NetWare network. Other provider DLLs are supplied by the appropriate network vendors.

Accessing a Remote File

When a process on a Windows NT computer tries to open a file that resides on a remote computer, the following steps occur.

First, the process calls the I/O Manager to request that the file be opened.

Then, the I/O Manager recognizes that the request is for a file on a remote computer, and passes the request to the redirector file-system driver.

Finally, the redirector passes the request to lower-level network drivers, which transmit it to the remote server for processing.

Workstation Service Dependencies

Configuration requirements for loading the Workstation service include:

- A protocol that exposes the TDI interface must be started.
- The MUP driver must be started.

The Server Service

Windows NT includes a second component, called the Server service. Like the redirector, the Server service sits above TDI, is implemented as a file system driver, and directly interacts with various other file-system drivers to satisfy I/O requests, such as reading or writing to a file.

The Server service supplies the connections requested by client-side redirectors and provides them with access to the resources they request.

When the Server service receives a request from a remote computer asking to read a file that resides on the local hard drive, the following steps occur.

- The low-level network drivers receive the request and pass it to the server driver (SRV).
- The Server service passes a read-file request to the appropriate local file-system driver.
- The local file-system driver calls lower-level, disk-device drivers to access the file.
- The data is passed back to the local file-system driver.
- The local file-system driver passes the data back to the Server service.
- The Server service passes the data to the lower-level network drivers for transmission back to the client computer.

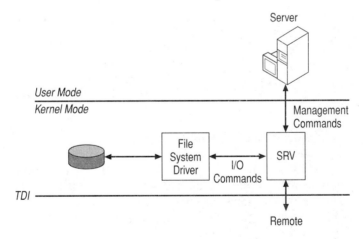

Figure 1.22   Server Service

Like the Workstation service, the Server service is composed of two parts.

- Server, a service that runs in the Services.exe, which is the Service Control Manager, where all services start. Unlike the Workstation service, the Server service is not dependent on the MUP service because the server is not a UNC provider. It does not attempt to connect to other computers, but other computers connect to it.

- Srv.sys, a file system driver that handles the interaction with the lower levels and directly interacts with various file system devices to satisfy command requests, such as file read and write.

Binding Options

Earlier in this chapter, we discussed how the Windows NT network architecture consists of a series of layers and how components in each layer perform specific functions for the layers above and below it. The bottom of the network architecture ends at the network adapter card, which moves information between computers that are part of the network.

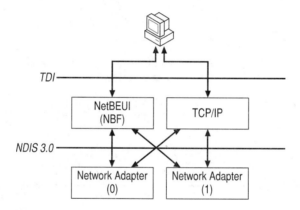

Figure 1.23   Network protocol bindings

The linking of network components on different levels to enable communication between those components is called *binding*. A network component can be bound to one or more network components above or below it. The services that each component provides can be shared by all the components bound to it.

When adding network software, Windows NT automatically binds all dependent components accordingly.

In the Network window, the **Bindings** tab displays the bindings of the installed network components, from the upper-layer services and protocols to the lowest layer of network adapter drivers. Bindings can be enabled and disabled, based on the use of the network components installed on the system.

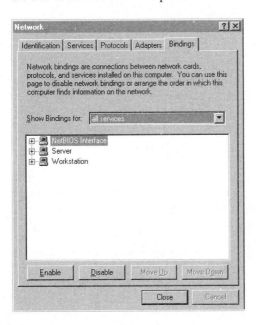

Figure 1.24   The Settings tab of the Network window

Bindings can be ordered or sequenced to optimize the system's use of the network. For example, if NetBEUI and TCP/IP are installed on a computer, and if most of servers that the computer connects to are running only TCP/IP, the Workstation bindings should be examined. The administrator of this computer would want to make sure that the Workstation is bound to TCP/IP first and that NetBEUI is at the bottom of the list.

In Windows NT 3.1, the redirector uses the following method to establish a connection.

- First, the redirector submits the connect request to the first protocol driver in the bindings order and waits for that protocol driver to complete the request and return.

- If the first protocol driver's return indicates that it could not connect to the specified server, then the redirector submits the connect request to the second protocol driver in the bindings order.

- This continues down the bindings order until a protocol-driver return indicates that the connection was successful or until all protocol drivers have been tried and have failed.

In Windows NT 3.5 and later, the redirector uses the following method to establish a connection.

- The redirector simultaneously submits the connect request to all protocol drivers.

- When one of the protocol drivers successfully completes the request, the redirector waits until all higher-priority protocol drivers, if there are any, have been returned. (The priority is based on the bindings order.)

- The redirector then proceeds to use the highest-priority protocol driver that returned with success status, and it disconnects all connections that may have been established through lower-priority protocol drivers.

Remote Access Service

The Windows NT Workstation and Windows NT Server RAS connects remote or mobile workers to corporate networks. Optimized for client/server computing, RAS is implemented primarily as a software solution, and is available on all Microsoft operating systems.

The distinction between RAS and remote control solutions (such as Cubix and pcANYWHERE) are important:

- RAS is a software-based multi-protocol router; remote control solutions work by sharing screen, keyboard, and mouse over the remote link.

- In a remote control solution, users share a CPU or multiple CPUs on the server. The RAS server's CPU is dedicated to communications, not to running applications.

Point-to-Point Protocol

The Windows NT operating system supports the Point-to-Point Protocol (PPP) in RAS. PPP is a set of industry-standard framing and authentication protocols. PPP negotiates configuration parameters for multiple layers of the OSI model.

PPP support in Windows NT 3.5 and later (and Windows 95) means that computers running Windows can dial into remote networks through any server that complies with the PPP standard. PPP compliance enables a Windows NT Server to receive calls from other vendors' remote-access software and to provide network access to them.

The PPP architecture also enables clients to load any combination of IPX, TCP/IP, and NetBEUI. Applications written to the Windows Sockets, NetBIOS, or IPX interfaces can now be run on a remote computer running Windows NT Workstation. The following figure illustrates the PPP architecture of RAS.

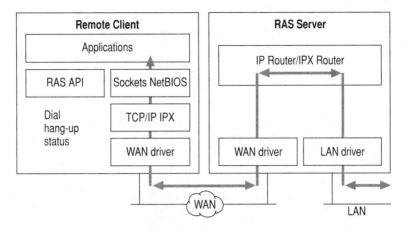

Figure 1.25   Point-to-Point Protocol

RAS Connection Sequence

The RAS connection sequence is key to understanding the PPP protocol. Upon connecting to a remote computer, the PPP negotiation begins.

- First, framing rules are established between the remote computer and server. This allows continued communication (frame transfer) to occur.

- Next, the RAS server uses the PPP authentication protocols (PAP, CHAP, SPAP) to authenticate the remote user. The protocols invoked depend on the security configurations of the remote client and server.

- Once authenticated, the Network Control Protocols (NCPs) are used to enable and configure the server for the LAN protocol that will be used on the remote client.

When the PPP connection sequence is successfully completed, the remote client and RAS server can begin to transfer data using any supported protocol, such as Windows Sockets, RPC, or NetBIOS. The following illustration shows where the PPP protocol is on the OSI model.

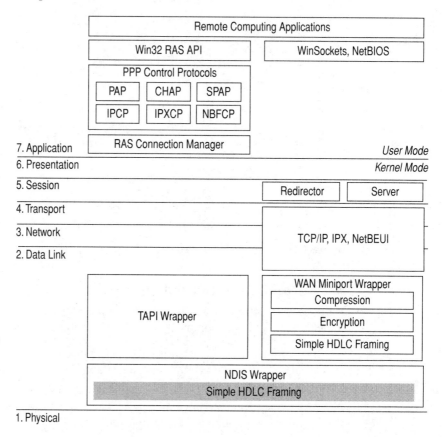

Figure 1.26   PPP within the OI model

If a remote client is configured to use the NetBIOS Gateway or Serial Line Internet Protocol (SLIP), this sequence is invalid.

Point-to-Point Tunneling Protocol

A RAS server is usually connected to a PSTN, ISDN, or X.25 network, allowing remote users to access a server through these networks. RAS now allows remote users access through the Internet by using the new Point-to-Point Tunneling Protocol (PPTP).

PPTP is a new networking technology that supports multiprotocol virtual private networks (VPNs), enabling remote users to access corporate networks securely across the Internet by dialing into an Internet Service Provider (ISP) or by connecting directly to the Internet. For more information, see the *Microsoft Windows NT Server Networking Supplement*, Chapter 11, "Point-to-Point Tunneling Protocol."

NetBIOS Gateway

Windows NT continues to support NetBIOS gateways, the architecture used in previous versions of the Windows NT operating system and LAN Manager. Remote users connect using NetBEUI, and the RAS server translates packets to IPX or TCP/IP, if necessary. This enables users to share network resources in a multiprotocol LAN, but prevents them from running applications that rely on IPX or TCP/IP on the client. The NetBIOS gateway is used by default when remote clients use NetBEUI. The following illustration shows the NetBIOS gateway architecture of RAS.

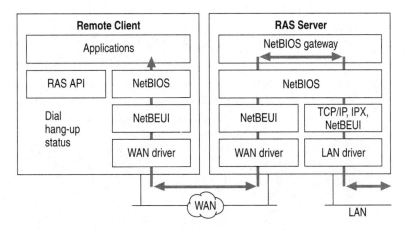

Figure 1.27   NetBIOS gateway architecture of RAS

An example of the NetBIOS gateway capability is remote network access for Lotus Notes users. While Lotus Notes does offer dial-up connectivity, dial-up is limited to the Notes application. RAS complements this connectivity by providing a low-cost, high-performance, remote-network connection for Notes users, which connects Notes and offers file and print services with access to other network resources.

Serial Line Internet Protocol

SLIP is an older communications standard found in UNIX environments. SLIP does not provide the automatic negotiation of network configuration and encrypted authentication that PPP can provide. SLIP requires user intervention. Windows NT RAS can be configured as a SLIP client, enabling users to dial into an existing SLIP server. RAS does not provide a SLIP server in Windows NT Server.

For more information about RAS issues, see the Rasphone.hlp online Help file on the Windows NT distribution disks (or, if RAS has been installed, see *systemroot*\System32).

Services for Macintosh

Through Windows NT Services for Macintosh, Macintosh users can connect to a Windows NT server in the same way they would connect to an AppleShare server. Windows NT Services for Macintosh will support an unlimited number of simultaneous AFP connections to a Windows NT server, and Macintosh sessions will be integrated with Windows NT sessions. The per-session memory overhead is approximately 15K.

Existing versions of LAN Manager Services for the Macintosh can be easily upgraded to Windows NT Services for Macintosh. OS/2-based volumes that already exist are converted with permissions intact. Graphical installation, administration, and configuration utilities are integrated with existing Windows NT administration tools. Windows NT Services for Macintosh requires System 6.0.7 or higher and is AFP 2.1-compliant; however, AFP 2.0 clients are also supported. AFP 2.1 compliance provides support for logon messages and server messages.

Support for Macintosh networking is built into the core operating system for Windows NT Server. Windows NT Services for Macintosh includes a full AFP 2.0 file server. All Macintosh file system attributes, such as resource data forks and 32-bit directory IDs, are supported. As a file server, all filenames, icons, and access permissions are intelligently managed for different networks. For example, a Word for Windows file will appear on the Macintosh with the correct Word for Macintosh icons. These applications can also be launched from the File Server as Macintosh applications. When files are deleted, no orphaned resource forks will be left to be cleaned up.

Windows NT Services for Macintosh fully supports and complies with
Windows NT security. It presents the AFP security model to Macintosh users
and allows them to access files on volumes that reside on CD-ROM or other read-
only media. The AFP server also supports both cleartext and encrypted passwords
at logon time. The administrator has the option to configure the server not to
accept cleartext passwords.

Services for Macintosh can be administered from Control Panel and can be
started transparently if the administrator has configured the server to use this
facility.

Macintosh-accessible volumes can be created in My Computer. Services for
Macintosh automatically creates a Public Files volume at installation time.
Windows NT file and directory permissions are automatically translated into
corresponding Macintosh permissions.

Windows NT Services for Macintosh has the same functionality as the LAN
Manager Services for Macintosh 1.0 MacPrint. Administration and configuration
are also easier. There is a user interface for publishing a print queue on AppleTalk
and a user interface for choosing an AppleTalk printer as a destination device.
The Windows NT print subsystem handles AppleTalk despooling errors, and uses
the built-in printer support in Windows NT. (The PPD file scheme of Macintosh
Services 1.0 is not used.) Services for Macintosh also has a PostScript-compatible
engine that allows Macintosh computers to print to any Windows NT printer as if
they were printing to a LaserWriter.

C H A P T E R 2

Network Security and Domain Planning

Network security refers to the protection of all components—hardware, software, and stored data—of a computer network from damage, theft, and unauthorized use. A computer security plan that is well thought out, implemented, and monitored makes authorized use of network computers easy and unauthorized use or accidental damage difficult or impossible.

Microsoft included security as part of the initial design specifications for Windows NT, and it is pervasive in the operating system. The security model includes components to control who accesses which objects (such as files and shared printers), which action an individual user can take on an object (such as write access to a file), and which events are audited.

Security over a Windows NT network incorporates domains and trust relationships to provide the most secure networking operating system available.

This chapter provides:

- An overview of the Windows NT security model and architecture.
- A description of how the features of the security model control access to resources.
- An overview of auditing security events.
- A description of how domains work to implement security over the network.
- Considerations for planning your domain structure, including a description of the Microsoft domain model.
- Troubleshooting.

This chapter presumes a good understanding of Windows NT domains. For background information about domains, see "Managing Windows NT Server Domains" in the *Microsoft Windows NT Server 4.0 Concepts and Planning Guide*.

Security Model Architecture

Figure 2.1 on the facing page shows the components of the Windows NT security model, which include:

- *Logon processes*, which accept logon requests from users. These include the initial interactive logon, which displays the initial logon dialog box to the user, and remote logon processes, which allow access by remote users to a Windows NT server process.

- *Local Security Authority (LSA)*, which ensures that the user has permission to access the system. This component is the center of the Windows NT security subsystem. It generates access tokens, manages the local security policy, and provides interactive user authentication services. LSA also controls audit policy and logs the audit messages generated by the Security Reference Monitor.

- *Security Account Manager (SAM)*, also known as the *directory database*, which maintains the user-accounts database. This database contains information for all user accounts and group accounts. SAM provides user validation services, which are used by LSA.

- *Security Reference Monitor*, which checks that the user has permission to access an object and perform whatever action the user is attempting. This component enforces the access validation and audit generation policy defined by LSA. It provides services to both kernel and user modes to ensure the users and processes attempting access to an object have the necessary permissions. This component also generates audit messages when appropriate.

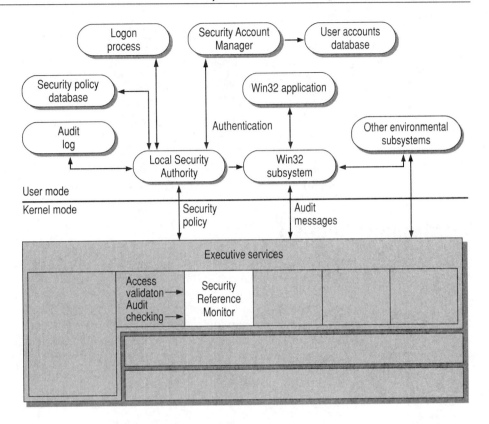

Figure 2.1   Windows NT Security Components

Together, these components are known as the security subsystem. This subsystem is called an *integral subsystem,* not an *environmental subsystem,* because it affects the entire Windows NT operating system.

The Windows NT security model is designed for C2-level security, as defined by the U.S. Department of Defense. Some of the most important requirements of C2-level security are:

- The owner of a resource (such as a file) must be able to control access to the resource.

- The operating system must protect objects so that they are not randomly reused by other processes.

  For example, the system protects memory so that its contents cannot be read after it is freed by a process. When a file is deleted, users must not be able to access the data from that file.

- Each user must identify himself or herself by typing a unique logon name and password before being allowed access to the system. The system must be able to use this unique identification to track the activities of the user.

- System administrators must be able to audit security-related events. Access to this audit data must be limited to authorized administrators.

- The system must protect itself from external interference or tampering, such as modification of the running system or of system files stored on disk.

For more information about C2-level security, see "Security Considerations and C2 Security Rating," later in this chapter.

Controlling Access

Windows NT Server provides control of what network computer users can and cannot do, while still giving them access to the resources they need. You can allow some users to connect to a resource (such as a printer) or perform an action (such as changing a file) while preventing others from doing so. You can even control access to system functions, such as setting a computer's system clock. This can be done for users working at the computer in which the resource is located and for users connecting to the resource over the network.

The following features allow and restrict access:

- User accounts
- User rights
- User groups
- Subjects and impersonations
- Security information about objects (permissions)

Implementing security over a network also involves the use of domains and domain controllers, which are presented in the section "Windows NT Server Domains" later in this chapter.

User Accounts

An individual who participates in a domain must have a user account to log on to the network and use domain resources, such as files, directories, and printers.

An administrator creates a user account by assigning a user name to an account, specifying the user's identification data, and defining the user's rights on the system. The account includes user information, group memberships, and security-policy information. Windows NT Server then assigns a unique security identifier (SID) to the new account.

Each SID is unique for all time. For example, suppose Sally, who has a Windows NT account, leaves her job at a company but later returns to a different job at the same company. When Sally leaves, the administrator deletes her account, and Windows NT no longer accepts her security ID as valid. When Sally returns, the administrator creates a new account, and Windows NT generates a new security ID for that account. The new security ID does not match the old one, so nothing from the old account is transferred to the new account.

When a user logs on, Windows NT creates a security-access token. This includes a security ID for the user, other security IDs for the groups to which the user belongs, and other information, such as the user's name and the names of the groups to which that user belongs. Every process that runs on behalf of this user will have a copy of his or her access token. For example, when Sally starts Notepad, the Notepad process receives a copy of Sally's access token.

Windows NT refers to the security IDs within a user's access token when he or she tries to access an object. The security IDs are compared to the list of access permissions for the object to ensure that the user has sufficient permission to access the object.

For more information about access tokens, see Chapter 6, "Windows NT Security Model," in the *Microsoft Windows NT Workstation 4.0 Resource Guide*.

User Rights

User rights are rules that determine the actions a user can perform. Unless the computer is a domain controller, they are computer-specific policies. If it is a domain controller, the computer policy extends to all domain controllers in the domain.

Note In the current release of Windows NT, the set of user rights is defined by the system and cannot be changed. Future versions of Windows NT may allow software developers to define new user rights appropriate to their application.

User rights can be assigned to individual user accounts, but are usually (and more efficiently) assigned to groups. Predefined (built-in) groups have sets of user rights already assigned. Administrators usually assign user rights by adding a user account to one of the predefined groups or by creating a new group and assigning specific user rights to that group. Users who are subsequently added to a group automatically gain all user rights assigned to the group account.

There are several user rights that administrators of high-security installations should be aware of and possibly audit. Of these, you might want to change the default permissions for two rights: **Log on locally** and **Shut down the system**.

Table 2.1   Default user rights that may require changing

User Right	Groups assigned this right by default	Recommended change
Log on locally Allows a user to log on at the computer, from the computer's keyboard.	Administrators, Backup Operators, Everyone, Guests, Power Users, and Users	Deny Everyone and Guests this right.
Shut down the system (SeShutdownPrivilege) Allows a user to shut down Windows NT.	Administrators, Backup Operators, Everyone, Power Users, and Users	Deny Everyone and Users this right.

The rights in the following table generally require no changes to the default settings, even in the most highly secure installations.

Table 2.2   Default user rights

Right	Allows	Initially assigned to
Access this computer from the network	A user to connect to the computer over the network.	Administrators, Everyone, Power Users
Act as part of the operating system (SeTcbPrivilege)	A process to perform as a secure, trusted part of the operating system. Some subsystems are granted this right.	(None)
Add workstations to the domain (SeMachineAccountPrivilege)	Nothing. This right has no effect on computers running Windows NT.	(None)
Back up files and directories (SeBackupPrivilege)	A user to back up files and directories. This right supersedes file and directory permissions.	Administrators, Backup Operators
Bypass traverse checking (SeChangeNotifyPrivilege)	A user to change directories and to access files and subdirectories, even if the user has no permission to access parent directories.	Everyone
Change the system time (SeSystemTimePrivilege)	A user to set the time for the internal clock of the computer.	Administrators, Power Users
Create a pagefile (SeCreatePagefilePrivilege)	Nothing. This right has no effect in current versions of Windows NT.	Administrators

Table 2.2   Default user rights *(continued)*

Right	Allows	Initially assigned to
Create a token object (SeCreateTokenPrivilege)	A process to create access tokens. Only the Local Security Authority can do this.	(None)
Create permanent shared objects (SeCreatePermanentPrivilege)	A user to create special permanent objects, such as \\Device, that are used within Windows NT.	(None)
Debug programs (SeDebugPrivilege)	A user to debug various low-level objects, such as threads.	Administrators
Force shutdown from a remote system (SeRemoteShutdownName)	A user to shut down a remote computer.	Administrators
Generate security audits (SeAuditPrivilege)	A process to generate security-audit log entries.	(None)
Increase quotas (SeIncreaseQuotaPrivilege)	Nothing. This right has no effect in current versions of Windows NT.	(None)
Increase scheduling priority (SeIncreaseBasePriorityPrivilege)	A user to boost the execution priority of a process.	Administrators, Power Users
Load and unload device drivers (SeLoadDriverPrivilege)	A user to install and remove device drivers.	Administrators
Lock pages in memory (SeLockMemoryPrivilege)	A user to lock pages in memory so they cannot be paged out to a backing store, such as Pagefile.sys.	(None)
Log on as a batch job	Nothing. This right has no effect in current versions of Windows NT.	(None)
Log on as a service	A process to register with the system as a service.	(None)
Log on locally	A user to log on at the computer from the computer keyboard.	Administrators, Backup Operators, Guests, Power Users, Users

Table 2.2   Default user rights *(continued)*

Right	Allows	Initially assigned to
Manage auditing and security log (SeSecurityPrivilege)	A user to specify what types of resource access (such as file access) are to be audited, and to view and clear the security log. This right does not allow a user to set system auditing policy using **Audit** on the User Manager **Policy** menu. Members of the Administrators group can always view and clear the security log.	Administrators
Modify firmware environment variables (SeSystemEnvironmentPrivilege)	A user to modify system-environment variables stored in nonvolatile RAM on systems that support this type of configuration.	Administrators
Profile single process (SeProfSingleProcess)	A user to perform profiling (performance sampling) on a process.	Administrators, Power Users
Profile system performance (SeSystemProfilePrivilege)	A user to perform profiling (performance sampling) on the system.	Administrators
Replace a process-level token (SeAssignPrimaryTokenPrivilege)	A user to modify a process's security-access token. This is a powerful right, used only by the system.	(None)
Restore files and directories (SeRestorePrivilege)	A user to restore backed-up files and directories. This right supersedes file and directory permissions.	Administrators, Backup Operators
Shut down the system (SeShutdownPrivilege)	A user to shut down Windows NT.	Administrators, Backup Operators, Power Users, Users
Take ownership of files or other objects (SeTakeOwnershipPrivilege)	A user to take ownership of files, directories, printers, and other objects on the computer. This right supersedes permissions protecting objects.	Administrators

Grouping Users with Similar Needs

Administrators typically group users according to the network access their jobs require. For example, most accountants working at a certain level will probably need access to the same servers, directories, and files. By using group accounts, administrators can simultaneously grant rights and permissions to multiple users. Other users can be added to an existing group account at any time, instantly gaining the rights and permissions granted to the group account.

There can be two types of group accounts:

- A *global group* consists of several user accounts from one domain, which are grouped together under an account name. A global group can contain user accounts from only a single domain: the domain in which the global group was created. *Global* signifies that the group can be granted rights and permissions to use resources in multiple (global) domains. A global group can contain only user accounts (not other groups). A global group cannot be created on a computer running Windows NT Workstation or on a computer set up as a member server.

  For more information about member servers see "Windows NT Server Domains" later in this chapter.

- A *local group* can include user accounts and global groups from one or more domains, grouped together under one account name. Users and global groups from outside the local domain can be added to the local group only if they belong to a trusted domain. *Local* signifies that the group can be granted rights and permissions to use resources in only a single (local) domain. A local group can contain users and global groups, but it cannot contain other local groups.

When working with groups, use these guidelines:

- It is best to grant rights and permissions to local groups and to use the global group as the method of adding users to the local groups.

  Global groups are the best method for simultaneously adding many users to another domain. The necessary rights and permissions are provided by the local group to which the global groups are added.

- Global groups are the most efficient way to add users to local groups.

- Global groups can be added to local groups in the same domain or in trusting domains, or to computers running Windows NT Workstation or Windows NT Server as a member server in either the same domain or a trusting domain.

Windows NT Server has built-in both local and global user groups. For more information about built-in groups, see "Working with User and Group Accounts" in the *Microsoft Windows NT Server 4.0 Concepts and Planning Guide*.

Subjects and Impersonation

One objective of the Windows NT security model is to ensure that the programs that a user runs have no more access to objects than the user does. That is, if a user is granted only read access to a file, then when he or she runs a program, that program cannot write to the file. The program, like the user, is granted read-only permission.

A *subject* is the combination of the user's access token and the program that is acting on the user's behalf. Windows NT uses subjects to track and manage permissions for the programs users run.

When a program or process runs on the user's behalf, it is said to be running in the *security context* of that user. The security context controls what access the subject has to objects and system services.

To accommodate the client/server model of Windows NT, there are two classes of subjects within the Windows NT security architecture:

- A *simple subject,* which is a process that was assigned a security context when the corresponding user logged on. It is not acting in the capacity of a protected server, which may have other subjects as clients.

- A *server subject,* which is a process implemented as a protected server (such as the Win32 subsystem), and which has other subjects as clients. In this role, a server subject typically has the security context of those clients available for use when acting on their behalf.

When a subject calls an object service through a protected subsystem, the subject's token is used within the service to determine who made the call and to decide whether the caller has sufficient access authority to perform the requested action.

Windows NT allows one process to take on the security attributes of another through a technique called *impersonation*. For example, a server process typically impersonates a client process to complete a task involving objects to which the server does not normally have access.

Security Information for Objects (Permissions)

All named objects in Windows NT and some unnamed objects can be secured. A *security descriptor* describes the security attributes for an object. An object's security descriptor includes four parts:

- An owner security ID, which indicates the user or group who owns the object. The owner of an object can change the access permissions for the object.

- A group security ID, which is used only by the POSIX subsystem and ignored by the rest of Windows NT.

- A discretionary access control list (ACL), which identifies the users and groups who are granted or denied specific access permissions. Discretionary ACLs are controlled by the owner of the object.

- A system ACL, which controls the auditing messages the system will generate. System ACLs are controlled by the security administrators.

For details and background information about security in Windows NT 4.0, see Chapter 6, "Windows NT Security," in the *Microsoft Windows NT Workstation Resource Guide*.

Types of Objects

The permissions that can be granted or denied for an object depends on the type of object. For example, you can specify permissions, such as Manage Documents and Print for a printer queue, and specify Read, Write, Execute for a directory.

Permissions of an object are also affected by whether that object is a container object or a noncontainer object. A *container object* is one that logically contains other objects; a *noncontainer object* does not contain other objects. For example, a directory is a container object that logically contains files and other directories. Files are noncontainer objects. This distinction between container and noncontainer objects is important because objects within a container object can inherit certain permissions from the parent container.

Note NTFS supports ACL inheritance from directory objects to file objects that are created within the directory. For more information about NTFS, see "Disk and File System Basics" and "Choosing a File System" in the *Microsoft Windows NT Workstation Resource Guide*.

Access Control Lists and Access Control Entries

Each ACL is made up of *access control entries* (ACEs), which specify access or auditing permissions to that object for one user or group. There are three ACE types: two for discretionary access control and one for system security.

The discretionary ACEs are AccessAllowed and AccessDenied. These explicitly grant and deny access to a user or group of users. The first AccessDenied ACE denies the user access to the resource, and no further processing of ACEs occurs.

Note There is an important distinction between a discretionary ACL that is empty (one that has no ACEs in it) and an object without any discretionary ACL. In the case of an empty discretionary ACL, no accesses are explicitly granted, so access is implicitly denied. For an object that has no ACL at all, there is no protection assigned to the object, so any access request is granted.

SystemAudit is a system security ACE that is used to keep a log of security events (such as who accesses which files) and to generate and log security audit messages.

Access Masks

Each ACE includes an *access mask*, which defines all possible actions for a particular object type. An access mask can be compared to a menu, from which you select permissions to grant or deny.

Specific types include access options that apply specifically to an object type. Each object type can have up to 16 specific access types. Collectively, the specific access types for a particular object type are called the *specific access mask*. These are defined when the object type is defined.

For example, Windows NT files have the following specific access types:

- ReadData
- WriteData
- AppendData
- ReadEA (Extended Attribute)
- WriteEA (Extended Attribute)
- Execute
- ReadAttributes
- WriteAttributes

Standard types apply to all objects and consist of these access permissions:

- SYNCHRONIZE, which is used to synchronize access and to allow a process to wait for an object to enter the signaled state.
- WRITE_OWNER, which is used to assign a write owner.
- WRITE_DAC, which is used to grant or deny write access to the discretionary ACL.
- READ_CONTROL, which is used to grant or deny read access to the security descriptor and owner.
- DELETE, which is used to grant or deny delete access.

Generic types are broad types of access used when protecting an object. Exact implementation of these is determined by the application defining an object. For example, an application that defines a voice-annotation object might define specific access rights by using VOICE_PLAY and VOICE_EDIT for playing and editing the object. It might set up a generic mapping structure in which GENERIC_EXECUTE maps to VOICE_PLAY and GENERIC_WRITE maps to both VOICE_PLAY and VOICE_EDIT.

The following table shows the generic types that are mapped from specific and standard types.

Table 2.3   Generic types of access masks

Generic type	Mapped from these specific and standard types
FILE_GENERIC_READ	STANDARD_RIGHTS_READ FILE_READ_DATA FILE_READ_ATTRIBUTES FILE_READ_EA SYNCHRONIZE
FILE_GENERIC_WRITE	STANDARD_RIGHTS_WRITE FILE_WRITE_DATA FILE_WRITE_ATTRIBUTES FILE_WRITE_EA FILE_APPEND_DATA SYNCHRONIZE
FILE_GENERIC_EXECUTE	STANDARD_RIGHTS_EXECUTE FILE_READ_ATTRIBUTES FILE_EXECUTE SYNCHRONIZE

Specific and standard types appear in the details of the security log. Generic types do not appear in the security log. Instead, the corresponding specific and standard types are listed.

Access Control Inheritance

When you create new objects within a container object, the new objects inherit permissions by default from the parent object.

In the case of files and directories, changing the permissions on a directory affects that directory and its files but does not automatically apply to existing subdirectories and their contents. They will do so if you select the **Replace Permissions On Existing Files** check box and the **Replace Permissions On Subdirectories** check box in the **Directory Permissions** dialog box.

Access Validation

When a user tries to access an object, Windows NT compares security information in the user's access token with the security information in the object's security descriptor.

A *desired access mask* for the subject is created, based on the type of access the user is attempting. This desired access mask, usually created by a program that the user is running, is compared with the object's ACL. (All generic access types in the ACL are mapped to standard and specific access types.) Each ACE in the ACL is evaluated as follows:

1. The security ID in the ACE is compared with the set of security IDs in the user's access token. If a match is not found, the ACE is skipped.

   Further processing is based upon the type of the ACE. AccessDenied ACEs are ordered (and therefore processed) before AccessAllowed ACEs.

2. If access is denied, the system checks whether the original desired access mask contained only a ReadControl and WRITE_DAC. If so, the system checks whether the requester is the owner of the object. If so, then access is granted.

3. For an AccessDenied ACE, the actions in the ACE access mask are compared with the desired access mask. If any access is found in both masks, access is denied. Otherwise, processing continues with the next requested ACE.

4. For an AccessAllowed ACE, the actions in the ACE are compared with those listed in the desired access mask. If all accesses in the desired access mask are matched in the ACE, no further processing is necessary, and access is granted. Otherwise, processing continues with the next ACE.

5. If the contents of desired access mask are still not completely matched at the end of the ACL, access is implicitly denied.

Auditing Security Events

Windows NT includes auditing features you can use to collect information about how your system is being used. These features also allow you to monitor events related to system security, to identify any security breaches, and to determine the extent and location of any damage. The level of audited events is adjustable to suit the needs of your organization. Some organizations need little auditing information, while others are willing to trade some performance and disk space for detailed information they can use to analyze their system.

Note When you enable auditing, remember that there is a small performance overhead for each audit check the system performs.

Windows NT can track events related to the operating system itself and to individual applications. Each application can define its own auditable events. Definitions of these events are added to the Registry when the application is installed on your Windows NT computer.

Audit events are identified to the system by the event source-module name (which corresponds to a specific event type in the Registry) and an event ID.

The security log in Event Viewer can list events by category and by event ID. The following categories of events are listed in the security log. (Those in parentheses are found in the **Audit Policy** dialog box in User Manager.)

Table 2.4   Security Events that can be audited

Category	Meaning
Account Management (User and Group Management)	These events describe high-level changes to the user-accounts database, such as User Created or Group Membership Change. Potentially, a more detailed, object-level audit is also performed. (See the "Object Access" category, below).
Detailed Tracking (Process Tracking)	These events provide detailed subject-tracking information, such as program activation, handle duplication, and indirect object access.
Logon/Logoff (Logon and Logoff)	These events describe a single logon or logoff attempt, whether successful or unsuccessful. Included in each logon description is an indication of what type of logon (that is, interactive, network, or service)was requested or performed.
Object Access (File and Object Access)	These events describe both successful and unsuccessful accesses to protected objects.
Policy Change (Security Policy Changes)	These events describe high-level changes to the security policy database, such as assignment of privileges or logon capabilities. Potentially, a more detailed, object-level audit is also performed. (See the "Object Access" category, above).
Privilege Use (Use of User Rights)	These events describe both successful and unsuccessful attempts to use privileges. The category also includes information about when some special privileges are assigned. These special privileges are audited only at assignment time, not at the time of use.
System Event (System)	These events indicate something occurred that affects the security of the entire system or audit log.

For more information about auditing security events, see "Windows NT Security" in the *Microsoft Windows NT Workstation Resource Guide*, and "Monitoring Events" in the *Microsoft Windows NT Server 4.0 Concepts and Planning Guide*.

Windows NT Server Domains

A *domain* is a logical grouping of network servers and other computers that share common security and user-account information. Within domains, administrators create one user account for each user. Users then log on to the domain, not to individual servers in the domain.

The term *domain* does not refer to a single location or specific type of network configuration. Computers in a single domain can share physical proximity on a small LAN or can be located in different parts of the world. They communicate over any of various physical connections, such as dial-up lines, ISDN, fiber, Ethernet, token ring, frame relay, satellite, and leased lines.

The domain structure provides the following advantages for maintaining a secure network:

- Single Logon Procedure

  Network users can connect to multiple servers by logging on to a single network.

- Universal Resource Access

  The user needs only one domain user account and password to use network resources.

- Centralized Network Administration

  A centralized view of the entire network from any workstation on the network provides the ability to track and manage information on users, groups, and resources in a distributed network. This single point of administration for multiple servers simplifies the management of a Windows NT Server–based network.

For detailed information about domains, see "Managing Windows NT Server Domains" in the *Microsoft Windows NT Server 4.0 Concepts and Planning Guide*.

The Directory Database

The *directory database*, SAM, stores all security and user-account information for a domain. The master copy of the directory database is stored on the primary server and is regularly replicated to backup servers to maintain centralized security. When a user logs on to a domain, the Windows NT Server software checks the user name and password against the directory database.

Domain Controllers

Domain controllers are computers running Windows NT Server that use one shared directory to store security and user-account information for the entire domain; they comprise a single administrative unit. Within a domain, domain controllers manage all aspects of user/domain interactions. Windows NT domain controllers use the information in the directory database to authenticate users logging on to domain accounts. There are two types of domain controllers:

- The *primary domain controller* (PDC), which tracks changes made to domain accounts and stores the information in the directory database. A domain has one PDC.

- A *backup domain controller* (BDC), which maintains a copy of the directory database. This is periodically synchronized with the directory database on the PDC. A domain can have multiple BDCs.

For more information about domain controllers, see "Managing Windows NT Server Domains" the *Microsoft Windows NT Server 4.0 Concepts and Planning Guide*.

Member Servers

Computers running Windows NT Server can be configured as *member servers,* which do not store copies of the directory data base and therefore do not authenticate accounts or receive synchronized copies of the directory database. These servers are dedicated to specific tasks, such as print or file servers, or to high-volume applications, such as databases.

Trust Relationships

Windows NT Server directory services provide security across multiple domains through trust relationships. A trust relationship is a link that combines two domains into one administrative unit that can authorize access to resources on both domains.

There are two types of trust relationships:

- In a *one-way trust relationship*, one domain trusts the users in the other domain to use its resources. More precisely, one domain trusts the domain controllers in the other domain to validate user accounts to use its resources. The resources that become available are in the *trusting* domain, and the accounts that can use them are in the *trusted* domain. If user accounts located in the trusting domain need to use resources located in the trusted domain, that requires a two-way trust relationship.

- A *two-way trust relationship* is two one-way trusts: Each domain trusts user accounts in the other domain. Users can log on to their domain account from computers in either domain. Each domain can have its own accounts and resources. Global user accounts and global groups can be used from either domain to grant rights and permissions to resources in either domain.

Note   Using resources located on any domain, trusting or otherwise, is always subject to permissions associated with the resources.

Through File Manager, users from the trusted domain can be given rights and permissions to objects in the trusting domain, as if they were members of the trusting domain. Users in the trusted domain can browse resources in the trusting domain, subject to account privilege.

For example, suppose the London domain trusts the Topeka domain of a corporate network. User EmilyP, who is a member of the Topeka domain, wants to access Myfile.txt, which is a file located on a computer in the London domain running Windows NT Server. When EmilyP attempts to log on to the server in London, her user account information is not transferred to the London domain's user database. Because London trusts Topeka, the London domain has access to user information in the Topeka domain's user-account database.

Domain Security Policies

Windows NT Server and Windows NT Workstation settings can provide different levels of security for user actions on the domain or computer, respectively.

You can define three security policies that apply to the domain as a whole:

- The *Account policy* controls how user accounts use passwords.
- The *Audit policy* controls the types of events the security log records.
- The *Trust Relationships policy* controls which domains are trusted and which domains are trusting domains. A trust relationship requires two or more single domains. This policy is available in a single-domain model (in which only one domain exists) only if the domain administering the computer is a domain controller.

The *User Rights policy* controls access rights given to groups and user accounts. User rights are applied at the domain level, and affect overall domain security.

For more information about the account policy, the audit policy, and the trust relationships policy, see "Managing Windows NT Server Domains" and for more information about the user-rights security policy, see "Working With User and Group Accounts," in the *Microsoft Windows NT Server 4.0 Concepts and Planning Guide*

Computer Accounts and Secure Communications Channels

Each computer running Windows NT Workstation and Windows NT Server that participates in a domain has its own account in the directory database, called a *computer account*. A computer account is created when the computer is first identified to the domain (rather than to a workgroup) during network setup at installation or when the administrator uses Server Manager to define the computer account.

When a computer running Windows NT Workstation or Windows NT Server logs on to the network, the NetLogon service on the client computer creates a secure communications channel with the NetLogon service on the server. A *secure communications channel* exists when computers at each end of a connection are satisfied that the computer on the other end has correctly identified itself. Computers identify themselves using their computer accounts. When the secure communications channel has been established, a communications session can begin between the two computers.

To maintain security during the communications session, internal trust accounts are set up between the workstation and the server, between the primary and backup domain controllers, and between domain controllers in both domains of a trust relationship.

Computer accounts and the secure channels they provide enable administrators to remotely manage workstations and member servers. They also affect the relationships between a workstation and domain servers, and between primary and backup domain controllers.

The computer account is part of an implicit one-way trust relationship between the client computer and the controllers in its domain. Workstations request logon authentication for a user account from a domain server in the same way a server in a trusting domain requests validation from a server in a trusted domain. This trust relationship enables administrators to select a workstation or member server for administration in the same way they select a domain.

When the computer account is created, the Domain Admins global group is automatically added to the workstation or member server's Administrators local group. Domain administrators can then use Windows NT Server utilities to remotely manage the computer's user and group accounts, including adding global groups to the computer's local groups. Domain administrators can perform any functions on the computer itself that are allowed by the Administrators local group.

For Windows NT Server domain controllers, computer accounts link the BDCs with the PDCs and pair up trusting and trusted domains. Server trust accounts, created while setting up the secure communications channel, allow BDCs to copy the master directory database from the PDC. Interdomain trust accounts allow domain controllers in a trusted domain to pass through authentication of user accounts to the trusting domain.

Security in Mixed Operating System Environments

Windows NT Server has an open networking architecture that allows flexibility in communicating with other network products. Client computers running operating systems other than Windows NT Workstation or Windows NT Server can interact with computers in a Windows NT Server domain. However, they do not have domain computer accounts and, therefore, do not have Windows NT Workstation logon security. Users running other operating systems can have user accounts stored in the directory database, but the computer itself does not have logon security to restrict access to its own resources.

Computers running Windows NT Workstation or Windows NT Server can also interact with servers and clients running other operating systems. Various protocols and other software that allows interoperability are either included with Windows NT Server or are available separately.

Workgroup Clients

A *workgroup* is a collection of computers (not users) that form an administrative unit and do not belong to a domain. In a workgroup, each computer tracks its own user- and group-account information and—in contrast to domain controllers— does not share this information with other workgroup computers.

Workgroup members log on only to workstation accounts and can view directories of other workgroup members over the network.

Computers running Windows NT Workstation, Windows NT Server, Windows for Workgroups, or Windows 95 can be configured to participate in either a domain or a workgroup. When setting up one of these computers for networking, you specify a computer name and a workgroup name. If the workgroup name matches a domain name, the computer name appears in the browse list for that domain. The computer can browse computers running Windows NT Server and Windows NT Workstation that participate in either a domain or a workgroup. You can specify whether the computer will log on to a Windows NT Server domain or a workgroup when you set up Windows NT.

Windows 95 Clients

Access to Windows NT Server networking is built in to Windows 95. Users with domain accounts who run Windows 95 can log on to their accounts the same way users running Windows NT Workstation do. Windows 95 user-account logons can be validated by both Windows NT Server domain controllers and LAN Manager 2.x domain controllers.

MS-DOS Clients

MS-DOS client computers running one of the following components can use shared network resources on the respective servers:

- Microsoft Network Client for MS-DOS version 3.0 enables computers running MS-DOS to interact with domain controllers running Windows NT Server and with computers running Windows NT Workstation or LAN Manager 2.x servers.

- Microsoft LAN Manager for MS-DOS version 2.2 enables computers running MS-DOS to interact with LAN Manager 2.x servers and Windows NT Server domain controllers.

Because computers running MS-DOS cannot store user accounts, they don't participate in domains the way Windows NT computers do. Each computer running MS-DOS usually has a default domain for browsing. An MS-DOS user with a domain account can be set up to browse any domain, not merely the domain containing the user's account.

LAN Manager 2.x Servers and Clients

Windows NT Server interoperates with Microsoft LAN Manager 2.x systems. Computers running LAN Manager workstation software on MS-DOS, Windows 3.1, or OS/2 can connect to servers running Windows NT Server. LAN Manager 2.x servers (on computers running either OS/2 or UNIX) can also work with servers running Windows NT Server—even in the same domain.

Microsoft LAN Manager for OS/2 version 2.2 is a component of Windows NT Server that enables computers running OS/2 version 1.3x to interact with LAN Manager 2.x servers and computers running Windows NT Workstation and Windows NT Server. If an OS/2 version 1.3x system is running these components, it can share network resources with the respective servers.

Novell NetWare Clients

You can connect computers running Windows NT Server to NetWare file and print resources by using NWLink protocol software and Gateway Service for NetWare. You can also enable a gateway to share NetWare file and print resources with Microsoft networking clients without NetWare client software.

NetWare client computers can also connect to file and print resources and server applications on computers running Windows NT Server.

Macintosh Clients

Microsoft Windows NT Server Services for Macintosh is a component of Windows NT Server that enables Windows clients and Apple Macintosh clients to share files and printers. With Services for Macintosh, one computer running Windows NT Server can act as a server for both types of computer, and Macintosh computers can share resources with any client supported by Windows NT Server, including MS-DOS and LAN Manager client computers.

Logon and Authentication Processes

Before doing anything on a Windows NT system, a user must log on to the system by supplying a username and password. Windows NT uses the username for identification and password for validation. Different processes at several levels protect resources, but logon security protects overall access to a domain or computer. The logon process requires users to identify themselves to the domain or the computer. The user name and password that the user types in the **Logon Information** dialog box are checked against either the computer directory database (if the user is logging on to a user account defined on the computer) or the domain directory database (if the user is logging on to a domain user account).

Once authenticated, an account is available for use with all Windows NT Server network services and compatible server applications, such as the Microsoft BackOffice™ suite of server products. Through directory services, authentication enables a user logging on to a single Windows NT Server domain to use other applications, such as Microsoft SQL Server and Microsoft Exchange Server, and network services, such as Services for Macintosh.

The initial logon process for Windows NT is *interactive*, meaning that the user must type information at the keyboard in response to a dialog box that appears on the screen. Windows NT grants or denies access based upon the information the user provides.

The steps included in the interactive logon and validation process are:

1. The user presses CTRL+ALT+DEL.

2. When the user provides a username and a password, the logon process calls the LSA.

3. The LSA runs the appropriate authentication package.

4. The authentication package checks the user-accounts database to see if the account is local. If it is, the username and password are verified against those held in the user accounts database. If not, the requested logon is forwarded to an alternate authentication package.

5. When the account is validated, SAM (which owns the user-accounts database) returns the user's security ID and the security IDs of any global groups to which the user belongs.

6. The authentication package creates a logon session and then passes the logon session and the security IDs associated with the user to LSA.

7. If the logon is rejected, the logon session is deleted, and an error is returned to the logon process.

   If the logon is not rejected, an access token, containing the user's security ID and the security IDs of Everyone and other groups, is created. It also contains the user rights (described in the next section) assigned to the collected security IDs. This access token is returned to the logon process with a Success status.

8. The logon session calls the Win32 subsystem to create a process and attach the access token to the process, thus creating a *subject* for the user account. (Subjects are described in the section called "Subjects and Impersonation," earlier in this chapter.)

9. For an interactive Windows NT session, the Win32 subsystem starts the desktop for the user.

After the validation process, a user's shell process (that is, the process in which the desktop is started for the user) is given an access token. The information in this access token is reflected by anything the user does or any process that runs on the user's behalf.

Note Windows NT has the ability to support multiple authentication packages that are implemented as DLLs. This flexibility allows third-party software vendors the opportunity to integrate custom authentication packages with Windows NT. For example, a network vendor might augment the standard Windows NT authentication package by adding one that allows users to log on simultaneously to Windows NT and to the vendor's network.

Interactive and Remote Logon

Two logon processes can start logon authentication:

- Interactive Logon
- Remote Logon

Interactive Logon Authentication

Interactive logon occurs when the user types information in the **Logon Information** dialog box displayed by the computer's operating system. In **Domain**, the user selects either the name of a domain or the name of the computer being used for logon, depending on where the user account being logged on to is defined. If the computer is a member of a workgroup and not of a domain, the **Logon Information** dialog box does not have a place for typing in the domain name.

The following table compares the logon options for a user on a computer running Windows NT in a workgroup, in a domain, and in a domain with a trust relationship. The unique identifier used by Windows NT after logon depends on the location of the database used to log on the user. The third column in this table describes the unique identifier used in each case. Any network connection requests sent elsewhere on the network include this unique identifier.

Table 2.5   Summary of Interactive Logon Authentication

Computer is in	User can logon at	Unique identifier
Workgroup	Local database	Computername and username
Domain	Local database Domain database	Computername and username Domain name and username
Domain with a trust relationship	Local database Home domain database Trusted domain database	Computername and username Domain name and username Trusted-domain name and username
Domain without a trust relationship	Local database	Computername and username Untrusting-domain name and username

Remote Logon Authentication

Remote logon takes place when a user is already logged on to a user account and makes a network connection to another computer. For example, the user connects to another computer using the **Map Network Drive** dialog box or the **net use** command.

A security-access token created at interactive logon is assigned to the initial process created for the user. When the user tries to access a resource on another computer, the remote server authenticates the user again and creates a security-access token for the user. The security-access token is placed in a table stored on the remote server. The server creates a user identifier (UID) for the user and maps it to the user's security-access token. This UID is sent back to the client redirector and is used in all further server-message-block (SMB) communication between the server and client. Subsequently, whenever a request for any resource on that server (and not just in the same share)comes in from the client, the UID identifies the user to the server process. The server checks the table and uses the security-access token stored for the UID.

For example, if a user attempts to connect to \\Myserver\share, a table entry on \\Myserver is set up with the user's SID. This is mapped to the user's access token. Later, if the user attempts to access a share called \art on \\Myserver, the original table entry will be used. The server examines the user's SID, locates an existing table entry, and validates (or denies) access to the files by comparing the access-token information to the access rights of the user. The attempt is successful in this example because the user had already established read access with the connection to \\Myserver\share.

If the user attempts to update information on \\Myserver\art and does not have write access to the share, access is denied. Even if the user is added to a group with write permissions, access will be denied because the one table entry still contains static information about the user's SID. The user must log off and log on again to create a new table entry. Then, the user will be able take advantage of the group's write permissions.

The server process creates a SID for the user and maps it to the user's security-access token. This SID is sent back to the client redirector and is used in all further server message block (SMB) communication between the server and client. Whenever a resource request comes in from the client, the SID identifies the user to the server process. The security-access token that maps to the user ID identifies the user to the remote security subsystem.

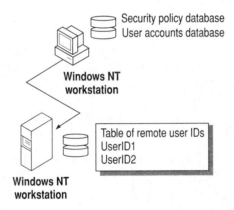

Figure 2.2   Remote logon authentication

The steps in a successful remote logon at a computer running Windows NT Workstation or Windows NT Server are:

1. The client computer sends the username, password, and domain name (the data entered in the **Begin Logon** dialog box) of the user to the remote Windows NT server.

2. The authenticating server compares the logon username and password with information in the user-accounts database.

3. If access is authorized, the server's LSA constructs an access token and passes it to the server process, which creates a user ID that refers to the access token.

4. The user ID is then returned to the client computer for use in all subsequent requests to the server.

After the session has been created, the client computer sends requests marked with the user ID it received during session setup. The server matches the user ID with the access token in an internal table. This access token at the server is used for access authentication.

The steps in a successful, remote logon at a Workgroup computer connecting to a computer running Windows NT in a domain are:

1. The local directory database performs interactive logon for the user at the workgroup computer (the client).

2. The client's username and a function of the password are passed to the specific server in the domain to which the client is trying to connect. This server checks the username and password with information in its local directory database. If there is a match, access to this server is allowed.

The steps in a successful remote logon at a domain computer connecting to a computer running Windows NT in the same domain are:

1. The domain's directory database performs interactive logon for the user at the client computer.

2. The client's domain name, username, and a function of the password are passed to the computer being accessed, which passes them to a computer running Windows NT Server in the domain.

3. The computer running Windows NT Server verifies that the domain name for the client matches this domain.

4. The computer running Windows NT Server checks the username and password against the domain's directory database. If there is a match, access is allowed.

The steps in a successful remote logon at a domain client in a trusted domain connecting to a Windows NT computer are:

1. The domain's directory database performs interactive logon for the user at the client computer.

2. The client's domain name, user name, and a function of the password are passed to the computer being accessed. That computer passes the logon information to a Windows NT Server in the domain.

3. The computer running Windows NT Server verifies that the client's domain is a trusted domain and then passes the client's identification information to a computer running Windows NT Server in the trusted domain.

4. A computer running Windows NT Server in the trusted domain (that is, in the same domain as the client computer) checks the user name and password against the domain's directory database. If there is a match, access is allowed.

The NetLogon Service

The NetLogon service provides users with a single access point to a domain's PDC and all BDCs.

The NetLogon service also synchronizes changes to the directory database stored on the PDC to all domain controllers. The size of the directory database is limited only by the number of registry entries permitted and by the performance limits of the computer.

The Windows NT Server NetLogon service automatically synchronizes the directory database. Based on settings in the registry, the PDC sends timed notices, which signal the BDCs to request directory changes from the PDC. The notices are staggered so that not all BDCs request changes at the same time. When a BDC requests changes, it informs the PDC of the last change it received, so the PDC is always aware of which BDC needs changes. If a BDC is up-to-date, the Net Logon service on the BDC does not request changes.

The Change Log

Changes to the directory database consist of any new or changed passwords, new or changed user and group accounts, and any changes in the associated group memberships and user rights.

Changes to the domain-directory database are recorded in the change log. The size of the change log determines how long changes can be held. The default NetLogon-service setting for updates is every five minutes, and the change log holds about 2,000 changes. As a new change is added, the oldest change is deleted. When a BDC requests changes, the changes that occurred since the last synchronization are copied to the BDC.

The change log keeps only the most recent changes. If a BDC does not request changes in a timely way, the entire domain directory database must be copied to that BDC. For example, if a BDC is offline for a time, more changes could occur during that time than can be stored in the change log.

Partial and Full Synchronization

Partial synchronization is the automatic, timed replication to all domain BDCs of directory database changes that have occurred since the previous synchronization.

Full synchronization is copying the entire directory database to a BDC. Full synchronization is automatically performed when changes have been deleted from the change log before replication takes place or when a new BDC is added to a domain.

The default NetLogon-service setting for update timing (every five minutes) and the size of the change log (about 2000 changes) ensure that full synchronization will not be required under most operating conditions.

The NetLogon service accepts logon requests from any client and provides complete authentication information from the directory database.

The NetLogon service runs on any Windows NT computer that is a member of a domain and requires the Workstation service. It also requires the Access This Computer from Network right, which is set in User Manager on computers running Windows NT Workstation, or in User Manager for Domains on domain controllers. A domain controller also requires that the Server service be running.

User Authentication

On a computer running Windows NT Workstation or a computer that is not a domain controller running Windows NT Server, the NetLogon service processes logon requests for the local computer and passes through logon requests to a domain controller.

The NetLogon service processes authenticates a logon request in three steps:

1. Discovery.
2. Secure channel setup.
3. Pass-through authentication (where necessary).

Discovery

When the computer starts up, it must determine the location of a domain controller within the domain and in each trusted domain. (There is an implicit trust between the workstation and domain controllers in the workstation's own domain.)

Locating the domain controller is called *discovery*. If the computer is part of a workgroup, rather than of a domain, the NetLogon service terminates. (If the workstation is not connected to a network, Windows NT treats it like a member of a workgroup consisting of one member.) Once a domain controller is discovered, it is used for subsequent user-account authentication.

When a domain controller starts up, the NetLogon service attempts discovery with all trusted domains. Discovery is not necessary on the domain controller's own domain, because it has access to its own directory database. Each domain is called three times in intervals of five seconds before discovery fails. If a trusted domain does not respond to a discovery attempt, the domain controller attempts another discovery every 15 minutes until it locates a domain controller on the trusted domain.

If the domain controller receives another request for authorization before discovery is successfully completed, it immediately attempts another discovery, no matter when discovery was last attempted.

Secure Communication Channel

The Net Logon services from each computer issue challenges to and receive challenges from every other computer, to verify the existence of their valid computer accounts. When verification is complete, a communication session is set up between the computers and used to pass user-identification data.

The NetLogon service maintains security on these communication channels by using user-level security to create the channel. The following special internal-user accounts are created:

- *Workstation trust accounts,* which allow a domain workstation to perform pass-through authentication for a computer running Windows NT Server in the domain, as described later in this chapter.
- *Server trust accounts,* which allow computers running Windows NT Server to get copies of the master-domain database from the domain controller.
- *Interdomain trust accounts,* which allow a computer running Windows NT Server to perform pass-through authentication to another domain.

The NetLogon service attempts to set up a secure channel when it is started and discovery is complete. If it fails, NetLogon retries every 15 minutes or whenever an action requiring pass-through authentication occurs. To reduce network overhead for trusted domains, the NetLogon service on a domain controller creates a secure channel only when it is needed.

The first time a user logs on to a domain account from a given workstation, a domain controller downloads validated logon information (from the domain directory database) to the workstation. This information is cached on the workstation. If a domain controller is not available on subsequent logons, the user can log on to the domain account using the cached logon information.

Computers running Windows NT Workstation and Windows NT Server store the information authenticating the last several (the default number is ten) users who logged on interactively. The credentials for users who log on to the local computer are also stored in that computer's local directory database.

Pass-through Authentication

Pass-through authentication occurs in the following cases:

- Case 1: An interactive logon in which a user logs on to a computer running Windows NT Workstation or to a computer running Windows NT Server as a member server, and the name in **Domain** in the **Logon Information** dialog box is not the computer name.

- Case 2: An interactive logon in which the computer being logged onto is a domain controller but the name in **Domain** is not the domain to which the controller belongs.

- Case 3: A remote logon (connecting to a computer over the network).

Note If the logon computer is not running Windows NT Workstation or Windows NT Server, domain controller authentication has no effect on the user's ability to use resources on the logon computer.

In case 1, the logon computer sends the logon request to a domain controller in the domain to which the computer account belongs. The controller first checks the domain name. If the domain names matches the controller's domain, the controller authenticates the logon credentials against its directory database and passes the account-identification information back to the logon computer, allowing the user to connect to resources on both the logon computer and the domain.

If the domain does not match the controller's domain, the controller checks whether the domain is a trusted domain. If it is, the domain controller passes the logon request through to a domain controller in the trusted domain. That domain controller authenticates the username and password against the domain directory database and passes the account-identification information back to the initial domain controller, which sends it back to the logon computer.

If the logon credentials supplied match the account-identification information, logon succeeds. If not, logon fails.

In case 2, the controller checks the domain name to see if it is a trusted domain. (The domain controller does not check for computer name because its directory database contains only domain accounts). If the domain is a trusted domain, the controller passes the logon information to a domain controller in the trusted domain for authentication. If the trusted domain controller authenticates the account, the logon information is passed back to the initial domain controller, and the user is logged on. If the account is not authenticated (is not defined in the trusted domain directory database), the logon fails.

If, in case 3, the user is logged on to a computer or domain account and then tries to make a network connection to another computer, pass-through authentication proceeds as in interactive logons. The credentials used at interactive logon are also used for pass-through authentication unless the user overrides those credentials by typing a different domain or computer name and user name in a dialog that appears under the following circumstances:

- When the user types an entry in **Connect As** in the **Map Network Drive** dialog box.

- When the user clicks **Start**, clicks **Run,** and types the UNC path at the prompt, using the syntax \\Servername\sharename.

The figure below illustrates pass-through authentication. In this example, AnnM wants to access a computer in the London domain. Because the London domain trusts AnnM's home domain, Topeka, it asks the Topeka domain to authenticate AnnM's account information.

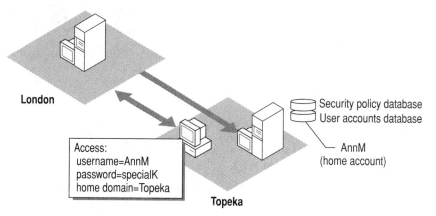

Figure 2.3   Pass-through authentication

If the user tries to make a network connection to a remote computer in an untrusted domain, the logon proceeds as if the user were connecting to an account on the remote computer. That computer authenticates the logon credentials against its directory database. If the account is not defined in the directory database but the Guest account on the remote computer is enabled, and if the Guest account has no password set, the user will be logged on with guest privileges. If the Guest account is not enabled, the logon fails.

For information about the Guest account, see the *Microsoft Windows NT Server 4.0 Concepts and Planning Guide*, Chapter 2, "Managing User and Group Accounts."

If the computer being connected to is a BDC in the domain in which the user account is defined, but the BDC fails to authenticate the user's password, the BDC passes through the logon request to the PDC in the same domain. For example, this happens if authentication is attempted after the password changes but before the BDC synchronizes with the PDC.

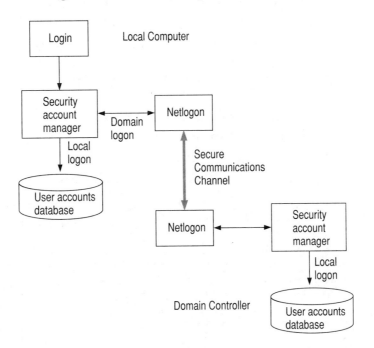

Figure 2.4   Passthrough authentication in Windows NT

Interdomain Trust Accounts

When one domain is permitted to trust another, User Manager for Domains creates an interdomain trust account in the directory database of the trusted domain. A trusted-domain object is created in the LSA of the trusting domain, and a secret object is created in the LSA of the trusting domain. This account is like any other global user account, except that the USER_INTERDOMAIN_TRUST_ACCOUNT bit in the control field for the account is set. The interdomain trust account is used only by the primary domain controller and is invisible in User Manager for Domains. The password is randomly generated and is maintained by User Manager for Domains.

When this trust relationship is established, the NetLogon service on the trusting domain attempts discovery on the trusted domain, and the interdomain trust account is authenticated by a domain controller on the trusted domain.

Similar accounts and procedures are used in the trust relationships between a PDC and a BDC, and between a domain controller running Windows NT and a computer running Windows NT Workstation in that domain.

In the following example, the trusted domain is referred to as *Master* and the trusting domain is referred to as *Resource*. The Master contains the user account information; the Resource trusts the Master to validate user access to its resources.

On each domain controller in RESOURCE, an LSA trusted-domain object represents the trust. This object contains the name of the trusted domain and the domain SID. The LSA trusted-domain object is replicated from the trusting domain PDC to each of the BDCs in the trusting domain.

On each domain controller in RESOURCE, a password is stored in an LSA secret object G$$<TrustedDomainName>, such as G$$MASTER. This object is stored in the registry key

HKEY_LOCAL_MACHINE\Security\Policy\Secrets

The LSA secret object for the trusted-domain trust relationship is replicated from the PDC in the trusting-domain to each of the trusting-domain BDCs.

On each domain controller in MASTER, the password is stored in the directory database user account marked as INTERDOMAIN_TRUST_ACCOUNT, such as RESOURCE$. This can be viewed in the registry path **\SAM\SAM\Domains\Account\Users\Names**

(HKEY_LOCAL_MACHINE subtree)

This account is replicated from the trusted-domain PDC to each of the trusted-domain BDCs.

These accounts are created when a trust is established. The administrator of the trusted domain, MASTER, permits RESOURCE to trust the MASTER accounts. When the domain is added in User Manager to the **Trust Relationships** dialog box, a hidden user account is created in the directory database for use by the trusting domain. The account contains the specified password, such as RESOURCE$.

For details on how to set up a trust relationship see "Managing Windows NT Server Domains" in Microsoft Windows NT Server 4.0 *Concepts and Planning* and online Help.

The administrator of the trusting domain establishes the trust. The administrator provides the password specified earlier, and User Manager creates the LSA secret object. The server in RESOURCE attempts to setup a session with the domain controller in MASTER, using the password RESOURCE$. The domain controller in MASTER responds with the error "0xc0000198, Status_Nologon_Interdomain_Trust_Account" because the special Interdomain Trust Account cannot be used in a normal session logon, and the session fails.

This error informs the domain controller in the RESOURCE domain that the trust account exists and a trust is possible. Upon receiving that response, it establishes a null session and then uses remote-procedure-call (RPC) transactions to call the remote APIs that establish the trusted domain relationship. A secure channel is set up later by the NetLogon service, using the trust information that was stored by the User Manager.

After the trust is established, the RESOURCE PDC changes the password for the trusted-domain object. All domain controllers in each domain receive the trust account objects through normal domain synchronization of the directory and the LSA databases. The domain controllers in RESOURCE receive the LSA secret object during the update of the LSA database, and the domain controllers in MASTER receive the account in the directory-database update. With these objects, any domain controller in the trusting domain can set up a secure channel to any domain controller in the trusted domain.

Maintenance of these accounts includes periodic password changes. Every seven days, the PDC of the trusting domain automatically changes the password of the trusted domain object by the following steps.

1. Setting the OldPassword field of the LSA secret object to the previous NewPassword field.

2. Selecting a new password.

3. Setting the NewPassword field in the LSA secret object to the selected password.

   This ensures that the domain controllers can always access a valid password in the event of a crash.

4. Sending an I_NetServerPasswordSet RPC call to a domain controller of the trusted domain, asking it to set the password in the directory-database-user trust account to the value of the NewPassword field in the LSA secret object of the trusting domain. The trusting PDC sends the RPC call to the trusted domain controller with which it established the secure channel. That domain controller passes the request through to the trusted PDC.

The password is now changed on both PDCs. Normal replication distributes the objects to the BDCs.

A domain controller of the trusted domain (MASTER) never initiates the password change. It is always initiated by the trusting domain PDC. Initiating the password change requires that the secure channel has been set up.

It is possible, but not likely, that the trusting domain controller will change the password without updating a domain controller in the trusted domain. For example, this might happen if the trusted domain controller failed during the process and did not received the updated password. As a safeguard, both the old and new passwords are kept in the LSA secret object on the trusting side. The PDC in the trusting domain never changes the new password unless it has successfully set up a secure channel using the current new password. If the secure-channel setup fails because the new password is invalid, the trusting PDC tries the old password. If a secure channel is established using the old password, it immediately (within 15 minutes) continues the password change algorithm with step 4 (above).

Planning Your Domain Design

The three domain models, single domain, single master domain, and multiple master domain, make use of trust relationships. The trust relationships provides flexibility. For detailed information about the three domain models, see "Managing Windows NT Server Domains" in the *Microsoft Windows NT Server 4.0 Concepts and Planning Guide*.

The domain model you select should match the way you want to manage your organization. The number of users in the organization, the topology, and the location will also influence how domains will be designed, implemented, and where the resources will be located. Because there are few limits imposed by Windows NT software, other aspects of the computing environment must be considered to provide guidelines for the decisions you make about your domain model.

The following assumptions are made:

- Unlike the Windows NT Server software, server hardware imposes limits on the number of users or sessions it can support.

  Unless otherwise noted, it is assumed that the Windows NT Server to be used as the PDC is a 486/33 machine (or higher) with 32 MB of physical RAM and a 1 GB hard disk. Test conditions at Microsoft included base Windows NT Server services, moderate file and print activity, Remote Access Service, SNA Server, and SQL Server.

- Real-life limits of the Windows NT Server system often go beyond the capacity of the server.

- The process of design and selection is recursive.

  Decisions made earlier in the process must be verified in light of information available later in the process. Therefore, you should anticipate making several passes through the process until all decisions at all steps match the available information.

There are many ways to implement your domain model. The following examples illustrate some of the flexibility of domains. These examples are followed by a list of business and equipment considerations that can affect your domain design.

Multiple Independent Lines of Business

Corporation with independent lines of business, such as a consulting division, a real estate division, and a retail sales division, may have separate marketing, sales, and data-processing groups within each of those divisions. At the center of the firm is a small group focused on functional services, such as accounting, finance, and human resources. Usually, users in a division need to access only the resources in their own division. There are times when an employee needs access to resources in another division, which requires that the master domains connect to each other.

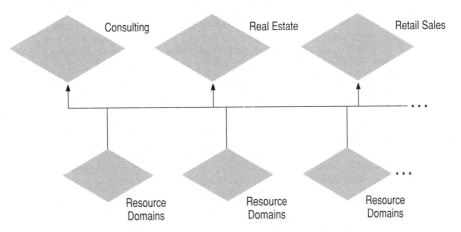

Figure 2.5   Multiple Independent Lines of Business domain model

A multiple master-domain model is the best choice for this case because the organization lacks a data-processing staff in its central division. The domain model can be constructed to acknowledge the data-processing autonomy of divisions as they exist. Trust relationships can be created between the master domains, as necessary.

A Large Organization

A large firm (approximately 100,000 employees) may have multiple locations. By using master domains, the number of users per master domain can be as high as 40,000 because the machine accounts are kept in the resource domains. The company can create three master domains of approximately 33, 000 users each or, to accommodate growth of the user base, four master domains of approximately 25,000 users each.

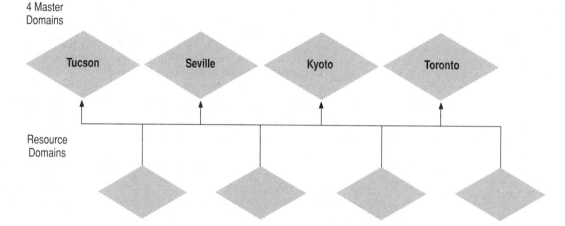

Figure 2.6   Large Organization domain model

The domain in which a user is defined can be based on any grouping or sequencing, such as alphabetical, divisional, departmental, or by location. Which domain is used in defining a particular user is unimportant because a trust relationship exists between each resource domain and each master domain.

Branch Offices

In a branch office, a single domain or single-master domain can usually be used. Companies with many small branch offices can group branch offices together into regional domains that will provide administration for the branches.

When the branch office is linked to the PDC by means of a communications link or modem, a BDC would be the on-site server. The BDC handles local authentication and local file and print services. A second BDC can be added for fault tolerance.

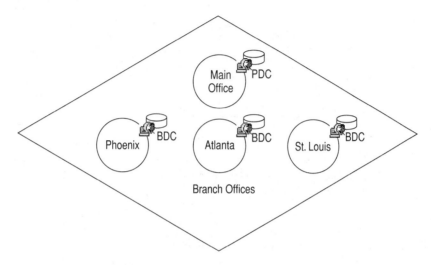

Figure 2.7   Branch Offices domain model

Secure Domains

In the multiple master-domain model, all master domains are linked to each other by trust relationships. Users in all domains can then access resources in any domain. However, some records should not be available for all employees to access, such as confidential financial records and personnel files. The solution is to create domains that are exclusively for the departments with confidential records, such as Finance and Human Resources. Those domains are trusted by the master MIS domain, but they do not trust other domains. Finance and HR users can then access MIS resources, but their own resources remain secure.

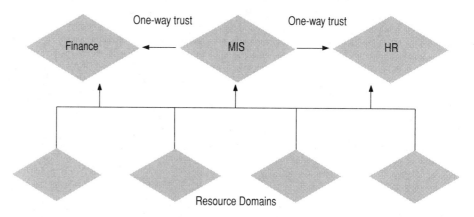

Figure 2.8   Secure domain model

Management and Administration Considerations

Windows NT enables you to manage user accounts either centrally or decentrally. With centralized management, there is usually one directory database and, therefore, one master domain, in which all user-account information is stored. Users are defined on the network only once and are given access permissions to resources based on their logon identity in the central user database. The single-domain model and single master-domain models are centrally managed. A multiple master-domain model can also be centrally managed by adding designated administrators to appropriate Admin groups.

With decentralized management, more than one directory database contains information about different user accounts in the organization. You can create trust relationships to enable domains to access resources in other domains. The multiple master-domain model and the single-domain models can use decentralized management.

In planning your domain model, you'll need to establish administrative policies and procedures for how you will:

- Manage and monitor domains and accounts.
- Manage and monitor resources.
- Establish addressing and naming conventions.

Location Considerations

The two most important location considerations are where to locate the BDCs that will act as account logon servers and how to plan account-synchronization traffic across wide area network (WAN) links. If your WAN speed or bandwidth is low, you will want users to log on at a local BDC.

The next consideration is whether your networked organization is in one site or in several sites, connected by WAN links. A *site* is a well-connected LAN and may communicate by fast links, such as bridges and routers, but not by asynchronous WAN links, such as T1, 56K, or ISDN. Sites generally correspond to physical locations, such as Seattle, Paris, and New York.

The physical distribution of BDCs is determined by several factors: line speed, link reliability, administrative access, protocol, user-authentication requirements, the number of users to be supported at a site, and locally available resources.

The diagram below shows part of a network topology that one of these domains services. The networked hub sites in London, Paris, and Warsaw, which all belong to a European domain.

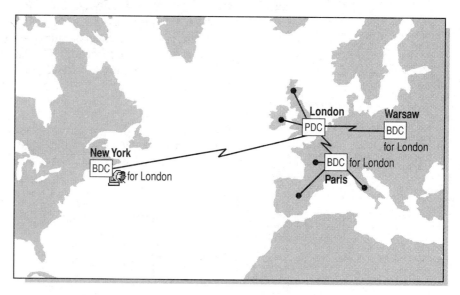

Figure 2.9   Locating domain controllers

The European PDC is in London, which is the network's main hub to Europe. The European PDC replicates to the BDCs at each site, including New York.

Synchronization over WAN and Remote Area Service

Consideration should be given to the amount of traffic that account synchronization places on WAN or Remote Access Service (RAS) dial-up lines. Avoid full synchronizations across WAN links. Full synchronizations are required when first setting up a new PDC or bringing a new location online. Full synchronizations are also initiated when more than 2,000 changes happen to users or groups within a short time (less than one hour). If you anticipate high change activity, you can increase the value for the size of the change log. If the above conditions do not exist, the synchronization process will include only the changes made in the directory database since the last time synchronization occurred.

BDC Over a RAS Link

A BDC can be connected to a remote domain using Windows NT, a modem, and the Windows NT Server RAS.

Using a RAS-connected BDC as a PDC

If a RAS-connected BDC is expected to be promoted to PDC at some time when it is remotely connected to the domain, this BDC should be set up as a dial-up networking client (RAS is not running on this computer). If you promote the dial-up networking client, NetLogon stops, changes roles, and restarts. RAS depends on NetLogon, so when NetLogon stops, you would lose your connection. By having the RAS client dial-out services on this remote BDC, it can function as a PDC because that functionality does not depend on NetLogon running constantly. If neither the RAS server (which could also be a BDC) nor the RAS-connected BDC are ever expected to serve as PDC, this is not an issue. A RAS-connected BDC that has been promoted to PDC will function as it should, but may respond more slowly, depending on line speed.

Partial Synchronization with a RAS-connected BDC

The default value for ChangeLogSize should be increased if either of the following conditions exist:

- A remote site has a RAS-connected BDC that dials in nightly to do a partial synchronization of any changes.
- Daily changes to the SAM/LSA database sometimes exceed 2,000.

Changing the default log size may also be necessary if many changes occur while a BDC is off-line. Otherwise, that BDC may be forced to do a full synchronization of the database.

If few changes occur during the time a BDC is not connected to the PDC, then the default size is sufficient. If an administrator notices a BDC doing full synchronizations, then it is probably a good idea to increase the ChangeLogSize. The default value for ChangeLogSize is 64K, which handles approximately 2,000 changes.

Calculating Replication Times

Managing the amount of network traffic so that response time remains acceptable is an important part of administration. When the PDC is located across a WAN or modem link, you can estimate the amount of traffic and time needed to replicate directory database changes to and from the PDC and then schedule this traffic to meet the needs of the site. The following chart helps you calculate the time needed for replication:

	Factors	
Password changes per month	Number of user accounts	A
	Passwords expire in how many (calendar) days	B
	Divide **B** by 30	C
	User account changes **A** + **C**	D
Additional changes per month	If number not knows, use 5% of **D**	E
	New user accounts	F
	Group changes * 4	G
	New machine accounts * 5	H
Amount of data to be replicated per month	**D** + **E** + **F** + **G** + **H**	I
Total monthly replication time	Compute throughput; modern/line speed in bps, If in KB, multiply by 1024 (i.e. 56KB = 57344 bps)	J1
	J1 * 8 bits/bytes =	J2
	J2 * 60 sec./min. =	J3
	J3 * 60 min./hour = total throughput	J
	I/J = total replication time (hours/month)	K

Figure 2.10   Job Aid to Calculate Monthly Replication Time

Security Considerations and C2 Security Rating

The National Computer Security Center (NCSC) was formed to help businesses and home users protect proprietary and personal data. The first goal of the NCSC was to create a document containing the technical standards and criteria to be used in evaluating computer systems. The NCSC also established a process by which software venders such as Microsoft could submit their security-related products for evaluation.

NCSC Security ratings range from "A" to "D," in which "A" represents the highest security. The "C" rating is generally applied to business software. Each rating is further divided into classes. For example, in the "C" division, software may be rated either "C2" or "C1," with "C2" representing the higher security. The most important feature requirements for operating systems rated "C2" focus on the following features.

- Discretionary access and control
- Identification and authentication
- Auditing
- Object reuse

An operating system must be able to define and control its users' access to objects (such as files and directories), provide a way for users to uniquely identify themselves, provide a way to audit security-related events and actions of individual users, and protect one process from accessing the data for another process.

For discretionary access and control, Windows NT enables an administrator or user to determine who can access files and how those files will be accessed. Other uses of Windows NT can be controlled, such as access to printers and network-server sharepoints.

Identification and authentication in Windows NT is achieved through the logon Secure Attention Sequence. All users must log on to start Windows NT. When a Windows NT users type their usernames and passwords to log on locally, they must first press CONTROL+ALT+DELETE to verify that no Trojan Horse programs are present. (A *Trojan Horse* is a program that can capture a user's logon information, thereby providing network access.) Because each user has a unique user name, domain name, and password combination, Windows NT can assure a user's unique identity.

Using Windows NT, a system administrator can audit all security events and user actions. The User Manager enables an administrator to specify which events (such as logon or file access) will be monitored. All audited information is stored in the Event Log, which can be viewed in Event Viewer.

One of the important issues in software security is object reuse. In a secure operating system, such as Windows NT, all allocation and deallocation of objects (such as files, directories, and memory) must be protected. Only users with proper access permissions should be allowed access. In Windows NT, this is achieved through a robust object manager that either initializes or zeros out objects before presenting them to a user.

The process of software evaluation is comprehensive. The NCSC evaluation is based on a series of standards published in the "Orange Book." Additional documents cover the evaluation process and are collectively referred to as the "Rainbow Series."

Microsoft Windows NT C2 Evaluation

The evaluation process begins when a software vendor presents a proposal to the NCSC, requesting the evaluation process. If approved, the software vendor must demonstrate to the NCSC that the product design and supporting documentation are complete. If satisfied, a team of NCSC evaluators are assigned to evaluate the new product. The most time-consuming part of the process is the evaluation itself. As part of the evaluation, the NCSC evaluators look at each aspect of the system to confirm that security has been properly implemented and to assess that security-testing of the system is complete. Once satisfied, the software is presented to the NCSC Technical Review Board for final approval. If approved, an entry is placed on the Evaluated Products List, indicating the success. The NCSC evaluation team releases a Final Evaluation Report, which covers all evaluated aspects of the software.

Microsoft began the process of the Windows NT Platform evaluation in 1991. In July 1995, Microsoft met its first milestone: a C2 Orange Book listing of the base operating system of the Windows NT Platform version 3.5 (with Service Pack 3).

The Windows NT operating system also received NCSC recognition for two B-level features: B2 Trusted Path and B2 Trusted Facility Management.

- The Trusted Path functionality prevents Trojan-horse programs from intercepting username and password information during initial logging on.
- The Trusted Facility Management functionality Windows NT supports separate account roles for operator and administrator functions.

  For example, Windows NT provides separate administrative roles for Administrators, users tasked with backups, users tasked with administrating printers, privileged Power Users, and Users.

Microsoft is currently involved in evaluating the Windows NT Platform version 4.0 to obtain the rating of C2 in a homogeneous networked environment. The NCSC publication "Trusted Network Interpretation," also called the "Red Book," serves as an interpretation of the Orange Book, as it applies to networking for this evaluation.

The typical NCSC security-evaluation cycle takes longer than the product release cycle of Windows NT. No significant changes have been made to the Windows NT security model from version 3.5 to versions 3.51 and 4.0.

The United Kingdom and Germany have an evaluation process similar to the one in the United States. This is the Information Technology Security Evaluation Criteria (ITSEC). In 1996, the Windows NT version 3.51 platform (in a homogeneous network environment) will complete its first ITSEC evaluation. Windows NT version 3.51 is seeking a C2 rating with an assurance rating of E3. In an ITSEC evaluation, the assurance rating given to a product indicates the level of analysis and supporting documentation used in developing the product. The greater the assurance rating, the higher the assurance. An E3 rating is typically mapped to the level of analysis performed in a "B" level evaluation.

In the Windows NT Final Evaluation Report, the NCSC security evaluators wrote, "One of the major initial design goals for Windows NT was to assure C2-level security through an integral, uniform protection mechanism. All system resources are treated as objects, and thus a single security 'gate' can be the protection component that all users must pass through to acquire system resources.

"This results in much greater assurance that the system meets the applicable security criteria, because a single security mechanism is easier to understand and to verify then multiple *ad hoc* mechanisms. When security is not an absolute requirement of the initial design, it is virtually impossible through later add-ons to provide the kind of uniform treatment to diverse system resources that Windows NT provides."

For more information on the security design of Windows NT, see Microsoft Windows NT 3.5 *Guidelines for Security, Audit, and Control,* published by Microsoft Press, and the Microsoft Web Server.

Domain-naming Conventions

When planning your domain, consideration needs to be given to the names of the domains. Once implemented, it is recommended that domain names not change. Changing domain names requires the reinstallation of every server that belongs to the renamed domain. For clarity, use domain names that reflect of the general business areas they serve.

Group-naming and Assignment Conventions

A corporation could create a global group for every resource domain. That group could include all those who use that domain as their primary resource base. Other global groups could be created for all departments or locations, and the members of each department could automatically be made members of their department groups. The group name should reflect the domain and the department For example, a Microsoft department in England might be named Mic-UK. Other groups may be created for job categories, such as Mic-UK-Managers.

Username Conventions

Ideally, one user ID and password would allow access to all of a user's resources. Microsoft Client Services for NetWare passes Windows NT usernames and passwords to NetWare. To take advantage of this, set up a user account on NetWare with the same account name and password as in Windows NT. Banyan VINES systems can also be configured in this way by setting the VINES username and password to match the ones in Windows NT and NetWare. Upon logging on, the user will also be logged on to VINES.

For details about configuring for Banyan VINES on a Windows NT network, see Chapter 5, "Network Services: Enterprise Level."

If the user's password cannot be sent to other systems, the next best thing is to have a consistent full-name property within each company organization.

Tools and Checklists for Domain Planning

For ease of administration, the preferred domain model is the single-domain model. If the single-domain model can not be used, the second choice should be the single master-domain model. If neither of these is acceptable, an administrator can use trust relationships to centralize all user administration into a single domain, eliminating the need to administer each domain separately.

The following sections contain tools and checklists to help you choose the proper domain model for your organization.

Domain Selection Matrix

It is useful to view the characteristics of the domain models side by side, to match the characteristics and benefits of each implementation model to the needs of your organization. If the needs of your organization change, you can review this matrix to determine the optimal implementation model.

If you have already established an implementation model, it is a good idea to review the following chart to see the benefits or trade-offs of other domain models.

Table 2.6   Domain Selection Matrix

Domain Attribute	Single Domain	Single Master Domain	Multiple Master Domain	Independent Single Domains with Trust relationships
Fewer than 40,000 users per domain	X	X	X	
More than 40,000 users per domain			X	
Centralized account management	X	X		
Centralized resource management	X		X	X
Decentralized account management			X	X
Decentralized resource management		X	X	
Central MIS	X	X		
No central MIS				X

*User account numbers are approximate. The exact SAM file size is dependent on the number of user accounts, computer accounts, and group accounts.

Location Considerations Checklist

Determine the location of the user community using the following checklist.

- Where will users log on?

  Ensure adequate access to an authenticating BDC.

- Do users need to be able to log on from more than one location?

  If so, their accounts cannot be tied to a location. Consider using a single master-domain or multiple master-domain model.

- What resource availability is required?

- Does a user need to be able to log on even when the WAN to the central location is down?

  Or, is all data central, so that no local processing can be done without the WAN?

- How fast are the WAN links?

  The speed of the links needed between locations should be determined by the resource usage across the links and by the frequency of changes to settings for users and groups.

Hardware Requirements

When selecting a computer for use as a PDC or BDC, use the hardware guidelines in Table 2.7, below. The table assumes that the computers will function only as PDCs and that no other major Windows NT operations will occur, such as moderate file server, SQL server, SNA server, and remote access server. All numbers are in megabytes (MB) and it is assumed that the computer's pagefile size is at least 250 MB.

Table 2.7   Domain Controller Hardware Requirements

# of User Accounts	SAM Size	Registry Size	Paged Pool	Minimum CPU Needed	Pagefile	RAM
Fewer than 3000	5	25 (default)	50 (default)	486dx/33	32	16
7500 (default)	10	25	50	486dx/33	64	32
10,000	15	25	50	Pentium, MIPS, Alpha AXP	96	48
15,000	20	30	75	Pentium, MIPS, Alpha AXP	128	64
20,000	30	50	100	Pentium, MIPS, Alpha AXP	256	128
30,000	45	75	128	Pentium, MIPS, Alpha AXP	332	166
40,000	60	102	128	SMP	394	197
50,000	75	102	128	SMP	512	256

For more information, refer to *Large Domain Testing Overview*, available from Microsoft Product Support Services.

Number of Domains Necessary

The number of users in a domain is a function of the size of the directory database. Figure 2.11 can help you determine the number of domains you need. The single-domain model and the single master-domain model can accommodate at least 26,000 user accounts if both user accounts and computer accounts are stored in the database.

Built-in local groups for a domain include Administrators, Domain Admins, Users, Domain Users, Guests, Domain Guests, Account Operators, Backup Operators, Print Operators, Server Operators, and Replicator.

	Factors	
Calculating SAM database size	Number of users, multiply by 1KB	A KB
	Number of machines , multiply by 0.5KB (workstations, servers, printers, etc.)	B KB
	Number of custom groups, multiply by 4 KB	C KB
	Built-in local groups	D 44KB
	Total SAM size: **A + B + C + D =**	E KB
	Convert SAM size to MB, multiply **E** by .001024	F
	Minimum # of domains = F / 401 (round up to the next whole number	

Figure 2.11   Job aide to calculate the number of master domains

---

[1] Maximum recommended SAM Database size is 40 MB.

Number of Trusted Domains

In the multiple master-domain model, user accounts are stored in master domains, and resources (machine accounts) are stored in all other domains. In this model, each resource domain trusts all master domains with a one-way trust.

On each domain controller in the resource domain, the existence of the trust relationship is represented by an LSA trusted-domain object. The object contains the name of the trusted domain and the domain security identifier (SID). The password associated with the trust link is stored in a LSA secret object, which is stored in the following registry key.

HKEY_LOCAL_MACHINE\Security\Policy\Secrets

In the Windows NT operating system, LSA secrets are used for other things and, until this version, the number of LSA secrets was fixed at 256. As a result, the recommended limit for trusted master domains was 128 per resource domain. This recommendation has been removed with the introduction of Windows NT 4.0 because the number of available LSA secrets has been significantly increased.

The second restriction limiting the number of master domains trusted by the resource domains is the nonpaged pool size of the domain controllers on which the resource domains are stored. When a domain controller starts, it attempts to discover domain controllers in each trusted domains by sending a message to each trusted domain. Each domain controller in the trusted domains responds with a message to the starting domain controller. The response is temporarily stored in the nonpaged pool until NetLogon can read it.

The RAM on your Windows NT computer is divided into two categories: nonpaged and paged. Nonpaged must stay in memory and cannot be written to or retrieved from peripherals. Peripherals include disks, the LAN, CD-ROMs, and other devices. Paged memory is RAM that the system can use and later reuse to hold different pages of memory from peripherals.

For more information on memory, see the *Microsoft Windows NT Workstation Resource Guide*, Chapter 12, "Detecting Memory Bottlenecks."

Windows NT Server 4.0 provides a default nonpaged pool size, which provides for a substantially higher number of trusted domains than earlier versions did. Table 2.8, below, lists the default nonpaged-pool size that is configured when Windows NT Server is installed on computers with different amounts of physical memory. The table also shows the recommended maximum number of trusted domains that will operate, based on the specified nonpaged pool size.

Table 2.8   Trusted domains needed for nonpaged-pool sizes

Nonpaged Pool Size	# of Trusted Domains	Total Physical Memory
1.2 MB	140	32 MB
2.125 MB	250	64 MB
4.125 MB	500	128 MB

Calculating Required Nonpaged and Paged Pool Sizes

Nonpaged and paged pool sizes are calculated from the physical memory on the computer when it starts up. Although the default nonpooled size is sufficient in most cases, you can approximate the values for an X86-based computer if you find it is necessary to change the nonpaged and paged pool size of your computer.

Table 2.9   Terms and values used to calculate the nonpaged pool size

Term	Value
Minimum Nonpaged Pool Size	256K
MinimumAdditionNonPagedPoolPerMb	32K
DefaultMaximumNonPagedPool	1MB
MaximumAdditionNonPagedPoolPerMb	400K
Pte_Per_Page	1024
Page_Size	4096

Calculating Nonpaged Pool Size

```
NonPagedPoolSize = MinimumNonpagedPoolSize + ((Physical MB-4) *
MinAdditionNonPagedPoolPerMb)
```

- *Example*:   On a 32 MB x86-based computer

```
MinimumNonPagedPoolSize = 256K
NonPagedPoolSize = 256K + ((32-4) * 32K) = 1.2 MB
```

```
MaximumNonPagedPoolSize = DefaultMaximumNonPagedPool; + ((Physical
MB-4) * MaxAdditionNonPagedPoolPerMb
```

```
IF: MaximumNonPagedPoolSize < (NonPagedPoolSize + Page_Size * 16)
THEN: MaximumNonPagedPoolSize = (NonPagedPoolSize + Page_Size *
16)
IF: NonPagedPoolSize >= 192 MB
THEN: NonPagedPoolSize = 192 MB
```

- *Example*:   On a 32 MB x86-based computer

```
MaximumNonPagedPoolSize = 1 MB + ((32 - 4) * 400K) = 12.5 MB
```

Calculating Paged Pool Size

```
Size = (2 * MaximumNonPagedPoolSize) / Page_Size
Size = (Size + Pte_Per_Page - 1)) / Pte_Per_Page
PagedPoolSize = Size * Page_Size * Pte_Per_Page
If PagedPoolSize >= 192 MB PagePoolSize = 192 MB
```

- *Example*:   On a 32 MB x86-based computer

```
Size = (2 * 12.5 MB) / 4096 = 6400
Size = (6400 + (1024 - 1)) / 1024 = 7.25
Paged Pool Size = 7.25 * 4096 * 1024 = 30 MB
```

Note If both the nonpaged and paged pool values are set to zero in the registry, then the paged pool size will approximately equal the memory size.

Changing Nonpooled and Pooled Page Size

Nonpooled and pooled page values can be changed in the registry. The page pooled memory management parameters are located in the following registry key.

HKEY_LOCAL_MACHINE\SYSTEM\CurrentControlSet\Control\Session \Memory Management Manager

---

Warning Using the Registry Editor incorrectly can cause serious, system-wide problems that may require you to reinstall Windows NT to correct them. Microsoft cannot guarantee that any problems resulting from the use of the Registry Editor can be solved. Use this tool at your own risk.

Increasing the size of NonPaged pool consumes physical memory that cannot be used for any other purpose.

Increasing the number of trusted domains increases the datagram traffic from each domain controller in the trusting domain.

Number of BDCs Necessary

The ratio of workstations to servers in a domain is a way to maintain responsiveness during logging on. More BDCs (also called *domain servers)* permit more users to log on simultaneously. One BDC can support up to 2,000 user accounts. The server configuration in Table 2.10 is for a 486/66 computer with 32 MB of RAM, running Windows NT Server.

Table 2.10   BDCs per number of user accounts

Number of workstations	Number of BDC servers
10	1
100	1
500	1
1,000	1
2,000	1
5,000	2
10,000	5
20,000	10
30,000	15

It is a good idea to perform the initial setup of all BDCs on site or over high-speed links because each new BDC will need a full synchronization with the PDC. Many companies set up their BDCs at the same site as the PDC and then ship them to their intended locations. This is the most efficient method for sites that have only low-speed or RAS access.

Microsoft Corporation Worldwide Network Background

Microsoft currently has approximately 16,000 user accounts and 35,000 network nodes worldwide. The Microsoft staff is evenly divided: About half the employees are located at or near the Redmond, Washington campus, and the rest are distributed among approximately 150 sites in 52 countries. All sites require full access to information and electronic mail.

In order to fulfill the goals of worldwide access to corporate information and to demonstrate its commitment to Windows NT Server technology, Microsoft designed its worldwide network around the Windows NT domain structure. The Microsoft worldwide-domain strategy includes the following goals.

- Optimum availability to all Microsoft sites

- Centralized support and administration

- The ability to recover from an extended WAN link interruption without requiring a full synchronization of the SAM to the PDC

To meet these goals, the Microsoft Information Technology Group (ITG) implemented a multiple master-domain model. The plan uses a relatively small number of first-tier, master-account domains (which are administered by ITG) and strategically placed PDCs and BDCs, to provide optimum availability and performance.

Many sites are connected to the network by (slower) 64K links. These are not yet cost-effective to upgrade and upgrades are not available in some locations. When requested, ITG will provide administration of second-tier domains.

Microsoft ITG worked to keep the number of master account domains as small as possible in order to achieve the following objectives.

- To keep administration centralized

- To make global groups feasible

Microsoft ITG chose to limit the number of departmental, site, and developer server domains because it is easier to divide large domains than to combine many small ones into a larger domain when needed. For example, there is one ITG-NETWORKS domain. All servers for the Corporate Networks department are maintained in this domain.

Implementation

Because every user and global group account in the company exists in one of the master-account domains, and because all domains trust every master-account domain in the company, every user and global group account in the company is functional in all domains.

In all cases, ITG has full administrative permissions on all the domains in the model. All domain controllers can be backed up, restored, and updated with current builds and new system-configuration files.

There are some disadvantages to the multiple master-domain model. The most challenging issue is administration of individualized global groups. Managing global groups becomes impractical unless it can be based on a database, against which data can be compared. In this way, a group would automatically be updated if an individual no longer requires membership in that group. ITG provides global groups (based on department accounts) and updates membership (based on HR records). Other global groups are reviewed by case. Users are added to a master-account domain based on their current geographic location. If a user moves to a different site within Microsoft (such as from Redmond to Northern Europe), the user will be removed from and added to the appropriate master-account domains. When the user account is recreated in another domain, the account SID changes, so account permissions must be reapplied.

Windows for Workgroup systems belong to a second-tier domain to ensure that they have full access to the domain model. They use their account on the master account domain and use the second-tier domain as their workgroup. This allows access to domain servers that are using Windows NT security.

All Windows NT Server-based systems running RAS are located in a second-tier domain. Because there is a trust relationship between all domains in the corporate model, a user can dial into a RAS server anywhere in the model without additional administration.

Administration

ITG has sole authority to establish a trust relationship between the master domains and another domain on the Microsoft corporate network. ITG can administer all servers running Windows NT Server in a trust relationship within the Microsoft domains structure. Microsoft ITG uses the following criteria to establish a trust relationship with a second-tier domain.

- Any product-development group is eligible to create one second-tier domain with trust relationships to the master account domains until every defined development business unit has a second-tier domain.

    For example, Apps-Word, Apps-Excel, Sys-WFW, or Sys-WinNT are second-tier domains.

- Every site outside the Redmond campus is eligible to create one resource domain with trust relationships with the master account domains.

    For example, USA-Atlanta, USA-Chicago, FRA-Paris, and GER-Munich are resources domains.

- ITG uses a standard administrative account that is part of the second-tier Domain Administrators group.

    This enables ITG to perform administrative duties and assist the domain administrator when needed. It also enables ITG to perform backups of domain servers.

The Microsoft Worldwide Domain Model

Master-user account domains contain all user accounts for the worldwide domain structure. Master-account-domain names represent the user's geographic location, to assist in distribution of BDCs.

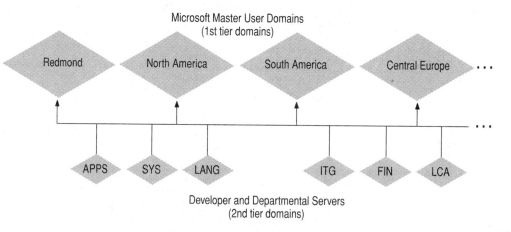

Figure 2.12   Microsoft worldwide domain model

The Microsoft network acknowledges two categories of administration. ITG is solely responsible for administration of some domains. Other domains are jointly administered by ITG and specific user groups, such as developers, sites, and others. Domain-administration permissions can be given to a group of users within their second-tier domain. ITG retains the option of allowing any of the departmental-server domains to have both their own domain administrators and ITG administration.

Domain Controller Locations

ITG provides master-account domains (first-tier), which are used by a specific set of sites. The name and size of these master-account domains are determined by geographic limitations, network topology, and the number of accounts to be supported. The PDC for the Redmond, NorthAmerica, and SouthAmerica master-account domains are located in Redmond. Others are located near the constituent users, where local data centers provide administrator resources. A BDC for the master-account domain is located at each remote site, for authentication of accounts at that site.

The European master account domain PDCs are in England, with a BDC for each European master account domain at each respective site.

Worldwide, a BDC for the global master account domain is also located at each network hub site.

Special Domain Considerations

Microsoft maintains two domains that, for security, have restricted access to and from the other domains. The groups using these special domains are the Microsoft Human Resources group and vendors who do business with Microsoft.

The Human Resources department maintains a secure network because of the confidential nature of its information. The HR master domain is isolated from the other domains on the network and is separately wired, so that it is not physically connected to the other network.

Vendors use the servers in the second restricted domain as a drop-off point. Microsoft employees can access the domain through a one-way trust relationship, but vendors are restricted to the vendor domain.

WAN Protocols

On the Microsoft corporate network, TCP/IP is used by Windows NT Server to forward authentication requests between domain controllers across a WAN. Every server in the master account domain can process logon requests from the domain user accounts.

Dynamic Host Configuration Protocol

Every server in the corporate domain runs TCP/IP. Adding Dynamic Host Configuration Protocol (DHCP) to the Microsoft network has significantly reduced administrative overhead for WAN management because individual machine TCP/IP addresses are configured automatically by DHCP.

Naming Conventions

Microsoft devised a naming convention for the corporate-domain structure to provide a consistent, worldwide interface to its users. The naming convention for second-tier domains is based on geographic location (USA-Atlanta), business (ITG-Networks), or development group (Apps-Word).

The following table shows some of the current domains. The rule is to use *{division}-{department}*. Another factor in establishing the domain name is to encompass the largest practical group.

Site domains are determined by *{country code}-{city name}*. Every site is permitted one resource domain in the corporate domain model.

Table 2.11   Microsoft first-tier and second-tier domain names

Master Account Domains (First-tier):

REDMOND	FAREAST	NORTHERNEUROPE	SOUTHPACIFIC
AFRICA	MIDDLEEAST	SOUTHAMERICA	
CENTRALEUROPE	NORTHAMERICA	SOUTHERNEUROPE	

Departmental and Site Resource Domains (Second-tier):

APPS-EXCEL	FRA-PARISEHQ	OPS-FACILITIES	SYS-BUSINESS
APPS-MULTIMEDIA	GER-BERLIN	OPS-MSPRESS	SYS-HARDWARE
APPS-POWERPOINT	GER-MUNICH	POL-WARSAW	SYS-MARKETING
APPS-WORD	ITG-APPS	PSS-BP	SYS-MSDOS-WIN
AT-RESEARCH	ITG-DEVELOPMENT	PSS-LP	SYS-WINNT
AUT-VIENNA	ITG-NETWORKS	PSS-RWG	USA-ATLANTA
FIN-ACCTSVRS	ITG-SQL	SWI-NYON	USA-DENVER

Troubleshooting Problems

This section discusses categories of typical problems users might face, such as the following situations.

- Problems viewing a server's shared resources
- Problems accessing a shared resource
- BDC failure to authenticate a user's password
- Problems caused by multiple PDCs in a domain
- Problems created by special characters in the domain name

Viewing a Server's Shared Resources

Suppose an employee named AnnM logs on to a Windows NT domain with her password, **Yippee**. She wants to view the shared resources on a server named \\Products, but her password there is **Hooray**. Ann will see the following message on screen:

```
Error 5: Access has been denied.
```

AnnM asks the administrator of \\Products to change her password, but the administrator leaves the **User Must Change Password At Next Logon** check box selected. When AnnM tries again to view the server's shared resources, she will see the following message displayed on the screen:

```
Error 2242: The password of this user has expired.
```

When the administrator of \\Products clears the **User Must Change Password At Next Logon** check box, AnnM will be able to see the server's shared resources.

Accessing a Server's Shared Resources

Two examples help explain some access issues.

- Suppose another employee, JeffH, wants to access a shared directory on \\Products but has no account on that domain. He is allowed access to this resource through the Guest account for \\Products and receives the associated permissions.
- Suppose AnnM is logged on to a Windows NT domain with the password **Yippee.** She wants to connect to the shared directory on \\Products, where her password is **Hooray**. Because there is an account for AnnM, she is not allowed to gain access by using the Guest account. Instead, Windows NT prompts AnnM for the valid password on \\Products.

BDC Failure to Authenticate the User's Password

If the computer being connected to is a BDC for the domain in which the user account is defined but the BDC fails to authenticate the user's password, this indicates that the password has changed but the BDC is not synchronized at the time the user logs on. In this case, the BDC passes the logon request through to the PDC in the same domain.

As a precaution, users who change their passwords should log on to all computers to which they have access within about 15 minutes of making the change. This ensures that the cached credentials are up-to-date on each machine and that the user will be able to log on with the cached credentials even if the PDC is unavailable during logon.

Avoiding Multiple PDCs in a Single Domain

Do not configure multiple PDCs on a single domain. The following scenario is an example of the problems involved.

Suppose a system administrator installs a computer running Windows NT Server. The computer is called \\Main_unit, which is designated during installation as the PDC of a domain called MyDomain.

Later, the system administrator shuts down \\Main_unit and turns off. Then, the system administrator installs another server, called \\Second_unit, which is also designated as the PDC for MyDomain. Because \\Main_unit is not currently on the network, the original MyDomain is not known, and the installation of \\Second_unit and creation of MyDomain proceeds without error. The two domains are not identical; they have different Security IDs.

When the system administrator turns \\Main_unit on again, the NetLogon service discovers another PDC on the network. NetLogon fails, and \\Main_unit can no longer participate in the domain.

The system administrator now has a serious problem. It is not possible to simply demote \\Main_unit from a PDC to a BDC and continue. The Security ID (SID) for \\Main_unit will not be recognized by the current PDC, \\Second_unit, and \\Main_unit cannot join MyDomain in any capacity.

This situation happens because a unique domain SID is created whenever a PDC is created. All BDCs and user accounts within the domain share this domain SID as a prefix to their own SIDs. When \\Second_unit is installed as a PDC, its SID prefix is different from the \\Main_unit prefix, and the two computers can never participate in the same domain.

The system administrator cannot change the name of \\Main_unit and rejoin MyDomain because the SID is fixed when Windows NT Server is installed. If \\Main_unit is to be the PDC of MyDomain, the system administrator must shut down both \\Main_unit and \\Second_unit, start up \\Main_unit, and then reinstall Windows NT Server on \\Second_unit, designating it as a BDC during setup.

To avoid this problem, \\Second_unit should be installed as a backup domain controller while \\Main_unit is running. Then, if \\Main_unit is taken offline, \\Second_unit can be promoted to PDC. When \\Main_unit is ready to go online again, \\Second_unit can be demoted to a BDC. The SID for \\Main_unit is recognized by \\Second_unit. When \\Main_unit is restarted, it becomes the PDC again.

(In general, it should not be necessary to designate a new PDC unless the original PDC is going to be down for a long time.)

Special Characters in Domain Names

The following special characters are illegal in domain names (in addition to * and space).

#define ILLEGAL_NAME_CHARS_STR TEXT ("\"/\\[]:|<>+=;,.?")
CTRL_CHARS_STR

Even though some special characters such as period (.) are valid, underscore (_) and dash (-) would be better choices as special characters in domain names.

C H A P T E R   3

Windows NT Browser Service

Users on a Windows NT network often need to know what domains and computers are accessible from their local computer. Viewing all the network resources available is called *browsing*. The Windows NT Browser service maintains a list (called the *browse list*) of all available domains and servers. The browse list can be viewed using Windows NT Explorer and is provided by a browser in the local computer's domain.

Note For the purposes of this discussion, the term *server* refers to any computer that can provide resources to the rest of the network. If a computer running Windows NT Workstation can share file or print resources with other computers on the network, it is considered a server in the context of the browser system. The computer does not have to be actively sharing resources to be considered a server.

This chapter includes descriptions of the following topics.

- The types of browser computers
- How browsers can work together to provide an accurate browser list, even if the master browser fails
- Master-browser elections
- The API calls used to register computers for the browser list and to receive the list from the master browser
- How browsing across domains is handled

The Windows NT Browser Service

Windows NT assigns browser tasks to specific computers on the network. The computers work together to provide a centralized list of shared resources, eliminating the need for all machines to maintain their own lists. This reduces the CPU time and network traffic needed to build and maintain the list.

The Windows NT Browser system consists of a master browser, backup browsers, and browser clients. The computer that is the master browser maintains the browse list and periodically sends copies to the backup browsers. When a browser client needs information, it obtains the current browse list by remotely sending a **NetServerEnum** application programming interface (API) call to either the master browser or a backup browser.

A *datagram* is a network message packet that can be sent to a mailslot on a specified computer (a *directed datagram)* or to a mailslot on any number of computers (a *broadcast datagram).* This centralized-browser architecture reduces the number of datagrams sent to produce the available resource list. The centralized-browser architecture also reduces demands on the client CPU and memory.

Specifying Browser Computers

When you start a computer running Windows NT Workstation or Windows NT Server, the Browser service looks in the registry for the configuration parameter **MaintainServerList** to determine whether or not a computer will become a browser. This parameter is found under:

\HKEY_LOCAL_MACHINE\System\CurrentControlSet\Services\Browser\Parameters

Table 3.1   Allowable Values for the MaintainServerList parameter

Parameter Value	Meaning
No	This computer will never participate as a browser.
Yes	This computer will become a browser. Upon startup, this computer attempts to contact the master browser to get a current browse list. If the master browser cannot be found, the computer will force a browser election. This computer will either be elected master browser or become a backup browser.
	Yes is the default value on a computer running Windows NT Server.
Auto	This computer, referred to as a *potential browser,* may or may not become a browser, depending on the number of currently active browsers. The master browser notifies this computer whether or not it will become a backup browser.
	Auto is the default value for computers running Windows NT Workstation.

On any computer with an entry of *Yes* or *Auto* for the **MaintainServerList** parameter, Windows NT Setup configures the Browser service to start automatically when the computer starts.

Another parameter in the registry, IsDomainMasterBrowser, helps to determine which servers become master browsers and backup browsers The registry path for this parameter is as shown below.

\HKEY_LOCAL_MACHINE\System\CurrentControlSet\Services\Browser\Parameters

Setting the IsDomainMasterBrowser parameter entry to *True* or *Yes* on a computer makes that computer a preferred master browser. A *preferred master browser* has priority over other computers in master browser elections. Whenever a preferred master browser starts, it forces a browser election.

Any computer running Windows NT Workstation or Windows NT Server can be configured as a preferred master browser. When the Browser service is started on the preferred master-browser computer, the Browser service forces an election. Preferred master browsers are given priority in elections, which means that if no other condition prevents it, the preferred master browser will always win the election. This gives an administrator the ability to configure a specific computer as the master browser.

To specify a computer as the preferred master browser, set the parameter entry for IsDomainMasterBrowser to True or Yes. Set the parameter in the following registry path:

\HKEY_LOCAL_MACHINE\System\CurrentControlSet\Services\Browser\Parameters

Unless the computer is configured as the preferred master browser, the parameter entry will always be False or No. There is no user interface for making these changes; the registry must be modified.

Browser System Roles

A computer running Windows NT 3.1, Windows NT Advanced Server 3.1, Windows NT Workstation 3.5 or later, Windows NT Server 3.5 or later, Windows for Workgroups 3.11, or Windows 95 can be browsers. There are five types of computers in the browser system:

- Non-browsers
- Potential browsers
- Backup browsers
- Master browsers
- Domain master browsers

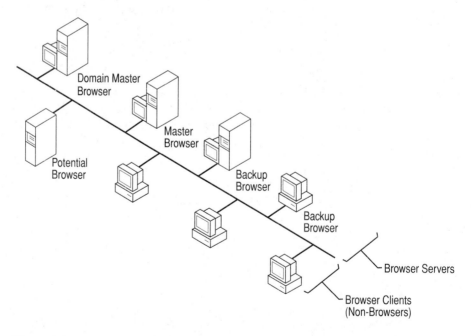

Figure 3.1   Browser and non-browser computers

Non-browser

A *non-browser* is a computer that has been configured not to maintain a network resource or browse list.

Potential Browser

A *potential browser* is a computer that is capable of a maintaining a network resource browse list and can be elected as a master browser. The potential browser computer can act as a backup browser if instructed to do so by the master browser.

Backup Browser

The *backup browser* receives a copy of the network-resource browse list from the master browser and distributes the list upon request to computers in the domain or workgroup. All Windows NT domain controllers are automatically configured as either master or backup browsers.

Computers running Windows NT Workstation, Windows for Workgroups, or Windows 95 can be backup browsers if there are fewer than three Windows NT Server computers performing backup-browser functions for the domain.

Backup browsers call the master browser every 15 minutes to get the latest copy of the browse list and a list of domains. Each backup browser caches these lists and returns the list of servers to any clients that send a remote **NetServerEnum** API call to the backup browser. If the backup browser cannot find the master browser, it forces an election of the master browser.

The data limit for the list of servers maintained on computers running a version of Windows NT prior to version 4.0, Windows for Workgroups, or Windows 95 is 64K. This limits the number of computers in a browse list for a single workgroup or domain to between 2,000 and 3,000 computers.

Master Browser

The *master browser* is responsible for collecting the information necessary to create and maintain the browse list. The browse list includes all servers in the master browser's domain or workgroup, and the list of all domains on the network.

Individual servers announce their presence to the master browser by sending a directed datagram called a *server announcement* to the domain or workgroup master browser. Computers running Windows NT Server, Windows NT Workstation, Windows for Workgroups, Windows 95, or LAN Manager send server announcements. When the master browser receives a server announcement from a computer, it adds that computer to the browse list.

When a domain spans more than one subnetwork, the master browser will do the following tasks:

- Maintain the browse list for the portion of the domain on its subnetwork
- Provide lists of backup browsers on the local subnetwork of a TCP/IP-based network to computers running Windows NT Server, Windows NT Workstation, and Windows for Workgroups

If a TCP/IP-based subnetwork is comprised of more than one domain, each domain has its own master browser and backup browsers. On networks using the NWLink IPX/SPX-compatible network protocols, name queries are sent across routers, ensuring that there is always only one master browser for each domain. NetBEUI Frame (NBF) is not designed for a routed network and requires a separate master browser per subnet.

When a computer starts and its **MaintainServerList** registry entry is set to Auto, the master browser must tell that computer whether or not to become a backup browser.

Domain Master Browser

The domain master browser is responsible for collecting announcements for the entire domain, including any network segments, and for providing a list of domain resources to master browsers. The domain master browser is always the primary domain controller (PDC) of a domain.

The PDC of a domain is given priority in browser elections to ensure that it becomes the master browser. The Windows NT Browser service running on a PDC has the special, additional role of being the domain master browser.

For a domain that uses TCP/IP and spans more than one subnetwork, each subnetwork functions as an independent browsing entity with its own master browser and backup browsers. NwLnkNb and NBF transports don't use the domain master browser role because those transports have only a single master browser for the entire network. Browsing across the wide area network (WAN) to other subnetworks requires at least one browser running Windows NT Server, Windows NT Workstation, or Windows For Workgroups 3.11b on the domain for each subnetwork. A PDC typically functions as the domain master browser on its subnetwork.

When a domain spans multiple subnetworks, the master browser of each subnetwork announces itself as the master browser to the domain master browser, using a directed MasterBrowserAnnouncement datagram. The domain master browser then sends a remote **NetServerEnum** API call to each master browser, to collect each subnetwork's list of servers. The domain master browser merges the server list from each subnetwork master browser with its own server list, forming the browse list for the domain. This process is repeated every 15 minutes to ensure that the domain master browser has a complete browse list of all the servers in the domain.

The master browser on each subnetwork also sends a remote **NetServerEnum** API call to the domain master browser to obtain the complete browse list for the domain. This browse list is available to browser clients on the subnetwork.

A single computer may play multiple browser roles. For example, the master browser may also be the domain master browser.

Note Windows NT workgroups cannot span multiple TCP/IP subnetworks. Any Windows NT workgroup that spans subnetworks actually functions as two separate workgroups with identical names.

Browser Elections

Browser elections occur to select a new master browser under the following circumstances.

- When a computer cannot locate a master browser
- When a preferred master browser comes online
- When a Windows NT domain-controller system starts

A computer initiates an election by sending a special datagram called an *election datagram*. All browsers can receive election datagrams. When a browser receives an election datagram, it examines that datagram's election criteria. If the browser has better election criteria than the sender of the election datagram, the browser will issue its own election datagram and enter what is called an *election in progress* state. If the browser does not have better election criteria than the sender of the election datagram, the browser attempts to determine which system is the new master browser.

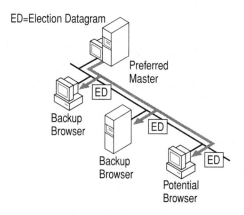

Figure 3.2   Browser election

The election criteria for a browser is based on the browser's current role in the domain and its current state, using the hierarchy in Table 3.2.

Table 3.2   The hierarchy of criteria for a browser election

Operating System Type	0xFF000000
Windows for Workgroups or Windows 95	0x01000000
Windows NT Workstation	0x10000000
Windows NT Server	0x20000000
Election Version	0x00FFFF00
Per Version Criteria	0x000000FF
PDC	0x00000080
WINS System	0x00000020L
Preferred Master	0x00000008
Running Master	0x00000004
MaintainServerList = Yes	0x00000002
Running backup browser	0x00000001

The browser will use all of the appropriate election criteria to determine the sending computer's election criteria.

The following criteria determine whether or not a browser has won an election.

- If the browser's election version is greater than the sender's election version, the browser wins. If not, the browser uses the next election criteria. The *election version* is a constant value that identifies the version of the browser-election protocol. The election version is the revision of the browser protocol and is not related to the operating-system version.
- If the browser's election criteria is greater than the sender's election criteria, the browser wins. If not, the browser uses the next election criteria.
- If the browser has been running longer than the sender, the browser wins. If not, the browser uses the next election criteria.
- If none of the criteria above have determined the election, then the server with the lexically (alphabetically, including numbers and symbols) lowest name wins. For example, a server named "A" will become master browser over a server named "X."

When a browser receives an election datagram indicating that it wins the election, the browser enters the *running election state*. While in this state, the browser sends out an election request after a delay, based on the browser's current role in the domain.

- Master browsers and the primary domain controllers delay for 100 microseconds (ms).
- Backup browsers and backup domain controllers randomly delay for 200 ms and 600 ms.
- All other browsers randomly delay between 800 ms and 3000 ms.

This delay occurs because Windows for Workgroups browsers go "deaf" for several hundred microseconds after sending an election datagram. This delay reduces the number of election datagrams sent. A browser winning an election may receive a different election datagram, causing it to lose an election later. By having less-likely winners delay longer, the less-likely winners typically don't send election datagrams.

The browser sends up to four election datagrams. If no other browser responds with an election criteria datagram that would win the election, the computer is promoted to master browser. If the browser receives an election datagram indicating that another computer will win the election, and the computer is currently the master browser, the computer will demote itself from master browser and become a backup browser.

To force an election, the client computer will broadcast an election datagram to the domain, indicating that an election should occur. This datagram is created to prevent the client that sends the datagram from winning the election.

When an election occurs, the Browser service on the computer that forced the election will log an event in the Event Viewer System log, indicating that it forced the election. An event is logged for each protocol on which the Browser service forces an election.

Browser Announcements

The Browser service must be notified by a resource when it is available for use on the Windows NT network. When a network computer running Windows for Workgroups, Windows 95, Windows NT Workstation, or Windows NT Server starts, it sends an announcement to the Browser service that it is an available resource.

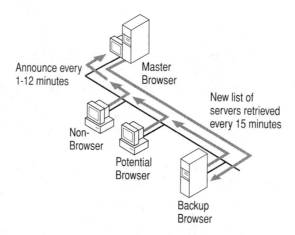

Figure 3.3   Browser announcements

Master browsers are responsible for receiving announcements from computers running any of the following software.

- Windows NT 3.1
- Windows NT 3.1 Advanced Server
- Windows for Workgroups
- Windows 95
- Windows NT Workstation 3.5, or later
- Windows NT Server 3.5, or later
- LAN Manager systems

Master browsers also return lists of backup browsers to computers running any of the following software.

- Windows NT 3.1
- Windows NT 3.1 Advanced Server
- Windows NT Workstation 3.5, or later
- Windows NT Server 3.5, or later
- Windows for Workgroups 3.11, or later
- Windows 95 clients

When a computer starts and its **MaintainServerList** parameter is set to Auto, the master browser is responsible for telling the system whether or not to become a backup browser.

When a computer becomes the master browser by winning an election, and the browse list is empty, the master browser forces all systems to announce. The master browser broadcasts a RequestAnnouncement datagram. All computers that receive this datagram must answer randomly within 30 seconds. This 30-second range for response prevents the master browser from becoming overloaded and losing replies, and protects the network from being flooded with responses.

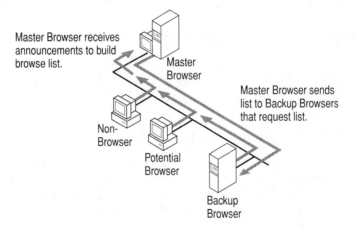

Figure 3.4   Browsing for Backup Lists

A master browser cannot be forced to rebuild the browse list for a workgroup or domain. However, shutting down and restarting a computer that is configured as the preferred master browser, or stopping and restarting the Browser service, forces the build of a new browse list. When a preferred master browser starts, it forces an election, which it will win. Because there is no browse list, it then forces all members of the domain or workgroup to announce themselves.

If a master browser receives an announcement from another computer that claims to be the master browser, the master browser will demote itself from master browser and force an election. This ensures that there is never more than one master browser in each workgroup or domain.

Non-browser Announcements

A non-browser computer periodically announces itself to the master browser by sending a directed datagram to the master browser on the network. Initially, each non-browser will announce itself every minute. The announcement interval will be extended to once every 12 minutes. The computer announces its availability in intervals of 1 minute, 2 minutes, 4 minutes, 8 minutes, 12 minutes, 12 minutes, and then announces to the master browser only every 12 minutes. If the master browser has not heard from the non-browser for three consecutive announcement periods, the master browser will remove the non-browser from the browse list.

Potential-browser Announcements

Most computers are potential browsers; that is, they are capable of becoming either backup browsers or master browsers. These computers announce themselves in the same manner as non-browsers.

Backup-browser Announcements

Backup browsers are a subset of potential browsers and announce themselves in the same manner as non-browsers. However, backup browsers participate in browser elections. Backup browsers call the master browser every 15 minutes to obtain updated network-resource browse lists and lists of workgroups and domains. The backup browser caches these lists and returns the browse list to any client that sends out a browse request by making a call, using the **NetServerEnum** API, to the backup browser. If the backup browser cannot find the master browser, it will force an election.

Because it can take up to 15 minutes for a backup browser to receive an updated browse list, it is possible that a computer will appear in the browse list for as long as 51 minutes after it is no longer an available resource on the network. The time period consists of 36 minutes, which is three 12-minute announcement cycles plus the 15 minutes for the backup browser to receive an updated list.

Configuring the Browser Announcement Time

You can change how often a browser client announces itself. In the registry path, under:

HKEY_LOCAL_MACHINE\System\CurrentControlSet\Services\ LanmanServer\Parameters

add the **Announce** parameter with a type of REG_DWORD, and set the number of seconds that the browser should wait between announcements. For example, if the default for **Announce** is 12 minutes, the length of time is set to 720.

The **Announce** value must be changed on all computers in the workgroup or domain before the new value can be used by all computers. As you decrease this value, announcement traffic increases. Increasing the **Announce** value reduces the amount of announcement traffic, but will increase the length of time that a shutdown computer will appear on the browse list.

Browser Requests

The purpose of the Browser service is to make a list of network resources available to users. To use this resource list, the client computer must know which computer to contact to request a copy of the list.

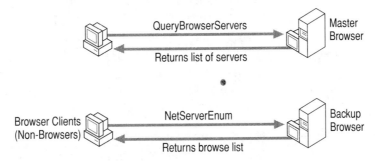

Figure 3.5   Flow of the Browser Request

The request issued to obtain the list of available network resources is a **NetServerEnum** API call. This request is sent when **net view** is entered at the command prompt or when the **Map Network Drive** dialog box lists the network resources. The client issues the **NetServerEnum** API call to a backup browser.

If this is the first time that a **NetServerEnum** API call is issued on the client computer, the computer must first find out which computers are the backup browsers for its workgroup or domain before it can send the API call. The client does this by issuing a GetBackupList datagram to the master browser.

The master browser receives and processes the GetBackupList request. The master browser returns a list of backup browsers active within the workgroup or domain being queried. The client selects the names of three backup browsers from the list and stores these names for future use. The **NetServerEnum** API call is sent to a backup browser randomly chosen from the three saved names.

If the master browser for the workgroup or domain being queried cannot be found after three attempts, the client will force the election of a new master browser in the domain. The client returns an ERROR_BAD_NETPATH message to the application, indicating that the master browser could not be found.

Number of Browsers in a Domain or Workgroup

The following rules determine the number of browsers in a domain or workgroup. In this discussion, the words *domain* and *workgroup* are used interchangeably.

If there is currently a PDC in the domain, it will be the master browser for the domain.

Every BDC in the domain will be a backup browser for the domain. The only exception to this is if the BDC is needed as a master browser because the PDC has failed. In that case, the BDC will be the master browser for the domain.

If a computer's **MaintainServerList** registry parameter is set to Yes, this computer will be a backup browser for the domain or TCP/IP subnet.

If no backup browsers are selected for the domain based on the preceding rules, the master browser determines the number of backup browsers for the domain. If a computer's **MaintainServerList** registry parameter is set to Auto, the master browser will select some of those computers to act as backup browsers based on the number of computers in the domain.

Table 3.3   Number of browsers in a domain or workgroup

Number of Computers	Number of Backup Browsers	Number of Master Browsers
1	0	1
2 to 31	1	1
32 to 63	2	1

For each additional 32 computers added to the domain, another backup browser is selected for the domain.

For the TCP/IP transport, each subnet independently enforces the preceding set of rules.

Browser Shutdown or Failure

If a backup browser shuts down properly, it sends an announcement to the master browser that it is shutting down. The backup browser does this by sending an announcement that does not include the Browser service in the list of running services.

If a Master Browser shuts down gracefully, it will send a ForceElection datagram so that a new master browser can be chosen.

If a computer does not shut down properly or if it fails for any reason, it must be removed from the browse list. The Browser service handles browser failures.

Non-browser Failure

When a non-browser fails, it stops announcing itself. The configured announcement period is between 1 and 12 minutes. If the non-browser has not announced itself after three announcement periods, the master browser removes the computer from the browse list. Therefore, it can take up to 51 minutes before all browsers know of a non-browser's failure. This figure includes up to 36 minutes for the master browser to detect the failure, and 15 minutes for all of the backup browsers to retrieve the updated list from the master browser.

Backup-browser Failure

As with a non-browser failure, when a backup browser fails, it may not be removed from the master-browser list for up to 51 minutes. If a browse list cannot be obtained from the missing backup browser, the client selects another backup browser from its cached list of three backups. If all of the client's known backup browsers fail, the client attempts to get a new list of backup browsers from the master browser. If the client is unable to contact the master browser, the client forces an election.

Master-browser Failure

When a master browser fails, a backup browser detects the failure within 15 minutes and forces an election of a new master browser.

If a client performs its browse request (using the **NetServerEnum** API call) after a master browser fails but before a backup browser detects the failure, the client forces an election. If a master browser fails and there are no backup browsers, browsing in the workgroup or domain will not function correctly.

During the gap between the master browser's failure and the election of a new master browser, the workgroup or domain can disappear from the lists that are visible to computers in other workgroups and domains.

Domain Master-browser Failures

If the domain master browser fails, the master browser for each network segment provides a browse list, containing only the servers in the local network segment. All servers that are not on the local network segment will eventually be removed from the browse list. Users will still be able to connect to servers on the other network segments if they know the name of the server.

Because a domain master browser is also a PDC, an administrator can correct the failure by promoting a BDC to PDC. A BDC can perform most PDC network tasks, such as validating logon requests, but does not promote itself to PDC and does not become domain master browser in the event of a PDC failure.

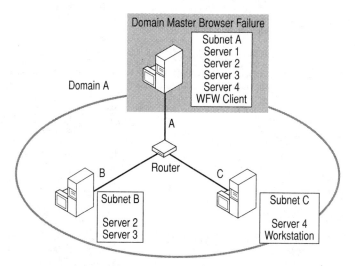

Figure 3.6   Master browser failure

Browse Service Across Multiple Workgroups and Domains

Users need to browse multiple workgroups and domains to retrieve a list of servers within their workgroup or domain and a list of other workgroups and domains.

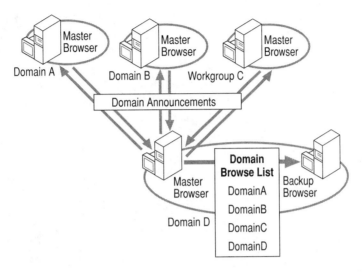

Figure 3.7   Browser service across multiple workgroups and domains

Upon becoming a master browser, each master browser in each workgroup and domain will broadcast a DomainAnnouncement datagram every minute for the first five minutes. After the first five minutes, the master browser will broadcast a DomainAnnouncement datagram once every 15 minutes. If a workgroup or domain has not announced itself for three announcement periods, the workgroup or domain will be removed from the list of workgroups and domains. Therefore, it is possible that a workgroup or domain will appear in the browse list 45 minutes after the workgroup or domain has failed or been shut down.

A DomainAnnouncement datagram contains the following information.

- The name of the domain
- The name of the master browser for that domain
- Whether the browser computer is running Windows NT Workstation or Windows NT Server

If the browser computer is running Windows NT Server, the DomainAnnouncement datagram will also specify whether or not the browser computer is the domain PDC.

Browse Service Across a Wide Area Network (WAN)

When using domains that are split across routers, each TCP/IP network segment functions as an independent browsing entity with its own master browser and backup browsers. Therefore, browser elections occur within each network segment.

Domain master browsers are responsible for spanning the network segments to collect computer-name information, in order to maintain a domain-wide browse list of available resources. The domain master browser and cooperating master browsers on each WAN segment provide browsing of domains that exist across multiple TCP/IP network segments. The domain master browser is the PDC of a domain. The master-browser computers on the subnets can be running Windows NT Server, Windows NT Workstation, Windows for Workgroups version 3.11b, or Windows 95.

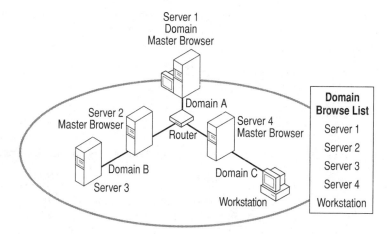

Figure 3.8   Browser service across a WAN

When a domain spans multiple network segments, the master browsers for each network segment use a directed datagram called a *MasterBrowserAnnouncement datagram* to announce themselves to the domain master browser. The MasterBrowserAnnouncement datagram notifies the domain master browser that the sending computer is a master browser in the same domain and that the domain master browser needs to obtain a copy of the master browser's browse list. When the domain master browser receives a MasterBrowserAnnouncement datagram, it sends a request to the network segment's master browser, which announced itself in order to collect a list of the network segment's servers.

The domain master browser then merges its own server list with the server list from the master browser that issued the announcement. This process is done every 15 minutes and guarantees that the domain master browser has a complete browse list of all the servers in the domain. When a client issues a browse request to a backup browser, the backup browser returns a list of all the servers in the domain, regardless of the network segment on which they are located.

Workgroup using Windows NT or Windows for Workgroups cannot span multiple network segments. Any workgroup of either kind that does span network segments will function as two separate workgroups with the same name.

Browse Service Across a WAN with TCP/IP

Currently, Browser-service communication relies almost entirely on broadcasts. In a WAN environment, such as TCP/IP, where domains are separated by routers, special broadcast problems can arise because broadcasts, by default, do not pass through routers. There are two issues to consider.

- How browsers separated by a router perform browser functions
- How local clients browse remote domains that are not on their local network segment

The following topics discuss three methods that can be used to set up WAN browsing with TCP/IP. They are presented in order of preference.

The Windows Internet Name Service (WINS)

The Windows Internet Name Service (WINS) resolves NetBIOS names to IP addresses so that datagrams can be sent to the targeted computer. Implementing WINS eliminates the need to configure the LMHOSTS file or to enable UDP port 137. Using WINS requires the following configuration.

- WINS is configured on a computer running Windows NT Server 3.5 or later.
- Clients are WINS-enabled.

  WINS clients can be configured with Windows NT 3.5 or later, Windows 95, Windows for Workgroups 3.11b running TCP/IP-32, LAN Manager 2.2c for MS-DOS, or Microsoft Network Client 3.0 for MS-DOS. The latter two are provided on the compact discs for versions 3.5 or later of Windows NT Server.

We usually recommend that you implement WINS for name resolution and browsing support. As an alternative, it is possible to have full domain browsing by using only LMHOSTS files on all computers, but this limits browsing to the local domain. Non-WINS clients still need the LMHOSTS file to browse a WAN, even if WINS has been implemented in the domain.

> **Note** A client will participate in domain browsing only when that client is using a workgroup name that is equivalent to the domain name (workgroup=domain). In the case of Windows NT computers, they can also join the domain to gain this functionality, instead of participating in a workgroup.

The LMHOSTS File

NetBIOS name resolution is typically performed through broadcasts, which will resolve names only on the local network segment. To resolve names of computers located on another network segment, the LMHOSTS file (located under \\<winnt_root>\System32\drivers\etc) must be configured. The LMHOSTS file must contain a NetBIOS name-to-IP address mapping for all computers that are not on the local network segment.

To implement communication between network segments and the domain master browser, the administrator must configure the LMHOSTS file with the NetBIOS names and IP addresses of all browsers. To ensure that the master browser for each network segment can access the domain's PDC, the PDC for each domain must exist in the LMHOSTS file on each master browser and have the #DOM tag.

The LMHOSTS file on each network segment's master browser should contain the following information.

- IP address and NetBIOS name of the domain master browser
- The domain name, preceded by the tags #PRE and #DOM, as in the following example

```
130.20.7.80 <Browser_name> #PRE #DOM:<domain_name>
```

To guarantee that the PDC can request the local browse list from the network segment's master browser, TCP/IP and all other WAN transports must cache the client's IP address.

UDP Port 137 (NetBIOS Name Service Broadcasts)

Not all WANs will have problems browsing. Some routers can be configured to forward specific types of broadcasts and filter out others.

All NetBIOS over TCP/IP (NetBT) broadcasts are sent to the UDP port 137, which is defined as the NetBT Name Service. This usage is defined by Request for Comment (RFC) 1001 and 1002. Routers normally filter out these frames because they are sent to the hardware and subnet broadcast addresses. However, some routers allow all frames sent to this particular UDP port—which is used only by NetBT—to be forwarded. As a result, the browser looks as if it is on one, big, network segment. All domains and computers within the network segments are seen by all computers, including Windows for Workgroups computers.

Windows for Workgroups and Windows 95 as Master Browsers

The Vserver.386 and Vredir files on the Windows NT Server versions 3.51 and 4.0 compact discs are different from the files of the same names on the Windows NT Server version 3.5 compact disc.

These two files have been modified so that computers running Windows for Workgroups 3.11b or Windows 95 can be master browsers for a network. This enables a computer on a network with computers running only Windows for Workgroups 3.11b and Windows 95 to browse Windows NT domains on other networks.

As the master browser for the network, a computer running Windows for Workgroups 3.11b or Windows 95 will communicate with the PDC of the domain to obtain the browse list for the entire domain.

The Windows for Workgroups 3.11b or Windows 95 master browser will function as if a Windows NT master browser were on the network. The Windows for Workgroups 3.11b or Windows 95 master browser will contact the PDC every 15 minutes to give it the local network's browse list and to obtain the domain-wide browse list.

The following conditions must exist for a computer running either Windows for Workgroups 3.11b or Windows 95 to function properly as a master browser.

- The computer must also be running TCP/IP.
- WINS must be used for name resolution.
- The domain's PDC must be a WINS client.
- The Windows for Workgroups 3.11b or Windows 95 client must be in a workgroup that has the same name as the domain, and must also be a WINS client.

Microsoft LAN Manager Interoperability

For interoperability between Windows NT Workstation or Windows NT Server and LAN Manager browsers, some configuration is required.

Selecting the **Make Browser Broadcasts to LAN Manager 2.x Clients** check box causes the browser to announce itself to LAN Manager 2.x computers using a LAN Manager-compatible server announcement. The default configuration is *not* to send announcements to LAN Manager 2.x computers.

▶ **To activate Make Browser Broadcasts to LAN Manager 2.x Clients**

1. Click **Start**, point to **Settings**, and click **Control Panel.**

2. Double-click **Network**.

3. Click the **Services** tab.

4. Double-click **Server**.

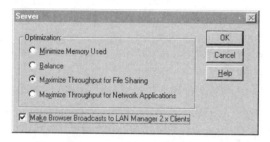

5. Select the **Make Browser Broadcasts to LAN Manager 2.x Clients** check box, and then click **OK**.

To configure this option on a Windows NT Workstation, change the **Lmannounce** parameter entry to 1 in the registry under the following path:

\HKEY_LOCAL_MACHINE\System\CurrentControlSet\Services\ LanmanServer\Parameters

Each computer can be configured to browse up to four other LAN Manager domains. These domains are the LAN Manager-only domains that the local computer is interested in browsing. If any other domains are configured on a domain master browser, the other domains are provided to all members of the domain.

To configure other domains, in the registry under:

\HKEY_LOCAL_MACHINE\System\CurrentControlSet\Services\ LanmanWorkstation\Parameters

add a value of OtherDomains with a type of REG_MULTI_SZ, and supply the other domain names.

Browser System Components

The Browser system consists of two components, the Browser service and the datagram receiver.

The Browser service is the user-mode portion of the Browser system and is responsible for maintaining the browse list, sending the API requests, and managing the various browser roles that a computer can have.

The Browser service actually resides within the Service Controller process (Lmsvcs.exe) and can be found under \<*winnt_root*>\system32. The Browser service is located in the registry path under the following key.

\HKEY_LOCAL_MACHINE\System\CurrentControlSet\Services\Browser

The datagram receiver is the kernel-mode portion of the Browser system and is simply a datagram and mailslot receiver. It receives directed and broadcast datagrams that are of interest to the Windows NT Workstation and Windows NT Server services. The datagram receiver also provides kernel-level support for the **NetServerEnum** API, support for remote mailslot reception (second-class, datagram-based, mailslot messages), and the request-announcement services.

In Windows NT 3.5 and later, the datagram receiver is implemented in the Windows NT redirector (Rdr.sys). In Windows NT 3.1, there is a separate driver, Browser.sys, for the datagram receiver.

Monitoring Browsers

The *Microsoft Windows NT Server Resource Kit 4.0* includes two utilities, Browmon.exe and Browstat.exe, that can be used to monitor the browsers within a workgroup or domain.

Browmon.exe

Browmon.exe is a graphical utility that can be used to view browsers—both the master and backups—for selected domains. It lists the browser servers for each protocol in use by computers in the domain.

You can click the **Properties** menu to see the servers in the browse list for the selected protocol and the domain browse list. In the **Properties** dialog box, click **Information** to open the **Information** dialog box, which shows the number of server announcements, domain announcements, election packets, and so forth.

Browstat.exe

Browstat.exe is a command-line utility that can be used to view the Browser servers—both the master and backups—in the specified workgroup or domain. Browstat.exe has some capabilities that Browmon.exe does not have, such as the ability to force an election and the ability to force a master browser to stop so that an election occurs.

Browstat.exe includes the following options.

```
Usage: BROWSTAT Command [Options | /HELP]
Where <Command> is one of:

ELECT       ( EL) - Force election on remote domain
 GETBLIST   ( GB) - Get backup list for domain
 GETMASTER  ( GM) - Get remote Master Browser name (using NetBIOS)
 GETPDC     ( GP) - Get PDC name (using NetBIOS)
 LISTWFW    (WFW) - List WFW servers that are actually running
                    browser
 STATS      (STS) - Dump browser statistics
 STATUS     (STA) - Display status about a domain
 TICKLE     (TIC) - Force remote master to stop
 VIEW       ( VW) - Remote NetServerEnum to a server or domain on
                    transport
```

How to Find the Master Browser: Example

To find the master browser for a domain, the following command line must be used.

```
browstat getmaster <transport> <domain_name>
```

Where *<transport>* is one of the protocols installed on the system, in the form reported by **net config rdr** on the following **Workstation active on** line.

```
NwlnkNb NetBT_Lance1 NetBT_EE162 Nbf_Lance1
```

For example, the following command could be used to find the master browser for a domain named *Seattle*.

```
browstat getmaster NetBT_Lance1 Seattle
```

Note When using Browstat.exe, you can use either the full command or the two- or three-character abbreviation, such as **gm** instead of **getmaster.**

PART II

Network Interoperability

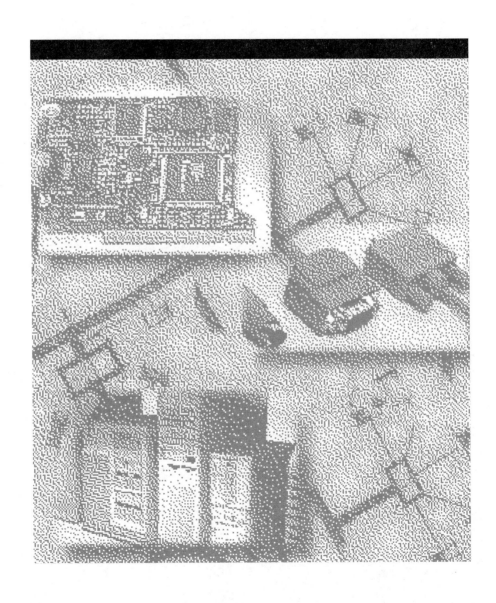

C H A P T E R   4

Terra Flora: A Fictitious Case Study

The following chapter is a preliminary draft of material that will appear in expanded form in the next edition of the Windows NT Server Resource Kit. *At that time, the case study will be further revised and expanded to include details about the Divisional, Department, and Desktop server services and other helpful information.*

In the early days of networking, there was only one type of network and operating system. Communication was not an issue: When the computers were connected, they communicated. It was relatively slow and very expensive, but it worked.

Today, corporate computer environments are often *heterogeneous*, that is, they have at least two different network operating systems on their standards list that must interoperate with both newer, intranet client/server environments and legacy computers and applications.

As network administrators attempt to make these systems work together, they find that the different network operating systems do not "speak" the same standard protocols and that there may be non-standard or proprietary protocols in use in various parts of their networks. They need to discover ways to connect these networks together, enabling them to interoperate and complement each other.

To illustrate problems and solutions for interoperability, we put together a real network for a fictitious company we call "Terra Flora, Incorporated." We imagined this company to be an international corporation in the floral industry. Terra Flora will serve as an example of a company with heterogeneous networks and of how to devise and implement a plan to bring these information systems together in a way that is consistent with the company's business operations and objectives.

Terra Flora is a totally fictitious corporation. The names of companies, products, people, characters, and data mentioned herein are fictitious and are in no way intended to represent any real individual, company, product, or event, unless otherwise noted.

Introducing Terra Flora

Terra Flora is an international corporation specializing in retail flower in the United States and Europe. The main business functions of Terra Flora are listed below.

- Operating nurseries that grow flowers, and purchasing exotic varieties of flowers from local growers under contract
- Manufacturing trademark "Terra Flora" brand terra cotta pots and vases
- Distributing the grown and purchased flowers and manufactured terra cotta products to the retail stores
- Obtaining and filling customer orders at the retail level
- Delivering flower orders

Terra Flora Corporate History

The business originally consisted of a single retail outlet, located in Sacramento, California, that began selling flowers in 1970.

The business grew significantly, so the company purchased other retail florist shops across the United States, including major retail stores in New York City and Los Angeles. These two stores installed order desks with toll-free phone lines. Customers could place orders by phone and have their purchases delivered anywhere in the United States, with guaranteed delivery times and schedules.

The flowers originally came from a local Sacramento nursery. As the company grew, it contracted with two European nurseries, in Amsterdam, The Netherlands, and Seville, Spain, to provide exotic flower varieties. The retail company purchased all three nurseries in 1988 and set up distribution procedures, which effectively turned the nurseries into supply and distribution centers.

In early 1990, the chain incorporated and offered ownership shares on the stock market. Using the capital generated from selling stock, the corporation purchased a manufacturing plant located in Sacramento that manufactured various styles of award-winning terra cotta pots and vases. The pots and vases have become the corporation's "signature" product and are used as part of the flower arrangements sold at the retail stores.

At the same time, the company began opening retail shops in upscale malls instead of purchasing existing florists. Currently, the company continues to focus on this strategy for expanding its business.

In December 1991, the corporation renamed itself "Terra Flora Incorporated."

In 1993, Terra Flora began selling flowers internationally. The corporation formalized the setup of supply and distribution centers in Amsterdam and Seville by purchasing office space near the supply farms. Terra Flora modeled the centers on the Sacramento operation, which had changed significantly over the years. More U.S. distribution centers were purchased in Dallas, Texas and Boston, Massachusetts.

Organization of Terra Flora

Terra Flora is now organized in three major divisions: Retail Services, Supply and Manufacturing, and Nursery Products. Corporate and divisional headquarters are all located in Sacramento. Each division has business operations in North American and European locations.

- The Retail Services division manages the operations of all Terra Flora retail stores. The division is also responsible for the regional retail-distribution service centers in Sacramento, Dallas, Boston, Seville, and Amsterdam, and for the major retail centers in Los Angeles, New York City, and London, England.

- The Supply and Manufacturing provides the terra cotta pots. The original manufacturing plant is in Sacramento, and a remote site is in Amsterdam.

- The Nursery Products division has remote sites in Seville and Amsterdam in addition to the Sacramento nursery.

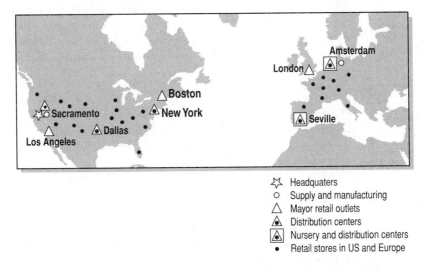

Figure 4.1   International locations of Terra Flora division sites

Until now, each division of Terra Flora operated as a separate company, implementing policies and procedures that the divisional managers felt were necessary to perform the various business functions. The autonomy of each division was the result of rapid growth and the fact that the procedures that were in place in each division worked well enough, in spite of some inefficiencies.

Each Terra Flora division also operates separate, heterogeneous computer environments that separately track and record various business functions, including sales, ordering, accounting, inventory, and division-specific information. Information is sent to division headquarters in Sacramento, where it is consolidated. None of the networks in any of the divisions communicate with the computers in other divisions. Consolidating information for the entire company means entering the same data several times into different computer systems.

The disadvantages of the situation are clear. It is costly, and information is redundant. Management reports are prone to error because synchronization of information is difficult. The heterogeneous networks must interoperate if the Terra Flora divisions are to merge and operate as a single business unit, relying on a centralized information database.

To meet this challenge, the company hired a new Chief Information Officer, who had managed the implementation of a similar strategic plan for another corporation before joining Terra Flora. As a first step, the CIO has asked each of the divisions to submit a list of the computer hardware and operating systems for analysis, along with descriptions of the major divisional business processes. The list would indicate the computer and manual interfaces into the processes. Each division has also been asked to supply network diagrams and brief descriptions of the databases and software applications that run on each computer. Analysis will be performed on each division in an attempt to decide which computer hardware and software from each division best fits the corporate strategy.

The immediate goal is to connect and maintain the existing systems necessary to continue business operations. In the long term, Terra Flora plans to migrate the existing systems applications to less costly and lower-maintenance client/server applications. More analysis of the custom applications must be done to determine the best features of those products and to create a plan for implementing the necessary client/server applications.

Retail Services Division

Because the Retail Services division grew by purchasing other florist shops, the division acquired those shops' computer equipment and software systems as part of the purchases. That computer equipment was then incorporated into the division's network.

The Retail Services Network

The network diagram below provides a representation of the computer equipment running in the Retail Services division.

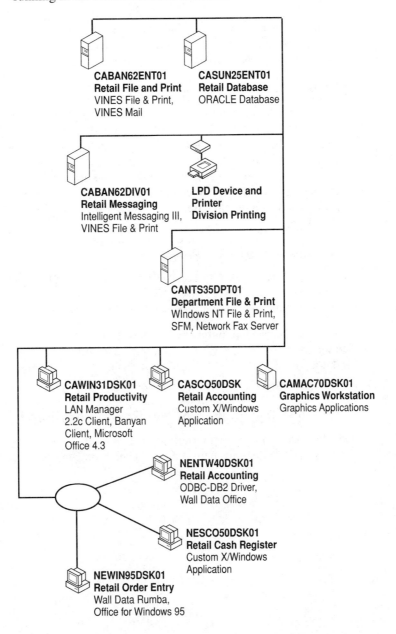

Figure 4.2   Retail Division network diagram before company-wide consolidation

The retail division was relatively slow to computerize. The division purchased the Sun server, currently named CASUN25ENT01, early in the 1980s. Custom applications were written, which are still updated and further customized as needed.

Distribution was incorporated into the Retail Services divisional operations when the distribution center in Dallas was purchased. A Banyan server was obtained as part of that purchase, which provides file and print services to the division.

Workings of the Sun Server

This server runs the Solaris SPARC version 2.5 operating system. The ORACLE database focuses on retail sales information, with emphasis on distribution and inventory information. Customized business application systems on the Sun server include an inventory-management system, accounting system, customer-ordering system, product-ordering system, point-of-sale application (including a custom exchange rate application to calculate the monetary differences in international customer orders and purchases), distribution software, and delivery-truck scheduling.

Workings of the Banyan Server

The Banyan server runs a Banyan VINES 6.22 network operating system. The server provides file and print services to the Retail Services division headquarters in Sacramento. Banyan mail messaging is provided through Beyond Mail.

Whenever Terra Flora purchased a retail store, the store was connected to the Sun server and then given access to appropriate information stored on the server. The retail stores are provided file and print services for management reports and sales tickets through printers on site in the stores.

Business Processes of the Retail Services Division

The business processes in Retail Services fall into two categories: dealings with consumers and dealings between the distribution centers and the retail stores.

Interactions with Consumers

1. The retail store receives customer orders in a number of ways:

   - A customer can walk into a retail store, place an order, and either take delivery or have the order delivered within a specified time.

   - A customer can phone or fax an order to the retail store and request delivery within a specified time.

   - A customer can phone in an order using the 1-800 phone lines. The order is forwarded to the appropriate retail store for delivery within the specified time.

2. Except for orders taken over the 1-800 lines, customer orders are entered into the system on the SCO computer, named CASC050DSK, which appears on the network diagram in the California domain at the Desktop level. This entry is made through an X/Windows front-end application. Orders that come in on the 1-800 phone line are entered on the SCO computer by the customer-service representative at the time the order is placed, while the customer is still on the phone.

3. The order data is posted to an ORACLE database running on the Sun server. This automatically triggers a division-wide examination and analysis of inventory and delivery schedules, and then triggers other business applications on other computers to perform the following functions:

   - If the customer order is placed in a retail store and the retail store can fill the order within the time frame specified by the customer, the inventory is relieved and a customer invoice is printed at the retail store on the local printer for delivery with the product.

   - If the customer order is placed in a retail store and the store cannot fill the order, the inventory of the retail stores in the area is examined. If an area retail store can fill the order, the order is forwarded to the delivery-schedule application of the area store for scheduling delivery within the customer-specified time frame. The inventory of the area store is relieved and a customer invoice prints on that store's local printer for delivery with the product.

   - If the customer order is placed in a retail store and neither the retail store or any area store can fill the order, the customer's order is placed on a product order to ensure that the order will arrive at the retail store and be delivered within the specified customer time frame.

   - If the customer order is placed over the 1-800 phone lines, the customer order is forwarded to a retail store that can fill the order within the customer's specified time frame. The inventory of the retail store is relieved and a customer invoice is printed on the local printer for delivery with the product or to give to the customer who chooses to pick up the product.

4. Standard accounting information is posted to the accounting database as a result of the customer order.

5. Automatic product orders are generated based on sales of product. The store manager reviews the order, accepts or changes the information on the order, and faxes the order to the proper distribution centers.

6. Delivery-truck schedules are produced and printed on local printers at the retail stores that are responsible for delivering customer orders.

Interactions Between Distribution Centers and Retail Stores

The Retail Services division is also responsible for the distribution of product from the distribution centers to the retail stores.

1. Each day, the ORACLE product-ordering database records the product received at the distribution center.

2. Distribution schedules are printed at corporate headquarters and the distribution sites, indicating which retail stores are to receive what products, based on the product orders submitted by the retail stores.

3. New product orders from the retail stores arrive by fax or telephone.

4. The product orders are entered into the ORACLE database on the Sun server.

5. Inventory is examined. If the products ordered are in stock, inventory is updated, product pick tickets are generated, and correct shipping labels and customs documents are printed at the proper printers in the distribution centers.

6. Accounting information in the ORACLE database is updated, as appropriate.

7. Orders for the flower products to be distributed are automatically generated and tracked in the ORACLE product-order database and then faxed or phoned to the proper nursery in the Nursery Products division or to the plant in the Supply and Manufacturing division.

Supply and Manufacturing Division

The Supply and Manufacturing division is responsible for the manufacturing of the signature terra cotta pots and other standard economy pots, as necessary. The division is also responsible for distributing the pots to the retail stores, based on stock and special orders placed by those stores.

The Supply and Manufacturing Network

The manufacturing plant was essentially an IBM shop when Terra Flora purchased it. The sale included the ES/9000, which was running various business-operations software. These software applications did not communicate with each other. The pot manufacturer had purchased an IBM AS/400 and had begun working on a plan to customize and migrate business operations from the ES/9000 to the AS/400.

Upon closer analysis, it was discovered that due to the specialized applications running on the ES/9000, such as the sophisticated money-exchange rate application, migration was not cost-effective. At that time, software was implemented on both servers to allow transfer of necessary information on a fixed schedule between the two machines.

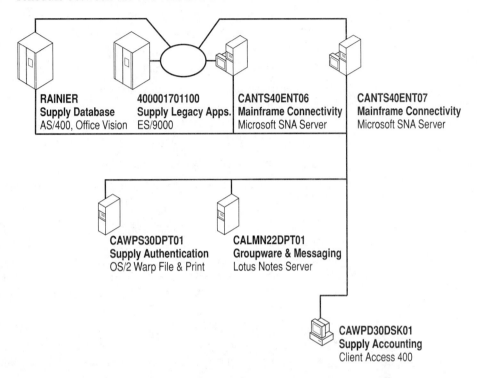

RAINIER
Supply Database
AS/400, Office Vision

400001701100
Supply Legacy Apps.
ES/9000

CANTS40ENT06
Mainframe Connectivity
Microsoft SNA Server

CANTS40ENT07
Mainframe Connectivity
Microsoft SNA Server

CAWPS30DPT01
Supply Authentication
OS/2 Warp File & Print

CALMN22DPT01
Groupware & Messaging
Lotus Notes Server

CAWPD30DSK01
Supply Accounting
Client Access 400

Figure 4.3   Supply and Manufacturing Division network diagram before company-wide consolidation

Functions of the ES/9000

The ES/9000 is running Virtual Machine/Enterprise Systems Architecture (VM/ESA). All the division's accounting applications and the sophisticated money exchange application run on the ES/9000.

Functions of the AS/400

The AS/400 is currently running V2R3 operating system; the databases for business operations are written in a combination of DB2 and RPG/400. The AS/400 runs applications including inventory management and control, a distribution-scheduling system, a production system, and the order system for raw materials for the production of the terra cotta pots and other lines of product.

Supply and Manufacturing Division's Business Processes

The business processes at the Supply and Manufacturing division are described below. Each process is numbered, and the process flow is documented using numbers and arrows on the network diagram.

1. The Supply and Manufacturing division receives product orders from their customers (the retail stores and distribution centers) by phone or fax.

2. An employee inputs the orders on a Warp client through a front-end application to a DB2 product-ordering database on the AS/400.

3. Exchange-rate information is automatically posted to the accounting database on the ES/9000.

4. A product order summary is printed, and the production manager schedules the production of pots for the day, based on the product orders received.

5. The production staff makes the scheduled product.

6. The daily production is entered into the production DB2 database on the AS/400.

7. The daily production is automatically posted to the accounting database on the ES/9000.

8. The production system on the AS/400 generates recommended stock orders, based on the raw materials used for the day's production. The orders are printed for the plant manager to review and, upon approval, are faxed to the suppliers of raw materials.

9. The production system updates the DB2 retail-store-customer ordering system. This updates on-hand inventory and then automatically recommends filling the outstanding product orders from the retail stores and distribution centers, based on production and the date on which the orders were submitted.

10. The retail-store-customer ordering system automatically sends appropriate accounting information to the accounting database on the ES/9000.

11. The retail-store-customer ordering system updates the DB2 distribution database about which orders are to be filled.

12. The distribution system prints product pick tickets, shipping labels, and necessary customs papers.

Nursery Products Division

Operations at the Nursery Products division are simpler because all the customers of the Nursery Products Division are in the Retail Services division.

The Nursery Products Network

When Terra Flora purchased the Sacramento nursery, a DECaxp150 running DEC UNIX and PATHWORKS version 5.0 was included in the purchase. All the applications are UNIX and include the following programs.

- Accounting
- A product-order system, for contacting the proper supplier for specific flowers
- A customer-order system, for tracking orders placed by the retail stores
- A delivery system, for tracking shipments to the retail stores and calculating the expected delivery of the products to the retail stores

The Sacramento nursery is the only one that is computerized.

All business operations for the Nursery Products division are tracked in databases on the DECaxp150 server running DEC UNIX, which are listed below.

- A customer-order database that lists the retail stores
- A product-order database, from which product orders are calculated
- Accounting
- An order-delivery database, which prints product pick tickets for the shipping department
- A labeling program, which prints package labels and international customs papers

The network diagram below represents the network computers used in the
Nursery Products division.

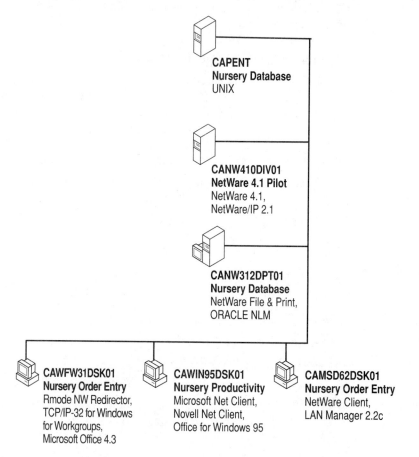

CAPENT
Nursery Database
UNIX

CANW410DIV01
NetWare 4.1 Pilot
NetWare 4.1,
NetWare/IP 2.1

CANW312DPT01
Nursery Database
NetWare File & Print,
ORACLE NLM

CAWFW31DSK01
Nursery Order Entry
Rmode NW Redirector,
TCP/IP-32 for Windows
for Workgroups,
Microsoft Office 4.3

CAWIN95DSK01
Nursery Productivity
Microsoft Net Client,
Novell Net Client,
Office for Windows 95

CAMSD62DSK01
Nursery Order Entry
NetWare Client,
LAN Manager 2.2c

**Figure 4.4   Nursery Products Division network diagram before company-wide
consolidation**

Nursery Products Division's Business Processes

The following list describes the process for the Nursery Products division.

1. Customer orders for products are received by phone or fax from retail stores.

2. The orders are input on any NetWare client into a front-end NetWare
   application.

3. Throughout the day, customer orders are processed by an ORACLE database
   on the DEC UNIX server.

4. A summary, based on the days orders, is printed and input into the accounting
   database on the UNIX server.

5. The bookkeeper posts the accounting information.

6. Inventory is checked, and those customer orders that can be filled are filled; then product pick tickets are printed and given to the shipping department.

7. Orders are boxed, and shipping labels and customs documents are typed on an IBM Selectric typewriter.

8. A daily summary of customer orders is printed for the nursery manager. Based on the inventory stocking levels, the manager phones the local or international farms to order enough stock to fill the retail customer orders.

9. The nursery manager records the items ordered from suppliers in the ORACLE product order database.

Reengineering the Terra Flora Network

Having summarized the main facts about the operations, current network usage, and business processes of each division, the CIO begins an analysis of the business and technical problems at Terra Flora and to create a plan. The planning will occur in three phases: studying the current network, organizing goals into priority levels, and developing a way to integrate the networks in a service-based model.

Understanding the Current Network

To understand the existing Terra Flora network, the newly hired CIO must go through the following steps.

- Identifying all hardware on the network, including clients, workstations, and servers. This information should be sufficiently detailed to help determine what equipment must be upgraded.

- Identifying the geographic extent of both the local area networks (LANs) and the wide area networks (WANs), including the media used for the LAN and to create the WAN.

- Identifying the location of the network components and operating systems.

- Identifying bandwidth information.

- Identifying specific user activities, the numbers of users doing those activities, and the usage patterns on the network.

- Identifying specific tasks, such as storing files, server backups, posting data to a database, data replication, and application distribution.

Realigning and Prioritizing the Goals

The business goals can be organized into the following priority levels.

- Business-critical goals
- Strategic goals
- User-benefit goals
- Wish-list goals

Business-critical Goals

Business-critical goals are goals that are required to do business. These goals must be accomplished as quickly as possible. Terra Flora identified the following business-critical goals, to be accomplished in no more than three months.

- To physically connect the three networks
- To migrate to the same network protocol
- To recognize security credentials, for authenticating network logons
- To allow users to share appropriate files and printers
- To integrate existing systems, for improving business processes
- To reduce training requirements
- To do business on the Internet

Strategic Goals

Strategic goals provide a clear benefit to the business. These goals can be accomplished within three to six months without harm or loss to the business. Terra Flora has the following strategic goals.

- To centralize user accounts
- To centralized network administration and backup
- To centralized application distribution
- To extend the Terra Flora network to all employees
- To create central information stores and applications
- To allow dynamic IP addressing in the network
- To give all employees electronic mail
- To electronically distribute corporate-wide information

User-benefit Goals

User-benefit goals provide a clear benefit to the user by enhancing productivity or increasing efficiency. These goals can be accomplished within six to twelve months without harm or loss to the business. Terra Flora has identified the following user-benefit goals.

- Internet access for Terra Flora employees
- Dial-up, telecommuting capabilities

Wish-list Goals

Goals on the wish list are amenities, but are not required. These goals can be accomplished at any time. Terra Flora has one item on its wish list, to integrate the DNS name space, using fully qualified domain names, such as mariag.terraflora.com.

Integrating the Networks Using a Services-based Model

The services provided on the network must be viewed independently of the divisional network structure. The integrated-network model groups the computers by the services they provide to the company rather than by division. The services can be grouped into four categories, called *layers:* Enterprise, Division, Department, and Desktop.

Table 4.1   Layers of the Services-based Network Model

Network Level	Services provided	Users
Enterprise	Support for the global network (such as centralized user accounts and network services) and providing master copies of common information across the organization	40,000
Division	Centralized file, print, and application services, focusing on business operations	100 to 1,000
Department	Local file, print, and application services	25 to 100
Desktop	Local file and application services	1 to 25

The new model also enables productive change in the following other areas.

- Integration of the information staff
- Centralization of network support
- Budgeting and tracking capital expenditures

The next sections describe the network services at each level and show how these will help create an efficient network at Terra Flora.

Enterprise Services

Servers at this level focus on supporting the global network (such as centralized user accounts and administration) and providing the master copy of common information across the organization. Enterprise servers are directly connected to the corporate or remote backbone, are kept in protected environments in the work area of the network administrators, and usually operate at 100 MB per second (such as by FDDI, CDDI, or Fast Ethernet). An Enterprise server might provide networking services for up to 40,000 users.

Local availability of the servers can affect which services exist at which level. When remote distances separate the servers and the users, backbone traffic can make timely access to these services difficult. Communications across WANs can be slow and costly. This makes direct, corporate-wide access to Enterprise services impractical. It makes sense to set up the servers at this top (Enterprise) level to maintain and update information, which users would access at lower levels.

For example, a server can be the master distribution point for site- or corporate-licensed software, standard corporate applications, and employee information. The master source servers would store the master copy, which would be used to replicate sources and download to servers on the Division level. This ensures that they are synchronized with the master corporate copy. Since Division-level servers are local to the users in the division, this replication and synchronization reduces both the network traffic on the corporate backbone and the cost of WAN communications.

Enterprise servers can also host the master copy of the distribution packages deployed by Microsoft Systems Management Servers.

The services typically offered at this level include the following items.

- Logon authentication

  This service ensures that users can log on to the network and perform the tasks for which they have permission. NetLogon is the Windows NT service that performs this function.

- Replicated user account database

  This service allows a copy of the Directory Database (formerly called SAM) to be replicated on other servers, effectively distributing the logon authentication process. Under Windows NT Server, NetLogon performs this function.

- Centralized network services

  These services allow an administrator to configure network services that affect the entire network and to make any administrative changes from one site.

  For example, a Dynamic Host Configuration Protocol (DHCP) server can be added to the network and configured to allow centrally defined global and subnet TCP/IP parameters for the entire internetwork. When a workstation computer moves between subnets, it is automatically reconfigured for TCP/IP at system startup.

- Name resolution

  This service centralizes the resolution of the unique user names and TCP/IP addresses that allow access to computer resources on the network.

  For example, a server running the Windows Internet Name Service (WINS) server software would perform this function. WINS servers maintain a database that maps computer names to IP addresses, allowing users to communicate with other computers and gain all the benefits of using TCP/IP.

  As another example, a DNS server also provides dynamic mapping of domain names to IP addresses and is the commonly used name-resolution service in environments running a UNIX operating system.

- Backup

  Servers at any level typically provide backup services for the next lower level of servers. Enterprise servers perform this function for the servers on the Division level, which, in turn, perform backups for the Department-level servers. Enterprise servers do not usually back up for the Department level.

- Limited protocol service support

  To reduce network traffic across the Enterprise backbone, servers at this level might support only one or two networking protocols. Frequently, the choice is the TCP/IP protocol.

- Internet Services (using the Internet Information Server service)

  These servers can be used to create web sites that the public can access for corporate information and customer-focused marketing.

- Intranet Services (using the Internet Information Server service)

  These servers store information that is to be available to all employees on the internal corporate network, but not to users outside of the company or organization. This might include corporate standards, employee benefits, corporate events, and other information, such as job listings. These Enterprise-level servers typically host references to the Division-level servers. For example, an Enterprise server might refer to a Division web site for the company's retail operations.

- Site

  These services affect organization sites but are hidden to the users. For example, the Enterprise servers can act as storage and master source for distribution of organization-supported software. The replicator service distributes the software to the Division level for distribution to the lower levels.

Division Services

This level typically contains the centralized file and print application, focusing on business operations. Division-level servers often provide networking services for up to 1,000 users, although they can be scaled to support larger numbers of users.

If the location of the division or region requires connecting over slower WAN links, then Enterprise services may be supplied at this level.

The Division level usually include the following services.

- Heterogeneous file and print interfaces

  These interfaces allow interoperability with other servers including UNIX, NetWare, LAN Server, and Banyan VINES.

- Integration

  This level may provide heterogeneous protocols, such as TCP/IP, IPX/SPX, SNA, and VINES IP, which allow integration with services offered on UNIX, NetWare, or mainframe Enterprise servers.

- Intranet Information services (using the Internet Information Server service)

  These servers provide corporate information that focuses on the division or region. For example, project plans, schedules, reviews, presentations, and background information for the division are stored here. Data sheets, product reviews, product comparisons, and product specification sheets may also be stored here for easy access and distribution to field sales and marketing personnel.

- Backup

  Servers at any level typically provide backup services for the next lower level of servers. For example, Division servers perform this function for servers on the Department level.

Department Services

Servers at this level focus on the business tasks. These servers provide local file, print, and application services. They also provide temporary file storage for workgroup projects, home directories, and scheduled-backup directories. In a typical scenario for this level, servers are organized by workgroups or departments to provide networking services for 25 to 100 users.

At the Enterprise level, a limited number of high-cost, high-performance servers address the centralized needs of the entire organization. At the Division level, less expensive servers provide adequate performance to a smaller group. At the Department level, a server may be a workstation-class machine, such as a 486 computer with 16 MB RAM running Windows NT Server.

Department-level servers typically provide the following services.

- Departmental or branch-office projects

  Information is stored about the department tasks and workgroup projects. Enterprise and Division servers can access this information to compile reports.

- Intranet Information services (using the Internet Information Server service)

  This information is specific to the Department. Status reports and the supporting information may be posted here for everyone to browse through at their convenience.

- Internet services (using the Internet Information Server service)

  At this level, project web sites may be created and posted to the Internet.

- Backup

  Servers at any level typically provide backup services for servers or computers on the next lower level. Department servers perform this function for Desktop computers.

Desktop Services

In most corporations, the desktop computer is the productivity platform, running either Windows 95 or Windows NT Workstation with various applications, such as Microsoft Office and custom programs for specific business needs. The focus here is to provide services to remote, mobile-networking, and desktop clients. The logical grouping of the desktop groups may include small departments of 5 to 20 people, or may include thousands of desktop computers. The services offered include the following functions.

- Local, personal file storage

  The Desktop provides local storage for personal files and application data for business applications.

- Local applications

  For productivity desktops, the local applications might include Microsoft Office Professional. For developer-class desktops, this might include Microsoft Visual C++® compilers and debug versions of the operation systems. For Internet Information Server service (IIS) developers, this might include IIS and SQL applications.

Creating the Information Plan

The 12-month objective at Terra Flora is to accomplish all the business-critical goals and as many as possible of the strategic goals.

Windows NT network services and some third-party services will be implemented to integrate the systems. Windows NT Workstation, Windows NT Server, or Windows 95 will be installed on any new equipment the company purchases, as appropriate to the role that the equipment will play in the Terra Flora network.

The information plan identifies the technical solutions for reaching the business goals as outlined in Table 4.2.

Table 4.2   Solutions for the Terra Flora Business Plan

Goal Priority	Business Goal	Technical Solutions for Information Plan
Business critical	Physically connect the three networks	Purchase routers and switches, as necessary to connect the network efficiently.
Business critical	Allow users to share files and printers as appropriate	Windows NT file and print (or, FPNW for NetWare clients; PCNFS for UNIX clients; Banyan File & Print for Windows NT for Banyan clients).
Business critical	Integrate all existing systems that facilitate business processes	Use SNA server to connect to the ES/9000 and AS/400. More analysis of the custom applications must be done for two reasons: to determine the best features of those products, and to create a plan for implementing the workstation and server applications necessary to effectively operate the business.
Business critical	Reduce training requirements	Provide a consistent, easy-to-use user interface for both desktop and server platforms. Allow connectivity to heterogeneous systems through a consistent interface.
Business critical	Do business on the Internet	The Terra Flora marketing department wants the corporation to create web pages for the Internet. These pages would feature images of popular floral arrangements. Customers would click an image to order it directly from the nearest retail order desk. Web pages would also list retail store locations and operating hours, the history of the company, product information, appropriate inventory data, and marketing information, such as seasonal specials. Internal departments responsible for maintaining web-page information would be given access to the pages.
Business critical	Migrate to the same network protocol	Install and configure TCP/IP on all platforms.
Business critical	Recognize security credentials and centrally authenticate network logons	Windows NT Network logon service will be used to authenticate credentials and provide single network log on.

Table 4.2   Solutions for the Terra Flora Business Plan *(continued)*

Goal Priority	Business Goal	Technical Solutions for Information Plan
Strategic	Centralized user accounts	Use Windows NT Server directory services to provide enterprise-wide user names and passwords.
		Trust relationships will be set up between domains, creating a single network logon.
Strategic	Centralized network administration and backup	Using Windows NT replication service for Enterprise-level databases, WINS, DNS, and DHCP services. For online backup, deploy Octopus for Windows NT. For the backup of data and software master copies, use Seagate Backup Exec for Windows NT.
Strategic	Extend the Terra Flora network to all employees	Use the built-in Windows NT RAS to connect mobile users.
		Use Windows NT Server PPTP to connect remote sites across the Internet, using a secure link.
		Create a secure communications link between the Seville site and headquarters in Sacramento.
Strategic	Create central information stores and applications	Analyze software applications to maintain the best ones, and program what is missing. Automate the manual tasks, as appropriate, such as the production line and distribution centers.
Strategic	Allow dynamic IP addressing in the network	Use Windows NT DHCP Server, and enable all capable DHCP clients.
Strategic	Give all employees electronic mail	Migrate to Microsoft Exchange.
Strategic	Electronically distribute corporate-wide information	Use Internet Information Server and Internet Explorer to distribute corporate-wide information.

Terra Flora Network Systems Diagram

The diagram inside the back cover of this book provides an illustration of the new network model for Terra Flora. All primary services and computers systems for Terra Flora are shown. For brevity, only a representative sample of worldwide retail operations is shown.

Naming Conventions

Each computer is labeled with a name that includes the following information.

- The computer name for the server
- The server IP address
- The services running on that computer

The first line below each computer icon lists the computer name, which has 12 characters. These follow specific naming conventions, with each character representing additional information about the computer.

- Characters 1 and 2

  The first two characters indicate the domain of which the computer is a part. Terra Flora uses the following domain symbols.
- CA, which represents the California domain
- NE, which represents the North East domain
- EU, which represents the Europe domain

- Characters 3-7

  The five characters following the domain symbol represent the operating system that the computer is running. Table 4.3 lists the five-character codes and the systems they represent.

  Table 4.3   Codes for Operating Systems

Operating System Code	Operating System Description
NTS40	Microsoft Windows NT Server 4.0
NTW40	Microsoft Windows NT Workstation 4.0
BAN62	Banyan 6.22
SUN25	SPARC 2.5
NW410	Novell NetWare 4.10
WPS30	IBM OS/2 Warp Connect Server 3.0
LMN22	Microsoft LAN Manager 2.2c
NTS35	Microsoft Windows NT Server 3.51
NW312	Novell NetWare 3.12
WIN31	Microsoft Windows 3.1
WIN95	Microsoft Windows 95
SCO50	Santa Cruz Operations Open Server 5.0
WPD30	IBM OS/2 Warp Desktop 3.0
MSD62	MS-DOS 6.22
MAC70	Macintosh Operating System 7.0
KIOSK	Santa Cruz Operations Open Desktop 5.0
CAPENT	DEC UNIX, with PATHWORKS 5.0
RAINIER	IBM AS/400
MAC 400001701100	ES/9000, with Virtual Machine Enterprise Systems Architecture (VM\ESA)

- Characters 8-10

  These represent a three-character code for the service level.

  - ENT, which represents the Enterprise level
  - DIV, which represents the Division level
  - DPT, which represents the Department level
  - DSK, which represents the Desktop level

- Characters 11 & 12

  These characters are the identification number for the computer. A computer number can be any number between 01 and 99.

Computer Software

Various software was installed on different computers. This software will be used to provide services to the computer network. The first text line in the diagram is reserved for the computer's name, and line two is reserved for the computer's IP address. The remainder of the text indicates the software loaded on each computer. The following table lists the codes and descriptions of the software represented by the code.

Table 4.4   Codes for Software

Software Code	Software Description
IIS (Internet)	Internet Information Server for connecting to the Internet.
PPTP	Point to Point Tunneling Protocol used to create secure communications over the Internet between Seville remote site and Sacramento site.
Deployment Server	A big server owned by the IS department of Terra Flora. It is typically used for projects. For example, all the documentation and files for the current migration project are stored on this server.
IIS (Intranet)	Microsoft Internet Information Server for Intranet internal, corporate network.
F&P	File and Print software. Specific to providers installed on the network.
Banyan F & P	Banyan VINES 6.2 allows file and print sharing with Microsoft Windows NT.
Banyan Vines Mail	Messaging service compatible with the Banyan Operating System.
Member Server	A server running Windows NT 4.0 that is neither a PDC or a BDC.
Backup RAS	A Microsoft Windows NT system running more RAS, fault tolerance, and authentication services, to relieve tasks from the primary RAS Server.
SNA	Protocol software used on the network to connect to the mainframe ES/9000 and AS/400.
SMS Central Site	Microsoft Systems Management Server 1.2 Central Site.
CA PDC	The California PDC which is used to authenticate logon access to the network and network resources.
DHCP	Dynamic Host Configuration Protocol, used to dynamically lease IP addresses to computers when they change subnets.
WINS	Windows Internet Name System, used to dynamically provide name resolution from NetBIOS names to TCP/IP addresses.

Table 4.4   Codes for Software *(continued)*

Software Code	Software Description
DNS	Domain Name Space, used to provide name resolution from fully qualified domain names to IP addresses.
CA BDC	The California Back up Domain Controller, used to provide fault tolerance and to replicate the directory services database through which users are authenticated. Also will perform logon authentication.
RAS	Remote Access Service provides secure dial-up access to internal network.
GSNW	Gateway Services for NetWare enables NetWare clients to access files from Microsoft Windows NT.
FPNW	File and Print Services for NetWare enables NetWare clients to share files and print resources on servers running Windows NT.
IM3	Intelligent Messaging mail service from Banyan.
Intranet Server	Internal corporate-network server used on corporate network to provide interactive information services to users through Internet protocols, such as HTTP, FTP, and Gopher.
Warp Authentication	Authentication for Warp Clients.
Lotus Notes Server	Groupware application.
Services for Macintosh	Allows Macintosh clients to authenticate to Windows NT directory services and access file and print services on Window NT Server.
ORACLE NLM	ORACLE NetWare Loadable Module.
LM 2.2 Client	LAN Manager 2.2c client software, providing network access to MS-DOS clients and MS-DOS-based Windows Operating systems. Also allows logon authentication to Microsoft Window NT Server Directory Services.
Banyan client	Client on the Banyan VINES Network.
TCP/IP-32 for WFW	32bit Protect mode stack for Window 3.11.
Rmode NW redir	Real mode NetWare redirector allows MS-DOS and Windows clients to access resources on NetWare servers.
MS Net Client	The generic network client allows basic network access to Microsoft Windows NT Services.
Novell Net Client	Novell network redirector for accessing File and Print Services on NetWare servers.
X/Windows	Windowing environment for UNIX systems in an alternate client/server model.
Warp Connect	Network enabled Warp server.
MS-DOS 6.22	Microsoft DOS version 6.22.

Table 4.4   Codes for Software *(continued)*

Software Code	Software Description
Microsoft Windows NTW	Microsoft Windows NT Workstation.
NFS Redir	Enables connectivity with a server providing access to the Network File System (NFS), typically UNIX Systems.
Extra! For NTW	Terminal-emulation application for mainframe host connectivity 3270/5250.
MPR	Multi-Protocol Routing allows IP packets to be routed across subnets.
NE BDC	North East backup domain controller used for authentication and replication of the directory database stored on the PDC.
EU BDC	Europe backup domain controller used for authentication and replication of the directory database stored on the PDC.

CHAPTER 5

Network Services: Enterprise Level

The following chapter is a tested but largely unedited draft of material that will appear in expanded form in the next update of the Windows NT Server Resource Kit. *At that time, the case study will be further revised and expanded to include details about the Divisional, Department, and Desktop server services and other helpful information.*

Chapter 4 introduced Terra Flora, a hypothetical case study of a fictitious company and of the challenges that company faces in bringing together its diverse, previously independent networks. The purpose of the case study is to show in real-world terms how network administrators and information officers can utilize Windows NT to integrate new and legacy hardware and software in a cost-effective way. The chapter further analyzed the Terra Flora case and developed a plan for interoperability. The next step for Terra Flora is to make choices about the Windows NT Server services and to configure those services.

Services will ultimately be configured on four defined levels of usage, depending on the scope of those services within the organization. These levels are, in order of increasingly narrow scope: Enterprise, Division, Department (or Branch Office), and Desktop. This chapter will deal with server services, but only on the Enterprise level. Detailed discussions of service configurations for the other three levels are not included in this edition of the Microsoft Windows NT 4.0 *Networking Guide.*

Enterprise-level server services are the those provided on a large scale to the entire network. These services primarily support the network itself; they are services that support other servers and keep the corporation-wide information synchronized on all areas of the network. These services include the following:

- Dynamic Host Configuration Protocol (DHCP)
- Windows Internet Name Service (WINS)
- Domain Name System (DNS)
- Network Logon Services
- Centralized Services
- Replication
- Backup
- Point-to-Point Tunneling Protocol

This chapter will make repeated references to the Terra Flora Network Diagram, printed on the inside back cover of this book. For convenience, open the diagram now so that you can easily refer to it as you read these discussions

Terra Flora is a totally fictitious company whose business operations and networking environment are being examined and used to demonstrate the functionality of Windows NT Server products throughout this Interoperability section. The names of companies, products, people, characters, and data mentioned herein are fictitious and are in no way intended to represent any real individual, company, product, or event, unless otherwise noted.

Preparations for Configuring Services

Before configuring services, Terra Flora needed to set up the hardware for these services and to adopt the protocols that the networks would use to communicate among themselves and with the Internet. The new protocols must then be installed and configured.

Selecting Protocol Standards

The first decision Terra Flora needs to make is which protocol to adopt as the protocol-of-choice for their network, which protocols to retain, and which to abandon.

Terra Flora's Choice of Protocols

Terra Flora elected to use Transmission Control Protocol/Internet Protocol (TCP/IP) as their network protocol of choice, while retaining Systems Network Architecture (SNA) protocols for connection to the legacy systems.

Why Terra Flora Chose TCP/IP as a Primary Standard

TCP/IP is a standard set of networking protocols that govern how data passes between the networked computers. With TCP/IP, Terra Flora networks will interoperate by using the Windows NT Workstation and Windows NT Server platforms with devices that use Microsoft Windows 95, other Microsoft networking products, and non-Microsoft operating systems, such as UNIX.

Many reasons supported the Terra Flora decision to use TCP/IP as the preferred network protocol.

TCP/IP is the primary protocol of the Internet and the World Wide Web. One of the primary goals of Terra Flora is to establish a presence on the Internet, allowing customers, nurseries, retail stores, and manufacturing sites to place orders directly. Terra Flora sees this as essential to keeping Terra Flora competitive.

TCP/IP is a very clean and efficient suite of standard protocols that can be used on both local and wide-area networks (WANs) to provide communications between all the basic operating systems on the network.

TCP/IP has the advantage of already being in place in parts of the Terra Flora network. TCP/IP currently supports communications between all UNIX-based systems and the AS/400 at Terra Flora, and is running on the following equipment.

- Computers running Windows NT Workstation and Windows NT Server
- Computers running Windows for Workgroups
- Computers running Windows 95
- Computers running LAN Manager

For a detailed discussion on TCP/IP see Chapter 6, "TCP/IP Implementation Details."

Why Terra Flora Chose SNA as a Secondary Standard

SNA Protocol enables communication between the department and divisions servers and the enterprise mainframe and AS/400 legacy application services. In the near future, SNA will remain, but Terra Flora plans to review the options of moving all the SNA dependent services to TCP/IP in a cost effective manner. If this is not an option, SNA will remain on the network as the protocol to access the legacy applications.

Why Terra Flora Rejected Other Protocol Options

Three other protocols are currently in place in various parts of the Terra Flora networks. The decisions to abandon these protocols as network standards were based on the reasons given in each case, as described below.

IPX/SPX

In the past, Terra Flora used the IPX/SPX protocol only in the Nursery Products division, to support NetWare services. IPX is easy to install and is dynamic in that it requires no configuration changes for either mobile or relocated network nodes.

Despite these advantages, the expense and performance degradation anticipated under this protocol for such a large and diverse network deterred Terra Flora from establishing IPX/SPX as a protocol standard. The protocol's reliance on network-wide broadcasts make overhead unreasonably high for effective WAN implementations.

IPX/SPX protocol depends on broadcasts of Service Advertising Protocol (SAP) and Routing Information Protocol (RIP) packets for network name-resolution services built into NetWare. SAP and RIP broadcasts are updated every sixty seconds by each server and sent to the entire network. These ongoing broadcasts are negligible within a local LAN environment. However, when IPX networks are connected in an enterprise manner, SAP and RIP broadcasts can dramatically erode the available bandwidth.

For the immediate future, Terra Flora will continue to use IPX/SPX for interchange of files between NetWare and other networking clients. Within the next year, Terra Flora aims to replace all hardware that depends on the IPX/SPX protocol with hardware that utilizes TCP/IP, and to phase out the IPX/SPX protocol.

AppleTalk

AppleTalk is a Macintosh-based protocol that runs primarily in peer-to-peer situations and has very limited support on other platforms.

At Terra Flora, AppleTalk has been used locally in the Retail Services division for graphics-art communications between Macintosh computers, which store the graphic software. Due to the small number of machines, the Macintosh computers were hooked together to form a peer-to-peer network.

Under the new Terra Flora plan, Windows NT Server Services for Macintosh will be added to the departmental servers running Windows NT Server, to provide file interchange and primary support for the Macintosh computers and the rest of the network. Although the Macintosh computers don't support TCP/IP, AppleTalk is enabled on the routers, allowing the Macintosh computers to communicate with the Department-level servers running Windows NT Server Services for Macintosh.

NetBEUI

NetBEUI is a non-routed, broadcast-based protocol. The master browser on TCP/IP networks cannot see or display computers that use NetBEUI to communicate with the network in the network browser list.

NetBEUI was used as a legacy protocol for networking between Windows 3.1 and MS-DOS clients. Terra Flora has already removed NetBEUI from all bridges and routed networks. Within the next six months, the Terra Flora client computers that rely on NetBEUI will be removed from the network or upgraded to Windows 95. The plan at Terra Flora is that no NetBEUI traffic will exist on any network segment after the next six months.

Installing and Configuring TCP/IP

Protocols are selected during the installation of a Windows NT operating system. The TCP/IP protocol must be configured differently for the various clients and client services.

The Terra Flora plan is to reduce network administration and improve performance by installing DHCP, WINS, and DNS to dynamically address computers, resolve names, and easily integrate with the existing UNIX environment. The installation of DHCP for dynamic addressing will decrease administration by lowering the number of entries necessary when the computers are moved from one physical location to another. The installation of WINS and DNS to resolve names will decrease the network traffic caused by computers announcing their presence to the network.

Configuring TCP/IP Clients

Only clients running an operating system software from the list below can be configured to act as a DHCP and WINS clients.

- Windows NT Workstation version 3.5 or higher
- Windows NT Server version 3.5 or higher
- Windows for Workgroups 3.11 with the Microsoft 32-bit TCP/IP VxD installed
- Microsoft Network Client for MS-DOS with real mode TCP/IP driver; this is one of the clients included on the Windows NT Server 3.5 or higher product
- LAN Manager 2.2x for MS-DOS, included on the Windows NT Server version 3.5 CD-ROM and in the Windows NT Server 4.0 product
- A Windows 95 computer

The configured clients can request DHCP IP addresses from computers running Windows NT Server DHCP service to communicate on the network with other computers. Configured clients can register their NetBIOS names with computers running Windows NT Server WINS service. The names and IP addresses will be passed to other computers to permit communications between the computers on the network. The configured clients can be located by computers running Windows NT Server DNS service and, therefore, communicate with other computers on the network.

Additional information on DHCP, WINS, and DNS appears later in this chapter and in Chapter 7 "Managing Microsoft DHCP Servers"; Chapter 8, "Managing Microsoft WINS Servers"; and Chapter 9, "Managing Microsoft DNS Servers."

The ability to use Windows NT Server DHCP service to obtain an address at startup is configured on the TCP/IP Properties dialog box, as illustrated on the **Microsoft TCP/IP Properties** dialog box below.

▶ **To open the TCP/IP Properties dialog box**

1. Click **Start**, point to **Settings**, and click **Control Panel**.

2. Double-click **Network**.

3. Click the **Protocols** tab.

4. In **Network Protocols**, click **TCP/IP Protocol**.

5. Click **Properties**.

   The **Microsoft TCP/IP Properties** dialog box appears.

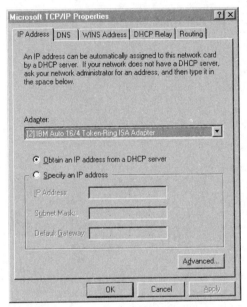

All three client services, DHCP, WINS, and DNS will be configured using this graphical interface.

Configuring the DHCP Client

A computer running Windows NT Server DHCP service can be configured to automatically provide IP addresses of the WINS and DNS servers used in the name resolution process. This removes the requirement of individually configuring each client with the WINS and DNS server IP addresses.

▶ **To configure a DHCP client**

- In the **IP Address** tab of the **Microsoft TCP/IP** Properties dialog box, click **Obtain an IP address from a DHCP server**, and then click **OK**.

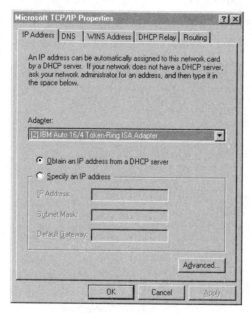

You must restart your computer for the new settings to take effect.

Notes

- During the setup of Windows NT Workstation, you can elect to receive an IP address from a DHCP server. If you select **Yes**, then **Obtain an IP address from a DHCP server** is set as the default, and the procedure above is unnecessary.

- The client computer will attempt to lease an IP address from the computer running Windows NT DHCP Server service. To obtain an address, the Scopes must be defined for the DHCP Server and addresses assigned to the Scopes for the client's subnet.

Configuring the WINS Client

A computer running Windows NT Server DHCP service can be configured to automatically provide IP addresses of the WINS and DNS servers used in the name resolution process. This removes the requirement of individually configuring each client with the WINS and DNS server IP addresses. The only requirement for the client is to click **Obtain an IP address from a DHCP server** in the **Microsoft TCP/IP Properties** dialog box.

The ability to use the Windows NT Server WINS service to resolve a client-computer request for other network computer names mapped to IP addresses is configured through TCP/IP. To do this, you need to know the following information.

- Primary WINS Server address. This is the IP address of the WINS server that the client will register its name and IP address with.
- Secondary WINS Server address. This is the WINS server that the client will register with and which will be used if the Primary WINS server is unavailable.

▶ **To configure a WINS client**

1. In the **Microsoft TCP/IP Properties** dialog box, click the **WINS Address** tab.
2. Type the appropriate server addresses in **Primary WINS** and **Secondary WINS**.
3. Set the following options.
    - To ensure that DNS servers will also be used to resolve client requests, select the **Enable DNS for Windows Resolution** check box.
    - To ensure that the LMHOSTS file will be used to resolve name requests from the client if WINS should fail, select the **Enable LMHOSTS Lookup** check box.

4. Click **OK** when all settings are entered, as shown in the dialog box below.

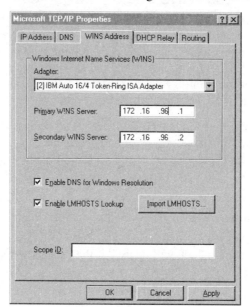

You must restart your computer for the new settings to take effect.

Configuring the DNS Client

A computer running Windows NT Server DHCP service can be configured to automatically provide IP addresses of the WINS and DNS servers used in the name resolution process. This removes the requirement of individually configuring each client with the WINS and DNS server IP addresses. The only requirement for the client is to click **Obtain an IP address from a DHCP server** in the **Microsoft TCP/IP Properties** dialog box.

The ability to use the Windows NT Server DNS service to resolve client requests for other network computer names is configured through TCP/IP.

▶ **To configure a DNS client**

1. In the **Microsoft TCP/IP Properties** dialog box, click the **DNS** tab.

2. In **Host Name**, type the client computer name.

3. In **Domain**, type the name of the authoritative domain.

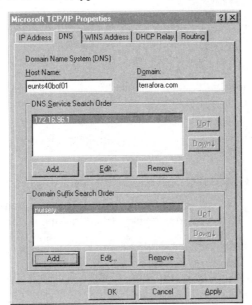

4. Under **Domain Service Search Order**, type the IP address of the server that will be used to resolve DNS name queries, and click **Add**.

   The **TCP/IP DNS Server** dialog box appears.

5. In **DNS Server IP address**, type the IP address of the DNS server that will be searched to resolve name-to-IP address queries, and click **Add**.

6. In **Domain Suffix Search Order**, type the domain suffix, click **Add**, and then click **OK**.

   You must restart your computer for the new settings to take effect.

Notes

- The domain name that would be entered for Terra Flora in step 3 of this procedure is Terraflora.com. For a complete discussion of domain names, see Chapter 3, "Implementation Considerations" of *the* Microsoft Windows NT Server 4.0 *Networking Supplement*.

- **DNS Service Search Order** contains the IP addresses of any DNS servers on the network (whether running Windows NT Server 4.0 DNS service or not).

- **Domain Suffix Search Order** indicated which subdomains will be searched to resolve the name queries.

Dynamic IP Addressing

All networked computers require both a unique name and address to communicate with any other networked computer. These addresses can be either dynamic or static.

- *Dynamic addressing* automatically assigns an address to a computer when the computer is turned on or is moved to a different location (subnet) on the network.

- *Static addressing* requires that an administrator configure new addresses.

Terra Flora's Choice of Addressing Services

Terra Flora has elected to use the Windows NT Dynamic Host Configuration Protocol (DHCP) to provide dynamic IP-addressing of the network computers.

Static configuration of client addresses can be expensive in terms of administrative effort and time. Currently, DHCP is the only open standard, which means it can interoperate with other operating systems. All other dynamic addressing products are proprietary.

Also, Terra Flora previously decided to standardize on the TCP/IP protocols with limited support for SNA protocol. The choice of DHCP helps keep the network administration costs down.

Other factors in the decision were Terra Flora's anticipated rate of corporate growth, the network requirements of traveling corporate personnel, and the requirements of the Internet. By setting up a dynamic system for addressing, Terra Flora can more easily accomplish its business goals in these areas.

Several tasks need to be accomplished to set up DHCP services for Terra Flora.

First, the servers that will become the DHCP servers need to be set up with static server addresses and then the DHCP Service must be installed on those servers.

Second, all the servers with DHCP enabled must be added to the DHCP Manager server list so that they can be administered.

Third, DHCP Scopes must be defined. This further involves establishing ranges of leased addresses for each subnet and configuring the optional configuration settings for those leases.

Fourth, Terra Flora will use DHCP Manager to reserve some IP addresses on the network for certain computers and devices.

Fifth, Terra Flora will configure a DHCP Relay Agent.

Administrative costs are reduced when network IP addressing tasks are performed by the servers instead of the administrative personnel; who are then free to perform other tasks. For example, the administrative task such as setup and maintenance of manual IP address tables to indicate which computer has which IP address will eliminated along with the need for administrators to travel to the physical location of computers to input or change the IP addresses.

Windows NT Server 4.0 supports DHCP to provide dynamic network addressing to clients. Currently it is the only open standard which can interoperate with other operating systems other products are proprietary.

Configuring DHCP

Procedures Used to Set Up DHCP

Computers running Windows NT Server are already placed throughout the Terra Flora network. On the Terra Flora network diagram, servers operating the DHCP service have been located in all three domains. In the California domain, CANTS40ENT03 is designated as a DHCP server. In the Northeast domain, NENTS40ENT01 plays that role, and in the Europe domain, it is EUNTS40ENT01. The DHCP service is part of the Windows NT Server product, and enabling the service is simple to do.

Configuring Static Server Addresses

A client computer obtains an address from a computer running the DHCP service when the client computer starts up. This depends on the client being able to locate the server responsible for leasing it an IP address. Because of this, the IP address of the server must not change; that is, the server running the DHCP service must have a static (unchanging) IP address.

▶ **To configure a static server address**

1. In the **Microsoft TCP/IP Properties** dialog box, click the **IP Address** tab.

2. In **Adapter**, select the network adapter for which you wish to specify an IP address (if necessary), and then click **OK**.

3. Click **Specify an IP address**.

   The settings in your dialog box will be similar to the following:

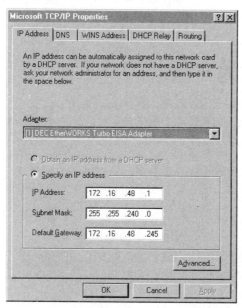

   You must restart the server for these settings to take effect.

   The option selected in the diagram is **Specify an IP address**. The administrator assigns a static IP Address, Subnet Mask, and Default Gateway address for the DHCP server.

Note If the administrator specified an IP address and IP address information during the setup of Windows NT Server, the above step can be skipped.

Installing the DHCP Service on the Windows NT Server

DHCP can be installed as part of Setup. If DHCP is not installed as part of Setup, it must be configured on at least one network computer running Windows NT Server.

▶ **To install the DHCP server service on a computer running Windows NT Server**

1. Click **Start**, point to **Settings**, and click **Control Panel**.
2. Double-click **Network**.
3. Click the **Services** tab.
4. Click **Add**.

   The **Select Network Services** dialog box appears.
5. In **Network Service**, click **Microsoft DHCP Server**.

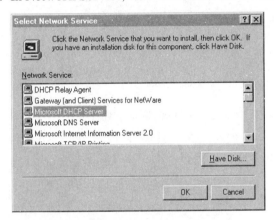

6. Click **OK** if loading from the network.

   Or, click **Have Disk** to load the software from disks or a CD-ROM.
7. Type the full path to the Windows NT Server DHCP files, and then click **OK**.

   You must restart the server for the changes to take effect.

Note You must be logged on as a member of the Administrators group to install the DHCP service.

Accessing the DHCP Manager

The addition of the DHCP service places DHCP Manager on the **Administrative Tools** menu. Once the installation is complete on the computer running Windows NT Server, use DHCP Manager to complete the configuration of the DHCP server.

▶ **To access DHCP Manager**

Click **Start**, point to **Programs**, point to **Administrative Tools**, and click **DHCP Manager**.

Adding Servers to the Server List

Using the DHCP Manager, the administrators at Terra Flora can configure, set up and maintain all the computers running Windows NT Server with the DHCP Server service enabled from a single computer or from any computer.

The DHCP Manager contains a list of the servers that it can administer. Initially, this list is empty. Until servers are added to the server list, the options provided with DHCP are not available. Even the first computer running Windows NT Server on which you install DHCP must be added to the server list before it can be administered. DHCP Manager.

▶ **To add a DHCP server to the Server List**

1. On the **Server** menu of DHCP Manager, click **Add**.

   The **Add DHCP Server to Server List** dialog box appears.

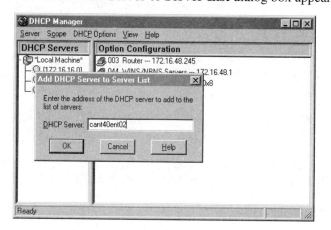

2. In **DHCP Server**, type the IP address of the DHCP server to be added to the list, and then click **OK**.

3. Repeat steps 1 and 2, if necessary, to add all the network computers running Windows NT Server with DHCP service enabled.

Note You cannot administer network servers running other dynamic addressing programs from a computer running Windows NT Server with DHCP service enabled.

Managing DHCP Scopes

On any given network, for clients to obtain dynamic IP addresses, there must be at least one computer running Windows NT Server DHCP service. Once the DHCP Server service is installed on a computer running Windows NT Server, and the Windows NT server is added to the server list, a DHCP scope must be created.

A *DHCP scope* consists of a pool of IP addresses on a given subnet, such as 223.223.223.1 to 223.223.223.200, that the DHCP Server can lease to DHCP Clients.

At Terra Flora, each computer running Windows NT Server DHCP service will store at least one scope containing the ranges of IP addresses that the Windows NT Server DHCP service can lease to requesting clients. Each scope will contain a unique pool of addresses from which to assign IP addresses.

Refer to the Terra Flora diagram. On the California domain PDC, a scope will be named CAPDCDHCP and will contain its own unique pool of IP addresses that will be assigned as clients start up. The scope on the BDC will be named CABDCDHCP and will also have a unique pool of addresses.

When the computer running Windows NT Server DHCP Service receives a request from a DHCP enabled client for an IP address, the DHCP server will select an available IP address from its pool of IP addresses and offer it to the DHCP client, along with other configuration information that can be displayed using various DOS commands.

The computers running Windows NT Server DHCP service will not only provide Terra Flora with the ability to dynamically configure clients IP addresses, but DHCP will, as part of the service it provides, record that address as leased to the client, eliminating the need for manual tracking of IP addresses. The DHCP leasing policy can be fully configured by administrators, eliminating any need for manual intervention.

The Windows NT Server DHCP service lease mechanism provides the following benefits:

- No need for user configuration.

  Users no longer need to acquire an IP address from an administrator to properly install and configure TCP/IP. When a client is configured to use automatic DHCP, it will automatically lease an IP address from a DHCP Server at start up.

- No more configuration errors.

  The Windows NT Server DHCP Service supplies all of the necessary configuration information to all of the DHCP-enabled clients and servers. As long as the DHCP Server maintains the correct configuration information, none of the clients or servers will ever be incorrectly configured. At Terra Flora, the difficulty of tracing network problems that resulted from incorrectly configured workstations and servers will be a thing of the past.

- Very little administrative overhead.

  Administrators define a pool of IP addresses that the Windows NT DHCP Service will lease to the DHCP clients. Administrators no longer need to keep track of which IP address are in use and which IP addresses are available.

- No need to reconfigure clients or servers that change subnets.

  When the client computer changes subnets and starts up on its new subnet, it will lease an IP address from a Windows NT Server running the DHCP Service that is appropriate for the subnet on which it is now located.

- DHCP client configurations automatically updated during the renewal process.

  For example, if you change a DNS server address, it gets distributed to the network client dynamically.

Note DHCP clients will cache their old IP addresses and will request the old IP addresses from the DHCP server if it is available. In most cases, the DHCP server will have the address available, as it assigns new addresses before scavenging old addresses.

A scope includes the following:

- A range of IP addresses that can be leased by DHCP clients, referred to as a *pool of IP addresses* or an *IP address pool*. Each DHCP scope will have a unique pool of IP addresses, which it can lease to DHCP clients. The IP addresses in the pool will not exist in a scope stored on any other network computer running Windows NT Server DHCP service.

- A valid Subnet Mask for the pool of IP addresses.

- Any IP addresses in the IP address pool range that need to be excluded so that they will not be leased to DHCP clients, such as the IP addresses of the other DHCP servers on the network, WINS and DNS servers, subnet addresses, router IP addresses, or any range that will be used on the network by devices requiring static IP addresses.

- The duration of the IP address lease, which defaults to three days.

   The maximum lease duration can be set to either 'Unlimited' or up to 999 days, 23 hours, and 59 minutes. For details on what happens when a lease expires, see Chapter 7, "Managing Microsoft DHCP Servers."

   The default length of an IP address lease can be configured to a longer or shorter amount of time by an administrator.

   Based on the number of available IP addresses in the DHCP scopes, how many of the scope's IP addresses will typically be in use by DHCP clients, and the frequency with which the DHCP clients will be rebooting or changing subnets, the lease duration for a DHCP Lease duration at Terra Flora will be configured at 7 days. This will provide a good balance between having too many addresses leased out to computers that are no longer on the network, and the renewal network traffic.

At Terra Flora, the guidelines for determining the appropriate lease duration were:

- Increasing the Lease Duration

   Terra Flora had to consider the number of IP addresses available in each DHCP scope. If there would be a large number of IP addresses available in the DHCP scope and relatively few DHCP clients, the lease duration should likely be increased in length. Increasing the lease duration would reduce the frequency that the DHCP clients will query the DHCP Server to renew their leases and therefore somewhat reduce network traffic.

- Reducing the Lease Duration

   If there was to be a limited number of IP addresses available in the DHCP scope, most of which will be in use at any given time, it would be desirable to reduce the lease duration. In addition, if DHCP clients on a given network would frequently be changing subnets and therefore requiring a different IP address, it would be beneficial to reduce the lease duration, especially if there are a limited number of IP addresses available. Reducing the lease duration would require DHCP clients to renew their leases more frequently, but would also ensure that any unused IP addresses in the pool are seen as available to lease by the DHCP server as soon as possible.

- The name of the scope, which is a maximum of 128 characters, and a descriptive comment about the DHCP Scope.

   At Terra Flora, the descriptive comment will be the name of the Domain on which the DHCP server resides.

The creation of DHCP servers scopes is performed from the DHCP Manager menu.

▶ **To create a scope**

1. Open DHCP Manager and double-click the DHCP server you want to manage.

2. On the **Scope** menu, click **Create**.

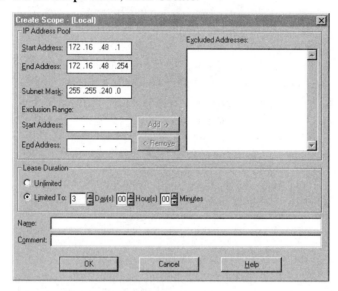

3. Under **IP Address Pool**, enter the server's beginning IP address in **Start Address**.

4. In **End Address**, enter the last IP address.

5. To add exclusion ranges, type a range in **Exclusion Range**, and click **Add**; then repeat for as many ranges as you want to set.

6. To remove exclusion ranges, click the range in **Excluded Address**, and then click **Remove**.

7. Under **Lease Duration**, click **Limited To** and enter the amount of time that the lease will last.

8. In **Name**, type the name of the scope.

9. If appropriate, type remarks in **Comment**, and then click **OK**.

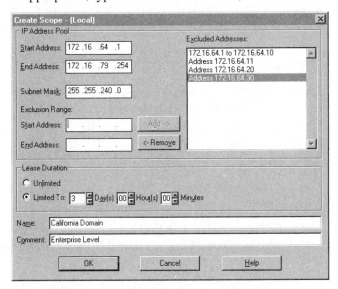

Terra Flora will configure a scope named "California" for the California Domain on the PDC. The Lease Duration at Terra Flora will be defined at seven days.

Note Once the administrative scope has been created, it must be activated before the DHCP Server will lease any IP addresses from the DHCP scope's IP address pool.

A DHCP scope is activated and deactivated from the DHCP Manager **Scope** menu. In DHCP Manager, active scopes will be preceded by a light bulb icon that looks as it is turned on and deactivated scopes will be preceded by a gray light bulb that looks as if it is turned off.

Once a DHCP scope has been created any of the scope's settings, such as the range of the IP address pool, it can be modified from the **Scope Properties** menu.

Reserving IP addresses

The DHCP Manager allows the reservation of a specific IP address for a computer. At Terra Flora, the plan is to reserve DHCP IP addresses on the network in the scope for the following devices and computers:

- Domain controllers (since the network also uses LMHOSTS files that define IP addresses for domain controllers).
- Clients that use IP addresses assigned by another TCP/IP configuration method, such as UNIX DNS and netware clients.
- Any DNS Servers on the network, whether running Windows NT Server 4.0 DNS service or not.
- Any Windows NT Server with WINS enabled.
- Any Routers used to direct network traffic between subnets.
- Any DHCP servers.

  The IP address for the DHCP servers were assigned during the Windows NT Server Setup. The addresses assigned to the DHCP servers will now be reserved for those servers.

The administrator will reserve IP addresses using **Add Reservations** on the DHCP Manager **Scope** menu. When the computer client requests an IP address from the DHCP Server, the DHCP Server will always return the reserved IP address.

Note The static addresses placed in Add Reservations will always override any configuration options specified using DHCP Manager.

▶ **To reserve a client address in DHCP:**

1. In DHCP Manager, double-click the DHCP server you want to manage.
2. Click the scope in which you want to add reservations.
3. On the **Scope** menu, click **Add Reservations**.

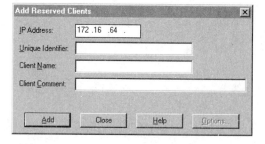

Two important entries in the dialog box are:

- **Unique Identifier**

  The *unique identifier* is the media access control (MAC) address for the DHCP client and can be obtained by typing the following command at the command prompt on the client computer for which the address will be reserved:

  - IPCONFIG -ALL.

  - Press ENTER.

  - The MAC address is the address labeled as the Physical Address.

- **Client Name**

  This entry should be the computer name of the DHCP client. The name is used only for identification purposes. This entry is not available when adding reservations for MS-DOS–based DHCP clients.

Notes It is critical that **Unique Identifier** entry be correct because the MAC address is sent as part of the DHCP client's request for an IP address to the DHCP Server. If this value is not correct, no match is found on the DHCP server, which means the DHCP Server will assign the client any available IP address instead of the reserved IP address.

On Windows 95 clients, you must run the program Winipcfg.exe to view the MAC or physical address.

Configuring DHCP Options

At a minimum, a DHCP server must provide the DHCP client with the following information:

- A valid IP address to lease (configured when the DHCP Scope is created).

- A Subnet Mask (configured when the DHCP Scope is created).

- A Default Gateway, which defaults to an IP address of 0.0.0.0 if not configured.

These items are referred to as *configuration parameters*. There are about 60 other predefined DHCP configuration parameters, called *options*, that an administrator can configure through the DHCP Manager for one or all scopes on a DHCP server. For a complete listing of the options and their meanings, see Chapter 7, "Managing Microsoft DHCP Servers"

There are four methods that can be used to set the DHCP Options:

- Global

  When you set a global DHCP option, the option takes affect for all DHCP scopes defined on the selected DHCP server. Global DHCP options appear in the DHCP Manager with a globe icon proceeding them.

- Scope

  Setting a scope DHCP option will set the option only for the selected scope on the **Options Scope** menu. DHCP options configured for a scope are displayed with a series of computer icons proceeding them in DHCP Manager.

- Default

  Setting a default DHCP option modifies the default value for one of the DHCP Options. When a default value is set, the default value becomes the default that was set during administration rather than the DHCP default that was set during installation of DHCP.

- Client

  This method can be used to configure one or more of the DHCP options for   a specific DHCP client. DHCP options can be set for a client only if the DHCP client has a reserved IP address. The only way to see if a DHCP option is set for a DHCP client is to view the properties of an active client lease on the **Scope Active Leases** menu and then clicking **Options**.

Configuring a Global, Scope, or Default DHCP Option

Configure a Global, Scope, or Default DHCP Option on the **DHCP Options** menu by clicking **Global**, **Scope**, or **Default**.

If **Scope** or **Global** is selected, the following dialog box appears, indicating which menu option was selected by printing the title of the menu option in the title bar.

▶ **To configure DHCP options globally or by scope**

1. In DHCP Manager, double-click the DHCP server you want to manage.

2. Click the scope for which you want to configure DHCP Options.

3. On the **DHCP Options** menu, click **Global** to change options globally.

   Or, click **Scope**, to change options by scopes.

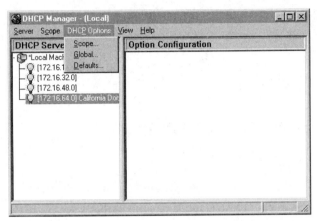

4. Click **Edit Array**.

   Enter the changes that you want for DHCP options.

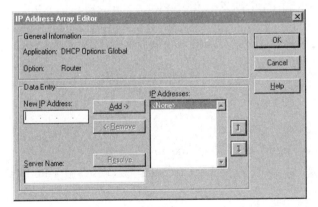

Using the dialog box, the administrator can change or add a new DHCP option to the list and configure it with the proper settings.

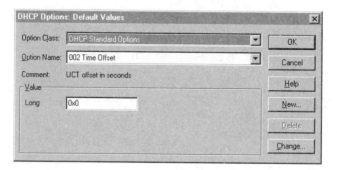

▶ **To configure Default DHCP Options**

1. If necessary, click the **DHCP Standard Options** default as the value in **Option Class**.

2. In **Option Name**, click **Change** to change the default.

   Or, click **New** to create a new default.

3. When the fields that need to be changed appear, enter the appropriate settings, and then click **OK**.

Configuring DHCP Options for a Particular Client

Configuring client options can be performed only if the IP address for the client has been reserved. Configuring client options is performed using a different graphical interface than was used to configure the Global, Scope or Default options.

For details about reserving addresses, see "Reserving IP addresses," earlier in this chapter.

▶ **To configure DHCP options for a particular client**

1. Click the server where the reserved client's IP address resides for which you want to enable options.

2. Click the scope that contains the client reservation.

3. On the **Scope** menu, click **Active Leases**.

4. Click the client that you want to configure.

5. Click **Properties.**

6. Click **Options**.

The **DHCP Options: Reservations** dialog box appears.

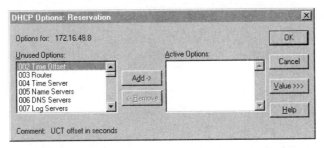

7. In **Unused Options**, click the option you want to add for the client, and then click **Add**.

8. To change or enter a value for the option, click it in **Active Options**, and then click **Value**.

9. Enter the appropriate value, and click **OK**.

For a complete description of the options available, see Chapter 7, "Managing Microsoft DHCP Servers."

Precedence of DHCP Options

If a DHCP option is set for more than one level, such as for both global and scope, precedence is in the following order:

- Client overrides both scope and global.
- Scope overrides global.
- If there is no client or scope setting for a DHCP option, then the global setting has precedence.

Benefits of DHCP Options

These include:

- Centrally administered network settings
- Dynamic updates
- No need for manual entry on every client

Commonly Configured DHCP Options

Some of the DHCP options administrators typically configure are:

- 003 Router

  The Router parameter requires the IP addresses for one or more routers and is the equivalent of the Default Gateway entry in the TCP/IP configuration dialog box.

- 006 DNS Servers

  The Domain Name Server parameter requires the IP addresses for one or more DNS servers.

- 015 Domain Name

  This option is used to specify DNS domain names to be used for host name resolution.

- 044 WINS/NBNS Servers

  The WINS/NBNS (NetBIOS Name Servers) Servers parameters requires IP addresses for one or more WINS/NBNS servers.

- 046 WINS/NBT node type

  This DHCP option can be used to configure the method that the DHCP client will use to resolve computer (NetBIOS) names: 0x1 (b-node), 0x2 (p-node), 0x4 (m-node), or 0x8 (h-node).

Note A computer running Windows NT Server DHCP service can be configured to automatically provide IP addresses of the WINS and DNS servers used in the name resolution process. This removes the requirement of individually configuring each client with the WINS and DNS server IP addresses. The only requirement for the client is to click Obtain an IP address from a DHCP server on the Microsoft TCP/IP Properties dialog box.

Configuring a DHCP Relay Agent

Computers running Windows NT Server DHCP service have the ability to use the bootP relay service which enables clients on one subnet to access a DHCP server on another subnet. Refer to the Terra Flora network diagram. In the Terra Flora California domain, all the servers running Windows NT Server DHCP service are located on the Enterprise level.

There are three subnets in the California domain, and only one subnet contains the servers running Windows NT Server DHCP service. The two subnets that do not contain computers running Windows NT Server DHCP service have a computer running Windows NT Workstation or Windows NT Server that acts as DHCP relay or bootP relay agent. The DHCP bootP relay agents are named CANTS40DIV03 and CANTS40DPT02.

When a dynamic client computer on the subnet where the bootP relay agent resides requests an IP address, the request is forwarded to the subnet's bootP relay agent. The bootP relay agent, in turn, is configured to forward the request directly to the correct computer running Windows NT Server DHCP service. The computer running Windows NT Server DHCP service returns an IP address directly to the requesting client.

For a detailed discussion on the bootP relay agents, see Chapter 7, "Managing Microsoft DHCP Servers."

Configuration of the DHCP bootP relay agent is a two-step process. The first step is to install the DHCP Relay Agent Service on the computer that will act as a bootP relay agent. The DHCP Relay Agent Service is a Windows NT Server service. The bootP agents can then be configured, using the **Microsoft TCP/IP Protocol Properties** dialog box, with the IP address of the computer running Windows NT Server DHCP, so the agent will know where to forward requests from clients for available IP addresses. Installing the service and configuring the agents are both performed using Network in Control Panel.

▶ **To install the DHCP Relay Agent Service**

1. In the **Network** dialog box, click the **Services** tab.

2. Click **Add**.

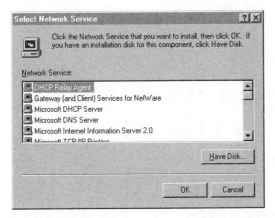

3. Under **Network Service**, click **DHCP Relay Agent**, and then click **Have Disk** if loading the software from disks or a CD-ROM.

   Or, click **OK** if loading from the network.

4. In the message that appears, type the full path to the Windows NT Server DHCP files, and click **OK**.

The DHCP service is installed.

5. Click **Close**.

Configuration and binding information is checked.

You must shut down and restart the computer before the new settings will take effect

Addition of the TCP/IP address of the computers running Windows NT Server DHCP service to the bootP relay agents is performed in the **TCP/IP Properties** dialog box.

▶ **To add an IP address to the bootP relay agent:**

1. In the **Network** dialog box, click the **Protocols** tab.
2. Click **TCP/IP Protocol,** and then click **Properties**.
3. Click the **DHCP Relay** tab.

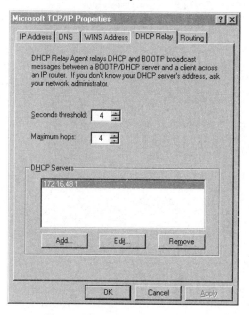

4. Check that the **Seconds threshold** and **Maximum hops** settings are set at 4.
5. Under **DHCP Servers**, type the IP address of the server that will provide the IP addresses to the subnet's requesting clients.
6. Click **Add**, and then click **OK**.

Name Resolution Using WINS and DNS

Due to the heterogeneity of the network at Terra Flora, administrators have decided to implement two Windows NT Server services to manage all name resolution issues. Windows Internet Name Service (WINS) and Domain Name System (DNS).

Terra Flora is interoperating several heterogeneous networks. To communicate, each computer needs a unique computer address and name. There are two types of names and both types exist on one or more of the small Terra Flora networks being merged into one large network. Windows NT network applications use a naming convention known as *NetBIOS*. In general, NetBIOS computer names consist of a single part.

In contrast, TCP/IP components rely on the DNS naming convention. DNS computer names consist of two parts: a *computer name* and a *domain name*, which combine to form the *fully qualified domain name* (FQDN).

NetBIOS computer names can be made compatible with DNS computer names, making interoperation possible between the two. Windows NT combines the NetBIOS computer name with the DNS domain name to form the FQDN.

Note Under Windows NT Server, the DNS host name defaults to the same name as the NetBIOS computer name. You can change this if you need separate names.

The Decision to Use WINS

As with dynamic addressing of computers, dynamic name registration and resolution of computers and associated addresses will reduce administrative costs at Terra Flora. If administrative tasks can automatically be performed by the computers running Windows NT Server with WINS enabled, administrators are free to perform other network administrative tasks.

A WINS server maintains a dynamic database that maps the NetBIOS computer names of WINS clients to their IP addresses. Both a computer name and IP address are necessary for network clients to communicate effectively on the enterprise network. At Terra Flora, clients are configured as both DHCP- and WINS-enabled.

The primary purpose of WINS is to respond to network clients that are trying to locate a computer on the network by using its' NetBIOS name. The WINS server responds to the network client with the IP address of the desired computer, thus enabling the client computer to connect to the desired computer via a TCP/IP session. To enable this functionality, the WINS clients register their NetBIOS names with the WINS server. The registered name is stored in a database on the server on a dynamic basis so the name can be reused later if the client stops using it.

A WINS client is responsible for maintaining the lease on its registered name and informing the WINS server periodically that it is still present on the network. When it shuts down, it also notifies the WINS server that the name is being released.

Terra Flora administrators decided to use WINS for the following reasons:

- Dynamic database maintenance will support computer name registration and name resolution. WINS provides dynamic name services, and it offers a NetBIOS name space, making it much more flexible than DNS for name resolution. The WINS and DNS servers will be integrated to serve all name resolution needs at Terra Flora.

- WINS centralizes management of the computer-name database and the database replication policies, which will alleviate the need for managing LMHOSTS files.

- Windows NT Server has been chosen as the integration tool to interoperate the heterogeneous networks at Terra Flora. Implementation of WINS will reduce the IP broadcast traffic while allowing client computers to easily locate remote systems across local or wide area networks.

Installing and Configuring WINS

A WINS server is a computer running Windows NT Server using the Microsoft TCP/IP protocol and the WINS server software. WINS servers maintain a database that maps computer names to IP addresses, allowing users to easily communicate with other computers while gaining all of the benefits of using TCP/IP.

For a complete discussion of the WINS service, see Chapter 8, "Managing Microsoft WINS Servers."

Installing WINS Servers

Installing a WINS server is part of the process of installing Microsoft TCP/IP in Windows NT Server. The following instructions assume you have already installed the Windows NT Server operating system on the computer.

You must be logged on as a member of the Administrators group to install WINS.

▶ **To install a WINS server**

1. Click **Start**, point to **Settings**, and click **Control Panel**.

2. Double-click **Network**.

3. Click the **Services** tab.

4. Click **Server**, and then click **Add**.

5. In the **Select Network Service** dialog box, click **Windows Internet Name Service**.

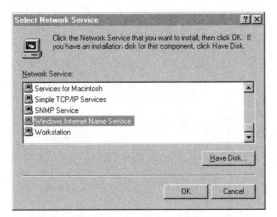

6. Click **Have Disk** if you are loading the software from disks or a CD-ROM.

   Or, click **OK** if loading from the network.

7. In the **Windows NT Setup** dialog box, type the full path to the Windows NT Server WINS files, and then click **Continue**.

   You must shut down and restart the computer before the new settings will take effect. The WINS Manager then appears on the **Administrative Tools (Common)** menu on the desktop.

Managing WINS Servers

The addition of the WINS service places the WINS Manager on the
Administrative Tools (Common) menu. Once the installation is complete on the
computer running Windows NT Server, use WINS Manager to complete the
configuration of WINS.

▶   **To start WINS Manager**

- Click **Start**, point to **Programs**, point to **Administrative Tools (Common)**,
  and click **WINS Manager**.

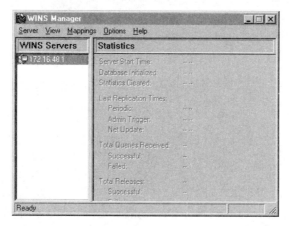

Adding WINS Servers

Before you can administer and manage WINS servers, you must add the WINS
servers to the Server List using the WINS Manager graphical interface. At Terra
Flora, all computers running Windows NT Server WINS service will be added to
the WINS Server List. Until the WINS servers are added to the list, no WINS
features are available. Once the servers are added to the list, administration of any
computer running Windows NT Server WINS Service can take place from any
other computer running Windows NT Server WINS Manager.

▶ **To Add a WINS server to the Server List**

   1. On the WINS Manager **Server** menu, click **Add**.

      The **Add WINS Server to Server List** dialog box appears.

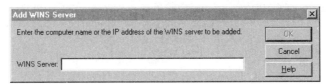

   2. In **WINS Server**, type the IP address of the DHCP server to be added to the list, and then click **OK**.

Once a WINS Server is added to the list, configuration of the server can take place.

Configuring WINS Servers

Terra Flora will configure multiple WINS servers to increase the availability and balance the load among servers. To configure a WINS server, you must be a member of the administrators group of that server.

▶ **To configure a WINS server**

   1. In WINS Manager, click the server you want to configure.

   2. On the **Server** menu, click **Configuration**.

      The **WINS Server Configuration** dialog box appears.

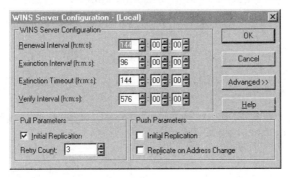

3. Select the configuration options you want.

- To specify how often a WINS client will renew its name registration with the WINS Server, type a value in **Renewal Interval**.

- To specify the interval between when an entry in the WINS database is marked as *released* (no longer registered) and when it is marked as *extinct,* type a value in **Extinction Interval**.

- To specify the interval between when an entry is marked extinct and when the entry is scavenged (removed) from the WINS database, type a value in **Extinction Timeout**.

- To specify when the WINS server will verify that old names it does not own (those replicated from other WINS servers) are still active, type a value in **Verify Interval**.

- To specify pull parameters, select the **Initial Replication** check box under **Pull**.

- To specify the number of times that the WINS server will attempt to contact a replication partner for pulling new WINS database entries, type a value in **Retry Count**.

- To have the WINS server notify its replication partners of the status of its WINS database when the system is initialized, select the **Initial Replication** check box under **Push Parameters**.

- To notify the replication partners of the WINS server when a name registration changes the WINS database status, select the **Replicate on Address Change** check box.

4. Click **Advanced** to configure other options.

- To specify logging of database changes to Jet.log, select the **Logging Enabled** check box.

- To log events in detail, select the **Log Detailed Events** check box.

- To replicate only WINS push or pull partners, select the **Replicate Only With Partners** check box.

- To automatically back up the database when WINS Manager stops, select the **Backup On Termination** check box.

  The database backup path must have a directory specified.

- To treat static unique and static multihomed records in the database as dynamic when they conflict with a new registration or replica, select the **Migrate On/Off** check box.

  This means that if they are no longer valid, they will be overwritten by the new registration or replica. By default, this option is not checked.

- To set the highest version ID number for the database, enter that number in **Starting Version Count**.

- To specify the directory where the WINS database backups will be stored, type the path in **Database Backup Path**.

5. When you have completed all changes in the **WINS Server Configuration** dialog box, click **OK**.

Notes

- Specify the %systemroot%\system32\wins directory. A subdirectory for the backup will be added to WINS directory.

- Logging events in detail requires considerable system resources and should be turned off if you are tuning for performance.

- If the **Replicate Only With Partners** check box is not selected, an administrator can ask a WINS server to pull or push from or to a non-listed WINS server partner. By default, this option is checked.

- Usually, you will not need to change the value in **Starting Version Count** unless the database becomes corrupted and needs to start fresh. In such a case, set this value to a number higher than appears as the version number counter for this WINS server on all the remote partners that earlier replicated the local WINS server's records. WINS may adjust the value you specify to a higher one to ensure that database records are quickly replicated to other WINS servers.

- If you specify a backup path, WINS automatically performs a full backup of its database to this directory every 24 hours. WINS uses this directory to perform an automatic restoration of the database in the event that the database is found to be corrupted when WINS is started. Do not specify a network directory.

Configuring Replication Partners

All of the WINS servers on a network can be configured to communicate with each other so that a name registered with one WINS server will eventually be known by all WINS servers. In addition to registration of all names on the network with all WINS servers, all WINS servers will eventually be notified when a name is released. Replication is carried out among replication partners, rather than by each server replicating to all other servers. Each WINS server must be configured with at least one other WINS server as its replication partner.

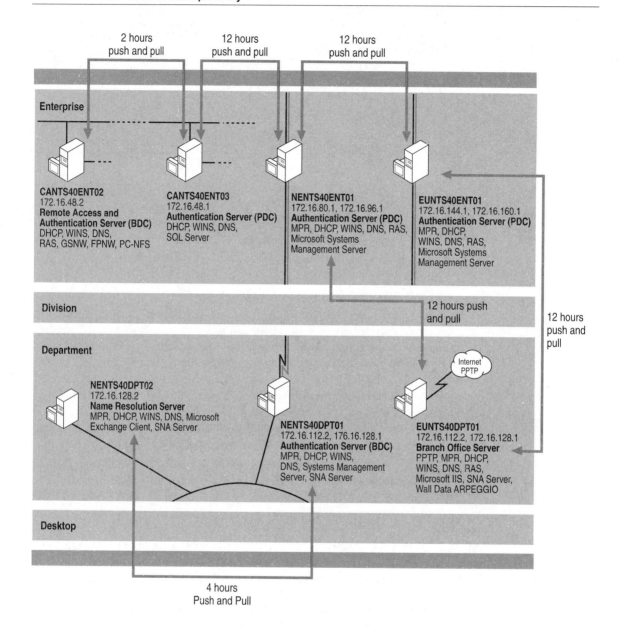

In Terra Flora's main California Domain, one WINS server will be designated as the central server, and all other WINS servers will be configured as both push and pull partners of this central server. A *pull partner* is a WINS server that pulls in replications of database entries from its partner by requesting and then accepting the replications. A *push partner* is a WINS server that sends update notification messages to its partner when its WINS database has changed. This configuration ensures that the WINS database on each server contains names addresses for every network computer.

The Terra Flora network diagram of the California domain shows only two of the WINS servers. At Terra Flora, WINS will be enabled on several computers running Windows NT at the Enterprise level. All of these computers running Windows NT Server WINS server will be configured as push and pull partners of each other.

The PDC will act as the central server. It will push changes made to its database to the next server in the line, which then pulls the changes from the PDC. This will continue down the line, with the server last on the line pushing back to the central server, which will pull in changes from the last server on the line. This ensures that all the databases on all WINS servers are replicated and up-to-date.

Additionally, the administrator can perform a replication immediately or at a specified time.

▶ **To add a replication partner to a WINS server**

   1. On the WINS Manager **Server** menu, click **Replication Partners**.

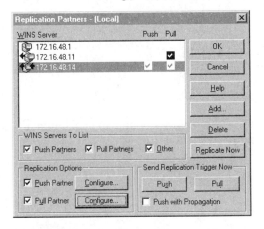

      The **Replication Partners** dialog box appears, showing all replication partners of the WINS server.

   2. Click **Add**.

   3. Type the IP address of the WINS server that is to be added as a push or pull partner.

      The added server can be configured as either a push or pull partner to the WINS server. The replication partner will automatically be added as both a push and pull partner of the server that is being configured. This can be changed.

▶ **To configure replication partners for a WINS server**

1. In **WINS Server** in the **Replication Partners** dialog box, click the server you want to configure.

2. Under **Replication Options**, select the **Push Partner** check box, the **Pull Partner** check box, or both, to indicate the appropriate replication partnership.

3. Under **Replication Options**, select the **Configure** check box for each of the appropriate settings.

   The **Push Partners Properties** or **Pull Partners Properties** dialog box appears.

▶ **To define pull partner properties**

1. In **Start Time** on the **Pull Partner Properties** dialog box, type a number to indicate when replication should begin, using any separator (such as AM or PM) for hours, minutes, and seconds.

2. In **Replication Interval**, type a time in hours, minutes, and seconds to indicate how often replications will occur.

   Or, to use values specified in the **Preferences** dialog box, click **Set Default Values**.

3. Click **OK**.

The AM and PM designators are part of your time setting in International (in Control Panel).

▶ **To define push partner properties**

1. In **Update Count** on the **Push Partner Properties** dialog box, type the number of additions and updates that can be made to records in the database before replication must take place.

   The minimum value is 20; replications that have been pulled in from partners do not count as insertions or updates in this context.

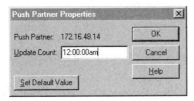

2. Click **OK**.

If you decide later to reset the values specified in the **Preferences** dialog box, you can reopen the **Push Partner Properties** dialog box and click **Set Default Values**.

Triggering Replication Between Partners

You can also immediately replicate the database between the partners, rather than waiting for the start time or replication interval specified in the **Preferences** dialog box. For details, see "Setting Preferences for WINS Manager" later in this chapter.

You probably want replication to begin immediately after you make a series of changes, such as entering a range of static address mappings.

▶ **To trigger replication**

1. On the **Server** menu of WINS Manager, click **Replication Partners.**

2. Click the WINS servers to which you want to send a replication trigger.

   Or, if you want the selected WINS server to propagate the trigger to all its pull partners, select the **Push With Propagation** check box.

3. Under **Send Replication Trigger Now**, click **Push** or **Pull**, depending on which partners you want to trigger.

   If **Push With Propagation** is not selected, the selected WINS server does not send the trigger to its other partners.

   If **Push With Propagation** is selected, the selected WINS server sends a propagate push trigger to its pull partners after it has pulled in the latest information from the source WINS server. If it does not need to pull in any replicas because it has the same or more up-to-date replicas than the source WINS server, it does not propagate the trigger to its pull partners.

▶ **To start replication immediately**

- In the **Replication Partners** dialog box, click **Replicate Now**.

Adding Static Mappings

Static mappings are permanent lists of computer name-to-IP address mappings. In the table, the administrator indicates the computer name and matches the IP address the computer. When a network client sends a name request to the WINS server, the WINS server will always respond with the name entered by the administrator. At Terra Flora, all DNS servers, DHCP servers and other WINS servers will be statically added to all WINS servers.

Note If DHCP is also used on the network, a reserved (or static) IP address will override any WINS server settings. Static mappings should not be assigned to WINS-enabled client computers.

You can add static mappings to the WINS database for specific IP addresses using two methods:

- Typing static mappings in a dialog box.
- Importing files that contain static mappings.

▶ **To type static mappings in a dialog box**

1. On the **Mappings** menu, click **Static Mappings**.

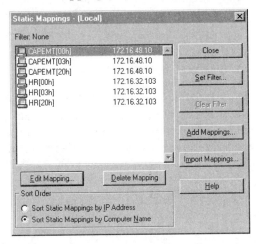

2. Click Add Mappings.

3. In **Name**, type the computer name of the system for which you are adding a static mapping.

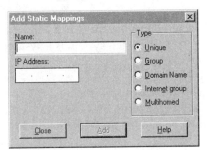

WINS Manager automatically adds the two backslashes (\\), which normally proceed the entry of a computer name.

4. In **IP Address**, type the address for the computer.

5. In **Type**, click to indicate whether this entry is a unique name or a group with a special name, and then click **Add**.

The mapping entry is immediately added to the database, and the check boxes are cleared so that you can add another static mapping entry.

The settings available under **Type** include the following:

- *Unique* is a unique name in the WINS database that permits only one address per name. The unique name is the WINS client's computer name.

- *Group* indicates a normal group for which the IP addresses of the individual clients are not stored. A normal group is the name to which broadcasts are sent and is the domain name used for browsing purposes. A normal group name has Ox1E as its 16th byte, which appears as a [1Eh] at the end of the name in Mappings, View Database option in WINS Manager. A normal group name does not have an IP address associated with it and can be valid on multiple networks and registered with multiple WINS Servers. When a WINS server receives a request for the group name, the WINS server returns the limited broadcast address *255.255.255.255,* which the WINS client will then use to broadcast to the network. For a description of the 16th byte fields, see Appendix G, "NetBIOS Names."

- *Internet Group* is a group that contains the IP addresses for up to 25 primary and backup domain controllers for the domain. An Internet group has a 0X1C as its 16th byte, which appears as a [1Ch] at the end of the name in Mappings, View Database option in WINS Manager. The Internet group name is another instance of the domain name being registered; however, this instance is used for the domain controllers in the domain to communicate with each other.

- *Multihomed* is similar to a unique name in that it is the WINS client's computer name; however, it can have up to 25 addresses and is for use by multihomed systems. A multihomed system is a system with more than one network interface and more than one IP address.

If **Internet Group** or **Multihomed** is selected under **Type**, the dialog box shows additional controls for adding multiple addresses. Click the down arrow (button) to move the address you type into the list of addresses for the group. Use the up-arrow button to change the order of a selected address in the list.

Entries for static mappings of unique and special group names can be imported from any file with the same format as the LMHOSTS file, which is described in Chapter 10 "Using LMHOSTS Files." Scope names and keywords other than #DOM are ignored. Static Mapping for normal group and multihomed names can be added only by typing entries in the **Add Static Mappings** dialog box.

Note For Internet group names defined in this dialog box (that is, added statically), make sure that the primary domain controller (PDC) for that domain is defined in the group if the PDC is running Windows NT Advanced Server version 3.1.

▶ **To import a file containing static mapping entries**

1. In the **Static Mappings** dialog box, click **Import Mappings**.

2. In the **Select Static Mapping File** dialog box, enter the name of the file containing the names to be mapped.

The specified file is read, and then a static mapping is created for each computer name and address. If the #DOM keyword is included for any record, an Internet group is created (if it is not already present), and the address is added to that group.

For more information on managing Static Mappings, see Chapter 8, "Managing Microsoft WINS Servers."

Setting Preferences for WINS Manager

Several options can be configured to administer WINS servers. The control preferences are on the **Options** menu.

▶ **To set preferences for WINS Manager**

1. On the **Options** menu, click **Preferences**.

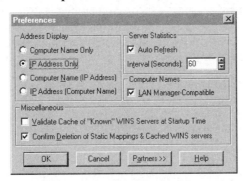

2. In the **Preferences** dialog box, specify the settings you want to change.

- To indicate how you want address information to be displayed throughout WINS Manager, click **Computer Name Only, IP Address Only,** or one of the ordered combinations: **Computer Name (IP Address)** or **IP Address (Computer Name.)**

- To automatically refresh the statistics in the WINS Manager window, select the **Auto Refresh** check box under **Server Statistics**, and then enter a number in **Interval (seconds)** to specify the time between refresh actions.

- To have computer names to adhere to the LAN Manager naming convention, select the **LAN Manager-Compatible** check box.

  This check box should be selected unless your network accepts NetBIOS name from other sources.

- To have the system query the listed servers each time the system starts to find out if each server is available, select the **Validate Cache Of "Known" WINS Servers At Startup Time** check box.

- To have a warning message appear each time you delete a static mapping or the cached name of a WINS server, select the **Confirm Deletion Of Static Mappings And Cached WINS Servers** check box.

- To specify the default for replication start time for new pull partners, type a time in **Start Time**, and then specify values in **Replication Interval** to indicate how often data replicas will be exchanged between the partners.

- To specify the default number of local registrations and changes that can occur before this server (as a push partner) sends a replication trigger, enter a number in **Update Count under New Push Partner Default Configuration.**

  The minimum value is 20.

3. Click **OK**.

WINS Manager also automatically refreshes the statistical display each time an action is initiated while you are working in WINS Manager.

LAN Manager computer names are limited to 15 characters, as compared to the 16-character NetBIOS names used by some other sources, such as Lotus Notes. In LAN Manager names, the 16th byte is used to indicate whether the device is a server, workstation, messenger, and so on. When this option is selected, WINS adds and imports static mappings with 0, 0x03, and 0x20 as the 16th byte.

All Windows–based networking, including Windows NT, follows the LAN Manager convention.

The replication interval should be equal to or less than the lowest refresh time interval that is set on any of the replicating WINS servers. The minimum value for the replication interval is 40 minutes.

The Decision to Integrate DNS with WINS

DNS is not dynamic, which means that administrative overhead is increased in a network like Terra Flora with the use of DNS. Administrators must update DNS computer files whenever a computer moves or a new computer is added to the network.

WINS was created to ease this type of administrative burden. Coupling DNS with WINS capitalizes on the strengths of each to provide a form of dynamic DNS. Windows NT 4.0 Server DNS Service provides a WINS lookup feature. If the name cannot be resolved using DNS, the name request is forwarded to WINS for resolution. It is this form of an integrated, dynamic, name-resolution feature that contributed to the decision at Terra Flora to migrate most of their DNS information and application to computers running Windows NT Server with the DNS service enabled. Terra Flora will use both DNS and WINS to resolve names.

It is clear to the CIO that the WINS Lookup feature provided as part of the Windows NT Server DNS service would help cut administrative costs by eliminating some of the manual name and address tracking administrative tasks associated with the current network DNS systems.

A key feature of the DNS service in Windows NT Server 4.0 is a graphical interface from which the database files can be managed. Use of this graphical tool should eliminate some of the error associated with making changes directly to a zone database file using an file editor.

Note This form of dynamic name resolution is only available on networks with computers running Windows NT Server with DNS and WINS enabled.

For a complete discussion of DNS and WINS integration, see Chapter 3, "Implementation Considerations" in the Microsoft Windows NT Server 4.0 *Networking Supplement*.

Implementation Plan for DNS

DNS is in use on many of the heterogeneous networks at Terra Flora. The plan to implement Windows NT Server DNS service was quite involved due to the fact that DNS is running without problems on the majority of the small, heterogeneous networks. However, the benefit of reduced administrative cost, combined with an integrated solution for the heterogeneous network was a compelling benefit to use Windows NT Server WINS and DNS services.

Before the merger of the heterogeneous networks, Terra Flora had four DNS zones. Terraflora.com was registered with Internet Network Information Center and operated as the authoritative domain. Three other zones were created on DNS servers, one for each of the company divisions, which were Nursery. Terraflora.com; Retail. Terraflora.com, and Supply.Terraflora.com.

The plan at Terra Flora includes replacing two of the three division's DNS systems with computers running Windows NT Server 4.0 DNS service. These two division are Supply.Terraflora.com and Nursery. Terraflora.com

The Sun server in the Retail Services division \\CASWN25ENT01 currently runs the key mission critical corporate application systems of Terra Flora. The plan for the current DNS system in the Retail. Terraflora.com zone is to incorporate a server running Windows NT Server 4.0 DNS service as a secondary server and track the performance of the server.

Then the Retail.Terraflora.com zone will be split. The new zone will be called NT.Retail.Terraflora.com and will consist of only computers running Windows NT Server 4.0 DNS service and no other DNS service. The servers will also be running WINS and DHCP and have the WINS Lookup feature enabled. The plan will be to eventually migrate all of the DNS functionality in the Retail Services division to Windows NT Server 4.0.

Note Domain: There are several meanings associated with Domain. In the DNS world a domain is the name and address of every machine associated with a group. Windows NT Server domains are defined as the logical grouping of network servers and other computers that share a common security and user account information. For this discussion, domains will be divided into two terms: DNS Domains and Windows NT Server Domains.

Replacing the Nursery and Supply Divisions DNS Systems

The plan at Terra Flora is to replace the DNS servers storing the zone information and files of Nursery.Terraflora.com and Supply.Terraflora.com with the Windows NT Server DNS service. To do this, the following steps must be performed:

- Windows NT Server 4.0 DNS service will be installed on primary and secondary servers running Windows NT Server DNS service in each zone. The graphical DNS manager tool is available on the Administrative Tools menu as a result of the installation of Windows NT 4.0 DNS Service.

- All the servers running Windows NT Server 4.0 with the DNS service enabled will be added to the server list using the graphical interface tool called DNS Manager. In this way, Terra Flora can administer all the computers running Windows NT Server 4.0 DNS service from any computer running Windows NT Server DNS service by using the DNS Manager graphical interface.

- The zone, boot and cache files for Nursery.Terraflora.com and Supply.Terraflora.com will be moved to the appropriate computer running Windows NT Server 4.0 with the DNS service enabled. The boot file will be changed to indicate the new information such as names and IP addresses of the zones.

- The database resource records will be changed to reflect these changes such as where zone files are located, the location of primary and secondary databases and static information about other DNS servers that are not running the Windows NT Server 4.0 DNS service.

- The static resource records of the servers which are not Windows NT Server 4.0 DNS servers will be added or updated as necessary to ensure that all DNS servers are checked for name resolution.

- The servers running Windows NT Server 4.0 DNS service will be enabled to participate in WINS Lookup.

Integrating the Retail DNS System with Windows NT Server DNS Service

For Retail.Terraflora.com, the plan is different. A server running Windows NT Server 4.0 DNS Service will be added as a secondary server to the existing DNS Zone which is installed on a computer not running Windows NT Server. The performance of Windows NT will be measured.

A key feature of the Windows NT Server 4.0 DNS is the WINS Lookup feature. The Retail.Terraflora.com zone will be split. A new subzone called NT.Retail.Terraflora.com will be set up on computers running Windows NT Server DNS service. The servers in the new subzone will be WINS lookup enabled. Migration to the servers running Windows NT Server DNS service will take place over the next several months. As applications requiring DNS services are changed, the DNS services will be moved to the servers running Windows NT Server 4.0 DNS. The following steps will be followed:

- Windows NT Server 4.0 DNS Service will be installed on all servers in the new split zone which will be created as NT.Retail.Terraflora.com.

- Using the graphical tool, all the Windows NT Server 4.0 DNS servers will be added to the Windows NT Server 4.0 DNS system, allowing administration from any server running Windows NT Server 4.0 DNS service.

- The new NT.Retail.Terraflora.com subzone will be configured as a primary and secondary zone. The secondary zone is a replicated copy of the primary subzone database.

- NS and A resource records will be added to the NT.Retail.Terraflora.com Windows NT Server 4.0 DNS database pointing to the Terraflora.com Windows NT Server 4.0 DNS database for name resolution.

- NS records will be added to the Terraflora.com Windows NT Server 4.0 DNS database pointing to the NT.Retail.Terraflora.com Windows NT Server 4.0 DNS database for name resolution.
- Static NS and A records will be added to the zone file for NT.Retail.Terraflora.com for all DNS servers that are running an operating system other than Windows NT Server 4.0 and for all workstations that are not Windows NT, Windows 95, Windows for Workgroups, and LanMan 2.*x*.
- All Windows NT Server 4.0 DNS servers will be WINS enabled.

Installing DNS Service

DNS is one of the Windows NT Server services. The instructions below assume you have already installed the Windows NT Server operating system. Terra Flora will install the DNS service on all computers running Windows NT Server service that will provide DNS services.

▶ **To install the DNS service**

1. Click **Start**, point to **Settings**, and click **Control Panel**.
2. Double-click **Network**.
3. Click the **Services** tab.
4. Click **Server**, and then click **Add**.
5. In the **Network Services** dialog box, click **Microsoft DNS Server**, and then click **Have Disk** if loading the software from disks or a CD.

   Or, select **OK** if loading from the network.
6. In the **Windows NT Setup** dialog box, type the full path to the Windows NT Server DNS files, and then click **OK**.
7. In the **Network Settings Change** dialog box, click **Yes** to restart the computer and complete the DNS installation.

Note   You must be logged on as a member of the Administrators group to install a DNS server.

Managing DNS Servers

Once a Windows NT Server DNS server is installed, DNS Manager is added to the Administrative Menu. Using DNS Manager, the administrator can add servers running Windows NT Server 4.0 DNS service to the server list. Once added, the administrator can view and change parameters of any of the Windows NT Server 4.0 DNS servers in the list.

▶   **To open the DNS Manager**

  • Click **Start**, point to **Programs**, point to **Administrative Tools**, and click **DNS Manager**.

    The Domain Name Service Manager window appears.

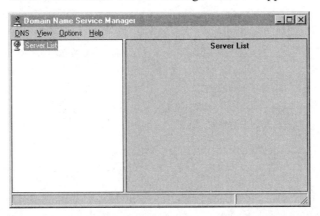

Add All Windows NT DNS Servers to the Server List

All of the servers running Windows NT Server 4.0 DNS service on the network can be administered and managed from any single computer running Windows NT Server DNS service, through the DNS Manager interface. To do this, the administrators at Terra Flora will add the servers to the server list using the DNS Manager interface. DNS features will not be available on any of the computers running Windows NT until the server is added to the server list.

▶ **To add a DNS server**

1. In Domain Name Service Manager, click **Server List**.

2. On the **DNS** menu, click **New Server**.

   The **Add DNS Server** dialog box appears.

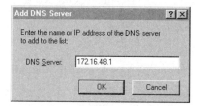

3. In **DNS Server**, type the IP address of the DNS server to be added to the server list, and then click **OK**.

   The server appears in the server list in Domain Name Service Manager.

Copy the Files

Three of the four existing zones will be moved to servers running Windows NT Server 4.0 DNS service.

The administers at Terra Flora will remove the appropriate zone, boot and cache files from the system servers which currently store the zones of Terraflora.com, Nursery.Terraflora.com and Supply.Terraflora.com. The files will then be placed in the SystemRoot\System32\DNS directory of the proper new server running Windows NT Server 4.0 DNS service which will, from that point forward, store the zone information.

The Terra Flora administrator will use the editor that they are familiar with to change the information about the zones in the boot file as appropriate.

Once the files are in the proper directory, the zone's structure can be viewed using the DNS Manager graphical interface. The administrators will be able to view the structure of the Nursery.Terraflora.Com and Supply.Terraflora.Com and Terraflora.Com zones.

Creating the New Zone

A zone is the administrative tool for information about the DNS domains. At Terra Flora, Terraflora.Com is the main authoritative DNS domain and the root zone. Three additional zones called Nursery.Terraflora.Com, Supply.Terraflora.Com and Retail.Terraflora.Com exist at Terra Flora. At Terra Flora, three of the zones have been moved to computers running Windows NT DNS Service. See the previous section "Copy the Files" for details.

Because of the mission critical nature of the applications in the retail division, the Retail.Terraflora.Com zone will be maintained. A fifth zone will be created to split the Retail.Terraflora.Com zone. This fifth zone will include only servers running Windows NT Server 4.0 DNS server. The zone will be set up as both primary and secondary in order for replication of the resource record database to take place. Two servers will store the zone information, one will store the primary zone information and one will store the secondary zone information.

▶ **To add the primary NT.Retail.Terraflora.Com zone**

1. In Domain Name Service Manager, click the server for which you will be creating the zone.

2. On the **DNS** menu, click **New Zone**.

   The **Create new zone for** *IP address of the server selected* dialog box appears.

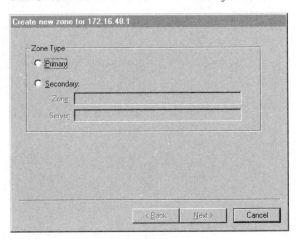

3. Click **Primary**.

4. Click **Next**.

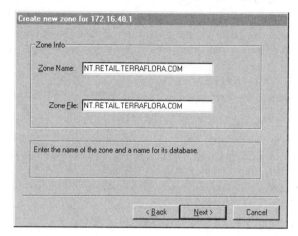

5. In **Zone Name**, type the name of the root domain within the zone.

6. If necessary, type the name of the database file in which you want the DNS resource records to be stored in **Zone File**.

7. Click **Next**.

8. Click **Finish**.

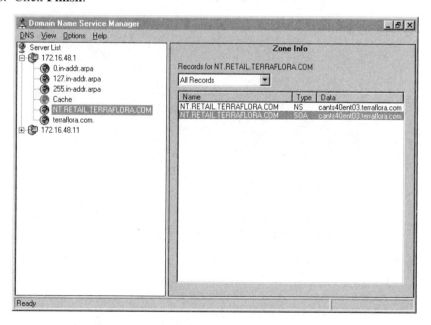

An SOA (Start of Authority) record is created in the database file entered in step 7. The SOA record indicates the Name Server which is the best source of information for supplying name resolution data.

NT.Retail.Terraflora.Com will also be set up as a secondary zone and the server assigned will be different than the one assigned for the Primary zone. If the server that stores the primary zone goes down, the server storing the secondary zone will be used for name resolution.

Selecting **Primary** as a zone type indicates that the zone does not obtain it's resource records from any other zone, the DNS Administrators are required to add, delete and modify all necessary resource records to the primary zone files.

The root domain is a DNS domain with multiple sections, each with a maximum of 63 characters and separated by a period (.). The zone name must be unique. The zone name will be NT.Retail.Terraflora.Com.

The default name of the **Zone File** will be the same name as entered in the **Zone Name** field.

▶ **To add the secondary NT.Retail.Terraflora.Com zone**

1. In Domain Name Service Manager, click the server for which you will be creating the secondary zone.

2. On the **DNS** menu, click **New Zone**.

   The **Create new zone for** *IP address of the server selected* dialog box appears.

3. Click **Secondary** as the **Zone Type**.

4. In **Zone**, type the name of the zone.

5. In **Server**, type the name of the server on which the primary zone information is stored, and then click **Next**.

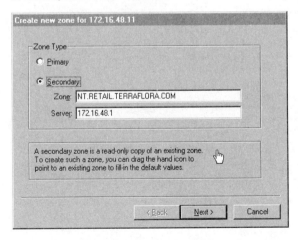

The secondary zone name appears in **Zone Name**.

6. In **Zone File**, type the name of the secondary database file you want the DNS resource records to be stored in, and then click **Next**.

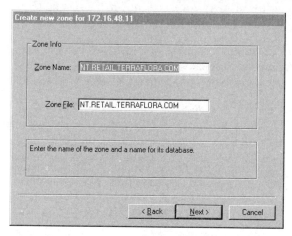

7. Click **Add**, and enter the IP address of the IP Master, which is the server on which the primary zone information is stored.

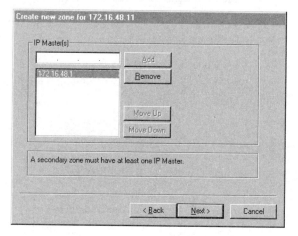

8. Click **Next**.

9. When a message appears, confirming that all the information for the new zone has been entered, click **Finish**.

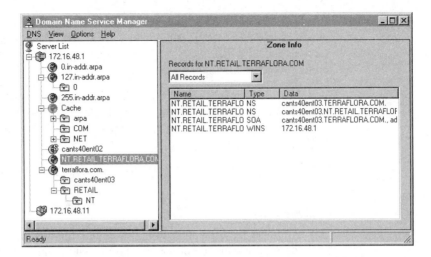

Selecting **Secondary** as the zone type indicates that the zone obtains its resource records from the primary zone. This means that the DNS Administrators are required to add, delete, and modify all resource records in the primary zone and not this secondary zone.

At Terra Flora, the zone name will be NT.Retail.Terraflora.Com, matching the primary name. The name should always be the primary zone name. When the secondary server starts, a query will be sent to the server specified as the *IP Master* for the zone file with the same primary name.

The default name in **Zone File** will be the name you entered in **Zone Name**.

Each secondary zone must have at least one IP master. You can add more than one IP master and move them in the list using the Move Up and Move Down buttons.

Adding and Changing Database Resource Records

During the process of creating the new NT.Retail.Terraflora.Com zone, Terra Flora specified the database file name and database server which would store the zone's database information. Resource records need to be added to the zone's database file that will indicate how computer names will be resolved.

Terra Flora has configured the DNS system so that when a client requests an IP address from the DNS server, the server on which the zone file for Terraflora.Com resides is examined first. If the name cannot be resolved within the Terraflora.Com file, the request is then forwarded to the servers on which the zone files for Retail.Terraflora.Com, Nursery.Terraflora.Com, and Supply.Terraflora.Com reside.

The resource records implementing this lookup already exist in all zones, except for the new NT.Retail.Terraflora.Com zone which was just created. New resource records must be put in the two zones Terraflora.Com and NT.Retail.Terraflora.Com.

Additionally, the resource records that exist in Nursery.Terraflora.Com and Supply.Terraflora.Com must be changed to reflect the information about the new server that now stores the zone files for Nursery.Terraflora.Com and Supply.Terraflora.Com.

The resource records that will be added to or changed for each of the zones are described below:

- Terraflora.Com

  An A (Address) record will be added supplying the host name and host address of NT.Retail.Terraflora.Com, which will indicate to other DNS servers and to the primary server storing the Terraflora.Com zone database file to search the NT.Retail.Terraflora.Com zone database file to resolve the clients name requests.

  An NS (Name Server) record will be added supplying the DNS Name Server name for the NT.Retail.Terraflora.Com zone, which will indicate to other DNS servers and to the server storing the Terraflora.Com zone database file to search the zone database file of NT.Retail.Terraflora.Com to resolve the request.

  The NS (Name Server) records will be changed to indicate the new DNS Name Server information for the Nursery.Terraflora.Com and Supply.Terraflora.Com zones.

  Other records can be added as necessary by the Terra Flora administrators, but these records are key in resolving name requests.

- NT.Retail.Terraflora.Com

  An A (Address) record will be added supplying the host name and host address of NT.Retail.Terraflora.Com to indicate to other DNS servers that the information stored in the NT.Retail.Terraflora.Com database should be examined for name resolution.

  An NS (Name Server) record will be added supplying the DNS Name Server name for the NT.Retail.Terraflora.Com zone to indicate to other DNS servers that the information stored in the NT.Retail.Terraflora.Com database should be examined for name resolution.

- Supply.Terraflora.Com and Nursery.Terraflora.Com

  The NS (Name Server) records will be changed supplying the new DNS Name Server name for the Supply.Terraflora.Com and Nursery.Terraflora.Com zone to indicate to other DNS servers that the information stored in the two zones should be examined for name resolution.

Other records can be added as necessary by the Terra Flora administrators, but these records are key in the continued use of DNS at Terra Flora.

▶ **To add a database resource record**

1. In Domain Name Service Manager, click the zone for which you will be creating the new record.

2. On the **DNS** menu, click **New Record**.

   The **New Resource Record** dialog box appears.

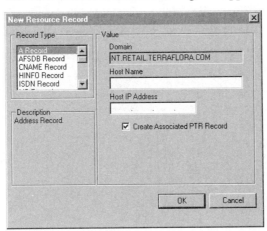

3. In **Record Type**, click the record you want to add.

   The dialog box changes, depending on which type of record you selected. For example, the **For Domain** name that is the zone name appears when you specify an NS record.

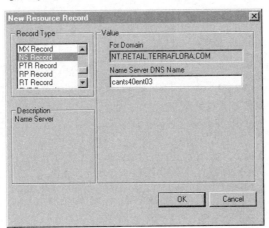

4. Under **Value**, type the necessary information, such as the **Name Server DNS Name** for NS records, which specifies the server name that will be used to resolve name requests.

5. Click **OK**.

▶ **To change a database resource record**

1. In Domain Name Service Manager, click the server that stores the zone with which you want to work.

2. Click the zone that contains the record you want to change.

3. In **Record for** *zone name*, click the record type you want to change.

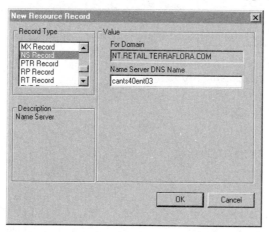

4. Double-click the record to be changed.

The dialog box changes, according to the kind of information required. For example, the Terra Flora administrator would type the name of the server which will now store the zone information for Nursery.Terraflora.Com in **Name Server DNS Name**.

5. To change another database resource record, repeat these steps.

For example, at Terra Flora, the administrator would repeat this procedure for Supply.Terraflora.Com.

6. When finished making changes, click **OK**.

At Terra Flora, the database resource records will need to be reviewed and changed as necessary.

In the case of Terraflora.Com, the administrator will be changing the NS record for Nursery.Terraflora.Com and Supply.Terraflora.Com. Consequently, the administer would complete the procedure for one record to step 5 and then repeat the procedure for the other record.

Static DNS Server Resource Records

At Terra Flora, there are DNS Servers that are not running Windows NT Server 4.0 in the Retail.Terraflora.Com zone that will be added to the zone files residing on the servers running Windows NT Server 4.0 DNS service. The static entry of the DNS servers ensures that all DNS servers will be searched in an attempt to map name and IP addresses. An A (Address) and NS (Name Server) resource record will be added to each zone for each DNS server that is to participate in name resolution.

WINS Lookup

When a server running Windows NT Server 4.0 DNS Service receives a DNS request to resolve a specified DNS name to an IP address, it will search its A (Address) resource records until it finds one whose DNS name matches the one specified in the request. It then returns the IP address stored in that A (Address) resource record to the requesting computer.

If the server cannot locate an A (Address) resource record for the requested DNS name, and if Use Wins Resolution is enabled, the DNS server will extract the host name, which is the text of the name, on the left hand side of the name, up to the first period, and send a request to a the specified WINS server asking it to map the host to an IP address. If the name was registered with WINS, WINS will return the associated IP address to the DNS server and the DNS server will return it in response to the original DNS request.

Any number of WINS servers can be specified for fault tolerance purposes. The server running Windows NT Server DNS service will try to locate the name by searching the WINS servers in the order listed.

▶ **To enable WINS Lookup**

1. In Domain Name Service Manager, click the zone for which you will be enabling WINS Lookup.

2. On the **DNS** menu, click **Properties**.

3. In the **Zone Properties** dialog box, click the **WINS Lookup** tab.

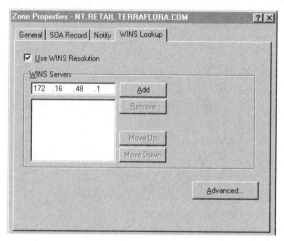

4. Select the **Use WINS Resolution** check box.

5. Under **WINS Servers**, type the WINS Server IP address that will be used for resolution.

6. Click **Add**.

You can repeat the procedure to add as many WINS servers for resolution as needed.

Integrating DHCP, WINS, and DNS in Heterogeneous Networks

Terra Flora has a difficult mix of disparate network operating systems, supporting multiple protocols, and different services with various administration tools. Most of them can support the TCP/IP protocol, and many of them can be dynamically configured with their IP address via the Dynamic Host Configuration Protocol, or DHCP.

However, there are legacy UNIX servers, and other network devices that use static IP addresses, and use the Domain Name Space (DNS) services to provide hostname-to-IP-address resolution. Therefore, they need to have a DNS servers in the environment as well.

The long range goals at Terra are to be able to handle an expanding network, and reduce costs. In addition, the types of network clients are changing, with portable and fully mobile networking requirements that break the previous networking models, and exceed the capabilities of the existing administrative mechanisms.

With that understanding, it becomes clear that Terra Flora needs to deploy DHCP services in their network environment to address the dynamic nature of the network clients and reduce the administrative costs of assigning and updating the host table information on the DNS servers. As DHCP only provides the dynamic IP address leasing, WINS services must also be deployed to provide the name resolution for these dynamic network clients. However, due to the presence and limitations of the existing legacy systems in the network, Terra Flora must continue to support DNS as well.

In order to meet the objectives, Terra Flora will deploy DHCP, WINS, and DNS services in their network environment. However, this does not mean that these technologies are islands unto themselves, where clients or servers using DNS can only access machines in the traditional DNS host tables, or where DHCP and WINS clients can only access computers similarly configured.

Windows NT Server 4.0 includes integrated name resolution server components, which allows both DNS and WINS-based clients to resolve names from both types of clients, while minimizing the impact on the existing network infrastructure.

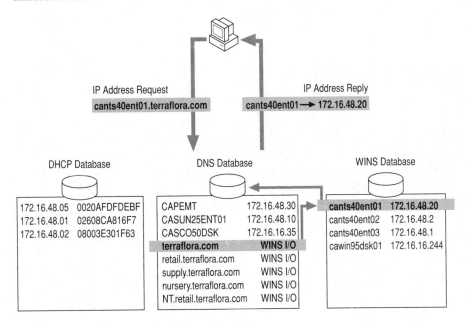

Using Windows NT Server 4.0 and integrating WINS, DNS and DHCP, the process of name and IP resolution becomes basically dynamic. A computer running Windows NT 4.0 will have a NetBIOS name. If a Windows NT, Windows 95 or Windows for Workgroups client sends a request for the IP Address location of a computer AshleyJ.Terraflora.com, and both computers are DHCP, WINS and DNS configured, the process of mapping the IP Address to the NetBIOS computer name of Ashleyj is as follows:

- A DHCP, WINS and DNS client computer requests the IP address of the NetBIOS named computer Ashleyj.

- The computer Ashleyj receives an IP address when it first starts up from DHCP.

- The IP address is registered with the WINS server, mapping the name Ashleyj to the IP address.

- The DNS server is able to resolve the Terraflora.Com portion of the name as a zone known to the WINS server.

- In configuring the Windows NT Server 4.0 DNS server, WINS servers were specified and associated to the zones. The NetBIOS portion of the name, which is the text up to the first period '.', will be sent by the server running Windows NT Server 4.0 DNS Service to the specified WINS servers.

- The WINS servers will be examined for the friendly name Ashleyj and the IP address. This information is sent back to the server running Windows NT Server 4.0 DNS service and then forwarded to the original requesting computer.

Network Logon Services

At Terra Flora, the logon services provided by the Windows NT operating system were selected to provide centralized network logon. This decision was made because Windows NT Server is the only product that provides the capability to log onto all the heterogeneous networks at Terra Flora. The Windows NT Server product provides users with the capability to sign onto all appropriate network resources using a single user account and password.

Note Password synchronization between network operating system platforms is not automatic for all platforms, but is a future technology for Windows NT Server (ODSI).

The Decision to Centralize Logon Services

Modern network server operating systems track user accounts in a secure and replicated database called a *directory*. The operating system services that facilitate the use of this database are called *Directory Services*. A *domain* is the administrative unit of Windows NT Server Directory Services. Within a domain, an administrator creates one user account for each user which includes user information, group memberships and security policy information.

Refer to the Terra Flora network diagram. At Terra Flora, three domains have been set up. They are the California Domain, the North East Domain and the Europe Domain.

Within each domain, *domain controllers* manage all aspects of user-domain interactions. Domain computers are computers running Windows NT Server that share one directory database to store security and user account information for the entire domain. Domain controllers use the information in the directory database to authenticate users logging on to domain accounts. Trust relationships are then set up between the domains to allow users in one domain to logon automatically to another domain. For details on how to manage the user work environment and domains, see Microsoft Windows NT Server 4.0 *Concepts and Planning*, Chapter 1, "Managing Windows NT Server Domains," Chapter 2, "Working with User Group Accounts" and Chapter 3, "Managing User Work Environments."

Currently, each of the heterogeneous networks in Terra Flora has its own security system through which the user signs onto the system and is authenticated to use the resources for which permissions are granted. One of the major complaints of network users is that they have to use multiple user accounts and passwords to sign onto different networks. Additionally, because there was no communications between networks, the users are required to log off one network to log onto another network.

At Terra Flora, the following steps have already been completed:

- PDC and BDCs for each Windows NT administrative domain have been properly configured. For details, see Start Here Installation and Basics Microsoft Windows NT Server, Version 4.0 and Microsoft Windows NT Server Concepts and Planning.
- The networks have been physically connected.
- User have been granted proper permissions and network access to all required network resources. For details on how to manage the user work environment and domains, see Microsoft Windows NT Server 4.0 *Concepts and Planning*, Chapter 1, "Managing Windows NT Server Domains," Chapter 2, "Working with User Group Accounts" and Chapter 3, "Managing User Work Environments."

Following the steps in the remainder of the chapter will provide the user with the ability to logon onto the network from any computer in the network and, if the accounts, passwords and permissions have been granted on all network platforms, will provide access to all the user's required network resources.

For the user, the single network logon will provide transparent, seamless access to the network resources. For example, a NetWare user will logon as usual to the NetWare network and be authenticated to the Windows NT network at the same time. It will just happen and the user will not know that a different network has been accessed. An additional benefit to the user is the ability to sign onto all appropriate network resources from any computer on the network.

For Terra Flora, this consistent interface helps to easily integrate the business processes available through applications stored on servers on different networks, reduces training and reduces support costs as it all appears to the user as the same network system, and reduces the administration costs associated with setting up and maintaining separate logon accounts and passwords on each separate network.

The following sections include information on installing and configuring network logon services to allow authentication of:

- UNIX Clients to Windows NT Servers
- Windows NT Clients to UNIX Servers
- Windows NT Clients to NetWare Servers
- NetWare Clients to Windows NT Servers
- Windows NT Clients to Banyan Servers
- Windows 3.1 Clients to Windows NT Servers
- MS-DOS Clients to Windows NT Servers
- Windows for Workgroups Clients to Windows NT Servers
- Windows 95 Clients to Windows NT Servers
- Macintosh Clients to Windows NT Servers

UNIX Clients Authenticating to Windows NT Servers

The UNIX operating systems support the Network File System (NFS). Terra Flora's Retail Services division uses as its primary divisional server a Sun server running the Solaris UNIX operating system. User names and passwords for authentication to the UNIX server are stored on the UNIX server, named CASUN25ENT01, (refer to the Terra Flora diagram) on the /etc directory in the Passwd file. At Terra Flora, a third party product by Intergraph called DiskShare will be installed on servers running Windows NT Server to allow UNIX clients access to Windows NT Servers.

Once Intergraph DiskShare is installed and configured, the existing UNIX /etc/Passwd file will be imported to the WINNT\System32\Drivers\Etc directory. Intergraph DiskShare provides a graphical interface through which the administrators can edit the password file. DiskShare provides a way to map UNIX names and passwords to the Windows NT user accounts and passwords so that UNIX users can have the same permissions as the Windows NT users to which they are mapped. Once the mapping is complete, users signing on to the Windows NT network will be simultaneously authenticated to the UNIX network.

Installing Intergraph DiskShare

Documentation is provided with the product. For installation instructions, see the Intergraph DiskShare *Quick Start Guide*. Additional information is provided in online Help files.

See the documentation accompanying the product for details on the various options provided.

Editing the Password File

The Passwd file is where the UNIX authentication information is stored. Using the graphical interface, administrators can add, change or delete the User Name, the User ID (UID), the user's group ID (GID) and the password.

The first step is for the administrator to copy the Passwd file from the /etc directory on the UNIX server to the WINNT\System32\Drivers\Etc directory on the computer running Windows NT Server. Once the file is in the right directory on the computer Windows NT server, it can be accessed by DiskShare to allow the necessary administration.

▶ **To access the Password File Editor**

1. Click **Start,** point to **Programs,** and click **DiskShare Server.**

2. On the Server menu, click Password File Editor.

    The **Password File Editor** dialog box appears.

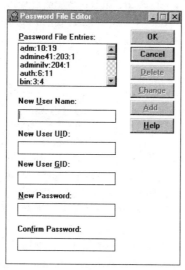

3. In **Password File Entries,** click the user you want to change or delete.

4. Type the appropriate information for the user name, user UID, user GID, and password in the spaces provided, and then do one of the following:

   - To add the user, click **Add**.

   - To enter changes for the user, click **Change**.

   - To delete the user, click **Delete**.

Mapping UNIX Passwords to Windows NT User Accounts

At Terra Flora, all user accounts, passwords and permissions have been set up on the computers running Windows NT Server. For details see, Microsoft Windows NT *Concepts and Planning,* Chapter 1, "Managing Windows NT Server Domains," Chapter 2, "Working with User and Group Accounts," and Chapter 3, "Managing User Work Environments."

Additionally, the UNIX /etc/Passwd file has been copied to the proper Windows NT directory WINNT\System32\Drivers\Etc, which makes it accessible to the graphical interface supplied in Integraph's DiskShare. The entries in the UNIX password file will be mapped or matched to user accounts created in Windows NT domains.

Mapping the UNIX user accounts and passwords to a Windows NT User account grants the UNIX user the same rights and permissions to the Windows NT server as the Windows NT user to whose account the UNIX account is mapped.

Note If the name and password are exactly the same in the UNIX /etc/Passwd file as that stored in the Windows NT Directory Database, mapping is automatic.

Without mappings, server resource access will default to whatever privileges are given to the Everyone user trying to access the group. See your UNIX documentation for more details on UNIX privileges.

▶ **To administer UNIX-to-NT user mappings**

1. Open the NFS Administrator.

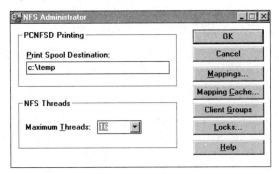

2. Click Mappings.

    In the **User Mappings** dialog box, the users that are currently mapped are listed in **NFS Mapped Users**.

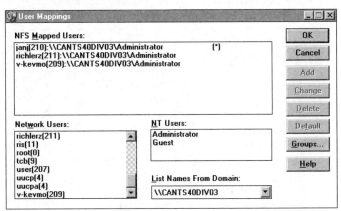

3. In **Network Users**, click the UNIX user to be mapped to the Windows NT user.

4. In **NT Users**, click the Windows NT user to which you want the UNIX Network user mapped.

5. Click **Add**.

The mapping appears in **NFS Mapped Users**.

Additional information that appears in the NFS Administrator window includes:

- **Network Users**, which list user names and user IDs (UIDs) in the format: network user name:UID. This information comes from the UNIX-style password file.

- **NT Users**, which lists Windows NT user accounts that are local to the domain controller of the specified NT domain.

- **List Names From Domain**, which lists all NT domains to which the local machine has access. It includes the local machine name, the primary domain, and any domains that trust the primary domain.

Note Changes made in this dialog box do not take effect until you click **OK**, to write the new information to the registry.

Online Help is part of the DiskShare product and explains mapping, such as how to map Windows NT User Groups to UNIX Groups and perform reverse mappings. These sections focus on administrative tasks specific to the Intergraph PC-NFS and DiskShare products.

Note Sharing and unsharing of NFS directories and files requires the same user permissions required by Windows NT Server and UNIX. The local user account must be logged on as a member of the Administrators, Server Operators, or Power Users groups.

Sharing NFS Server Resources

Two separate and complimentary mechanisms govern file access through the NFS server. The first is the NFS administrator's ability to control both which server resources are made available as network resources and what access clients within the network will have to the data. The second is the security administration performed by the underlying server file system itself. Effective access permission granted to any user is the more restrictive of these two mechanisms.

Share permissions are the first line of defense for the NFS server. Using share permissions, an administrator can control which network NFS client nodes have read and/or write access to NFS Shared resources. Four levels of access are available depending on the type of object selected, as follows:

- No Access

This prevents all *mount* or connection requests for the share except for those individual client nodes or client groups that have a type of access specified.

- Read-Only

  The client is allowed to mount and read the shared resource, but cannot alter it.

- Read-Write

  The client may mount, read and write the shared resource.

- Root

  The client may mount, read, write, and perform "superuser" type operations on the file system assuming the requesting User ID is correct for the operation, and that is maps to the Administrator privilege. This access level can only be assigned to individual client nodes or client groups.

To determine if sufficient permission is available for the NFS request, the Global Permission is checked first. If this is not sufficient, an individual client's permission entry is checked. If no individual client permissions are present, then permission is given based on client group access.

File permissions within NFS are very much like those in a UNIX system. Under UNIX, every file belongs to a single user and group; the user must be a member of the group that owns the file. More precisely, a file has a single user ID and a single group ID. Because several different user accounts can have the same user ID, and several groups the same group ID, it may be ambiguous to speak of a particular user or group. The following criteria, in order of decreasing precedence, govern access to files:

- Access granted to the owner of the file, a user with the same effective user ID as the file owner ID.

- Access granted to members of the group to which the file belongs, users can belong to several groups simultaneously.

- Access to granted to all others, such as those who do not own the file and are not members of the group to which the file belongs.

Each permission category controls three modes of access:

- *Read*, which is the ability to open the file for read access and examine its contents without altering it in any way.

- *Write*, which is the ability to open the file with write access and update its contents.

- *Execute*, which is the ability to load the file into the system and run it. For directory files, execute access is interpreted as search permission.

Understanding the Security Descriptor

Intergraph DiskShare uses the Windows NT security descriptor when implementing NFS access permissions. The security descriptor is the structure that governs security within Windows NT. The security descriptor contains the following components:

- File owner.
- File group.
- System Access Control List (SACL). The SACL is used for auditing and does not affect file permissions.
- Discretionary Access Control List (DACL).

The following is an example of a security descriptor:

Owner: spike

Group: UtilGroup

DACL: spike   Read (R)

UtilGroup   Read (RX)

Everyone   Read (RX)

In this example, the file owner is spike, the file group is UtilGroup, and the DACL shows the permissions given to spike, UtilGroup, and Everyone.

Within the security descriptor, the file owner and file group are pointers to Security Identifiers (SIDs). The SID can be thought of as the internal representation for an individual user or group. The primary reason for using SIDs is to distinguish between accounts across different domains that may share the same account name. Even though the names are the same, they represent different accounts and can thus be given different access rights to the same file.

Understanding the DACL

The Discretionary Access Control List (DACL) within the security descriptor provides the core of Windows NT security. The DACL is a list of entries that grants or denies certain rights to specific users or groups. A list entry is called an Access Control Entry (ACE). Each ACE consists of the following:

- A Security Identifier (SID) to identify a particular user or group.
- An access list specifying the rights allowed or denied for the user or group.

The following is an example of a DACL:

DACL: mrjones   Full Control (All)

ToolGroup   Read (RX)

Everyone   Read (RX)

In this DACL, mrjones has read, write, and execute access to the file; members of the group ToolGroup have read and execute access, and members of the group Everyone (all other users) have read and execute access.

The following rules govern access to a file:

- If no DACL is present, everyone is granted full access.
- If a DACL is present, but contains no entries, everyone is denied any access.
- The file owner always has the ability to change the DACL.

Reverse Mapping Permissions

The function of Intergraph DiskShare is to translate between a security descriptor on the computer running Windows NT Server and Intergraph DiskShare and a (UID, GID, mode) triplet on the NFS client.

Intergraph DiskShare controls permission translation with reverse mapping. Intergraph DiskShare's NFS Administrator program allows the DiskShare administrator to specify a mapping between NFS User and Group IDs and their corresponding Windows NT users and groups.

- A given UID can be mapped to any Windows NT user.

  Because multiple UIDs can be mapped to the same Windows NT user, one of the mappings will be marked as the default mapping. The default mapping is the UID to be returned when the mapped Windows NT user is found to be the file owner.

  If the given UID is not mapped, the ANONYMOUS LOGON account will be used. This can have some undesirable results, so we recommend that all UIDs be mapped to a valid Windows NT account.

- A given GID can be mapped to any Windows NT group.

Note   If the given GID is not mapped, no group will be assigned, and no group entry will be placed in the DACL.

You can use the reverse mapping feature when mapping from NFS to Windows NT, or from Windows NT to NFS.

Sharing Files and Directories on a NFS Server

Once the DiskShare product is installed, the ability to share the NFS server files and directories and grant permissions to the users is provided through the computer running Windows NT Server.

▶ **To share files and directories on a NFS Server**

1. Click Start, and then click **Run**.

2. In **Open,** type **winfile**, and then click **OK**.

3. On the **Disk** menu, click **Share as**.

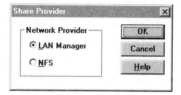

4. Click **NFS**, and then click **OK**.

5. In the **New NFS Share** dialog box, type the path of the file you want to share.

6. Click **Permissions**.

   The **NFS Share Permissions** dialog box appears.

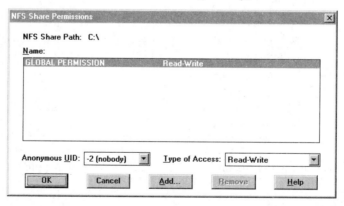

7. Enter the settings you want for **Anonymous UID** and **Type of Access**, and then click **Add**.

8. Under **Names** in the **Add Clients and Client Groups** dialog box, click the user to be granted access.

9. In **Type of Access**, click the setting you want, and then click **OK**.

UNIX Client Sign On

Once the above steps are performed, the UNIX client is mapped with the proper permissions to the computer running Windows NT Server. When the UNIX client signs onto the server, authentication is provided via pcnfsd on the UNIX server to Windows NT User Account.

From the UNIX client, create a local directory as a mount point. Then mount the exported directory to a local directory.

Windows NT Clients Authenticating to UNIX Servers

At Terra Flora, a third party product called Intergraph PC-NFS for Windows NT will be installed on all computers running Windows NT Workstations and client computers running Windows NT that need access to UNIX servers. When the Windows NT client computer starts, a login screen will display. The user logs into the NFS authenticating server and can access the resources for which permissions have been granted.

A new product called Intergraph DiskAccess will replace the product Intergraph PC-NFS for Windows NT. It is scheduled to ship 30 days after the Windows NT Server 4.0 product ships. The current product of Intergraph PC-NFS for Windows NT can be used with server versions of the Windows NT product which proceeded the 4.0 version, and operates fine with version 4.0. The major difference between Intergraph's DiskAccess and PC-NFS will be changes to the graphical interface.

The users at Terra Flora have been granted permissions and the user accounts and passwords have been entered in the /etc/Passwd file of the authenticating UNIX server.

Installing Intergraph PC-NFS for Windows NT

Intergraph PC-NFS for Windows NT is to be installed on the computers running Windows NT Workstation and Windows NT Server, which will require client access to UNIX servers. For instructions on installing Intergraph PC-NFS for Windows NT, see the documentation provided with the product titled *PC-NFS for Windows NT Quick Start Guide*. Once installed, the product provides File Manager functions, a Control Panel-based configuration program and various utility programs.

Configuring PC-NFS

Configuration of the product can be performed to customize PC-NFS to fit your network environment.

▶ **To start PC-NFS Config**

1. Click **Start**, point to **Settings** and click **Control Panel**.
2. Double-click **PC-NFS Config**.

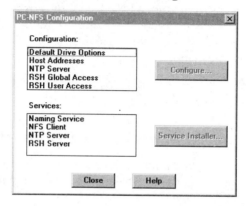

See online Help for details about using PC-FNS Config.

Logging onto a UNIX Server Using PC-NFS

Once the above steps are complete, computers running Windows NT Workstation and Server that will require client access to UNIX servers can logon to Windows NT and be authenticated to the UNIX servers in the same step. When a user logs into the system and starts a Windows NT session, by default the PC-NFS Login dialog box appears to indicate that PC-NFS software is running.

Authentication establishes UNIX-style user and group permissions for UNIX clients on the network and is necessary if the NFS server restricts entry by user name. You do not have to use the PC-NFS Login dialog box to log in to the server before connecting to network-based NFS resources. However, if you do not do so, you may find that an NFS server restricts or denies access to some or all of its resources.

▶ **To log on as a Windows NT client to a UNIX server**

1. Click **Start**, point to **Programs**, point to **PC-NFS for Windows NT**, and then click **PC-NFS Login**.

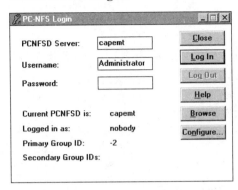

2. In **PCNFSD**, type the name of the NFS authenticating server.

   This can be any computer running NFS, such as a UNIX server for which the user has permissions.

3. In **Username**, type your user name for login purposes.

4. In **Password**, type your password.

5. Click **Log In**.

Mounting Remote Resources

To mount or connect to a resource, use the Windows NT Explorer. Remote NFS resources mounted through PC-NFS software appear as virtual disk drives on your computer and display as network drives in Windows NT Explorer.

▶ **To Mount Remote Resources**

1. Click **Start**, point to **Programs**, and then click **Windows NT Explorer**.

2. On the **Tools** menu, click **Map Network Drive**.

   The **Map Network Drive** dialog box appears.

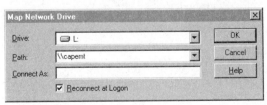

3. In **Drive**, click the drive you want to use.

4. In **Path**, type the path to the remote device to which you want to attach.

5. To map to another network drive using a different user account or group account ID, enter than information in **Connect As**.

6. Click **OK**.

Windows NT Clients Authenticating to NetWare Servers

On Terra Flora's network, there are existing installations of Novell NetWare, which are primarily used for file and print services. User accounts and privileges are stored in the NetWare *Bindery*, which is Novell's equivalent of the Windows NT directory. Access is validated based on user accounts and passwords in a Windows NT domain via the directory database, or on a Novell NetWare server via the bindery.

Novell uses the IPX/SPX protocol as their primary network protocol. In order for Windows NT Workstations or Windows NT Servers to communicate with the NetWare services, Microsoft developed NWLINK, an IPX/SPX-compatible protocol. NWLINK is the fundamental building block for the NetWare-compatible services on the Windows NT platform, and by itself, NWLINK does provide connectivity for database access to databases running as NetWare Loadable Modules on NetWare servers. So, for example, a Visual Basic application running on Windows NT Workstation can access an Oracle database running on a NetWare server, through ODBC and the NWLINK components.

Client Service for NetWare (CSNW)

The Client Service for NetWare installed on a computer running Windows NT Workstation provides basic file and print connectivity for that client to a NetWare 3.*x* server, or a NetWare 4.*x* server which includes the functionality of CSNW on the server platform. A different service, Gateway Service for NetWare (GSNW), provides access for computers running Windows NT Server to NetWare Servers.

▶ **To add CSNW**

1. Click **Start**, point to **Settings**, and click **Control Panel**.

2. Double-click **Network**.

3. Click the **Services** tab.

4. Click **Add**.

5. Click Client Services for NetWare, and click OK.

6. Type the path to the CSNW files, and click **Continue**.

7. In the **Client Services for NetWare Dialog** box, type the name of the NetWare Server that will be used for authentication, click **OK**, and then click **Close**.

You must restart the computer to complete the installation. Click **Yes** and the computer will restart to complete the process.

Configuration of CSNW is necessary for the Windows NT Client to be able to connect to the NetWare server. A preferred server is selected when the CSNW service is added to the computer running Windows NT Workstation. In addition, as a result of adding CSNW, a CSNW icon is added to the Control Panel.

▶ **To activate and configure CSNW**

1. Click **Start**, point to **Settings**, and click **Control Panel**.

2. Double-click **CSNW**.

3. In the **Current Preferred Server** dialog box, select a server, if necessary, and then click **OK**.

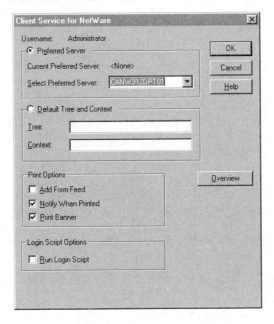

The Preferred Server setting performs the Attach command to the NetWare server and thus provides authentication to the NetWare server providing that the user and privileges have been added to the NetWare Bindery on the server that the user is trying to access.

Gateway Service for NetWare (GSNW)

The Gateway Service for NetWare (GSNW) provides computers running Windows NT Server all support necessary to connect to NetWare servers, plus the additional capability to re-share the network connections from a NetWare server. The service allows the computers running Windows NT Server to access the NetWare servers as if they were just another client and, in addition, allows the network clients to access files on a NetWare server without having to have a NetWare client redirector on an IPX/SPX protocol stack loaded.

Gateway Service for NetWare depends on and works with two other NetWare compatibility features of Windows NT Server; the NWLink protocol, and NWLink NetBIOS. NWLink is an implementation of the internetworking packet exchange (IPX) and sequenced packet exchange (SPX) transport protocols used by the NetWare network. NWLink NetBIOS is a Microsoft-enhanced implementation of Novell NetBIOS, and transmits Novell NetBIOS packets between a NetWare server running Novell NetBIOS and a Windows NT computer, or between two Windows NT computers. The Microsoft implementations of the IPX, SPX, and Novell NetBIOS compatible protocols can seamlessly coexist with other protocols on the same network adapter card.

The computer running Windows NT Server establishes a network connection to the NetWare server, similar to any network client connection.

Gateway Service for NetWare is installed from the Windows NT Server CD-ROM.

Note Before you install the Gateway Service, you must remove any existing NetWare redirectors, such as NetWare Services for Windows NT from Novell, and then restart your computer.

▶ **To remove existing NetWare redirector installations**

1. Click **Start**, point to **Settings**, and click **Control Panel**.
2. Double-click **Network**.
3. Click the **Services** Tab.
4. Click the existing NetWare redirector software, and click **Remove**.
5. When prompted to confirm your choice, click **Yes**.

You must restart your computer to complete the removal process.

You are now ready to install the Gateway Service on a computer running Windows NT Server. You must be logged on as a member of the Administrators group for the local computer to install and configure the Gateway Service for your Windows NT computer. When you install the Gateway Service on a computer running Windows NT Server, the NWLink transport protocol is also installed if it is not already on your computer.

Activating a Gateway

Before enabling a gateway on a computer running Windows NT Server:

- A user account must be set up on the NetWare network with the necessary rights for the resources you want to access.

- The NetWare server must have a group named NTGATEWAY with the necessary rights for the resources you want to access.

- The NetWare user account you use must be a member of the NTGATEWAY group.

By controlling membership in the NTGATEWAY group, the administrator can control which Windows NT Server computers can be gateways to the NetWare server, and what kind of access to what files each user account has.

The administrator has total control over whether the gateway allows access to files and print queues on the NetWare server. With a gateway, the network administrator can control access to NetWare network resources either over the gateway or directly on the NetWare network:

- On the Windows NT Server computer acting as a gateway, the administrator can restrict access by limiting which network users or groups have access to gateway shares. Using multiple share restrictions through a gateway, the Windows NT administrator can control which network users and groups can access files through the gateway.

- Using NTGATEWAY special gateway group created on the NetWare file, the administrator can set trustee rights on the directories and files to which users and groups are allowed access through the gateway. There is no auditing of gateway access.

▶ **To make a NetWare server available to a gateway account**

1. Use the NetWare **syscon** utility to create the NTGATEWAY group account on the NetWare file server.

2. Use **syscon** to create a NetWare user account with the same name and password the user will use to log on from the Windows NT Server computer.

3. Add the gateway account to the NTGATEWAY group.

4. Establish trustee rights for the NTGATEWAY group.

For detailed information on the **syscon** utility and NetWare user accounts and trustee rights, see your NetWare documentation.

If you want to control user access, you can set permissions for the share when you create it, or later if your needs change.

Install Gateway Services for NetWare

Once the user gateway and information is added to the NetWare server, you are ready to install GSNW on the computer running Windows NT Server.

▶ **To install GSNW**

1. Click **Start**, point to **Settings**, and click **Control Panel**.

2. Double-click **Network**.

3. Click the **Services** tab.

4. Click **Server**, and then click **Add**.

5. Click **Gateway Services for NetWare**, and click **OK**.

6. Type the path to the source files, and click **Continue**.

7. In the **Gateway Services for NetWare** dialog box, enter the name of the NetWare server to which the computer running Windows NT Server will connect.

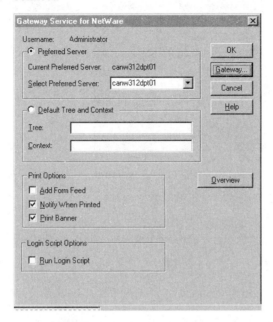

8. Click **Gateway**.

9. Select the **Enable Gateway** check box.

10. Type the NetWare user account created to logon to the NetWare server from a computer running Windows NT Server, and click **Add**.

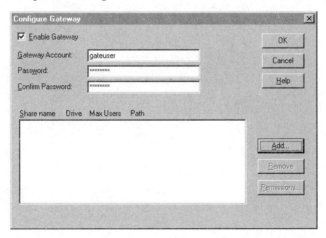

11. In the **New Share** dialog box. type the Share name of the gateway on the NetWare server.

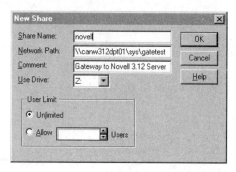

12. Type the full path to the new share on the NetWare server.

13. Type an entry in **Comment**, if you want one.

14. Enter a letter for the drive on which the new share will reside.

15. If necessary, enter a value to limit the number of users.

16. Click **OK**.

The GSNW option is added to Control Panel and is used to activate the gateway.

Limitations of the Gateway Service for NetWare

GSNW is not designed to be a high bandwidth, user intensive, high performance gateway. It is designed to meet the needs of the customers who desire to have casual access to files that exist on a NetWare server, from a Windows Networking, or remote client.

Accessing Shared Resources on the NetWare Server

To access shared resources on a NetWare server, use the **Map Network Driver** option in the Explorer. You can map to both print and file servers. Again, this assumes that the proper privileges are assigned to the user when the connection is attempted.

▶ **To access shared resources**

1. Click Start, point to Programs, and click Windows NT Explorer.

2. On the **Tools** menu, click **Map Network Drive**.

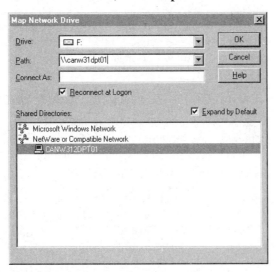

3. In **Drive**, confirm that the drive displayed is the one that is mapped to the server you want to access.

4. In **Path**, type the path to the resource to which you are trying to connect.

5. To connect to the specified drive on start up, select the **Reconnect at Logon** check box.

6. Click **OK**.

Commands to View and Find NetWare Servers

From the command line you can view your existing network connections, and their network providers.

▶ **To view network connections**

1. Click **Start**, point to **Programs**, and click **Command Prompt**.

2. Type **Net Use**, and press ENTER.

You can also browse the network to specifically find NetWare servers.

▶   **To browse for NetWare Servers**

1. Click **Start**, point to **Programs**, and click **Command Prompt**.

2. Type **Network:NW**, and press ENTER.

Windows NT Client Logon to NetWare

Logging onto the NetWare network is accomplished through Windows NT. When the user starts a computer running Windows NT Server or Workstation and the steps outlined above are complete, the **Begin Logon** dialog box appears. The user then supplies the ALT+CTRL+DEL key sequence and the **Logon Information** dialog box appears. When the user provides the logon information, the user is authenticated to the Windows NT network. At the same time, the user is authenticated to the NetWare network and has access to all NetWare resources for which they have been granted permissions.

NetWare Clients Authenticating to Windows NT Servers

At Terra Flora, the NetWare clients are, in most cases, configured with only the NetWare client software, including the IPX/SPX stack, and the NCP protocol. For many reasons, including limited conventional memory, or other incompatibilities, the users simply cannot run multiple protocol stacks on their client machines.

It is easy to justify a business case for connecting the NetWare clients to the Windows NT Servers. This connection would allow the computers running Windows NT Server to absorb the additional file and print load on the network and save Terra Flora the expense of investing in additional NetWare systems.

In the past, Terra Flora has been reluctant to take this step because completing the connection of the NetWare clients to computers running Windows NT Server would have required adding SMB networking support to and changing the configuration on each NetWare client, which just did not make cost-effective sense.

Now using the File and Print Services for NetWare, network clients can directly access information on a Windows NT Server without changing any of the client-side software or configuration information.

The File and Print Services for NetWare uses an NCP-compatible protocol to support file and print services to NetWare clients, using either the NETX or VLM redirectors. To the NetWare client, the Windows NT Server looks like a NetWare 3.12 server, providing both file and print resources via the same dialogs as the NetWare servers themselves.

▶ **To install FPNW on a computer running Windows NT Server**

1. Click **Start**, point to **Programs**, and click **Control Panel**.

2. Double-click **Network**.

3. Click the **Services** tab.

4. Click **Have Disk**, and then type the path to the FPNW files, which are shipped on disks or a CD-ROM as part of a separate Microsoft product called Services for NetWare.

5. Click **OK**.

6. In the **Select OEM Option** dialog box, click **File and Print Services for NetWare**, and then click **OK**.

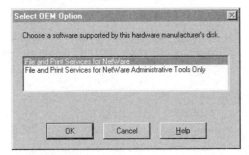

7. In the **Install File and Print Services for NetWare** dialog box, type the location for the SYSVOL directory that will be the equivalent of the NetWare SYS: volume in **Directory for SYS Volume**.

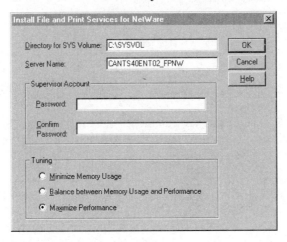

8. In **Server Name**, type the computer name that the NetWare client computers will use to access the server.

9. Type a password for the Supervisor's account in **Supervisor Account**, and then type the same password in **Password** and **Confirm Password**.

10. In **Tuning**, click an option for tuning server performance.

11. If you are installing File and Print Services for NetWare on a domain controller, enter a password for the FPNW Service Account when prompted.

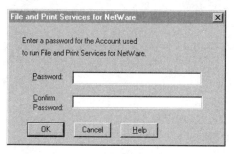

You must restart the computer to complete the installation. The FPNW icon will then appear in Control Panel; a check box and **NW Compat** option are added to the **New User** dialog box for User Manager for Domains.

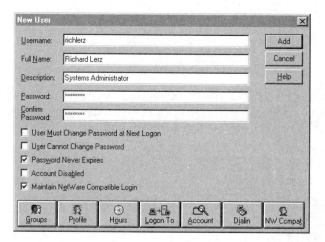

The network administrator can then select the **Maintain NetWare Compatible Login** check box to allow the user to log on to File and Print Services for NetWare.

Notes

- In step 7 of the procedure above, it is recommended that you specify a directory on an NTFS partition to be the equivalent of the NetWare SYS: volume. If you specify a directory on a non-NTFS partition, you lose the security features that NTFS provides and will not be able to set or enforce file or directory security settings. SYS is the volume that is traditionally created.

- In step 8, above, the **Server Name** must be typed in all capital letters. The default is the server's computer name with "FPNW" appended, but can be any NetWare-compatible name that does not conflict with any other NetWare server names.

- In step 9, above, the password can be as many as 14 characters, and is case-sensitive.

- If you install File and Print Services for NetWare on multiple domain controllers in a domain, you must specify the same password for this account on each domain controller on which you install the utility.

Security access to FPNW on the Windows NT server is specified in the user's User Account. For information on setting up User Accounts, see *Concepts and Planning*.

NetWare Client Logon to Windows NT

Logging onto the Windows NT network is accomplished through NetWare. When the user starts the NetWare client, the user provides the necessary information to log onto the NetWare network. At the same time that the user is authenticated to the NetWare network, the user is also authenticated to the Windows NT network and has access to all Windows NT resources for which they have been granted permissions.

Windows NT Clients Authenticating to Banyan Servers

Windows NT Clients can authenticate to Banyan servers using the Banyan Enterprise Client for Windows NT version 5.56. The Windows NT clients will be able to access file and print resources on Vines server using this product.

Installing Banyan Enterprise Client for Windows NT

Banyan provides a product called Banyan Enterprise Client for Windows NT which enables the computers running Windows NT server or workstation to connect as clients to the Banyan servers.

At Terra Flora, user accounts and passwords are set up on the Banyan server that match the user accounts and passwords set up in the Directory Services of Windows NT.

▶ **To install Banyan Enterprise Client for Windows NT**

1. Click Start, point to Programs, and click Windows NT Explorer.

2. Select the letter of the drive that contains the setup files.

3. Double-click **Setup.exe**.

4. In the **Network Communications** dialog box, select the **Enable IP Encapsulation** check box, and then click **Advanced**.

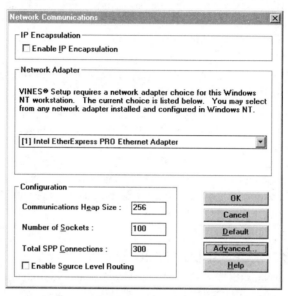

5. In the **VINES Workstation Configuration** dialog box, select the settings you want, if necessary, and then click **Continue**.

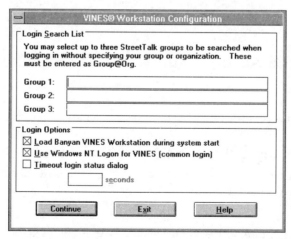

6. In the **VINES Desktop Configuration** dialog box, select the options shown in the following illustration.

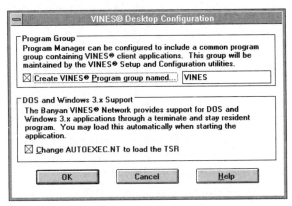

7. Select the **Create VINES Program group named** check box and enter the name of the VINES program as you want it to appear under Programs on the Start menu.

8. Select the **Change AUTOEXEC.NT** check box to load the TSR, and then click **OK**.

9. In the **Configure Network Computer Name** dialog box, type the name of the computer on which you are installing Banyan Enterprise Client for Windows NT, and then click **Continue**.

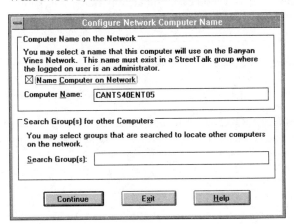

You must restart the computer to complete the procedure.

Notes

- You are not required to use **Log In Search**, but if the groups are set up on the Banyan server, you can use this feature. The groups specified in the Search List will be searched to see if the user that is attempting to log in is a member of that group and what the permissions are associated with the user. You can specify up to three groups. When the user attempts to log on, the first group is checked, if no information about the user is located, the second group is checked. If no information about the user is found, the third group is checked. If no user information is found, the log in attempt fails.

- The **Load Banyan VINES Workstation during system start** check box must be selected if the computer running Windows NT is to authenticate to the Banyan server automatically during logon.

- The **Use Windows NT Logon for VINES** (common login) option creates a common login for both Windows NT and Banyan VINES. This requires that the user account and password on both machines be the same.

- You can specify the log in attempt seconds before the result is a time out failure.

- Step 10, above, allows MS-DOS applications to recognize the Banyan connections. This is required since most administrative applications running on the Banyan server are MS-DOS based.

- In step 11, above, the Name must be included in a group in Street Talk on the Banyan server. You can indicate any name that is included in the group but the default will be the name of computer on which you are installing the product.

If the Banyan Enterprise Client for Windows NT is configured as described, login will take place when the Windows NT client starts up. When the user logs into the Windows NT network, authentication to the Banyan server also occurs.

If you elect not to configure automatic log in to the Banyan server because use is infrequent, the users can sign onto the Banyan server from the Windows NT Start menu.

▶ **To log into the Banyan server**

1. Click **Start**, point to **Programs**, and click VINES (the program group name will appear as entered in the Vines Workstation Configuration dialog box).

2. Double-click Login.

3. In the VINES Login dialog box, type the user's account name and password that is configured on the Banyan server, and then click OK.

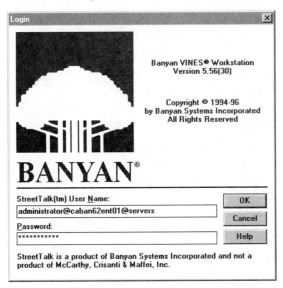

The **VINES Login Status** dialog box appears. Once this dialog box is closed, the Windows NT **Start** menu dialog box appears.

Banyan Clients Authenticating to Windows NT Servers

Banyan Systems Inc. has announced their StreetTalk Access for Windows NT which allows Banyan clients to directly access file and print resources on Windows NT servers. For more information, please contact Banyan Systems Inc. at http://www.banyan.com.

Windows 3.1 Clients Authenticating to Windows NT Servers

In order for a Windows 3.1 client to connect to a network, network software such as LAN Manager or Microsoft Networking Clients must be installed and configured. See the user documentation accompanying the LAN Manager or Microsoft Networks product for installation instructions. At Terra Flora, LAN Manager 2.2c is the product that will be installed to allow the Windows 3.1 clients to access the network.

Once LAN Manager is installed, the Config.sys and Windows\system.ini files will be updated and the network will start up automatically when the client running Windows 3.1 is started.

In addition, for a user to log onto a computer running Windows NT Server the user's account with necessary permissions must exist on the computer running Windows NT Server. For information on creating the user account and assigning permissions to access resources, see Microsoft Windows NT Server 4.0 *Concepts and Planning*, Chapter 1, "Managing Windows NT Server Domains," Chapter 2, "Working with User and Group Accounts," and Chapter 3, "Managing User Work Environments."

Once LAN Manager is installed, the LAN Manager Logon will display every time the Windows 3.1 client starts up.

If a User Account and permissions have been set up on the Windows NT Server, the user is authenticated to the Windows NT network. To access the file and print servers, the user supplies the network path and connects to the required Windows NT resources.

▶ **To connect to Windows NT resources**

1. On Program Manager, click **LAN MAN**.

2. Click Net Admin.

3. Double-click **Network**.

   The **Drives - Network Connections** dialog box appears.

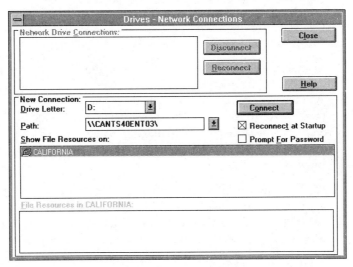

4. Select the **Drive Letter** for the connection.

5. In **Path**, type the path to the Windows NT Resources to which you want to connect.

6. To connect to the Windows NT Resources each time the computer starts up, select the **Reconnect at Startup** check box.

7. Click **Connect**.

Note The user can connect to the network using **File Manager**. On the **Disk** menu, click **Connect Network Drive** and enter the path of the network resource to which you want to connect.

MS-DOS Clients Authenticating to Windows NT Servers

In order for a DOS client to connect to a network, network software such as LAN Manager or Microsoft Networks must be installed and configured. See the user documentation accompanying the selected product for installation. At Terra Flora, LAN Manager 2.2c is the product that will be installed to allow the MS-DOS clients to access the Windows NT network.

Once LAN Manager is installed, the Autoexec file is changed and the network will start up automatically when the client running DOS is started.

In addition, for a user to log onto a computer running Windows NT Server the user's account with necessary permissions must exist on the computer running Windows NT Server. For information on creating the user account and assigning permissions to access resources, see Microsoft Windows NT Server 4.0 *Concepts and Planning*, Chapter 1, "Managing Windows NT Server Domains," Chapter 2, "Working with User and Group Accounts," and Chapter 3, "Managing User Work Environments."

When the network starts, the user types the Net Use command at the prompt and supplies the server name and share to which they want to connect. In the example below, the user wants to connect to payroll share on the Supply and Manufacturing payroll department server. At the prompt, the user would type:

```
Net Use * \\CAWPS30DPT01\Payroll
```

When ENTER is pressed, an available drive letter is assigned and connection to the server is completed.

Windows For Workgroups Clients Authenticating to Windows NT Servers

At Terra Flora, the clients running Windows for Workgroups are already configured and working together in workgroups. The workgroups are defined by task. For example, one of the payroll workgroups consists of all those responsible for entering hours worked into the payroll system. Since all the computers running Windows for Workgroups are already connected as workgroups, it is a simple configuration task to the computers to access other network computers running Windows NT Server.

Before the users of the computer running Windows for Workgroups can logon to the computer running Windows NT Server, the user's accounts and passwords must be set up and proper permissions assigned to the user on the Windows NT Server. For details, see *Microsoft Windows NT Concepts and Planning,* Chapter 1, "Managing Windows NT Server Domains," Chapter 2, "Working with User and Group Accounts," and Chapter 3, "Managing User Work Environments."

▶ **To make sure TCP/IP is enabled**

1. On the **Program Manager**, double-click **Network**.

2. Double-click Network Setup.

3. In the Network Setup dialog box, make sure that Microsoft TCP/IP-32 3.11b is one of the drivers selected, and then click OK.

   If the driver is not selected or is not available, see your Windows For Workgroups documentation for instructions on how to select the driver.

Note The driver is located on the NT Server CD and can be selected from the \Clients\TCP32WFW directory.

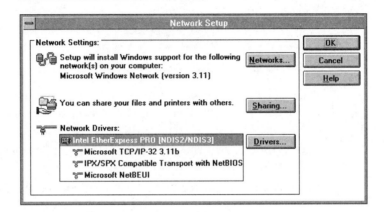

At Terra Flora, the Windows for Workgroups client will log on onto the computer running Windows NT Server. In order to accomplish this task, the computer running Windows for Workgroups needs to be properly configured.

▶ **To configure the computer running Windows for Workgroups to join the Windows NT domain**

1. On the **Program Manager**, double-click **Main**.

2. Double-click **Control Panel**.

3. Double-click **Network**.

4. In the **Microsoft Windows Network** dialog box, make sure the computer name appears in **Computer Name**.

5. In **Workgroup**, click the domain the user will log on to.

6. In **Default Logon Name**, type the user account, as set up on the Computer running Windows NT Server.

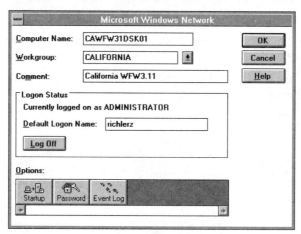

7. Click **Startup**, and then specify settings in the **Startup Settings** dialog box for how logon will occur when you start the computer running Windows for Workgroups.

8. Under **Options for Enterprise Networking**, select **Log On to Windows NT or LAN Manager Domain**.

9. Make sure the setting for **Domain Name** is correct, and then click **Set Password**.

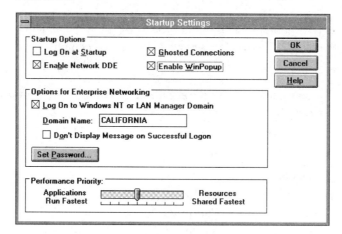

10. In the **Change Domain Password** dialog box, make sure the information displayed is correct, or change the password, and then click **OK**.

The password must match the user account information set up on the computer running Windows NT Server.

When the user starts up the computer, the **Welcome to Windows for Workgroups** dialog box appears.

If the Logon Name is correct, the user types the password, clicks **OK**, and is authenticated to the Windows NT Network. The information can be changed.

Windows 95 Clients Authenticating to Windows NT Servers

At Terra Flora, Windows 95 clients have been configured and are in use throughout the Terra Flora Network. Configuration of each Windows 95 client is required for the client to access the Windows NT Domain.

During Windows 95 setup, information is supplied which will be reviewed during the configuration process. Additional information will be configured about the Windows NT Domain and the Windows NT client.

Prior to configuring the Windows 95 clients, the Terra Flora administrators set up user accounts on the Windows NT servers, granting the proper permissions to each user that will access the computers running Windows NT Server. For details, see *Microsoft Windows NT Concepts and Planning*, Chapter 1, "Managing Windows NT Server Domains," Chapter 2, "Working with User and Group Accounts," and Chapter 3, "Managing User Work Environments."

▶ **To configure the Windows 95 client requiring access to a computer running Windows NT Server**

1. Click Start, point to **Settings**, and click **Control Panel**.

2. Double-click **Network**.

3. In the Network dialog box, click the **Configuration** tab, which displays information that was input during the setup of Windows 95.

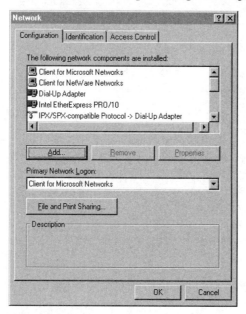

4. Click **Client for Microsoft Networks**, and then click **Properties**. The dialog box appears.

5. Enter settings in the **Client for Microsoft Networks Properties** dialog box, as illustrated below, substituting the name of your Windows NT domain in **Windows NT domain**, and then click **OK**.

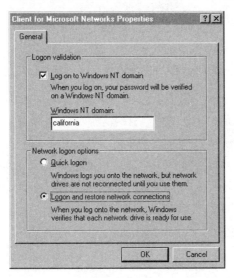

6. Click **TCP/IP** and the installed net card, and then click **Properties**.

7. Verify that the **IP address information** is correct.

8. Verify the information contained on the other TCP/IP tabs: **DNS Configuration**, **WINS Configuration**, **Gateway**, **Bindings**, and **Advanced**, and then click **OK**.

    Refer to the *Windows 95 Resource Kit* for more information about these options, if necessary.

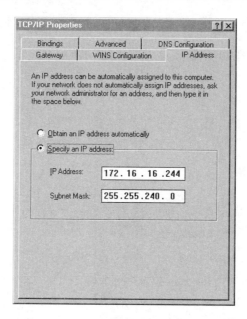

9. In the **Network Dialog** box click the **Identification** tab.

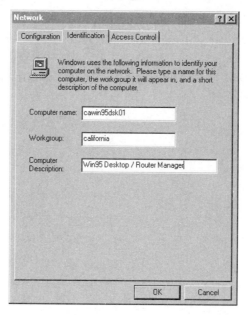

10. Type the name of the computer, the NT domain name, and a description of the client, and then click **OK**.

You must restart the computer for the changes to take effect.

When the client starts Windows 95, the **Enter Network Password** dialog box appears. To log on to the network, the user enters the **User Name** and **Password** that match the ones set up for the user on the computer running Windows NT Server.

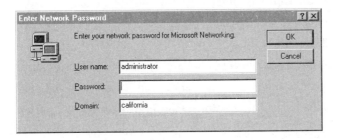

Macintosh Clients Authenticating to Windows NT Servers

Microsoft Windows NT Server Services for Macintosh is a thoroughly integrated component of Microsoft Windows NT Server, making it possible for computers running Windows NT Server and Apple Macintosh clients to share files and printers.

With Services for Macintosh, Macintoshes need only the Macintosh operating system software to function as clients; no additional software is required. You can, however, set up the optional user authentication module, which is software that provides a secure logon to the Windows NT Server.

For complete information on planning and setting up the Macintosh network, see the Microsoft Windows NT Server 4.0 *Networking Supplement*.

Installing Services for Macintosh

Terra Flora is using Macintosh clients to produce some of the necessary graphical marketing materials. At Terra Flora, they will enable Services for Macintosh on the computers running Windows NT Server using the Network icon in the Control Panel and the Windows NT Server distribution disk.

When Services for Macintosh are installed, the AppleTalk Protocol, File Server for Macintosh, and Print Server for Macintosh are automatically started, or enabled. An explanation of these services is provided in the Microsoft Windows NT Server 4.0 *Networking Supplement*, Chapter 15, "Introduction to Services for Macintosh."

In addition, setting up Services for Macintosh creates an icon in Control Panel, which gives the administrator the same server administration capabilities as the MacFile menu, excluding volume management, for the local computer.

▶   **To set up Services for Macintosh**

Services for Macintosh are loaded through the Network Icon on the Control Panel from the CD ROM accompanying the Windows NT Server product.

1. On the **Control Panel**, click the **Network** icon.

2. Click the **Services** tab.

3. Click **Add**.

4. On **Network Service**, click to **Services for Macintosh**, and click **OK**.

5. Type the full path of the Services for Macintosh, and click **Continue**.

6. In the AppleTalk **Protocol Configuration** dialog box, enter the changes you want, such as selecting a new zone, a different network, or enabling AppleTalk routing.

   For details about this configuration, see, Microsoft Windows NT Server 4.0 *Networking Supplement*, Chapter 16, "How Services for Macintosh Works," Chapter 18, "Setting Up Services for Macintosh" and Chapter 21, "Working with Macintosh-Accessible Volumes." Choose **OK** or Cancel if you don't want to change the configuration.

The computer must be restarted for the changes to take effect.

Authentication Services for Macintosh Client Software

Microsoft authentication is an extension to AppleShare, which provides a more secure logon session to a computer running Windows NT Server. It encrypts passwords and stores them on the computer running Windows NT Server. Administrators can either set up or instruct Macintosh users to set up the authentication file on their Macintoshes via the network.

With Microsoft authentication, users can also specify a domain when they log on or change their passwords. So if there are multiple domains on the network, the user's account domain will be used.

Note Because the Apple System software up to version 7.1 does not fully support custom user authentication modules, Microsoft encourages the installation of Microsoft Authentication (MS UAM) only if increased security is necessary on the network computers running Windows NT Server.

A user authentication module (UAM) is a software program that prompts users for an account name and password before they log on to a server. Apple's Chooser has a standard UAM built in, which uses the clear-text password method of security. Microsoft Authentication offers an additional level of security because it encrypts, or scrambles, a password so it cannot be monitored when it is sent over the network. At Terra Flora, the administrators have determined that encryption is an important security measure, and will require use of Microsoft Authentication when the user logs on to the computer running Windows NT Server.

▶ **To gain access to the authentication files**

1. On the Macintosh Apple menu, click **Chooser**.

   The **Chooser** dialog box appears.

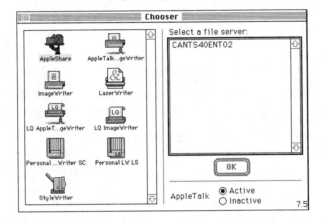

2. Click the **AppleShare** icon, and then click the AppleTalk zone in which the computer running Windows NT Server resides.

3. Click the name of the Windows NT Server, and then click **OK**.

   A sign-in dialog box appears.

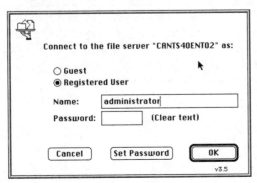

4. Click **Registered User** or **Guest**, as appropriate, and then click **OK**.

A server dialog box appears.

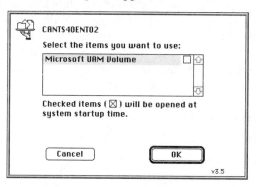

5. Click **Microsoft UAM Volume**, and then click **OK**.

▶ **To install the authentication files on the Macintosh client**

1. From the **Macintosh Desktop**, double-click the **Microsoft UAM Volume**.

The Microsoft **UAM Volume** window appears.

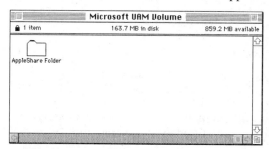

2. Drag the **AppleShare Folder** to the **System Folder** on your hard disk.

Note If the Macintosh client already has an AppleShare Folder in the System Folder, you will see a message that asks whether you want to overwrite the folder. You should not overwrite it because it may contain other UAMs, such as the NetWare UAM. If you want to maintain the files in the original AppleShare Folder, simply open the AppleShare Folder in the Microsoft UAM Volume, and drop the MS UAM file into your existing AppleShare Folder in your System Folder.

Configuring Services for Macintosh

Apple Talk Protocol is a stack of protocols that Services for Macintosh uses to route information and configure zones. It works behind the scenes to ensure that computers on the network can talk to one another. The Apple Talk Protocol is configured accessing Services for Macintosh located under the Network option of the Control Panel.

▶ **To configure Services for Macintosh**

1. In **Control Panel**, click **Network**.

2. In the Services tab, select Services For Macintosh and click Properties.

   The **Microsoft AppleTalk Protocol Properties** dialog box appears.

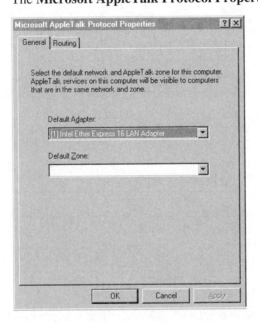

3. Select a default network from a list of adapter cards bound to the AppleTalk Protocol.

For details, see the *Microsoft Windows NT Server Networking Supplement*, Chapter 19, "Configuring Services for Macintosh."

How Files Are Shared

With Services for Macintosh, Macintosh users can easily share files stored on the computer running Windows NT Server. On a computer running Services for Macintosh, files are stored in shared directories or in Macintosh volumes.

With Services for Macintosh, Macintosh users cannot automatically gain access to all shares. To make a directory, and consequently its subdirectories, which may or may not be shared on the Windows NT system network, available to Macintosh users, the administrator must designate the directory as a *Macintosh-accessible volume*. For details, see the *Microsoft Windows NT Server 4.0 Networking Supplement*, Chapter 21, "Working with Macintosh-Accessible Volumes."

Creating Volumes

All Macintosh-accessible volumes must be created on an NTFS partition. Similar to creating a share (shared directory) for PC users, you can designate a directory as a Macintosh-accessible volume. If the directory is to be accessed by PC clients as well as Macintosh clients, make sure you share the directory using the Share As command on the Disk menu and designate it as a Macintosh-accessible.

Note You cannot give a directory Macintosh-accessible volume status if it is a subdirectory of another directory that has Macintosh-accessible volume status. For specifics, see *Microsoft Windows NT Server Networking Supplement*, Chapter 21, "Working with Macintosh-Accessible Volumes."

You can designate a directory as a Macintosh-accessible volume using the Create Volume command on the MacFile menu. From the Create Volume dialog box, you can create the volume by accepting the default settings, or may customize by changing the options.

To create a Macintosh-accessible volume

1. In **File Manager**, select the directory that you want to designate as a Macintosh-accessible volume.

2. On the **MacFile** menu, click **Create Volume**.

3. Type a name in **Volume Name**, which will be the name Macintosh users will see when they log on.

4. To accept the default options (listed below in Table 5.1), click **OK**.

   Or, go to step 5.

5. Enter the settings you want to change from the default settings.

   Refer to Table 5.2, below, for descriptions of the options.

6. Click **Permissions** to set directory permissions for Macintosh users, and then click **OK**.

The Macintosh-accessible volume automatically inherits the permissions of the corresponding directory, although you may change these. See Setting Permissions for Volumes and Folders later in this section.

Table 5.1.   The default settings for the Create Volume **dialog box**

Option	Default Setting
Volume name	Same as the directory name. The character limit is 27.
Path	Same as the directory path.
Password/Confirm Password	No password.
This volume is read-only	This option is Off.
Guests can use this volume	This option is On (Yes).
User Limit	Unlimited.
User Permissions	Current directory permissions.

Table 5.2   Alternate settings for the Create Volume **dialog box**

Option	Description
Password	Enter the password for this volume. When Macintosh users try to mount this volume, they will be asked for this password.
Confirm Password	Confirm the password just entered.
This volume is read-only	This volume and all of its contents have read-only access. This option supersedes all directory permissions set with the Permission button. In other words, if you give this volume read-only access, the permissions of directories with less restrictive access will not be honored.
Guests can use this volume	Guests can have access to this volume. If not selected, guests do not have access.
User Limit	Number of clients that can simultaneously mount the volume on the respective desktops. Select Unlimited or Allow and specify the number of users.
Permissions	Set access permissions on this volume. See Setting Permissions for Volumes and Folders later in this section.

Creating Folders in a Volume

You can create subdirectories for a Macintosh-accessible volume from the computer running Windows NT Server or folders from the Macintosh clients. In either case, the procedure for creating the directories or folders is no different than it is for creating other directories or folders on the respective systems.

On the computer running Windows NT Server, the folders appear in the File Manager's directory tree as subdirectories of the directory. To create another subdirectory, you select the directory in which it will appear and choose Create Directory from the File menu.

On the Macintosh, you create folders using the New Folder command on the File menu. You can view and use the folders in the Macintosh-accessible volume just organized by Name, Date, Icon, Size, and so forth.

Note You cannot designate the subdirectory or folder as another Macintosh-accessible volume when the directory is already designated as a Macintosh-accessible volume.

Network Security

Services for Macintosh translates user identification, authentication (passwords), and permissions so that the security of the server is maintained regardless of the type of client used.

Services for Macintosh uses the same user accounts database as Windows NT Server. Therefore, if you already have Windows NT Server accounts created for the people who will be using Macintoshes on the network, you don't need to create additional accounts.

One aspect of Windows NT Server user accounts, the user's primary group, applies only to Services for Macintosh. The *user's primary group* is the group the user works with most, and it should be the group with which the user has the most resource needs in common. When a user creates a folder on a server, the user becomes the owner. The owner's primary group is set as the group associated with the folder. The administrator or owner can change the group associated with the folder.

Passwords

Macintosh users are logged on to a computer running Windows NT Server in one of three possible scenarios:

- Guest Logons

  Using Services for Macintosh, you can set up guest logons, which allow users without accounts to log on to the server using a Macintosh. You can specify what access to resources guest logon users have; administrators typically grant guest users fewer permissions than users who have accounts on the server. If the guest logon option is enabled, the server always approves the logon request without requiring a password. For information on setting up Guest Logons, see the *Microsoft Windows NT Server Concepts and Planning Guide.*

- Cleartext Passwords

  Cleartext password protection is part of the AppleShare client software on Macintoshes. It provides less security than encrypted password protection because the passwords are sent over computer lines and can be detected by "sniffers," which are network monitors that can look for passwords. Moreover, the AppleShare passwords can be no longer than eight characters. This method of protection is offered for Macintosh users who use the standard AppleShare client software or System 7 File Sharing.

- Encrypted Passwords

  An encrypted, or encoded, password is more secure than the cleartext password type of security. Windows NT Server encodes passwords and stores them so that they cannot be directly stolen from the client itself. Encrypted passwords can be as long as 14 characters. Services for Macintosh offers encrypted passwords to Macintosh clients.

For more information about security, see *Windows NT Server Services for Macintosh, Microsoft Windows NT Server 4.0 Networking Supplement* and the *Windows NT Server System Guide.*

Volume Passwords

Services for Macintosh provides an extra level of security through Macintosh-accessible *volume passwords*. A volume password is a password you assign to a Macintosh-accessible volume when configuring it. Any Macintosh user who wants to use the volume must type the volume password. Volume passwords are case-sensitive. Volume passwords are optional; when you create a new Macintosh-accessible volume, the default is to have no volume password.

Note   Because of a constraint with the System 6 and 7 Finder, you cannot automatically mount a volume with a volume password at startup or by double-clicking an alias. You also cannot automatically mount a volume if the user originally connected to the volume with Microsoft Authentication.

Permissions

Access to network files and directories is controlled with *permissions*. With the Windows NT security system, you specify which users can use which shares, directories, and files, and how they can use those files. The Macintosh-style permissions differ in that they can be set for folders (directories) only—not files.

The Windows NT Server Administrator account always has full permissions on Services for Macintosh volumes.

Macintosh users set Macintosh-style permissions on the folders they create. In Windows NT, new files and new subdirectories inherit permissions from the directory in which they are created.

Macintosh files effectively inherit the permissions set on folders. Even though the Macintosh doesn't have file permissions, any Windows NT permission specified for a file will be recognized by the File Server for Macintosh, even though the Macintosh user won't see any indication in the Finder that these permissions exist. The Macintosh has the following four types of permissions for a folder:

- See Files, which lets a user see what files are in the folder and read those files

- See Folders, which lets a user see what folders are contained in the folder

- Make Changes, which lets a user modify the contents of files in the folder, rename files, move files, create new files, and delete existing files

- Cannot Move, Rename, or Delete, which prohibits these actions on a folder

The Macintosh security scheme is based on the idea that every folder on a server falls into one of three types: private information, accessible only by a single person, the owner of the folder; group information, accessible by a single workgroup; and public information, accessible by everyone.

For example, there can be a folder containing information that all members of a certain group should see, but that only one person can change. The person allowed to change the information should be the owner of the folder and should have See Files, See Folders, and Make Changes permissions. The workgroup that uses the folder should be the group associated with the folder and should have only See Files and See Folders permissions. Because no one else needs to see the folder's contents, the Everyone category should not be selected.

Although a folder's owner will often be a member of the group associated with the folder, this is not required.

With both Macintosh-style and Windows NT Server-style permissions, users' access to folders can be defined differently for each directory and subdirectory within a directory tree. For example, you could give a user See Files, See Folders, and Make Changes permissions for one folder, only the See Files permission for a subfolder of that folder, and no permissions at all for another subfolder.

The Macintosh does not support file-level permissions. When a file has file-level permissions, those permissions apply to Macintosh users only if the permissions are more restrictive than those assigned for the directory that contains the file.

Setting Permissions for Volumes and Folders

You control who can use Macintosh-accessible volumes by setting permissions. Permissions also control what kind of access is granted to users. For example, permissions dictate which users can make changes to a folder, and which ones can read the content of the folder but not alter it.

▶ **To set Macintosh-style permissions on a Macintosh-accessible volume or folder**

1. In **File Manager,** click the directory you've designated as a Macintosh-accessible volume or a subdirectory that represents a folder in the volume.

2. On the **MacFile** menu, click **Permissions**.

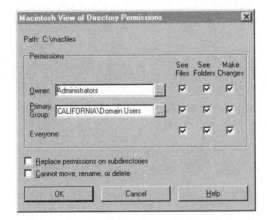

3. Select or click to clear the **See Files**, **See Folders**, and **Make Changes** check boxes, as appropriate, for **Owner**, **Primary Group**, and **Everyone**.

   Refer to Table 5.3, below, to help you decide which permissions to set.

Table 5.3   Options for Permissions

Permission	Description
See Files	Allows the owner, primary group, or everyone to see and open files in this folder.
See Folders	Allows the owner, primary group, or everyone to see and open folders in this folder.
Make changes	Allows the owner, primary group, or everyone to add or delete files and folders, and save changes to files in this folder.

4. To copy the permissions you set to all folders within this volume or folder, select the **Replace permissions on subdirectories** check box.

5. To prevent Macintosh users from moving, renaming, or deleting the volume or folder, select the **Cannot move, rename, or delete** check box.

Printing

When you set up a printer on the AppleTalk network to be used with Services for Macintosh, you can specify whether Services for Macintosh will capture the printer. This means that the printer will not accept print jobs from any source other than the print server, thus giving Windows NT Server administrators complete control over the printer.

In general, it is best to always capture a printer, unless a source other than the print server prints jobs on the printer. If a printer won't be used by anything other than Windows NT Server, Microsoft recommends that you capture it. Doing so ensures that users don't accidentally bypass the print server and send print jobs directly to the printer or reset the printer, which may cause spooler problems.

If a printer is not captured and both Windows NT Server and another source send jobs to the printer, no jobs will be interrupted; however, while the printer is printing a job from one source, it will appear busy to the other sources.

For information about how to capture AppleTalk printers, see the *Networking Supplement*.

Before setting up printers, it's important to understand the distinction between a printing device and a printer that you create using the Add Printer wizard.

- A printing device is the hardware that actually does the printing, such as a Hewlett-Packard LaserJet.

- A printer you create using Windows NT Server is a software interface between the document and the printing device. You create a printer using the Add Printer wizard, and each printer sends jobs to the printing device, according to the specified priority—for example, on a first-come, first-served basis.

These concepts and others are explained more fully in the *Windows NT Server Concepts and Planning Guide* and the *Windows NT Networking Supplement*.

When Services for Macintosh (SFM) is set up, several AppleTalk services are integrated into Windows NT Server. The print server, called *Print Server for Macintosh*, is integrated into the Windows NT Server Printers folder. The print server makes printers connected to the computer running Windows NT Server available to Macintosh clients, and it makes AppleTalk PostScript printers (with LaserWriter drivers) available to PC clients.

When the print server receives print jobs from the print server, it sends them to a spooler, which is a portion of the hard disk. The spooler then sends the print job to the specified printing device—for example, to a printing device on the AppleTalk network. This enables Macintosh users, as well as PC users, to submit print jobs and continue working on their computers without waiting for the print job to complete.

The print server also translates all incoming PostScript files if the print request is to a non-PostScript printer attached to the computer running Windows NT Server. So, a Macintosh client (but not a Windows NT client) can send a PostScript job to any Windows NT Server printer.

Note This implementation of Postscript RIP for SFM supports 300 dpi and Postscript level 1.

Stopping and Restarting the Print Server

When you set up SFM, all services are automatically started, including the print server. You might want to stop and restart the print server if, for example, you must remove a printing device. You stop and restart the Print Server for Macintosh using the Services icon in Control Panel.

▶ **To stop and restart Print Server for Macintosh**

1. In Control Panel, click **Services**.
2. In **Service**, click **Print Server For Macintosh**.
3. Click **Stop** or **Start**, as appropriate, and then click.
4. To change options at startup, click **Startup**.
5. Click **Close**.

Creating a Printer on a Computer Running Windows NT Server

After you have physically attached a printing device to a computer running Windows NT Server (either directly or on a network), use the Add Printer wizard to create a printer that represents it. You can create more than one printer representing the same printing device.

For example, if you have a printing device in your office but also share it with others over the network, you might want to create two printers representing the printing device. You can create a printer for yourself that is not shared over the network and a second printer that is shared. Then it's easy to control the use of the shared printer. You can set permissions on the shared printer, ensuring that only members of your department can print to it. Or you can set a low priority for it, ensuring that documents you send to the printer will always print before documents sent by those who share it.

Another common example is to create a printer that spools to a printing device at night and another printer that spools to the same printing device during the day.

To create a printer, you must be logged on with sufficient permissions. Administrators, Server Operators, and Print Operators can create printers.

▶ **To create a printer**

1. Click **Start**, point to **Settings**, and then click **Printers**.
2. In the **Printers** dialog box, click **Add Printer**.
3. Follow the Add Printer wizard to choose the printer ports, printer driver, and printer name. You can also set printer properties, such as location and scheduling information.

See the online Help during setup for more information.

Note The printer name can be up to 32 characters in length. This name will appear in the title bar of the printer window. By default, it is the name that network users (except MS-DOS users) will see when you share the printer.

Choose the **Share this printer** option during setup. In the Share Name box, specify the printer name that you want MS-DOS clients to see.

When you are selecting a destination, if the printing device is physically connected to the Windows NT Server computer, then select the appropriate port. If the printing device is on the network, click **Add Port**. Choose **AppleTalk Printing Devices** from the **Printer Ports** dialog box and click **OK**. From the **Available AppleTalk Printing Devices** dialog box, select a zone and a printer, and click **OK**.

Setting Up a User Account for Macintosh Print Jobs

After setting up Services for Macintosh, you should create an account that will be used by all Macintosh clients when printing jobs to captured AppleTalk printing devices or to other devices on the computer running Windows NT Server. You should also configure Print Server for Macintosh to use this account.

After it is created, the user account (for example, MACUSERS) appears in the list of names that appears when you choose **Permissions** from the **Security** menu in Print Manager. You can give specific rights to this user account, just as you would any user account, including Print and No Access.

For more information about permissions, see *Networking Supplement*, Chapter 22, "Managing the File Server." For information on creating a user account and more specific information for configuring it to run with a service (such as Print Server for Macintosh), see the *Windows NT Server Concepts and Planning Guide*.

▶ **To configure the Print Server for Macintosh service to use a user account**

1. In Control Panel, double-click **Services**.

2. Click **Print Server For Macintosh**.

3. Click **Startup**.

4. In the **Print** Server **For Macintosh** dialog box, click **This Account** and type the user account.

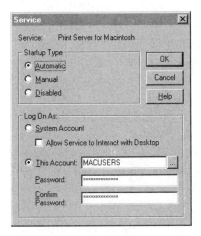

5. To require Macintosh users of the computer running Windows NT Server to use a password , type a password in **Password** and in **Confirm Password**.

6. Click **OK**.

Enabling Clients to Use Printers on the AppleTalk Network

With SFM, both PC and Macintosh clients can send print jobs to printing devices or spoolers on the AppleTalk network.

The printing device must appear as a LaserWriter in the Chooser, and there must be a Windows NT print driver for the printing device.

Macintosh clients use printers just as they normally do—through the Chooser. If an AppleTalk printer has been set up through Print Manager, it can be captured so that Macintosh clients cannot access it directly. This causes Macintosh print jobs go through the computer running Windows NT Server and be spooled along with print jobs from PC clients.

You can disable the capture setting. Doing so enables any Macintosh client to print to an AppleTalk printer directly. There are a few problems with this scenario, the most important being that the jobs will not be under the administrator's control.

▶ **To release or recapture an AppleTalk printing device**

1. In **Printers**, select an AppleTalk printing device.

2. On the **File** menu, click **Properties**.

3. Click the **Ports** tab, and then click **Configure Port**.

   A dialog box appears, asking if you want to capture this AppleTalk printing device.

4. Click **Yes** to capture it.

   –Or–

   Click **No** to release it.

5. Click **OK**.

When an AppleTalk printer is released, any Macintosh user on the AppleTalk network can use the device directly.

A printing device on AppleTalk can be captured when SFM is set up and a printer is created for it. It must remain captured so that all Macintosh clients send print jobs through the computer running Windows NT Server. If a printing device has been released for some reason, you can recapture it.

You can select another spooler instead of an actual device. Use this type of configuration with caution. It is possible to create an endless loop of print spooling with this method.

Centralized Services

At Terra Flora, the goal of centralizing administrative services was achieved with the installation of Windows NT Server as the common platform from which to interoperate their heterogeneous networks. Use of the Windows NT network operating system has provided Terra Flora with the ability to administer all clients and servers running operating systems other than Windows NT from one client computer. Several sessions can be started on any computer running Windows NT Server or Workstation so the administrator can view and monitor all network computers.

Though there are some limitations to the extent of administrative functionality, Windows NT Server was the most flexible and functional solution to the challenges presented to Terra Flora's plan to centrally administer the different network operating systems.

The Decision to Centralize Administrative Tasks

To Terra Flora, one of the major benefits of installing and configuring Windows NT Server services is the ability to administer all clients and servers on the network from a central point, regardless of the geographic location of the computer or which operating system is running.

Additionally, all the servers can be administrated on one client running Windows NT Workstation or Server because the computer will support the running of multiple sessions as illustrated below.

Novell Netware Administration Utilities

UNIX Administration Utilities x/Windows Support

BANYAN Administration Utilities

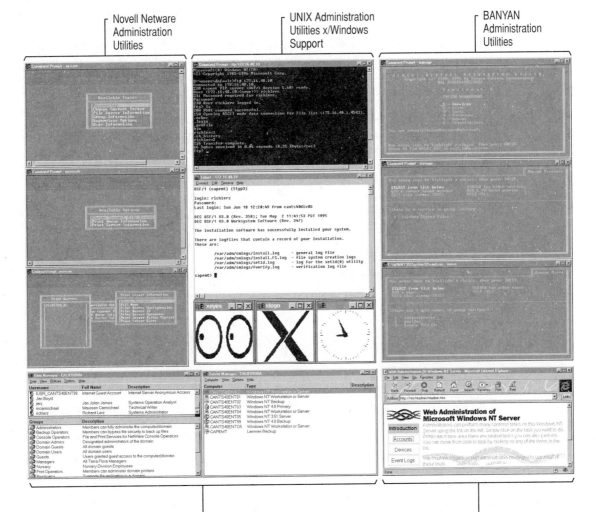

NT Server Administration Utilities

NT Web-based Administration Utilities

Most of the administration of all network servers will be performed by the network administration staff located in Sacramento, California. The administration may not be performed on a single computer, but the ability to do so provides greater flexibility to the network administrators. Occasionally, the administrators will want to sign onto machines while visiting remote sites and administer computers located at corporate headquarters or at the remote sites. At some remote sites administration may be localized to reduce excessive wide area network (WAN) traffic.

The administrative tasks necessary to manage the clients and servers are the same regardless of the operating system that is being run on the computer. For example, administrators set up and maintain user accounts and grant permissions to users or groups of users on Windows NT Servers as well as on UNIX and NetWare servers. Administrative tools are supplied with each operating system and the idea of interoperability includes the ability to sign onto any computer in the network and run any administrative tools on any network computer. Windows NT provides this capability.

This ability will reduce the administrative costs associated with managing a network the size of Terra Flora's. This eliminates the need for administrators to be located at remote sites, the need for administrators to travel to remote sites to perform routine administrative tasks and eliminates some of the wide area network (WAN) traffic that would occur administering files remotely.

The following table provides examples of which administrative tools are provided by which operating systems to remotely administer the servers at Terra Flora. This section will focus on the ability to connect to the administrative tool from Windows NT. The details of how to use each of the administrative tools is provided in the documentation accompanying the operating system.

Operating System	Administrative Tools (not all-inclusive)	Use of the Tool
UNIX	FTP	Allows users to connect to the UNIX remote hosts (computers) to transfer files such as /etc/passwrd, /etc/hosts, etc.
	Telnet	In many UNIX-oriented environments, administrative functions are performed via a remote console command-line interface, known as Telnet. Telnet is a simple UNIX remote command line window to the remote host server. Windows NT Workstation and Windows NT Server have a graphical Telnet application in the Program Manager's Accessories group.
	X/Windows	Provides access to graphical programs running on UNIX servers. The XWindows client acts as a UNIX display server. The Windows NT client can run both character bit DOS applications and XWindows graphical interface applications.
NetWare	Syscon	The primary NetWare administration tool used to set up and maintain user accounts, policies and resource permissions.
	RConsole	Provides remote connection of a network client to the NetWare network as a remote system console.
	PConsole	Provides the tools necessary to manage print servers.

Operating System	Administrative Too(not all-inclusive)	Use of the Tool
Banyan	Manage.com	Provides a menu from which Banyan administrators can choose the administration tool with which they want to work.
	Mservice.com	Allows the user to add services with which they will administrate Banyan servers to a menu to select from and run.
	Muser.com	Allows administration of Banyan user accounts.
Windows NT	User Manager	Allows the management of user and group accounts which grant access to the Windows NT network resources.
	Server Manager	Server Manager is used to manage Windows NT domains and computers.
	Internet Homepage	The Catapult server provides centralized access to the Internet and acts as an Internet proxy server.

UNIX Administration

Two additional services need to be added to the computers running Windows NT Workstation or Server in order to use computers running Windows NT Workstation or Server to administer UNIX servers, *FTP* and *Telnet*.

File Transfer Protocol

File Transfer Protocol (FTP) allows users to connect to the remote computers to transfer files. What this means to the administrator is that, for example, files stored on a remote UNIX computer can be transferred to a local Windows NT computer, administrative changes can be made to the files, and the files transferred back to the remote computer for continued storage.

FTP is widely used on the Internet for transferring files. Terra Flora is anticipating that over time, this file download process will be hidden by world wide web (WWW) browsers that will perform the transfer operations in the background as required by the applications.

FTP Server

FTP Server capabilities are built into Windows NT Server. This provides capabilities for UNIX clients or windows sockets-based UNIX oriented applications to perform file transfer. Files can be transferred to the UNIX server for administration or transferred from a UNIX server for administration.

Note   One of the limitations of the FTP server is that the password to the FTP server is sent over the wire in clear text, meaning that the password is not encrypted or otherwise protected on the network. Any person on the network with a network sniffer can capture the password packets and know the password for the specified user.

Due to the clear-text password limitation, most FTP servers are configured to only allow anonymous connections. *Anonymous* is a specific user name which is used for non-secure sessions. Anonymous is used to prevent anyone from accidentally using a valid user name and password to gain server access. Once the user is connected to the server using the anonymous user name and password, the user is prompted for their domain name service (DNS) name as the password, such as johndoe@terraflora.com to provide an audit of the user's access and hits on specific files stored on the FTP server.

Installing FTP Server

FTP Server is installed when you install the Internet Information Server. Once the FTP server is installed, there is a graphical interface that provides the connection to the server that stores the files you want to transfer.

▶   **To install the FTP Server service**

1. Click **Start**, point to **Settings**, and click **Control Panel.**
2. Double-click **Network**.
3. Click the **Services** tab.
4. Click **Add**.
5. In the **Select Network Service** dialog box, click **Microsoft Internet Information Server 2.0 (IIS).**
6. Click **Have Disk**, and enter the path to the Windows NT CD-ROM or disks that contain the services.

7. Click **OK**.

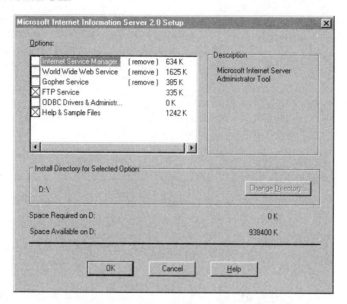

8. If you are not using IIS and are installing it only to access FTP, click to clear the following check boxes in the **Microsoft Internet Information Server 2.0 Setup** dialog box:

   - **Internet Information Service**
   - **World Wide Web Services**
   - **Gopher Service**

9. Click **OK**.

Transferring Files Using FTP

This example illustrates how files would be transferred from a UNIX server using FTP. The files would be transferred to a Windows NT Server and the administrator could make changes to the files and transfer the files back to the UNIX server on which they are normally stored. The administrators at Terra Flora use FTP to transfer remote server files on a regular basis to avoid editing the files remotely over the WAN. At Terra Flora, the UNIX server is named CAPWKSENT01. Using the procedure below, FTP will be used to transfer the files from the UNIX server to the Windows NT Server.

▶ **To transfer files from the Terra Flora UNIX server, the administrator will**

1. Click **Start**, point to **Programs**, and click **Command Prompt**.

2. Type **FTP** and the host name or IP address of the server from which files will be transferred.

3. If you are using FTP to access an UNIX server, you must provide the UNIX user-account and password information, as shown in the following illustration.

Once you connect to the UNIX server, you can use standard FTP commands, such as **Get** and **Put**, to transfer files, as if you were running FTP on the UNIX server.

Telnet Client

At Terra Flora as in many UNIX environments, administrative functions are often performed on a remote *console*, which is a control client computer through which a user communicates with a server. The administrator uses a command-line interface available on the client, known as *Telnet*, which is a simple UNIX remote command line window to access the remote server. Windows NT Workstation and Windows NT Server provide a graphical Telnet application. The application allows the computer running Windows NT Workstation or Windows NT Server to connect to the UNIX server and use the Telnet commands to administer the server. The computer running Windows NT Server or Workstation connects to the UNIX server as just another remote client.

Note Windows NT does allow administrative commands to be issued through the command-line interface, however, it is not the preferred method of administration.

Windows NT Server does not contain a Telnet server, but Telnet servers are available as shareware on the Internet.

The Telnet client service is installed as part of the installation TCP/IP services on of either computers running Windows NT Workstation or Server.

▶ **To run the Telnet service on the computer running Windows NT Workstation or Server**

1. Click **Start**, point to **Programs**, point to **Accessories**, and then click **Telnet**.

2. On the **Connect** menu, click **Remote System**.

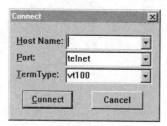

3. In **Host Name**, type the name of the UNIX computer on which the files you want to administer are stored.

4. Click Connect.

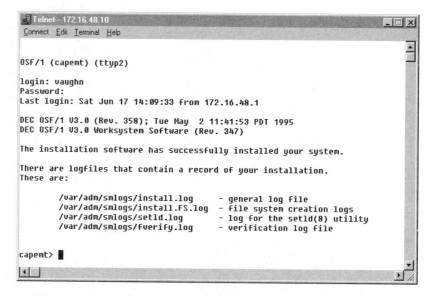

5. If the client is not already connected to the UNIX server, type the user-account and password-login information required to access the UNIX server when prompted.

Once logged onto the UNIX server, you can administer the UNIX files stored on the server.

For UNIX clients to communicate with Windows NT Servers, Integraph's DiskShare product was installed on the computers running Windows NT Server. Once installed, the UNIX clients were able connect to the Windows NT server, once a user account had been set up and proper permissions on the Windows NT server granted to the user of the UNIX client. For details, see "UNIX Clients Authenticating to Windows NT Servers," earlier in this chapter. The UNIX client can then administer the Windows NT Servers.

Access to the UNIX servers by Windows NT clients can now be performed because Integraph's PC-NFS was installed on the Windows NT client computers. Again, since proper permissions have been granted to the user on the UNIX server, the Windows NT client can administer the UNIX servers. For complete instructions on the installation, configuration and use of Integraph PC-NFS and DiskShare, see the earlier topics in this chapter, "UNIX Clients Authenticating to Windows NT Servers" and "Windows NT Clients Authenticating to UNIX Servers."

Once the connection is made between the computers running UNIX and Windows NT, administration can be performed using the additional services of FTP and Telnet as described above.

X/Windows Support

Client/server graphical application support for UNIX-based applications has evolved around the X/Windows interface. The X/Windows application programming interfaces (APIs) help to span the different variations of UNIX implementation in various networking environments by providing a common application interface programming model for applications.

In the popular PC-based computing circles, a *client* computer refers to the end-node machines sitting on the desktops, while the *server* computer is a powerful processing "workhorse" computer which makes resources available to a large number of clients.

In X/Windows, and UNIX, terminology, the X/Windows server is really the X/Windows display server which provides the services to display the graphical interface application to the user and resides on the desktop machines. The X/Windows client is the is the processing engine for the X/Windows application. For those readers familiar with the PC-based nomenclature, simply reverse the typical definitions when thinking about the X/Windows environment.

X/Windows is different than typical PC-based client server models. In X/Windows, the server application executes the instructions on the network server known as the X/Client. The network server executes the applications, and sends the commands to draw the appropriate graphical images on the screen. The user mouse clicks and keyboard commands are sent across the network to the X/Client application, and are processed remotely. In essence, X/Windows applications that are viewed on the desktop are actually running on the remote network server, and the graphical information, as well as the user input are relayed across the network to the display client.

Applications written to the common X/Windows specifications will run on many different versions of UNIX, however, some of their version-specific functionality may not be available on all platforms.

X/Windows Server

Terra Flora, with its mixed networking environment, has made use of the traditional UNIX computing model which is a workstation computer (server) running a version of UINX connected to a mainframe or minicomputer (client) for, as an example, statistical sales analysis.

However, as the PC-based computing environment has spanned the enterprise, the ease of use and powerful graphical productivity applications have moved into sales and accounting areas by necessity to communicate with the rest of the corporation, as well as provide a common platform for document creation, charting, and integrated analysis.

At Terra Flora, this has also led to the dual-computer desktops in many work areas. One workstation running UNIX with X/Windows applications for statistical sales analysis work, and another desktop running the Windows interface for document creation, charting and integrated analysis presented in graphical format. The problem with this solution is that it is expensive, both in hardware costs and administration. Additionally, it is difficult to get information from one system to another. There is a solution for this problem, X/Windows servers for Windows NT.

In the previous section, an example was presented illustrating how a computer running Windows NT Server or Workstation can become a remote console to administer files on, for example, a UNIX server. The interface presented to the client computer is a *character mode* interface. There is no access to the graphical applications on the UNIX server.

At Terra Flora, an X/Windows product from Hummingbird Communications, Ltd called eXceed, version 5, will be installed on all computers running Windows NT Workstation or Server that will act as remotes consoles connecting to the UNIX servers. By installing the X/Windows product, the client will be able to access a DOS character mode interface and access the graphical interface applications.

▶ **To install X/Windows**

1. Click **Start**, and then click **Run**.

2. Follow instructions provided in the Exceed 5 documentation about the information to be entered on the command line and other installation details.

Below are samples of the graphical interface demo files loaded on all UNIX servers. The demo files are all loaded on a single Windows NT computer to illustrate the ability to use both graphical applications and character bit applications.

The first shot is the graphical application called Xeyes.

The second screen shot is of the UNIX graphical application called Xclock.

The third screen shot is of the graphical application called calculator.

As demonstrated in the screen shot below, the Windows NT client can be used to run multiple sessions. Any variety of the graphical applications can be run from a single station. On a single workstation, both Windows-based applications and X/Windows applications are accessible, and information interchange is relatively easy. The cost reduction is significant, as Windows NT Workstations are typically less expensive than UNIX workstations, plus the second desktop machine is no longer required.

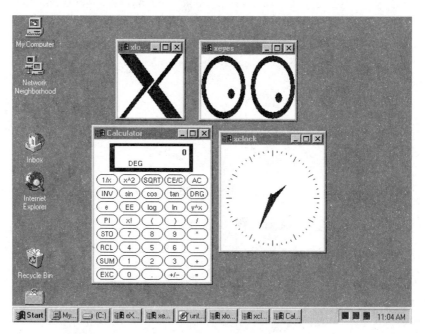

NetWare Administration

NetWare servers cannot be administered directly. Instead a NetWare client acts as the system console and controls the administration of the NetWare server. A computer running Windows NT Server with the Gateway Services for NetWare (GSNW) enabled or a computer running Windows NT Workstation with the Client Services for NetWare (CSNW) enabled, can act as a NetWare client and connect to the NetWare Environment.

For complete instructions on installing and configuring CSNW and GSNW, see the earlier topics in this chapter, "Windows NT Clients Authenticating to NetWare Servers" and "NetWare Clients Authenticating to Windows NT Servers."

NetWare Administration Using a Windows NT Computer

At Terra Flora, CSNW or GSNW has been installed on all computers running Windows NT Workstation or Server that are going to function as NetWare clients to administrate NetWare servers. For a detailed explanation of CSNW and GSNW, installation and configuration instructions, see the earlier topics in this chapter, "Client Service for NetWare" and "Gateway Service for NetWare."

Now that the two systems can interoperate, any computer running Windows NT can act as a system console and run the NetWare Administration utilities, examples of which would be Syscon, PConsole and RConsole. For details on the use and operation of the NetWare Administration utilities, see the NetWare documentation.

Access to the NetWare environment as a NetWare client is accomplished through Windows NT using either the CSNW or GSNW service. When the computer running Windows NT Server or workstation with either the CSNW or GSNW service installed starts up, the Begin Logon dialog box appears. The user then logs into the Windows NT Network as normal, supplying the user account and password for Windows NT set up by the administrator. If the CSNW or GSNW service is correctly configured, the user is authenticated not only to the Windows NT network, but to the NetWare network at the same time.

Access to Syscon, RConsole and PConsole is accomplished on the Windows NT client as if the Windows NT client were a NetWare client. In a NetWare environment, the primary administration tool called System Console (Syscon) is used to set up user accounts, define policies, and grant user access permissions to the NetWare network.

The screen shot of Syscon below was captured on a computer running
Windows NT Workstation or Windows NT Server connecting as a NetWare client
to the NetWare environment.

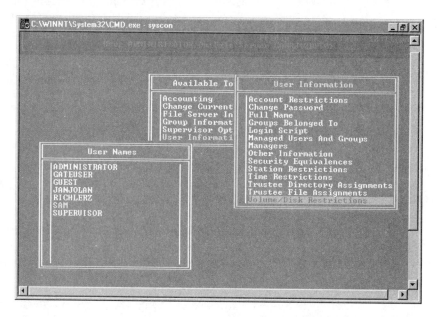

RConsole provides a remote view of the NetWare system console. The console
functions can be performed on the remote console. The screen shot of RConsole
below was captured on a computer running Windows NT Workstation or
Windows NT Server connecting as a NetWare client to the NetWare environment.

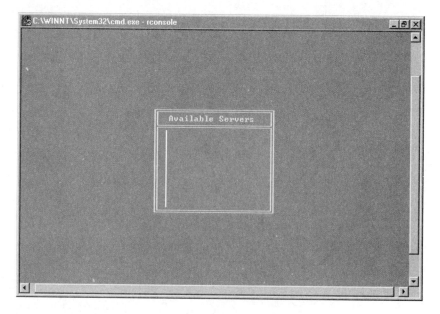

PConsole provides the administrator with the tools necessary to manage print servers. The screen shot of PConsole below was captured on a computer running Windows NT Workstation or Windows NT Server connecting as a NetWare client to the NetWare environment.

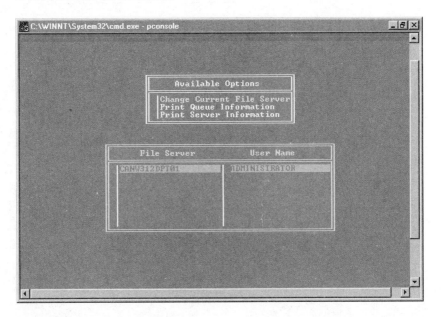

Multiple sessions of the administration tools can be run on a single Windows NT client. The information about each of the servers to which the client is connected will be displayed in a separate window on the client. This is a major benefit of using computers running Windows NT. The result is the ability to monitor all of the NetWare servers from one system console, which is not possible on computers running other operating systems such as MS-DOS.

▶ **To connect to additional NetWare servers**

1. Click **Start**, point to **Programs**, and click **Windows NT Explorer**.

2. On the **Tools** menu, click **Map Network Drive**.

3. In **Drive**, enter a drive letter, if necessary.

4. In **Path**, type the path to the NetWare server.

5. To connect to the NetWare server using another user account and password, type the information in **Connect As** (optional).

6. Click **OK**.

Note Although Windows NT Workstation and Windows NT Server versions 4.0 support connections to NetWare Directory Services (NDS), they do not support administration of NDS trees at this time.

The screen shot below displays multiple sessions of the administration tools running on one Windows NT client.

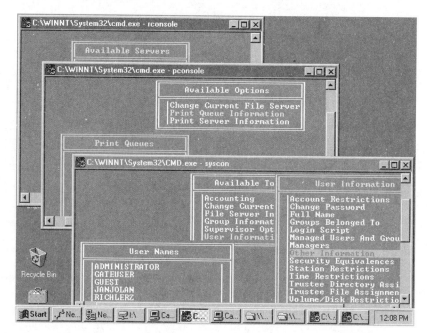

Administrating Windows NT Servers Using NetWare Clients

For a NetWare client to access and administer a Windows NT Server, File and Print Services for NetWare must be installed on the computer running Windows NT Server. Once FPNW is installed and configured, a NetWare client can sign onto the computer running Windows NT Server and perform administration tasks. For instructions on installing and configuring FPNW, see "NetWare Clients Authenticating to Windows NT Servers," earlier in this chapter. For details on the use of the administration tools, see online Help.

Banyan Administration

As part of the Terra Flora strategy to provide centralized network services, Terra Flora has installed Banyan Enterprise Client for Windows NT on all computers running Windows NT Server or Workstation that will be required to function as Banyan clients. Banyan servers cannot be directly administered. Instead as with NetWare and UNIX, server administration is performed on clients functioning as system consoles.

Installation of the Banyan Enterprise client for Windows NT allows the computer running Windows NT Server or Workstation to connect to the Banyan network as a system console. The system console has access to the administration tools on the Banyan server that allow the management of user accounts and other networking services.

When a computer running Windows NT Server or Workstation that will function as a Banyan client starts, the user supplies the same user account and password normally used to log on to Windows NT and is authenticated to the Windows NT network.

Logon to the Banyan server may be configured as automatic, which means that the configuration of the Banyan Enterprise client for Windows NT is set up so that authentication to the Banyan server is accomplished when the user supplies their user account and password for logging onto the Windows NT network. For information on installation and configuration of Banyan Enterprise Client for Windows NT on the on computers running Windows NT Server and Workstation, the section titled, "Windows NT Clients Authenticating to Banyan Servers," earlier in this chapter.

During Banyan logon, the redirector will map the system files volume to the default Z drive. The user can then select the administration tools they want to work with from drive Z.

From the DOS prompt, type Manage.com. Press ENTER. The Manage.com menu appears. From the menu, the user selects the type of administration that they want to do. See your Banyan documentation for details on the administration utilities available on the Manage.com menu. The screen shot of Manage.com below was captured on a computer running Windows NT Server connecting as a Banyan client to the Banyan server.

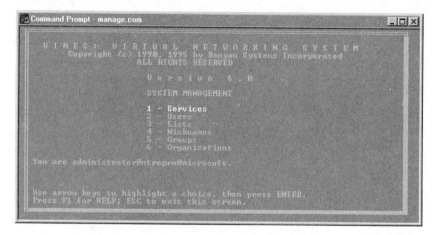

The first two menu options are the ones that we will focus on for the remainder of this section. Services (Mservice) allows the Banyan Administrator to administer the server using various services that can be specified on the menu. See your Banyan documentation for details on the use of Services options.

Services can be accessed in two ways.

- At the DOS prompt, after connecting to the Banyan Server from a computer running Windows NT Workstation or Server, type Mservice.com and press ENTER.

- Additionally, as is illustrated in this example, you can select option 1 Services on the Manage.com menu.

The screen shot of MService below was captured on a computer running Windows NT connecting as a Banyan client to the Banyan server.

Option 2 on the Manage.com menu allows the user to administer user accounts on the Banyan server. For detailed instructions on how to use the User option, see your Banyan documentation.

There are two ways to access Users:

- At the DOS prompt, after connecting to the Banyan Server from a computer running Windows NT Workstation or Server, type Muser.com and press ENTER.

- Additionally, you can select option 2 Services on the Manage.com menu.

The screen shot of MUser below was captured on a computer running Windows NT connecting as a Banyan client to the Banyan environment.

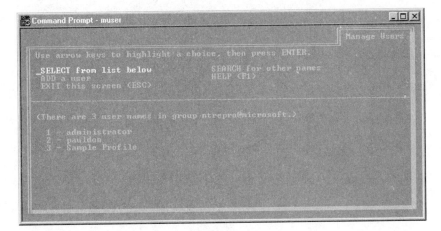

Multiple sessions of the administration tools can be run on a single computer running Windows NT Workstation or Server acting as a client connected to a Banyan client. The information about each of the servers to which the client is connected will be displayed in a separate window on the client. This is a major benefit of using computers running Windows NT. The result is the ability to monitor all of the Banyan servers from one computer running Windows NT Workstation or Server acting as a system console. This feature also exists in a limited fashion on computers running Windows 95, but is not a feature that is available on computers running other operating systems such as MS-DOS.

The screen shot below displays multiple sessions of the administration tools running on one Windows NT client.

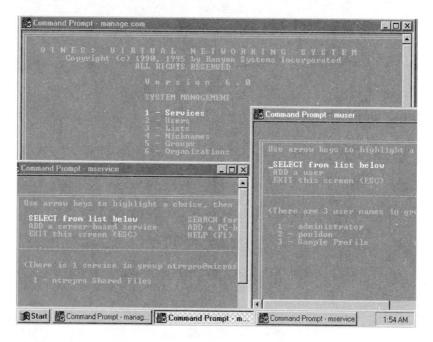

Windows NT Connectivity and Administration

Computers running Windows NT Workstation or Windows NT Server can be administered from any other computer running Windows NT Server or Workstation. Additionally, most computers operating in a heterogeneous network can be used to connect and in some cases administer computers running Windows NT Workstation or Windows NT Server.

- By installing and configuring Intergraph DiskShare on the computers running Windows NT Server, UNIX clients can connect to connect to computers running Windows NT Server for access to file services.

- By installing and configuring File and Print Services for NetWare on the computer running Windows NT Server, NetWare clients can be used to connect to computers running Windows NT Server.

- By installing and configuring network software such as LAN Manager or Microsoft Works, Windows 3.1 clients and DOS clients can be used to connect to and administer Windows NT servers.

- By installing and configuring Services for Macintosh, Macintosh clients can be used to connect to computers running Windows NT Server.

- Computers running Windows for Workgroups and Windows 95 can be configured to authenticate automatically to the Windows NT network and can be used to administer the Windows NT servers.

For complete instructions on how to install and configure the software required for interoperating the different operating systems referenced above, see "Network Logon Services," earlier in this chapter.

User Manager for Domains

User Manager for Domains is used to administer user and group accounts which allow users to participate in a Windows NT domain and access the domain's resources. Additionally with User Manager for Domains, rights and permissions can be granted to the user and group accounts providing the appropriate amount of access and restrictions to network resources in the Windows NT domain.

Once a client computer accesses the Windows NT Server with the proper permissions, the client can administer the server. For complete instructions on how to install and configure the software required for interoperating the different operating systems referenced above, see "Network Logon Services," earlier in this chapter.

▶ **To run User Manager**

- Click Start, point to Programs, point to Administrative Tools (Common), and then click User Manager for Domains.

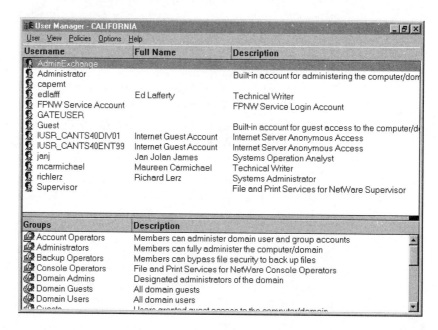

For complete instructions on the use of User Manager for Domains, see the *Windows NT Server Concepts and Planning Guide*, Chapter 2, "Working with User and Group Accounts." See Chapter 3, "Manager User Work Environments," for complete instructions on managing User Profiles and System Policies.

Server Manager

Client computers connected to the computer running Windows NT Server can be used to administer the computers running Windows NT Server by connecting to the servers. For complete instructions on how to install and configure the software required for interoperating the different operating systems referenced above, see "Network Logon Services," earlier in this chapter.

Server Manager is the tool used to manage domains and computers. With Server Manager you can:

- Select a Windows NT domain, workgroup or computer for administration.
- Manage a computer including viewing a list of connected users, viewing shared and open resources, managing services and shared directories and sending messages to connected users.
- Manage a domain including promoting a backup domain controller to the primary domain controller (PDC), synchronizing servers with primary domain controllers and adding computers to and removing computers from the domain.

Once a client computer accesses the Windows NT Server, the client can administer the server. For complete instructions on how to install and configure the software required for interoperating the different operating systems referenced above, see "Network Logon Services," earlier in this chapter.

▶ **To run Server Manager**

- Click Start, point to Programs, point to Administrative Tools (Common), and then click Server Manager.

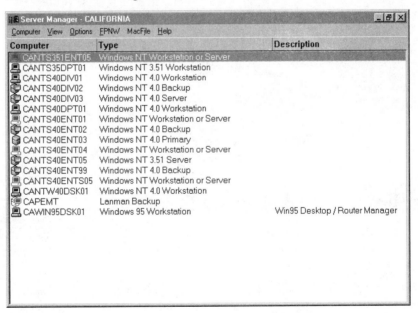

For complete instructions on the use of Server Manager, see the Help file.

Internet Service

At Terra Flora, a server has been installed to provide a proxy agent to the Internet and prevent unauthorized access to or from the network. What happens is that network users communicate with the proxy agent server that acts as a *fire wall* to the network and the proxy agent server then communicates with the Internet. By the same token, users accessing the Terra Flora network from the Internet communicate with the proxy agent server acting as a fire wall and protecting the network from unauthorized access. There is no actual access to the Internet from the network and there is no access from the Internet to the network except through the proxy fire wall server, which will authenticate requested user access.

Additionally, the Internet server provides a central access point to the Internet. All users either exiting the network to the Internet or entering the network from the Internet will pass through this central server.

Replication and Backup Services

At Terra Flora, the Windows NT Replication service will be used to ensure that all crucial Enterprise level databases are replicated to other computers running Windows NT Server. These include WINS and DNS.

Terra Flora has elected to use a flexible back up strategy for the data that exists on their servers, at all levels. Third party software will be incorporated for online backups and to protect master copies of distributed databases and other software.

The business reasons for replicating and backing up the business applications and databases are fairly obvious, to protect the business critical applications and ensure that should servers fail, recovery is quick and accurate.

Terra Flora's Decisions About Replication

On servers running Windows NT Server, replication of the Enterprise databases are configured at the time that the Enterprise level service is installed. For example the WINS and DNS databases were configured to replicate on backup servers during configuration. Additionally, the primary domain controller (PDC) will replicate the directory services to the backup domain controller (BDC), ensuring fault tolerance and providing another server which can authenticate users of the Windows NT services.

DHCP is a database that is not automatically replicated. For this reason, Terra Flora will use the Replicator service, which is a service that is part of Windows NT Workstation and Server, to backup the DHCP database and files to another server, ensuring that should the primary server fail, DHCP information can be recovered and dynamic network addressing of clients and servers continue.

Terra Flora's Decisions About Backup

Terra Flora has elected to use a flexible back up strategy for the data that exists on their servers, at all levels. Regularly scheduled backup of the WINNT, data and software master copy directories will be performed using third party software which works in conjunction with Windows NT. For daily, weekly and disaster recovery, Terra Flora will use the Seagate, (formerly Arcada) BackUp Exec for Windows NT, Single Server/Enterprise Edition - Version 6 Product.

Seagate Backup Exec for Windows NT is a proven 32-bit backup that protects the entire network. With centralized administration and its exclusive ExecView monitoring console, Backup Exec provides client/server functionality for Windows NT data protection. Backup Exec supports any combination of clients on any platform, on the Windows NT network. The documentation accompanying the product will explain setup and configuration of backup service.

For online backups, Terra Flora uses Octopus for Windows NT to provide data fault tolerance and real time data protection between the Enterprise/Enterprise Remote servers and for designated data directories on the divisional/regional servers such as project directories. *Online* backups are backups that occur as data in a file or database is added, changed or deleted.

Octopus mirrors files and/or directories rather than disks and will be set up on the computers running Windows NT Server. *Source* servers are the computers where the data to be backed up resides and *target* servers are the computers where the mirrored data will be stored. Any changes to the source files are mirrored and sent over the network to the target computers. Documentation accompanying the Octopus product explains setup and configuration of backup services.

At the Terra Flora Enterprise/Enterprise Remote level, the computers running Windows NT Server will back up their own servers as well as back up data directories on the Division/Region servers. The Division/Region servers will backup their own servers as well as back up the data directories on the Department/Branch Office servers. The Department/Branch servers will backup their own servers and users of the Desktop workstations will be responsible for backing up the necessary information on the workstations.

Backup of the DHCP Directory and Files

Replication of the WINS and DNS databases is an automatic feature of both the Windows NT Server WINS and DNS services and is configured during the installation process of WINS and DNS. At Terra Flora, replication of these databases has been configured to replicate on different servers in the network. The DHCP service, while it does provide a backup of the database and files in the System32\DHCP\Backup directory, cannot automatically be configured to replicate to different servers. An additional step is required.

The System 32\DHCP\ Backup directory is stored on the same physical drive as the DHCP database directory. At Terra Flora, the plan is to backup the DHCP directory to a different physical device on the same computer running the Windows NT Server DHCP service and then replicate the backup to another server. This plan provides a backup DHCP database copy should either the physical drive on which the DHCP database is stored or the computer running Windows NT Server DHCP service fail. The backup plan for the DHCP servers is as follows:

1. The Registry will be edited to allow backup of the DHCP database to another physical drive on the DHCP server.
2. Additionally, each DHCP database and associated files will be replicated to an Enterprise/Enterprise level server that is not running DHCP.
3. The Replicator service will be used to back up the necessary file stored in the System32\DHCP\Backup directory to an Enterprise/Enterprise Remote server which is not running the DHCP service.

Refer to Terra Flora's network diagram, one DHCP database directory on the server named CANTS40ENT03 will be replicated to CANT40ENT01 and the other DHCP directory on the server named CANT40ENT02 will be replicated on CANT40ENT05.

Editing the Registry

At Terra Flora, the Registry Editor will be changed to ensure that backup is made to a different physical device on the DHCP server that stores the database and files.

▶ **To edit the registry**

1. At the command prompt, type **Regedt32**, and press ENTER.
2. Double-click HKEY_LOCAL_MACHINE.
3. Double-click System.
4. Double-click CurrentControlSet.
5. Double-click Services.
6. Double-click DHCP Server.
7. Double-click Parameters.
8. Double-click Backup Database Path.
9. Change the first part of the line to indicate a different physical drive on the server, such as **D:\System32\dhcp\backup**.

    The information will then be backed up to the physical drive indicated.

You can now use the Replicator Service to copy that directory to a backup server.

Managing Directory Replication

Backing up a directory to a different server is a task performed by Windows NT Server Directory Replicator service. The server on which the DHCP directory is stored will be configured as an *export* server. The server which will store the backup copy of the DHCP directory and files is the *import* server.

When you update a file in the directory tree on one server (the export server), the updated file is automatically copied to all the other computers (the import computers). Only servers running Windows NT Server can be export servers; import computers can run either Windows NT Server or Windows NT Workstation.

How Directory Replication Works

Directory replication is initiated and carried out by the *Directory Replicator service*. This service operates on each export server and import computer that participates in replication. The service on each computer logs on to the same user account, which you create for this purpose.

You set up an export server and import computers to send and receive updated files. An export directory on the export server contains all the directories and subdirectories of files to be replicated, and when changes are saved to files in these directories, the files automatically replace the existing files on all the import computers.

You can also specify whether to have the export server send changes out as soon as a file has changed or, to prevent exporting partially changed trees, to wait until one export subdirectory has been stable before exporting. See "Managing Exported Subdirectories," later in this chapter.

In addition, you can lock a particular export or import directory, when needed. Changes to the locked directory are not exported or imported until you unlock the directory.

On the export server, you also designate which computers or domains are to receive replicated copies of the directories this server is exporting.

An export server has a default export path:

   C:*systemroot*\\SYSTEM32\\REPL\\EXPORT

All directories to be replicated are exported as subdirectories in the export path. Subdirectories created in the export path, and files placed in those subdirectories, are automatically exported. Export servers can replicate any number of subdirectories (limited only by available memory), with each exported subdirectory having up to 32 subdirectory levels in its tree.

An import computer has a default import path:

   C:*systemroot*\\SYSTEM32\\REPL\\IMPORT.

Imported subdirectories and their files are automatically placed here. You do not need to create these import subdirectories. They are created automatically when replication occurs.

Replication Prerequisites

Before a computer can participate in replication, you must create a special user account. Then for each computer in a domain that will participate in replication, configure its Directory Replicator service to log on using that special account:

- In User Manager for Domains, create a domain user account for the Directory Replicator service to use when logging on. Be sure the user account has the **Password Never Expires** option selected, all logon hours allowed, and membership in the domain's Backup Operators group. See online Help and Microsoft Windows NT Server 4.0 *Concepts and Planning*, Chapter 2, "Working with User and Group Accounts" and Chapter 3, "Managing User Work Environments" for details.

- After the user account is created for each computer that will be configured as an export server or an import computer, use Server Manager or the Services option in Control Panel to configure the Directory Replicator service to start up automatically and to log on under that user account. Be sure the password for that user account is typed correctly. See online Help for details.

Setting Up an Export Server

Any computer running Windows NT Server can be set up as an export server. (A computer running Windows NT Workstation cannot.)

Before you set up an export server, you must perform these tasks on the export server:

- Assign a logon account to the Directory Replicator service of the export server.
- Create the directories to be exported. They must be subdirectories of the replication export path (usually C:*systemroot*\ SYSTEM32\REPL\EXPORT).

Use the **Directory Replication** dialog box to set up an export server.

Managing Exported Subdirectories

By clicking **Manage** under **Export Directories** in the **Directory Replication** dialog box, you can manage certain features of subdirectory replication by the export server:

- You can *lock* a subdirectory to prevent it from being exported to any import computers. For example, if you know a directory will be receiving a series of changes that you do not want partially replicated, you can put one or more locks on the subdirectory in the export path. Until you remove the lock or locks, the subdirectory will not be replicated. The date and time the lock was placed is displayed so that you know how long a lock has been in force.

- When you *stabilize* a subdirectory, the export server waits two minutes after changes before exporting the subdirectory. The waiting period allows time for subsequent changes to take place so that all intended changes are recorded before being replicated.

- You specify whether the entire *subtree* (the export subdirectory and all of its subdirectories) or just the first-level subdirectory in the export directory path is exported.

Setting Up an Import Computer

Both Windows NT Server and Windows NT Workstation computers can be set up as import computers. A computer running Windows NT Server that is configured as an export server can also be configured as an import computer.

Before you set up an import computer, you must assign a logon account to the Directory Replicator service of the import computer.

On the import computer you do not need to create the imported subdirectories. A subdirectory is automatically created the first time it is imported.

Use the **Directory Replication** dialog box to set up an import computer. The Windows NT Server version of the **Directory Replication** dialog box is slightly different from the Windows NT Workstation version of this dialog box. The Windows NT Workstation version contains only the items related to imported directories.

Tip You can set up a server to replicate a directory tree to itself (from its export directory to its import directory). This replication can provide a local backup of the files, or you can use the import version of these files as another source for users to access, while preserving the export version of the files as a source master.

Managing Locks and Viewing Import Subdirectory Status

You can use locks to prevent imports to subdirectories on an import computer. Import of a locked subdirectory to that import computer is prevented until the lock is removed. Locking a subdirectory on an import computer affects replication to only that computer, not to other import computers.

You can manage locks on subdirectories and also view the status of each subdirectory by clicking **Manage** under **Import Directories** in the **Directory Replication** dialog box.

The **Status** column can have one of four entries:

- OK indicates that the subdirectory is receiving regular updates from an export server and that the imported data is identical to that exported.

- No Master indicates that the subdirectory is not receiving updates. The export server might not be running, or a lock might be in effect on the export server.

- No Sync indicates that although the subdirectory has received updates the data is *not* up-to-date. This could be due to a communications failure, open files on the import computer or export server, the import computer not having access permissions at the export server, or an export server malfunction.

- No entry (blank) indicates that replication never occurred for that subdirectory. Replication may not be properly configured for this import computer, for the export server, or both.

The **Last Update** column shows the date and time of the latest change to the import subdirectory or to any of its subdirectories.

Point-to-Point Tunneling Protocol (PPTP)

With the release of Windows NT Server 4.0, the ability to communicate securely over the Internet has become a reality. At Terra Flora, this will mean that Seville, Spain will be able to communicate with corporate headquarters using the Internet. Terra Flora will install computers running Windows NT at remote sites including Seville, Spain. Seville, Spain will be configured to use PPTP through a dial up Remote Access Service (RAS) connection to the Internet Information Server (IIS) at the Enterprise level named CANTS40ENT04.

The Decision to Use PPTP

The Seville, Spain site is a Nursery growing plants for distribution to the retail stores. It has become, by necessity, a distribution site, implementing the same distribution procedures as other distribution sites. Basically, a computer running Windows NT Server will be installed at the Seville, Spain site, along with other computers running Windows NT Workstation, in order to computerize the manual processes. Computerizing the Seville, Spain site will also allow Nursery personnel to focus on tasks other than the tasks performed by the computers at other nursery and distribution sites.

Remote Access Service (RAS) has been offered with Windows NT Server since the product was introduced. A RAS server is usually connected to a PSTN, ISDN or X.25 line allowing remote users to access a various network servers. RAS now allows remote users access through the Internet by using the new Point-to-Point Tunneling Protocol (PPTP). For detailed information on RAS, see the Microsoft Windows NT Server 4.0 *Networking Supplement*, Chapter 5, "Understanding Remote Access Service," Chapter 6, "Installing and Configuring Remote Access Service" and Chapter 7, "RAS Security."

At Terra Flora, PPTP will be installed to enable remote users to access corporate networks securely across the Internet by dialing into an Internet Service Provider (ISP) or by connecting directly to the Internet. PPTP offers the following advantages:

- Lower Transmission Costs

  PPTP uses the Internet as a connection instead of a long-distance telephone number or 800 service. This can greatly reduce transmission costs.

- Lower Administrative Overhead

  With PPTP, network administrators centrally manage and secure their remote access networks at the RAS server. They need to manage only user accounts instead of supporting complex hardware configurations.

- Enhanced Security

  Above all, the PPTP connection over the Internet is encrypted and secure, and it works with any protocol (including, IP, IPX, and NetBEUI).

Applications for PPTP

PPTP provides a way to route Point-to-Point Protocol (PPP) packets over an IP, IPX or NetBEUI network. Since PPTP allows multiprotocol encapsulation, Terra Flora can send any type of packet over the network.

PPTP treats the existing corporate network as a PSTN, ISDN, or X.25 network. This virtual WAN is supported through public carriers, such as the Internet.

Compare PPTP to the other WAN protocols: When using PSTN, ISDN, or X.25, a remote access client establishes a PPP connection with a RAS server over a switched network. After the connection is established, PPP packets are sent over the switched connection to the RAS servers to be routed to the destination LAN.

In contrast, when using PPTP instead of a switched connection to send packets over the WAN, a transport protocol such as TCP/IP is used to send the PPP packets to the RAS server over the virtual WAN.

The end benefit for the corporation is a savings in transmission costs by using the Internet rather than long distance dial-up connections.

Secure Access to Corporate Networks over the Internet

A RAS client that has PPTP as its WAN protocol can access resources on a remote LAN by connecting to a Windows NT RAS server through the Internet. There are two ways to do this: By connecting directly to the Internet or by dialing an Internet Service Provider (ISP) as shown in the following examples.

The client that is directly connected on the Internet dials the number for the RAS server. PPTP on the client makes a tunnel through the Internet and connects to the PPTP enabled adapter on the RAS server. After authentication, the client can access the corporate network, as shown in the figure below.

Note   Connecting directly to the Internet means direct IP access without going through an ISP. (For example, some hotels allow you to use an Ethernet cable to gain a direct connection to the Internet.)

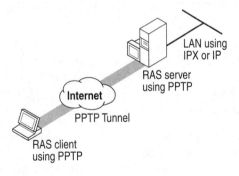

The same functionality is achieved by calling an ISP instead of being directly connected to the Internet. The client first makes a call to the ISP. After that connection is established, the client makes another call to the RAS sever located anywhere on the Internet or the ISP and that establishes the PPTP tunnel.

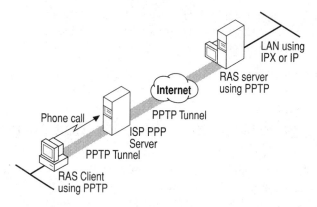

At Terra Flora, the clients are directly connected to the Internet, no ISP is used. The RAS servers at headquarters and Seville will dial directly into the Internet.

Security Considerations

Data sent across the PPTP tunnel is encapsulated in PPP packets. Because RAS supports encryption, the data will be encrypted. RAS supports bulk data encryption using RSA RC4 and a 40-bit session key that is negotiated at PPP connect time between the RAS client and the Windows NT RAS server.

PPTP uses the Password Authentication Protocol and the Challenge Handshake Authentication Protocol encryption algorithms.

In addition to supporting encrypted PPP links across the Internet, a PPTP-based solution also enables the Internet to become a network backbone for carrying IPX and NetBEUI remote-access traffic. PPTP can transfer IPX traffic because it encapsulates and encrypts PPP packets so that they can ride TCP/IP. Thus, a solution does not depend only on TCP/IP LANs.

This technology gives Terra Flora the opportunity to send sensitive materials over the Internet, an option that they haven't had previously. They will use this connection to collect general ledger information from Seville and to provide to Seville marketing information such as product special pricing and corporate advertisements which will be incorporated into network web pages.

Installing PPTP

You must have the PPTP protocol installed on the RAS servers and on the client or communications servers.

▶   **To Install PPTP**

1. Click **Start**, point to **Settings**, and click **Control Panel**.
2. Double-click **Network**.
3. Click the **Protocols** Tab.
4. Select **Point-to-Point Protocol,** and then click **Add**.
5. Click **Have Disk** if loading the software from disks or a CD.

    Or, click **OK** if loading from the network.
6. When prompted, type the full path to the Windows NT Server PPTP files, and then click **OK**.
7. Enter the number of connections you want available to PPTP (that is, for Virtual Private Networks).

8. RAS setup will start and add the PPTP protocol to RAS.

You must restart your computer to complete the installation.

Protecting a RAS Server from Internet Attacks

If PPTP filtering is selected, the selected network adapter for all other protocols is effectively disabled. Only PPTP packets will be allowed in.

Terra Flora will want to do this on all multihomed computers with one network adapter (with PPTP filtering enabled) connected to the Internet and another network adapter connected to the internal corporate network. Clients outside the corporate network can use PPTP to connect to the computer from across the Internet and gain secure access to the corporate network. Thus, the only traffic that can access the corporate network is PPTP packets from clients who have been authenticated using RAS authentication.

Note The RAS client can either be connected to the Internet directly or to a service provider. It is not necessary to be connected to both to use PPTP.

▶ **To install PPTP filtering for protection**

1. Click **Start**, point to **Settings**, and click **Control Panel**.

2. Double-click **Network**.

3. Click the **Protocols** tab.

4. Click **TCP/IP Protocol**.

5. Click **Properties**.

6. Click the **IP Address** tab, if necessary, and then click **Advanced**.

7. In Adapter, click the network adapter for which you want to specify PPTP filtering.

   The PPTP filtering settings in this dialog box are defined only for the selected network adapter.

8. To enable PPTP filtering, click **Enable PPTP Filtering**.

You must restart the computer to have the settings take effect.

For more information about advanced TCP/IP configuration, see the topic "To Configure Advanced TCP/IP Options" in the TCP/IP online Help file.

P A R T   I I I

TCP/IP

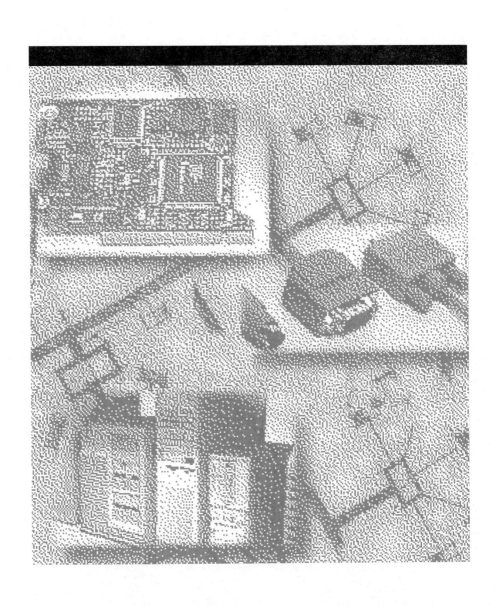

C H A P T E R   6

TCP/IP Implementation Details

The Transmission Control Protocol/Internet Protocol (TCP/IP) suite is a set of networking transports that govern how data passes between networked computers. Microsoft has adopted TCP/IP as the strategic enterprise network transport for its platforms. Microsoft 32-bit TCP/IP for Windows NT is a high-performance, portable, 32-bit implementation of the industry-standard TCP/IP protocol.

This chapter is intended for network engineers and support professionals who are already familiar with TCP/IP or who have read the TCP/IP chapters in the *Networking Supplement* for Windows NT Server version 4.0. This chapter provides additional technical detail about Microsoft 32-bit TCP/IP as implemented in Windows NT.

This chapter discusses the following topics:

- Microsoft TCP/IP architectural model
- Microsoft Network Driver Interface Specification (NDIS)
- Core TCP/IP protocol stack components
- Transport driver interface (TDI)
- Network application interfaces and Microsoft TCP/IP
- Windows NT client/server programs that use TCP/IP

This chapter concludes with a summary of TCP/IP changes in Windows NT Server version 4.0.

Network traces are used throughout this chapter to help illustrate concepts. These traces were gathered and formatted using Microsoft Network Monitor, a software-based protocol tracing and analysis tool included in the Microsoft Systems Management Server product. All the IP addresses in these traces have been replaced with the IP addresses for the fictitious company Terra Flora.

Note The base code described in this chapter is shared by all Microsoft 32-bit TCP/IP protocol stacks, including TCP/IP for Windows NT Server, Windows NT Workstation, and Windows 95. However, there are small differences in implementation, configuration methods, and available services. This chapter describes the implementation, configuration, and available services for Microsoft 32-bit TCP/IP for Windows NT.

Architecture of Microsoft TCP/IP for Windows NT

TCP/IP is the primary protocol of the Internet and intranets (networks that connect enterprise-wide local area networks). You can communicate with computers running under Windows NT, with devices that use other Microsoft networking products, and with computers running under non-Microsoft operating systems using TCP/IP (such as UNIX computers).

The TCP/IP protocol suite in Windows NT Server and Windows NT Workstation was completely redesigned beginning with Windows NT version 3.5. It is a high-performance, portable, 32-bit implementation of the industry-standard TCP/IP protocol suite and is easy to administer. Microsoft 32-bit TCP/IP for Windows NT provides support for standard TCP/IP features including:

- Logical multihoming
- Internal IP routing capability
- IP multicasting support using the Internet Group Management Protocol (IGMP)
- Duplicate IP address detection
- Multiple default gateways
- Dead gateway detection
- Automatic discovery when using Path Maximum Transfer Unit (PMTU)

The TCP/IP protocol suite for Windows NT Server and Windows NT Workstation is comprised of:

- Core protocol elements
- Windows NT–based services
- Interfaces between the protocol elements and services

The Windows NT–based networking services include, but are not limited to, the following:

- Windows Internet Name Service (WINS), used for NetBIOS name resolution services
- Domain Name System (DNS), used for host and domain name resolution services
- Point-to-Point (PPP) and Serial Line IP (SLIP), used for Remote Access Service (RAS)
- Point-to-Point Tunneling Protocol (PPTP), used for virtual private remote networks
- TCP/IP network printing (lpr/lpd)
- SNMP agent
- NetBIOS interface
- 32-bit Windows Sockets interface
- Remote Procedure Call (RPC)
- Network Dynamic Data Exchange (NetDDE)
- WAN (wide area network) browsing support
- High-performance Internet Information Server with Web, FTP, and GOPHER services
- TCP/IP connectivity utilities, including **finger**, **ftp**, **rcp**, **rexec**, **rsh**, **telnet**, and **tftp**
- Server software for simple network protocols, including Character Generator, Daytime, Discard, Echo, and Quote of the Day
- TCP/IP management and diagnostic tools, including **arp**, **hostname**, **ipconfig**, **nbtstat**, **netstat**, **nslookup**, **ping**, **route**, and **tracert**

The following figure illustrates the Windows NT TCP/IP architecture model and shows the core protocol elements and the interfaces between protocol elements and services.

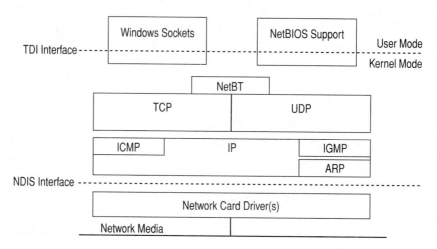

Figure 6.1   The Windows NT TCP/IP Architecture Model

Note   Specifications and programming information for Microsoft 32-bit TCP/IP are included in the Windows NT Device Driver Kit (DDK). The Transport Driver Interface (TDI) and the Network Driver Interface Specification (NDIS) are public specifications available from Microsoft.

Network Driver Interface Specification

Microsoft networking protocols (including TCP/IP) communicate with network card drivers using the Network Driver Interface Specification (NDIS). Windows NT Server version 4.0 uses NDIS version 4.0. The following figure illustrates the NDIS interface and the layers below the NDIS interface.

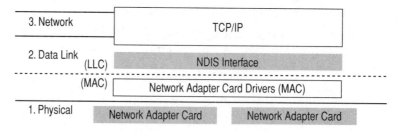

Figure 6.2   NDIS Interface

The NDIS interface (Ndis.sys) provides basic services used by the protocol modules. The protocol driver uses the NDIS interface to send raw data packets over a network device and to receive notification of incoming packets received by the NIC. NDIS allows the protocol components to function independently of the NIC.

Any NDIS-compliant protocol driver can communicate with any NDIS-compliant NIC.

Network Adapter Card Bindings

The NDIS layer supports *binding*, a process that establishes the communication channel between a protocol driver (such as TCP/IP) and a network card, in the following ways:

- Multiple protocol drivers of different types binding to a single NIC driver
- A single protocol driver binding to multiple NIC drivers

The NDIS specification describes the communications technique known as *multiplexing,* which allows transmitting a number of separate signals simultaneously over a single channel or line and which supports the different ways of binding a protocol driver and network card.

To improve networking performance, you can manually change the default bindings on a computer running under Windows NT by using the **Bindings** tab in the **Control Panel—Network** dialog box. You can choose to disable a binding, enable a binding, or redefine the default binding search order.

Media Access Control Layer

Because the NDIS interface handles raw packets, the protocol stack is normally responsible for building each frame, including Media Access Control (MAC) layer headers. This means that the protocol stack must explicitly support each media type. Microsoft 32-bit TCP/IP for Windows NT versions 4.0 and 3.5x provides support for:

- Ethernet (and 802.3 SNAP)
- FDDI
- Token Ring (802.5)
- ARCNET
- WAN (switched virtual circuit wide area media, such as ISDN, X.25, and dial-up or dedicated asynchronous lines)

In addition, there are now asynchronous transfer mode (ATM) adapters available for Windows NT. The drivers for these adapters use "LAN emulation" to appear to the protocol stack as a supported media type, such as Ethernet.

Link Layer

Link layer functionality is divided between the combination (binding) of the NIC driver and the low-level protocol stack driver. The binding of the NIC driver and low-level protocol stack driver creates filters based on the destination MAC address of each frame. Normally, the hardware filters out all incoming frames except those containing one of the following destination addresses:

- The address of the adapter
- The IP broadcast address (255.255.255.255)
- Multicast addresses which a protocol driver on this host has registered interest in by using a fundamental NDIS primitive command

Because this first filtering decision is made by the hardware, all frames not meeting the filter criteria are discarded by the NIC without any CPU processing. All frames (including broadcasts) that *do* pass the hardware filter are passed up to the NIC driver through a hardware interrupt.

A NIC driver is software on the local computer, and any frames that reach the NIC require some CPU time to process. The NIC driver brings the frame into system memory from the NIC. Then the frame is passed up to the appropriate bound transport drivers, in this case, TCP/IP. The NDIS specification provides more detail on this process.

Most NICs can be selectively configured in a non-selective mode. A NIC in non-selective mode does not perform any address filtering on frames that appear on the media. Instead, it passes upward every frame that passes the cyclic redundancy check (CRC). This feature is used by some protocol analysis software—for example, Microsoft Network Monitor.

Frames are passed upward to all bound transport drivers, in the order of the binding. By default, the binding order is the alphabetical order of their key names in the Registry.

As a frame traverses a network or series of networks, the source MAC address is always that of the NIC that placed it on the media, and the destination MAC address is that of the NIC that is intended to pull it off the media. This means that in a routed network, the source and destination MAC addresses change with each "hop" through a network-layer device (router).

Maximum Transfer Unit

Each media type has a maximum frame size that cannot be exceeded. The link layer is responsible for discovering this maximum transfer unit (MTU) and reporting it to the protocols above. NDIS drivers can be queried for the local MTU by the protocol stack. The upper layer protocols, such as TCP, use the MTU to automatically optimize packet sizes for each media. See the section "Internet Control Message Protocol" later in this chapter for related information about path maximum transfer unit (PMTU) discovery.

If a NIC driver such as an ATM driver is using LAN-emulation mode, it may report that it has an MTU higher than what is expected for that media type. For example, it may emulate Ethernet but report an MTU of 9180 bytes. Windows NT accepts and uses the MTU size reported by the adapter even when it exceeds the normal MTU for a given media type.

Core Protocol Stack Components

The following figure illustrates the core protocol stack components in the Tcpip.sys driver which exists between the NDIS and TDI interfaces.

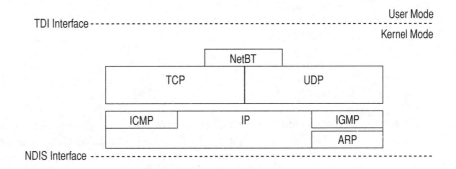

Figure 6.3   Core Protocol Stack Components

Address Resolution Protocol

Address Resolution Protocol (ARP) performs IP address-to-MAC-address resolution for outgoing packets. As each outgoing IP datagram is encapsulated into a frame, source and destination MAC addresses must be added. Determining the destination MAC address for each frame is the responsibility of ARP.

ARP compares the destination IP address on every outbound IP datagram to the *ARP cache* for the NIC which that frame will be sent over. If there is a matching entry, then the MAC address is retrieved from the cache. If not, ARP broadcasts an *ARP Request Packet* onto the local subnet, requesting that the owner of the IP address in question reply with its MAC address. If the packet is going through a router, ARP resolves the MAC address for that next-hop router rather than for the final destination host. When an ARP reply is received, the ARP cache is updated with the new information, and it is used to address the packet at the link layer.

ARP Cache

You can view, add, or delete entries in the ARP cache using the **arp** utility (see the following examples). Entries added manually are static, and do not get aged out of the cache like dynamic entries do.

To view the ARP cache, type the following command; you will get results similar to those in the following example:

```
C:\>arp -a

Interface: 172.16.112.123
Internet Address    Physical Address    Type
172.16.112.1        00-00-0c-1a-eb-c5   dynamic
172.16.112.124      00-dd-01-07-57-15   dynamic

Interface: 172.16.113.190
Internet Address    Physical Address    Type
172.16.113.138      00-20-af-1d-2b-91   dynamic
```

In these examples, the computer is *multihomed*, meaning that it has multiple NICs, so there is a separate ARP cache for each interface. The **arp-s** command can be used to add a static entry to the ARP cache used by the second interface, for the host whose IP address is 172.16.90.32 and whose NIC address is 00608C0E6C6A, as shown in the following example:

```
C:\>arp -s 172.16.90.32 00-60-8c-0e-6c-6a 172.16.48.190

C:\>arp -a

Interface: 172.16.112.123
  Internet Address    Physical Address    Type
  172.16.112.1        00-00-0c-1a-eb-c5   dynamic
  172.16.112.124      00-dd-01-07-57-15   dynamic

Interface:172.16.48.190
  Internet Address    Physical Address    Type
  172.16.113.138      00-20-af-1d-2b-91   dynamic
  172.16.90.32        00-60-8c-0e-6c-6a   static
```

ARP Cache Aging

Windows NT versions 4.0 and 3.5*x* adjust the size of the ARP cache automatically. Entries are aged out of the ARP cache if they are not used by any outgoing datagrams for two minutes. Entries that are being referenced get aged out of the ARP cache after 10 minutes. Entries added manually are not aged out of the cache. A new registry parameter, **ArpCacheLife,** was added to allow more administrative control over aging. This parameter is described in online Registry Help.

Entries can be deleted from the cache using **arp -d** as shown next:

```
C:\>arp -d 172.16.90.32

C:\>arp -a

Interface: 172.16.112.123
  Internet Address    Physical Address    Type
  172.16.112.1        00-00-0c-1a-eb-c5   dynamic
  172.16.112.124      00-dd-01-07-57-15   dynamic

Interface: 172.16.113.190
  Internet Address    Physical Address    Type
  172.16.113.138      00-20-af-1d-2b-91   dynamic
```

ARP will queue one outbound IP datagram to a given destination address while that IP address is being resolved to a MAC address. If a UDP–based program sends multiple IP datagrams to a single destination address without any pauses between them, some of the datagrams may be dropped if there is no ARP cache entry already present.

Internet Protocol

Internet Protocol (IP) is the "mailroom" of the TCP/IP stack, where packet sorting and delivery takes place. At this layer, each incoming or outgoing packet is known as a *datagram*. Each IP datagram bears the source IP address of the sender and the destination IP address of the intended recipient. Unlike the MAC addresses, the IP addresses in a datagram remain the same throughout a packet's journey across an internetwork. The following sections describe the IP layer functions.

Routing

Routing is the primary function of IP. Datagrams are handed to the IP protocol from UDP and TCP above, and from the NIC(s) below. Each datagram is labeled with a source and destination IP address. The IP protocol examines the destination address on each datagram, compares it to a locally maintained route table, and decides what action to take. There are three possibilities for each datagram:

- It can be passed up to a protocol layer above IP on the local host.
- It can be forwarded by using one of the locally attached NICs.
- It can be discarded.

The route table maintains four different types of routes. They are listed here in the order in which they are searched for a match:

1. Host (a route to a single, specific destination IP address)
2. Subnet (a route to a subnet)
3. Network (a route to an entire network)
4. Default (used when there is no other match)

You can view the route table from the command prompt, as shown in the following example of the command and its results.

```
C:\>route print
```

Network Address	Netmask	Gateway Address	Interface	Metric
0.0.0.0	0.0.0.0	172.16.112.1	172.16.112.123	1
127.0.0.0	255.0.0.0	127.0.0.1	127.0.0.1	1
172.16.112.0	255.255.255.0	172.16.112.123	172.16.112.123	1
172.16.112.123	255.255.255.255	127.0.0.1	127.0.0.	1
172.16.112.255	255.255.255.255	172.16.112.123	172.16.112.123	1
224.0.0.	224.0.0.0	172.16.112.123	172.16.112.123	1
255.255.255.255	255.255.255.255	172.16.112.123	172.16.112.123	1

The preceding route table is for a computer with the class C IP address 172.16.112.123. It contains seven entries, as follows:

- The first line, to address 0.0.0.0, is the default route.
- The second line is the loopback address, 127.0.0.0.
- The third line is a network route, for the network 172.16.112. The local interface is specified as the path to this network.
- The fourth line is a host route for the local host. Note that it specifies the loopback address, which makes sense because a datagram bound for the local host should be handled internally.

- The fifth line is the subnet broadcast address (again specifying the local interface).
- The sixth line is the IP multicast address.
- The seventh line is for limited broadcast address.

On this host, if a packet is sent to 172.16.112.122, the table is first scanned for a host route (not found), then for a subnet route (not found), then for a network route (that is found). The packet is sent by using the local interface 172.16.112.123. If a packet is sent to 172.17.1.1, the same search is used, and no host, subnet, or network route is found. In this case, the packet is directed to the default gateway, by inserting the MAC address of the default gateway into the destination MAC address field.

The route table is maintained automatically in most cases. When a host initializes, entries for the local network(s), loopback, multicast, and configured default gateway are added. More routes may appear in the table as the IP layer learns of them. For example, a computer may receive a message from the default gateway that indicates (using ICMP, as explained later) a better route to a specific network, subnet, or host. Routes also may be added manually by using the **route** command. In Windows NT versions 4.0 and 3.5*x*, the *-p (persistent)* switch can be used with the **route** command to specify permanent routes. Permanent routes are stored in the Registry under:

```
HKEY_LOCAL_COMPUTER\SYSTEM\CurrentControlSet\Services\Tcpip\Parameters\
PersistentRoutes
```

Note In Windows NT version 3.5, manually-added routes were treated as temporary files and the routes were deleted from the table when the computer was restarted.

Most routers use a protocol such as RIP (Routing Information Protocol) or OSPF (Open Shortest Path First) to exchange routing tables with each other.

Multi-Protocol Router

The Multi-Protocol Router (MPR) in Windows NT consists of the following:

- Routing Information Protocol (RIP) for TCP/IP
- RIP for Internetwork Packet Exchange (IPX)
- Boot Protocol (BOOTP) relay agent for DHCP

Routers use RIP to dynamically exchange routing information. Windows NT routes the RIP protocols and dynamically exchanges routing information with other routers running the RIP protocol.

The Windows NT router uses the BOOTP relay agent to forward DHCP requests to DHCP servers on other subnets. This allows one DHCP server to service multiple IP subnets.

Note By default, computers running under Windows NT do not behave as routers. You must install MPR after installing TCP/IP on your computer. MPR is included with Windows NT Server and Windows NT Workstation version 4.0. MPR for Windows NT version 3.51 is available from **ftp.microsoft.com**, and is included with Service Pack 3 and later under the "MPR" directory. Windows NT version 3.5 or earlier, when used as a router, does not include support for RIP.

Routing for Multiple Logical Subnets

When running multiple logical subnets on the same physical network, use the following command to tell IP to treat all subnets as local and to use ARP directly for the destination:

route add 0.0.0.0 MASK 0.0.0.0 <my local ip address>

Thus, packets destined for "non-local" subnets will be transmitted directly onto the local media instead of being sent to a router. In essence, the local interface card can be designated as the default gateway. This might be useful where several class "C" networks are being used on one physical network with no router to the outside world.

Duplicate IP Address Detection

Duplicate address detection is an important feature. When the stack is first initialized, a "gratuitous" ARP Request is broadcast for the IP address(es) of the local host. If another computer replies, the IP address is already in use. When this happens, the Windows NT computer will still start; however, IP on the offending interface is disabled, a system log entry is generated, and a popup error message is displayed. If the computer that is "defending" the address is also a Windows NT computer, a system log entry is generated and a popup error message is displayed there; however, its interface will continue to operate. After transmitting the ARP reply, the "defending" computer ARPs for its own address again so that other hosts on the network will maintain the correct mapping for the address in their ARP caches.

A computer using a duplicate IP address may be started while it is not attached to the network, in which case no conflict would be detected at that point. However, if it is then plugged into the network, the first time that it ARPs for another IP address, any Windows NT computer with a conflicting address will detect the conflict. The computer detecting the conflict will display a popup error message and log a detailed event in the system log. The following is a sample event log entry:

```
** The system detected an address conflict for IP address 172.16.48.123
with the system having network hardware address 00:DD:01:0F:7A:B5.
Network operations on this system may be disrupted as a result. **
```

Multihoming

When a computer is configured with more than one IP address, it is known as a *multihomed* computer. The different types of multihoming are:

- Multiple IP addresses per NIC.

  Five addresses per card may be configured using Control Panel; however, more may be added in the Registry. For details, see the **IPAddress** registry parameter in online Registry Help.

  NetBT (NetBIOS over TCP/IP per RFC 1001/1002) binds to only one IP address per interface card. When a NetBIOS name registration is sent, it contains the first IP address in the list of addresses assigned to the NIC.

- Multiple NICs per physical network.

  No restrictions other than hardware.

- Multiple networks and media types.

  No restrictions other than hardware and media support as described in the section "Network Driver Interface Specification" earlier in this chapter.

Note   Under Windows NT version 3.51, NetBT did not bind to a NIC that had more than 16 to 20 IP addresses associated with it.

When an IP datagram is sent from a multihomed host, it will be handed down to the interface card with the best apparent route to the destination. Accordingly, the datagram may bear the source IP address of one interface in the multihomed host, yet be placed on the media by a different NIC. The source MAC address on the frame will be that of the NIC that actually transmitted the frame onto the media, and the source IP address will be the one that the sending application sourced it from, not necessarily one of those associated with the sending NIC in the configuration screens in the network control panel.

Routing problems may arise when a computer is multihomed with NICs attached to *disjoint networks* (networks that are separate from and unaware of each other, such as one connected by using RAS). In this scenario, it is often necessary to set up static routes to remote networks.

More details on name registration and resolution with multihomed computers are provided in the section "NetBIOS over TCP/IP" later in this chapter.

Classless Interdomain Routing

Classless Interdomain Routing (CIDR), also known as *supernetting,* can be used to consolidate several class C network addresses into one logical network. CIDR is described in RFC 1518/1519. To use supernetting, the IP network addresses that are to be combined must share the same high-order bits, and the subnet mask is "shortened" to take bits away from the network portion of the address and add them to the host portion.

This is best explained with an example. The class C network addresses 199.199.5.0, 199.199.6.0, and 199.199.7.0 can be combined by using a subnet mask of 255.255.252.0 for each:

```
NET     199.199.5       (1100 0111 . 1100 0111 . 0000 0101.0000 0000)
NET     199.199.6       (1100 0111 . 1100 0111 . 0000.0110.0000 0000)
NET     199.199.7       (1100 0111 . 1100 0111 . 0000.0111.0000 0000)
MASK    255.255.252.0   (1111 1111 . 1111 1111 . 1111 1100.0000 0000)
```

When routing decisions are made, only the bits covered by the subnet mask are used, thus making these addresses all appear to be part of the same network for routing purposes. Any routers in use must also support CIDR and may require special configuration.

IP Multicasting

IP multicasting is used to provide efficient multicast services to clients that may not be located on the same network segment. Windows Sockets programs can join a multicast group. For more information, see the section "Using IP Multicasts with Windows Sockets Programs," later in this chapter.

Windows NT versions 4.0 and 3.5*x* are level-2 (send and receive) compliant with RFC 1112. IGMP is the protocol used to manage IP multicasting.

Internet Control Message Protocol

Internet Control Message Protocol (ICMP) is a maintenance protocol specified in RFC 792 and is normally considered to be part of the IP layer. ICMP messages are encapsulated within IP datagrams, so they can be routed throughout an internetwork. ICMP is used by Windows NT to:

- Build and maintain route tables.
- Assist in Path Maximum Transfer Unit (PMTU) discovery.
- Diagnose problems (using the utilities **ping** and **tracert**).
- Adjust flow control to prevent link or router saturation.

Maintaining Route Tables

When a Windows NT computer is initialized, the route table normally contains only a few entries. One of those specifies a *default gateway*. Datagrams that have a destination IP address with no match in the route table are sent to the default gateway.

However, because routers share information about network topology with each other, the default gateway may know of a better route to a given address. When this is the case, upon receiving a datagram that could be taking the better path, the router forwards the datagram normally, then advises the sender of the better route using an *ICMP redirect* message.

These messages can specify redirection for one host, a subnet, or for an entire network. When a Windows NT computer receives an ICMP redirect, a check is performed to be sure that it came from the first-hop gateway in the current route, and that the gateway is on a directly connected network. If so, the route table is adjusted accordingly.

If the ICMP redirect did not come from the first-hop gateway in the current route, or if that gateway is not on a directly connected network, then the ICMP redirect is ignored.

Path Maximum Transfer Unit Discovery

TCP uses Path Maximum Transfer Unit (PMTU) discovery. The mechanism relies on ICMP destination unreachable messages.

Using ICMP to Diagnose Problems

The **ping** utility is used to send ICMP echo requests to an IP address, and wait for ICMP echo responses. **Ping** reports on the number of responses received and the time interval between sending the request and receiving the response. There are many different options that can be used with the **ping** utility.

Tracert is a route-tracing utility that can be very useful. **Tracert** works by sending ICMP echo requests to an IP address, while incrementing the time-to-live (TTL) field in the IP header by one starting at 1, and analyzing the ICMP errors that get returned. Each succeeding echo request should get one hop further into the network before the TTL field reaches 0 and an ICMP Time Exceeded error is returned by the router attempting to forward it. **Tracert** simply prints out an ordered list of the routers in the path that returned these error messages. If the *-d* switch is used (meaning do not do a DNS lookup on each IP address), then the IP address of the near-side interface of the routers is reported.

Adjusting Flow Control by Using ICMP

If a host is sending datagrams to another computer at a rate that is saturating the routers or links between them, it may receive an *ICMP Source Quench* message asking it to slow down. The TCP/IP stack in Windows NT honors a source quench message as long as it contains the header fragment of one of its own datagrams from an active TCP connection. If a Windows NT computer is being used as a router, and it is unable to forward datagrams at the rate they are arriving, it drops any datagrams that cannot be buffered but does not send ICMP source quench messages to the senders.

Internet Group Management Protocol

Windows NT versions 4.0 and 3.5*x* provide level-2 (full) support for IP multicasting as specified in RFC 1112. The introduction to RFC 1112 provides a good overall summary of IP multicasting. The text reads:

IP multicasting is the transmission of an IP datagram to a "host group", a set of zero or more hosts identified by a single IP destination address. A multicast datagram is delivered to all members of its destination host group with the same "best-efforts" reliability as regular unicast IP datagrams, i.e., the datagram is not guaranteed to arrive intact at all members of the destination group or in the same order relative to other datagrams.

The membership of a host group is dynamic; that is, hosts may join and leave groups at any time. There is no restriction on the location or number of members in a host group. A host may be a member of more than one group at a time. A host need not be a member of a group to send datagrams to it.

A host group may be permanent or transient. A permanent group has a well-known, administratively assigned IP address. It is the address, not the membership of the group, that is permanent; at any time a permanent group may have any number of members, even zero. Those IP multicast addresses that are not reserved for permanent groups are available for dynamic assignment to transient groups that exist only as long as they have members.

Internetwork forwarding of IP multicast datagrams is handled by "multicast routers" that may be co-resident with, or separate from, Internet gateways. A host transmits an IP multicast datagram as a local network multicast that reaches all immediately-neighboring members of the destination host group. If the datagram has an IP time-to-live greater than 1, the multicast router(s) attached to the local network take responsibility for forwarding it towards all other networks that have members of the destination group. On those other member networks that are reachable within the IP time-to-live, an attached multicast router completes delivery by transmitting the datagram as a local multicast.

IP/ARP Extensions for IP Multicasting

To support IP multicasting, an additional route is defined. The route (added by default) specifies that if a datagram is being sent to a multicast host group, it should be sent to the IP address of the host group by using the local interface card, not forwarded to the default gateway. The following route (which can be seen with the **route print** command) illustrates this:

Network Address	Netmask	Gateway Address	Interface	Metric
224.0.0.0	224.0.0.0	172.16.80.138	172.16.80.138	1

Host group addresses are easily identified, because they are from the class D range, 224.0.0.0 to 239.255.255.255. These IP addresses all have "1110" as their high-order 4 bits.

To send a packet to a host group using the local interface, the IP address must be resolved to a MAC address. From RFC 1112:

An IP host group address is mapped to an Ethernet multicast address by placing the low-order 23 bits of the IP address into the low-order 23 bits of the Ethernet multicast address 01-00-5E-00-00-00 (hex). Because there are 28 significant bits in an IP host group address, more than one host group address may map to the same Ethernet multicast address.

For example, a datagram addressed to the multicast address 225.0.0.5 would be sent to the (Ethernet) MAC address 01-00-5E-00-00-05. This MAC address is formed by the junction of 01-00-5E and the 23 low-order bits of 225.0.0.5 (00-00-05).

Because more than one host group address might map to the same Ethernet multicast address, the NIC may indicate up some multicasts for a host group for which no local programs have registered interest. These extra multicasts are discarded.

Finally, the protocol stack must provide a means of joining and leaving host groups.

Using IP Multicasts with Windows Sockets Programs

IP multicasting is currently supported only on AF_INET sockets of type SOCK_DGRAM. By default, IP multicast datagrams are sent with a time-to-live (TTL) of 1. The setsockopt() call can be used by a program to specify a TTL. By convention, multicast routers use TTL thresholds to determine how far to forward datagrams. The following table lists the TTL thresholds that are used to determine how far to forward multicast datagrams.

Table 6.1   Time-to-Live Thresholds for Windows Sockets Programs

TTL Threshold	Description
TTL equal to 0	Restricted to the same host
TTL equal to 1	Restricted to the same subnet
TTL equal to 32	Restricted to the same site
TTL equal to 64	Restricted to the same region
TTL equal to 128	Restricted to the same continent
TTL equal to 255	Unrestricted in scope

Use of IGMP by Windows NT Components

At the time of this writing. the only Windows NT component that uses IGMP is Windows Internet Name Service (WINS), which attempts to locate replication partners by using multicasting.

Transmission Control Protocol

Transmission Control Protocol (TCP) provides a connection-based, reliable, byte-stream service to programs. Microsoft networking relies upon the TCP transport for logging on, file and print sharing, replication of information between domain controllers, transfer of browse lists, and other common functions. TCP can only be used for one-to-one communications. TCP uses a checksum on both the headers and data of each segment to reduce the chance of network corruption going undetected.

Size Calculation of the TCP Receive Window

The TCP receive window size is the amount of receive data (in bytes) that can be buffered at one time on a connection. The sending host can send only that amount of data before waiting for an acknowledgment (ACK) and window update from the receiving host.

The TCP/IP stack is designed to self-tune itself in most environments. Instead of using a hard-coded default receive window size, TCP adjusts to even increments of the *maximum segment size* (MSS) negotiated during connection setup.

Matching the receive window to even increments of the MSS increases the percentage of full-sized TCP segments used during bulk data transmission. The following defaults are used for receive window size: TCPWindowSize = 8K rounded up to the nearest MSS increment for the connection; if that is not at least 4 times the MSS, then it's adjusted to 4 times the MSS, with a maximum size of 64K.

Note The maximum window size is 64K because the field in the TCP header is 16 bits in length. RFC 1323 describes a TCP window scale option that can be used to obtain larger receive windows; however Windows NT TCP/IP does not yet implement that option.

For Ethernet, the window will normally be set to 8760 bytes (8192 rounded up to six 1460-byte segments); for 16/4 Token Ring or FDDI, it will be around 16K. These are default values and it's not generally advisable to alter them; however, you can either change the registry parameter **TcpWindowSize** to globally change the setting for the computer, or use the setsockopt() Windows Sockets call to change the setting on a per-socket basis.

Delayed Acknowledgments

Per RFC 1122, TCP uses delayed acknowledgments to reduce the number of packets sent on the media. The Microsoft stack takes a common approach to implementing delayed acknowledgments. The following conditions cause an acknowledgment to be sent as data is received by TCP on a given connection:

- No ACK is sent for the previous received segment.
- Segment is received, and no other segment arrives within 200ms for that connection.

In summary, normally an ACK is sent for every other TCP segment received on a connection, unless the delayed ACK timer (200ms) expires. There is no configuration parameter to disable delayed ACKs.

PMTU Discovery

RFC 1191 describes PMTU discovery. When a connection is established, the two hosts involved exchange their TCP MSS values. The smaller of the two MSS values is used for the connection. The MSS for a computer is usually the MTU at the link layer minus 40 bytes for the IP and TCP headers.

When TCP segments are destined to a non-local network, the "don't fragment" bit is set in the IP header. Any router or media along the path may have an MTU that differs from that of the two hosts.

If a media is encountered with an MTU that is too small for the IP datagram being routed, the router will attempt to fragment the datagram accordingly. Upon attempting to do so, it will find that the "don't fragment" bit in the IP header is set. At this point, the router should inform the sending host with an *ICMP destination unreachable* message that the datagram can't be forwarded further without fragmentation. Most routers will also specify the MTU that is allowed for the next hop by putting the value for it in the low-order 16 bits of the ICMP header field that is labeled "unused" in the ICMP specification. See RFC 1191, section 4, for the format of this message.

Upon receiving this ICMP error message, TCP adjusts its MSS for the connection to the specified MTU minus the TCP and IP header size, so that any further packets sent on the connection will be no larger than the maximum size that can traverse the path without fragmentation. The minimum MTU permitted by RFCs is 68 bytes, and this limit is enforced by Windows NT TCP.

Some non-compliant routers may silently drop IP datagrams that cannot be fragmented, or may not correctly report their next-hop MTU. If this occurs, it may be necessary to make a configuration change to the PMTU detection algorithm. There are two registry changes that can be made to the TCP/IP stack to find and correct errors caused by these problematic routers:

- **EnablePMTUBHDetect**: adjusts the PMTU discovery algorithm to attempt to detect these "black hole" routers. Black hole detection is disabled by default.

- **EnablePMTUDiscovery**: completely enables or disables the PMTU discovery mechanism. When PMTU discovery is disabled, an MTU of 576 bytes is used for all *non-local* destination addresses. PMTU discovery is enabled by default.

The PMTU between two computers can be discovered by manually using **ping** with the *-f (do not fragment)* switch as follows:

```
ping -f -n <number of pings> -l <size> <destination ip address>
```

In the preceding example, the *size* parameter can be varied until the MTU is found. Note that the size parameter used by **ping** is the size of the data buffer to send, not including headers. The ICMP header consumes 8 bytes, and the IP header would normally be 20 bytes. In the following case (Ethernet), the link layer MTU is the maximum-sized **ping** buffer plus 28, or 1500 bytes:

```
C:\temp>ping -f -n 1 -l 1472 172.16.48.03
Pinging 172.16.48.03 with 1472 bytes of data:
Reply from 172.16.48.03: bytes=1472 time<10ms TTL=30

C:\temp>ping -f -n 1 -l 1473 172.16.48.03
Pinging 172.16.48.03 with 1473 bytes of data:
Packet needs to be fragmented but DF set
```

In the preceding example, the router returned an ICMP error message which **ping** interpreted for us. If the router had been a "black hole" router, the **ping** would simply not be answered once its size exceeded the MTU that the router could handle. **Ping** can be used in this manner to detect such a router.

A sample ICMP destination unreachable error message is as follows:

```
+ FRAME: Base frame properties
+ FDDI: Length = 77
+ LLC: UI DSAP=0xAA SSAP=0xAA C
+ SNAP: ETYPE = 0x0800
+ IP: ID = 0x0; Proto = ICMP; Len: 56
  ICMP: Destination Unreachable, Destination: 172.16.112.125
    ICMP: Packet Type = Destination Unreachable
    ICMP: Unreachable Code = Fragmentation Needed, DF Flag Set
    ICMP: CheckSum = 0x8ABF
    ICMP: Data: Number of data bytes remaining = 28 (0x001C)


00000: 50 00 60 8C 14 C7 0E 00 00 0C 1A EB C0 AA AA 03
00010: 00 00 00 08 00 45 00 00 38 00 00 00 00 FF 01 D3
00020: 36 C7 C7 2C 01 C7 C7 2C FE 03 04 8A BF 00 00 05
00030: C7 45 00 05 F8 55 24 40 00 1F 01 1B D7 C7 C7 2C
00040: FE C7 C7 28 7D 08 00 00 75 01 00 63 00
```

Network Monitor did not parse the MTU suggestion in this frame, but it is shown underlined in the hex portion of the trace. This error is generated by using *ping -f -l 2000* on an FDDI-based host to send a large datagram through a router to an Ethernet host. When the router tried to place the large frame onto the Ethernet segment, it found that fragmentation is not allowed, and so it returned the error message indicating the largest datagram that could be forwarded is 0x5c7, or 1479 bytes.

Dead Gateway Detection

Microsoft TCP/IP provides dead gateway detection. Dead gateway detection allows TCP to detect failure of the default gateway and to make an adjustment to the IP routing table to use another default gateway.

Dead gateways are detected by using TCP retries. Microsoft TCP/IP stack uses the triggered reselection method as described in RFC 816.

TCP will attempt to send a packet to the default gateway configured on a computer until it receives an acknowledgment or until one-half of the **TcpMaxDataRetransmissions** registry parameter is reached. If no response is received from the default gateway and multiple gateways are configured on the computer, TCP requests that IP switch to the next default gateway in the list.

Note If the computer running Windows NT Server or Windows NT Workstation is a DHCP client, the default gateway is automatically configured on the computer.

▶ **To add additional default gateways or to configure gateways for non-DHCP configured computers**

1. Click **Start**, point to **Settings**, and click **Control Panel**.
2. Double-click **Network**, and then click the **Protocol** tab.
3. Under **Network Protocols**, click **TCP/IP**, and then click **Properties**.
4. If necessary, click the **IP Address** tab, and then click **Advanced**.
5. You can add additional gateways under **Gateway** in the **Advanced IP Addressing** dialog box.

IP utilities such as **ping** do not trigger the dead gateway detection process. They use the current default gateway. If TCP detects a dead gateway and selects a new one, the IP utilities will then function using the new gateway. By default, dead gateway detection is set to "on" when you configure a computer running under Windows NT with the IP address of more than one gateway.

Retransmission Behavior

TCP starts a retransmission timer when each outbound segment is handed down to IP. If no acknowledgment has been received for the data in a given segment before the timer expires, then the segment is retransmitted, up to the value of the **TcpMaxDataRetransmissions** registry parameter. The default value for this parameter is 5.

The retransmission timer is initialized to three seconds when a TCP connection is established; however it is adjusted "on the fly" to match the characteristics of the connection using smoothed round trip time (SRTT) calculations as described in RFC 793. The timer for a given segment is doubled after each retransmission of that segment. Using this algorithm, TCP tunes itself to the "normal" delay of a connection. TCP connections over high-delay links will take much longer to time out than those over low-delay links.

Note   Adding [1] to the registry parameter **TcpMaxDataRetransmissions** approximately doubles the total retransmission time-out period for all connections.

The following trace clip shows the retransmission algorithm for two hosts connected over Ethernet on the same subnet. An FTP file transfer was in progress when the receiving host was disconnected from the network. Since the SRTT for this connection is very small, the first retransmission is sent after about one-half second. The timer is then doubled for each of the retransmissions that followed. After the fifth retransmission, the timer is once again doubled, and if no acknowledgment is received before it expires, the transfer is aborted.

Delta	Source Ip	Dest Ip	Pro	Flags	Description
0.000	172.16.90.32	172.16.80.138	TCP	.A....	, len: 1460, seq: 8043781, ack: 8153124, win: 8760
0.521	172.16.90.32	172.16.80.138	TCP	.A....	, len: 1460, seq: 8043781, ack: 8153124, win: 8760
1.001	172.16.90.32	172.16.80.138	TCP	.A....	, len: 1460, seq: 8043781, ack: 8153124, win: 8760
2.003	172.16.90.32	172.16.80.138	TCP	.A....	, len: 1460, seq: 8043781, ack: 8153124, win: 8760
4.007	172.16.90.32	172.16.80.138	TCP	.A....	, len: 1460, seq: 8043781, ack: 8153124, win: 8760
8.130	172.16.90.32	172.16.80.138	TCP	.A....	, len: 1460, seq: 8043781, ack: 8153124, win: 8760

TCP Keepalive Messages

A TCP keepalive packet is simply an ACK with the sequence number set to one less than the current sequence number for the connection. A computer receiving one of these ACKs should respond with an ACK for the current sequence number. Keepalives can be used to verify that the computer at the remote end of a connection is still available. TCP keepalives can be sent once every *KeepAliveTime* (defaults to 7,200,000 milliseconds or two hours), if no other data or higher level keepalives have been carried over the TCP connection. If there is no response to a keepalive, it is repeated once every *KeepAliveInterval* seconds. KeepAliveInterval defaults to one second. NetBT connections, such as those used by many Microsoft networking components, send NetBIOS keepalives more frequently, and so normally no TCP keepalives will be sent on a NetBIOS connection. TCP keepalives are disabled by default, but Windows Sockets programs may enable them using setsockopt().

Slow Start Algorithm and Congestion Avoidance

When a connection is initially established, TCP processes at a slow rate to assess the bandwidth of the connection and to avoid overflowing the receiving host or any other devices or links in the path. The send window is set to two TCP segments.

If the TCP/IP segments are acknowledged, the send window is incremented again, and so on until the amount of data being sent per burst reaches the size of the receive window on the remote host. At that point, the slow start algorithm is no longer in use and flow control is governed by the receive window on the remote host.

However, at any time during transmission, congestion could still occur on a connection. If this happens (evidenced by the need to retransmit), a congestion avoidance algorithm is used to reduce the send window size temporarily, and then to slowly increment the send window back towards the receive window size.

Note   Slow start and congestion avoidance are discussed in RFC 1122.

Silly Window Syndrome

Silly Window Syndrome (SWS) is described in RFC 1122 as follows:

> In brief, SWS is caused by the receiver advancing the right window edge whenever it has any new buffer space available to receive data and by the sender using any incremental window, no matter how small, to send more data [TCP:5]. The result can be a stable pattern of sending tiny data segments, even though both sender and receiver have a large total buffer space for the connection.

TCP/IP for Windows NT implements SWS avoidance per RFC 1122 by not sending more data until there is a sufficient window size advertised by the receiving end to send a full segment. It also implements SWS on the receive end of a connection by not opening the receive window in increments of less than a TCP segment.

Nagle Algorithm

TCP/IP for Windows NT Server and Windows NT Workstation implements the Nagle algorithm described in RFC 896. The purpose of this algorithm is to reduce the number of "tiny" segments sent, especially on high-delay (remote) links. The Nagle algorithm allows only one small segment to be outstanding at a time without acknowledgment. If more small segments are generated while awaiting the ACK for the first one, then these segments are coalesced into one larger segment. Any full-sized segment is always transmitted immediately, assuming there is a sufficient receive window available. The Nagle algorithm is effective in reducing the number of packets sent by interactive programs, such as Telnet, especially over slow links.

The following trace captured by using Microsoft Network Monitor shows the Nagle algorithm at work. The trace was captured by using PPP to dial up an Internet provider at 9600 bps. A Telnet (character-mode) session is established, then the "y" key is held down on the Windows NT Workstation. At all times, one segment is sent, and further "y" characters were held by the stack until an acknowledgment is received for the previous segment. In this example, three to four "y" characters were saved up each time and sent together in one segment. The Nagle algorithm resulted in a huge savings in the number of packets sent—it is reduced by a factor of about three.

Time	Source IP	Dest IP	Prot	Description
0.644	172.16.16.243	172.16.144.0	TELNET	To Server From Port = 1901
0.144	172.16.144.0	172.16.16.243	TELNET	To Client With Port = 1901
0.000	172.16.16.243	172.16.144.0	TELNET	To Server From Port = 1901
0.145	172.16.144.0	172.16.16.243	TELNET	To Client With Port = 1901
0.000	172.16.16.243	172.16.144.0	TELNET	To Server From Port = 1901
0.144	172.16.144.0	172.16.16.243	TELNET	To Client With Port = 1901

Each segment contained several of the "y" characters. Following is the first segment shown more fully parsed, and the data portion is pointed out in the hex at the bottom.

Time	Source IP	Dest IP	Prot	Description

```
0.644 172.16.48.1  172.16.112.0  TELNET  To Server From Port = 1901
+ FRAME: Base frame properties
+ ETHERNET: ETYPE = 0x0800 : Protocol = IP: DOD Internet Protocol
+ IP: ID = 0xEA83; Proto = TCP; Len: 43
+ TCP: .AP..., len:   3, seq:1032660278, ack: 353339017, win: 7766, src:
        1901 dst:  23 (TELNET)
 TELNET: To Server From Port = 1901
   TELNET: Telnet Data
D2 41 53 48 00 00 52 41 53 48 00 00 08 00 45 00    .ASH..RASH....E.
00 2B EA 83 40 00 20 06 F5 85 CC B6 42 53 C7 B5    .+..@. .....BS..
A4 04 07 6D 00 17 3D 8D 25 36 15 0F 86 89 50 18    ...m..=.%6....P.
1E 56 1E 56 00 00 79 79 79                         .V.V..yyy
                                                        ^^^
                                                        data
```

Windows Sockets programs can disable the Nagle algorithm for their connection(s) by setting the TCP_NODELAY socket option. However, this practice should be avoided unless absolutely necessary because it increases network usage. Some network programs may not perform well if their design does not take into account the effects of transmitting large numbers of small packets and the Nagle algorithm.

Throughput Considerations

TCP is designed to provide optimum performance over varying link conditions. Actual throughput for a link is dependent on a number of variables, but the most important factors are:

- Link speed (bits per second that can be transmitted)

- Propagation delay

- Window size (amount of unacknowledged data that may be outstanding on a TCP connection)

- Link reliability

- Router congestion

TCP throughput calculation is discussed in detail in Chapters 20 through 24 of *TCP/IP Illustrated,* by W. Richard Stevens. The following are some key considerations:

- The capacity of a pipe is (bandwidth * round-trip time). This is known as the bandwidth-delay product. If the link is reliable, for best performance the window size should be greater than or equal to the capacity of the pipe. The largest window size that can be specified is 65535 due to its 16-bit field in the TCP header. RFC 1323 describes a Window Scale option; however, it has not yet been implemented by Windows NT TCP.
- Throughput will never exceed (window size / round-trip time).
- If the link is unreliable (or badly congested) and packets are being dropped, using a larger window size may not improve throughput.
- Propagation delay depends on the speed of light and latencies in transmission equipment, and so on.
- Transmission delay depends on the speed of the media.
- For a given path, propagation delay is fixed, but transmission delay depends on the packet size.
- At low speeds, transmission delay is the limiting factor. At high speeds, propagation delay may become the limiting factor.

To summarize, Windows NT TCP/IP will adapt to most network conditions and dynamically provide the best throughput and reliability possible on a per-connection basis. *Attempts at manual tuning are often counter-productive* unless a qualified network engineer performs careful study of data flow.

User Datagram Protocol

User Datagram Protocol (UDP) provides a connectionless, unreliable transport service. It is often used for one-to-many communications, using broadcast or multicast IP datagrams. Because delivery of UDP datagrams is not guaranteed, programs using UDP must supply their own mechanisms for reliability if needed. Microsoft networking uses UDP for logon, browsing, and name resolution.

UDP and Name Resolution

UDP is used for (1) NetBIOS name resolution by using unicast to a NetBIOS name server (such as WINS) or subnet broadcasts, and (2) for DNS host name and IP address resolution. NetBIOS name resolution is accomplished over UDP port 137. DNS queries use UDP port 53. Because UDP itself does not guarantee delivery of datagrams, both of these services use their own retransmission schemes if they receive no answer to queries. Broadcast UDP datagrams are not usually forwarded over IP routers, and so NetBIOS name resolution in a routed environment requires a name server of some type, or the use of static database files.

Mailslots over UDP

Many NetBIOS programs use mailslot messaging. A 2nd class mailslot is a simple mechanism for sending a message from one NetBIOS name to another over UDP. Mailslot messages may be broadcast on a subnet, or may be directed to the remote computer. In order to direct a mailslot message to another computer, there must be some method of NetBIOS name resolution available. The WINS server running under Windows NT Server provides this service.

TCP/IP Security Filters

Security filtering for TCP/IP allows you to control the type of network traffic passed up the TCP/IP protocol stack to upper-layer protocols and programs. Security filters are one of the security mechanisms typically used on Internet servers.

TCP/IP security filters control the ports on which TCP connections and UDP datagrams are accepted (For more information ,see Appendix B, "Port Reference for MS TCP/IP.") The filters also control which IP protocol can be assessed by using raw sockets.

If TCP/IP security filters are configured on a computer running under Windows NT, incoming connection requests and datagrams are accepted or rejected based on the configured security filters. Outgoing connection requests and datagrams are not affected.

Security filters are configured separately for each network adapter to which TCP/IP is bound. Filters are applied to network traffic based on the adapter that received the traffic.

For specific information about configuring advanced TCP/IP security, see Microsoft TCP/IP Help.

NetBIOS over TCP/IP

The following TCP and UDP ports are used in NetBT, the Windows NT implementation of NetBIOS over TCP/IP.

- UDP port 137 (name services)
- UDP port 138 (datagram services)
- TCP port 139 (session services)

NetBIOS over TCP/IP is specified by RFC 1001 and RFC 1002. The Netbt.sys driver is a kernel-mode component that supports the TDI interface. Services such as Windows NT Workstation and Windows NT Server services use the TDI interface directly, while traditional NetBIOS programs have their calls mapped to TDI calls by using the Netbios.sys driver. Using TDI to make calls to NetBT is a more difficult programming task, but can provide higher performance and freedom from historical NetBIOS limitations.

See the section "Network Application Interfaces" later in this chapter for more information about NetBIOS.

Transport Driver Interface

Microsoft developed the transport driver interface (TDI) to provide greater flexibility and functionality than provided by existing interfaces such as NetBIOS and Windows Sockets. The TDI interface is exposed by all Windows NT transport providers. The TDI interface specification describes the set of primitive functions by which transport drivers and TDI clients communicate, and the call mechanisms used for accessing them. Currently, the TDI Interface is *kernel-mode* only.

The Windows NT redirector and server both use TDI directly, rather than going through the NetBIOS mapping layer. By doing so, they are not subject to many of the restrictions imposed by NetBIOS, such as the 254 session limit.

TDI may be the most difficult to use of all the Windows NT network APIs. It is a simple conduit, so the programmer must determine the format and meaning of messages.

Note More information on the TDI interface is available in the Windows NT Device Driver Kit (DDK).

The following features are part of the Windows NT implementation of TDI.

- Support for all Windows NT transports excluding the DLC protocol
- An open naming and addressing scheme
- Message and stream mode data transfer
- Asynchronous operation
- Support for unsolicited indication of events
- Extensibility—clients can submit private requests to a transport driver that can process the requests
- Support for limited use of standard kernel-mode I/O functions to send and receive data
- 32-bit addressing and values

Network Application Interfaces

There are a number of ways that network programs can communicate by using the TCP/IP protocol stack. Some of them, such as named pipes, go through the network redirector, which is part of the Workstation service. Many older programs were written to the NetBIOS interface, which is supported by NetBIOS over TCP/IP. Windows Sockets is used in many programs.

The network application programming interfaces (APIs) discussed in this section are:

- Windows Sockets
- NetBIOS over TCP/IP

Windows Sockets Interface

Windows Sockets is an API used for sending and receiving data on a network. Originally designed as the top-level interface for TCP/IP network transport stacks, the Windows Sockets API provides a standard Windows interface to many transports with different addressing schemes, including, for example, TCP/IP and IPX.

Windows Sockets specifies a programming interface based on the "socket" interface from the University of California at Berkeley. It includes a set of extensions designed to take advantage of the message-driven nature of Microsoft Windows. Windows Sockets is an open, industry-standard specification and Microsoft is one member of the group that originally defined Windows Sockets.

There are many Windows Sockets programs available. A number of the utilities that ship with Windows NT are Windows Sockets–based; for example, the DHCP client/server program.

Note   Windows NT version 4.0 implements 32-bit Windows Sockets version 2.0. Earlier versions of Windows NT implemented 32-bit Windows Sockets version 1.1. See Appendix D, "Windows Sockets," for a list of Microsoft and other Internet sites from which you can receive Windows Sockets specifications.

Name and Address Resolution

Windows Sockets programs generally use the gethostbyname() call to resolve a host name to an IP address. The gethostbyname() call uses the following (default) name lookup sequence:

1. Check local computer host name.
2. Check the HOSTS file for a matching name entry.
3. If a DNS server is configured, query it.
4. If no match is found, try the NetBIOS name resolution.

Some programs use the gethostbyaddr() call to resolve an IP address to a host name. The gethostbyaddr() call uses the following sequence:

1. Check local computer host name.
2. Check the HOSTS file for a matching address entry.
3. If a DNS server is configured, query it.
4. If no match is found, send a NetBIOS Adapter Status Request to the IP address being queried, and if it responds with a list of NetBIOS names registered for the adapter, parse it for the computer name.

Support for IP Multicasting

The Windows Sockets API has been extended to provide support for IP multicasting. The extensions, and a sample program, *party.exe,* that illustrates usage, are available from **ftp.microsoft.com**. IP multicasting is currently supported only on AF_INET sockets of type SOCK_DGRAM.

The Backlog Parameter

Windows Sockets server programs generally create a socket and then use *listen( )* to listen on it for connection requests. One of the parameters passed when calling *listen( )* is the *backlog* of connection requests that the program would like Windows Sockets to queue for it.

Windows NT Server version 4.0 allows a backlog maximum of 200. Windows NT Workstation version 4.0 supports only a maximum allowable value of 5.

Note Earlier versions of Windows NT based on the Windows Sockets 1.1 specification used the specified maximum allowable value (5) for *backlog*.

FTP or Web servers that are heavily used may benefit from increasing the backlog to a larger number than the default. Microsoft Internet Information Server allows the backlog parameter to be specified by using a registry setting.

PUSH Bit Interpretation

By default, Windows NT versions 4.0 and 3.5*x* complete a recv() call when:

- Data arrives with the PUSH bit set.
- The user recv() buffer is full.
- 0.5 seconds have elapsed since any data arrived.

If a client program is run on a computer with a TCP/IP implementation that does not set the PUSH bit on-sends, response delays may result. It's best to correct this on the client side; however, a configuration parameter (IgnorePushBitOnReceives) is added to Afd.sys to force it to treat all arriving packets as though the PUSH bit were set.

NetBIOS Interface

Network Basic Input/Output System (NetBIOS) defines a software interface and a naming convention, not a protocol. The NetBEUI protocol, introduced by IBM in 1985, provided a protocol for programs designed around the NetBIOS interface. However, NetBEUI is a small protocol with no networking layer and because of this, it is not a routable protocol suitable for medium-to-large intranets.

NetBIOS over TCP/IP (NetBT) provides the NetBIOS programming interface over the TCP/IP protocol, extending the reach of NetBIOS client/server programs to the WAN and providing interoperability with various other operating systems. NetBT and NetBIOS are illustrated in the following figure.

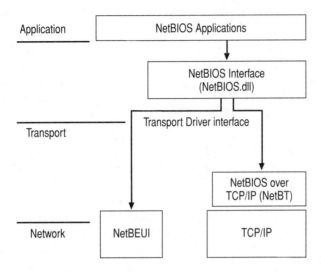

Figure 6.4   NetBIOS over TCP/IP (NetBT) Component

The Windows NT Workstation service, Server service, Browser, Messenger, and Netlogon services are all direct NetBT clients that use the TDI to communicate with NetBT. Windows NT also includes a NetBIOS emulator. The emulator takes standard NetBIOS requests from NetBIOS programs and translates them to equivalent TDI primitives.

NetBIOS Names

The NetBIOS namespace is flat, meaning that all names within a network must be unique. NetBIOS names are 16 characters in length. Resources are identified by NetBIOS names that are registered dynamically when computers start, services start, or users log on. Names can be registered as unique (one owner) or as group (multiple owner) names. A NetBIOS Name Query is used to locate a resource by resolving the name to an IP address.

Microsoft networking components, such as Windows NT Workstation and Windows NT Server services, allow the first 15 characters of a NetBIOS name to be specified by the user or administrator, but reserve the 16th character of the NetBIOS name to indicate a resource type (00-FF hex). See Appendix G, "NetBIOS Names."

▶ **To identify the names registered on your local computer**

1. Click **Start**, and then click **Run**.

2. In **Open**, type **nbtstat** *-n*.

NetBIOS Scope

NetBIOS Scope, also known as TCP/IP Scope, provides a method for adding a second element to the single-element NetBIOS computer name. The scope ID is a character string value that is appended to the NetBIOS name and is used for all NetBT communications from that computer. The character string can be multi-part—for example, "mydomain.mycompany.com".

Note Use of NetBIOS Scope is strongly discouraged if you are not already using it, or if you use Domain Name System (DNS) on your network.

By installation default, the NetBIOS Scope value is NULL. You can change the default value by entering a character string in the **Scope ID** on the **WINS Address** tab on the **Microsoft TCP/IP Properties page**. Note that the maximum length of the combined NetBIOS name and NetBIOS Scope ID is limited to 256 characters.

Note NetBIOS Scope should not be confused with DHCP Scope, which defines the group of IP addresses that the DHCP server can lease to client computers.

The effect of using a NetBIOS Scope ID, other than the default NULL value, is to isolate a group of computers on the network that can communicate only with other computers that are configured with the identical NetBIOS Scope ID. *Use NetBIOS Scope only when it is necessary to isolate a group of computers that cannot communicate with other computers on the intranet.*

Once configured on the local computer, NetBIOS Scope is automatically attached to all NetBIOS commands on that local computer. In other words, NetBIOS programs started on a computer using NetBIOS Scope ID cannot "see" (receive or send messages) NetBIOS programs started by a process on a computer configured with a different NetBIOS Scope ID.

Several Windows NT-based programs, such as net logon and domain controller pass-through authentication, use NetBIOS names. Therefore, consider the effect of NetBIOS Scope ID if you decide to change the default NetBIOS Scope ID. Use the following guidelines:

1. All Windows NT Workstation, Windows NT Server, and Windows 95 computers in the same Windows NT domain that are using the same NetBIOS Scope ID can communicate and connect with each other.

2. However, no pass-through authentication can occur between domains that are configured with different NetBIOS Scope IDs. In other words, using NetBIOS Scope ID can break the trust between domains.

3. Users cannot log on to their assigned domain from Windows 95 and Windows NT Workstation computers if the scope on the computer is different from the NetBIOS Scope configured on the domain controller in the user's assigned domain.

4. Users cannot log on to any computer on which the configured NetBIOS scope is not the same as the NetBIOS Scope ID configured on the domain controller for the selected domain.

5. Users cannot connect, either by the command window or by using a program that issues a **net use** command, to a server whose NetBIOS Scope is different from the scope assigned to the domain controllers in the domain the user is logged on to, or the domain specified in the **Connect** dialog box.

NetBIOS Name Registration and Resolution

Windows NT versions 4.0 and 3.5*x* computers use several methods for locating NetBIOS resources:

- NetBIOS name cache
- NetBIOS name server
- IP subnet broadcasts
- Static LMHOSTS files
- Static HOSTS files
- DNS servers

Earlier implementations used only cache, broadcasts, and LMHOSTS files; however, in Windows NT versions 4.0 and 3.5*x*, a NetBIOS name server—the WINS server—was implemented, and modifications were made to allow NetBIOS programs to query the DNS namespace by appending configurable domain suffixes to a NetBIOS name.

NetBIOS name resolution order depends on the node type and computer configuration. The following node types are supported:

- b-node—uses broadcasts for name registration and resolution.
- p-node—uses only point-to-point name queries to a NetBIOS name server (in this case WINS servers) for name registration and resolution.
- m-node—uses broadcasts for name registration; for name resolution, tries broadcasts first, but switches to p-node if no answer is received.
- h-node—uses NetBIOS name server for both registration and resolution; however, if no name server can be located, it switches to b-node. Continues to poll for nameserver and switches back to p-node when one becomes available. By default, WINS clients are configured as h-node.
- Microsoft-enhanced—local LMHOSTS files or WINS proxies plus Windows Sockets gethostbyname() calls (using standard DNS and local HOSTS files) in addition to standard node types.

The many configurable options sometimes make it difficult to determine what name resolution methods to choose, and what name resolution order each configuration will use. The following flowcharts illustrate name resolution for the various node types and the relationships between the different Windows NT name resolution services.

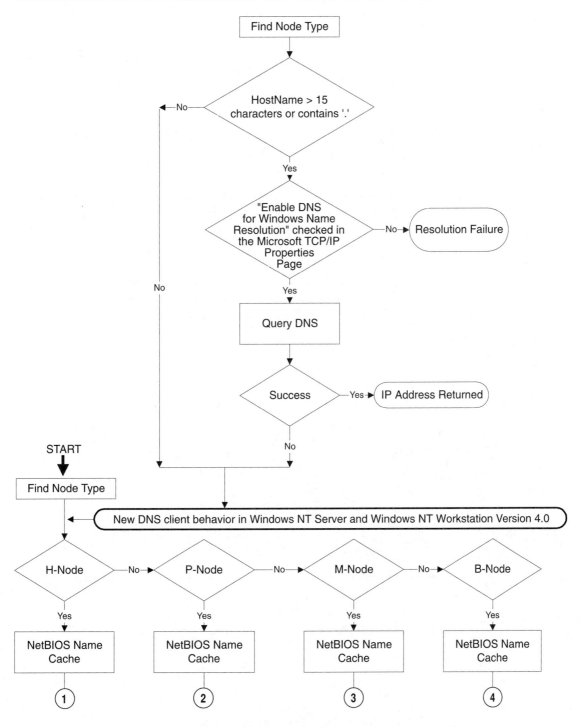

Figure 6.5   NetBIOS Name Resolution Flowchart (part 1 of 3)

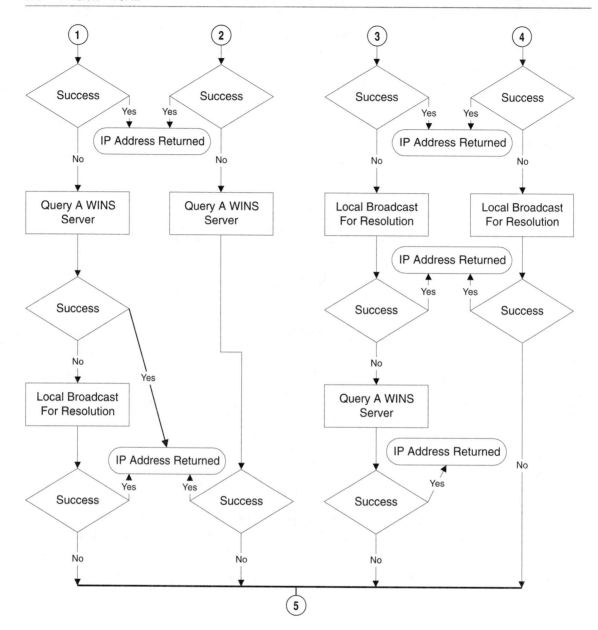

Figure 6.6   NetBIOS Name Resolution Flowchart (part 2 of 3)

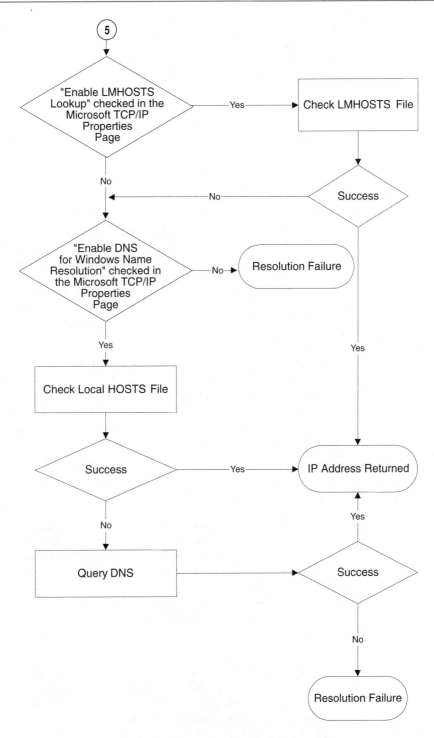

Figure 6.7   NetBIOS Name Resolution Flowchart (part 3 of 3)

The NetBIOS name server provided with Windows NT Server is the Windows Internet Name Service (WINS) server. Most WINS clients are set up as h-nodes; in other words, they first attempt to register and resolve names by a using WINS server, and if that fails they try local subnet broadcasts. Using a name server to locate resources is generally preferable to broadcasting, for two reasons:

- Broadcasts are not usually forwarded over routers.

- Broadcasts are received by all computers on a subnet, requiring processing time at each one.

NetBT and DNS

It has always been possible to connect from one Windows NT computer to another using NetBT over the Internet and other TCP/IP networks. To do so, some means of *name resolution* (associating a name with the appropriate IP address) is used because an IP address is required to establish a connection.

NetBT is the name resolution service for Windows-based networking in TCP/IP. DNS is the traditional and widely used name resolution service for the Internet and other TCP/IP networks. Windows NT Server version 4.0 has expanded support for DNS by implementing a DNS server.

A DNS name is similar to a NetBIOS name in that it is a "friendly" name for a computer or other network device. However, the DNS name is based on a hierarchical naming structure (also known as the name space) that is more flexible than the flat structure of NetBIOS names. DNS computer names consist of two parts: a *host name* and a *domain name*, which when combined, form the *fully qualified domain name (FQDN)*.

NetBIOS computer names are analogous to DNS host names, however a DNS name can be as long as 255 characters while the NetBIOS name is limited to 15 user-definable characters.

Note Under Windows NT, the DNS host name defaults to the NetBIOS computer name. Windows NT combines the NetBIOS computer name with the DNS domain name to form a FQDN by removing the 16th character in the NetBIOS name and appending a dot and the DNS domain name. If you want to change the default host name from the NetBIOS computer name, reconfigure TCP/IP by selecting the **DNS** page on the **Microsoft TCP/IP Properties** dialog box and changing the host name displayed on the **DNS** page.

It is now possible, in Windows NT 4.0, to connect to a NetBT resource by using an IP address, FQDN, or NetBIOS computer name. For example, if using the Event Viewer, when prompted to "select computer," you now can choose to enter an FQDN or IP address or NetBIOS computer name.

NetBIOS Name Registration and Resolution for Multihomed Computers

As mentioned earlier, NetBT only binds to one IP address per physical network interface. From the NetBT viewpoint, then, a computer is multihomed only when it has more than one NIC installed. When a name registration packet is sent from a multihomed computer, it is flagged as a "multihomed name registration" so that it will not conflict with the same name being registered by another interface in the same computer.

When a broadcast name query is received by a multihomed computer, all NetBT interface bindings receiving the query will respond with their address and, by default, the client will choose the first response and connect to the address supplied by it. This behavior can be controlled by the **RandomAdapter** registry parameter described in online Registry Help.

When a directed name query is sent to a WINS server, the WINS server will respond with a list of all IP addresses that were registered with WINS by a multihomed computer.

Choosing the "best" IP address to connect to on a multihomed computer is a client function. Currently, the following algorithm is employed, in the order listed:

1. If one of the IP addresses in the name query response list is on the same logical subnet as the *calling binding of NetBT* on the local computer, then that address is selected. If more than one of the addresses meet this criteria, one is picked at random from those that match.

2. If one of the IP addresses in the list is on the same logical subnet as any binding of NetBT on the local computer, then that address is selected. If more than one of the addresses meet this criteria, one is picked at random from those that match.

3. If none of the IP addresses in the list is on the same subnet as any binding of NetBT on the local computer, then an address is selected at random from the list.

This algorithm provides a reasonably good way of balancing connections to a server across multiple NICs, while still favoring direct connections when they are available.

Note   The current implementation of NetBT does not attempt to "walk the list" of returned addresses if a connection attempt to the first choice fails. This enhancement has been requested and is under review.

NetBT Sessions

NetBIOS sessions are established between two names. For example, when a Windows NT Workstation makes a file sharing connection to a server, the following sequence of events takes place:

1. The NetBIOS name for the server is resolved to an IP address.
2. A TCP connection is established from the workstation to the server, using port 139.
3. The workstation sends a NetBIOS session request to the server name over the TCP connection. Assuming the server is listening on that name, it will respond affirmatively and a session is established.

Once the NetBIOS session has been established, the workstation and server negotiate a higher level protocol to use over it. Microsoft networking uses only one NetBIOS session between two names at any point in time. Any additional file or print sharing connections made after the first one are multiplexed over that same NetBIOS session.

NetBIOS keepalives are used on each connection to verify that the server and workstation are both still up and able to maintain their session. This way, if a workstation is shut down ungracefully, the server will eventually clean up the connection and associated resources, and vice versa. NetBIOS keepalives are controlled by the **SessionKeepAlive** registry parameter and default to once per hour.

If LMHOSTS files are used and an entry is misspelled, it is possible to attempt to connect to a server using the correct IP address but an incorrect name. In this case, a TCP connection will still be established to the server. However, the NetBIOS session request (using the wrong name) will be rejected by the server, because there is no listen posted on that name. Error 51, "remote computer not listening," will be returned.

NetBT Datagram Services

Datagrams are sent from one NetBIOS name to another over UDP port 138. The datagram service provides the ability to send a message to a unique name or to a group name. Group names may resolve to a list of IP addresses or to a broadcast. For example, the command **net send** */d:mydomain test* would send a datagram containing the text "test" to the group name <mydomain>[03]. The <mydomain>[03] name would resolve to an IP subnet broadcast, and so the datagram would be sent with the following characteristics:

- Destination MAC address: broadcast (255.255.255.255)
- Source MAC address: The NIC address of the local computer
- Destination IP address: The local subnet broadcast address

- Source IP address: The IP address of the local computer
- Destination name: <mydomain>[03] (the Messenger service on the remote computers)
- Source name: <localcomputer>[03] (the Messenger service on the local computer)

All hosts on the subnet would pick up the datagram and process it at least to the UDP protocol. On hosts running a NetBIOS datagram service, UDP would hand the datagram to NetBT on port 138. NetBT would check the destination name to see if any program had posted a datagram receive on it, and if so would pass the datagram up. If no receive is posted, the datagram is discarded.

TCP/IP Client/Server Programs

This chapter is intended to provide an overview of the Windows NT versions 4.0 and 3.5x implementation of the TCP/IP stack, not the many clients and services that are shipped with the product or are available from third parties. However, there are a few client/server programs that are critical to the configuration and operation of the TCP/IP protocol suite. These client/programs are briefly described in the following sections and then explained in detail in:

- Chapter 7, "Managing Microsoft DHCP Servers"
- Chapter 8, "Managing Microsoft WINS Servers"
- Chapter 9, "Managing Microsoft DNS Servers"
- Chapter 11, "Using SNMP for Network Management"
- Appendix E, "RAS Reference"

Dynamic Host Configuration Protocol

The Dynamic Host Configuration Protocol (DHCP) client/server is a Windows Sockets program that is used to provide automatic and dynamic configuration of various TCP/IP protocol components. The server is configured with "scopes," which are ranges of IP addresses, to distribute to network clients as they start on the network. The DHCP server can also provide the additional configuration parameters that are associated with the IP addresses. For example, a scope that includes a specific range of IP addresses may also be associated with default gateway, DNS server, and NetBIOS Name Server (WINS), with which the DHCP clients can be configured.

Obtaining Configuration Parameters Using DHCP

When a DHCP-enabled client starts for the very first time, it broadcasts a *DHCP Discover* request onto the local subnet. Any DHCP server that receives the request may respond with a *DHCP Offer* that contains proposed configuration parameters.

The client can evaluate the offer, and respond with a *DHCP request* to accept it. The server finalizes the transaction with a *DHCP ACK*. The following example explains this sequence.

First, the DHCP Discover is sent as the stack initializes:

Time	Source IP	Dest IP	Prot	Description
0.000	0.0.0.0	255.255.255.255	DHCP	Discover (xid=68256CA8)

```
+ FRAME: Base frame properties
 ETHERNET: ETYPE = 0x0800 : Protocol = IP: DOD Internet Protocol
  + ETHERNET: Destination address : 255.255.255.255
  + ETHERNET: Source address : 00DD01075715
   ETHERNET: Frame Length : 342 (0x0156)
   ETHERNET: Ethernet Type : 0x0800 (IP: DOD Internet Protocol)
   ETHERNET: Ethernet Data: Number of data bytes remaining = 328
          (0x0148)
 IP: ID = 0x0; Proto = UDP; Len: 328
   IP: Version = 4 (0x4)
   IP: Header Length = 20 (0x14)
  + IP: Service Type = 0 (0x0)
   IP: Total Length = 328 (0x148)
   IP: Identification = 0 (0x0)
  + IP: Flags Summary = 0 (0x0)
   IP: Fragment Offset = 0 (0x0) bytes
   IP: Time to Live = 32 (0x20)
   IP: Protocol = UDP - User Datagram
   IP: CheckSum = 0x99A6
   IP: Source Address = 0.0.0.0
   IP: Destination Address = 255.255.255.255
   IP: Data: Number of data bytes remaining = 308 (0x0134)
 UDP: IP Multicast: Src Port: BOOTP Client, (68); Dst Port: BOOTP
      Server (67); Length = 308 (0x134)
   UDP: Source Port = BOOTP Client
   UDP: Destination Port = BOOTP Server
   UDP: Total length = 308 (0x134) bytes
   UDP: CheckSum = 0x4A0E
   UDP: Data: Number of data bytes remaining = 300 (0x012C)
 DHCP: Discover      (xid=68256CA8)
   DHCP: Op Code      (op)   = 1 (0x1)
   DHCP: Hardware Type   (htype) = 1 (0x1) 10Mb Ethernet
   DHCP: Hardware Address Length (hlen) = 6 (0x6)
   DHCP: Hops        (hops) = 0 (0x0)
   DHCP: Transaction ID  (xid)  = 1747283112 (0x68256CA8)
   DHCP: Seconds      (secs) = 0 (0x0)
   DHCP: Flags       (flags) = 0 (0x0)
     DHCP: 0............... = No Broadcast
   DHCP: Client IP Address (ciaddr) = 0.0.0.0
   DHCP: Your  IP Address (yiaddr) = 0.0.0.0
```

```
DHCP: Server IP Address  (siaddr) = 0.0.0.0
DHCP: Relay IP Address   (giaddr) = 0.0.0.0
DHCP: Client Ethernet Address (chaddr) = 00DD01075715
DHCP: Server Host Name (sname) = <Blank>
DHCP: Boot File Name  (file)  = <Blank>
DHCP: Magic Cookie = [OK]
DHCP: Option Field   (options)
   DHCP: DHCP Message Type  = DHCP Discover
   DHCP: Client-identifier  = (Type: 1) 00 dd 01 07 57 15
   DHCP: Host Name      = DAVEMAC4
   DHCP: End of this option field
```

There are several interesting points to note in the DHCP discover packet. First, it is sent as a broadcast at both the link layer and the IP layer. Second, the DHCP broadcast flag is set to 0, indicating that the client is capable of receiving a response that is directed to its MAC address (indicated by chaddr). This means that the DHCP server is not required to broadcast the response.

Note Windows NT version 3.5 computers required a broadcast response and did not set this flag to 0.

Finally, note that there is a transaction ID (XID) used to track each configuration sequence. Any response to this discover packet should reference the same XID.

A DHCP offer follows:

Time	Source IP	Dest IP	Prot	Description
0.165	172.16.113.254	172.16.112.13	DHCP	Offer (xid=68256CA8)

```
+ FRAME: Base frame properties
 ETHERNET: ETYPE = 0x0800 : Protocol = IP: DOD Internet Protocol
  + ETHERNET: Destination address : 00DD01075715
  + ETHERNET: Source address : 00000C1AEBC5
   ETHERNET: Frame Length : 590 (0x024E)
   ETHERNET: Ethernet Type : 0x0800 (IP: DOD Internet Protocol)
   ETHERNET: Ethernet Data: Number of data bytes remaining = 576
          (0x0240)
 IP: ID = 0x906; Proto = UDP; Len: 576
   IP: Version = 4 (0x4)
   IP: Header Length = 20 (0x14)
  + IP: Service Type = 0 (0x0)
   IP: Total Length = 576 (0x240)
   IP: Identification = 2310 (0x906)
  + IP: Flags Summary = 0 (0x0)
   IP: Fragment Offset = 0 (0x0) bytes
   IP: Time to Live = 31 (0x1F)
   IP: Protocol = UDP - User Datagram
```

```
     IP: CheckSum = 0xAF0D
     IP: Source Address = 172.16.113.254
     IP: Destination Address = 172.16.112.13
     IP: Data: Number of data bytes remaining = 556 (0x022C)
   UDP: Src Port: BOOTP Server, (67); Dst Port: BOOTP Client (68); Length
       = 556 (0x22C)
  DHCP: Offer         (xid=68256CA8)
    DHCP: Op Code       (op)    = 2 (0x2)
    DHCP: Hardware Type    (htype) = 1 (0x1) 10Mb Ethernet
    DHCP: Hardware Address Length (hlen) = 6 (0x6)
    DHCP: Hops        (hops)  = 0 (0x0)
    DHCP: Transaction ID  (xid)   = 1747283112 (0x68256CA8)
    DHCP: Seconds       (secs)  = 0 (0x0)
    DHCP: Flags         (flags) = 0 (0x0)
       DHCP: 0............... = No Broadcast
    DHCP: Client IP Address (ciaddr) = 0.0.0.0
    DHCP: Your  IP Address (yiaddr) = 172.16.112.13
    DHCP: Server IP Address (siaddr) = 0.0.0.0
    DHCP: Relay IP Address (giaddr) = 172.16.112.1
    DHCP: Client Ethernet Address (chaddr) = 00DD01075715
    DHCP: Server Host Name (sname) = <Blank>
    DHCP: Boot File Name  (file)  = <Blank>
    DHCP: Magic Cookie = [OK]
    DHCP: Option Field   (options)
       DHCP: DHCP Message Type  = DHCP Offer
       DHCP: Subnet Mask      = 255.255.255.0
       DHCP: Renewal Time Value (T1) = 1 Days, 12:00:00
       DHCP: Rebinding Time Value (T2) = 2 Days, 15:00:00
       DHCP: IP Address Lease Time = 3 Days, 0:00:00
       DHCP: Server Identifier   = 172.16.113.254
       DHCP: End of this option field
```

The DHCP offer is also interesting. The XID is the same as that in the discover packet. It is a directed offer, not sent as a broadcast, and it is directed to the MAC address of the client and to the *proposed* IP address for the client. The source address is from a different subnet (172.16.113) than the subnet that the client is attached to, indicating that both the discover and the offer must have traversed a router. This can be verified by checking the DHCP "giaddr" field, that is set to 172.16.112.1. As you might suspect, a router is configured to forward DHCP broadcasts from this subnet to the one where the DHCP server is located. DHCP forwarding is discussed in RFC 1542, and routers used for this purpose must explicitly support the RFC and be configured accordingly.

Next, the client accepts the offer:

Time	Source IP	Dest IP	Prot	Description
0.172	0.0.0.0	255.255.255.255	DHCP	Request (xid=08186BD1)

```
+ FRAME: Base frame properties
+ ETHERNET: ETYPE = 0x0800 : Protocol = IP: DOD Internet Protocol
+ IP: ID = 0x100; Proto = UDP; Len: 328
+ UDP: IP Multicast: Src Port: BOOTP Client, (68); Dst Port: BOOTP
       Server (67); Length = 308 (0x134)
 DHCP: Request        (xid=08186BD1)
   DHCP: Op Code        (op)    = 1 (0x1)
   DHCP: Hardware Type   (htype) = 1 (0x1) 10Mb Ethernet
   DHCP: Hardware Address Length (hlen) = 6 (0x6)
   DHCP: Hops          (hops)  = 0 (0x0)
   DHCP: Transaction ID (xid)   = 135818193 (0x8186BD1)
   DHCP: Seconds        (secs)  = 0 (0x0)
   DHCP: Flags         (flags) = 0 (0x0)
     DHCP: 0.............. = No Broadcast
   DHCP: Client IP Address (ciaddr) = 0.0.0.0
   DHCP: Your   IP Address (yiaddr) = 0.0.0.0
   DHCP: Server IP Address (siaddr) = 0.0.0.0
   DHCP: Relay IP Address (giaddr) = 0.0.0.0
   DHCP: Client Ethernet Address (chaddr) = 00DD01075715
   DHCP: Server Host Name (sname) = <Blank>
   DHCP: Boot File Name  (file)  = <Blank>
   DHCP: Magic Cookie = [OK]
   DHCP: Option Field   (options)
     DHCP: DHCP Message Type   = DHCP Request
     DHCP: Client-identifier   = (Type: 1) 00 dd 01 07 57 15
     DHCP: Requested Address   = 172.16.112.13
     DHCP: Server Identifier   = 172.16.113.254
     DHCP: Host Name        = DAVEMAC4
     DHCP: Parameter Request List = (Length: 7) 01 0f 03 2c 2e 2f 06
     DHCP: End of this option field
```

The request is again broadcast, and the proposed IP address from the server is referenced. The request is broadcast for a reason—the client could have received more than one offer and, by broadcasting its request, it allows the other DHCP servers to see that it isn't going to use their offers.

Finally, the client acknowledges that it will accept the lease:

Time	Source IP	Dest IP	Prot	Description
0.061	172.16.113.254	172.16.112.13	DHCP	ACK (xid=08186BD1)

```
+ FRAME: Base frame properties
+ ETHERNET: ETYPE = 0x0800 : Protocol = IP: DOD Internet Protocol
+ IP: ID = 0xA06; Proto = UDP; Len: 576
+ UDP: Src Port: BOOTP Server, (67); Dst Port: BOOTP Client (68);
       Length = 556 (0x22C)
 DHCP: ACK         (xid=08186BD1)
   DHCP: Op Code        (op)   = 2 (0x2)
   DHCP: Hardware Type   (htype) = 1 (0x1) 10Mb Ethernet
   DHCP: Hardware Address Length (hlen) = 6 (0x6)
   DHCP: Hops          (hops)  = 0 (0x0)
   DHCP: Transaction ID  (xid)  = 135818193 (0x8186BD1)
   DHCP: Seconds        (secs)  = 0 (0x0)
   DHCP: Flags          (flags) = 0 (0x0)
     DHCP: 0.............. = No Broadcast
   DHCP: Client IP Address (ciaddr) = 0.0.0.0
   DHCP: Your  IP Address (yiaddr) = 172.16.112.13
   DHCP: Server IP Address (siaddr) = 0.0.0.0
   DHCP: Relay IP Address (giaddr) = 172.16.112.1
   DHCP: Client Ethernet Address (chaddr) = 00DD01075715
   DHCP: Server Host Name (sname) = <Blank>
   DHCP: Boot File Name  (file)  = <Blank>
   DHCP: Magic Cookie = [OK]
   DHCP: Option Field   (options)
     DHCP: DHCP Message Type   = DHCP ACK
     DHCP: Renewal Time Value (T1) = 1 Days, 12:00:00
     DHCP: Rebinding Time Value (T2) = 2 Days, 15:00:00
     DHCP: IP Address Lease Time = 3 Days, 0:00:00
     DHCP: Server Identifier   = 172.16.113.254
     DHCP: Subnet Mask       = 255.255.255.0
     DHCP: Domain Name       = (Length: 22) 63 73 77 61 74 63 70 2e 6d
           69 63 72 6f 73 6f 66 ...
     DHCP: Router          = 172.16.112.1
     DHCP: NetBIOS Name Service = 172.16.113.254
     DHCP: NetBIOS Node Type  = (Length: 1) 08
     DHCP: End of this option field
```

The acknowledgment is the final packet of the transaction, and it contains all of the configuration parameters that the client will use.

Lease Expiration and Renewal

DHCP-supplied configurations are "leased" from the server. Periodically, the client will contact the server to renew the lease. The protocol and implementation are very robust and configurable, and short-term server or network outages do not generally affect lease renewal. For example, DHCP clients start to try to renew their lease when 50 percent of the lease time has expired. Repeated attempts are made to contact the DHCP server and renew the lease, until 87.5 percent of the lease time has expired. At this point, the client attempts to get a new lease from any available DHCP server.

When a DHCP client is rebooted, it attempts to verify that the lease it holds is valid for the current subnet. If it is moved to another subnet and rebooted, the following sequence takes place:

Source	Destination	Source IP	Destination IP	Pro	Description
davemacp	*BROADCAST	0.0.0.0	255.255.255.255	DHCP	Request (xid=6E3A2E74)
router	*BROADCAST	10.57.8.1	255.255.255.255	DHCP	NACK (xid=6E3A2E74)
davemacp	*BROADCAST	0.0.0.0	255.255.255.255	DHCP	Discover (xid=51CA7FED)
router	davemacp	10.57.8.1	10.57.13.152	DHCP	Offer (xid=51CA7FED)
davemacp	*BROADCAST	0.0.0.0	255.255.255.255	DHCP	Request (xid=2081237D)
router	davemacp	10.57.8.1	10.57.13.152	DHCP	ACK (xid=2081237D)

In this example the portable computer "davemacp" is moved to a new subnet and re-started. It broadcasts a DHCP request for renewal of its old parameters, but the DHCP server responsible for the new subnet recognized that these were invalid for the subnet and NAK'd them. The DHCP client software automatically went through a normal discovery process to get reconfigured with parameters that are valid for the new location. For additional information on DHCP, see Chapter 7, "Managing Microsoft DHCP Servers."

Windows Internet Name Service

Windows Internet Name Service (WINS) is a NetBIOS name service as described in RFC 1001 and RFC 1002. When a Windows NT computer is configured as h-node (default for WINS clients), it attempts to use a WINS server for name registration and resolution first and, if that fails, it resorts to subnet broadcasts.

WINS Name Registration and Resolution

Using WINS for name services dramatically reduces the number of IP broadcasts used by Microsoft network clients. The following portion of a trace illustrates name registration and resolution traffic caused by starting a Windows NT workstation.

Source IP	Destination IP	Prot	Description
172.16.112.124	172.16.113.254	NBT	NS: MultiHomed Name Registration req. for DAVEMAC4<00>
172.16.113.254	172.16.112.124	NBT	NS: Registration resp. for DAVEMAC4<00>, Success
172.16.112.124	172.16.113.254	NBT	NS: Registration req. for DAVEMACD<00>
172.16.113.254	172.16.112.124	NBT	NS: Registration resp. for DAVEMACD<00>, Success
172.16.112.124	172.16.113.254	NBT	NS: Query req. for DAVEMACD<1C>
172.16.113.254	172.16.112.124	NBT	NS: Query resp. for DAVEMACD<1C>, Success
172.16.112.124	172.16.113.254	NBT	NS: MultiHomed Name Registration req. for DAVEMAC4<03>
172.16.113.254	172.16.112.124	NBT	NS: Registration resp. for DAVEMAC4<03>, Success

This trace shows that the starting client (172.16.112.124) sends a single name registration request to the WINS server, asking to register the computer name (DAVEMAC4<00>) as a unique name for a multihomed host. The WINS server responds affirmatively. Next, the domain name (DAVEMACD<00>) is registered as a group name. Then a name query is sent to the WINS server, requesting a list of domain controllers (who all register the <domain>[1C] name) so that a logon server can be contacted. One more registration is shown, for DAVEMAC4<03>, which is the name registered by the Messenger service. The fully parsed version of the domain name registration follows:

Source IP	Destination IP	Prot	Description
172.16.112.124	172.16.113.254	NBT	NS: Registration req. for DAVEMACD<00>

```
+ FRAME: Base frame properties
+ ETHERNET: ETYPE = 0x0800 : Protocol = IP: DOD Internet Protocol
+ IP: ID = 0x300; Proto = UDP; Len: 96
+ UDP: Src Port: NETBIOS Name Service, (137); Dst Port: NETBIOS Name
        Service (137); Length = 76 (0x4C)
 NBT: NS: Registration req. for DAVEMACD<00>
   NBT: Transaction ID = 32770 (0x8002)
   NBT: Flags Summary = 0x2900 - Req.; Registration; Success
     NBT: 0.............. = Request
     NBT: .0101.......... = Registration
     NBT: .....0......... = Non-authoritative Answer
     NBT: ......0........ = Datagram not truncated
     NBT: .......1....... = Recursion desired
     NBT: ........0...... = Recursion not available
     NBT: .........0..... = Reserved
     NBT: ..........0.... = Reserved
     NBT: ...........0... = Not a broadcast packet
     NBT: ............0000 = Success
   NBT: Question Count = 1 (0x1)
   NBT: Answer Count = 0 (0x0)
   NBT: Name Service Count = 0 (0x0)
   NBT: Additional Record Count = 1 (0x1)
   NBT: Question Name = DAVEMACD<00>
```

```
NBT: Question Type = General Name Service
NBT: Question Class = Internet Class
NBT: Resource Record Name = DAVEMACD<00>
NBT: Resource Record Type = NetBIOS General Name Service
NBT: Resource Record Class = Internet Class
NBT: Time To Live = 300000 (0x493E0)
NBT: RDATA Length = 6 (0x6)
NBT: Resource Record Flags = 57344 (0xE000)
  NBT: 1............... = Group NetBIOS Name
  NBT: .11............. = Reserved
  NBT: ...0000000000000 = Reserved
NBT: Owner IP Address = 172.16.112.13
```

Because the domain name is a group name, any number of hosts are allowed to register it.

WINS in a DHCP Environment

WINS is especially helpful on DHCP-enabled networks. One of the DHCP-provided parameters can be the address of a WINS server, and so as soon as the client is configured by DHCP, it registers its name(s) and address with the WINS server, and can then be easily located by the other computers on the network. This combination of DHCP and WINS is ideal for dynamic situations.

For additional information on WINS, see Chapter 8, "Managing Microsoft WINS Servers."

Domain Name System

Windows NT Server version 4.0 includes an RFC-compliant Domain Name System (DNS) server. DNS servers are defined in RFCs 1034 and 1035.

DNS is a global, distributed database based on a hierarchical naming system. The naming system was developed to provide a method for uniquely identifying hosts (computers and other network devices) on the Internet and other TCP/IP networks. The root of the DNS database is managed by the Internet Network Information Center. The top-level domains are assigned by organization and by country.

The DNS name consists of two parts—the domain name and the host name—known together as the fully qualified domain name (FQDN). For example, using the fictional domain name of Terra Flora, an FQDN for a workstation in the nursery division could be: jeff.nursery.terraflora.com. Note that the DNS name can actually be multi-part with each part of the name separated by a period (.).

DNS uses a client/server model. The DNS name server contains information about a portion of the global DNS name space, such as a private intranet. Client computers can be configured to query the DNS server for host name-to-IP-address mapping as needed to connect to the Internet or an intranet TCP/IP network resource.

Integration of Windows NT DNS and WINS Servers

The Windows NT–based DNS server provides connectivity between WINS and DNS. In addition to providing an RFC-compliant DNS service, the Windows NT Server-based DNS server can pass through an unresolved DNS name query to a WINS server for final name resolution.

This occurs transparently and the client need not be aware of whether a DNS or WINS server processed the name query. In a Windows NT–based network running both DNS and WINS servers, you can perform forward look-up—which is IP address resolution by using a friendly (NetBIOS or DNS) name, and reverse look-up—which is (NetBIOS or DNS) name resolution by using an IP address.

Dynamic WINS and Static DNS

WINS provides a dynamic, distributed database for registering and querying dynamic NetBIOS computer name-to-IP-address mappings. DNS provides a static, distributed database for registering and querying static FQDN name-to-IP-address mappings.

DNS depends on static files for name resolution and does not yet support dynamic updates of name and IP address mapping. In other words, DNS requires static configuration of IP addresses to perform name-to-IP-address mapping, WINS supports DHCP dynamic allocation of IP addresses and can resolve a NetBIOS computer name to a dynamic IP address mapping.

Note Dynamic DNS is currently under discussion by the Internet Engineering Task Force (IETF).

For information about installing a Microsoft DNS server, see online Help. For information about configuration of the DNS server and using the DNS Manager, see online DNS Manager Help.

Note Microsoft first included a Beta version of a DNS server for Windows NT 3.5x in the Windows NT 3.5x Resource Kits. You can upgrade the Beta version to Microsoft DNS server under Windows NT Server version 4.0. See the topic "To Upgrade a Windows NT 3.51 Resource Kit DNS Server" in Microsoft TCP/IP Help.

For additional information on DNS, see Chapter 9, "Managing Microsoft DNS Servers."

The Browser

The Browser service (not to be confused with a Web browser) was originally designed to be a simple workgroup enumeration tool, but has been enhanced significantly over time. The Browser service supports browsing computers on the network and being browsed by other computers.

It is the service that gathers and organizes the list of computers and domains that is displayed in **Network Neighborhood.** (You can also see the browse list by typing **net view** in the command window.) The Browser maintains an up-to-date list of computers and provides this information to programs that require it.

Note   Under Windows NT version 3.5*x*, use the File Manager **Connect Network Drive** dialog box to view the computer browser list.

Master Browser Elections

The Primary Domain Controller (PDC) for a domain always functions as the Domain Master Browser and is responsible for replicating the browse lists to all Master Browsers within the domain. A Master Browser is elected on each subnet within the domain.

Each domain has one Master Browser per subnet that contains computers listening for server announcements. The Master Browser maintains lists of available resources that can be requested by client computers.

As the number of hosts on a subnet grows, the Master Browser will start to replicate the browse list to Backup Browsers. If the Master Browser is shut down, an election takes place to determine the new Master Browser. Existing Backup Browsers have an advantage in the election. For this process, workgroups and domains function alike, except that all Windows NT Servers are either a Master Browser or Backup Browser, and Windows NT Workstation and Windows for Workgroups computers are not allowed to become Backup or Master browsers unless specifically configured.

Master Browser elections take place over the special <domain>[1E] NetBIOS name using subnet broadcasts (without using WINS). The election is fully automatic and takes into consideration a number of heuristics: operating system, version number, uptime, role (Workstation, Backup Domain Controller, Primary Domain Controller), etc. In general, the most robust computer on the network wins. Elections are forced when:

- A client cannot find its Master Browser at startup.
- A client detects that a Master Browser has disappeared.
- A Windows NT Server starts on the network.

Maintaining Browse Lists

File servers periodically (once every 12 minutes) announce their presence to the special <domain>[1D] NetBIOS name in an IP subnet broadcast. The Master Browser builds a list from these broadcasts. In addition, all Master Browsers register a group name \0x01\0x02__MSBROWSE__\0x02\0x01on the local subnet (not with WINS). Periodically the Master Browsers in the domains and workgroups announce their presence to this special name. Thus, in addition to the workgroup or domain membership lists, Master Browsers also maintain lists of other domains with their associated Master Browsers.

Requesting Browse Lists

When a browse request is made from a client, a "GetBackupListRequest" is sent to the <domain>[1D] name (the Master Browser) that returns a list of Browser servers for the local subnet. The "GetBackupListRequest" is also unicast to the Domain Master Browser, which handles the case in which the queried domain has no members on the subnet. The client Browser service selects three of the browsers from the list and stores them for future use. Then when further browsing is done, by calling the *NetServerEnum* API, one of the three saved names is contacted by the client.

When a client queries its workgroup or domain browser, it first gets back a list of all of the domains and workgroups that the browser has learned about through the \0x01\0x02__MSBROWSE__\0x02\0x01 name as well as the name of the Master Browser for each. When the user expands a domain or workgroup into a membership list, the client sends a request to <domain>[1D] to get to the list (this is translated to a local subnet broadcast by WINS). If this fails, it contacts the Master Browser for the particular domain or workgroup and fetches the membership list.

The Domain Master Browser

As mentioned earlier, the PDC always acts as the Domain Master Browser. Because each locally-elected Master Browser will only hear local membership announcements, there needs to be a mechanism to consolidate all of the members into a single list. This is the role of the Domain Master Browser.

Periodically, all of the locally-elected Master Browsers contact the PDC and replicate their membership lists to it. The PDC merges the list with the "master" list for the whole domain and replicates the master list back down.

The replication algorithm is "smart" in that the local Master Browsers only replicate the members that they have learned about locally to the domain master. This whole mechanism allows members in a domain to span subnets and, for all clients (eventually), to be able to get complete membership lists.

On WINS-enabled networks, the browser code in Windows NT versions 4.0 and 3.5x periodically connects to WINS and learns all of the computers that have registered any <domain>[1B] names. The Browser then does a GetDCName() on each of the <domain>[1B] names (followed by an attempt on <domain>[1C]), and adds the <domain name> <master browser name> to its domain/workgroup list. This allows members of one domain to locate the Master Browser for another domain even when it is on another subnet and the two domains have no "broadcast area" in common.

Browsing for Other Windows-based Computers

Browser code for Windows for Workgroups computers has been enhanced several times to reduce the dependency on having a BDC per subnet. The updated files are available from **ftp.microsoft.com**. Windows 95 computers also contain enhanced browsing code.

Windows NT Workstation and Windows NT Server Services

The Workstation and Server services are used for file and print sharing. Both use NetBIOS over TCP/IP to communicate with each other; however, they are not NetBIOS programs. They are written to talk directly to NetBT over the TDI interface. Being direct TDI clients, they are high performance and *not* subject to limitations of the NetBIOS interface, such as the 254 session limit. The Server Message Block (SMB) protocol is used to send commands and responses between clients and servers. Public SMB specifications are available from **ftp.microsoft.com**.

Logging On

When a user logs on to a Windows NT domain, the following sequence of events occurs:

1. If the computer is WINS-enabled, a name query for the NetBIOS <domain>[1C] name is sent to the WINS server.

2. The WINS server responds with a list of up to 25 IP addresses corresponding to domain controllers for the specified domain name. One of the IP addresses in the list will always be the Primary Domain Controller.

3. A \MAILSLOT\NET\NTLOGON request is broadcast on the local subnet. If a response to the local subnet broadcast is received, then the logon process contacts the responding domain controller to attempt a logon.

4. Otherwise, the logon process sends a directed datagram to each of the addresses returned in the list from the WINS server, and attempts to log on to the first domain controller to respond.

5. All domain controllers register this <domain>[1C] name on the network, typically with the WINS database. All password information is encrypted before being transmitted on the network.

Connecting to Network Resources

When a workstation attempts to connect to a shared resource on the network, the resource is "called" by its NetBIOS name. The name-to-IP-address resolution is done in the manner illustrated in the NetBIOS Name Resolution Flowchart (Figures 6.5 through 6.7) in the section "NetBIOS Interface" earlier in this chapter.

Once the IP address of the target host is known, a standard TCP/IP connection is set up, and a NetBIOS session is established over that connection. The user is authenticated using encrypted passwords, and then client/server messages are exchanged using the SMB protocol. The workstation and server use sophisticated caching mechanisms to reduce network traffic and provide high performance. When WINS is used, there is no reliance on IP broadcasts, with the single exception of ARPs.

Optimizations

The Windows NT Workstation and Windows NT Server services were designed with many optimizations to minimize network traffic and maximize throughput. The network redirector works closely with the Windows NT Cache Manager to provide read-ahead caching, write-behind caching, and search caching. Various file locking schemes, such as opportunistic locking and local file lock optimization, help to reduce network traffic. The SMB protocol which is used supports compound commands and responses, such as *LockAndRead* and *WriteAndUnlock*.

Microsoft Remote Access Service

Windows NT Remote Access Service (RAS) is a networking service that connects remote or mobile workers to corporate networks. RAS uses the following remote access protocols for RAS server and client services:

- Point-to-Point Protocol (PPP)
- Serial Line IP (SLIP)
- Microsoft RAS Protocol (asynchronous NetBEUI)

Note   Remote access protocols control the transmission of data over wide area networks (WANs). Protocols such as TCP/IP, IPX, and NetBEUI are considered local area network (LAN) protocols. The focus of this chapter is TCP/IP; for detailed information about RAS and the other LAN protocols, see the *Networking Supplement* for Windows NT Server version 4.0.

RAS Servers

RAS servers act as a "proxy" for TCP/IP clients. RAS servers use proxy ARP to respond to ARP requests from dial-up networking clients and also set up the network host routes to each dial-up client. RAS servers may obtain configuration parameters for their clients from a DHCP server, and then use PPP IPCP (Internet Protocol Control Protocol), as defined in RFC 1332, to dynamically configure their clients with these parameters over the RAS link.

When a RAS server is configured to use DHCP to obtain TCP/IP configuration parameters for its clients, a pool of leased addresses is obtained from the DHCP server and managed locally by the RAS server. If more addresses are needed, or leases need to be renewed, the RAS server will contact the DHCP server; however, it does not check with the DHCP server each time a dial-up networking client starts. If the RAS server is moved to another subnet, it may have a pool of leases that are not valid for the new subnet still stored in the registry until they expire.

Dial-up Clients

RAS clients using TCP/IP can be configured to use the default gateway on the remote network while they are connected to a RAS server. This default gateway overrides any local network default gateway while the RAS connection is established. The override is accomplished by manipulating the IP route table. Any local routes, including the default gateway, get their metric (hop count) incremented by one, and a default route with a metric of 1 hop is dynamically added for the duration of the connection. One-hop routes are also added for the IP multicast address (224.0.0.0), for the local WAN interface, and for the network that the PPP server is attached to.

This can present a problem connecting to resources by using the local network default gateway, unless static routes are added at the client. The following are sample route tables for a computer running Windows NT Workstation or Windows NT Server before and after connecting to a remote network using PPP.

Route table before dialing a PPP Internet provider:

Network Address	Netmask	Gateway Address	Interface	Metric
0.0.0.0	0.0.0.0	172.16.112.1	172.16.112.11	1
127.0.0.0	255.0.0.0	127.0.0.1	127.0.0.1	1
172.16.112.0	255.255.255.0	172.16.112.11	172.16.112.11	1
172.16.112.11	255.255.255.255	127.0.0.1	127.0.0.1	1
172.16.112.255	255.255.255.255	172.16.112.11	172.16.112.11	1
224.0.0.0	224.0.0.0	172.16.112.11	172.16.112.11	1
255.255.255.255	255.255.255.255	172.16.112.11	172.16.112.11	1

Route table after dialing a PPP Internet provider:

Network Address	Netmask	Gateway Address	Interface	Metric
0.0.0.0	0.0.0.0	172.16.112.1	172.16.112.11	2
0.0.0.0	0.0.0.0	172.16.16.243	172.16.16.243	1
127.0.0.0	255.0.0.0	127.0.0.1	127.0.0.1	1
172.16.112.0	255.255.255.0	172.16.112.11	172.16.112.11	2
172.16.112.11	255.255.255.255	127.0.0.1	127.0.0.1	1
172.16.112.255	255.255.255.255	172.16.112.11	172.16.112.11	1
204.182.66.0	255.255.255.0	172.16.16.243	172.16.16.243	1
172.16.16.243	255.255.255.255	127.0.0.1	127.0.0.1	1
224.0.0.0	224.0.0.0	172.16.16.243	172.16.16.243	1
224.0.0.0	224.0.0.0	172.16.112.11	172.16.112.11	1
255.255.255.255	255.255.255.255	172.16.112.11	172.16.112.11	1

Secure Internet Transport with TCP/IP and PPTP

Windows NT-based RAS is based on PPP, the industry-standard for dial-up access services and includes industry-standards for authentication and encryption. PPTP, which is used to create virtual private networks (VPNs), uses PPP to provide compressed and encrypted RAS communication. PPTP technology enables RAS user access to private networks by using the Internet instead of long distance telephone lines (thus reducing transmission costs). RAS users can use PPTP over the Internet by either:

- Connecting directly to the Internet
- Dialing into an Internet Service Provider (ISP)

PPTP provides multi-protocol support for IP, IPX, and NetBEUI protocols. For example, RAS clients using PPTP and the Internet (as a network backbone) can send and receive IPX and NetBEUI packets.

Note Because the Internet is a TCP/IP-based network, you must install and bind TCP/IP to the network card that will be used for RAS and PPTP communications. To select the network card (adapter) and to enable PPTP filtering, open the **Microsoft TCP/IP Properties** page, and click **Advanced** to open the **Advanced TCP/IP Properties** page. For specific instructions, see online Help.

The following figure illustrates the implementation of PPTP. Note that after processing a packet (from an IP, IPX, or NetBEUI transport), PPTP sends the packet to the top of the TCP/IP protocol stack. The TCP/IP protocol stack then sends the packet across the Internet. (At the receiving end of a packet transmission, the PPTP packet must be decoded by another PPTP service.)

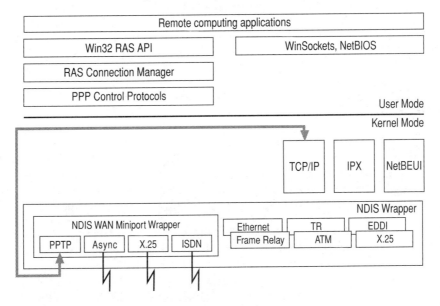

Figure 6.8   Using RAS with PPTP and TCP/IP

For detailed information about PPTP, see the chapter "Point-to-Point Tunneling Protocol" in the *Networking Supplement* for Windows NT Server version 4.0.

Bandwidth Considerations

By default, RAS uses effective compression methods to increase the amount of data that can be pumped over a serial link. Bandwidth planning is important when designing and installing computers and services using RAS. As a rule of thumb, transfer rates can be estimated using the 10-bit byte to allow for protocol and timing overhead. For example, 9600 BPS (without compression) is approximately 1 Kbyte/second, 60Kbytes/minute, and 3.5Mbytes/hour. If the data being transferred compresses fairly well, 5-8 Mbytes per hour throughput might be expected. While this may be an adequate rate for a single workstation, it probably is not feasible as an inter-site link for most programs. ISDN (128Kbits/second or 45 Mbytes/hour, not including compression) might be more realistic. ISDN service in the United States has recently become more available and economical to install and use.

Simple Network Management Protocol

The Simple Network Management Protocol (SNMP) agent in Windows NT provides some programmatic access to the TCP/IP protocol stack and can be used to get information about the performance and usage of network components. The SNMP agent supports network management programs provided by Microsoft and third-party vendors. For more information about SNMP, see Chapter 11, "Using SNMP for Network Management," and Appendix C, "MIB Object Types for Windows NT." For information about installing and configuring SNMP, see Microsoft TCP/IP Help.

TCP/IP Printing

Line printer (LPR) is one of the network protocols and utilities of the TCP/IP protocol suite and is defined in RFC 1179. LPR provides a standard for transmitting TCP/IP print jobs between computers. With the LPR protocol, a client can send a print job to a print spooler service on another computer running the print spooler service known as line-printer daemon (LPD).

Windows NT provides both the LPR and LPD services for TCP/IP printing. In general, Windows NT supports TCP/IP printing as documented in RFC 1179. However, because RFC 1179 describes an existing print server protocol that is widely used on the Internet, but which is not an Internet standard, changes to printing under Windows NT 4.0 is somewhat different than printing described in RFC 1179. The following TCP/IP print enhancements were added to Windows NT version 4.0.

- Support for multiple data files per control file
- When used in "print through" mode as an intermediate spooler, the host name parameter is passed through the Windows printing subsystem
- LPR jobs are sourced from any reserved port between 512 and 1023

Note Under Windows NT version 3.5x, all TCP/IP print jobs *sent from* a Windows NT computer were sourced from TCP ports 721 through 731, and, if many jobs were sent in quick succession, the ports could be "used up," causing a pause in printing until one of them passed through the TCP TIME_WAIT state.

Microsoft Internet Information Server

Internet Information Server (IIS) is a powerful Web, FTP, and GOPHER server designed specifically for Windows NT. It uses a worker thread model (as opposed to a "thread per client" model) to provide the ability to service an extremely large number of connections with high performance. It also takes advantage of the new performance-boosting Microsoft Internet API set, which includes calls such as TransmitFile() and AcceptEx().

All three services run from within the same process (inetinfo.exe) and share resources such as worker threads and cached file handles. IIS has configurable logging that supports both text files and logging directly to a database by using ODBC. IIS also supports the use of sophisticated databases on the "backend" so that access to a database can be achieved by using a standard Web browser. In many cases a database is easier to maintain than a large number of static HTML files.

IIS ships with Windows NT Server 4.0, and versions for Windows NT Server 3.51 are available from **www.microsoft.com**. Microsoft Internet Information Server is not designed (or licensed) to run on Windows NT Workstation. More details are available from the Microsoft Web site.

Summary of Changes

As a convenient reference, the following sections list recent changes in Microsoft 32-bit TCP/IP for Windows NT.

Service Enhancements

- Domain Name System (DNS) server (added in Windows NT 4.0)
- NetBT and DNS Enhancements (added in Windows NT 4.0)
- Nslookup utility added to TCP/IP utilities for troubleshooting DNS (added in Windows NT 4.0)
- MPR (Multi-Protocol Router) support (added in Windows NT 3.51 Service Pack 2)
- TCP/IP printing support enhancements (added in Windows NT 4.0)
- Point-to-Point Tunneling Protocol enhancement (added in Windows NT 4.0)

Additional or Changed TCP/IP Registry Parameters

- **Afd.sys** Registry Key
- **IgnorePushBitOnReceives** (changed in Windows NT 4.0 and Windows NT 3.51 Service Pack 5)
- **ArpCacheLife** (new in Windows NT 4.0 and Windows NT 3.51 Service Pack 4)
- **ArpTRSingleRoute** (new in Windows NT 4.0 and Windows NT 3.51 Service Pack 5)
- **DefaultTTL** for IP changed from 32 to 128 (changed in Windows NT 4.0)
- **EnableSecurityFilters** (new in Windows NT 4.0)
- **MaxForwardBufferMemory** (new in Windows NT 3.51 Service Pack 2)
- **MaxForwardPending** (new in Windows NT 3.51 Service Pack 2)
- **MaxNumForwardPackets** (new in Windows NT 3.51 Service Pack 2)
- **MaxUserPort** (new in Windows NT 4.0 and Windows NT 3.51 Service Pack 5)
- **PersistentRoutes** (The primary route metric is added as the fourth parameter in the **PersistentRoutes** key; new in Windows NT 3.51 Service Pack 2)
- **RawIpAllowedProtocols** (new in Windows NT 4.0)
- **TcpAllowedPorts** (new in Windows NT 4.0)
- **TcpTimedWaitDelay** (new in Windows NT 4.0 and Windows NT 3.51 Service Pack 5)
- **UdpAllowedPorts** (new in Windows NT 4.0)

C H A P T E R   7

Managing Microsoft DHCP Servers

Dynamic Host Configuration Protocol (DHCP) is an open, industry standard that is designed to reduce the complexity of Transmission Control Protocol/Internet Protocol (TCP/IP) network administration. DHCP specifies methods for simplified and dynamic configuration of computers on TCP/IP networks, and reduces the administrative burden of adding, moving, and configuring computers on TCP/IP networks.

DHCP is specified by Internet Engineering Task Force (IETF) Requests for Comments (RFCs) 1533, 1534, 1541, and 1542.

The information in this chapter is intended for network administrators and support personnel who need to manage and support Microsoft DHCP servers. This chapter includes the following topics:

- Introduction to Dynamic Host Configuration Protocol (DHCP)
    - Microsoft DHCP server
    - DHCP clients
    - DHCP/BOOTP relay agents
- Planning for Microsoft DHCP server implementation
    - Planning for small networks
    - Planning for routed networks
    - Planning for DHCP server and client traffic
    - Setting local policies
    - Partitioning the Microsoft DHCP server address pool
    - Using Microsoft DHCP with Domain Name System (DNS) servers
- Using DHCP Manager
- Managing the DHCP server database
- Troubleshooting DHCP services

Introduction to Dynamic Host Configuration Protocol

Every computer on a TCP/IP internetwork must be given a unique computer name and IP address. The IP address identifies both the computer and the subnetwork to which it is attached. When the computer is moved to a different subnetwork, the IP address must be changed to reflect the new subnetwork ID.

DHCP is designed to reduce the complexity of configuring computers for TCP/IP networks. RFC 1541 specifies two major components needed for DHCP services: a protocol for communicating TCP/IP configuration parameters between a DHCP server and a DHCP client, and a method for allocating IP addresses to the DHCP client.

Understanding IP Addresses

To receive and deliver packets successfully between computers, TCP/IP requires that three values be provided by the network administrator: an IP address, a subnet mask, and a default gateway (router).

IP Addresses

Every device attached to a TCP/IP network is identified by a unique *IP address*. (If a computer has multiple network adapters, each adapter will have its own IP address.) This address is typically represented in dotted-decimal notation—that is, with the decimal value of each octet (8 bits, or 1 byte) of the address separated by a period. The following is a sample IP address:

```
172.16.48.1
```

Important Because IP addresses identify devices on a network, each device on the network must be assigned a unique IP address.

Network ID and Host ID

Although an IP address is a single value, it contains two pieces of information: the network ID and the host ID of your computer.

- The *network ID* identifies the systems that are located on the same physical network. All systems on the same physical network must have the same network ID, and the network ID must be unique to the internetwork.

- The *host ID* identifies a workstation, server, router, or other TCP/IP device within a network. The address for each device must be unique to the network ID.

A computer connected to a TCP/IP network uses the network ID and host ID to determine which packets it should receive or ignore and to determine the scope of its transmissions. (Only computers with the same network ID accept each other's IP-level broadcast messages.)

Note Networks that connect to the public Internet must obtain an official network ID from the Internet Network Information Center (InterNIC) to guarantee the uniqueness of the IP network ID. For more information, visit the InterNIC home page on the Internet at **http://www.internic.net/**

After receiving a network ID, the local network administrator must assign unique host IDs for computers within the local network. Although private networks not connected to the Internet can use their own network identifier, obtaining a valid network ID from InterNIC allows a private network to connect to the Internet in the future without reassigning addresses.

The Internet community has defined address *classes* to accommodate networks of varying sizes. The address class can be discerned from the first octet of an IP address. Table 7.1 summarizes the relationship between the first octet of a given address and its network ID and host ID fields. It also identifies the total number of network IDs and host IDs for each address class that participates in the Internet addressing scheme. The example in Table 7.1 uses w.x.y.z to designate the bytes of the IP address.

Table 7.1   IP Address Classes

Class	w values [1,2]	Network ID	Host ID	Available networks	Available hosts per network
A	1–126	w	x.y.z	126	16,777,214
B	128–191	w.x	y.z	16,384	65,534
C	192–223	w.x.y	z	2,097,151	254

[1] Inclusive range for the first octet in the IP address.

[2] The address 127 is reserved for loopback testing and interprocess communication on the local computer; it is not a valid network address. Addresses 224 and above are reserved for special protocols (Internet Group Management Protocol multicast and others), and cannot be used as host addresses.

Subnet Masks

Subnet masks are 32-bit values that allow the recipient of IP packets to distinguish the network ID portion of the IP address from the host ID. Subnet masks are created by assigning 1s to network ID bits and 0s to host ID bits. The 32-bit value is then converted to dotted-decimal notation, as shown in Table 7.2.

Table 7.2   Default Subnet Masks for Standard IP Address Classes

Address class	Bits for subnet mask	Subnet mask
Class A	11111111 00000000 00000000 00000000	255.0.0.0
Class B	11111111 11111111 00000000 00000000	255.255.0.0
Class C	11111111 11111111 11111111 00000000	255.255.255.0

For example, when the IP address is 172.16.16.1 and the subnet mask is 255.255.0.0, the network ID is 172.16 and the host ID is 16.1.

Because the class of a host is easily determined, configuring a host with a subnet mask might seem redundant. But subnet masks are also used to further segment an assigned network ID among several local networks. Sometimes only *portions* of an octet need to be segmented, using only a few bits to specify subnet IDs.

Important To prevent addressing and routing problems, all computers on a logical network must use the same subnet mask and network ID.

Microsoft DHCP Server

Microsoft DHCP server provides a reliable and flexible alternative to manual TCP/IP configuration. Microsoft DHCP server includes a graphical administrative tool—DHCP Manager—that allows you to define DHCP client configurations, and a database for managing assignment of client IP addresses and other optional TCP/IP configuration parameters.

You can use Microsoft DHCP server to automatically and dynamically assign TCP/IP configuration parameters to computers that start on the network. TCP/IP configuration parameters that can be dynamically assigned by a Microsoft DHCP server include:

- IP addresses for each network adapter card in a computer.
- Subnet masks that identify the portion of an IP address that is the physical segment (subnet) network identifier.
- Default gateway (router) that connects the subnet to other network segments.
- Additional configuration parameters that can be optionally assigned to DHCP clients, such as domain name.

A Microsoft DHCP server database is automatically created when the Microsoft DHCP server is installed on a computer running Windows NT Server and the TCP/IP protocol. You add data to the DHCP server database by defining DHCP scopes and DHCP options when using DHCP Manager.

DHCP Scopes

A DHCP scope is an administrative grouping that identifies the configuration parameters for all DHCP clients grouped together on a physical subnet. The scope must be defined before DHCP clients can use the DHCP server for dynamic TCP/IP configuration.

To create a DHCP scope, you must use DHCP Manager to enter the following required information:

- Scope name assigned by the administrator when the scope is created
- Unique subnet mask used to identify the subnet to which an IP address belongs
- Range of IP addresses contained within the scope
- Time interval (known as lease duration) that specifies how long a DHCP client can use an assigned IP address before it must renew its configuration with the DHCP server

---

Note   Each subnet can have only one scope with a single continuous range of IP addresses. To use several address ranges within a scope, create a continuous range that encompasses all of the address ranges; then manually exclude the addresses that fall between the specific address ranges. See the section "Using DHCP Manager" later in this chapter for additional information.

In addition to the required DHCP scope information, you can define individual scope options by using DHCP Manager. The following table lists additional scope options:

Table 7.3   Additional Scope Options

Option	Description
Deactivate	You can release an IP address if a computer is removed from a network.
Renewal	You can change the renewal period for IP-address leases. By installation default, DHCP clients begin the renewal process when 50 percent of the IP address lease time has expired.
Reserve	You can reserve a specific IP address for a DHCP client, such as an Internet Information Server or WINS server. An IP address can also be reserved if a computer on the network is not DHCP-enabled. Also, for TCP/IP security, computers designated as network firewalls are configured with reserved IP addresses.

DHCP Options

Other options, known as DHCP options, can also be configured on the DHCP server by using DHCP Manager. In addition to defining the required DHCP Scope configuration parameters, you can use Microsoft DHCP server to automatically assign advanced TCP/IP configuration options, such as a Windows Internet Name Service (WINS) server and a Domain Name System (DNS) server, to DHCP clients. To do this, you select one or more DHCP options when using DHCP Manager.

Microsoft DHCP options can be selected and assigned to a selected scope or to all scopes by clicking either **Scope** or **Global** on the **DHCP Options** menu. When using DHCP options, keep in mind the following guidelines:

- Active global options always apply unless overridden by Scope options or by manual configuration of a DHCP client.

- Active options for a scope apply to all computers in that scope, unless overridden by manual configuration of a DHCP client.

Microsoft DHCP server provides the ability to configure many standard DHCP options as defined by RFC 1541. The following table lists the standard DHCP options available when using Microsoft DHCP server.

Note You can use Microsoft DHCP server to set any of the options described in this table. However, Windows-based and Windows NT-based DHCP clients support only the options whose code and option name are listed in bold type. (If you use Microsoft DHCP server to administer third-party DHCP clients, you can use any option listed in this table that is supported on the third-party DHCP client.)

Table 7.4   Default DHCP Options as Defined by RFC 1541

Code	Option name	Meaning
0	Pad	Causes subsequent fields to align on word boundaries.
255	End	Indicates end of options in the DHCP packet.
1	**Subnet mask**	Specifies the subnet mask of the client subnet. This option is defined in the DHCP Manager **Create Scope** or **Scope Properties** dialog box. It cannot be set directly in the **DHCP Options** dialog box.
2	Time offset	Specifies the Universal Coordinated Time (UCT) offset in seconds.
3	**Router**	Specifies a list of IP addresses for routers on the client's subnet.[1]

Table 7.4   Default DHCP Options as Defined by RFC 1541 *(continued)*

Code	Option name	Meaning
4	Time server	Specifies a list of IP addresses for time servers available to the client.[1]
5	Name servers	Specifies a list of IP addresses for name servers available to the client.[1]
6	**DNS servers**	Specifies a list of IP addresses for DNS name servers available to the client.[1] Multihomed computers can have only one list per computer, not one per adapter card.
7	Log servers	Specifies a list of IP addresses for MIT_LCS User Datagram Protocol (UDP) log servers available to the client. [1]
8	Cookie servers	Specifies a list of IP addresses for RFC 865 cookie servers available to the client. [1]
9	LPR servers	Specifies a list of IP addresses for RFC 1179 line-printer servers available to the client. [1]
10	Impress servers	Specifies a list of IP addresses for Imagen Impress servers available to the client. [1]
11	Resource Location servers	Specifies a list of RFC 887 Resource Location servers available to the client. [1]
12	Host name	Specifies the host name of up to 63 characters for the client. The name must start with a letter, end with a letter or digit, and have as interior characters only letters, numbers, and hyphens. The name can be qualified with the local DNS domain name.
13	Boot file size	Specifies the size of the default boot image file for the client, in 512-octet blocks.
14	Merit dump file	Specifies the file and directory where the client's core image is dumped if a crash occurs.
15	**Domain name**	Specifies the DNS domain name that the client should use for DNS host name resolution.
16	Swap server	Specifies the IP address of the client's swap server.
17	Root path	Specifies the ASCII path for the client's root disk.
18	Extensions path	Specifies a file that can be retrieved by using Trivial File Transfer Protocol (TFTP). This file contains information interpreted the same as the vendor-extension field in the BOOTP response, except that the file length is unconstrained and references to Tag 18 in the file are ignored.
19	IP layer forwarding	Enables or disables forwarding of IP packet for this client. 1 enables forwarding; 0 disables it.

Table 7.4   Default DHCP Options as Defined by RFC 1541 *(continued)*

Code	Option name	Meaning
20	Nonlocal source routing	Enables or disables forwarding of datagrams with non-local source routes. 1 enables forwarding; 0 disables it.
21	Policy filter masks	Specifies policy filters that consist of a list of pairs of IP addresses and masks specifying destination/mask pairs for filtering nonlocal source routes. Any source-routed datagram whose next-hop address does not match a filter will be discarded by the client.
22	Max DG reassembly size	Specifies the maximum size datagram that the client can reassemble. The minimum value is 576.
23	Default time-to-live	Specifies the default time-to-live (TTL) that the client uses on outgoing datagrams. The value for the octet is a number between 1 and 255.
24	Path MTU aging timeout	Specifies the timeout in seconds for aging Path Maximum Transmission Unit (MTU) values (discovered by the mechanism defined in RFC 1191).
25	Path MTU plateau table	Specifies a table of MTU sizes to use when performing Path MTU Discovered as defined in RFC 1191. The table is sorted by size from smallest to largest. The minimum MTU value is 68.
26	MTU option	Specifies the MTU discovery size for this interface. The minimum MTU value is 68.
27	All subnets are local	Specifies whether the client assumes that all subnets of the client's internetwork use the same MTU as the local subnet where the client is connected. 1 indicates that all subnets share the same MTU; 0 indicates that the client should assume some subnets might have smaller MTUs.
28	Broadcast address	Specifies the broadcast address used on the client's subnet.
29	Perform mask discovery	Specifies whether the client should use Internet Control Message Protocol (ICMP) for subnet mask discovery. 1 indicates that the client should perform mask discovery; 0 indicates that the client should not.
30	Mask supplier	Specifies whether the client should respond to subnet mask requests using ICMP. 1 indicates that the client should respond; 0 indicates that the client should not respond.
31	Perform router discovery	Specifies whether the client should solicit routers using the router discovery method specified in RFC 1256. 1 indicates that the client should perform router discovery; 0 indicates that the client should not use it.

Table 7.4   Default DHCP Options as Defined by RFC 1541 *(continued)*

Code	Option name	Meaning
32	Router solicitation address	Specifies the IP address to which the client submits router solicitation requests.
33	Static route	Specifies a list of IP address pairs that indicate the static routes the client should install in its routing cache. Any multiple routes to the same destination are listed in descending order or priority. The routes are destination/router address pairs. (The default route of 0.0.0.0 is an illegal destination for a static route.)
34	Trailer encapsulation	Specifies whether the client should negotiate use of trailers (RFC 983) when using the Address Resolution Protocol (ARP). 1 indicates that the client should attempt to use trailers; 0 indicates that the client should not use trailers.
35	ARP cache timeout	Specifies the timeout in seconds for ARP cache entries.
36	Ethernet encapsulation	Specifies whether the client should use Ethernet (as specified by RFC 894) or IEEE 802.3 (RFC 1042) encapsulation if the interface is Ethernet. 1 indicates that the client should use RFC 1042 encapsulation; 0 indicates that the client should use RFC 894 encapsulation.
37	Default time-to-live	Specifies the default TTL that the client should use when sending TCP segments. The minimum value of the octet is 1.
38	Keepalive interval	Specifies the interval in seconds that the client TCP should wait before sending a keepalive message on a TCP connection. A value of 0 indicates that the client should not send keepalive messages on connections unless specifically requested by an application.
39	Keepalive garbage	Specifies whether the client should send TCP keepalive messages with an octet of garbage data for compatibility with older implementations. 1 indicates that a garbage octet should be sent; 0 indicates that it should not be sent.
40	NIS domain name	Specifies the name of the Network Information Service (NIS) domain as an ASCII string.
41	NIS servers	Specifies a list of IP addresses for NIS servers available to the client.[1]
42	NTP servers	Specifies a list of IP addresses for Network Time Protocol (NTP) servers available to the client.[1]

Table 7.4   Default DHCP Options as Defined by RFC 1541 (*continued*)

Code	Option name	Meaning
43	Vendor-specific information	Binary information used by clients and servers to exchange vendor-specific information. Servers not equipped to interpret the information ignore it. Clients that don't receive the information attempt to operate without it.
44	**WINS/NBNS servers**	Specifies a list of IP addresses for NetBIOS name servers (NBNS).[1]
45	NetBIOS over TCP/IP NBDD	Specifies a list of IP addresses for NetBIOS datagram distribution servers (NBDD).[1]
46	**WINS/NBT node type**	Allows configurable NetBIOS over TCP/IP (NetBT) clients to be configured as described in RFC 1001/1002, where 1 = b-node, 2 = p-node, 4 = m-node, and 8 = h-node. On multihomed computers, the node type is assigned to the entire computer, not to individual adapter cards.
47	**NetBIOS scope ID**	Specifies a text string that is the NetBIOS over TCP/IP Scope ID for the client, as specified in RFC 1001/1002. On multihomed computers, the scope ID is assigned to the entire computer, not to individual adapter cards.
48	X Window system font	Specifies a list of IP addresses for X Window font servers available to the client.[1]
49	X Window system display	Specifies a list of IP addresses for X Window System Display Manager servers available to the client.[1]
51	**Lease time**	Specifies the time in seconds from address assignment until the client's lease on the address expires. Lease time is specified in the DHCP Manager **Create Scope** or **Scope Properties** dialog box. It cannot be set directly in the **DHCP Options** dialog box.
58	**Renewal (T1) time value**	Specifies the time in seconds from address assignment until the client enters the renewing state. Renewal time is a function of the lease time option, which is specified in the DHCP Manager **Create Scope** or **Scope Properties** dialog box. It cannot be set directly in the **DHCP Options** dialog box.
59	**Rebinding (T2) time value**	Specifies the time in seconds from address assignment until the client enters the rebinding state. Rebinding time is a function of the lease time option, which is specified in the DHCP Manager **Create Scope** or **Scope Properties** dialog box. It cannot be set directly in the **DHCP Options** dialog box.

Table 7.4   Default DHCP Options as Defined by RFC 1541 *(continued)*

Code	Option name	Meaning
64	NIS + Domain Name	Network Information Service (previously known as Yellow Pages) domain name.
65	NIS + Servers	Network Information Service (previously known as Yellow Pages) server name.
66	Boot Server Host Name	Identifies a Trivial File Transfer Protocol (TFTP) server.
67	Bootfile Name	Identifies the file that is to be used as the bootfile.
68	Mobile IP Home Agents	Can be used to list (in order of preference) IP addresses that identify mobile IP home agents.

[1] List is specified in order of preference.

Boldface type indicates those options that Windows-based and Windows NT-based clients support

The Microsoft DHCP network packet allocates 312 bytes for DHCP options. This is more than enough space for most option configurations. With some DHCP servers and clients, you can allocate unused space in the DHCP packet to additional options. This feature, called *option overlay,* is not supported by Microsoft DHCP server or client. If you attempt to use more than 312 bytes, some options settings will be lost. In that case, you should delete any unused or low-priority options.

Tip   If you are using Microsoft DHCP server to configure computers that should use the services of a WINS server, be sure to use option #44, WINS Servers, and option #46, Node Type. These DHCP options automatically configure the DHCP client as an h-node computer that directly contacts WINS servers for name registration and name query instead of using broadcasts (b-node.)

You can also add custom parameters to be included with DHCP client configuration information and change values or other elements of the predefined DHCP options, as needed.

DHCP Clients

To configure a computer running Windows NT Server or Windows NT Workstation as a DHCP client, select the **Obtain an IP address from a DHCP server** check box on the **IP Address** tab of the **Microsoft TCP/IP Properties** page. A DHCP server can also be used to configure computers running under following operating systems:

- Windows 95
- Windows for Workgroups version 3.11 with the Microsoft 32-bit TCP/IP VxD installed
- Microsoft–Network Client version 3.0 for MS-DOS with the real-mode TCP/IP driver installed
- LAN Manager version 2.2c

Table 7.5 describes the basic TCP/IP configuration parameters that a DHCP server must provide to DHCP clients.

Table 7.5   Required TCP/IP Configuration Parameters for DHCP Clients

Basic TCP/IP configuration parameters	Description
IP address	Every device attached to a TCP/IP network is identified by a unique IP address. (If the computer has multiple network adapter cards, it will require multiple IP addresses.) The IP address is a numeric identifier comprised of four 8-bit octets separated by periods. (This number is generally shown in dotted-decimal notation, for example, 172.16.32.1) The IP address is actually two parts: the first part represents a network ID and the second part represents a host (computer) ID.
Subnet mask	Used to identify the part of the unique IP address that is the network identifier and the part that is the host identifier. Subnet masks are created by assigning 1s to network ID bits and 0s to the host ID bits of the IP address.
Default gateway	The computer (router) connected to the local subnet and other subnets that is used to pass IP packets from one subnet to another. (A default gateway is required only when the client is located on a routed TCP/IP network.)

Initial DHCP Client Configuration

When a DHCP client computer is started on a TCP/IP network, it communicates with a DHCP server to get its TCP/IP configuration information. The following table describes the DHCP message types exchanged between client and server.

Table 7.6   DHCP Message Types

Message type	Description
Dhcpdiscover	The first time a DHCP client computer attempts to start on the network, it requests IP address information from a DHCP server by broadcasting a Dhcpdiscover packet. The source IP address in the packet is 0.0.0.0 because the client does not yet have an IP address.
Dhcpoffer	When the DHCP server receives the request, it selects an unleased IP address from the range of available IP addresses and offers it to the DHCP client. In most cases, the DHCP server also returns additional TCP/IP configuration information, such as the subnet mask and default gateway in a Dhcpoffer packet. More than one DHCP server can respond with a Dhcpoffer packet, and the client accepts the first Dhcpoffer it receives.
Dhcprequest	When a DHCP client receives a Dhcpoffer packet, it responds by broadcasting a Dhcprequest packet that contains the offered IP address.
Dhcpdecline	A message from the DHCP client to the server indicating that the offered configuration parameters are invalid.
Dhcpack	The DHCP server acknowledges the client Dhcprequest for the IP address by sending a Dhcpack packet.
Dhcpnack	If the IP address cannot be used by the client because it is no longer valid or is now used by another computer, the DHCP server will respond with a Dhcpnack packet.
Dhcprelease	A message from the DHCP client to the server that releases the IP address and cancels any remaining lease.

When the DHCP server receives the request from the DHCP client computer, it dynamically assigns an IP address to the requesting computer from the range of valid IP addresses contained within the DHCP scope. The DHCP server allocates the IP address with a *lease* that defines how long the IP address is usable by the client computer. The DHCP server can also establish other configuration parameters, such as subnet mask and DNS and WINS server identification, for the client computer.

If the DHCP client has previously been assigned an IP address by the DHCP server or by manual configuration, the client sends a Dhcprequest packet. The following figure illustrates this process.

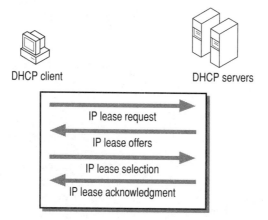

Figure 7.1   DHCP Client and Server Interaction During System Startup

---

Note The client accepts the first offer it receives, regardless of whether the offer came from a DHCP server on the local subnet or from a DHCP server on a different subnet.

When a client accepts an IP address, and any other configuration information offered by the DHCP server, the client saves the configuration in the following Registry keys:

```
HKEY_LOCAL_MACHINE\SYSTEM\CurrentControlSet\Services:
    Network interface specific: <adapter>\parameters\Tcpip
    General: Dhcp\parameters\options\*
```

IP addressing information is leased to a client until the client manually releases the address, or until the DHCP server cancels the lease and makes the address available to other computers on the network.

If a client does not receive a Dhcpoffer packet from a DHCP server, it will broadcast a request four times, at 2- ,4- ,8- , and 16-second intervals (plus a random amount between 0 and 1,000 milliseconds). If the client does not receive a response after four attempts, it will cease trying and retry again in five minutes. In the case where the DHCP server is unavailable or there is no available IP addressing information to lease to a client computer, the client is unable to bind to TCP/IP.

Restarting a DHCP Client

When a client computer restarts and logs on to the network, it broadcasts a Dhcprequest packet instead of a Dhcpdiscover packet. The Dhcprequest packet contains a request for the previously assigned IP address. The DHCP server will attempt to allow the client to retain the same IP address, and will respond with a Dhcpack packet. If the IP address cannot be used by the client because it is no longer valid, or is now used by another computer, the DHCP server will respond with a Dhcpnack packet. The client that receives a Dhcpnack response must restart the configuration process by sending a Dhcpdiscover request.

DHCP/BOOTP Relay Agents

TCP/IP networks are interconnected by routers that connect network segments (subnets) and pass IP packets between the subnets. As mentioned earlier, one of the major components of the DHCP specification is the DHCP protocol for communications between DHCP servers and clients.

A DHCP server can provide IP addresses to clients in multiple subnets if the router that connects the subnets is an RFC 1542-compliant router. RFC 1542 specifies the DHCP/BOOTP relay agent. If the router cannot function as a relay agent, each subnet that has DHCP clients requires a DHCP server.

A *relay agent* is a program used to pass specific types of IP packets between subnets. A DHCP/BOOTP relay agent is simply a hardware or software program that can pass DHCP/BOOTP messages (packets) from one subnet to another subnet according to the RFC 1542 specification.

Planning for DHCP Implementation

This section describes how to develop strategies for implementing DHCP servers in small LANs or large routed networks. Most network administrators implementing DHCP will also be planning a strategy for implementing WINS servers. The planning tasks described here also apply to WINS servers. In fact, the administrator will probably want to plan DHCP and WINS implementation in tandem.

Note If you use DHCP servers, you must use WINS servers so that the dynamic IP addressing of DHCP clients can be dynamically updated in name-to-IP-address mappings.

Before you install Microsoft DHCP servers on your network, consider the following recommendations:

- The general guideline for determining how many DHCP servers are needed in a network is that one online DHCP server and one backup DHCP server (a hot standby) can support 10,000 clients. However, when deciding how many DHCP servers you will need, consider the location of routers on the network and whether you will want a DHCP server in each subnet.

- To determine where to install the DHCP servers, use the physical characteristics of your LAN or WAN infrastructure and not the logical groupings defined in the Windows NT domain concepts. When subnets are connected by RFC 1542-compliant routers, DHCP servers are not required on every subnet on the network. Note that DHCP servers can be administered remotely from a computer running under Windows NT Server that is DHCP- or WINS-enabled.

- Compile a list of requirements including:
    - Client support (numbers and kinds of systems to be supported)
    - Interoperability with existing systems (including your requirements for mission-critical accounting, personnel, and similar information systems)
    - Hardware support and related software compatibility (including routers, switches, and servers)
    - Network monitoring software, including Simple Network Management Protocol (SNMP) and other tools

- Isolate the areas of the network where processes must continue uninterrupted, and then target these areas for the last stages of implementation.

- Review the geographic and physical structure of the network to determine the best plan for defining logical subnets as segments of the intranet.

- Define the components in the new system that require testing, and then develop a phased plan for testing and adding components

  For example, the plan could define the order for types of computers to be phased in (including Windows NT servers and workstations, Microsoft RAS servers and clients, Windows for Workgroups computers, and MS-DOS clients).

- Create a pilot project for testing.

- Create a second test phase, including tuning the DHCP (and WINS) server-client configuration for efficiency.

  This task can include determining strategies for backup servers and for partitioning the address pool at each server to be provided to local versus remote clients.

- Document all architecture and administration issues for network administrators.

Planning for Small Networks

In a small LAN that does not include routers and subnetting, a single DHCP server could be used to service all DHCP clients as illustrated in the following figure.

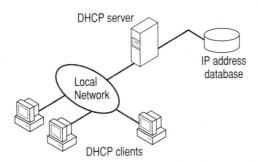

Figure 7.2   A Single Local Network Using Automatic TCP/IP Configuration with DHCP

Before installing the DHCP server you will need to identify:

- The hardware and storage requirements for the DHCP server.

- Which computers can immediately be configured as DHCP clients for dynamic TCP/IP configuration and which computers should be manually configured with static TCP/IP configuration parameters including static IP addresses.

- The DHCP option types and their values to be predefined for the DHCP clients.

Planning for DHCP in Routed Networks

A router is a TCP/IP gateway computer that has two or more network adapter cards (NICs). Each adapter is connected to a different physical network (a subnet). A router device provides services that are determined by the hardware and software configuration of the computer that serves as the router.

Routers that implement the DHCP/BOOTP relay agent as specified by RFC 1542 can be used to route traffic between DHCP servers and clients located on different subnets. The relay agent on the router forwards requests from local DHCP clients to the remote DHCP server and subsequently relays the DHCP server responses back to the DHCP clients. The following figure illustrates an example of a routed network with DHCP server and DHCP clients.

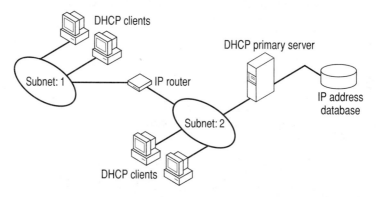

Figure 7.3   An Internetwork Using Automatic TCP/IP Configuration with DHCP

Windows NT Server version 4.0 includes Multi-Protocol Router (MPR), which is a software router that can be configured on a general purpose computer to provide DHCP/BOOTP relay agent support. MPR includes:

- BOOTP relay agent for DHCP
- Routing Information Protocol (RIP) for TCP/IP
- Routing Information Protocol for IPX

Note Windows NT supports DHCP but does not support BOOTP. You can use Microsoft DHCP server on the same network with clients and servers running BOOTP. The Windows NT-based DHCP servers simply ignore any BOOTP client packets that they may receive from the network. You must make sure, however, that the BOOTP server and the DHCP server do not manage leases for the same IP addresses. The best way to ensure that there is no overlap in managed addresses is to define the scope of the DHCP server as the entire address range that is managed by both the DHCP server and the BOOTP server, and then exclude the address range that is managed by the BOOTP server. As BOOTP clients are dropped or upgraded to DHCP, the exclusion range can be adjusted accordingly.

Additional planning issues for a large enterprise network are:

- Ensuring the compatibility of hardware and software routers with DHCP.
- Planning the physical subnetting of the network and relative placement of DHCP servers. This includes planning for placement of DHCP (and WINS) servers among subnets in a way that reduces b-node broadcasts across routers.
- Specifying the DHCP option types and their values to be predefined per scope for the DHCP clients. This might include planning for scopes based on the needs of particular groups of users. For example, for a marketing group that uses portable computers docked at different stations, or for a unit that frequently moves computers to different locations, shorter lease durations can be defined for the related scopes. This way, frequently changed IP addresses can be freed for reuse.

As one example of planning for a large enterprise network, the segmenting of the WAN into logical subnets could match the physical structure of the internetwork. Then one IP subnet can serve as the backbone, and off this backbone each physical subnet would maintain a separate IP subnet address.

In this case, for each subnet a single computer running Windows NT Server could be configured as both the DHCP and WINS server. Each server would administer a defined number of IP addresses with a specific subnet mask, and would also be defined as the default gateway. Because the server is also acting as the WINS server, it can respond to name resolution requests from all systems on its subnet.

These DHCP and WINS servers can in turn be backup servers for each other. The administrator can partition the address pool for each server to provide addresses to remote clients.

There is no limit to the maximum number of clients that can be served by a single DHCP server. However, your network can have practical constraints based on the IP address class, and server configuration issues such as disk capacity and CPU speed.

Planning for DHCP Traffic

DHCP client and server TCP/IP configuration traffic does not use significant network bandwidth during normal periods of usage. However, there are two phases of DHCP client configuration that do generate some network traffic load. These phases are:

- IP Address Lease
- IP Address Renewal

IP Address Lease

When a new client initializes TCP/IP for the first time (and is configured as a DHCP client), its first step is to acquire an IP address using DHCP. This process results in a conversation between the DHCP client and server consisting of four packets, the first of which is the client computer broadcasting a Dhcpdiscover packet in an attempt to locate a DHCP server.

DHCP Discover

The Dhcpdiscover frame will be either 342 or 590 bytes total. (Older versions of Windows for Workgroups TCP/IP stack, TCP/IP-32 3.11a, as well as Windows NT 3.5, used 590-byte frames.) The first 14 bytes constitute the Ethernet header portion of the packet. The first distinguishing characteristic is the destination address, which is the Ethernet broadcast address of 255.255.255.255. The client computer has no knowledge of where any DHCP servers reside, and so it initiates a broadcast which is an Ethernet Type 0800 frame (IP).

The next 20 bytes are the IP header portion of the packet. The interesting things to note are the source and destination addresses. The source address is 0.0.0.0; because the client does not yet have a valid IP address, it initializes with an address of 0.0.0.0. The destination address is 255.255.255.255, which is the IP network broadcast address. As with the Ethernet header, the client does not know the location or address of any DHCP servers, and so it initiates an IP broadcast.

DHCP is a UDP-based protocol, and so the next 8 bytes are the UDP header. The UDP source and destination ports are both BOOTP (68 and 67, respectively). DHCP is an extension of the BOOTP protocol, and thus uses its ports for messaging.

The remainder of the frame contains the Dhcpdiscover packet components. The majority of the remaining fields are either zeros or blank, because the client has no knowledge of any IP addresses or parameters. Upon examining the DHCP Option Field section, you will notice the Client Identifier, which is its MAC address, and its Host name. These are added to the frame in the event that a DHCP server may have a reserved address for the client which is identified by its MAC address.

The host will broadcast up to four Dhcpdiscover messages in an attempt to find a DHCP server. If, after four attempts, a server cannot be located, the computer will cease trying, and then attempt to locate a DHCP server every five minutes until it is successful.

DHCP Offer

Once a DHCP server has received the Discover packet, and determined that it can accommodate the client's request, it responds with a Dhcpoffer message. The Dhcpoffer frame is 342 bytes total. The first 14 bytes constitute the Ethernet header portion of the packet. The first distinguishing characteristic is the destination address, which is the Ethernet broadcast address of 255.255.255.255. The server responds to the client with a broadcast which is an Ethernet Type 0800 frame (IP).

The next 20 bytes are the IP header portion of the packet. The interesting things to note are the source and destination addresses. The source address is that of the DHCP server, and the destination address is 255.255.255.255, which is the IP network broadcast address. As with the Ethernet header, the client responds with an IP broadcast.

DHCP is a UDP-based protocol, and so the next 8 bytes are the UDP header. The UDP source and destination ports are both BOOTP (67 and 68, respectively).

The remainder of the frame (300 bytes) contains the Dhcpoffer packet components. The new items configured are Your IP address, which is set to the proposed address for the client, and proposals for the IP address lease time (including renewal periods). The DHCP server's IP address is also listed here.

DHCP Request

The Dhcprequest frame will be either 342 or 590 bytes total, depending on the size of the Dhcpdiscover message. The first 14 bytes constitute the Ethernet header portion of the packet. The first distinguishing characteristic is the destination address, which is the Ethernet broadcast address of 255.255.255.255. The client computer knows the address of the server it is accepting its address from, but responds with a broadcast to let all DHCP servers know that it has selected an address from a specific server. It is an Ethernet Type 0800 frame (IP).

The next 20 bytes are the IP header portion of the packet. The interesting things to note are the source and destination addresses. The source address is 0.0.0.0; because the client does not yet have a valid IP address, it initializes with an address of 0.0.0.0. The destination address is 255.255.255.255, which is the IP network broadcast address. As with the Ethernet header, the client initiates an IP broadcast to let all DHCP servers accept the frame, and learn that it has accepted an offer.

DHCP is a UDP-based protocol, and so the next 8 bytes are the UDP header. The UDP source and destination ports are both BOOTP (68 and 67, respectively).

The remainder of the frame contains the Dhcprequest packet components. The majority of the remaining fields are either zeros or blank, because the client has no knowledge of any IP addresses or parameters. Upon examining the DHCP Option Field section, you will notice the Requested address, which is the IP address the client is requesting, and a Server Identifier (IP address of the server the request is being made of). These are added to the frame so that other DHCP servers are notified that the client has accepted an offer from a specific server, and they can offer the address they offered to this client to another DHCP client.

DHCP ACK

Once a DHCP server has received the Request packet, it responds with a Dhcpack message. The Dhcpack frame is 342 bytes total. The first 14 bytes constitute the Ethernet header portion of the packet. The first distinguishing characteristic is the destination address, which is the Ethernet broadcast address of 255.255.255.255. The server responds to the client with a broadcast. It is an Ethernet Type 0800 frame (IP).

The next 20 bytes are the IP header portion of the packet. The interesting things to note are the source and destination addresses. The source address is that of the DHCP server, and the destination address is 255.255.255.255, which is the IP network broadcast address. As with the Ethernet header, the client responds with an IP broadcast.

DHCP is a UDP-based protocol, and so the next 8 bytes are the UDP header. The UDP source and destination ports are both BOOTP (67 and 68, respectively).

The remainder of the frame contains the Dhcpack packet components. Your IP address, which is set to the proposed address for the client, is still configured, and parameters, such as IP Lease Time, and renewal and rebinding times, as well as other DHCP options, such as Router, NetBIOS Name Server address, NetBIOS Node Type, and so on, are listed in the Option Field portion of the frame. This portion will be variable, depending on the options requested from the client and those returned by the server.

IP Address Renewal

Whenever a DHCP client starts, it must renew its IP address with its DHCP server. When renewing an IP address using DHCP, the conversation is a simple one consisting of the last two packets of the IP address lease phase. The client computer will request a renewal of its current IP address with a Dhcprequest packet and, if successful, the DHCP server responds with a Dhcpack packet.

The only difference between the Dhcprequest and Dhcpack packets for a renewal and those of the acquisition is that the conversation is directed, and not broadcast, because the client and server already know about each other. Additionally, any new DHCP options, such as Domain Name Server address, that have been configured since the client acquired the IP address lease, are now sent to the client computer.

DHCP clients also renew their IP address lease at one-half of the TTL, which is a configurable length. At this time, the client issues a Dhcprequest packet to its DHCP server, and the server will respond with a Dhcpack, if the address is still valid for the client.

The DHCP client will retry its renewal attempt one time. If unsuccessful, it will try again at the next renewal period.

Summary of DHCP Traffic

To recap, the entire process of acquiring an IP address lease through DHCP takes a total of four packets, varying between 342 and 590 bytes in size. This process, on a clean network (no other network traffic using bandwidth), takes less than 1 second (about 300 milliseconds).

DHCP conversations generally occur in the following instances:

- When a DHCP client initializes for the first time (all four frames).
- When an automatic renewal, which is only done every one-half lease life (three days by default, so every 18 hours), takes two packets (Dhcprequest and Dhcpack) and approximately 200 milliseconds.
- When a client is moved to a new subnet (Dhcprequest, Dhcpnack, then the four frames as if it is a new client).
- When a DHCP client replaces its network adapter card (all four frames).
- Whenever a client manually refreshes or releases its address by using the **ipconfig** utility.

This process should not have a significant effect on network traffic, even if multiple DHCP clients are acquiring or renewing addresses simultaneously.

Planning Guideline for DHCP Traffic

DHCP does not normally have a big impact on network traffic. If you wish to reduce the amount of traffic generated by DHCP, it is possible to adjust the lease duration for IP address leases. This is done using DHCP Manager, and adjusting **Lease Duration** in the **Scope Properties** dialog box.

As noted earlier, the default lease duration is three days, which would cause each client to attempt to renew their lease every 18 hours from the time the client acquired the address. A lease renewal is only two packets, with a maximum totoal size of 932 bytes.

Setting Local Policies

This section provides some suggestions for setting lease options, dividing the free address pool among DHCP servers, and preventing DNS naming problems.

Managing DHCP Addressing Policy

Allocation of IP addresses for distribution by DHCP servers can be done dynamically or manually. These methods use the same DHCP client-server protocol, but the network administrator manages them differently at the DHCP server end.

Dynamic Allocation of IP Addresses

Dynamic allocation enables a client to be assigned an IP address from the free address pool. The lease for the address has a lease duration (expiration date), before which the client must renew the lease to continue using that address. Depending on the local lease policies defined by the administrator, dynamically allocated addresses can be returned to the free address pool if the client computer is not being used, if it is moved to another subnet, or if its lease expires. Any IP addresses that are returned to the free address pool can be reused by the DHCP server when allocating an IP address to a new client. Usually, the local policy ensures that the same IP address is assigned to a client each time that it starts.

After the renewal time of the lease duration has passed, the DHCP client enters the *renewing* state. The client sends a request message to the DHCP server that provided its configuration information. If the request for a lease extension fits the local lease policy, the DHCP server sends an acknowledgment that contains the new lease and configuration parameters. The client then updates its configuration values and returns to the bound state.

When the DHCP client is in the renewing state, it must release its address immediately in the rare event that the DHCP server sends a negative acknowledgment. The DHCP server sends this message to inform a client that it has incorrect configuration information, forcing it to release its current address and acquire new information.

If the DHCP client cannot successfully renew its lease, the client enters a *rebinding* state. At this stage, the client sends a request message to all DHCP servers in its range, attempting to renew its lease. Any server that can extend the lease sends an acknowledgment containing the extended lease and updated configuration information. If the lease expires or if a DHCP server responds with a negative acknowledgment, the client must release its current configuration, and then return to the *initializing* state. (This happens automatically, for example, for a computer that is moved from one subnet to another.)

If the DHCP client uses more than one network adapter to connect to multiple networks, this protocol is followed for each adapter that the user wants to configure for TCP/IP. Windows NT allows multihomed systems to selectively configure any combination of the system's interfaces. You can use the **ipconfig** utility to view the local IP configuration for a client computer.

When a DHCP-enabled computer is restarted, it sends a message to the DHCP server with its current configuration information. The DHCP server either confirms this configuration or sends a negative reply so that the client must begin the initializing stage again. System startup might, therefore, result in a new IP address for a client computer, but neither the user nor the network administrator has to take any action in the configuration process.

Before loading TCP/IP with an address acquired from the DHCP server, DHCP clients check for an IP address conflict by sending an Address Resolution Protocol (ARP) request containing the address. If a conflict is found, TCP/IP does not start, and then the user receives an error message. The conflicting address should be removed from the list of active leases or it should be excluded until the conflict is identified and resolved.

Managing Lease Options

To define appropriate values for lease duration, consider the frequency of the following events for your network:

- Changes to DHCP options and default values
- Network interface failures
- Computer removals for any purpose
- Subnet changes by users because of office moves, laptop computers docked at different workstations, and so on

All of these types of events cause IP addresses to be released by the client or cause the leases to expire at the DHCP server. Consequently, the IP address is returned to the free address pool to be reused.

If many changes occur on your internetwork, you should assign short lease times, such as two weeks. This way, the addresses assigned to systems that leave the subnet can be reassigned quickly to new DHCP client computers requesting TCP/IP configuration information.

Another important factor to consider is the ratio between connected computers and available IP addresses. For example, the demand for reusing addresses is low on a network where 40 systems share a class C address (with 254 available addresses). A long lease time, such as two months, would be appropriate in such a situation. However, if 230 computers share the same address pool, demand for available addresses is much greater, and so a lease time of a few days or weeks is more appropriate.

Notice, however, that short lease durations require that the DHCP server be available when the client seeks to renew the lease. Backup servers are especially important when short lease durations are specified.

Although infinite leases are allowed, they should be used with great caution. Even in a relatively stable environment, there is a certain amount of turnover among clients. At a minimum, portable computers might be added and removed, desktop computers might be moved from one office to another, and network adapter cards might be replaced. If a client with an infinite lease is removed from the network, the DHCP server is not notified, and then the IP address cannot be reused. A better option is a very long lease duration, such as six months. A long lease duration ensures that addresses are ultimately recovered.

Partitioning the Address Pool

You will probably decide to install more than one DHCP server, so that the failure of any individual server will not prevent DHCP clients from starting. However, DHCP does not provide a way for DHCP servers to cooperate in ensuring that assigned addresses are unique. Therefore, you must divide the available address pool among the DHCP servers to prevent duplicate address assignment.

A typical scenario is where a local DHCP server maintains TCP/IP configuration information for two subnets. For each DHCP server, the network administrator allocates 70 percent of the IP address pool for local clients and 30 percent for clients from the remote subnet, and then configures a relay agent to deliver requests between the subnets.

This scenario allows the local DHCP server to respond to requests from local DHCP clients most of the time. The remote DHCP server will assign addresses to clients on the other subnet only when the local server is not available or is out of addresses. This same method of partitioning among subnets can be used in a multiple subnet scenario to ensure the availability of a responding server when a DHCP client requests configuration information.

Using DHCP with DNS Servers

Domain Name System (DNS) servers can be used to provide names for network resources. However, there is no current IETF specification for dynamically updating DNS servers such as when a DHCP client is dynamically configured with an IP address and other TCP/IP configuration parameters. Therefore, DNS naming conflicts can occur if you are using a DHCP server for dynamic assignment of client IP addresses.

This problem primarily affects systems that extend internetworking services to local network users. For example, a server acting as an anonymous FTP server or as an electronic mail gateway might require users to contact it using DNS names. In such cases, clients should have reserved leases with an unlimited duration.

For workstations in environments that do not require the computers to register in the DNS name space, DHCP dynamic allocation can be used without problems.

Using DHCP Manager

When you install Microsoft DHCP server, the graphical user-interface, DHCP Manager, is automatically installed and added to the **Administrative Tools (Common)** programs group. You use DHCP Manager to configure and monitor remote and local DHCP servers.

You can use DHCP Manager to view and change parameters for Microsoft DHCP servers on the network for which you have administrator privileges. DHCP Manager Help is organized to provide information for each of the specific administration and configuration tasks that you need to perform to manage DHCP servers. See DHCP Manager Help for specific tasks details.

▶ **To start DHCP Manager**

- Click **Start,** point to **Programs**, point to **Administrative Tools (Common)**, and then click **DHCP Manager**.

Managing the DHCP Server Database

The DHCP server database under Windows NT Server version 4.0 uses the performance-enhanced Exchange Server storage engine version 4.0. When you install Microsoft DHCP server, the files shown in the following table are automatically created in the *systemroot*\System32\Dhcp directory.

Table 7.7   Microsoft DHCP Server Database Files

File	Description
Dhcp.mdb	The DHCP server database file.
Dhcp.tmp	A temporary file used by the DHCP database as a swap file during database index maintenance operations. This file may remain in the *systemroot*\System32\Dhcp directory after a crash.
J50.log and J50#####.log	A log of all database transactions. This file is used by the DHCP database to recover data if necessary.
J50.chk	A checkpoint file.

Important The J50.log file, J50#####.log file, Dhcp.mdb file, and Dhcp.tmp file should not be removed or tampered with in any manner.

As previously discussed, the DHCP server database is a dynamic database that is updated as DHCP clients are assigned, or release, their TCP/IP configuration parameters. Because the DHCP database is not a distributed database like the WINS server database, maintenance of the DHCP server database is less complex.

The DHCP database and related Registry entries are backed up automatically at a specific interval (15 minutes by installation default). This installation default can be changed by changing the value of the Registry parameter **BackupInterval** in the Registry key:

```
SYSTEM\current\currentcontrolset\services\DHCPServer\Parameters
```

Troubleshooting DHCP Server

The following error conditions indicate potential problems with the DHCP server:

- The administrator can't connect for a DHCP server by using DHCP Manager. The message that appears might be "The RPC server is unavailable."
- DHCP clients cannot renew the leases for their IP addresses. The message that appears on the client computer is "The DHCP client could not renew the IP address lease."
- The DHCP Client service or Microsoft DHCP Server service might be stopped and cannot be restarted.

The first troubleshooting task is to make sure that the DHCP services are running. Open **Services** in **Control Panel** to verify that the DHCP services are running. "Started" should appear in the Status column for the DHCP Client service and "Started" should appear in the Status column for the Microsoft DHCP Server service. If the appropriate service is not started, start the service.

In rare circumstances, a DHCP server cannot start or a STOP error might occur. If the DHCP server is stopped, complete the following procedure to restart it.

▶ **To restart a DHCP server that is stopped**

1. Turn off the power to the server, and then wait about one minute.
2. Turn on the power, start Windows NT Server, and then log on under an account with Administrator rights.
3. At the command prompt, type **net start dhcp**, and then press ENTER.

Note Use Event Viewer in the Administrative tools to find the possible source of problems with DHCP services.

Using IPCONFIG

Ipconfig is a TCP/IP utility that you can use at the command prompt. You can use the **ipconfig** command to get information about the configured TCP/IP parameters.

For more information on how to use the **ipconfig** command, see the topic "TCP/IP Procedures Help" in Control Panel Help.

Upgrading the DHCP Database to Windows NT Server Version 4.0

When upgrading a Windows NT Server version 3.51 (or earlier) release to Windows NT 4.0, the DHCP database must be converted to the new database format. This is required because the services now use an improved database engine that is faster and that compacts automatically to prevent fragmentation and consequent growth of the database. The database conversion procedure happens automatically as part of an upgrade installation.

Database Conversion Procedure

When the DHCP service first starts after an upgrade to Windows NT 4.0, it detects that the database needs to be converted. It then starts a conversion process, Jetconv.exe. (If Jetconv.exe has already been started by another service, a second Jetconv.exe process is not started.) Prior to conversion, the user is notified that the conversion process is about to start and is asked for confirmation. If the user clicks **OK**, the DHCP service terminates and the conversion begins. Jetconv.exe converts the databases of all the installed services (DHCP and if installed WINS and RPL) to the new Windows NT 4.0 database format.

After the DHCP database is converted successfully, the DHCP Server service is automatically restarted.

Before starting the conversion process, note the following guidelines:

- Prior to upgrading to Windows NT Server 4.0, bring the Windows NT 3.51 databases for the DHCP server to a consistent state. Do this by terminating the services, either by using **Service** in **Control Panel** or by using the **net stop service** command. This is recommended because it prevents the Jetconv.exe conversion from failing due to an inconsistent Windows NT 3.51 database.

- The conversion requires approximately the same amount of free disk space as the size of the original database and log files. You should have at least 5 MB free for the log files for each database.

- The conversion process preserves the original database and log files in a subdirectory named *351db* under the same directory where the original database and log files were located. On the DHCP server, this is the *systemroot*\System32\dhcp\351db\ directory. The administrator can later remove these files to reclaim the disk space.

The database conversion can take anywhere from a minute to an hour depending on the size of the database. The user must not try to restart the services while the databases are being converted. To check the status of the conversion, the user should watch the Application Event Log of the Jetconv.exe process by using Event Viewer.

In case this automatic procedure of converting databases fails for some reason (as can be determined from the event logs), the database that couldn't be converted can be converted manually using *winntdir*\system32\upg351db.exe. At the command line, type **upg351db -?** for instructions.

Note the following information:

- You cannot convert the new database back to the previous database format.
- The converted database will not work with Windows NT 3.51 or earlier services.
- The new database engine uses log files named by using the prefix *J50*.

Restoring the DHCP Database

If you determine that the DHCP services are running on both the client and server computers but the error conditions described earlier under "Troubleshooting DHCP Server" persist, then the DHCP database is not available or has become corrupted. If a DHCP server fails for any reason, you can restore the database from a backup copy.

▶ **To restore a DHCP database**

1. Before starting, make a copy of the DHCP server database files.
2. In the *systemroot*\System32\Dhcp directory, delete the J50.log, J50#####.log, and Dhcp.tmp files.
3. Copy an uncorrupted backup version of the Dhcp.mdb to the *systemroot*\System32\Dhcp directory.
4. Restart the Microsoft DHCP Server service.

Restarting and Rebuilding a Stopped DHCP Server

In rare circumstances, the DHCP server may not start or a STOP error might occur. If the DHCP server is stopped, use the following procedure to restart it.

▶ **To restart a DHCP server that is stopped**

1. Turn off the power to the server and wait at least 15 seconds.
2. Turn on the power, start Windows NT Server, and then log on under an account with Administrator rights.
3. At the command prompt, type the **net start dhcp** command, and then press ENTER.

If the hardware for the DHCP server is malfunctioning or other problems prevent you from running Windows NT, you must rebuild the DHCP database on another computer.

▶   **To rebuild a DHCP server**

1. If you can start the original DHCP server by using the **net start** DHCP command, use a copy command to make backup copies of the files in the *systemroot*\System32\Dhcp directory. If you cannot start the computer at all, you must use the last backup version of the DHCP database files.

2. Install Windows NT Server and Microsoft TCP/IP to create a new DHCP server using the same hard-drive location and *systemroot* directory.

    That is, if the original server stored the DHCP files on C:\Winnt\System32\Dhcp, then the new DHCP server must use this same path to the DHCP files.

3. Make sure the Microsoft DHCP Server service on the new server is stopped, and then use the Registry Editor to restore the DHCP keys from backup files.

4. Copy the DHCP backup files to the *systemroot*\System32\Dhcp directory.

5. Restart the new, rebuilt DHCP server.

Moving the DHCP Server Database

You may find a situation where you need to move a DHCP database to another computer. To do this, use the following procedure.

▶   **To move a DHCP database**

1. Stop the Microsoft DHCP Server on the current computer.

2. Copy the \System32\Dhcp directory to the new computer that has been configured as a DHCP server.

    Make sure the new directory is under exactly the same drive letter and path as on the old computer.

    If you must copy the files to a different directory, copy Dhcp.mdb, but do not copy the .log of .chk files.

3. Start the Microsoft DHCP Server on the new computer.

    The service automatically starts using the .mdb and .log files copied from the old computer.

When you check **DHCP Manager**, the scope still exists because the Registry holds the information on the address range of the scope, including a bitmap of the addresses in use. You need to reconcile the DHCP database to add database entries for the existing leases in the address bitmask. As clients renew, they are matched with these leases, and eventually the database is once again complete.

▶   **To reconcile the DHCP database**

1. On the **Scope** menu, click **Active Leases**.

2. In the **Active Leases** dialog box, click **Reconcile**.

Although it is not required, you can force DHCP clients to renew their leases in order to update the DHCP database as quickly as possible. To do so, type **ipconfig/renew** at the command prompt.

Compacting the DHCP Server Database

Windows NT Server 4.0 is designed to automatically compact the DHCP database and normally you should not need to run this procedure. However, if you are using Windows NT Server versions 3.51 or earlier, after DHCP has been running for a while, the database might need to be compacted to improve DHCP performance. You should compact the DHCP database whenever it approaches 30 MB.

You can use the Jetpack.exe utility provided with Windows NT Server version 3.5 and 3.51 to compact a DHCP database. Jetpack.exe is a command-line utility that is run in the Windows NT Server command window. The utility is found in the \%*Systemroot*\System32 directory.

The Jetpack.exe syntax is:

Jetpack.exe <*database name*> <*temp database name*>

For example:

```
> CD %SYSTEMROOT%\SYSTEM32\DHCP
> JETPACK DHCP.MDB TMP.MDB
```

In the preceding example, Tmp.mdb is a temporary database that is used by Jetpack.exe. Dhcp.mdb is the DHCP server database file.

When Jetpack.exe is started, it performs the following tasks:

1. Copies database information to a temporary database file called Tmp.mdb.
2. Deletes the original database file, Dhcp.mdb.
3. Renames the temporary database file to the original filename.

▶ **To compact the DHCP database**

1. In Control Panel, double-click Services.
2. Under Service, click Microsoft DHCP Server.
3. Click Stop, and then click Close. (Alternatively, you can type net stop DHCP at the command prompt.)
4. At the command prompt, run the Jetpack.exe program as previously described.
5. Restart the DHCP Server service by using the **Services** dialog box.

C H A P T E R   8

Managing Microsoft WINS Servers

Microsoft Windows Internet Name Service (WINS) is an RFC-compliant NetBIOS name-to-IP-address mapping service. WINS allows Windows-based clients to easily locate resources on Transmission Control Protocol/Internet Protocol (TCP/IP) networks. WINS servers maintain databases of static and dynamic resource name—to-IP-address mappings. Because the Microsoft WINS database supports dynamic name and IP address entries, WINS can be used with Dynamic Host Configuration Protocol (DHCP) services to provide easy configuration and administration of Windows-based TCP/IP networks.

The information in this chapter is intended for network administrators and support personnel who need information about WINS and how to plan, manage, and troubleshoot WINS services. The following topics are included in this chapter:

- Introduction to Windows Internet Name Service (WINS)
  - Microsoft WINS servers
  - Microsoft WINS server push and pull partners
  - Microsoft WINS clients
  - Microsoft WINS proxies
- Planning for Microsoft WINS server implementation
- Using WINS Manager
  - Viewing WINS server operational status
  - Configuring WINS server and WINS client behavior
  - Managing static NetBIOS computer name—to-IP-address mappings
  - Special names for static entry types
  - Managing the WINS server database
- Troubleshooting WINS servers and databases

Introduction to Windows Internet Name Service

NetBIOS is a session-level interface used by programs to communicate over NetBIOS-compatible transports, including TCP/IP. One function of the NetBIOS interface is to establish logical names for networking programs.

Microsoft Windows Internet Name Service (WINS) is compliant with RFC 1001 and RFC 1002. Microsoft WINS is designed to provide a flexible solution to the problem of locating NetBIOS resources in routed, TCP/IP-based networks.

When using TCP/IP to communicate on a network, a "friendly" Windows-based NetBIOS computer name, such as "mycomputer," must be resolved to an IP address. This is necessary because TCP/IP requires an IP address, such as 172.16.48.1, to establish a connection to a network device. Several different name resolution methods provide NetBIOS name resolution. These methods include:

- IP broadcasts
- Static mapping files (LMHOSTS and DNS-based HOSTS files)
- NetBIOS name server (in Windows NT-based networks, this is the Microsoft WINS server)
- Domain Name System server (in Windows NT-based networks, this is the Microsoft DNS Server)

Microsoft WINS Servers

WINS servers are designed to prevent the administrative difficulties that are inherent in the use of both IP broadcasts and static mapping files such as LMHOSTS files. Microsoft WINS is designed to eliminate the need for IP broadcasts (which use valuable network bandwidth and cannot be used in routed networks), while providing a dynamic, distributed database that maintains computer name-to-IP-address mappings.

WINS servers use a replicated database that contains NetBIOS computer names and IP address mappings (database records). When Windows-based computers log on to the network, their computer name and IP addressing mapping are added (registered) to the WINS server database, providing support for dynamic updates. The WINS server database is replicated among multiple WINS servers in a LAN or WAN. One of the benefits of this database design is that it prevents different users from registering duplicate NetBIOS computer names on the network.

WINS servers provide the following benefits:

- Dynamic database that supports NetBIOS computer name registration and name resolution in an environment where the dynamic TCP/IP configuration of DHCP-enabled clients is dynamically configured for TCP/IP.
- Centralized management of the NetBIOS computer name database and its replication to other WINS servers.
- Reduction of NetBIOS name query IP broadcast traffic.
- Support for Windows-based clients (including Windows NT Server, Windows NT Workstation, Windows 95, Windows for Workgroups, and LAN Manager 2.*x*).
- Support for transparent browsing across routers for Windows NT Server, Windows NT Workstation, Windows 95, and Windows for Workgroups clients.

The following figure illustrates an intranet with multiple WINS servers in a routed network. The components of a WINS system are shown in the illustration and are discussed in the following sections:

- Microsoft WINS server push and pull partners
- WINS clients, referred to as WINS-enabled computers
- WINS proxy and non-WINS enabled computers

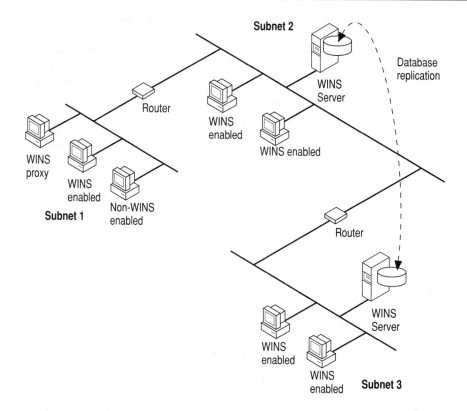

Figure 8.1   WINS Servers and WINS Clients in a Routed TCP/IP Network

Microsoft WINS Server Push and Pull Partners

A given network should have one or more WINS servers that WINS clients can contact to resolve a computer name to an IP address. It is desirable to have multiple WINS servers installed on an intranet for the following reasons:

- To distribute the NetBIOS computer name query and registration processing load

- To provide WINS database redundancy, backup, and disaster recovery

Microsoft WINS servers communicate with other Microsoft WINS servers to fully replicate their databases with each other. This ensures that a name registered with one WINS server is replicated to all other Microsoft WINS servers within the intranet, providing a replicated and enterprise-wide database.

When multiple WINS servers are used, each WINS server is configured as a *pull* or *push* partner of at least one other WINS server. The following table describes the pull and push partner types of replication partners.

Table 8.1   WINS Server Replication Partners

Type	Description
Pull partner	A pull partner is a WINS server that pulls (requests) WINS database entries from its push partners. The pull partner pulls new WINS database entries by requesting entries with a higher version number than the last entry it received during the last replication from that push partner. A pull partner can notify push partners that replication is needed by using either of the following:
	▪ An arbitrary time interval, as configured by the WINS administrator. This is called the *time interval*.
	▪ Immediate replication, initiated by the WINS administrator by using the WINS Manager.
Push partner	A push partner is a WINS server that sends a message to its pull partners that the WINS database has changed. When the pull partners respond to the message with a replication request, the push partner sends a copy of its new WINS database entries to the pull partners. The push partner notifies pull partners of replication requirements by using any of the following:
	▪ An arbitrary number of WINS updates, as configured by the WINS administrator. This is referred to as the *update count*.
	▪ Immediate replication, initiated by the WINS administrator by using WINS Manager.

It is always a good idea for replication partners to be both push and pull partners of each other. The primary and backup WINS servers *must* be both push and pull partners with each other to ensure that the primary and backup databases are consistent.

Replication is triggered when a WINS server polls another server to get replicated information. This can begin when the WINS server is started, and is repeated based on the configured update count or time interval, or by using WINS Manager to start immediate replication.

Microsoft WINS Clients

WINS clients, referred to as *WINS-enabled* clients, are configured to use the services of a WINS server.

Windows NT-based clients are configured with the IP address of one or more WINS servers by using the **WINS Address** tab on the **Microsoft TCP/IP Properties** page in **Control Panel – Network**. The following figure illustrates this configuration page.

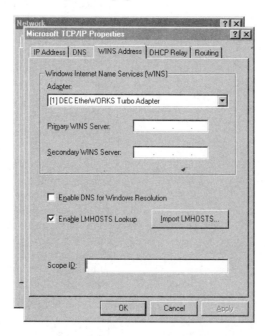

Figure 8.2   Enabling the WINS Service on a WINS Client

The WINS-enabled client communicates with the WINS server to:

- Register the client names in the WINS database.
- Get mappings for user names, NetBIOS names, DNS names, and IP addresses from the WINS database.

How WINS Clients Register Their Names

When a WINS-enabled computer is started, the WINS client service attempts to directly contact the WINS server (by using point-to-point communication) to register the client names and corresponding IP address. The type of message the client sends is referred to as a *name registration request*. The WINS client sends one name registration request (which includes the computer IP address) for the computer, logged-on user, and networking services running on the computer.

Note The IP address is dynamically assigned by a DHCP server if the client is DHCP-enabled. If DHCP is not used, the IP address is a statically assigned number which you must get from a network administrator and manually configure on the computer.

When the WINS server receives a name registration request, it checks the WINS database to ensure that the name in the request is unique and does not exist in the WINS database. The WINS server responds with either a positive or negative *name registration response*. The following table describes the processing that occurs for each type of WINS server name registration response.

Table 8.2 WINS Server Response to Name Registration Request

WINS server name registration response	WINS client behavior
No response	The WINS client sends another name registration request.
Positive	The WINS server responds with a positive name registration response if there is not a duplicate name in the WINS database. The response includes a time-to-live (TTL) value that indicates how long the client can own that name. The client must renew the name registration before the TTL expires.
Negative	If there is an existing registration for the name in the WINS database, the WINS server sends a challenge, referred to as a *name query request*, to the currently registered owner of the name.
	The WINS server sends the challenge three times, waiting 500 milliseconds between attempts. If the computer is multihomed, the WINS server tries each IP address it has for the computer until the WINS server receives a response or until all of the IP addresses have been tried.
	If the WINS server receives a response from the current owner, it sends a negative name registration response to the WINS client attempting to register the name, by using the IP address included in the client registration request.

The following figure illustrates the flow of name registration request and name response.

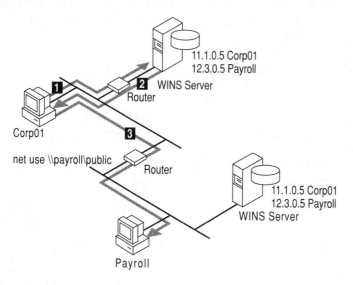

Figure 8.3   WINS Client Name Registration

How WINS Clients Renew Their Names

WINS clients must renew their name registrations before the time-to-live (TTL) value expires. The TTL value indicates how long the client can own that name.

When a WINS client renews its name registration, it sends a *name refresh request* directly (point-to-point) to the WINS server. The name refresh request includes the WINS client's IP address and the name that the client is requesting to have refreshed. The WINS server responds to the name refresh request with a *name refresh response* that includes a new TTL for the name.

A WINS client first attempts to refresh its name registrations after one-half of the TTL is expired. If the WINS client does not receive a name refresh response from the WINS server, it sends name refresh requests every two minutes, until one-half of the TTL is expired.

If the WINS client does not receive a name refresh response and one-half of the TTL is expired, the WINS client begins sending name refresh requests to a secondary WINS server if the computer is configured with an IP address for a secondary WINS server. The WINS client attempts to refresh its registrations with the secondary WINS server as if it were the first refresh attempt—n time increments equal to one-eighth of the TTL. The WINS client sends the name refresh requests until it successfully receives a name refresh response, or one-half of the TTL is expired. If the WINS client cannot contact the secondary WINS server by the time half of the TTL has expired, it reverts back to the primary WINS server. After a WINS client has successfully refreshed its name registrations, it does not start subsequent name registration requests until one-half of the TTL is expired.

How WINS Clients Release Their Names

When a WINS-enabled computer is correctly stopped, the WINS client sends a *name release request* to the WINS server. A name release request is sent for each name associated with the computer, logged-on user, and network client service that is registered with the WINS server. The name release request includes the computer IP address and the name that should be released (deleted) from the WINS server database.

Because the WINS-enabled client is configured with the IP address of the WINS server, the name release requests are sent directly to the WINS server. When the WINS server receives a name release request, the WINS server checks the WINS database for the specified name.

Based on the results of the database check, the WINS server sends a positive or negative *name release response* to the WINS client and removes the specified name from the WINS database. The name release response contains the name released and a TTL of 0 (zero).

Table 8.3   WINS Server Response to Name Release Request

WINS server name release response	WINS client behavior
No response	The WINS client waits to receive the response, and if it does not receive one, it sends another name release request.
Positive	The WINS client releases the name and stops. Microsoft WINS clients ignore the contents of the name release response.
Negative	The WINS client releases the name and stops. Because Microsoft WINS clients ignore the contents of the name release response when the WINS server sends a negative name release response, the server does not prevent the client from releasing the name and stopping.
	The WINS server sends a negative name release response only if it encounters a WINS database error or if the address of the WINS client does not match the address stored in the WINS database.

How WINS Clients Perform Name Resolution

WINS clients perform NetBIOS computer name-to-IP-address mapping resolution by using the NetBIOS over TCP/IP (NetBT) component. A Windows NT-based computer is automatically configured to use one of four different NetBT name resolution modes (methods), based on how TCP/IP is configured on the computer. The following table describes the computer (referred to as a node) configuration and its associated NetBT name resolution mode.

Table 8.4   Description of NetBIOS Node Types

NetBIOS name resolution node type	Description
b-node	Uses IP broadcast messages to register and resolve NetBIOS names to IP addresses. Windows NT-based computers can use *modified b-node* name resolution.
p-node	Uses point-to-point communications with a NetBIOS name server (in Windows NT-based networks, this is the WINS server) to register and resolve computer names to IP addresses.
m-node	Uses a combination (mix) of b-node and p-node communications to register and resolve NetBIOS names. M-node first uses b-node; then, if necessary, p-node. M-node is typically not the best choice for larger networks because its preference for b-node broadcasts increases network traffic.
h-node	Uses a *hybrid* combination of b-node and p-node. When configured to use h-node, a computer always tries p-node first and uses b-node *only* if p-node fails. When a Windows NT-based computer is configured as a WINS client, it is by default configured as h-node. To further lessen the potential for IP broadcasts, Windows NT-based computers are configured, by installation default, to use an LMHOSTS file to search for name-to-IP-address mappings before using b-node IP broadcasts.

Note   Use the **ipconfig /all** command to display the TCP/IP configuration, including node type, of your computer. For example, on a computer that is configured as a WINS client, the node type Hybrid appears when the **ipconfig /all** command is entered.

The following figure illustrates the name resolution processes between a WINS client (h-node) and a WINS server.

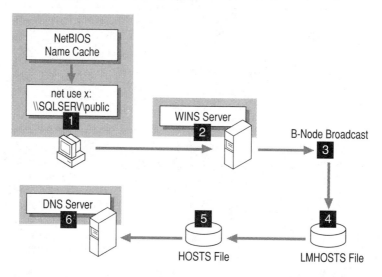

Figure 8.4   H-Node Name Resolution for WINS Clients

Microsoft WINS Proxy

A WINS proxy is a WINS-enabled computer that helps resolve name queries for non-WINS enabled computers in routed TCP/IP intranets. By default, non-WINS enabled computers are configured as b-node which use IP broadcasts for name queries. The WINS proxy computer listens on the local subnet for IP broadcast name queries.

When a non-WINS enabled computer sends an IP name query broadcast, the WINS proxy accepts the broadcast and checks its cache for the appropriate NetBIOS computer name-to-IP-address mapping. If the WINS proxy has the correct mapping in its cache, the WINS proxy sends this information to the non-WINS computer. If the name-to-IP-address mapping is not in cache, the WINS proxy queries a WINS server for the name-to-IP-address mapping.

If a WINS server is not available on the local subnet, the WINS proxy can query a WINS server across a router. The WINS proxy caches (stores in memory) computer name-to-IP-address mappings it receives from the WINS server. These mappings are used to respond to subsequent IP broadcast name queries from b-node computers on the local subnet.

The name-to-IP-address mappings that the WINS proxy receives from the WINS server are stored in the WINS proxy cache for a limited time. (By installation default this value is 6 minutes. The minimum value is 1 minute.)

When the WINS proxy receives a response from the WINS server, it stores the mapping in its cache and responds to any subsequent name query broadcasts with the mapping received from the WINS server.

The role of the WINS proxy is similar to that of the DHCP/BOOTP relay agent which forwards DHCP client requests across routers. Because the WINS server does not respond to broadcasts, a computer configured as a WINS proxy should be installed on subnets which contain computers that use broadcasts for name resolution.

Note To configure a computer as a WINS proxy, you must manually edit that computer's registry. The registry parameter **EnableProxy** must be set to 1 (REG_DWORD). This parameter is located in the following Registry key:

`HKEY_LOCAL_MACHINE\SYSTEM\CurrentControlSet\Services\Netbt\Parameters`

Planning for Microsoft WINS Server Implementation

The number of Windows NT-based WINS servers that an enterprise requires is based on the number of WINS client connections per server and the network topology. The number of users that can be supported per server varies according to usage patterns, data storage, and processing capabilities of the WINS server computer.

Planning for WINS server implementation on the network typically requires consideration of the issues presented in the following table.

Table 8.5   Network Configuration Planning Issues for WINS Servers

Planning issue	Guideline
How many WINS servers are required to ensure distribution of name query and name registration loads throughout the network?	One WINS server can handle NetBIOS name resolution requests for 10,000 computers. However, the location of routers on the network and the distribution of clients in each subnet should be considered when deciding how many WINS servers are required. See the following sections: "Planning for WINS Server Performance," "Planning for WINS Client Network Traffic," and "Planning for Replication Partners and Proxies."
Is the WAN bandwidth sufficient to support WINS server and WINS client name registration traffic?	See the next section, "Planning for WINS Client Network Traffic."
How many WINS servers are needed for disaster recovery, backup, and redundancy requirements?	See the following sections: "Planning for WINS Server Fault Tolerance" and "Planning for WINS Server Performance."
How can a planned distribution of WINS servers throughout the network be validated before installation?	When planning a network configuration, a generally accepted approach is to consider the consequences of two simultaneous failures at different points on the network.

See the following section, "Planning for WINS Server Fault Tolerance." |

Other planning issues for WINS servers can be similar to those for implementing Microsoft DHCP servers, as described in Chapter 7, "Managing Microsoft DHCP Servers."

Planning for WINS Client Network Traffic

WINS clients generate the following types of network traffic:

- Name registration
- Name refresh
- Name release
- Name query

When a WINS-enabled client starts on the network, it sends a name registration request for the computer name, user name, domain name, and any additional Microsoft network client services running on the computer. In other words, when a WINS client starts on the network, it generates a minimum of three name registration requests and three entries in the WINS database.

A Windows NT Server-based WINS client usually registers more NetBIOS names than other WINS-enabled clients. The name registration requests generated by a computer running under Windows NT Server include the following:

- Server component
- Domain names
- Replicator service name
- Messenger service name
- Browser service name
- Additional network program and service names

WINS Client Traffic on Routed Networks

When planning for WINS client traffic on large routed networks, consider the effect of name query, registration, and response traffic routed between subnets. Name requests and responses that occur at the daily startup of computers must pass through the traffic queues on the routers, and may cause delays at peak times.

Daily Startup of WINS Clients

An active WINS client name registration in a WINS server database is replicated to all pull partners configured on that WINS server. After some time, the active name registration is replicated to all WINS servers on the network.

When the WINS client is turned off at the end of the day, it releases the name. When the computer is started the next morning, the WINS client registers the name again with the WINS server, and receives a new version ID. This new, active name registration entry is replicated to the WINS server's pull partners as on the previous day.

Therefore the number of name registration entries that are replicated each day is roughly equivalent to the number of computers started each day times the number of NetBIOS names registered at each computer.

On large networks (50,000 or more computers), the biggest traffic load may be the name registration requests generated when WINS clients start on the network.. Fortunately, the difference in time zones in large enterprise networks provides some distribution of this WINS client startup load.

Roving User

When a user stops the computer and then moves and starts the computer on a different subnet with another primary WINS server, name challenge traffic is generated. Typically, the name registration request is answered with a Wait for Acknowledgment message (100 bytes), and the new WINS server (assuming the active entry was replicated) challenges the IP address that is currently in its database for this name (Name Query packet, 92 bytes). When there is no reply, as can be expected in this case, the WINS server repeats the challenge two more times and then updates the name registration entry with the new IP address and a new version ID. The new version ID indicates that the entry must be replicated from its new "owning" WINS server to other WINS servers on the network.

Estimating WINS Client Traffic

You can estimate WINS client traffic based on the behavior of the WINS clients as described in the preceding sections. However, when estimating WINS client traffic, you must also consider the network topology and the design or configuration of the routers in the network. In some cases it may not always be possible to predict the traffic load on a specific network router because the routers may be designed, or configured, to autonomously route traffic based on factors other than traffic load.

Planning for WINS Server Replication Across Wide Area Networks

The frequency of WINS database replication between WINS servers is a major planning issue. The WINS server database should be replicated frequently enough that the down-time of a single WINS server does not affect the reliability of the mapping information in the database of other WINS servers. However, when planning WINS database replication frequency, you do not want frequency of database replication to interfere with network throughput, which could happen if replication frequency is set to a small time interval.

Consider the network topology when planning for replication frequency. For example, if your network has multiple hubs connected by relatively slow wide-area-network (WAN) links, you can configure WINS database replication between WINS servers on the slow links to occur less frequently than replication on the local area network or on fast WAN links. This reduces traffic across the slow link and reduces contention between replication traffic and WINS client name queries.

For example, WIN servers at a central local-area-network site may be configured to replicate every 15 minutes, while database replication between WINS servers in different WAN hubs might be scheduled for every 30 minutes, and replication between WINS servers on different continents might be scheduled to replicate twice a day. The following figure illustrates this example of variation in replication frequency.

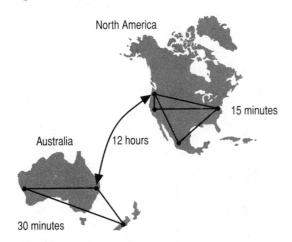

Figure 8.5   Enterprise Network Configuration and WINS Server Replication

Planning for Replication Convergence Time

The time needed to replicate a new entry in a WINS database from the WINS server that owns the entry to all other WINS servers on the network is called *convergence time*. When planning for WINS servers, you need to decide what is acceptable as the convergence time for your network.

This following figure illustrates an example network installation of WINS servers and the database replication interval between each WINS server. This example network configuration is presented to show how replication interval between WINS servers affects the convergence time.

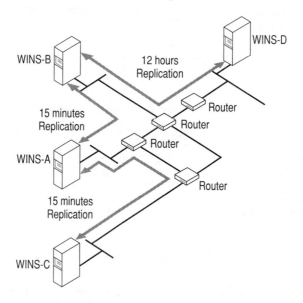

Figure 8.6   Replication Intervals Between WINS Servers in a Routed TCP/IP Network

If a WINS client registers its name with the WINS server labeled WINS_C in the figure, other WINS clients can query WINS_C for this name and get the name-to-IP-address mapping. WINS clients that query any of the other WINS servers shown in the figure (WINS_A, WINS_B, and WINS_D) do not get a positive response until the entry is replicated from the WINS_C server to WINS_A, WINS_B, and WINS_D. WINS_C is configured to start replication when the push *Update Count threshold* is exceeded or when the pull *Replication Interval* expires on its WINS pull partner, WINS_A. (For this example, WINS_A is configured with a replication interval of 15 minutes.)

Only when the pull Replication Interval expires is the entry replicated, but queries for the new name to WINS servers B and D may still not be successful. The time interval for replication to server B is 15 minutes; to server D, it is 12 hours. The convergence time is calculated as:

```
12 hours + 2x (15 minutes) = 12.5 hour
```

Name query requests may, in reality, succeed before the convergence time has passed. This would happen if the entries have to be replicated over a shorter path than the worst case path. And it would also happen when an Update Count threshold would be passed before the Replication Interval would expire; this would result in earlier replication of the new entry. The longer the replication path, the longer the convergence time.

Planning for WINS Server Fault Tolerance

There are two basic types of WINS server failures:

- A WINS server may crash, or be stopped to do maintenance.
- Network failures including failures of routers and link stations.

In Figure 8.6, a failure of WINS-A or WINS-B would segment the distribution of WINS server services. Entries would no longer be replicated from WINS-C to WINS-D, and vice versa. Because the IP address and name would no longer match for updated clients, other clients would not be able to connect to the updated computers. Adding replication between WINS-B and WINS-C would improve the configuration for cases in which WINS-A fails. Adding replication between WINS-D and WINS-C would improve fault tolerance in a case where the WINS-B server fails.

Failure of one of the links between A, B, and C could be tolerated because the underlying router network would reroute the traffic. Failure of the link between B and D, however, would segment the communication between WINS servers and would make other network traffic impossible should there be an on-demand backup link between D and C. The WINS replication traffic would then be rerouted by the underlying router infrastructure.

Planning for WINS Server Performance

A WINS server can typically service:

- 1,500 name registrations per minute.
- 4,500 queries per minute.

A conservative recommendation is that you plan to install one WINS server and a backup server for every 10,000 computers on the network, based on these numbers and the possibility for large-scale power outages that would cause many computers to re-start simultaneously.

Two factors enhance WINS server performance. WINS server performance can be increased almost 25 percent on a computer with two processors. WINS server name replication response time can be measurably improved by using a dedicated disk.

After you establish WINS servers on the intranet, you can adjust the time between a WINS client name registration and name renewal. This is referred to as the *Renewal Interval*. Setting this interval to reduce the numbers of registrations can help tune server response time. (The Renewal Interval is specified when configuring the WINS server.)

Planning for Replication Partners and Proxies

Choosing whether to configure another WINS server as a push partner or pull partner depends on several considerations, including the specific configuration of servers at your site, whether the partner is across a wide area network (WAN), and how important it is to distribute changes throughout the network. Only one computer configured as a WINS proxy should be installed on each subnet. (Configuring more than one WINS proxy per subnet can overload the WINS servers on the same subnet.)

In one possible configuration, one WINS server can be designated as the central server, and all other WINS servers can be configured as both push partner and pull partner of this central server. Such a configuration ensures that the WINS database on each server contains addresses for every node on the WAN.

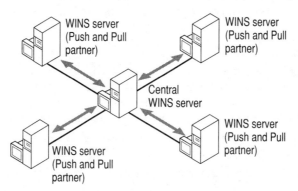

Figure 8.7   WINS Servers Replication by using a Central WINS Server

Another option is to set up a chain of WINS servers, where each server is both the push partner and pull partner with a nearby WINS server. In such a configuration, the two servers at the ends of the chain would also be push and pull partners with each other.

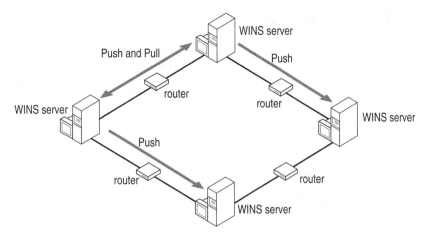

Figure 8.8   WINS Servers Replication in a Chained Network Configuration

Other replication partner configurations can be established for your site's needs. For example, in the following illustration, Server1 has only Server2 as a partner, but Server2 has three partners. So, for example, Server1 gets all replicated information from Server2, but Server2 gets information from Server1, Server3, and Server4.

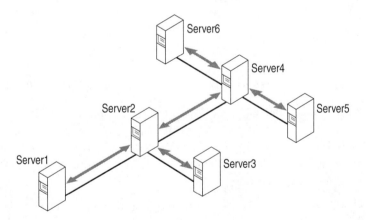

Figure 8.9   WINS Server Replication in a T Network Configuration

- If Server2, for example, needs to perform pull replications with Server4, make sure it is a push partner of Server1 and Server3.
- If Server2 needs to push replications to Server3, it should be a pull partner of Server1 and Server4.

Fine-tuning WINS Server Replication Traffic

Fine-tuning the Replication Intervals may save some bandwidth on WAN links. Figure 8.10 illustrates a network configuration based on the network configuration first illustrated in Figure 8.6. The network configuration in Figure 8.6 was changed to the configuration shown in Figure 8.10 to illustrate one possible method for reducing convergence time.

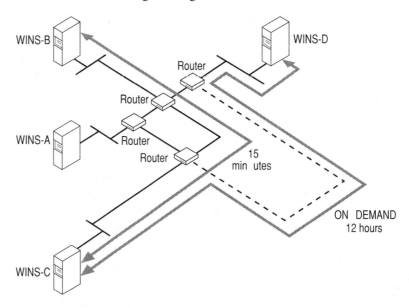

Figure 8.10   Reducing WINS Server Replication Convergence Time

By keeping the pull Replication Intervals between WINS-C and WINS-B short (15 minutes), WINS servers A, B, and C can be reasonably synchronized. Replicas are never pulled in twice; only replicas with a higher version ID are copied. When WINS-B has an entry directly from WINS-C, it does not pull that entry from WINS-A.

However, under the example configuration there is the chance that both WINS-D and WINS-B can pull replicas from WINS-C by using the link between WINS-B and WINS-C. The resultant load on the link between WINS-B and WINS-C would increase.

In the example, this problem can be avoided if WINS-D is configured to pull replicas from WINS-B first and then check WINS-C. The pull Replication Interval between WINS-D and WINS-C would typically be the same 12 hours. Remember to configure push Update Counts (on WINS-D and WINS-C) to correspond to the 12 hours pull Replication Interval; otherwise unexpected replication is triggered by the Update Count threshold and not by the pull Replication Interval.

Using WINS Manager

When you install a WINS server, the **WINS Manager** graphic administration tool is added to the **Administrative Tools (Common)** Programs group on the **Start** menu.

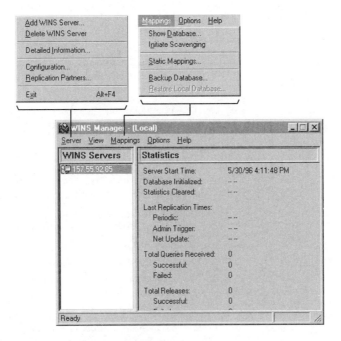

Figure 8.11   Using WINS Manager

Use WINS Manager to view and change parameters for WINS servers on the network for which you have administrator privileges. WINS Manager Help is organized to provide information for each of the specific administration and configuration tasks that you need to perform to manage WINS servers. See WINS Manager Help for specific task lists and instructions.

Note   Other tools you can use to manage WINS servers include the Performance Monitor and SNMP agent service. Use Performance Monitor to monitor WINS server performance. Use the SNMP service to monitor and configure WINS servers by using third-party SNMP manager tools. Note that when using a third-party SNMP manager tool, some WINS queries may time out; if so, you should increase the time-out on the SNMP tool you are using.

Viewing WINS Server Operational Status

WINS Manager allows you to view administrative and operational information about WINS servers. When you open WINS Manager, it displays basic statistics about the selected WINS server in the right pane of the WINS Manager window. The following table describes these basic statistics for WINS servers.

Table 8.6   Statistics in WINS Manager

Statistic	Description
Database Initialized	The last time static mappings were imported into the WINS database.
Statistics Cleared	The time when statistics for the WINS server were last cleared with the **Clear Statistics** command from the **View** menu.
Last Replication Times	The times at which the WINS database was last replicated.
Periodic	The last time the WINS database was replicated based on the replication interval specified in the **Preferences** dialog box.
Admin Trigger	The last time the WINS database was replicated because the administrator clicked the **Replicate Now** button in the **Replication Partners** dialog box.
Net Update	The last time the WINS database was replicated as a result of a network request, which is a push notification message that requests propagation.
Total Queries Received	The number of name query request messages received by this WINS server. Successful indicates how many names were successfully matched in the database, and Failed indicates how many names this WINS server could not resolve.
Total Releases	The number of messages received that indicate a NetBIOS program has stopped. Successful indicates how many names were successfully released, and Failed indicates how many names this WINS server could not release.
Total Registrations	The number of messages received that indicate name registrations for clients.

You can display additional statistics by clicking **Detailed Information** on the **Server** menu. The following table describes these detailed information statistics.

Table 8.7   Detailed Information Statistics for WINS Manager

Statistic	Meaning
Last Address Change	Indicates the time at which the last WINS database change was replicated.
Last Scavenging Times	Indicates the last times that the database was cleaned for specific types of entries. (For information about database scavenging, see "Managing the WINS Server Database" later in this chapter.)
Periodic	Indicates when the database was cleaned based on the renewal interval specified in the **WINS Server Configuration–(Local)** dialog box.
Admin Trigger	Indicates when the database was last cleaned because the administrator chose **Initiate Scavenging**.
Extinction	Indicates when the database was last cleaned based on the Extinction interval specified in the **WINS Server Configuration** dialog box.
Verification	Indicates when the database was last cleaned based on the verify interval specified in the **WINS Server Configuration** dialog box.
Unique Registrations	Indicates the number of name registration requests that have been accepted by this WINS server.
Unique Conflicts	The number of conflicts encountered during registration of unique names owned by this WINS server.
Unique Renewals	The number of renewals received for unique names.
Group Registrations	The number of registration requests for groups that have been accepted by this WINS server. (For information about groups, see Table 8.10 later in this chapter.)
Group Conflicts	The number of conflicts encountered during registration of group names.
Group Renewals	The number of renewals received for group names.

Configuring WINS Server and WINS Client Behavior

Use WINS Manager to configure WINS server management of WINS client mappings by using the configuration options in the **WINS Server Configuration - (Local)** dialog box. The configuration options allow you to specify time intervals that govern WINS client behavior as described in the following table.

Table 8.8   Configuration Options for WINS Server

Configuration option	Description
Renewal Interval	Specifies how often a client reregisters its name. The default is six days.
Extinction Interval	Specifies the interval between when an entry is marked as *released* and when it is marked as *extinct*. The default is dependent on the renewal interval and, if the WINS server has replication partners, on the maximum replication time interval. Maximum allowable value is six days.
Extinction Timeout	Specifies the interval between when an entry is marked *extinct* and when the entry is finally scavenged from the database. The default is dependent on the renewal interval and, if the WINS server has replication partners, on the maximum replication time interval. The default is six days.
Verify Interval	Specifies the interval after which the WINS server must verify that old names it does not own are still active. The default is dependent on the extinction interval. The maximum allowable value is 24 days.

The extinction interval, extinction timeout, and verify interval are derived from the renewal interval and the partner replication interval. The WINS server adjusts the values specified by the administrator to keep the inconsistency between a WINS server and its partners as small as possible.

You can run the Registry Editor program at the command prompt to configure a WINS server by changing the values of the Registry parameters listed in the following table.

Table 8.9   Advanced WINS Server Configuration Options

Configuration option	Description
Logging Enabled	Specifies whether logging of database changes to J50.log files should be turned on.
Log Detailed Events	Specifies whether logging events is verbose mode. (This requires considerable computer resources and should be turned off if you are tuning for performance.)
Replicate Only With Partners	Specifies that replication occurs only with configured WINS pull or push partners. If this option is not checked, an administrator can ask a WINS server to pull or push from or to a non-listed WINS server partner. By default, this option is checked.
Backup On Termination	Specifies that the database is backed up automatically when WINS Manager is stopped, except when the computer is stopped.
Migrate On/Off	Specifies that static unique and multihomed records in the database are treated as dynamic when they conflict with a new registration or replica. This means that if they are no longer valid, they are overwritten by the new registration or replica. Check this option if you are upgrading non-Windows NT-based computers to Windows NT. By default, this option is not checked.
Starting Version Count	Specifies the highest version ID number for the database. Usually, you do not need to change this value unless the database becomes corrupted and needs to start fresh. In such a case, set this value to a number higher than appears as the version number counter for this WINS server on all the remote partners that earlier replicated the local WINS server's records. WINS may adjust the value you specify to a higher one to ensure that database records are quickly replicated to other WINS servers. The maximum allowable value is $2^{31} - 1$. This value can be seen in the **View Database** dialog box in WINS Manager.
Database Backup Path	Specifies the directory where the WINS database backup is stored. If you specify a backup path, WINS automatically performs a full backup of its database to this directory every 24 hours. WINS uses this directory to perform an automatic restoration of the database in the event that the database is found to be corrupted when WINS is started. Do not specify a network directory.

Managing Static NetBIOS Name-to-IP-Address Mappings

Static mappings are non-dynamic database entries of NetBIOS computer name-to-IP address mappings for computers on the network that are not WINS-enabled or special groups of network devices.

Click **Static Mappings** on the **Mappings** menu in WINS Manager to view, add, edit, import, or delete static mappings.

Once entered to the WINS server database, static name-to-IP-address mappings cannot be challenged or removed, except by an administrator who manually removes the specific mapping by using WINS Manager to remove the entry from the WINS server database. All changes made to the WINS server database by using WINS Manager take effect immediately.

Important A DHCP reserved (or static) IP address for a unique name in a multihomed computer overrides an obsolete WINS static mapping if the WINS server advanced configuration option **Migration On/Off** is checked "on."

Static NetBIOS name mappings can be any of the types listed in the following table.

Table 8.10   Types of Static NetBIOS Name Mappings

Type option	Description
Unique	A unique name that maps to a single IP address. Contrast with multihomed type.
Group	Also referred to as a "Normal" Group. When adding an entry to Group by using WINS Manager, you must enter the computer name and IP address.
	However, the IP addresses of individual members of Group are not stored in the WINS database. Because the member addresses are not stored, there is no limit to the number of members that can be added to a Group.
	Broadcast name packets are used to communicate with Group members. Contrast with Internet group type.
Domain	A NetBIOS name-to-IP-address mapping that has 0x1C as the 16th byte. A domain group stores up to a maximum of 25 addresses for members. For registrations after the 25th address, WINS overwrites a replica address or, if none is present, it overwrites the oldest registration.

Table 8.10   Types of Static NetBIOS Name Mappings *(continued)*

Type option	Description
Internet group	Internet groups are user-defined groups that allow you to group resources, such as printers, for easy reference and browsing. The default 16th byte of an Internet group name is set equal to 0x20. An Internet group can store up to a maximum of 25 *addresses* for members. When you add a Internet group three unique records are added: • InternetGroupName<0x20> • InternetGroupName<0x3> • InternetGroupName<0x0> This is similar to the domain group. Internet group members can be added as the result of dynamic group registrations. A dynamic member, however, does not replace static member added by using WINS Manager or importing the LMHOSTS file. Contrast with Group type.
Multihomed	A unique name that can have more than one address. This is used for multihomed computers. The maximum number of addresses that can be registered as multihomed is 25. For registrations after the 25th address, WINS overwrites a replica address or, if none is present, it overwrites the oldest registration. Contrast with Unique type.

Managing the WINS Server Database

The WINS database under Windows NT Server 4.0 uses the performance-enhanced Exchange Server Storage engine version 4.0.

There is no built-in limit to the number of records that a WINS server can replicate or store. The size of the database is dependent upon the number of WINS clients on the network. The WINS database grows over time as a result of clients starting and stopping on the network.

The size of the WINS database is not directly proportional to the number of active client entries. Over time, as some WINS client entries become obsolete, and are deleted, there remains some unused space.

To recover the unused space, the WINS database is compacted. Under Windows NT Server 4.0, WINS server database compaction occurs as an automatic background process during idle time after a database update.

Because the WINS server database compaction occurs while the database is being used, you do not need to stop the WINS server to compact the database.

Note Under Windows NT Server 3.51 or earlier, you must manually compact the WINS server database. See the topic "Compacting the WINS Server Database" in the section "Troubleshooting the WINS Server Database" later in this chapter. In most cases there is no need to manually compact the WINS server database under Windows NT Server 4.0. However, if you decide to do so, use this same procedure.

The following database files are stored in the \%*systemroot*%\System32\Wins directory.

Table 8.11   Microsoft WINS Server Database Files

File	Description
J50.log and J50#####.log	A log of all transactions done with the database. This file is used by WINS to recover data if necessary.
J50.chk	A checkpoint file.
Wins.mdb	The WINS server database file which contains two tables: ■ IP address-Owner ID mapping table ■ Name-to-IP-address mapping table
Winstmp.mdb	A temporary file that is created by the WINS server service. This file is used by the database as a swap file during index maintenance operations and may remain in the %*systemroot*%\System32\Wins directory after a crash.

Important The J50.log, J50#####.log, Wins.mdb, and Winstmp.mdb files should not be removed or tampered with in any manner.

WINS Manager provides the tools you need to maintain, view, back up, and restore the WINS server database. For example, you use the WINS Manager to back up the WINS server database files, and this administrative task should be done when you back up other files on the WINS server.

Backing Up the Database

WINS Manager provides backup tools so that you can back up the WINS database. After you specify a backup directory for the database, WINS performs complete database backups every three hours, by installation default.

For specific instructions on how to back up and restore the WINS database, see the Help topic "Backing Up and Restoring the Database" in WINS Manager Help.

You should also periodically back up the Registry entries for the WINS server.

Scavenging the Database

Scavenging the WINS server database is an administrative task related to backing up the database. Like any database, the WINS server database of address mappings needs to be periodically cleaned and backed up.

The local WINS server database should periodically be cleared of released entries and old entries that were registered at another WINS server and replicated to the local WINS server, but for some reason did not get removed from the local WINS database when the entries were removed from the remote WINS server database.

This process, called *scavenging*, is done automatically over intervals defined by the relationship between the Renewal and Extinct intervals defined in the **Configuration** dialog box. You can also clean the database manually.

The following table describes the results of scavenging the WINS database.

Table 8.12   Scavenging the WINS Database

State before scavenging	State after scavenging
Owned active names for which the Renewal interval has expired	Marked *released*
Owned released name for which the Extinct interval has expired	Marked *extinct*
Owned extinct names for which the Extinct timeout has expired	Deleted
Replicas of extinct names for which the Extinct timeout has expired	Deleted
Replicas of active names for which the Verify interval has expired	Revalidated
Replicas of extinct or deleted names	Deleted

Troubleshooting WINS Servers

This section describes some basic troubleshooting steps for common problems. It also describes how to restore or rebuild the WINS database.

The following error conditions can indicate potential problems with the WINS server:

- The administrator can't connect to a WINS server by using WINS Manager and receives an error message when attempting to do so.
- The WINS client service or Windows Internet Name Service might be down and cannot be restarted.

Verifying WINS Service Status

The first troubleshooting task is to make sure the appropriate services are running.

▶ **To ensure that the WINS services are running**

1. Use the **Services** option in **Control Panel** to verify that the WINS services are running.

   In the **Services** dialog box for the client computer, "Started" should appear in the Status column for the WINS client service. For the WINS server itself, "Started" should appear in the Status column for the Windows Internet Name Service.

2. If a necessary service is not started on either computer, start the service.

Resolving Common WINS Errors

▶ **To resolve "duplicate name" error messages**

- Check the WINS database for the entries for that name that have a static name-to-IP-address mapping. If there is a static address record, delete it from the WINS server database.

  Or, set the value of **MigrateOn** in the Registry equal to 1, so that the static records in the database can be updated by dynamic registrations (after the WINS server successfully challenges the old address).

▶ **To locate the source of "network path not found" error messages on a WINS client**

- Check the WINS database for the name. If the name is not present in the database, check whether the destination or target computer uses b-node name resolution. If so, add a static mapping for it in the WINS database.

  If the computer is configured as p-node, m-node, or h-node, and if its IP address is different from the one in the WINS database, then it may be that its address changed recently and the new address has not yet replicated to the local WINS server. To get the latest records, ask the WINS server that registered the address to perform a push replication with propagation to the local WINS server.

▶ **To discover why a WINS server cannot pull or push replications to another WINS server**

1. Use the **ping** utility to verify that each WINS server is running and can be connected to.

2. Ensure that each server is correctly configured as both a pull and push partner.
   - If ServerA needs to perform pull replications with ServerB, make sure it is a push partner of ServerB.
   - If ServerA needs to push replications to ServerB, it should be a pull partner of ServerB.

   To determine the configuration of a replication partner, check the values under the **Pull** and **Push** keys in the Registry.

▶ **To determine why WINS backup fails**

- Make sure the path for the WINS backup directory is on a local disk on the WINS server.

  WINS cannot back up its database files to a remote drive.

Troubleshooting the WINS Server Database

This section describes how to restore, rebuild, or move the WINS database. Also provided is a procedure for compacting the WINS database for Windows NT Server version 3.51 or earlier. (Microsoft WINS running under Windows NT Server version 4.0 provides automatic compacting of the WINS database.)

Restoring a WINS Server Database

If you have determined that the Windows Internet Name Service is running on the WINS server, but you cannot connect to the server using WINS Manager, then the WINS database is not available or has become corrupted. If a WINS server fails for any reason, you can restore the database from a backup copy.

You can use WINS Manager to restore the WINS database, or you can manually restore the database. For information about using WINS Manager to restore a WINS database, see the topic "Backing Up and Restoring the Database" in WINS Manager Help.

▶ **To restore a WINS database manually**

1. Before starting, make a copy of the WINS database files.

2. In the \%*Systemroot*%\System32\Wins directory, delete the J50.log, J50#####.log, and Wins.tmp files.

3. Copy an uncorrupted backup version of Wins.mdb to the *Systemroot*\System32\Wins directory.

4. Restart the WINS service on the WINS server, using the procedure in the next section.

Restarting and Rebuilding a Stopped WINS Server

In rare circumstances, the WINS server may not start or a STOP error might occur. If the WINS server is stopped, use the following procedure to restart it.

▶ **To restart a WINS server that is stopped**

1. Turn off the power to the server and wait at least 15 seconds.

2. Turn on the power, start Windows NT Server, and then log on under an account with Administrator rights.

3. At the command prompt, type **net start wins**, and then press ENTER.

If the hardware for the WINS server is malfunctioning or other problems prevent you from running Windows NT, you must rebuild the WINS database on another computer.

▶ **To rebuild a WINS server**

1. If you can start the original WINS server using MS-DOS, use MS-DOS to make backup copies of the files in the *Systemroot*\System32\Wins directory.

   If you cannot start the computer with MS-DOS, you must use the last backup version of the WINS database files.

2. Install Windows NT Server and Microsoft TCP/IP to create a new WINS server using the same hard drive location and *Systemroot* directory.

   That is, if the original server stored the WINS files on C:\Winnt35\System32\Wins, then the new WINS server must use this same path to the WINS files.

3. Make sure the WINS services on the new server are stopped, and then use the Registry Editor to restore the WINS keys from backup files.

4. Copy the WINS backup files to the *Systemroot*\System32\Wins directory.

5. Restart the new, rebuilt WINS server.

Moving the WINS Server Database

You may find a situation where you need to move a WINS database to another computer. To do this, use the following procedure.

▶ **To move a WINS database**

1. Stop the Windows Internet Name Service on the current computer, using the procedure in the preceding section.

2. Copy the \System32\Wins directory to the new computer that has been configured as a WINS server.

   Make sure the new directory is under exactly the same drive letter and path as on the old computer.

   If you must copy the files to a different directory, copy Wins.mdb, but do not copy the checkpoint (.chk) or log files.

3. Start the Windows Internet Name Service on the new computer.

   The service automatically starts using the .mdb and .log files copied from the old computer.

Compacting the WINS Server Database

Windows NT Server version 4.0 is designed to automatically compact the WINS database, and you should normally not need to run this procedure. However, if you are using Windows NT Server version 3.51 or earlier, after WINS has been running for a while, the database might need to be compacted to improve WINS performance. You should compact the WINS database whenever it approaches 30 MB.

You can use the Jetpack.exe utility provided with Windows NT Server version 3.5 and 3.51 to compact a WINS database. Jetpack.exe is a command-line utility that is run in the Windows NT Server command window. The utility is found in the \%*Systemroot*\System32 directory.

The Jetpack.exe syntax is:

Jetpack.exe <*database name*> <*temp database name*>

For example:

```
> CD %SYSTEMROOT%\SYSTEM32\WINS
> JETPACK WINS.MDB TMP.MDB
```

In the preceding examples, Tmp.mdb is a temporary database that is used by Jetpack.exe. Wins.mdb is the WINS database file. When Jetpack.exe is started, it performs the following sequential tasks:

1. Copies database information to a temporary database file called Tmp.mdb.
2. Deletes the original database file, Wins.mdb.
3. Renames the temporary database file to the original filename.

▶ **To compact the WINS database**

1. In Control Panel, on the local WINS server computer, double-click **Services**.
2. Under Service, click **Windows Internet Name Service**.
3. Click **Stop,** and then click **Close**. (Alternatively, you can type **net stop wins** at the command prompt.)
4. Click **Start**, and then click **Run**.
5. In **Open**, type **Jetpack.exe**, and then click **OK**.
6. Restart the Windows Internet Name Service by using the **Services** dialog box.

C H A P T E R   9

Managing Microsoft DNS Servers

The Domain Name System (DNS) is a set of protocols and services for Transmission Control Protocol/Internet Protocol (TCP/IP) networks. DNS enables you to use hierarchical "friendly" names to easily locate computers and other resources on a network. Microsoft DNS server is a new service in the family of TCP/IP networking services provided by Windows NT Server version 4.0. It enables you to provide and manage DNS services for your private TCP/IP networks and for users who connect to the public Internet. Microsoft DNS server is based on a client/server architecture that enables Microsoft DNS servers to maintain DNS name data and process DNS client name queries.

This chapter is for network administrators and support personnel who need to understand and administer DNS services. It includes the following topics:

- Introduction to the Domain Name System
- Microsoft DNS server
  - DNS server database
  - Primary and secondary DNS servers
- Microsoft DNS clients
- Planning for Microsoft DNS server implementation
  - Using Microsoft DNS server to connect to the Internet
  - Planning for Microsoft DNS and Microsoft WINS integration
- Using DNS Manager
  - Adding DNS servers
  - Creating zones
  - Adding and Modifying DNS resource records
  - The zone transfer

- Troubleshooting DNS server
  - Using the DNS diagnostic utility—**Nslookup**
  - Refreshing DNS server statistics
  - Resolving slow DNS zone transfer
  - Resolving zone wizard errors
  - Porting data files from other DNS servers

Introduction to Domain Name System

The Domain Name System (DNS) is used extensively on the Internet and in many private enterprises today. Computers running TCP/IP and connected to the Internet can have one or more IP addresses associated with each network adapter card in the computer. DNS is designed so that people do not have to remember IP addresses, but can instead use "friendly" names to locate and connect to remote computers and other network devices on TCP/IP networks. DNS is used on private TCP/IP-based intranets as well as the Internet.

Before the implementation of DNS, the use of names to locate resources on TCP/IP networks was supported by using a name resolution method based on files known as HOSTS files. Each HOSTS file contained a list of host (computer or other TCP/IP network device) names and their associated IP addresses. As the number of computers and users on the Internet grew, the HOSTS file method of name resolution became an unmanageable solution.

DNS is designed to replace the HOSTS file with a distributed database that implements a conceptual naming system. This naming system allows for growth on the Internet and the creation of host names that are unique throughout the Internet and private TCP/IP-based intranets.

The conceptual naming system on which DNS is based is a hierarchical and logical tree structure called the *domain name space*. The root (the top-most level) of the domain name space is managed by the Internet Network Information Center (InterNIC) (**http://www.internic.net**). InterNIC is responsible for delegating administrative responsibility for portions of the domain name space to organizations and enterprises that connect to the Internet.

These organizations and enterprises then employ DNS servers to manage the name-to-IP-address mappings for computers and network devices contained within their *authoritative* domain. The DNS servers that are used at the upper levels of the DNS hierarchy and at private domain nodes lower down in the DNS hierarchy are referred to as the *authoritative name servers*.

To understand how the conceptual domain name space is used to create unique names for computers on TCP/IP networks, you need to understand the top-down structure of DNS. The top level of the domain name space is managed by InterNIC and is divided into three main areas:

- Organizational domains—these are named by using a 3-character code that indicates the primary function or activity of the enterprises contained within the domain. Most organizations and enterprises located in the United States are contained within one of these organizational domains, as shown in Table 9.1.

- Geographical domains—these are named by using the 2-character country codes established by ISO 3166. These codes are used primarily for international organization and enterprise domains.

- Reverse domain—this is a special domain, named *in-addr.arpa*, that is used for IP-address-to-name mappings (referred to as *reverse name lookup*.)

The most commonly used top-level DNS name components for organizations and institutions in the United States are described in the following table and in Figure 9.1.

Table 9.1   Top-level Name Component of the DNS Hierarchy

Top-level name component	Description	Example domain name
.com	InterNIC assigns portions of the domain name space under this level to commercial organizations, such as the Microsoft Corporation.	microsoft.com
.edu	InterNIC assigns portions of this domain name space to educational organizations, such as the Massachusetts Institute of Technology.	mit.edu
.gov	InterNIC assigns portions of this domain name space to governmental organizations, such as the White House in Washington, D.C.	whitehouse.gov
.int	InterNIC assigns portions of this domain name space to international organizations, such as the North Atlantic Treaty Organization.	nato.int

Table 9.1   Top-level Name Component of the DNS Hierarchy *(continued)*

Top-level name component	Description	Example domain name
.mil	InterNIC assigns portions of the domain name space to military operations, such as the Defense Date Network.	ddn.mil
.net	InterNIC assigns portions of the domain name space to networking organizations, such as the the National Science Foundation.	nsf.net
.org	InterNIC assigns portions of the domain name space to noncommercial organizations, such as the Center for Networked Information Discovery and Recovery.	cnidr.org

As mentioned earlier, InterNIC manages the assignment of domain names to organizations, private enterprises, and institutions. The organizations and enterprises to which InterNIC assigns a portion of the domain name space are then responsible for naming the computers and network devices within their assigned domain and its subdivisions.

The following figure illustrates the DNS naming conventions described in Table 9.1 by using a fictional domain named TerraFlora that contains a host (computer) named 'mfgserver'.

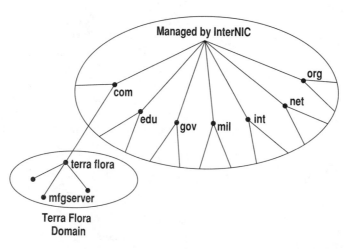

Figure 9.1   Domain Name System

A DNS-based name for the server in the TerraFlora domain is constructed as *mfgserver.terraflora.com*, which is the concatenation of the host name (mfgserver) with the domain name (terraflora) and the upper-level name (com) separated by the dot "." character at each point of concatenation. This name is referred to as the *Fully Qualified Domain Name (FQDN)*.

Note In general, domain names and host names have restrictions in their naming which only allow the use of characters a-z, A-Z, 0-9, and the dash or minus sign (-). The use of characters such the slash (/), period (.), and underscore (_) is not allowed by specification. However, Microsoft DNS server does allow the use of underscore (_) in a name. This is done to support BIND versions earlier than BIND version 4.94

The preceding figure presents a simple view of a domain. In actuality, domains can contain both hosts (computers) and other domains (referred to as zones, sub-zones, or domains). Each organization assigned authority for a portion of the domain name space is responsible for administering, subdividing, and naming the zones, sub-zones, domains, and computers within the domain for which they are "authoritative" by InterNIC assignment.

Subdividing is an important concept in DNS. Creating subdivisions of the domain name space and private TCP/IP network domains supports new growth on the Internet and the ability to continually expand name and administrative groupings.

For example, the Terraflora domain could contain groups such as retail, manufacturing, and so on. A DNS administrator of the Terraflora domain could subdivide the domain to create host names that reflect these groupings. For example, Terraflora's Internet server could be named www.terraflora.com and their retail departmental server could be named ntserver.retail.terraflora.com, and so on.

Microsoft DNS Server

Microsoft DNS server running under Windows NT Server version 4.0 is an RFC-compliant DNS name server that you use to manage and administer DNS services on your TCP/IP network. Microsoft DNS server supports RFCs 1033, 1034, 1035, 1101, 1123, 1183, and 1536, and is also compatible with the Berkeley Internet Name Domain (BIND) implementation of DNS.

Note BIND is a popular implementation of DNS originally developed at Berkeley for the 4.3 BSD UNIX operating system.

Because Microsoft DNS server is an RFC-compliant DNS server, it creates and uses standard DNS database files and record types. These are referred to as resource record types. Microsoft DNS server is interoperable with other DNS servers and can be managed by using the standard DNS diagnostic utility, **nslookup**. (**Nslookup** is included with the TCP/IP utilities provided with Windows NT Server version 4.0.)

Microsoft DNS server also has features above and beyond those specified in the RFCs, such as tight integration with Microsoft Windows Internet Name Service (WINS) and ease-of-administration through the use of the graphical user interface, DNS Manager.

Integration of DNS and WINS services is an important feature that allows interoperability between non-Microsoft and Microsoft Windows-based TCP/IP network clients. DNS and WINS integration provides a method to reliably resolve name queries for Windows-based computers that use dynamic (DHCP-based) IP addressing and NetBIOS computer names.

The other important new feature of the Microsoft DNS server implementation is DNS Manager, a graphical user interface that you use to manage local and remote Microsoft DNS servers and database files.

Microsoft DNS server allows you to use a computer running under Windows NT Server version 4.0 to administer an entire domain or subdivisions of the domain referred to as zones, sub-zones and domains. These subdivisions are dependent on your enterprise requirements for name and administrative groupings of computers, integration of Windows NT-based domains into the DNS domain model, or your role as an Internet Service Provider (ISP) to other enterprises.

Note In existing TCP/IP networks that are administratively organized by using Windows NT-based domain concepts, it is recommended that you use, or realign, your Windows NT-based domains with the DNS domain and subdivisions you have or may create. For additional information, see the topic "Planning for Microsoft DNS and Microsoft WINS Integration" later in this chapter.

The main administrative grouping by which a computer running Microsoft DNS server manages DNS services is the zone. A *zone* is an administrative portion (in small enterprises it can be the entire portion) of a DNS domain, referred to as the zone's *root domain*. (This root domain is generally the domain for which your organization is authoritative.) You can install Microsoft DNS servers in the root domain, zone, and zone subdivisions of a TCP/IP network— wherever you need a DNS server to manage your DNS data and DNS name query traffic.

The following figure illustrates an example deployment of Microsoft DNS servers based on the domain and zone concepts.

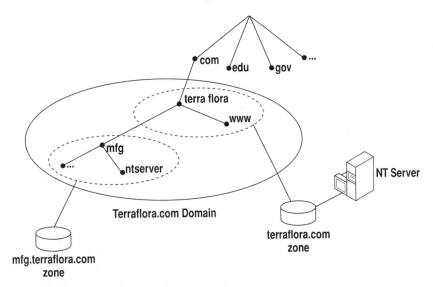

Figure 9.2   DNS Zones

A single Microsoft DNS server can be configured to manage one or multiple zones. You can also use multiple DNS servers to administer a zone and its subdivisions, as shown in the preceding figure. Dividing a domain into multiple zones can be done to distribute administrative tasks to different groups and to provide efficient data distribution by using the data replication method referred to as a *zone transfer*.

Microsoft DNS Server Database

The Microsoft DNS server database is a set of files that contain the host name-to-IP-address mappings and other DNS information data for the computers on your TCP/IP network. These data records are referred to as *resource records* and are contained in the zone, cache, reverse-lookup, and arpa-127 files in the \%systemroot%\Winnt\System32\Dns directory.

The following table describes the different types of resource records that may be used to provide DNS-based data about computers on a TCP/IP network.

Table 9.2   DNS Resource Record Types

Record type	Description
A	An address record that maps a host name to an IP address in a DNS zone. Its counterpart, the PTR resource record, is used to map an IP address to a host name in a DNS reverse zone (those in the *in-addr.arpa.* DNS domain).
AFSDB	Gives the location of either an Andrew File System (AFS) cell database server, or a DCE (Distributed Computing Environment) cell's authenticated name server. The AFS system uses DNS to map a DNS domain name to the name of an AFS cell database server. The Open Software Foundation's DCE Naming service uses DNS for a similar function.
CNAME	The canonical name resource record creates an alias (synonymous name) for the specified host name. You can use CNAME records to hide the implementation details of your network from the clients that connect to it. For example, ftp.terraflora.com is an alias (CNAME) for the real name of the computer that runs the FTP server. This alias also allows the FTP server to be moved to a different computer; only the CNAME record needs to change.
HINFO	The host information resource record identifies a host's hardware type and operating system. The CPU Type and Operating System identifiers should come from the computer names and system names listed in RFC 1700.
ISDN	The Integrated Services Digital Network (ISDN) resource record is a variation of the A (address) resource record. Rather than mapping a host name to an IP address, the ISDN record maps the name to an ISDN address. An ISDN address is a phone number that consists of a country code, an area code or country code, a local phone number, and, optionally, a subaddress. The ISDN resource record is designed to be used in conjunction with the RT (route through) resource record.
MB	The mailbox resource record is an experimental record that specifies a DNS host with the specified mailbox. Other related experimental records are the MG (mail group) resource record, the MR (mailbox rename) resource record, and the MINFO (mailbox information) resource record.
MG	The mail group resource record is an experimental record that specifies a mailbox that is a member of the mail group (mailing list) specified by the DNS domain name. Other related experimental records are the MB (mailbox) resource record, the MR (mailbox rename) resource record, and the MINFO (mailbox information) resource record.

Table 9.2 DNS Resource Record Types *(continued)*

Record type	Description
MINFO	The mailbox information resource record is an experimental record that specifies a mailbox that is responsible for the specified mailing list or mailbox. Other related experimental records are the MB (mailbox) resource record, the MG (mail group) resource record, and the MR (mailbox rename) resource record.
MR	The mailbox rename resource record is an experimental record that specifies a mailbox that is the proper rename of the other specified mailbox. Other related experimental records are the MB (mailbox) resource record, the MG (mail group) resource record, and the MINFO (mailbox information) resource record.
MX	The mail exchange resource record specifies a mail exchange server for a DNS domain name. A mail exchange server is a host that will either process or forward mail for the DNS domain name. Processing the mail means either delivering it to the addressee or passing it to a different type of mail transport. Forwarding the mail means sending it to its final destination server, sending it using Simple Message Transfer Protocol (SMTP) to another mail exchange server that is closer to the final destination, or queuing it for a specified amount of time.
NS	The name server resource record identifies the DNS server(s) for the DNS domain. NS resource records appear in all DNS zones and reverse zones (those in the *in-addr.arpa* DNS domain).
PTR	The pointer resource record maps an IP address to a host name in a DNS reverse zone (those in the *in-addr.arpa* DNS domain). Its counterpart, the A (address) resource record, is used to map a host name to an IP address in a DNS zone.
RP	The responsible person resource record indicates who is responsible for the specified DNS domain or host. You can specify multiple RP records for a given DNS domain or host. The record has two parts: an electronic mail address (in the same DNS format as the one in the SOA resource record), and a DNS domain name that points to additional information about the contact.
RT	The route through resource record specifies an intermediate host that routes packets to a destination host. The RT record is used in conjunction with the ISDN and X25 resource records. It is syntactically and semantically similar to the MX record type and is used in much the same way.
SOA	The start of authority resource record indicates that this DNS server is the authoritative source of information for the data within this DNS domain. It is the first record in each of the DNS database files. The SOA resource record is created automatically by DNS Manager when you create a new DNS zone.

Table 9.2   DNS Resource Record Types *(continued)*

Record type	Description
TXT	The text resource record associates general textual information with an item in the DNS database. A typical use is for identifying a host's location (for example, Location: Building 26S, Room 2499). The text string must be less than 256 characters, but multiple TXT resource records are allowed.
WINS	A record that contains the IP address of the WINS server configured on the DNS Server for WINS name resolution. This record is automatically created when WINS lookup is enabled on the DNS server, and is not a record that can be manually created by using **Add Record** in DNS Manager.
WINS_R	This record instructs Microsoft DNS server to use a NetBIOS node adapter status (nbtstat) command to resolve a DNS client reverse-lookup query. The reverse-lookup query requests the name of a computer identified only by an IP address. This record is automatically created when WINS reverse lookup is enabled on the DNS server, and is not a record that can be manually created by using **Add Record** in DNS Manager.
WKS	The well-known service resource record describes the services provided by a particular protocol on a particular interface. The protocol is usually UDP or TCP, but can be any of the entries listed in the PROTOCOLS file (\%systemroot%\system32\drivers\etc\protocol). The services are the services below port number 256 from the SERVICES file (\%systemroot%\system32\drivers\etc\services).
X.25	The X.25 resource record is a variation of the A (address) resource record. Rather than mapping a host name to an IP address, the X.25 record maps the name to an X.121 address. X.121 is the International Standards Organization (ISO) standard that specifies the format of addresses used in X.25 networks. The X.25 resource record is designed to be used in conjunction with the RT (route through) resource record.

The following sections describe the DNS files that contain DNS resource records and that you create and use as the Microsoft DNS server database files.

Zone Files

A zone file contains *resource records* (described in the preceding table) for computers within the zone for which the DNS server is authoritative. A Microsoft DNS server zone file can contain multiple resource records of different types, depending on the information you enter about the computers in the zone.

A zone file is automatically created when you create a zone by using DNS Manager. The DNS Manager zone wizard prompts you for the needed information and then automatically creates a file named *zonename*.dns in the \%systemroot%\System32\Dns directory. You then use DNS Manager to add resource records to the *zonename*.dns file.

Note   If you want to create a new zone file or reuse an existing zone file by using a text editor, rather than by using DNS Manager, see the sample zone files in the \%systemroot%\System32\Dns\Sample directory.

Cache File

The cache file contains name-to-IP-address mappings for the Internet root DNS servers and is used by the Microsoft DNS server to resolve name queries for computers that are located outside the enterprise network on the Internet.

When you install Microsoft DNS server, a cache file with current Internet root DNS mappings is automatically installed in the \%systemroot%\System32\Dns directory.

If you plan to use the Internet, you can use this cache file or you can obtain a copy from **ftp://rs.internic.net/domain/named.cache**.

If you do not connect to resources on the Internet, you should delete this file and create a new cache file that contains the host name-to-IP-address mappings for the DNS servers that are authoritative for the root of your private TCP/IP network. Replace the existing cache file in the \%systemroot%\System32\Dns directory with the new cache file.

Reverse Lookup Files

This file contains IP-address-to-host-name mappings (PTR records) that are used when a program or user has only the IP address of a remote computer but needs the host name associated to that IP address. This reverse lookup file is important for programs that implement security based on the connecting host name, and is also used for TCP/IP network troubleshooting.

There is no direct correlation between the conceptual model used to create IP addresses and the hierarchical structure of domain names. To provide a conceptual structure to manage IP-address-to-host-name mappings by using DNS servers, a special domain named *in-addr.arpa* was created. Nodes in the *in-addr.arpa* domain are named by using the numbers that comprise the dotted-octet representation of IP addresses, and IP-address-to-host-name mappings are mapped to these node numbers.

This is a somewhat complex mapping because IP addresses get more specific from left to right and domain names get less specific from left to right. The order of IP address octets must be reversed when building the *in-addr.arpa* top-down hierarchy (or tree). However, by using this method, administration of lower levels of the *in-addr.arpa* domain can be managed by using DNS servers and zones based on the class A, B, or C subnet addresses assigned to an enterprise.

You use the zone wizard in DNS Manager to create the reverse-lookup zone and files. DNS Manager automatically creates a reverse-lookup zone when the zone name that you enter is some form of *nnn.nnn.nnn.in-addr.arpa*.

After the reverse-lookup zone is created, you can add PTR records for the IP addresses contained within that zone. (The PTR record is analogous to the A record in the other zone files.) Reverse-lookup files also contain SOA and name server (NS) records as do other zone files.

Note In a PTR record, the IP address is actually written in reverse order and the text "in-addr.arpa." is appended to the end of the IP address to create the pointer. For example, the pointer for a computer with the static IP address 172.16.48.1 would be entered as "1.48.16.172.in-addr.arpa".

Boot Files

Although a boot file is not needed for Microsoft DNS server, it is described here for completeness. This file is not required by RFC and is actually a feature of DNS servers running under a BIND implementation of DNS. You would only use a boot file on a Microsoft DNS server if you want to port an existing BIND boot file to the Microsoft DNS server. For more information about using a BIND boot file, see the topic "Porting Data Files from Other DNS Servers" in the section "Troubleshooting DNS Server" later in this chapter.

Primary and Secondary Servers

The Microsoft DNS server can be either a *primary* or *secondary* DNS server to another Microsoft DNS server or to a DNS server running under another operating system (such as UNIX or other vendor's Windows NT implementation).

A *primary name server* is a DNS server that gets the data for its zones from the local DNS database files. When a change is made to the zone data, such as delegating a portion of the zone to another DNS server or adding hosts in the zone, these changes must be made on the primary DNS server so that the new information is entered in the local zone file.

A *secondary name server* gets its zone data file from the primary DNS server that is authoritative for that zone. The primary DNS server sends a copy of the zone file to the secondary DNS server in a process referred to as a *zone transfer*.

The minimum number of DNS servers you need in order to serve each zone is two —a primary and a secondary. Both a primary and a secondary server are required to provide database redundancy and a degree of fault tolerance. Generally, plan to install the primary and secondary servers on different subnets to provide continual support for DNS name queries if one subnet should go down. (Note that Microsoft DNS server automatically makes a zone backup by creating a local DNS backup directory the first time a zone is created on the computer running Microsoft DNS server.)

When a DNS server receives a DNS name query, it attempts to locate the requested information by retrieving data from its local zone files. If this fails because the server is not authoritative for the domain requested and thus does not have the data for the requested domain, the server can communicate with other DNS servers to resolve the request.

Caching-only Servers

Although all DNS servers cache queries that they have resolved, *caching-only servers* are DNS servers that only perform queries, cache the answers, and return the results. In other words, they are not authoritative for any domains and only store data that they have cached while resolving queries.

When trying to determine when to use such a server, keep in mind that when the server is initially started it has no cached information and must build up this information over time as it services requests. The benefit of using a caching-only server is that it does not generate zone transfer network traffic.

Microsoft DNS Clients

A DNS client (sometimes called a *resolver*) uses a DNS server to resolve name queries and to locate resources on TCP/IP networks.

Note Computers running under Windows NT Workstation or Windows NT Server version 4.0 automatically use DNS name resolution when a name query contains a name that is greater than 15 characters in length. If the name is less than or equal to 15 characters, either NetBIOS or DNS name resolution may be attempted. See Chapter 6, "TCP/IP Implementation Details," for additional details about DNS and NetBIOS name resolution.

There are three types of name queries that a DNS client can make. These types of name queries are *recursive*, *iterative*, and *reverse* (also called *inverse*).

A *recursive name query* is one in which the DNS client requires that the DNS server either respond to the client with the requested name-to-IP-address mapping or an error message stating that the data or domain name does not exist. The DNS server can *not* just refer the DNS client to a different DNS server.

Recursive name queries are generally made by a DNS client to a DNS server or by a DNS server that is configured to pass unresolved name queries to another DNS server. (Keep in mind that a DNS server can be a client to another DNS server.)

An *iterative name query* is one in which the queried DNS server returns the best answer it can give based on its cache or zone data. What this means is that if the queried DNS server does not have an exact match for the queried name, the best possible information it can return is a pointer to an authoritative DNS server in a higher level of the domain name space. This process will continue up through the DNS hierarchy to the next authoritative DNS server until the query reaches a DNS server that can provide a referral down the hierarchy to a lower-level DNS server in a different branch of the domain name space, until a DNS server is located that has data that is an exact match for the queried name, or an error or timeout condition is met.

This process is sometimes referred to as "walking the tree" and this type of query is typically initiated by a DNS server that attempts to resolve a recursive name query for a DNS client.

A *reverse name query* is one in which the DNS client provides the IP address and requests the name that matches that IP address. For example, to find a host name for the IP address 172.16.48.1, the DNS client would query the DNS server for a PTR record for *1.48.16.172.in-addr.arpa*. If this IP address is outside the local domain, the DNS server would need to connect to the *in-addr.arpa* root server and sequentially resolve the *in-addr.arpa* domain nodes until it locates the DNS server that is authoritative for that IP address.

Planning for Microsoft DNS Server Implementation

You will want to install a Microsoft DNS server if the following conditions exist on your network:

- You have established your own domain on the Internet and need a DNS name server.
- Your enterprise needs to implement DNS names on a TCP/IP-based intranet.
- You need a DNS name server that provides a GUI-based administration tool.
- You need to migrate existing non-Microsoft DNS name services to the Windows NT-based DNS server.

The number and location of computers running Microsoft DNS server that are needed to effectively manage DNS name data and name query traffic within your enterprise is a function of the size (number of hosts and their locations) of your network, the links between network subnets, and your network's security requirements.

When planning for the installation of Microsoft DNS server in your enterprise, there are several choices you can make. One option is to create one DNS zone that contains your entire enterprise domain.

The minimum number of DNS servers needed to serve each zone is two—a primary and a secondary—to provide database redundancy. As with any fault tolerant system, the computers should be as independent as possible, for example, by placing the primary and secondary servers on different subnets.

There are some disadvantages to using a single zone. One of the disadvantages is that the primary DNS server may have a problem responding to polling from secondary DNS servers. There are several ways to resolve this problem, such as increasing the secondary refresh interval, configuring some of the secondaries to obtain zone data from other secondaries, and configuring DNS servers in remote locations (or on the far side of a slow network link) as caching-only servers. (Caching-only servers allow you to avoid the overhead of zone transfers to remote locations or over slow network links.)

Large networks which span multiple sites should not use a single zone but instead use multiple zones to manage their DNS services. This implementation would consist of one root domain with (1) a primary DNS server and one or more secondary DNS servers and (2) one or more zones (and sub-zones as needed), each with a primary DNS server and one or more secondary DNS servers.

A network architect usually breaks up a corporate DNS domain into multiple subdivisions to distribute the administration of parts of the domain to various entities within the enterprise.

Whenever possible, plan to align your Windows NT domains with the organizational structure of your DNS domain, zones, and subdomains.

Using Microsoft DNS Server to Connect to the Internet

Many enterprises today are connecting their private, internal networks to the Internet to provide access to external resources on the Internet. Although this is an important capability, it is one that must be well planned to avoid possible security risks by exposing the internal network to users outside the enterprise.

One common way to provide protection is to use a computer that is referred to as a firewall. A *firewall* is a computer or network device that allows only certain authorized operations or programs to be run between internal networks and the Internet.

A firewall configuration can be very simple or extremely complex depending on the particular requirements of the enterprise. This chapter is not designed to provide an exhaustive description of firewalls but will briefly discuss how the Microsoft DNS server can be used on a network that uses the services of a firewall to provide security for the network.

The following figure illustrates a typical network architecture that includes a multihomed computer running as an Internet firewall.

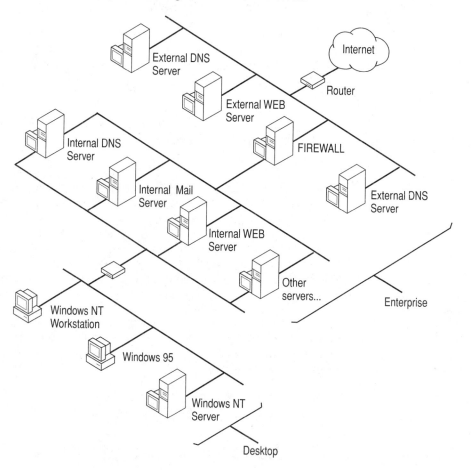

Figure 9.3   A Typical Network with a Firewall

As is illustrated in the Figure, the firewall protects the internal network from computers on the Internet that may attempt to access the internal network, while allowing computers on the internal network to access Internet resources. The example network design also includes computers that are configured as WWW and FTP servers that are *external* to the firewall.

The external servers allow computers from outside the internal network to access resources provided as public services, but these external servers must be closely monitored and secured because they are connected directly to the Internet network and do not use the firewall for access control. A router that is configured to control the type of packets allowed to pass through the router (referred to as *packet filtering*) can provide some additional access control.

The DNS services for the external and internal networks should be entirely isolated from one another to prevent computers outside the internal network from obtaining the names and IP addresses for resources located on the internal side of the firewall. This will help ensure that the only externally available information are the names and IP addresses of the external servers that are configured to provide external public services. These services include electronic mail, WWW, and FTP servers.

When internal network computers require access to computers outside the internal network, DNS name resolution typically requires interaction with DNS servers located on the public Internet. For this reason, you may want to allow only certain DNS servers to communicate outside the internal enterprise network. A DNS server that can communicate outside of the private network to resolve a DNS name query is referred to as *forwarder*.

After one or more DNS servers are designated as a forwarder, all other DNS servers on the internal network should be configured to use the forwarder for name resolution outside the internal network. The following figure illustrates this concept.

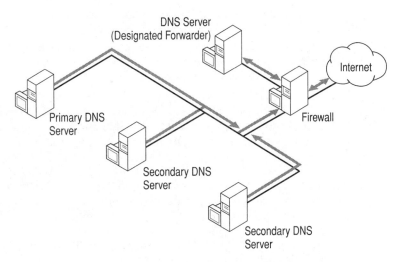

Figure 9.4   Using a DNS Forwarder and a Firewall

When a DNS server which is configured to use forwarders receives a DNS request that it is unable to resolve (through its own zone files), it passes the request to one of the designated forwarders. The forwarder then carries out whatever communication is necessary to resolve the request and returns the results to the requesting server, which, in turn, returns the results to the DNS client. If the forwarder is unable to resolve the query, the DNS server attempts to resolve the query on its own as normal.

▶ **To configure a Microsoft DNS server to use a forwarder**

1. In **DNS Manager**, right-click the appropriate server icon, and then click **Properties**.

2. In the **Server Properties** dialog box, click the **Forwarders** tab and enter the IP address of the forwarder.

Planning for Microsoft DNS and Microsoft WINS Integration

You can configure Microsoft DNS servers to use a Microsoft WINS server for host name resolution (remember that the host name portion of a fully qualified domain name (FQDN) is analogous to a NetBIOS computer name.) Microsoft DNS server includes support for inter-operation with the NetBIOS naming system of traditional Microsoft networking by delegating part of the name resolution process to computers running Microsoft WINS server. DNS names and NetBIOS computer names can be integrated as complementary naming schemes by using Microsoft WINS servers and Microsoft DNS servers.

A Microsoft DNS server can be configured to resolve the upper layers of a FQDN and, if necessary, to pass the final part of name resolution, the host name portion of the FQDN, to a Microsoft WINS server. The Microsoft WINS server can then use the host name (if it is the same as the NetBIOS computer name) to find the correct name-to-IP-address mapping. Once the WINS server finds the correct mapping, it then returns this information to the DNS server. The DNS server then sends the information to the DNS client; the interaction between the WINS server and the DNS server is transparent to the DNS client to whom it appears as though the DNS server handled the entire name resolution process.

Using Microsoft WINS and Microsoft DNS on a TCP/IP network allows network clients to use either a NetBIOS name or a DNS name to find, communicate with, and connect to network resources. When both Microsoft WINS and Microsoft DNS are enabled on a computer, the order of name resolution is as follows:

1. A name query that contains a name greater than 15 characters is first sent to the DNS server for name resolution.

2. If the name is less than or equal to 15 characters, the name query is sent to the WINS server. If the WINS server cannot resolve the name, the name query is forwarded to the DNS server.

By integrating Microsoft WINS and Microsoft DNS, you can use the dynamic names services of Microsoft WINS and reduce the number of static resource records you would normally have to maintain in a DNS database file. Note that this support is available only for Windows NT-based and Windows-based computers that are configured to use DHCP and Microsoft WINS servers.

You can install Microsoft WINS server and Microsoft DNS server on the same computer or on different computers running under Windows NT Server version 4.0.

When configuring TCP/IP on a computer running Microsoft WINS server under Windows NT Server, consider the following recommendations:

- When determining the physical location of Microsoft WINS and DNS servers, use the physical characteristics of your LAN or WAN infrastructure and not the logical groupings defined in the Windows NT (or DNS) domain concepts.

- Manually assign an IP address, subnet mask, default gateway, and other TCP/IP parameters on the computer. Do not configure the computer as a DHCP client. Enter the Microsoft WINS server's static IP address into the DHCP server database as a reserved IP address (using DHCP Manager) to prevent assigning the IP address to another computer.

▶ **To configure TCP/IP on a computer running Microsoft WINS server under Windows NT server**

1. Click **Start**, point to **Settings**, and then click **Control Panel**.

2. Double-click **Network**.

3. On the **Protocols** tab, select **TCP/IP Protocol**, and click **Properties**.

4. Click the **WINS Address** tab.

5. Select the **Enable DNS for Windows Resolution** checkbox.

6. Click the **DNS** tab.

7. In the **DNS Service Search Order** list, type the IP address of the DNS server that is geographically (physically) closest to the WINS server.

   You can enter multiple DNS servers in this list.

When configuring TCP/IP on a computer running Microsoft DNS Server under Windows NT Server, consider the following recommendations:

- Manually assign an IP address, subnet mask, default gateway, and other TCP/IP parameters on the Microsoft DNS server. Enter the DNS server's static IP address into the DHCP server database as a reserved IP address (using DHCP Manager) to prevent assigning the IP address to another computer.

- Use DNS Manager to configure the Microsoft DNS server to pass unresolved name queries to WINS servers, referred as *WINS Lookup*. See online Help in DNS Manager for detailed DNS server configuration tasks. (Microsoft DNS server can also be configured to perform *Reverse WINS Lookup,* which refers to obtaining an NetBIOS name by IP address query.)

- After you have configured TCP/IP on the Microsoft DNS server, create a zone for each group of computers where name resolution can be performed by using a WINS server.

Capacity Planning and Performance

Microsoft DNS server keeps track of a number of server usage statistics and displays these statistics in the right pane of the DNS Manager window. These statistics are cumulative; in other words they are started when the DNS server is started and are not cleared until the DNS server is stopped.

These statistics are useful for comparing relative name query traffic and load on each DNS server to determine how many name queries each DNS server is servicing. If one DNS server is busier than other DNS servers, you can direct some of the name query traffic away from the overloaded server to another server that is not as heavily loaded. For example if you have a primary and two secondaries, you can balance the load on the primary by configuring some of the DNS clients to point to one DNS secondary and other clients to point to the other DNS secondary. This reconfiguration can be done by using the DHCP server to change the DNS server which DHCP clients are configured to use, or by manually reconfiguring TCP/IP on non-DHCP enabled clients.

For capacity planning purposes, it is important to periodically compare the level of growth in usage of the DNS server versus the memory, disk, network, and CPU capabilities of the computer running the DNS server. If you feel that a DNS server is not responding as fast as it should, look first at the following performance monitor counters on that server. If any of the thresholds described in the following table are being met, there may be room to improve performance on the DNS server.

Table 9.3   Using Performance Monitor Counters to Monitor DNS Server

Object	Counter	Threshold	Notes
processor	%processor time	> 80%	
memory	available bytes	< 1 MB	
physical disk	%disk time	> 67%	only available if you start the counters from the command line with diskperf -y, and reboot
network segment	% network usage	> 40%	only available if Network Monitor Agent is installed

If memory is an issue, then check the 'process' object, 'DNS' instance, 'Private Bytes' counter. If this counter is high, then the DNS service is causing the memory available bytes counter to be low. If this is the case, add more memory or possibly investigate which records are currently active in the DNS cache and find out the TTL associated with each.

If processor is an issue , check the 'process' object, 'DNS' instance, '%processor time' counter. If this is > 80 %, consider running the DNS server on a more powerful server. If this is not high, and processor '%processor time' is still high, look at all the other processes and determine which process is requiring large amounts of CPU time.

On a DNS server, physical disk '%disk time' should not be a problem, unless the system has started paging for lack of memory. If this is the case, treat this as a memory issue.

If network use is a problem, find out if it is the DNS server that is causing all of the traffic or another server on the same segment. To do this, use the **Network Monitor** utility to examine the traffic that is received and sent by the server.

DNS Server Memory Usage

Microsoft DNS server cache memory is different than processing of resource records. Virtual (pageable) memory is allocated for cached data as needed (remember, as a DNS server performs name resolution for a name query, it caches a copy of the data which is retained for the time period specified by the TTL). If the DNS server requires more than the normal amount of cache memory, this memory is taken from the local computer page file and is usually slower than cache memory.

Using DNS Manager

DNS Manager is the graphical user interface that is automatically installed and added to **Administrative (Tools)** on the **Program** menu when you install Microsoft DNS server on a computer running under Windows NT Server 4.0. You can use DNS Manager to administer local and remote Microsoft DNS servers and database files.

Note Keep in mind that you cannot administer non-Microsoft DNS servers by using DNS Manager.

DNS Manager provides menus and options that enable you to add and configure DNS servers, and a zone wizard that enables you to create the zones and sub-zones managed by each DNS server. Once you have added DNS servers and their zones, you can then administer the local and remote DNS servers and add, view, and edit DNS resource records that comprise the database files for each zone and DNS server.

▶   **To start DNS Manager**

- Click **Start**, point to **Programs,** point to **Administrative Tools**, and click **DNS Manager**.

The following sections provide introductory information about the basic tasks you perform to start using Microsoft DNS server. For a complete task list and detailed task instructions, see DNS Manager Help.

Tip When you make a change to DNS server and zone data by using DNS Manager, click **DNS** on the menu bar, then click **Update Server Data Files** to immediately write the changed information to the DNS database files.

Adding DNS Servers

Use DNS Manager to add the local and remote Microsoft DNS servers to be managed by using the local computer running Microsoft DNS server.

▶ **To add a Microsoft DNS server**

1. In DNS Manager, click the **Server List** icon.

2. Click **New Server**, and enter either the DNS server host name or the IP address in the **Add DNS Server** dialog box.

3. Click **OK**.

DNS Manager will automatically display a server icon for the new server and automatically create the following zones:

- Cache— contains the records needed to connect to the Internet root DNS name servers.

- 0.*in-addr.arpa*—used to prevent passing reverse-lookup queries for the IP address 0.0.0.0 to the root DNS server.

- 127.*in-addr.arpa*—used to prevent passing reverse-lookup queries for the loopback address name queries to the root DNS server.

- 255.*in-addr.arpa*—used to prevent passing broadcast name queries to the root DNS server.

After you have added a server, you can then configure the server and create the zone or zones to be managed by the server.

▶ **To configure the server**

1. Right-click the server icon, and click **Properties**.

2. In the **Server Properties** dialog box, add the IP address (or IP addresses for a multihomed computer) and forwarder information as needed.

Creating Zones

After you have added and configured a server by using DNS Manager, you create the zone or zones managed by that server. Remember that you will need to create a zone for each group of WINS-enabled computers where you want to use both DNS and NetBIOS name resolution. Before creating a zone, make sure that you have correctly configured TCP/IP on the DNS server and that you have entered the DNS server host name and domain name on the **DNS** tab on the **Microsoft TCP/IP Properties** page.

▶ **To add a Primary zone**

1. Right-click the appropriate server icon, and click **New Zone** to start the zone wizard.

2. Click **Primary**, and then click **Next**.

The zone wizard will prompt you for additional information and then automatically create the zone, zone file, and the SOA, NS, and server A data records.

Tip To create a reverse-lookup zone, use this same procedure and use a zone name that complies with the reverse-lookup name format (*nnn.nnn.nnn.in-addr.arpa*). For example, the reverse-lookup zone that could contain PTR records for IP addresses 172.16.16.1 through 172.16.224.254 would be named *.16.172.in-addr.arpa*. Whenever possible, create reverse-lookup zones before adding host data so that you can use the automatic **Create PTR Record** option in the **Add Host** dialog box.

After you have created the primary zone, you can create secondary zones by using the same procedure.

▶ **To add a Secondary zone**

1. Right-click the secondary server icon, and click **New Zone** to start the zone wizard.

2. Click **Secondary**, and enter the requested information.

3. Click **Next**.

   The zone wizard will prompt you for additional information and then automatically create the zone, zone file, and the SOA, NS, and server A data records.

After a zone is created, you can further subdivide that zone as described in the following procedure.

▶ **To create a subdomain (a domain contained within a zone)**

1. Right-click the appropriate zone folder.

2. Click **New Domain**.

3. Type the domain name in **Domain Name**, and then click **OK**.

After you have successfully added a zone, you can configure and modify the zone properties. To do this, select and right-click the zone icon to display the **Zone Properties** dialog box. You can use the **Zone Properties** dialog box to perform the following actions:

- Change the zone from a primary to secondary, or vice versa, by using the **General** tab.

- Modify the default server TTL values and the values used to determine refresh and zone transfer rates by using the **SOA Record** tab.

- Identify the secondary DNS servers that should be notified of changes in the zone by using the **Notify** tab.

- Configure the zone server to use WINS for host name resolution by using the **WINS Lookup** tab (on a reverse-lookup zone, this tab is labeled **WINS Reverse Lookup**.)

The following figure illustrates the **Zone Properties** dialog box for a normal zone.

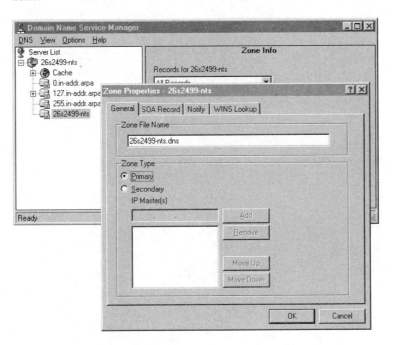

Figure 9.5   Zone Properties dialog box

The only difference in the **Zone Properties** dialog box for a reverse-lookup zone is the text on the **WINS Lookup** tab, as illustrated in the following figure.

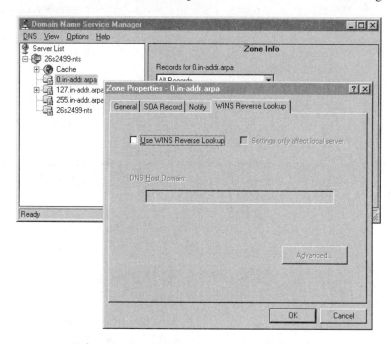

Figure 9.6   Zone Properties dialog box for Reverse-Lookup Zone

Adding and Modifying DNS Resource Records

DNS Manager makes it easy to add data to both local and remote Microsoft DNS servers because you can create and edit all DNS resource records by using DNS Manager. After you create a zone, you can select and right-click the zone to display a menu of actions that you can perform on the zone. The following figure illustrates this menu.

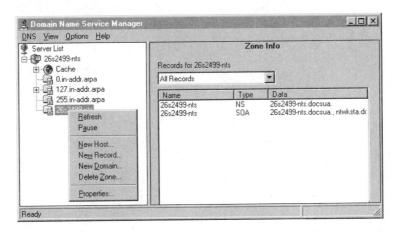

Figure 9.7   Zone menu

The two menu choices that you use to add information about the computers in the zone are **New Host** and **New Record**.

You will want to use the **New Host** option to add the A and PTR records for the computers in the zone that are not DHCP- or WINS-enabled. The following figure illustrates the **Add New Host** dialog box.

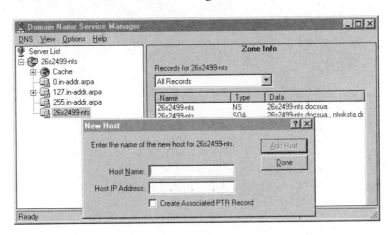

Figure 9.8   New Host dialog box

Additionally you will want to use **New Resource Record** to add other DNS information about a computer, such as alias (Cname), mail server, and so on. (Refer back to Table 9.2 for descriptions of the different types of resource records you can create.)

The following figure illustrates the **New Resource Record** dialog box.

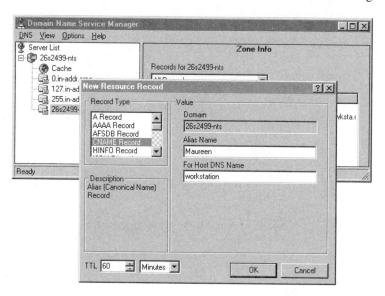

Figure 9.9   **New Resource Record dialog box**

Note   You can use existing resource records in the DNS database files from other DNS servers. For more information about this topic, see "Porting Data Files from Other DNS Servers" in the section "Troubleshooting DNS Server" later in this chapter.

The Zone Transfer

How often zone transfers should occur is a function of how often names and IP address mappings change within your domain. Note that unnecessary zone transfer could cause unnecessary network and server loads.

A zone transfer is nothing more than a file copy procedure. The entire contents of the database are copied from the primary (or master) to the secondary each time the secondary is 'notified' by the primary (or master) that there has been a change in the zone data.

You configure primary and secondary zones with the information needed to initiate and request zone transfers by using the **SOA Record** and **Notify** tabs of the **Zone Properties** dialog box. You can change the default zone transfer timers by using the **SOA Record** tab. You can change the following values that affect zone transfer:

- Serial Number

- Refresh Interval

- Retry Interval

- Expire Time

- Minimum Default TTL

The following figure illustrates the SOA Record tab.

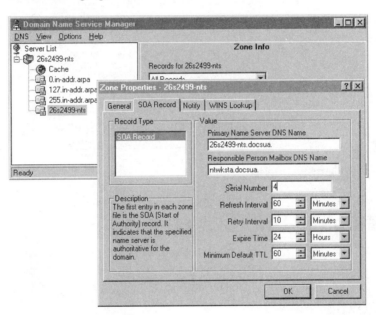

Figure 9.10   SOA Record tab

On the primary zone, use the **Notify** tab of the **Zone Properties** dialog box to identify the secondary or secondaries to notify for the zone transfer. The following figure illustrates the **Notify** tab.

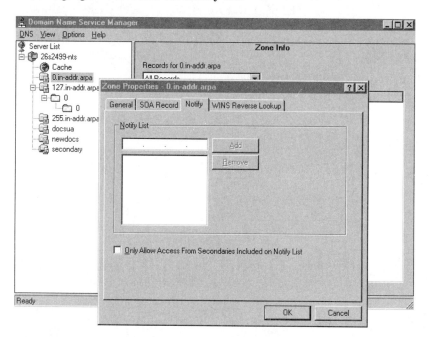

Figure 9.11   Notify Tab

Troubleshooting DNS Server

The following sections provide information about problems you might encounter when using Microsoft DNS server and the tools or procedures that you can use.

Using Nslookup

Nslookup is a TCP/IP utility that you can use at the command prompt. Use the **nslookup** command to get information about hosts in a domain or to set configuration parameters on a Microsoft DNS server.

For more information on how to use the **nslookup** command, see the topic "TCP/IP Procedures Help" in Control Panel Help.

Clearing DNS Server Statistics

DNS Manager displays statistics about the traffic received on the computer running Microsoft DNS server. These statistics are automatically started and displayed in the right pane of DNS Manager after you add a server and create at least one zone on that server. By default, these statistics are cumulative and are not normally cleared until the computer running Microsoft DNS server is stopped.

You can use the **dnsstat.exe** utility provided in the Windows NT Server version 4.0 Resource Kit to clear the statistics without stopping the Microsoft DNS server.

This command-line utility provides a dump of statistics about traffic received on a computer running Microsoft DNS server. You can also use **dnsstat** to clear these statistics without stopping the DNS server. By default, these statistics are cumulative and are not normally cleared until the computer running Microsoft DNS server is stopped.

dnsstat syntax

dnsstat {*servername* | *IP address*} [{*-c* | */c* | *-clear* | */clear*}]

Where *servername* returns all DNS server statistics on the server named *servername*. *IP address* returns all DNS server statistics on the server with the IP address indicated. The options *-c* or */c* or *-clear* or */clear* clear clearable DNS statistics on the server indicated.

▶ **To clear the Microsoft DNS server statistics by using the dnsstat command**

1. Click **Start**, and then click **Run**.
2. In **Open**, type **dnsstat** <*servername*> **-c** or **dnsstat** <*servername*> **/c**, and then click **OK**.

    This will reset the value the DNS statistics to zero. Open DNS Manager to verify that the statistics have been cleared and restarted.

For detailed information about using this utility, see Resource Kit Tools Help.

Resolving Slow DNS Zone Transfer to non-Microsoft DNS Servers

Slow DNS zone transfers may occur when your secondary DNS server is a non-Microsoft DNS server. By default, the Microsoft DNS server performs zone transfers to non-Microsoft DNS secondaries by sending one resource record per message. This behavior enables Microsoft DNS server to work with DNS servers running under an implementation of BIND earlier than BIND version 4.9.4. (Only BIND version 4.9.4 and later use a faster, high compression method that allows multiple resource records to be sent per message.)

If you are running a secondary non-Microsoft DNS server under BIND version 4.9.4 or higher, you can increase the speed of the zone transfer by creating a new parameter **BindSecondaries** of type DWORD with Value=0 in the following Registry key:

```
\HKEY_LOCAL_MACHINE\SYSTEM\CurrentControlSet\Services\DNS\Parameters
```

▶   **To add the BindSecondaries parameter**

1. Click **Start**, and then click **Run**.

2. In **Open**, type **regedit**, and then click **OK**.

3. Open the following key folder:

```
\HKEY_LOCAL_MACHINE\SYSTEM\CurrentControlSet\Services\DNS\Parameters
```

4. On the **Edit** menu, click **New**, and then click **Key**.

5. Type **BindSecondaries**, and then press ENTER.

6. On the **Edit** menu, click **New**, and then click **DWORD Value**.

7. Type 0 or 1 in the value box, and press ENTER.

Note   Use value = 0 if you have no BIND secondaries or if all BIND secondaries are running under BIND version 4.9.4 or later. Use value = 1 if you have BIND secondaries running under a BIND implementation earlier than BIND version 4.9.4.

---

8. Stop and restart the Microsoft DNS server by using **Services** in **Control Panel**.

Note   Zone transfers between computers running Microsoft DNS server are automatically performed using the faster, high compression transfer method and are not affected by the **BindSecondaries** parameter.

Zone Wizard Did Not Correctly Autocreate SOA, NS, or A Record

The DNS zone wizard retrieves information from your user logon information and the TCP/IP configuration on the DNS server in order to create a zone. For example, the DNS zone wizard uses your logon name in the **Responsible Party Mailbox Name** field of the SOA Record dialog box.

If you are creating a zone that has the same name as your domain and you do not enter the domain name on the **DNS** page in the **Microsoft TCP/IP Properties** dialog box, the DNS zone wizard cannot create the A record. To add the domain name, use the **Network** applet in **Control Panel** to display and configure TCP/IP properties. Type the domain name on the **DNS** page of the **Microsoft TCP/IP properties** dialog box and then stop and restart the Microsoft DNS server by using the **Services** applet in **Control Panel**.

Note If you are creating a zone whose name is *not* the same as your domain name, you must manually add the SOA, A, and NS records in order to create the records with the new domain name and not the domain name configured on the local DNS server.

Porting Data Files from Other DNS Servers

You can use the boot, zone, cache, and other files from non-Microsoft RFC-compliant DNS servers. To do this, you must install these files in the \%systemroot\System32\DNS directory, and then stop and restart the DNS server.

Before installing files from other DNS servers on a Microsoft DNS server, you must edit the file name and directory location text in the ported files and make additional changes as described in this section.

The boot file will be used to load the data files you want to port into a Microsoft DNS server. A boot file is actually a file that controls the startup behavior of DNS servers running under a BIND implementation of DNS. It is a BIND-specific feature and not a requirement of the DNS RFCs. Microsoft DNS server's ability to use a boot file on initial startup is provided to support migration of data from BIND-based DNS servers to Microsoft DNS servers.

Although Microsoft DNS server will support a boot file, you must install the edited boot file before using DNS Manager. Starting DNS Manager configures the Microsoft DNS server to use the Windows NT Server Registry instead of the boot file.

If you need port data files after starting DNS Manager, you must change the value of the **EnableRegistryBoot** parameter from 1 to 0. The **EnableRegistryBoot** parameter is located in the following key:

\HKEY_LOCAL_MACHINE\SYSTEM\CurrentControlSet\Services\DNS\Parameters

▶ **To change the value of the EnableRegistryBoot parameter**

1. Click **Start**, and then click **Run**.

2. In **Open**, type **regedit**, and then press ENTER.

3. Open the following key folder:

   `\HKEY_LOCAL_MACHINE\SYSTEM\CurrentControlSet\Services\DNS\Parameters`

4. Select the EnableRegistryBoot parameter in the right pane of the Registry Editor, and then select **Edit**.

5. Click **Modify**, and type **0**.

6. Click **OK**, and return to the menu bar and click **Edit**.

7. Select **New**, and then click **DWORD Value**.

8. Type **0** in the value box, and press ENTER.

9. Stop and restart the Microsoft DNS server by using **Services** in **Control Panel**.

The following table describes the format of boot file commands. You can use any text editor to edit or create a boot file. Commands must start at the beginning of a line and no spaces may precede the commands. This table shows the order in which the Microsoft DNS server supported boot commands must appear in the file, and gives the syntax for each command.

Table 9.4   BIND Boot File Commands

Command	Description	Syntax
Directory	Specifies a directory where other files referred to in the boot file can be found.	directory <directory>
Cache	Specifies a file used to help the DNS service contact DNS servers for the root domain. This command and the file it refers to *must* be present.	cache <filename>
Primary	Specifies a domain for which this DNS server is authoritative, and a database file which contains the resource records for that domain in the zone file. Multiple primary command records can be entered in the boot file.	primary <domain> <filename>
Secondary	Specifies a domain for which this DNS server is authoritative, and a list of master server IP addresses from which to attempt downloading the zone information.	secondary <domain> <hostlist> <local filename>

CHAPTER 10

Using LMHOSTS Files

Windows NT supports several different name resolution services to locate, communicate with, and connect to resources on the network. For example, a command to connect to an application server by using the server name must be resolved to an IP address in TCP/IP networks before the command can be successfully completed. This is referred to as *name resolution*.

If WINS servers are available on the network, the LMHOSTS file can be used to support the subnets that do not have a WINS server, and to provide a backup name resolution service in case the WINS server is not available. The LMHOSTS file provides a NetBIOS name resolution method that can be used for small networks that do not use a WINS server.

This chapter provides information about the following topics:

- Using LMHOSTS files to find remote computers and services
- Creating the LMHOSTS file
- Configuring TCP/IP to use LMHOSTS name resolution
- Maintaining the LMHOSTS file
- Troubleshooting the LMHOSTS file

Using LMHOSTS File to Find Computers and Services

Windows NT versions 4.0 and 3.5x provide name resolution services for both NetBIOS computer names and Domain Name System (DNS) host names on TCP/IP networks. For an overview of all the Windows NT name resolution services for TCP/IP networks, refer to the chapter "Implementation Considerations" in the *Windows NT Server Networking Supplement*.

The LMHOSTS file is one method of name resolution for NetBIOS name resolution for TCP/IP networks. The other NetBIOS over TCP/IP (NetBT) name resolution methods that are used, depending on the computer's configuration, are:

- NetBIOS name cache
- IP subnet broadcasts
- WINS NetBIOS name server

Note NetBT is defined by RFCs 1001 and 1002. These RFCs define the different configurations—b-node, p-node, m-node, and h-node—that define how a computer attempts to resolve NetBIOS names to IP addresses.

By installation default, a Windows NT-based computer not configured as a WINS client or WINS server, is a *b-node* computer. A b-node computer is one that uses IP broadcasts for NetBIOS name resolution.

IP broadcast name resolution can provide dynamic name resolution. However, the disadvantages of broadcast name queries include increased network traffic and ineffectiveness in routed networks. Resources located outside the local subnet do not receive IP broadcast name query requests because, by definition, IP-level broadcasts are not passed to remote subnets by the router (default gateway) on the local subnet.

As an alternate method to IP broadcasts, Windows NT enables you to manually provide NetBIOS name and IP address mappings for remote computers by using the LMHOSTS file. Selected mappings from the LMHOSTS file are maintained in a limited cache of NetBIOS computer names and IP address mappings. This memory cache is initialized when a computer is started. When the computer needs to resolve a name, the cache is examined first and, if there is no match in the cache, Windows NT uses b-node IP broadcasts to try to find the NetBIOS computer. If the IP broadcast name query fails, the complete LMHOSTS file (not just the cache) is parsed to find the NetBIOS name and the corresponding IP address. This strategy enables the LMHOSTS file to contain a large number of mappings, without requiring a large chunk of static memory to maintain an infrequently used cache.

The LMHOSTS file can be used to map computer names and IP addresses for computers outside the local subnet (an advantage over the b-node broadcast method). You can use the LMHOSTS file to find remote computers for network file, print, and remote procedure services and for domain services such as logons, browsing, replication, and so on.

The Windows NT-based LMHOSTS method of name resolution is compatible with Microsoft LAN Manager 2.*x* TCP/IP LMHOSTS files.

Locating Remote Computers

Computer names can be resolved outside the local broadcast subnet if the remote computer name and IP address mappings are specified in the LMHOSTS file. For example, suppose your computer, named ClientA, is configured without the WINS client service, but you want to use TCP/IP to connect to a computer, named ServerB, that is located on another TCP/IP subnet. By default, your computer is a b-node computer that uses NetBIOS cache and IP broadcasts, and is enabled for LMHOSTS file lookup, by using an LMHOSTS file provided by your network administrator.

At system startup, the name cache on ClientA is preloaded only with entries from the LMHOSTS file, defined as preloaded by a special keyword, the #PRE keyword. For this example, ServerB is on a remote subnet outside of your local subnet IP broadcast area and is *not* one of the entries in preloaded cache. A strict b-node IP broadcast (as defined in RFCs 1001 and 1002) fails by timing out when no response is received. In this example, ClientA's IP broadcast to locate ServerB will time out, because ServerB is located on a remote subnet and does not receive ClientA's broadcast requests.

This example is summarized in the following steps:

1. ClientA enters a Windows NT command, such as a print file command, using the NetBIOS name of ServerB.

2. The NetBIOS name cache on ClientA is checked for the IP address that corresponds to the NetBIOS name of ServerB.

3. Because ServerB was not preloaded, its NetBIOS name is not found in the name cache, and ClientA broadcasts a name request with the NetBIOS name of ServerB.

4. Because ServerB is on a remote network, ClientA does not receive a reply to its name request broadcast because IP broadcasts are not routed to remote subnets. (If ServerB were on the local network, ClientA would receive a response to its broadcast and the response would contain the IP address of ServerB.)

5. Because the LMHOSTS method has been enabled on ClientA, Windows NT continues to attempt to resolve the NetBIOS name to an IP address. The LMHOSTS file in the *%systemroot%*\System32\Drivers\Etc directory is examined to find the NetBIOS name, ServerB, and its corresponding IP address. If the NetBIOS name is not found in the LMHOSTS file, and no other name resolution method is configured on ClientA, an error message appears.

Specifying Domain Controllers

The most common use of the LMHOSTS file is to locate remote servers for file and print services. But the LMHOSTS file can also be used to find domain controllers providing domain services on routed TCP/IP networks. Examples of such domain controller activities include domain controller pulses (used for account database synchronization), logon authentication, password changes, master browser list synchronization, and other domain management activities.

Windows NT primary domain controllers (PDCs) and backup domain controllers (BDCs) maintain the user account security database and manage other network-related services. Because large Windows NT domains can span multiple IP subnets, it is possible that routers could separate the domain controllers from one another or separate other computers in the domain from the domain controllers. In a network that does not use WINS servers, LMHOSTS name resolution can be used to allow client computers to connect to domain controllers located across routers on different subnets.

Using Centralized LMHOSTS Files

The primary LMHOSTS file on each computer is always located in the *%systemroot%*\System32\Drivers\Etc directory. With Microsoft TCP/IP, you can include other LMHOSTS files from local and remote computers.

Network administrators can manage the LMHOSTS files used by computers on the network by providing one or more global LMHOSTS files on a central server. Windows NT-based computers on the network can be configured to import the correct and up-to-date computer name-to-IP-address mappings.

Users can import the LMHOSTS file from remote computers on the network by using #INCLUDE statements in the LMHOSTS file or by clicking **Import LMHOSTS** on the **WINS Address** tab of the **Microsoft TCP/IP Properties** dialog box. See Figure 10.1 in the section "Configuring TCP/IP to Use LMHOSTS Name Resolution" later in this chapter.

Alternatively, an administrator can use the replicator service to distribute multiple copies of the global LMHOSTS file to multiple servers.

Note If network clients access a central LMHOSTS file, the computer on which the file is located must include the Registry parameter **NullSessionShares** for the LMHOSTS location. The **NullSessionShares** parameter is in the Registry key:

```
HKEY_LOCAL_MACHINE\SYSTEM\CurrentControlSet\Services\LanManServer\
Parameters
```

For detailed information on Registry parameters, see online Help.

Creating the LMHOSTS File

Before configuring a computer to use the LMHOSTS file, you must create the primary LMHOSTS file on each computer, name the file LMHOSTS, and save the file in the %*systemroot*%\System32\Drivers\Etc directory.

You can create the file by using a text editor—for example, Notepad—to create, and change the LMHOSTS file because it is a simple text file. (An example of the LMHOSTS format is provided in the file named LMHOSTS.sam in the Windows NT %*systemroot*%\System32\Drivers\Etc directory. This is only an example file; do not use this file as the primary LMHOSTS file.)

The following sections describe the different types of entries that can be created and edited in the LMHOSTS file.

Creating Entries in the LMHOSTS File

Use the following rules to create and to edit entries in the LMHOSTS file:

- Each entry must be on a separate line. The final entry in the file must be terminated by a carriage return.

- Enter the IP address in the first column, followed by the corresponding computer (NetBIOS) name.

> **Caution**   You cannot add an LMHOSTS entry for a computer that is a DHCP client, because the IP addresses of DHCP clients change dynamically. To avoid problems, make sure that the computers whose names are entered in the LMHOSTS files are configured with static IP addresses.

- The address and the computer name must be separated by at least one space or tab.

- NetBIOS names can contain uppercase and lowercase characters and special characters. If a name is placed between double quotation marks, it is used exactly as entered. For example, `"AccountingPDC"` is a mixed-case name, and `"HumanRscSr    \0x03"` generates a name with a special character.

- Every NetBIOS name is 16 characters long. The user-definable portion of the NetBIOS name is the first 15 characters. The 16th character is reserved to identify the network client service that registered the name. The most familiar example of a NetBIOS name is the computer name on any Windows-based computer. When the computer is started, the Microsoft Network Client services are started and register their names, which consist of the computer name plus a unique 16th character. For example, the name <computer_name[0x00]> is the Microsoft Workstation service; the name <computer_name[0x20]> is the Microsoft Server service. As you can see, the only difference between these two names is the 16th character. The 16th character makes it possible to uniquely identify each of the Network Client services running on the computer. For more information, see Appendix G, "NetBIOS Names."

- Entries in the LMHOSTS file can represent Windows NT Server computers, Windows NT Workstation computers, Windows 95 computers, LAN Manager servers, or Windows for Workgroups 3.11 computers running Microsoft TCP/IP. There is no need to distinguish between different platforms in LMHOSTS.

- The number sign (#) character is usually used to mark the start of a comment. However, it can also designate special keywords, as described in Table 10.1.

The keywords listed in the following table can be used in the LMHOSTS file for Windows NT-based computers. (LAN Manager 2.*x*, which also uses LMHOSTS for NetBT name resolution, treats these keywords as comments.)

Table 10.1   LMHOSTS Keywords

Keyword	Description
\0x*nn*	Support for nonprinting characters in NetBIOS names. Enclose the NetBIOS name in double quotation marks and use \0x*nn* notation to specify a hexadecimal value for the character. This enables custom applications that use special names to function properly in routed topologies. However, LAN Manager TCP/IP does not recognize the hexadecimal format, and so you surrender backward compatibility if you use this feature.
	Note that the hexadecimal notation applies only to one character in the name. The name should be padded with blanks so that the special character is last in the string (character 16).
#BEGIN_ALTERNATE	Used to group multiple #INCLUDE statements. Any single successful #INCLUDE statement causes the group to succeed.
#END_ALTERNATE	Used to mark the end of an #INCLUDE statement grouping.
#DOM:*<domain>*	Part of the computer name-to-IP-address mapping entry that indicates that the IP address is a domain controller in the domain specified by *<domain>*. This keyword affects how the Browser and Logon services behave in routed TCP/IP environments. To preload a #DOM entry, you must *first* add the #PRE keyword to the line. #DOM groups are limited to 25 members.
#INCLUDE *<filename>*	Forces the system to seek the specified *<filename>* and parse it as if it were local. Specifying a Uniform Naming Convention (UNC) *<filename>* allows you to use a centralized LMHOSTS file on a server. If the server on which the specified *<filename>* exists is outside of the local broadcast subnet, you must add a preloaded entry for the server before adding the entry in the #INCLUDE section.
#MH	Part of the computer name-to-IP-address mapping entry that defines the entry as a unique name that can have more than one address. The maximum number of addresses that can be assigned to a unique name is 25. The number of entries is equal to the number of network cards in a multihomed computer.

Table 10.1   LMHOSTS Keywords *(Continued)*

Keyword	Description
#PRE	Part of the computer name-to-IP-address mapping entry that causes that entry to be preloaded into the name cache. (By default, entries are not preloaded into the name cache but are parsed only after WINS and name query broadcasts fail to resolve a name.) The #PRE keyword must be appended for entries that also appear in #INCLUDE statements; otherwise, the entry in the #INCLUDE statement is ignored.
#SG	Part of the computer name-to-IP-address mapping entry that associates that entry with a user-defined special (Internet) group specified by *<name>*. The #SG keyword defines Internet groups by using a NetBIOS name that has 0x20 in the 16TH byte. A special group is limited to 25 members.

The following example shows how all of these keywords are used:

```
102.54.94.102    "appname      \0x14"              #special app server
102.54.94.123    printsrv      #PRE                #source server
102.54.94.98     localsrv      #PRE
102.54.94.97     primary       #PRE #DOM:mydomain  #PDC for mydomain

#BEGIN_ALTERNATE
#INCLUDE \\localsrv\public\lmhosts     #adds LMHOSTS from this server
#INCLUDE \\primary\public\lmhosts      #adds LMHOSTS from this server
#END_ALTERNATE
```

In the preceding example:

- The servers named `printsrv`, `localsrv`, and `primary` are defined by using the #PRE keyword as entries to be preloaded into the NetBIOS cache at system startup.

- The servers named `localsrv` and `primary` are defined as preloaded and also identified in the #INCLUDE statements as the location of the centrally maintained LMHOSTS file.

- Note that the server named `"appname       \0x14"` contains a special character after the first 15 characters in its name (including the blanks), and so its name is enclosed in double quotation marks.

The following sections further explain the use of the keywords #PRE, #DOM, #INCLUDE, and #SG.

Adding Remote System Names by Using #PRE

Using #PRE entries improves access to the identified computers because name and IP address mappings are contained in the computer's cache memory. However, by default, Windows NT limits the preload name cache to 100 entries. (This limit affects only entries marked with the #PRE keyword.)

If you specify more than 100 #PRE entries, only the first 100 #PRE entries are preloaded into the computer's cache. Any additional #PRE entries are ignored at startup and are used only if name resolution by the cache and IP broadcast fails. Windows NT then parses the complete LMHOSTS file which contains all the entries, including the #PRE entries that exceeded the cache limit of 100.

You can change the default maximum allowed #PRE entries by adding a **MaxPreLoads** value entry to the Registry. This value entry must be added to the following Registry key:

```
HKEY_LOCAL_MACHINE\SYSTEM\CurrentControlSet\Services\Netbt\Parameters
```

For example, the LMHOSTS file could contain the following information:

```
102.54.94.91    accounting              #accounting server
102.54.94.94    payroll                 #payroll server
102.54.94.97    stockquote     #PRE     #stock quote server
102.54.94.102   printqueue              #print server in Bldg 7
```

In this example, the server named stockquote is preloaded into the name cache, because it is tagged with the #PRE keyword. The servers named accounting, payroll, and printqueue would be resolved only after the cache entries failed to match and after broadcast queries failed to locate them. After non-preloaded entries are resolved, their mappings are cached for a period of time for reuse.

Adding Domain Controllers by Using #DOM

The #DOM keyword can be used in LMHOSTS files to distinguish a Windows NT domain controller from other computers on the network. To use the #DOM tag, follow the name and IP address mapping in LMHOSTS with the #DOM keyword, a colon, and the domain in which the domain controller participates. For example:

```
102.54.94.97 primary    #PRE#DOM:mydomain    #The mydomain PDC
```

Using the #DOM keyword to designate domain controllers adds entries to a *domain name cache* that is used to contact available controllers for processing domain requests. When domain controller activity such as a logon request occurs, the request is sent to the domain group name. On the local subnet, the request is broadcast and is picked up by any local domain controllers. However, if you use the #DOM keyword to specify domain controllers in the LMHOSTS file, Microsoft TCP/IP uses datagrams to also forward the request to domain controllers located on remote subnets. Adding more domain controllers in the LMHOSTS file will help distribute the load on all the controllers.

The following list contains guidelines for mapping important members of the domain by using the #DOM keyword.

- It is recommended that the #DOM entries be pre-cached by using the #PRE keyword. Note that the #PRE keyword must precede the #DOM keyword.

- For each local LMHOSTS file on a Windows NT computer that is a member in a domain, there should be #DOM entries for all domain controllers in the domain that are located on remote subnets. This ensures that logon authentication, password changes, browsing, and so on, all work properly for the local domain. These are the necessary minimum entries.

- For local LMHOSTS files on all servers that can be backup domain controllers, there should be mappings for the primary domain controller's name and IP address, plus mappings for all other backup domain controllers. This ensures that promoting a backup to primary domain controller status does not affect the ability to offer all services to members of the domain.

- If trust relationships exist between domains, all domain controllers for all trusted domains should also be listed in the local LMHOSTS file.

- For domains that you want to browse from your local domain, the local LMHOSTS files should contain at least the name and IP address mapping for the primary domain controller in the remote domain. Again, backup domain controllers should also be included so that promotion to primary domain controller does not impair the ability to browse remote domains.

Names that appear with the #DOM keyword in the LMHOSTS file are placed in a special domain name list in NetBT. When a datagram is sent to this domain using the DOMAIN<1C> name, the name is resolved first by using WINS or IP broadcasts. The datagram is then sent to all the addresses contained in the list from LMHOSTS, and there is also a broadcast on the local subnet.

Adding User-defined Special Groups by Using #SG

You can group resources such as printers, or computers that belong to groups on the intranet, for easy reference, browsing, or broadcasting, by using the #SG keyword to define a special group in the LMHOSTS file. Special groups are limited to a total of 25 members. (If you are using WINS, they can also be defined by using the WINS Manager.)

Specify the name just as you would a domain name except that the keyword portion of the entry is #SG. For example:

```
102.54.94.99 printsrvsg     #SG:mycompany   #Specialgroup of computers
```

The preceding example results in a special group being created. In some cases you may want to just specify the name of a special group without specifying an IP address. This can be done by giving the name of the group preceded by #SG. For example:

```
printsrvsg     #SG:mycompany   #Specialgroup of computers
```

Addresses entered by using the LMHOSTS file become permanent addresses in the special group and can be removed only by using the WINS Manager.

Adding Multihomed Devices by Using #MH

A multihomed device is a computer with multiple network interface cards (NICs). A multihomed device can be defined by a single, unique name with which multiple IP addresses are associated.

You can provide multihomed name-to-IP-address mappings in the LMHOSTS file by creating entries that are specified by using the keyword #MH. An #MH entry associates a single, unique NetBIOS computer name to an IP address. You can create multiple entries for the same NetBIOS computer name for each NIC in the multihomed device, up to a maximum of 25 different IP addresses for the same name.

The format of the LMHOSTS entry that is used to specify name-to-IP-address mappings for multihomed devices is the same as the other keyword entries. For example, the entries required to map name to IP address for a multihomed device with two NICs are:

```
102.54.94.91 accounting          #accounting server NIC 1
102.54.94.91 accounting          #accounting server NIC 2
```

Defining a Central LMHOST File by Using #Include

For small- to medium-sized networks with fewer than 20 domains, a single common LMHOSTS file usually satisfies all workstations and servers on the intranet. An administrator can:

- Use the Windows NT Replicator service to maintain synchronized local copies of the global LMHOSTS file.

- Use centralized LMHOSTS files, as described in this section.

Use the #BEGIN_ALTERNATE and #END_ALTERNATE keywords to provide a list of servers maintaining copies of the same LMHOSTS file. This is known as a *block inclusion*, which allows multiple servers to be searched for a valid copy of a specific file. The following example shows the use of the #INCLUDE and #_ALTERNATE keywords to include a local LMHOSTS file (in the C:\Private directory):

```
102.54.94.97primary        #PRE  #DOM:mydomain      #primary DC
102.54.94.99backupdc       #PRE  #DOM:mydomain      #backup DC
102.54.94.98localsvr       #PRE  #DOM:mydomain

#INCLUDE     c:\private\lmhosts                #include a local lmhosts

#BEGIN_ALTERNATE
#INCLUDE     \\primary\public\lmhosts          #source for global file
#INCLUDE     \\backupdc\public\lmhosts         #backup source
#INCLUDE     \\localsvr\public\lmhosts         #backup source
#END_ALTERNATE
```

Important This feature should never be used to include a remote file from a redirected drive because the LMHOSTS file is shared between local users who have different profiles and different logon scripts. Even on single-user systems, redirected drive mappings can change between logon sessions.

In the preceding example, the servers primary and backupdc are located on remote subnets from the computer that owns the file. The local user has decided to include a list of preferred servers in a local LMHOSTS file located in the C:\Private directory. During name resolution, the Windows NT computer first includes this private file, then gets the global LMHOSTS file from one of three locations: primary, backupdc, or localsvr. All names of servers in the #INCLUDE statements must have their addresses preloaded using the #PRE keyword; otherwise, the #INCLUDE statement is ignored.

The block inclusion is satisfied if one of the three sources for the global LMHOSTS file is available and none of the other servers is used. If no server is available, or for some reason the LMHOSTS file or path is incorrect, an event is added to the event log to indicate that the block inclusion failed.

Configuring TCP/IP to Use LMHOSTS Name Resolution

By default, the LMHOSTS name resolution method is enabled when TCP/IP is installed on a computer. You can disable LMHOSTS name resolution by clicking to clear the **Enable LMHOSTS Lookup** check box on the **WINS Address** tab of the **Microsoft TCP/IP Properties** dialog box. It is recommended that you do not disable LMHOSTS name resolution because it provides a backup name service for WINS servers that are off-line or unavailable.

To use an LMHOSTS file from a remote computer or different directory on the local computer, click **Import LMHOSTS** as illustrated in the following figure.

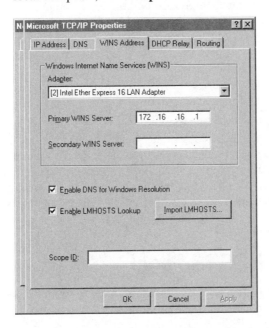

Figure 10.1   Configuring TCP/IP to Enable LMHOSTS Lookup

Maintaining the LMHOSTS File

When you use an LMHOSTS file, be sure to keep it up-to-date and organized. Use the following guidelines:

- Update the LMHOSTS file whenever a computer is changed or removed from the network.

- Because LMHOSTS files are searched one line at a time from the beginning, list remote computers in priority order, with the ones used most often at the top of the file, followed by remote systems listed in #INCLUDE statements.

- Use #PRE statements to preload into the local computer's name cache frequently accessed workstations and servers listed in the #INCLUDE statements. #PRE keyword entries should be entered at the end of the file, because these are preloaded into the cache at system startup time and are not accessed later. This increases the speed of searches for the entries used most often. Because each line is processed individually, any comment lines that you add will increase the parsing time.

- Use the **nbtstat** command to remove or correct preloaded entries that might have been typed incorrectly or any names cached by successful broadcast resolution. You can reprime the name cache by using the **nbtstat -R** command to purge and reload the name cache, reread the LMHOSTS file, and then insert entries tagged with the #PRE keyword. For more information about using the **nbtstat** command, see the Help topic "TCP/IP Procedures Help" or refer to Appendix A, "TCP/IP Utilities Reference."

Troubleshooting LMHOSTS Files

When using the LMHOSTS file, problems such as failure to locate a remote computer can occur because one or more of the following errors are present in the LMHOSTS file:

- The LMHOSTS file does not contain an entry for the remote server.

- The computer (NetBIOS) name in the LMHOSTS file is misspelled. (Note that LMHOSTS names are automatically converted to uppercase.)

- The IP address for a computer name in the LMHOSTS file is not valid.

- The required carriage return at the end of the last entry in the LMHOSTS file is missing.

C H A P T E R   1 1

Using SNMP for Network Management

Simple Network Management Protocol (SNMP) is a network management standard widely used in TCP/IP networks and, more recently, with Internet Package Exchange (IPX) networks. Windows NT Server and Windows NT Workstation 4.0 include an SNMP service that allows Windows NT–based computers to be managed by using SNMP network management programs.

The information in this chapter is for the administrator who needs to understand SNMP and the SNMP-based service running under Windows NT 4.0.

This chapter begins with a review of basic SNMP concepts, and provides a glossary of the network management terms that are used throughout this chapter. The next two sections describe the SNMP network management standard and the Windows NT implementation of SNMP. The remaining sections in the chapter provide information about using and troubleshooting the SNMP service running under Windows NT. At the end of the chapter there is a list of reference materials that provide detailed information about SNMP, TCP/IP, and IPX.

Overview of SNMP

Simple Network Management Protocol (SNMP) is a network management protocol frequently used in TCP/IP networks to monitor and manage computers and other devices (such as printers) connected to the network. SNMP is supported in Windows NT Server and Windows NT Workstation by the SNMP service.

As part of the Internet TCP/IP protocol suite, SNMP is defined in the Internet Engineering Task Force (IETF) Request for Comments (RFCs) 1155, 1157, and 1213. The following table describes these RFCs.

Table 11.1   Titles and Descriptions of RFCs Defining SNMP

RFC #	Title	Description
1155	Structure and Identification of Management Information for TCP/IP-based Internets	Defines the structure used to define data objects in a MIB.
1157	Simple Network Management Protocol (SNMP)	Defines SNMP communication formats and operations.
1213	Management Information Base for Network Management of TCP/IP-based Internets: MIB-II	Defines basic and industry-common types of managed-objects.

Requirements for Network Management

The term *network management* generally refers to specific administrative functions and the ability to perform these functions from a centralized computer, often referred to as a *management console*.

To perform centralized network management, the managing computer must be able to get data from other computers on the network, including the following:

- Network protocol identification and statistics
- Dynamic identification of computers attached to the network (referred to as *discovery*)
- Hardware and software configuration data
- Computer performance and usage statistics
- Computer event and error messages
- Program and application usage statistics

How SNMP Uses the Registry

The Registry, the operating system database on each Windows NT-based computer, contains information that is needed for network management. The SNMP service accesses the Registry and converts the information into a format that can be used by third-party SNMP network management programs.

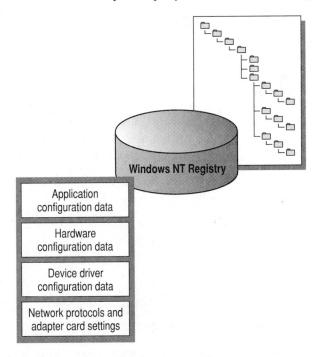

Figure 11.1   The Windows NT Registry

The following sections—"Management Information Base," "Agents," and "Managers"—provide a high-level overview of the major software components of SNMP. Windows NT implements SNMP-based MIBs and an SNMP agent component to provide the necessary framework for SNMP network management.

SNMP uses a glossary of network management terms that may be unfamiliar to some readers. The following SNMP network management terminology is used in this chapter.

- A *host* is any network device, including workstation and server computers.

- *Managed-objects* are host hardware and software resources, such as a computer disk partition, that can be monitored (managed) by a network administrator at another computer on the network.

- Each SNMP host (computer) has one or many *management information bases* (MIBs) that contain information about the managed-objects on that computer.

- A *manager* is a software program that sends requests for data to other computers on the network. Typically, the manager includes a user interface (UI) for displaying status and data retrieved from the network computers and devices.

- An *SNMP management console* is any computer running SNMP manager software.

- An *agent* is a software program that processes manager requests for data by retrieving data from managed-objects on the computer. The agent program is part of the SNMP service running under Windows NT.

Management Information Base

A management information base (MIB) is a data file containing the managed-object descriptions and object values. Each host that is to be managed by SNMP must have a MIB that describes the manageable objects on that host.

Basically, a MIB will define the following for every object contained within that MIB:

- the association between (1) the host hardware or software component (object) and (2) an object name and an object identifier.

- A definition of the data type used to define the object.

- A textual description of the object.

- An index method used for objects that are a complex data type.

- The read or write access that is allowed on the object.

RFC 1213 defines an industry-standard SNMP MIB referred to as MIB-II. Industry vendors, such as Microsoft, can define additional MIBs that allow unique hardware or software services developed by the vendor to be monitored and managed by SNMP management consoles.

Note Additional MIBs that are supported by Windows NT Server are described in Appendix C, "MIB Object Types for Windows NT."

Object Identifiers

Each object in a MIB is identified by a universally unique label referred to as an *object-identifier* (OID). The object name space is implemented as a multi-part, hierarchical, naming scheme. A hierarchical naming scheme can be viewed as an inverted tree with the branches pointing downward. Each point where a new branch is added is referred to as a *node*. This OID is internationally accepted and allows developers and vendors to create new components and resources and assign a unique OID to each new component or resource.

The OID naming scheme is governed by the Internet Engineering Task Force (IETF). The IETF grants authority for parts of the name space to individual organizations, such as Microsoft. For example, Microsoft has the authority to assign the OIDs that can be derived by branching downward from the node in the MIB name tree that starts at 1.3.6.1.4.1.311.

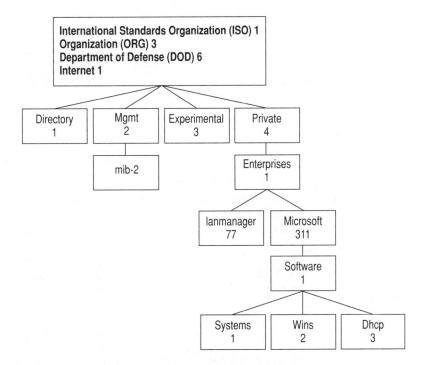

Figure 11.2   A Managed-object Name Hierarchy

SNMP programs use the OID to identify the objects on each computer that can be managed by using SNMP. For example, when a network administrator requires information about managed-objects from some computer on the network, the SNMP management program sends a message over the network that requests information about the object as identified by the OID. The computer that receives the message can use the OID to retrieve information from the specific object on the computer and send the information back to the SNMP management program.

Agents

An agent is an SNMP program that must be installed on each managed computer in an SNMP-managed network. The Windows NT-based SNMP service includes an SNMP agent.

The agent program provides an interface to the MIBs and managed-objects installed on the computer. SNMP management programs send management requests to the computers on the network. The agent program on the computer receives the requests and processes them by retrieving information from the MIBs on the computer. The agent then sends the requested information back to the SNMP manager program that initiated the request.

The Windows NT-based SNMP service is an optional service that is installed after TCP/IP is installed on a Windows NT-based computer. After the SNMP service is installed on a computer, it automatically starts each time the computer is started.

When the agent program is started on a computer, it waits for SNMP requests from a manager program on the network management console (computer). When an agent program receives an SNMP message, it performs the requested **get**, **get-next**, and **set** operations.

The only operation that an agent spontaneously starts is a **trap** operation to alert the SNMP manager program that the computer has started, stopped, or is experiencing an extraordinary event (such as disk-full) on some managed-object on the computer.

In summary, the agent program performs the following operations:

- The **get** operation retrieves a specific value about a managed-object, such as available hard disk space, from the host MIB.
- The **get-next** operation returns the "next" value by traversing the MIB database of managed-object variables.
- The **set** operation changes the value of a managed-object variable. Only variables whose object definitions allow read/write access can be set.
- The **trap** operation sends messages to the SNMP management console when a change or error occurs in a managed-object.

Note By installation default, the computer software port 161 is used to listen for SNMP messages and port 162 is used listen for SNMP traps. If you need to run multiple SNMP agents, you can change these port settings in the *systemroot*\System32\Drivers\Etc\Service\Service file.

Managers

SNMP management programs are referred to as *managers*. Managers obtain data about network devices and make this information available to a network administrator through textual, graphical, or object-oriented user interfaces. The manager program sends SNMP messages to network hosts. These messages are received by the agent on the host, and initiate the **get**, **get-next**, and **set** operations. The manager program waits (listens) for the SNMP messages from the agent that contain the results of the operation, and displays the information on the SNMP-management console or saves the data in a specified file or database.

As noted earlier, the SNMP service running under Windows NT is an SNMP agent, which is the necessary framework needed for network management. However a separate SNMP manager program is needed to perform management operations.

There are several SNMP manager utilities provided with the Windows NT Server Resource Kit compact disc. Other network management software can be obtained from Microsoft or from third-party vendors.

Windows NT-based Implementation of SNMP

The SNMP service running under Windows NT implements SNMP version 1 and provides an SNMP agent that allows remote, centralized SNMP management of:

- Windows NT Server computers
- Windows NT Workstation computers
- Windows NT-based WINS server computers
- Windows NT-based DHCP server computers
- Windows NT-based Internet Information Server computers
- LAN Manager server computers

Note Network Driver Interface Specification (NDIS) 4.0-compliant peripheral devices attached to a Windows NT-based computer are also manageable by using the Windows NT-based SNMP service. If the device is to be managed by using SNMP, the device vendor must provide a device .inf file that can be registered in the Windows NT-based Registry.

The Windows NT-based SNMP agent is implemented as a service and can be installed on Windows NT-based computers that use the TCP/IP and IPX protocols. The TCP/IP protocol must be installed before installing SNMP. For more information about installing SNMP, see TCP/IP Help.

Note You must install TCP/IP to be able to install the SNMP service, even if IPX is installed as the main network protocol.

The SNMP service is implemented as a Windows 32-bit service by using Windows Sockets over both TCP/IP and IPX/SPX. The additional Microsoft MIBs for DHCP, WINS, and the Internet Information Server, extend SNMP management to these Windows NT-based services. The agent programs that implement these additional MIBs are referred to as *extension-agents*. The extension-agent programs work with the master Windows NT-based agent program. These Windows NT-based extension-agents are implemented as Windows 32-bit dynamic-link libraries (DLLs).

The following diagram shows a simple interaction between an SNMP manager computer and a Windows NT-based computer with an SNMP agent program.

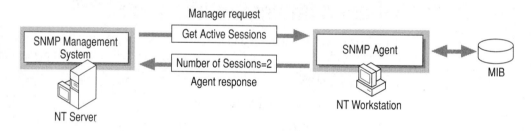

Figure 11.3   SNMP Manager and SNMP Agent Interaction

Windows NT SNMP Files

The following table describes the files that are installed on a Windows NT computer with the SNMP service installed.

Table 11.2   SNMP Service Files

File name	Description
Dhcpmib.dll	DHCP MIB extension-agent DLL is available only when the DHCP server is installed on a computer running Windows NT Server.
Iis.dll	Internet Information Server DLL is available only if the Internet Information Server is installed on a computer running Windows NT Server.
Inetmib1.dll	MIB-II extension-agent DLL.
Lmmib2.dll	LAN Manager extension-agent DLL.
Mgmtapi.dll	A Windows NT-based SNMP manager API that listens for manager requests, and sends the requests to and receives responses from SNMP agents.
Mib.bin	Installed with the SNMP service and used by the management API, Mgmtapi.dll, to map text-based object names to numerical OIDs.
Snmp.exe	SNMP agent service, a master (proxy) agent that accepts manager program requests and forwards the requests to the appropriate sub-agent-extension DLL for processing.
Snmptrap.exe	Receives SNMP traps from the SNMP agent and forwards them to the SNMP manager API on the management console. A background process, Snmptrap.exe is started only when the SNMP manager API receives a manager request for traps.
Winsmib.dll	WINS MIB extension-agent DLL, available only when the WINS server is installed on a computer running Windows NT Server.

MIB Implementation Notes

The Windows NT-based SNMP service includes MIB-II, based on RFC 1213, LAN Manager MIB-II, and Microsoft proprietary MIBs for DHCP, Internet Information Server, and WINS servers. Appendix C, "MIB Object Types for Windows NT," contains information about the Windows NT-based MIBs, and a description of each object in the MIB.

The Windows NT-based SNMP service supports multiple MIBs through an agent application programming interface (API). The separate extension-agent DLL is used to access the Windows NT-based MIBs. When the SNMP service is started, it loads the SNMP extension-agent DLLs. The extension-agent DLLs must be defined in the Registry in order to be loaded.

This use of DLLs in the SNMP service architecture allows new MIBs to be easily added. Microsoft and third-party developers can develop MIBs for new hardware and software components and easily integrate the new functionality by using SNMP.

The MIB name space assigned to Microsoft by the IETF starts at the node labeled *1.3.6.1.4.1.311*. Microsoft has the authority to assign objects and OIDs to all objects that are developed below that node.

The following table identifies the Windows NT-based MIBs and top-most object (base object) from which all other objects in the MIB are derived. When the SNMP service is started, each extension-agent sends the OID for the base object in its MIB to the master agent program. This process identifies to the master agent the MIBs and managed objects that are actually installed on the computer.

Table 11.3   Base Object Identifiers

MIB name	Base object name	Base object identifier (OID)	Description
Internet MIB-II	iso.org.dod.internet. mgmt.mib-2	1.3.6.1.2.1	Defines objects essential for either configuration or fault analysis. Internet MIB-II is defined in RFC 1213.
LAN Manager MIB-II	iso.org.dod.internet. private.enterprise. lanmanager	1.3.6.1.4.1.77	Defines objects that include such items as statistical, share, session, user, and logon information.
Microsoft DHCP server MIB	iso.org.dod.internet. private.enterprise. microsoft.software. dhcp	1.3.6.1.4.1.311.1 .3	Contains statistics for the DHCP server, and DHCP scope information.
Microsoft Internet Information Server MIB	iso.org.dod.internet. private.enterprise. microsoft.software. iis	1.3.6.1.4.1.311.1 .7	The FTP, Gopher, and HTTP server MIBs are derived from the Internet Information Server base object.
Microsoft WINS server MIB	iso.org.dod.internet. private.enterprise. microsoft.software. wins	1.3.6.1.4.1.311.1 .2	Contains information about the WINS server, including statistics, database information, and push and pull data.

SNMP Security Implementation Notes

The SNMP security service is referred to as an *authentication* service. Simply put, a management request contained within an authenticated SNMP message is processed; a message that cannot be authenticated is not processed.

SNMP uses *community names* to authenticate messages. The community name can be thought of as a password shared by the SNMP management consoles and the SNMP managed hosts. All SNMP messages must contain a community name. The SNMP agent that receives an SNMP message checks (authenticates) the community name with the community name or names with which the SNMP service is configured. If the message contains a known community name, the message is processed. If the message contains a community name that is not configured on the host, the message is rejected and the host (optionally) sends a trap message to an SNMP management console. The trap message alerts the SNMP management console that a message authentication failure occurred at that host.

The default community name when the SNMP service is installed on a Windows NT-based computer is "public." Additional community names can be added or removed by selecting **SNMP Service** from the **Network Services** tab.

If you remove all the community names, including the default name, Public, the SNMP service on that Windows NT-based computer will authenticate and process SNMP messages containing *any* community name. This may or may not be desirable, but is expected behavior, as described in RFC 1157:

> An SNMP message originated by an SNMP application entity that in fact belongs to the SNMP community named by the community component of said message is called an authentic SNMP message. The set of rules by which an SNMP message is identified as an authentic SNMP message for a particular SNMP community is called an authentication scheme. An implementation of a function that identifies authentic SNMP messages according to one or more authentication schemes is called an authentication service.

> Clearly, effective management of administrative relationships among SNMP application entities requires authentication services that (by the use of encryption or other techniques) are able to identify authentic SNMP messages with a high degree of certainty. Some SNMP implementations may wish to support only a trivial authentication service that identifies all SNMP messages as authentic SNMP messages.

When there are no community names identified, the SNMP service implements the behavior as described in the preceding selection from RFC 1157.

Planning for SNMP Installation

Before installing the SNMP service, an administrator must identify the following information:

- The contact person and location for the administrator of the local computer.
- Community names that can be shared by hosts on the network.
- IP address, IPX address, or network computer name of the SNMP management console, or consoles, that will be the destination for trap messages generated by computers within a specific community. (Not all SNMP management consoles must also be trap destinations.)

Agent Configuration

You configure the SNMP agent by selecting the **Agent** tab on the **Microsoft SNMP Properties** page. By default, the optional agent configuration options are checked, as illustrated in the following figure. You only need to add the name of the person to contact, such as the network administrator, and the location of the contact.

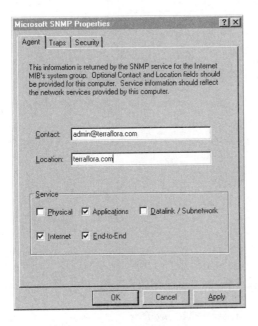

Figure 11.4   Configuring the SNMP Agent

Community Names

Community names provide a rudimentary security scheme for the SNMP service. You can add and delete community names by using the **Security** tab on the **Microsoft SNMP Properties** page. You can also filter the type of packets that the computer will accept. The following figure shows the **Security** tab.

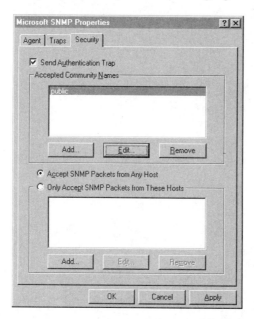

Figure 11.5   Configuring SNMP Security

You must configure the SNMP service with at least one community name. The installation default is the Public community name. You can delete or change the default community name and add multiple community names.

There is no relationship between community names and domain or workgroup names. Community names serve as a shared password for groups of hosts on the network and should be selected and changed as you would any other password. Members of a community (hosts that share the same community name) are typically grouped by their physical proximity.

When the SNMP agent receives an SNMP request that does not contain the correct community name or that came from an unknown host, the SNMP agent can send a trap to one or more trap destinations (SNMP manager programs). The trap message indicates that the request failed authentication.

In the following example, there are two communities—Terraflora and Public.

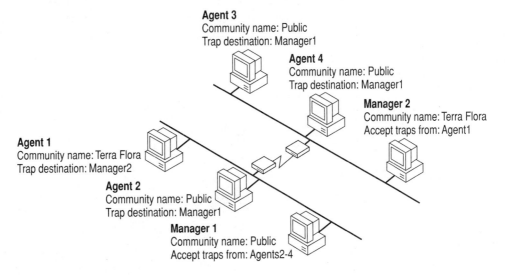

Agent 3
Community name: Public
Trap destination: Manager1

Agent 4
Community name: Public
Trap destination: Manager1

Manager 2
Community name: Terra Flora
Accept traps from: Agent1

Agent 1
Community name: Terra Flora
Trap destination: Manager2

Agent 2
Community name: Public
Trap destination: Manager1

Manager 1
Community name: Public
Accept traps from: Agents2-4

Figure 11.6   SNMP Community Names

Only the agents and managers that are configured with the same community name can communicate with each other.

- Agent 1 can send traps and other messages to Manager 2 because they are both members of the Terra Flora community.

- Agent 2 through Agent 4 can send traps and messages to Manager 1 because they are all members of the Public (default) community.

The community names that are configured by using the **Security** tab are used when configuring Trap Destinations.

Trap Destinations

The SNMP agent generates trap messages, which are sent to an SNMP management console, the trap destination. Trap messages can be generated for changes such as host system startup, shutdown, or password violation. Trap destinations can be configured by a user, but the occurrences which generate a trap message are internally defined by the SNMP agent.

Trap destinations are identified by a computer name, IP address, or IPX address of the host or hosts on the network to which you want the trap messages sent. The trap destination must be a host that is running an SNMP manager program.

You configure the trap destination on a Windows NT-based computer by using the **Traps** tab on the **Microsoft SNMP Properties** page to enter the host name, IP address, or IPX address of the computer or computers running an SNMP manager program. The following figure shows the **Traps** tab of the **Microsoft SNMP Properties** page.

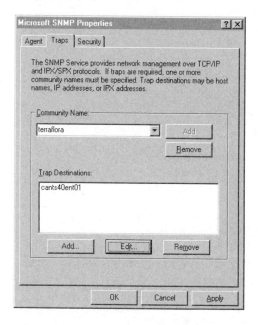

Figure 11.7   Configuring SNMP Traps

Using SNMP

When the SNMP service is installed, a network administrator can:

- View and change parameters in the LAN Manager and MIB-II MIBs by using SNMP manager programs.

- Monitor and configure parameters for any WINS servers on the network by using SNMP manager programs.

- Monitor DHCP servers by using SNMP manager programs.

- Use Performance Monitor to monitor TCP/IP-related performance counters which are ICMP, IP, Network Interface, TCP, UDP, DHCP, FTP, WINS, and Internet Information Server performance counters.

- Use the Windows NT Server Resource Kit utilities to perform simple SNMP manager functions.

The following table describes SNMP-related utilities and files provided on the Resource Kit compact disc.

Table 11.4   SNMP-related Utilities and Files on theWindows NT Server Resource Kit Compact Disc

File name	Description
Dhcp.mib	DHCP server objects. See Appendix C, "MIB Object Types for Windows NT."
Wins.mib	Microsoft WINS server managed-objects. See Appendix C, "MIB Object Types for Windows NT."
Inetsrv.mib	Internet Information Server managed-objects. See Appendix C, "MIB Object Types for Windows NT."
FTP.mib	FTP server managed-objects. See Appendix C, "MIB Object Types for Windows NT."
Gopherd.mib	Gopher server managed-objects. See Appendix C, "MIB Object Types for Windows NT."
Http.mib	HTTP server managed-objects. See Appendix C, "MIB Object Types for Windows NT."
Lmmib2.mib	LAN Manager MIB-II. See Appendix C, "MIB Object Types for Windows NT."
Mib_ii.mib	MIB-II. See Appendix C, "MIB Object Types for Windows NT."
Smi.mib	Structure of Management Information MIB, as specified in RFC 1155. This file contains the global definitions used to define the objects in the other MIBs.
Mibcc.exe	SNMP MIB compiler used to produce a new Mib.bin that includes additional MIBs, for example, the Wins.mib.
Perf2mib.exe	MIB builder tool. See the section "Using Performance Monitor Counters with SNMP" later in this chapter.
Snmputil.exe	A simple SNMP browser manager application that implements **Get**, **Get Next**, **Walk**, and **Trap** network management operations to obtain information from Windows NT-based hosts. This application is also provided in the Windows 32-bit SDK.
Snmpmon.exe	SNMP Monitor is a utility that can monitor SNMP MIB objects on any number of remote hosts, and optionally log the results in an ODBC database. Snmpmon.exe uses an .ini file, for example Perfmib.ini.

For information on how to use any of the Windows NT-based Resource Kit utilities, see Resource Kit Tools Help.

Starting and Stopping the SNMP Service

After the SNMP service has been installed, it automatically starts when the computer is started and so you will usually not need to start the SNMP service. However, if you stop SNMP, you must then restart it because it does not automatically restart. Stopping a service cancels any network connections the service is using.

You can start and stop the SNMP service at the command prompt by typing the commands **net start snmp and net stop snmp.** You can also point to **Control Panel** and double-click the **Services** icon, then select **SNMP** and click the **Start** or **Stop** service buttons.

You must stop and restart the SNMP service to add new extension-agent DLLs and MIBs.

Note The syntax for the **net start snmp** and **net stop snmp** commands has changed in Windows NT 4.0. SNMP error logging parameters are not supported and have been replaced by improved SNMP error handling in the Windows NT Event Log. The syntax for these commands is:

net start snmp

net stop snmp

Using SNMP to Manage DHCP, WINS, and Internet Information Servers

If you have installed the DHCP server, Internet Information Server, or WINS server software on a Windows NT-based computer on the network, you can monitor the DHCP, Internet Information Server, or WINS services by using an SNMP manager program.

The Windows NT-based DHCP server objects and Internet Information Server server objects can be monitored, but not configured, using SNMP.

WINS server objects can be configured and monitored by using SNMP. All but a few of the WINS configuration parameters that can be set by editing the Registry can also be set by using SNMP. For information about which WINS parameters can be set by using SNMP, refer to the description of the WINS MIB in Appendix C, "MIB Object Types for Windows NT." WINS objects that are defined with *Access read-write* can be configured by using SNMP.

Using Performance Monitor Counters with SNMP

All Performance Monitor counters installed on a computer can be viewed by using SNMP. To do this, use the Perf2MIB utility provided on the Windows NT Server Resource Kit compact disc to create a new MIB file which enumerates the counters in which you are interested. For additional information on how to use the Perf2mib.exe utility, see Resource Kit Tools Help.

Troubleshooting SNMP

This section discusses problems that you might encounter using SNMP, and what to do to resolve them.

Using the Event Viewer to Find SNMP Errors

SNMP error handling has been improved in Windows NT Server and Windows NT Workstation version 4.0. Manual configuration of SNMP error-logging parameters has been replaced by improved error handling that is integrated with the Event Viewer. Use the Event Viewer if you suspect a problem with the SNMP Service.

Note Refer to the *Windows NT Server Resource Guide* for detailed information about using the Event Viewer.

▶ **To use Event Viewer**

1. From the **Start** menu, point to **Programs**.

2. Click Administrative Tools on the Programs menu.

3. Double-click **Event Viewer** to display the System Log.

4. If any is any event is identified as SNMP in the Source column, double-click that row to display the **Event Detail**.

The following figure illustrates an SNMP event display in the **Event Viewer**.

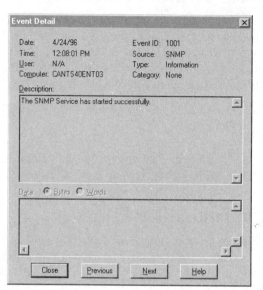

Figure 11.8   SNMP Event Message

Modifying SNMP Parameters in the Registry

SNMP parameters and information about the SNMP extension-agent DLLs are contained in the Registry. You can view or change this information by using the Registry Editor (Regedt32.exe).

▶ **To start the Registry Editor**

1. Click the **Start** button and click **Run**.

2. Type **regedt32** in the command line box.

Warning Using Registry Editor incorrectly can cause serious, system-wide problems that may require you to reinstall Windows NT to correct them. Microsoft cannot guarantee that any problems resulting from the incorrect use of the Registry Editor can be solved.

Windows NT-based SNMP parameters are contained in the Registry in the following key:

```
HKEY_LOCAL_MACHINE\System\CurrentControlSet\Services\SNMP\Parameters
```

The following table describes the SNMP parameters contained in the Registry.

Table 11.5   SNMP Parameters Contained in the Registry

Registry parameter	Description
EnableAuthenticationTraps Units: Boolean Range: 0 (Off) or 1 (On) Default: On	A value of On (1) indicates that the SNMP service sends a trap whenever it receives a request that does not match any community name or host filter in its lists. Off (0) indicates that the SNMP service does not send a trap when this occurs.
ExtensionAgents	Contains information about each of the extension-agent DLLs to load.
ValidCommunities Units: names Range: — Default: public	Specifies one or more community names defining groups of hosts from which the SNMP service will accept requests.
TrapConfiguration Units: name Range: — Default: —	Specifies one or more host names, IP addresses, or IPX addresses defining hosts to which the SNMP service sends traps. Under the **TrapConfiguration** key, there is a key for each community. Under the **ValidCommunities** key, there are trap destination values for that community.

Timeout on WINS Server Queries

When querying a WINS server, it might be necessary to increase the SNMP timeout period on the SNMP management system. If some WINS queries work and others time out, increase the timeout period.

No Counters Appear in Performance Monitor

You must install the SNMP service to see any of the TCP/IP, Internet Control Message Protocol (ICMP), Network Interface, or UDP performance counters in Performance Monitor. When the SNMP service is installed, the following TCP/IP-related counters are added to Performance Monitor:

- ICMP
- IP
- Network Interface
- TCP
- UDP

SNMP is not automatically installed when you install TCP/IP. See TCP/IP Help for information about installing and configuring SNMP on your local computer.

For more information about Performance Monitor and counters, refer to the *Windows NT Server Resource Guide.*

Note When the IPX protocol is used as the main network protocol, the TCP/IP objects that can be monitored by using SNMP are null.

Error Using an IPX Address as a Trap Destination

If you enter an IPX address as a trap destination when installing the SNMP service, the following error message may appear when you restart your computer:

```
Error 3
```

This problem occurs if the IPX address has been entered incorrectly, using a comma or hyphen to separate a network number and a MAC address. For example, an SNMP manager program such as HP OpenView may normally accept an address such as this: 00008022,0002C0-F7AABD. However, the Windows NT-based SNMP agent does not recognize an address using a comma or hyphen between the network number and MAC address.

The address used for a trap destination must use the "8.12" format for the network number and Media Access Control (MAC) address.

To correct this problem, enter the IPX address for the trap destination in the 8.12 format. For example, the following format is valid:

xxxxxxxx.yyyyyyyyyyyy

where *xxxxxxxx* is the network number and *yyyyyyyyyyyy* is the MAC address.

Reference Materials

The following books contain more information about SNMP.

Network Management: A Practical Perspective
    by Allan Leinwand and Karen Fang
    Addison-Wesley Publishing Company, Inc 1993
    ISBN 0-201-52771-5

SNMP, SNMPv2, and CMIP: The Practical Guide to Network-Management Standards
    by William Stallings
    Addison-Wesley Publishing Company, Inc 1993
    ISBN 0-201-63331-0

The Simple Book: An Introduction to Management of TCP/IP-based Internets
  by Marshall T. Rose
  Prentice-Hall, Inc., 1994
  ISBN 0-13-177254-6

Internetworking with TCP/IP
  Volume 1: Principles, Protocols, and Architecture (third edition)
  by Douglas E. Comer
  Prentice-Hall, Inc., 1991
  ISBN 0-13-468505-9

The following Requests for Comments (RFCs) are published by the Internet Engineering Task Force (IETF) and other working groups. The RFCs that define SNMP are listed in the following table.

Table 11.6   RFC Specifications about SNMP

RFC	Title
1155	Structure and Identification of Management Information for TCP/IP-based Internets
1157	Simple Network Management Protocol
1213	Management Information Base for Network Management of TCP/IP-based internets: MIB-II

RFCs can be obtained via FTP from:

- **nis.nsf.net**
- **nisc.jvnc.net**
- **venera.isi.edu**
- **wuarchive.wustl.edu**
- **src.doc.ic.ac.uk**
- **ftp.concert.net**
- **ds.internic.net**, or
- **nic.ddn.mil**

C H A P T E R   1 2

Troubleshooting Tools and Strategies

Many excellent network troubleshooting tools are available for Windows NT Server and Windows NT Workstation. Most are included with the product or in the Windows NT Server and Windows NT Workstation Resource Kits. Microsoft Network Monitor is an excellent network tracing tool that is included in the Microsoft Systems Management Server product.

When troubleshooting any problem, it is helpful to use a logical approach. Some questions to ask are:

- What does work?
- What doesn't work?
- How are the things that do and don't work related?
- Have the things that don't work ever worked on this computer and network?
- If so, what has changed since they last worked?

Troubleshooting a problem "from the bottom up" is often a good way to quickly isolate it. The troubleshooting tasks discussed in this chapter are organized using this "bottom up" approach.

The first section of this chapter gives an overview of TCP/IP troubleshooting tools. The next section discusses various TCP/IP troubleshooting tasks, followed by a section on using Performance Monitor and Network Monitor to analyze network behavior. The final section of this chapter provides information about common TCP/IP networking problems.

Overview of TCP/IP Troubleshooting Tools

The following table lists the diagnostic utilities included with Microsoft TCP/IP that can be used to identify or resolve TCP/IP networking problems.

Table 12.1   TCP/IP Diagnostic Utilities

Utility	Used to
arp	View the ARP (address resolution protocol) table on the local computer to detect invalid entries.
hostname	Print the name of the current host.
ipconfig	Display current TCP/IP network configuration values, and update or release TCP/IP network configuration values.
nbtstat	Check the state of current NetBIOS over TCP/IP connections, update the LMHOSTS cache, and determine the registered name and scope ID.
netstat	Display protocol statistics and the state of current TCP/IP connections.
nslookup	Check records, domain host aliases, domain host services, and operating system information by querying Internet domain name servers.
ping	Verify whether TCP/IP is configured correctly and that a remote TCP/IP system is available.
route	Print the IP route table, and add or delete IP routes.
tracert	Check the route to a remote system.

For complete details about the TCP/IP utilities, see Appendix A, "TCP/IP Utilities Reference."

These additional Windows NT tools can be used for TCP/IP troubleshooting:

- Microsoft SNMP service—provides statistical information to SNMP management systems
- Event Viewer—tracks errors and events
- Performance Monitor—analyzes TCP/IP and WINS server performance
- Registry Editor— allows viewing and editing of Registry parameters

In general, when troubleshooting it is usually best to first verify that the computer TCP/IP configuration is correct, and then verify that a connection and route exist between the computer and network host by using **ping**, as described in the section "Test Connection to the TCP/IP Network by Using Ping" later in this chapter.

Compile a list of what works and what doesn't work, and then study the list to help isolate the failure. If link reliability is in question, try a large number of pings of various sizes at different times of the day, and plot the success rate. When all else fails, using a protocol analyzer, such as Microsoft Network Monitor, can be helpful.

Identify the TCP/IP Configuration by Using IPConfig

When troubleshooting a TCP/IP networking problem, begin by checking the TCP/IP configuration on the computer experiencing the problem. Use the **ipconfig** command to get the host computer configuration information, including the IP address, subnet mask, and default gateway. **Ipconfig** is a command-line utility that prints out the TCP/IP-related configuration of the local computer.

Note   Windows 95 users use **winipcfg** in place of **ipconfig**.

When **ipconfig** is used with the */all* switch, it produces a detailed configuration report for all interfaces, including any configured serial ports (RAS). **Ipconfig** output may be redirected to a file and pasted into other documents. This output of **ipconfig** can be reviewed to find any problems in the computer network configuration. For example, if the computer has been configured with an IP address that is a duplicate of an existing IP address, the subnet mask will appear as 0.0.0.0.

The following example illustrates the results of an **ipconfig/all** command on a computer that is configured to use a DHCP server for automatic TCP/IP configuration, and WINS and DNS servers for name resolution:

```
Windows NT IP Configuration
    Host Name . . . . . . . . . : davemac1.terraflora.com
    DNS Servers . . . . . . . . : 172.16.48.03
    Node Type . . . . . . . . . : Hybrid
    NetBIOS Scope ID. . . . . . :
    IP Routing Enabled. . . . . : No
    WINS Proxy Enabled. . . . . : No
    NetBIOS Resolution Uses DNS : No
```

```
Ethernet adapter Elnk31:
    Description . . . . . . . . : ELNK3 Ethernet Adapter.
    Physical Address. . . . . . : 00-20-AF-1D-2B-91
    DHCP Enabled. . . . . . . . : Yes
    IP Address. . . . . . . . . : 172.16.48.10
    Subnet Mask . . . . . . . . : 255.255.248.0
    Default Gateway . . . . . . : 172.16.48.03
    DHCP Server . . . . . . . . : 172.16.48.03
    Primary WINS Server . . . . : 172.16.48.03
    Secondary WINS Server . . . : 172.16.48.03
    Lease Obtained. . . . . . . : Sunday, June 25, 1996 11:43:01
    PM
    Lease Expires . . . . . . . : Wednesday, June 28, 1996
    11:43:01 PM

Ethernet adapter NdisWan5:
    Description . . . . . . . . :
    Physical Address. . . . . . : 00-00-00-00-00-00
    DHCP Enabled. . . . . . . . : No
    IP Address. . . . . . . . . : 0.0.0.0
    Subnet Mask . . . . . . . . : 0.0.0.0
    Default Gateway . . . . . . :
```

If no problems appear in the TCP/IP configuration, the next step is to test the ability to connect to other host computers on the TCP/IP network.

Test Connection to the TCP/IP Network by Using Ping

Ping is a tool that helps to verify IP-level connectivity. When troubleshooting, the **ping** command is used to send an ICMP echo request to a target host name or IP address. Use **ping** whenever you need to verify that a host computer can connect to the TCP/IP network and network resources. You can also use the **ping** utility to isolate network hardware problems and incompatible configurations.

It is usually best to verify that a route exists between the local computer and a network host by first using **ping** and the IP address of the network host to which you want to connect. First try pinging the IP address of the target host to see if it will respond, because this is the simplest case. The command syntax is:

ping *IP_address*

Perform the following steps when using **ping**:

1. Ping the loopback address to verify that TCP/IP is installed and configured correctly on the local computer.

   `Ping 127.0.0.1`

2. Ping the IP address of the local computer to verify that it was added to the network correctly.

   `Ping IP_address_of_local_host`

3. Ping the IP address of the default gateway to verify that the default gateway is functioning and that you can communicate with a local host on the local network.

   `Ping IP_address_of_default_gateway`

4. Ping the IP address of a remote host to verify that you can communicate through a router.

   `Ping IP_address_of_remote_host`

Ping uses Windows Sockets-style name resolution to resolve a computer name to an IP address, so if pinging by address succeeds, but fails by name, then the problem lies in address or name resolution, not network connectivity. Refer to the section "Test IP-address-to-MAC-address Resolution by Using ARP" later in this chapter.

If you cannot use **ping** successfully at any point, check the following:

- The computer was restarted after TCP/IP was installed and configured.
- The local computer's IP address is valid and appears correctly in the **IP Address** tab of the **Microsoft TCP/IP Properties** dialog box.
- IP routing is enabled and the link between routers is operational.

Type **ping -?** to see what command-line options are available. For example, **ping** allows you to specify the size of packets to use, how many to send, whether to record the route used, what time-to-live (TTL) value to use, and whether to set the "don't fragment" flag.

The following example illustrates how to send two pings, each 1450 bytes in size, to address 172.16.48.10:

```
C:\>ping -n 2 -l 1450 172.16.48.10
Pinging 172.16.48.10 with 1450 bytes of data:

Reply from 172.16.48.10: bytes=1450 time=10ms TTL=32
Reply from 172.16.48.10: bytes=1450 time=10ms TTL=32
```

By default, **ping** waits only 750 ms for each response to be returned before timing out. If the remote system being pinged is across a high-delay link such as a satellite link, responses could take longer to be returned. The **-w (wait)** switch can be used to specify a longer timeout.

Understanding Address and Name Resolution

TCP\IP under Windows NT allows a computer to communicate over a network with another computer by using any of the following:

- IP address
- Host name
- NetBIOS name

If you get the correct response when using **ping** with an IP address but an incorrect response when using **ping** with the host name or NetBIOS name, you have a *name resolution* problem. The following sections describe the processes that occur when using a host name or a NetBIOS name, instead of an IP address, to connect with hosts on a TCP/IP network.

Host Name Resolution

A DNS server or the HOSTS file is used when you use the TCP/IP utilities, such as **ping**. You can find the HOSTS file in the winnt\system32\drivers\etc directory. This file is *not* dynamic; entries are made manually. The format of the file is the following:

IP Address   Friendly Name

```
172.16.48.10jsmith_nt    # Remarks are denoted with a #.
```

Host Name Resolution Using a HOSTS File

The general process that occurs when using the HOSTS file for name resolution is summarized in the following steps.

1. Computer A enters a command using the host name of Computer B.

2. The HOSTS file on Computer A (in the \Systemroot\System32\Drivers\Etc directory) is parsed. When the host name of Computer B is found, it is resolved to an IP address.

3. The Address Resolution Protocol (ARP) is then used to resolve the IP address of Computer B to its hardware address. If Computer B is on the local network, its hardware address will be obtained by using the ARP cache or by sending a local broadcast asking for a reply from Computer B with its hardware address. If Computer B is on a remote network, ARP will determine the hardware address of the default gateway for routing to Computer B.

Note Host name resolution using a Domain Name System (DNS) server is similar to the preceding steps. Instead of parsing the HOSTS file in Step 2, the DNS server looks up the host name of Computer B in its database and resolves it to an IP address.

The following types of problems can occur because of errors related to the HOSTS file:

- The HOSTS file or the DNS server does not contain the particular host name.

- The host name in the HOSTS file or in the command is misspelled.

- An invalid IP address is entered for the host name in the HOSTS file.

- The HOSTS file contains multiple entries for the same host on separate lines; if so, the first entry is the one that is used.

- A mapping for a computer name-to-IP-address was mistakenly added to the HOSTS file (rather than LMHOSTS).

Troubleshoot NetBIOS Name Resolution by Using NBTStat

NetBIOS over TCP/IP (NetBT) resolves NetBIOS names to IP addresses. TCP/IP provides many options for NetBIOS name resolution, including local cache lookup, WINS server query, broadcast, DNS server query, and LMHOSTS and HOSTS lookup.

Nbtstat is a useful tool for troubleshooting NetBIOS name resolution problems. The **nbstat** command allows for removing or correcting preloaded entries.

- **nbtstat -*n*** displays the names that were registered locally on the system by applications such as the server and redirector.

- **nbtstat -*c*** shows the NetBIOS name cache, which contains name-to-address mappings for other computers.

- **nbtstat -*R*** purges the name cache and reloads it from the LMHOSTS file.

- **nbtstat -*a* <*name*>** performs a NetBIOS adapter status command against the computer specified by ***name.*** The adapter status command returns the local NetBIOS name table for that computer plus the MAC address of the adapter card.

- **nbtstat -*S*** lists the current NetBIOS sessions and their status, including statistics, as shown in the following example:

```
NetBIOS Connection Table

Local Name     State      In/Out Remote Host   Input   Output
---------------------------------------------------------------
DAVEMAC1 <00> Connected  Out    CNSSUP1<20>   6MB     5MB
DAVEMAC1 <00> Connected  Out    CNSPRINT<20>  108KB   116KB
DAVEMAC1 <00> Connected  Out    CNSSRC1<20>   299KB   19KB
DAVEMAC1 <00> Connected  Out    STH2NT<20>    324KB   19KB
DAVEMAC1 <03> Listening
```

Test IP-address-to-MAC-address Resolution by Using ARP

TCP\IP under Windows NT allows a computer to communicate over a network with another computer by using either an IP address, a host name, or a NetBIOS name. However, when one computer attempts to communicate with another computer using one of these three naming conventions, that name must ultimately be resolved to a hardware address, the medium access control (MAC) address.

The Address Resolution Protocol (ARP) allows a host to find the MAC address of a destination host on the same physical network, given the destination host's IP address. To make ARP efficient, each computer caches IP-to-MAC address mappings to eliminate repetitive ARP broadcast requests.

The **arp** command allows a user to view and modify the ARP table entries on the local computer. The **arp** command is useful for viewing the ARP cache and resolving address resolution problems.

Understanding IP Routing for Windows NT

Windows NT supports routing on both single- and multi-homed computers with, and without, the Multi-Protocol Router (MPR). MPR includes Routing Information Protocol (RIP) for TCP/IP and RIP for IPX. Routers use RIP to dynamically exchange routing information. RIP routers broadcast their routing tables every 30 seconds by default. Other RIP routers will listen for these RIP broadcasts and update their own route tables.

This section provides information about the Windows NT-based route table as used on single- and multi-homed computers with, and without, MPR. This background information will help with TCP/IP troubleshooting.

The Route Table

Even a single-homed TCP/IP host has to make routing decisions. The route table controls these routing decisions. You can display the route table by typing **route print** at the command prompt. The following is an example route table from a single-homed machine. Windows NT automatically builds this simple route table based on the IP configuration of your host.

Network Address	Netmask	Gateway Address	Interface	Metric
0.0.0.0	0.0.0.0	172.16.16.1	172.16.48.169	1
127.0.0.0	255.0.0.0	127.0.0.1	127.0.0.1	1
172.16.16.0	255.255.248.0	172.16.16.169	172.16.16.169	1
172.16.48.169	255.255.255.255	127.0.0.1	127.0.0.1	1
172.16.255.255	255.255.255.255	172.16.48.169	172.16.48.169	1
224.0.0.0	224.0.0.0	172.16.48.169	172.16.48.169	1
255.255.255.255	255.255.255.255	172.16.48.169	172.16.48.169	1

Network Address

The network address in the route table is the destination address. The network address column can contain:

- Host address
- Subnet address
- Network address
- Default gateway

Netmask

The netmask defines which portion of the network address must match in order for that route to be used. When the mask is written in binary, a 1 is significant (must match) and a 0 need not match. For example, a 255.255.255.255 mask is used for a host entry.

The mask of all 255s (all 1s) means that the destination address of the packet to be routed must exactly match the network address in order for this route to be used. For another example, the network address 172.16.48.0 has a netmask of 255.255.192.0. This netmask means that the first two octets must match exactly, the first 2 bits of the third octet must match (192=11000000), and the last octet does not matter. Because 18 in the decimal number system is equivalent to 00110000 in binary, a match would have to start with 0011. Thus, any address of 172.16 and the third octet of 48 through 255 (255=11111111) will use this route. This is a netmask for a subnet route and is therefore called the *subnet mask*.

Gateway Address

The gateway address is where the packet needs to be sent. This can be the local network card or a gateway (router) on the local subnet.

Interface

The interface is the address of the network card over which the packet should be sent out. 127.0.0.1 is the software loopback address.

Metric

The metric is the number of hops to the destination. Anything on the local LAN is one hop, and each router crossed after that is an additional hop. The metric is used to determine the best route.

Multihomed Router

The following is the default route table of a multihomed Windows NT host:

Network Address	Netmask	Gateway Address	Interface	Metric
0.0.0.0	0.0.0.0	172.16.24.1	172.16.24.193	1
0.0.0.0	0.0.0.0	172.16.40.1	172.16.40.139	1
127.0.0.0	255.0.0.0	127.0.0.1	127.0.0.1	1
172.16.24.0	255.255.248.0	172.16.24.193	172.16.24.193	1
172.16.24.193	255.255.255.255	127.0.0.1	127.0.0.1	1
172.16.40.0	255.255.255.0	172.16.40.139	172.16.40.139	1
172.16.40.139	255.255.255.255	127.0.0.1	127.0.0.1	1
172.16.40.255	255.255.255.255	172.16.40.139	172.16.40.139	1
224.0.0.0	224.0.0.0	172.16.24.193	172.16.24.193	1
224.0.0.0	224.0.0.0	172.16.40.139	172.16.40.139	1
255.255.255.255	255.255.255.255	172.16.40.139	172.16.40.139	1

To enable routing, check **Enable IP Forwarding** on the **Routing** tab of the **Microsoft TCP/IP Properties** dialog box. At this point, Windows NT will route between these two subnets.

A note on default gateways: in the TCP/IP configuration, you can add a default route for each network card. This will create a 0.0.0.0 route for each. However, only one default route will actually be used. In this case, the 199.199.40.139 is the first card in the TCP/IP bindings, and therefore the default route for this card is used. Because only one default gateway will be used, configure only one card to have a default gateway. This will reduce confusion and ensure the results you intended.

If the Windows NT router does not have an interface on a given subnet, it will need a route to get there. This can be done by adding static routes or by using MPR.

Adding a Static Route

The following is an example route.

```
Route Add 199.199.41.0 mask 255.255.255.0 199.199.40.1 metric 2
```

The route in this example means that to get to the 199.199.41.0 subnet with a mask of 255.255.255.0, use gateway 199.199.40.1, and that the gateway is 2 hops away. A static route will also need to be added on the next router, telling it how to get back to subnets reachable by the first router. With a network of a few routers or more, static routes can become very complicated.

Examine the Route Between Network Connections by Using Tracert

Tracert is a route tracing utility. **Tracert** uses the IP TTL field and ICMP error messages to determine the route from one host to another through a network. Sample output from the **tracert** command is shown in the ICMP section of this chapter.

Examine the Route Table by Using Route

Route is used to view or modify the route table. **Route print** displays a list of current routes known by IP for the host, including routes that Windows NT creates by default and routes learned by running RIP. Sample output is shown in the IP section of this chapter. **Route add** is used to add routes to the table, and **route delete** is used to delete routes from the table. Note that routes added to the table are not made permanent unless the *-p* switch is specified. Non-persistent routes last only until the computer is restarted.

In order for two hosts to exchange IP datagrams, they must both have a route to each other, or use default gateways that know of a route. Normally, routers exchange information with each other using a protocol such as RIP.

Display Current TCP/IP Connections and Statistics by Using Netstat

Netstat displays protocol statistics and current TCP/IP connections. **Netstat -a** displays all connections, and **netstat -r** displays the route table plus active connections. The **-n** switch tells **netstat** not to convert addresses and port numbers to names. The following is sample output:

```
C:\>netstat -e
Interface Statistics

                          Received       Sent
Bytes                     3995837940     47224622
Unicast packets           120099         131015
Non-unicast packets       7579544        3823
Discards                  0              0
Errors                    0              0
Unknown protocols         363054211


C:\>netstat -a

Active Connections

   Proto Local Address        Foreign Address      State
   TCP   davemac1:1572        172.16.48.10:nbsession ESTABLISHED
   TCP   davemac1:1589        172.16.48.10:nbsession ESTABLISHED
   TCP   davemac1:1606        172.16.105.245:nbsession ESTABLISHED
   TCP   davemac1:1632        172.16.48.213:nbsession ESTABLISHED
   TCP   davemac1:1659        172.16.48.169:nbsession ESTABLISHED
   TCP   davemac1:1714        172.16.48.203:nbsession ESTABLISHED
   TCP   davemac1:1719        172.16.48.36:nbsession ESTABLISHED
   TCP   davemac1:1241        172.16.48.101:nbsession ESTABLISHED
   UDP   davemac1:1025        *:*
   UDP   davemac1:snmp        *:*
   UDP   davemac1:nbname      *:*
   UDP   davemac1:nbdatagram *:*
   UDP   davemac1:nbname      *:*
   UDP   davemac1:nbdatagram *:*


C:\>netstat -s
```

IP Statistics

Packets Received	= 5378528
Received Header Errors	= 738854
Received Address Errors	= 23150
Datagrams Forwarded	= 0
Unknown Protocols Received	= 0
Received Packets Discarded	= 0
Received Packets Delivered	= 4616524
Output Requests	= 132702
Routing Discards	= 157
Discarded Output Packets	= 0
Output Packet No Route	= 0
Reassembly Required	= 0
Reassembly Successful	= 0
Reassembly Failures	= 0
Datagrams Successfully Fragmented	= 0
Datagrams Failing Fragmentation	= 0
Fragments Created	= 0

ICMP Statistics

	Received	Sent
Messages	693	4
Errors	0	0
Destination Unreachable	685	0
Time Exceeded	0	0
Parameter Problems	0	0
Source Quenchs	0	0
Redirects	0	0
Echos	4	0
Echo Replies	0	4
Timestamps	0	0
Timestamp Replies	0	0
Address Masks	0	0
Address Mask Replies	0	0

TCP Statistics

Active Opens	= 597
Passive Opens	= 135
Failed Connection Attempts	= 107
Reset Connections	= 91
Current Connections	= 8
Segments Received	= 106770
Segments Sent	= 118431
Segments Retransmitted	= 461

```
UDP Statistics

Datagrams Received    = 4157136
No Ports              = 351928
Receive Errors        = 2
Datagrams Sent        = 13809
```

Using Performance Monitor

The Windows NT Server and Windows NT Workstation Performance Monitor can be used to view many different TCP/IP-related counters. Because it accesses statistics that have been gathered by the SNMP service, the SNMP service must be installed on Windows NT-based computers where TCP/IP statistics are to be monitored. Performance Monitor counters are available for NIC, IP, ICMP, UDP, TCP, and NetBT.

One of the features of Performance Monitor is that it allows counters from various systems to be monitored from a single management window. It also supports setting alert levels for the counters being monitored.

Using the Microsoft Network Monitor

Microsoft Network Monitor is a tool developed by Microsoft to make the task of troubleshooting complex network problems much easier and more economical. It is packaged as part of the Microsoft Systems Management Server product but can be used as a stand-alone network monitor.

In addition, Windows NT Server, Windows NT Workstation, and Windows 95 distribution media include the Network Monitor Agent software. Stations running Network Monitor can attach to stations running the agent software over the network or using dial-up (RAS) to perform monitoring or tracing of remote network segments. This can be a very useful troubleshooting tool.

Network Monitor works by setting the NIC to allow you to capture traffic to and from the local computer. Capture filters can be defined so that only specific frames are saved for analysis. Filters can be defined based on source and destination NIC addresses, source and destination protocol addresses, and pattern matches. Once a capture has been obtained, display filtering can be used to further narrow down a problem. Display filtering allows specific protocols to be selected as well.

Once a capture has been obtained and filtered, Network Monitor protocol parsing interprets the binary trace data into readable terms using parsing DLLs. The following sample Server Message Block (SMB) frame is shown fully parsed:

```
***********************************************************************
Frame Time  Src Other Addr Dst Other Addr Protocol Description
7     0.020 172.16.48.36    172.16.48.10   SMB      C get attributes,
File = \temp


 FRAME: Base frame properties
   FRAME: Time of capture = Jun 27, 1995 8:11:11.636
   FRAME: Time delta from previous physical frame: 3 milliseconds
   FRAME: Frame number: 7
   FRAME: Total frame length: 106 bytes
   FRAME: Capture frame length: 106 bytes
   FRAME: Frame data: Number of data bytes remaining = 106 (0x006A)
 ETHERNET: ETYPE = 0x0800 : Protocol = IP: DOD Internet Protocol
   ETHERNET: Destination address : 00608C0E6C6A
     ETHERNET: .......0 = Individual address
     ETHERNET: ......0. = Universally administered address
   ETHERNET: Source address : 0020AF1D2B91
     ETHERNET: .......0 = No routing information present
     ETHERNET: ......0. = Universally administered address
   ETHERNET: Frame Length : 106 (0x006A)
   ETHERNET: Ethernet Type : 0x0800 (IP: DOD Internet Protocol)
   ETHERNET: Ethernet Data: Number of data bytes remaining = 92 (0x005C)
 IP: ID = 0x4072; Proto = TCP; Len: 92
   IP: Version = 4 (0x4)
   IP: Header Length = 20 (0x14)
   IP: Service Type = 0 (0x0)
     IP: Precedence = Routine
     IP: ...0.... = Normal Delay
     IP: ....0... = Normal Throughput
     IP: .....0.. = Normal Reliability
   IP: Total Length = 92 (0x5C)
   IP: Identification = 16498 (0x4072)
   IP: Flags Summary = 2 (0x2)
     IP: .......0 = Last fragment in datagram
     IP: ......1. = Cannot fragment datagram
   IP: Fragment Offset = 0 (0x0) bytes
   IP: Time to Live = 32 (0x20)
   IP: Protocol = TCP - Transmission Control
   IP: CheckSum = 0xC895
   IP: Source Address = 09.48.16.172
   IP: Destination Address = 172.16.48.10
   IP: Data: Number of data bytes remaining = 72 (0x0048)
 TCP: .AP..., len:  52, seq: 344830227, ack:  2524988, win: 8166, src:
1677 dst: (NBT Session)
   TCP: Source Port = 0x068D
   TCP: Destination Port = NETBIOS Session Service
```

```
TCP: Sequence Number = 344830227 (0x148DB113)
TCP: Acknowledgment Number = 2524988 (0x26873C)
TCP: Data Offset = 20 (0x14)
TCP: Reserved = 0 (0x0000)
TCP: Flags = 0x18 : .AP...
   TCP: ..0..... = No urgent data
   TCP: ...1.... = Acknowledgement field significant
   TCP: ....1... = Push function
   TCP: .....0.. = No Reset
   TCP: ......0. = No Synchronize
   TCP: .......0 = No Fin
TCP: Window = 8166 (0x1FE6)
TCP: CheckSum = 0xC072
TCP: Urgent Pointer = 0 (0x0)
TCP: Data: Number of data bytes remaining = 52 (0x0034)
NBT: SS: Session Message, Len: 48
  NBT: Packet Type = Session Message
  NBT: Packet Flags = 0 (0x0)
     NBT: .......0 = Add 0 to Length
  NBT: Packet Length = 48 (0x30)
  NBT: SS Data: Number of data bytes remaining = 48 (0x0030)
SMB: C get attributes, File = \temp
  SMB: SMB Status = Error Success
    SMB: Error class = No Error
    SMB: Error code = No Error
  SMB: Header: PID = 0xCAFE TID = 0x0800 MID = 0x43C0 UID = 0x0800
    SMB: Tree ID   (TID) = 2048 (0x800)
    SMB: Process ID (PID) = 51966 (0xCAFE)
    SMB: User ID   (UID) = 2048 (0x800)
    SMB: Multiplex ID (MID) = 17344 (0x43C0)
    SMB: Flags Summary = 24 (0x18)
       SMB: .......0 = Lock & Read and Write & Unlock not supported
       SMB: ......0. = Send No Ack not supported
       SMB: ....1... = Using caseless pathnames
       SMB: ...1.... = Canonicalized pathnames
       SMB: ..0..... = No Opportunistic lock
       SMB: .0...... = No Change Notify
       SMB: 0....... = Client command
    SMB: flags2 Summary = 32771 (0x8003)
       SMB: ...............1 = Understands long filenames
       SMB: ..............1. = Understands extended attributes
       SMB: ..0............. = No paging of IO
       SMB: .0.............. = Using SMB status codes
       SMB: 1............... = Using UNICODE strings
  SMB: Command = C get attributes
    SMB: Word count = 0
    SMB: Byte count = 13
    SMB: Byte parameters
    SMB: Path name = \temp
```

```
00000:  00 60 8C 0E 6C 6A 00 20 AF 1D 2B 91 08 00 45 00    .`..lj. ..+...E.
00010:  00 5C 40 72 40 00 20 06 C8 95 9D 39 09 8A 9D 39    .\@r@. ....9...9
00020:  0D 98 06 8D 00 8B 14 8D B1 13 00 26 87 3C 50 18    ...........&.<P.
00030:  1F E6 C0 72 00 00 00 00 00 30 FF 53 4D 42 08 00    ...r.....0.SMB..
00040:  00 00 00 18 03 80 00 00 00 00 00 00 00 00 00 00    ................
00050:  00 00 00 08 FE CA 00 08 C0 43 00 0D 00 04 5C 00    .........C....\.
00060:  74 00 65 00 6D 00 70 00 00 00                      t.e.m.p...
```

The preceding parsed output example consists of three sections:

- summary window
- detailed description window
- hex output

If you are sending traces to support personnel at Microsoft, they are most useful in electronic form rather than printed form, because they can be manipulated and scanned electronically. Large printed traces are time-consuming to read.

Using the Microsoft Knowledge Base

The Microsoft Knowledge Base (KB) is an excellent source of information on all aspects of Windows NT Server and Windows NT Workstation. It contains thousands of articles written by the support professionals in the Corporate Network Systems unit at Microsoft. Articles are updated daily, and topics include:

- Installation and configuration information
- Status on known problems and fixes
- Service Pack updates
- Technology discussions
- Troubleshooting tips
- Hardware-specific information

For example, to find additional information about the LMHOSTS file in Windows NT, query on the following words in the Microsoft Knowledge Base:

```
lmhosts and windows and nt
```

The Microsoft KB is available from many different sources, including the Internet (full-text search capabilities for WWW browsers on **www.microsoft.com**), several on-line services, and CD-ROM subscription services, such as Microsoft TechNet.

Troubleshooting Other Connection Problems

This section presents some possible TCP/IP symptoms with recommendations for using the diagnostic utilities to determine the source of the problems.

Error 53

▶ **To determine the cause of Error 53 when connecting to a server**

1. If the computer is on the local subnet, confirm that the name is spelled correctly and that the target computer is running TCP/IP as well. If the computer is not on the local subnet, be sure that its name and IP address mapping are available in the LMHOSTS file or the WINS database.

    Error 53 is returned if name resolution fails for a particular computer name.

2. If all TCP/IP elements appear to be installed properly, use **ping** with the remote computer to be sure that its TCP/IP software is working.

Long Connect Times When Using LMHOSTS for Name Resolution

▶ **To determine the cause of long connect times after adding an entry to LMHOSTS**

- Because this behavior can occur with a large LMHOSTS file with an entry at the end of the file, mark the entry in LMHOSTS as a preloaded entry by following the mapping with the #PRE tag. Then use the **nbtstat -R** command to update the local name cache immediately.

    Or, place the mapping higher in the LMHOSTS file.

    As discussed in Chapter 10, "Using LMHOSTS Files," the LMHOSTS file is parsed sequentially to locate entries without the #PRE keyword. Therefore, you should place frequently used entries near the top of the file and place the #PRE entries near the bottom.

Cannot Connect to a Specific Server

▶ **To determine the cause of connection problems when specifying a server name**

- Use the **nbtstat -n** command to determine what name the server registered on the network.

  The output of this command lists several names that the computer has registered. A name resembling the computer's computer name should be present. If not, try one of the other unique names displayed by **nbtstat**.

  The **nbtstat** utility can also be used to display the cached entries for remote computers from either #PRE entries in LMHOSTS or recently resolved names. If the name the remote computers are using for the server is the same, and the other computers are on a remote subnet, be sure that they have the computer's mapping in their LMHOSTS files.

Cannot Connect to Foreign Systems When Using Host Name

▶ **To determine why only IP addresses but not host names work for connections to remote computers**

1. Make sure that the appropriate HOSTS file and DNS setup have been configured for the computer by checking the host name resolution configuration using the **Network** icon in **Control Panel** and then choosing the **DNS** tab in the **Microsoft TCP/IP Properties** dialog box.

2. If you are using a HOSTS file, make sure that the name of the remote computer is spelled the same in the file and by the application using it.

3. If you are using DNS, be sure that the IP addresses of the DNS servers are correct and in the proper order. Use **ping** with the remote computer by typing both the host name and IP address to determine whether the host name is being resolved properly.

TCP/IP Connection to Remote Host Appears To Be Hung

▶ **To determine why a TCP/IP connection to a remote computer is not working properly**

- Use the **netstat -a** command to show the status of all activity on TCP and UDP ports on the local computer.

  The state of a good TCP connection is usually established with 0 bytes in the send and receive queues. If data is blocked in either queue or if the state is irregular, there is probably a problem with the connection. If not, you are probably experiencing network or application delay.

Troubleshooting Telnet

▶ **To determine why the banner displayed with Telnet identifies a different computer, even when specifying the correct IP address**

1. Make sure the DNS name and HOSTS table are up to date.

2. Make sure that two computers on the same network are not mistakenly configured with the same IP address.

   The Ethernet and IP address mapping is done by the ARP module, which believes the first response it receives. Therefore, the impostor computer's reply sometimes comes back before the intended computer's reply.

   These problems are difficult to isolate and track down. Use the **arp -g** command to display the mappings in the ARP cache. If you know the Ethernet address for the intended remote computer, you can easily determine whether the two match. If not, use **arp -d** to delete the entry; then use **ping** with the same address (forcing an ARP), and check the Ethernet address in the cache again by using **arp -g**.

   Chances are that if both computers are on the same network, you will eventually get a different response. If not, you might have to filter the traffic from the impostor host to determine the owner or location of the system.

Troubleshooting Gateways

▶ **To determine the cause of the message, "Your default gateway does not belong to one of the configured interfaces..." during Setup**

- Find out whether the default gateway is located on the same logical network as the computer's network adapter by comparing the network ID portion of the default gateway's IP address with the network ID(s) of any of the computer's network adapters.

   For example, a computer with a single network adapter configured with an IP address of 102.54.0.1 and a subnet mask of 255.255.0.0 would require that the default gateway be of the form 102.54.$a.b$ because the network ID portion of the IP interface is 102.54.

Troubleshooting TCP/IP Database Files

The following table lists the UNIX-style database files that are stored in the
systemroot\System32\Drivers\Etc directory when you install Microsoft TCP/IP:

Table 12.2   UNIX-style Database Files

File name	Use
HOSTS	Provides host name-to-IP-address resolution for Windows Sockets applications
LMHOSTS	Provides NetBIOS name-to-IP-address resolution for Windows-based networking
Networks	Provides network name-to-network ID resolution for TCP/IP management
Protocols	Provides protocol name-to-protocol ID resolution for Windows Sockets applications
Services	Provides service name-to-port ID resolution for Windows Sockets applications

To troubleshoot any of these files on a local computer:

- Make sure the format of entries in each file matches the format defined in the sample file originally installed with Microsoft TCP/IP.
- Check for spelling or capitalization errors.
- Check for invalid IP addresses and identifiers.

Reinstalling TCP/IP

When you attempt to reinstall a TCP\IP service, the following error message may
appear:

```
The Registry Subkey Already Exists.
```

To correct this problem, ensure that all the components of a given TCP\IP service
are properly removed and then remove the appropriate registry subkeys.

Warning Using Registry Editor incorrectly can cause serious, system-wide
problems that may require you to reinstall Windows NT to correct them.
Microsoft cannot guarantee that any problems resulting from the incorrect use of
Registry Editor can be solved. Use this tool at your own risk.

Connectivity Utilities

If you have removed the TCP/IP service components, you must also remove the following registry subkeys:

```
HKEY_LOCAL_MACHINE\Software\Microsoft\NetBT
HKEY_LOCAL_MACHINE\Software\Microsoft\Tcpip
HKEY_LOCAL_MACHINE\Software\Microsoft\TcpipCU
HKEY_LOCAL_MACHINE\SYSTEM\CCS\Services\DHCP
HKEY_LOCAL_MACHINE\SYSTEM\CCS\Services\LMHosts
HKEY_LOCAL_MACHINE\SYSTEM\CCS\Services\'NetDriver'\Parameters\Tcpip
HKEY_LOCAL_MACHINE\SYSTEM\CCS\Services\NetBT
```

SNMP Service

If you have removed the SNMP service components, you must also remove the following registry subkeys:

```
HKEY_LOCAL_MACHINE\Software\Microsoft\RFC1156Agent
HKEY_LOCAL_MACHINE\Software\Microsoft\Snmp
HKEY_LOCAL_MACHINE\System\CCS\Services\Snmp
```

TCP/IP Network Printing Support

If you have removed the LPDSVC line printer service components, you must also remove the following registry subkeys:

```
HKEY_LOCAL_MACHINE\Software\Microsoft\Lpdsvc
HKEY_LOCAL_MACHINE\Software\Microsoft\TcpPrint
HKEY_LOCAL_MACHINE\SYSTEM\CCS\Services\LpdsvcSimple TCP\IP Services
```

If you have removed the simple TCP/IP services components, you must also remove the following registry subkeys:

```
HKEY_LOCAL_MACHINE\Software\Microsoft\SimpTcp
HKEY_LOCAL_MACHINE\SYSTEM\CCS\Services\SimpTcp
```

DHCP Server Service

If you have removed the DHCP Server service components, you must also remove the following registry subkeys:

```
HKEY_LOCAL_MACHINE\Software\Microsoft\DhcpMibAgent
HKEY_LOCAL_MACHINE\Software\Microsoft\DhcpServer
HKEY_LOCAL_MACHINE\SYSTEM\CCS\Services\DhcpServer
```

WINS Server Service

If you have removed the WINS Server service components, you must also remove the following registry subkeys:

```
HKEY_LOCAL_MACHINE\Software\Microsoft\Wins
HKEY_LOCAL_MACHINE\Software\Microsoft\WinsMibAgent
HKEY_LOCAL_MACHINE\SYSTEM\CCS\Services\Wins
```

Cannot Ping Across a Router when Using TCP/IP as a RAS Client

This problem occurs if you have **Use default gateway on remote network** selected under **TCP/IP settings** in the **RAS Phonebook**. This feature adds a route to the route table, and the new route allows IP addresses that are not resolved by other entries in the route table to be routed to the gateway on the RAS link. However, to use Internet utilities, such as a WEB browser or FTP, this feature must be enabled.

▶   **To ping or otherwise connect to computers in a remote subnet across a router while you are connected as a RAS client to a remote Windows NT RAS Server**

   • Use the **route add** command to add the route of the subnet you are attempting to use and tie that route to the local LAN gateway by adding the appropriate subnet mask.

PART IV

Using Windows NT Server Networking

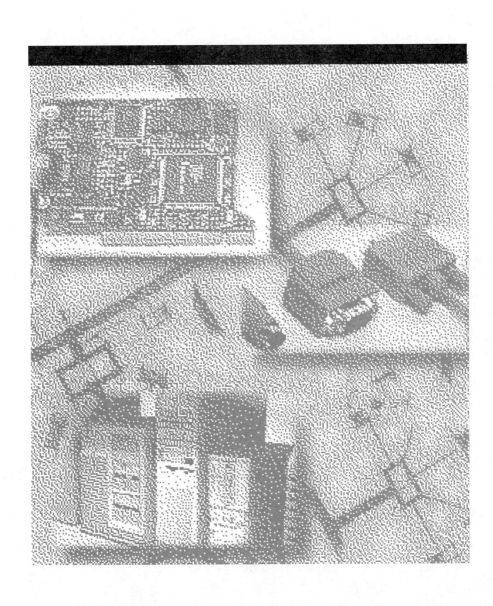

C H A P T E R   1 3

Using NetBEUI with Windows NT

The NetBEUI protocol was one of the earliest protocols available for use on networks composed of personal computers. In 1985, IBM introduced NetBEUI to provide a protocol that could be used with software programs designed around the Network Basic Input/Output System (NetBIOS) interface.

NetBEUI was designed as a small, efficient protocol for use in department-sized local area networks (LANs) of 20 to 200 computers that do not need to be routed to other subnets. Today, NetBEUI is used almost exclusively on small, non-routed networks composed of computers running under a variety of operating systems that can include Microsoft Windows NT Server 3.5 and later, Windows NT Workstation version 3.5 and later, Microsoft LAN Manager, Windows for Workgroups, Windows 3.1, Windows NT version 3.1, and LAN Manager for UNIX as well as IBM PCLAN and LAN Server.

Windows NT-based NetBEUI, also referred to as NBF because it uses NetBEUI Frame (NBF), implements the IBM NetBIOS Extended User Interface (NetBEUI) 3.0 specification. This protocol provides compatibility with existing LANs that use the NetBEUI protocol and is compatible with the NetBEUI protocol driver shipped with past Microsoft networking products.

This chapter describes Windows NT-based NetBEUI and how it interfaces with the architecture of Windows NT Server and Windows NT Workstation to support connection-oriented and connectionless data transfer and to support a virtually infinite number of network *sessions* (logical connections between networked computers).

The information presented in this chapter is intended for the network administrator and support personnel who need to understand NetBEUI and to manage computers that connect to the network by using the NetBEUI protocol. You should be familiar with the architecture of Windows NT Server and Windows NT Workstation to understand the information discussed in this chapter. For information about the architecture of Windows NT Server, refer to Chapter 1,"Windows NT Networking Architecture" in this book. For information about the architecture of Windows NT Workstation, refer to the *Windows NT Workstation Resource Guide*.

Overview of Windows NT NetBEUI

The Windows NT-based implementation of NetBEUI, referred to as NBF throughout the remainder of this chapter, does the following:

- Uses the Windows NT-based Transport Driver Interface (TDI) which provides an emulator for interpretation of NetBIOS network commands.
- Uses the Windows NT-based Network Device Interface Specification (NDIS) version 3.0 with improved transport support and a full 32-bit asynchronous interface.

Note Developers who require detailed information about the NDIS 4.0 specification should see the Windows NT Device Driver Kit (DDK).

- Removes the NetBIOS session number limit.
- Uses memory dynamically to provide automatic memory tuning.
- Supports dial-up client communications with Remote Access Service (RAS) services.
- Provides connection-oriented and connectionless data transfer services.

Interoperability Using NBF

NBF provides compatibility with computers running under the earlier operating systems of Microsoft LAN Manager and MS-Net, and IBM LAN Server. NBF can be used to connect LAN workstation and server computers, and to connect remote and dial-up clients, including laptop computers, to computers running the Windows NT-based RAS.

NBF can be used with programs that implement a variety of services based on the following application programming interfaces (APIs):

- NetBIOS
- Named Pipes
- Mailslot
- Network DDE (dynamic data exchange)
- Remote Procedure Call (RPC) over NetBIOS
- RPC over Named Pipes

NBF is most efficient when used for computers connecting to small to medium-sized, single-location networks. NBF is not a routable protocol like TCP/IP or IPX, although NBF does support a form of routing known as Token Ring routing, available only on IBM Token Ring networks. Additionally, NBF uses a single part naming scheme that does not support network segmentation used in most large networks.

Architecture of NBF

NBF is a transport driver that is composed of the following layers:

LLC802.2 Protocol
> Corresponds to the Open Systems Interconnect (OSI) Logical Link Control (LLC) layer. It performs code, address, and control frame flow, and provides connectionless data transfer.

NetBIOS Frame Protocol (NBFP)
> Corresponds to the OSI Transport and Session layers. It performs session establishment, multiplexing, and termination. It also performs message segmentation, delimiting, assembly, and acknowledgment.

Figure 13.1 shows the components of NBF and their relation to the OSI model.

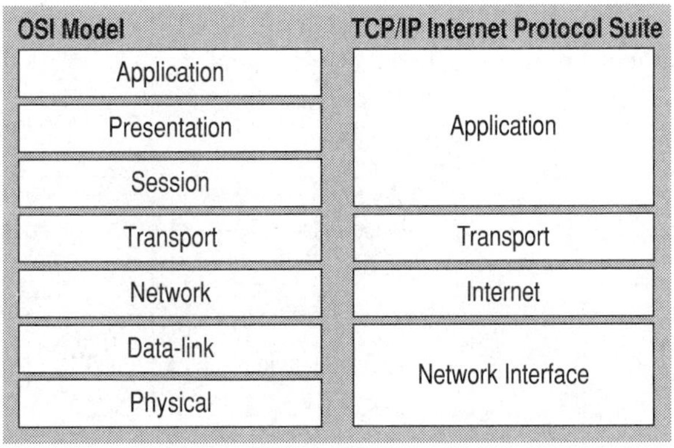

OSI Model	TCP/IP Internet Protocol Suite
Application	Application
Presentation	Application
Session	Application
Transport	Transport
Network	Internet
Data-link	Network Interface
Physical	Network Interface

Figure 13.1   The OSI Model and the Architecture of NBF

Notice that the upper edge of NBF, the NBFP component, connects to the bottom edge of the Windows NT-based Transport Driver interface (TDI). The lower edge of NBF, the LLC component, connects to the Network Driver Interface (NDIS).

Note In the preceding illustration, the Network layer between NBFP and LLC is intentionally empty. In the OSI model, the Network layer lies between the Transport and LLC layers. However, NetBEUI uses IBM Token Ring source routing to perform network layer functions. Token Ring source routing conforms to a different standard, the IEEE 802.5 standard, and logically corresponds to the OSI Physical layer, not the OSI Network layer.

The following sections describe the NBF functions at its upper and lower edges:

- "NBF's Interface to the Upper OSI Layers—The TDI Interface"
- "NBF's Interface to the Lower OSI Layers—The NDIS Interface"

NBF's Interface to the Upper OSI Layers—The TDI Interface

Software programs that rely on NBFP for network communication require a transport driver that exposes the NetBIOS interface. However, the Windows NT-based transport drivers for NBF, IPX, and TCP/IP do not expose a NetBIOS interface; instead they expose the more flexible Windows NT TDI, as illustrated in both Figure 13.1 and Figure 13.2.

The Windows NT TDI provides a NetBIOS emulator that maps NetBIOS commands to TDI commands to support applications designed for use with NBFP. Note that Figure 13.2 illustrates how both NetBIOS-based and Windows Sockets-based applications use the TDI.

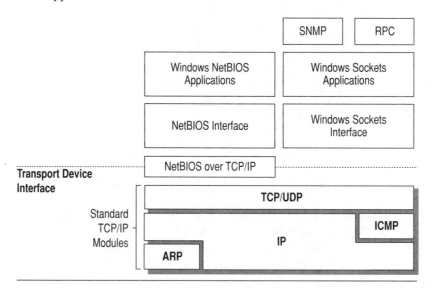

Figure 13.2   The Transport Driver Interface (TDI) and NBF

Note In the preceding figure, the term "transport providers" refers to the binding of a specific transport driver, such as NBF, to a specific underlying NIC driver. Computers in which multiple NIC cards are installed will have multiple bindings.

This is how the TDI supports NetBIOS-based applications: NetBIOS commands are formatted as network control blocks (NCBs). When a program running on a Windows NT-based computer creates an NCB, the NetBIOS command is first processed by the Windows NT-based NetBIOS driver (Netbios.sys). Netbios.sys processes the NCB by mapping it to the corresponding TDI command or commands, and sends the TDI command to the Windows NT-based NetBEUI driver (Nbf.sys). (TDI calls implement the same general semantics as NetBIOS NCBs, but are optimized for a 32-bit kernel interface.)

In other words, unlike 16-bit Windows and MS-DOS transport clients which send NCBs directly to a NetBEUI driver, the NetBIOS network applications running on a Windows NT-based computer must direct the NCBs to a NetBIOS emulator. The NetBIOS emulator creates TDI requests and sends the TDI requests to the NBF transport driver.

NBF's Interface to the Lower OSI Layers — The NDIS Interface

The NBF transport driver processes the TDI requests as frames that are to be sent out on the network in the Logical Link Control (LLC) layer. This lower edge, the LLC layer, is the NBF layer that receives frames sent from a remote computer on the network.

NBF conforms to the IEEE 802.2 LLC protocol standard and performs the following functions:

- Link establishment (connection-oriented data transfer)
- Maintenance and termination
- Frame sequencing and acknowledgment
- Frame flow control
- Connectionless data transfer

At the LLC layer, NBF binds, receives, and sends packets to the underlying NIC drivers by using the NDIS 4.0 interface. (See the earlier note about the term "transport providers.")

Communication within the LLC layer is based on *service access points*, *links*, and *link stations*. Each LLC client program identifies itself by registering a unique *service access point* (SAP). A SAP is actually a mechanism by which the layer above can programmatically access a particular service implemented by the layer below. A SAP can also be thought of as the address of a software port as defined by the OSI model. There are well-known SAPs, similar to the well-known ports of TCP/IP. Because NBF is a NetBIOS implementation, it uses the well-known NetBIOS SAP (0xF0). This is illustrated in Figure 13.3, which shows the relationship of the SAP to the LLC Layer.

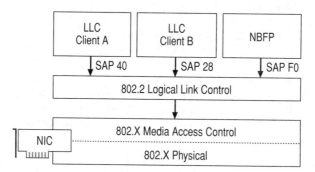

Figure 13.3   The NBF LLC Layer and NDIS Interface to the Physical Layers

When a network client program uses LLC to send a frame on to the network, LLC specifies the client SAP as well as the destination SAP in the header of the LLC frame. The header of an LLC frame thus identifies the:

- Source service access point (SSAP)—the LLC client on the sending computer that created the frame.

- Destination service access point (DSAP)—the LLC client on the receiving computer that should receive the frame.

The SSAP, DSAP, and NIC address of the destination client are all that is needed for *unreliable connectionless* data transfer, in which NBF transmits the message once or a specified number of times and is responsible only for ensuring that the frame is properly transmitted on the network medium. No acknowledgment from the destination client is required.

Reliable connection-oriented data transfer service requires establishment of a *link* between the sending and receiving LLC clients in which NBF is responsible for transferring the frame from the source client to the destination client and which requires an acknowledgment from the destination client that the frame is received. The link is established by using the sending client SAP, the destination client SAP, and the NIC address of the remote computer. Note that the NIC address of the receiving client can be specified as:

- An individual computer's NIC address where the LLC frame is received by a single LLC client that registered the destination SAP.

- A NetBIOS multicast address where the LLC frame is received by all LLC clients that have registered the multicast destination SAP.

NBF Removes the NetBIOS Session Limit

Early versions of NetBEUI used a 1-byte (8-character binary) number with a maximum decimal value of 254 to identify NetBIOS sessions. Session numbers were assigned per computer. That is, a computer using NetBEUI could support a maximum of 254 network connections.

NBF is not constrained by the session limitation of earlier versions of NetBEUI. NBF uses the TDI and a TDI 32-bit handle composed of the session number and the network address of the remote computer. This allows a virtually limitless range of unique numbers that can be used to uniquely identify sessions.

Using NBF, it is possible for a Windows NT Server with a single network adapter card to support simultaneous sessions that exceed the previous NetBEUI session limit of 256. For example, a Windows NT Server running NBF with a single network adapter card is able to support sessions with more than 1,000 clients.

The following figure illustrates the differences between NBF and other non-Windows implementations of NetBEUI.

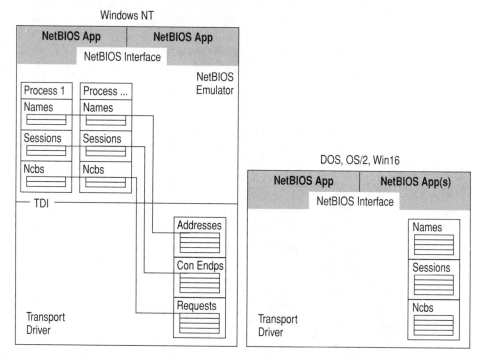

Figure 13.4   Comparison between NetBEUI and Windows NT NBF Session Limits

NBF Dynamically Allocates Memory

A Windows NT-based computer running NBF automatically allocates the memory necessary to process the requests made by session clients. This means that NBF uses memory only when needed. For example, on a Windows NT-based computer that does not have an active network connection, very little memory will be used by the NBF protocol stack.

Because of this dynamic memory management, installing NBF on a Windows NT-based computer is easily done. It does not require additional configuration for number of sessions, packets, or buffers.

NBF Supports RAS Clients

NBF is used by remote computers that need to connect to a computer running Windows NT Server with RAS server. Because NBF dynamically allocates memory and is self-tuning, no configuration is required on the computer running the RAS client service. However, the **WanNameQueryRetries** parameter in the Registry can be changed to fine-tune RAS name query performance by using the Registry Editor. (This parameter is the WAN equivalent of the **NameQueryRetries** parameter.)

Connection-oriented and Connectionless Data Transfer

NBF supports both unreliable connectionless and reliable connection-oriented data transfer. Unreliable connectionless data transfer is also called *datagram*, or *Type 1*, operation.

Unreliable connectionless communication is similar to sending a letter in the mail. No response is generated by the receiver of the letter to tell the sender that the letter made it to its destination.

Note Connectionless communications can be either *unreliable* or *reliable*. NBF provides only unreliable connectionless communications. Reliable connectionless communications is like a registered letter whose sender is notified that the letter arrived.

In unreliable connectionless communicaton, the transport protocol driver transmits the message once or a specified number of times, ensuring only that the message was properly transmitted to the network medium. The message can only be a single frame. Acknowledgment from the destination computer is not required.

Note If reliable connectionless communication is required, NBF can be configured for certain communication commands to send a number of frames that will allow time for the destination computer to respond to the message. The number is based on *retry* Registry value entries, such as **NameQueryRetries**. The time between sending each frame is determined by *timeout* Registry entries, such as **NameQueryTimeout**.

Reliable connection-oriented communication is also called *session*, or *Type 2*, operation. Reliable connection-oriented communication provides reliable communications between two computers in a way that is analogous to a phone call where two callers connect, a conversation occurs, and then the connection is dropped when the conversation ends. A reliable connection requires more overhead than connectionless communications do.

In reliable connection–oriented communications, the transport protocol driver assumes responsibility for transferring the entire message from source to destination, and within an acceptable time period. Sequencing is provided; a message that is larger than the maximum transmit frame size can be broken down into multiple frames, sent across the network, and properly reassembled at the receiving computer.

Connectionless Traffic

Three types of NetBIOS commands generate connectionless traffic:

- Name claim and resolution
- Datagrams
- Miscellaneous commands

These commands are sent as Unnumbered Information (UI) frames at the LLC sublayer.

To understand how Windows NT Server and Windows NT Workstation use retry and timeout values, consider what happens when the Windows NT-based computer running NBF registers its NetBIOS computer name. The Windows NT-based computer sends a multicast message containing an ADD_NAME_QUERY frame on to the network. Other computers on the network running NBF can retrieve and process the ADD_NAME_QUERY message. The multicast frames are sent a total of **AddNameQueryRetries** times at time intervals of **AddNameQueryTimeout.** This allows computers on the network enough time to inform the sending computer whether the name is already registered as a unique computer name or as a group name on the network.

Note All Registry values discussed in this chapter are found under the following Registry path:

```
HKEY_LOCAL_MACHINE\SYSTEM\CurrentControlSet\Services\Nbf
```

Connection-oriented Traffic

The **net use** command is an example of a connection-oriented communication, as illustrated in Figure 13.5.

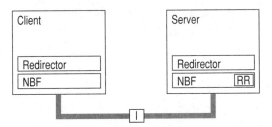

Figure 13.5   Connection-oriented Network Traffic

When a user types **net use** at the command line to connect to a shared resource, NBF must first locate the server by sending UI-frames, and then initialize the link. This is handled by the redirector when it makes a connection to the NBF drivers by using the TDI interface. NBF begins the sequence by generating a NetBIOS Find Name frame. Once the server is found, a session is set up with Class-II frames which contain timing parameters following the 802.2 protocol standard (802.2 governs the overall flow of data).

The client computer sends a Set Asynchronous Balance Mode Extended (SABME) frame, and the server returns an Unnumbered Acknowledgment (UA) frame. Then the client sends a Receive Ready (RR) frame, notifying the server that it is ready to receive Informational (I) frames whose sequence number is currently 0. The server acknowledges this frame.

Once the LLC-level session is established, additional NetBEUI-level information is exchanged. The client sends a Session Initialize frame, and then the server responds with a Session Confirm frame. At this point, the NetBEUI-level session is ready to handle application-level frames (Server Message Blocks, or SMBs).

Reliable transfer is achieved with link-oriented frames by numbering the I-frames. This allows the receiving computer to determine whether the frames were lost and in what order they were received.

NBF improves performance for connection-oriented traffic through two techniques: use of adaptive sliding windows and use of link timers. The next two sections describe these techniques.

Adaptive Sliding Window Protocol

NBF uses an adaptive sliding window algorithm to improve performance while reducing network congestion and providing flow control. A sliding window algorithm allows the Windows NT-based computer using NBF to dynamically tune the number of LLC frames sent before an acknowledgment is requested. Figure 13.6 shows frames traveling through a two-way pipe.

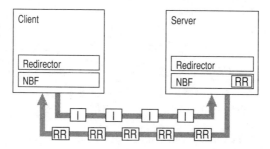

Figure 13.6   Adaptive Sliding Window

If the sending computer could send only one frame on to the network and then had to wait for an acknowledgment (ACK), the sending computer would be underused. The frames would travel forward, and then ACKs for the received frames would have to travel back to the sending computer before it could send another frame. The number of frames that the sender is allowed to send before it must wait for an ACK is referred to as the *send window*.

The number of frames that a receiving computer is allowed to receive before sending an ACK to the sending computer is referred to as a *receive window*. In general, *NBF has no receive window*, unless it detects that the remote sending computer is running a version of IBM NetBEUI which does not support polling; in this case, NBF uses a receive window based on the value of **MaximumIncomingFrames** in the Registry.

The default value for **MaximumIncomingFrames** is 2 and this value does *not* dynamically change. It must be manually changed by using the Registry Editor. For additional information about the receive window, refer to "Using Windows NT NetBEUI in IBM LAN Server Networks" in the section "Troubleshooting NetBEUI" later in this chapter.

The adaptive sliding window protocol tries to determine the best sizes for the send window based on current network conditions. Ideally, the windows should be big enough so that maximum throughput can be realized. However, if the window gets too big, the receiving computer could get overloaded and drop frames.

Dropped frames cause significant network traffic because more frames have to be retransmitted. Dropped frames might be a problem on slow links or when frames have to pass over multiple hops to find the destination computer. Dropped frames coupled with large send windows generate multiple retransmissions. This traffic overhead might make an already congested network worse. Limiting the send window size can improve performance by reducing network traffic.

Link Timers

NBF uses three timers to help regulate network traffic: the response timer (T1), the acknowledgment timer (T2), and the inactivity timer (Ti). These timers are controlled by the values of the Registry parameters **DefaultT1Timeout**, **DefaultT2Timeout**, and **DefaultTiTimeout**, respectively.

The response timer is used to determine how long the sender should wait before it assumes that the I-frame is lost. After T1 milliseconds, NBF sends an RR frame and doubles the value for T1. If the RR frame is not acknowledged after the number of retries defined by the value of **LLCRetries**, the link is dropped.

Where the return traffic does not allow the receiver to send an I-frame within a legitimate time period, the acknowledgment timer begins, and then the ACK is sent. The value for this timer is set by the T2 variable, with a default value of 150 milliseconds. If the sender has to wait until the T2 timer starts in order to receive a response, the link might be underused while the sender waits for the ACK. This rare situation can occur over slow links. On the other hand, if the timer value is too low, the timer starts and sends unnecessary ACKs, generating excess traffic. NBF is optimized so that the last frame that the sender wants to send is sent with the POLL bit turned on. This forces the receiver to send an ACK immediately.

The inactivity timer, Ti, is used to detect whether the link has gone down. The default value for Ti is 30 seconds. If Ti milliseconds pass without activity on the link, NBF sends an I-frame for polling. This is then ACKed, and the link is maintained.

Note   Remember that T2 is less than or equal to T1, which is less than or equal to Ti.

The T1 parameter is tuned dynamically on a per-link basis, based on link conditions and throughput. The value of the T1 parameter as specified in the Registry is used as the starting value for how long the process should wait for a response. This registry parameter can be changed. For example, if you know that the computer connects to the network on a slow link, the T1 registry parameter value can be increased. However, even if this parameter is not changed, NBF can detect the slow link quickly and automatically tune the T1 registry parameter value.

T2 and Ti are not adapted dynamically.

NBF Sessions

Each process that uses Windows NT-based NetBIOS can communicate with up to 254 different computers. Earlier implementations of NetBIOS supported only 254 sessions *for the entire computer*, including the workstation and server components.

The implementation of NetBIOS under Windows NT requires that an application do a few more things than have traditionally been required in other NetBIOS implementations, but the capacity for maintaining up to 254 sessions *from within each process* by using Windows NT-based NetBIOS is well worth the price.

Note that the 254-session limit does not apply to the default workstation or server components of Windows NT. The workstation and server services avoid the session limit problem completely by writing directly to the TDI, which is a 32-bit handle-based interface, instead of writing directly to the NetBIOS interface.

NBF also has a unique method of handling resources to create a virtually infinite (local computer memory permitting) number of connections, as described in the next section.

Session Limits

The 254-session limit is based on a key variable in the NetBIOS architecture called the *Local Session Number* (LSN). This is a 1-byte number (0 to 255) with several numbers reserved for system use. When two computers establish a session via NBF, there is an exchange of LSNs.

The LSNs on the two computers might be different. They do not have to match, but a computer always uses the same LSN for a given session. This number is assigned when a program issues a call for a Network Control Block (CALL NCB). The number is actually shared between the two computers in the initial frame sent from the calling computer to the listening computer. Figure 13.7 shows this session-creation frame exchange.

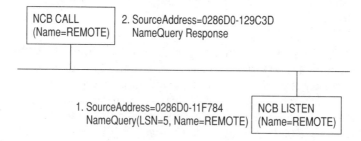

Figure 13.7   Multicast of NameQuery

The initial frame is a NameQuery frame. In earlier implementations of NBF, this frame was broadcast onto the network. All computers read the frame and check to see if they have the name in their name space and if there is a LISTEN NCB pending on the name. If there is a LISTEN NCB pending, the computer assigns a new LSN for itself. It adds the LSN to the response frame, satisfying the LISTEN NCB which now contains just the LSN used on that computer. Even though each computer knows the LSN of the other, the information is not used. The more important information for the two communicating partners is the network addresses that are part of the frames. As the frames are exchanged, each partner picks up the address of the other in the source address component of the frame received. The NBF protocol keeps the network address of the remote partner so that subsequent frames can be addressed directly.

Note   This process applies only to NBF connections. NetBIOS connections established by using NetBIOS over TCP/IP (NetBT) are handled differently.

Windows NT has to use the same NameQuery frame to establish connections with remote computers via NBF; otherwise, it would not be able to talk to existing workstations and servers. The NameQuery frame transmitted must contain the 1-byte-wide LSN to be used.

For example, suppose a computer running Windows NT Server and NBF assigns a session number of 1 to identify the session between itself and Computer A and also assigns the number 1 for the simultaneous session with Computer B. The computer running Windows NT Server can identify the different sessions because it uses the computer network address as part of the TDI handle to further identify each session. When the computer running Windows NT Server sends a session frame to either Computer A or Computer B, it uses the network address to direct the frame across the network. Therefore, Computer A does not receive the frames addressed to Computer B, and vice versa. However, if the computer running Windows NT Server and NBF establishes another session with Computer A, it must use a session number other than 1 to uniquely identify the second session.

A Windows NT Server computer running NBF can do this only when it is able to determine beforehand which adapter the session connection is going to be made to. Consider the following three scenarios:

1. A client connecting to a Windows NT computer running NBF.

   When a client connects to a computer running NBF, NBF can inspect the incoming frame to determine the remote adapter's address and assign a session number for that adapter.

2. NBF connecting to a remote client with a unique NetBIOS name.

   When NBF is connecting to a remote client, it first sends a FINDNAME frame. A response from the remote client means that the name is a unique name. NBF can then look at the remote adapter address in the response and assign a session number for that adapter because it knows that only that remote client owns this name.

3. NBF connecting to a remote client with a group NetBIOS name.

   If the FINDNAME response indicates that the connection is being made to a group name, NBF has no way of knowing which adapter belonging to the group will respond when it tries to connect, and so it has to assign a session number on a global basis, just as NetBEUI did for all connections.

These scenarios show that NBF has no limit on sessions, unless it is establishing connections to group names, in which case the old NetBEUI limit still applies. To be accurate, if you have n group name connections, then you can have $254-n$ connections to any given remote client. If n is 0, then you can have a full 254 connections to a remote. If n is 253, you can still have 1 connection to each remote, but if n is 254, then no connections can be made until one of the existing ones is disconnected.

Breaking the 254-session Limit

NBF breaks the 254-session barrier by using a combination of two matrices, one maintained by NBF and one maintained by NetBIOS.

The matrix maintained by NBF is two-dimensional, as shown in Figure 13.8.

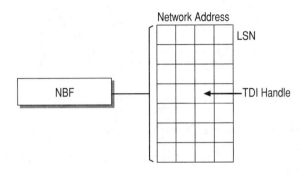

Figure 13.8   NBF and Its LSN Matrix

Along the side of this matrix are the LSN numbers 1 to 254. Across the top are the network addresses for the different computers that it has sessions with. In the cell defined by the intersection of the LSN and network address is the TDI handle, which relates back to the process that established the connection (either the CALL or LISTEN).

Note   The matrix concept and its contents are for illustration purposes only. The physical storage algorithm and exact contents are beyond the scope of this chapter.

The NameQuery frame from Windows NT contains the LSN number associated with the TDI handle that satisfies either the NCB CALL or the LISTEN. In the case of a CALL, it is not broadcast but is addressed directly to the remote computer.

The remaining question is how NBF gets the network address of the remote computer to add to its matrix to be used when doing the CALL. (It's easy on the LISTEN side because the address is in the NameQuery frame received.)

Figure 13.9 illustrates the NCB CALL and NCB LISTEN frames.

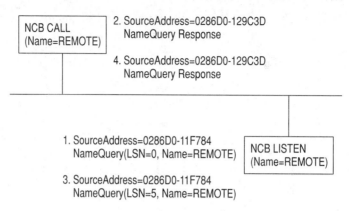

Figure 13.9   NameQuery Frames in NBF

The numbered items in Figure 13.9 represent the following:

1. The first frame (1) is the FindName frame of the NameQuery.
   However, an LSN of 0 is special; it indicates that it is a FindName frame. The
   FindName frame is broadcast on the network; when a remote computer
   responds to the frame, NBF on the local computer receives the network
   address of the remote computer.

2. The second frame (2) of the NameQuery is then sent directly to the remote
   computer by using the network address and a LSN value that indicates it is a
   CALL command. The remote client returns a successful FindName frame,
   even if no LISTEN NCB is posted against the name.

3. If no LISTEN NCB is posted against the name, frame (3) is sent.

4. The same frame is responded to by frame (4).

NBF must also address another problem—the LSN from the NBF matrix cannot
be the one returned to the process issuing the CALL or LISTEN commands. NBF
may have established connections with multiple remote computers with LSN=5,
for example. Windows NT must return to each process an LSN number that
uniquely defines its session.

As stated earlier, NBF uses the TDI handle to know which LSN and network
address to send frames to, and each process has its own set of LSNs available to
it. Therefore, there must be a component between the originating process and the
TDI interface of NBF that translates a process ID and an LSN into a TDI handle.
The component in the middle is Netbios.sys.

Figure 13.10 illustrates the Netbios.sys matrix, which is 254 LSNs per LAN
adapter number per process. (In Windows NT, the LANA number identifies a
unique binding of a protocol driver and one network adapter (NIC) driver.) In
reality, each process can have up to 254 sessions per LANA number, not just a
total of 254 sessions.

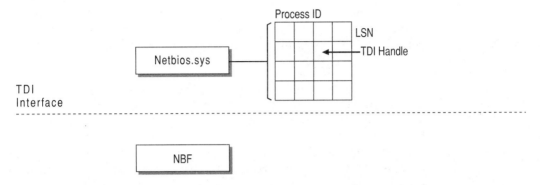

Figure 13.10   Netbios.sys Matrix

Netbios.sys builds a second matrix that has LSNs down the side, process IDs
along the top, and TDI handles in the cells. It is the LSN from this table that is
passed back to the originating process.

To further understand how Netbios.sys uses this matrix, suppose a process needs
to establish a session with a remote computer. Before the process can issue the
CALL NCB, it must issue a RESET NCB. This command signals Netbios.sys to
allocate space in its TDI handle table, among other things. Once the RESET is
satisfied, the process issues a CALL NCB to make a connection with a specific
remote computer. This NCB is directed down to the Netbios.sys device driver.
The driver opens a new TDI handle to NBF and sends the command to NBF.

NBF issues the first NAME_QUERY with LSN=0 to find the remote computer.
When the remote computer responds, the network address is extracted from the
frame, and a column in the NBF table is created. The second NAME_QUERY
with an LSN is sent directly to the remote computer. When that frame is returned
successfully, NBF returns from the TDI call to the Netbios.sys driver with a
successful status code.

Netbios.sys then fills in the LSN from its table into the NCB and sends it back to
the calling process.

Limited Network Routing Using NBF

Multi-location networks, such as a wide area network (WAN), require routing capabilities, while single-location, small- to medium-sized local area networks (LANs) generally do not require the overhead of a routing protocol.

NBF is not a routable protocol. It uses a single-part naming scheme which cannot be used to differentiate between computers belonging to multiple interconnected networks. NBF can provide a simple form of routing known as Token Ring source routing, and it can only be implemented on Token Ring networks.

Token Ring source routing occurs when NBF broadcasts a name query frame on a local token ring; if it doesn't receive a response in a set period of time, it enables source routing fields in the name query ring frame that force source routing bridges to receive and process the frame. The source routing bridges add additional routing information to the frame and send it to all other rings to which the bridge is connected. When the name query frame reaches the desired computer, that computer sends its computer name in the return message frame, using the routing information from the query to send the message directly to the originating computer. The originating computer caches the routing information and uses the cache to address subsequent frames.

Troubleshooting NetBEUI

This section discusses problems that you might encounter on a Windows NT-based computer on which the NetBEUI protocol is installed and running.

Note NBF is the underlying implementation of the NetBEUI protocol installed on a computer running Windows NT Server or Windows NT Workstation. Most users are more familiar with the term NetBEUI. When troubleshooting, it is more common to use the term NetBEUI, rather than NBF.

Tuning NetBEUI Using Registry Parameters

When NetBEUI is installed on a Windows NT-based computer, it is installed with default configurations. Because NBF is largely self-tuning, no configuration is required when installing NetBEUI on a Windows NT–based computer.

If desired, however, you can change the default values for NetBEUI registry parameters. The NetBEUI startup parameters are found under the following subkey:

```
HKEY_LOCAL_MACHINE\SYSTEM\Services\NBF\Parameters
```

Warning Using Registry Editor incorrectly can cause serious, system-wide problems that may require you to reinstall Windows NT to correct them. Microsoft cannot guarantee that any problems resulting from the incorrect use of Registry Editor can be solved. Use this tool at your own risk.

Changing a NetBEUI Binding

You can manually change the NetBEUI bindings. The changes you can make are:

- Enable a binding
- Disable a binding
- Move the order (priority) of the bindings up or down

▶ **To change a NetBEUI binding**

1. Click **Start**, point to **Settings**, and click **Control Panel**.
2. Double-click **Network**.
3. Click the **Bindings** tab.
4. In **Show Bindings for**, click **all protocols**.
5. Double-click **NetBEUI Protocol** to display a list of bindings.
6. Select the binding you want to change and then click the appropriate action button.
7. Click **OK**.

Source Routing Not Supported in FDDI Network

Source routing is only supported for Token Ring networks. A network using a fiber data distributed interface (FDDI) for network communications cannot use NBF for source routing. To correct this problem, use transparent source routing or transparent bridging.

No Session Alive Frames

NBF does not use NetBIOS session alive frames to determine if the remote client is up. Instead, it sends LLC poll frames, which serve the same purpose. NBF will respond correctly to session alive frames, so this should cause no interoperability problems with other implementations of NetBEUI.

Using Windows NT NetBEUI in IBM LAN Server Networks

In general, NBF has no receive window, unless it detects that the remote sending computer is running a version of IBM NetBEUI which does not use network polling—for example, IBM LAN Server. NBF initiates a link with a remote computer in the same manner as IBM NetBEUI; however, NBF looks for a *poll* bit in received frames. If a frame is received that does not have the poll bit set, the Windows NT-based computer will wait until T2 expires before sending a frame ACK.

Note When the poll bit is set in a received frame, NBF ignores the receive window and immediately sends an ACK.

For example, an IBM LAN Server computer is a non-polling system that may have a send window set to 1. If this the case, the registry parameter **MaxIncomingFrames** should be decreased from its default of 2 to 1. If not, the non-Windows NT-based computer will wait for an ACK from the Windows NT-based computer, which in this case will be sent only when the T2 time limit expires.

NBF uses a receive window based on the value of **MaximumIncomingFrames** in the Registry. The default value for **MaximumIncomingFrames** is 2, and this value does *not* dynamically change. It must be manually changed by changing the parameter default value in the Registry.

Note   When a Windows NT-based computer is using the **MaxIncomingFrames** receive window, it may not always send an acknowledgment frame after receiving exactly **MaxIncomingFrames** packets. This is because NBF will also wait until it receives an NDIS **ProtocolReceiveComplete** before sending the ACK. However, when the Windows NT-based computer receives POLL frames, it will ACK immediately (typically on return from **NdisTransferData** (synchronous communications) or within **ProtocolTransferDataComplete** (asynchronous communications).

NetBEUI Browser Does Not See TCP/IP Clients

Browsing on a computer running under Windows NT is based on a per protocol basis. In other words, there is a master browser for each protocol. Computers running only the NetBEUI protocol register with the master browser computer running the NetBEUI protocol. Computers running only NetBEUI get the master browser list from the master browser running NetBEUI. Because computers running only the TCP/IP protocol register with a master browser running TCP/IP, these computers will not be on the master browser list from a computer running only NetBEUI.

C H A P T E R   1 4

Using DLC with Windows NT

A Data Link Control (DLC) protocol interface device driver is included in Windows NT Workstation and Windows NT Server version 4.0. The DLC protocol is traditionally used to provide connectivity to IBM mainframes. It is also used to provide connectivity to local area network print devices that are directly attached to the network instead of to a specific computer. The DLC protocol is not designed to be a primary protocol for use between personal computers, and it needs to be installed only on computers performing the above-mentioned tasks and not on other computers on the network.

This chapter provides information for the network administrator and support personnel who need information about using the DLC protocol device driver for Windows NT to connect to IBM mainframes or to use print devices that are directly attached to the network. The following topics are discussed in this chapter:

- Overview of Data Link Control (DLC) protocol
- Installing the DLC protocol
- DLC driver parameters in the Registry
- Communicating with System Network Architecture (SNA) hosts using DLC
- Changing the locally administered address
- Using DLC to connect to Hewlett-Packard print devices

Overview of Data Link Control

The Data Link Control (DLC) protocol is a special purpose, non-routable protocol provided with Windows NT. Windows NT–based DLC provides applications only with direct access to the data link layer.

Windows NT–based DLC does not support the TDI interface as do other Windows NT–based transport protocols. Because DLC does not support the TDI, it cannot be used for communication with TDI client applications, such as the Windows NT redirector and server. Because the redirector cannot use DLC, this protocol is not used for normal session communication between Windows NT–based computers.

The DLC protocol driver provided with Windows NT enables the computer to communicate with other computers running the DLC protocol stack (for example, an IBM mainframe) and other network peripherals (for example, print devices such as a Hewlett-Packard HP 4Si that use a network adapter card (NIC) to connect directly to the network.)

The DLC protocol driver provides access to IEEE 802.2 class I and class II services. It also provides the direct interface to send and to receive raw 802.5, 802.3, and Ethernet type network frames. The interface consists of a dynamic-link library and a device driver.

Windows NT DLC contains an 802.2 Logical Link Control (LLC) Finite State Machine, which is used when transmitting and receiving type 2 connection-oriented frames. DLC can also transmit and receive type 1 connectionless frames, such as Unnumbered Information (UI) frames. Type 1 and 2 frames can be transmitted and received simultaneously.

Windows NT–based DLC works with either token ring or Ethernet Media Access Control (MAC) drivers and can transmit and receive Digital.Intel.Xerox (DIX) format frames when bound to an Ethernet MAC.

The DLC interface can be accessed from 32-bit Windows NT–based programs and from 16-bit MS-DOS-based and 16-bit Windows–based programs. The 32-bit interface conforms largely to the CCB2 interface, the segmented 16-bit pointers being replaced with flat 32-bit pointers. The 16-bit interface conforms to the CCB1 interface.

Note For definitions of the CCB interfaces, see the *IBM Local Area Network Technical Reference.*

Installing the DLC Protocol

By default, the DLC protocol is not installed during Windows NT Setup. The DLC driver can be loaded when the system is first installed, or at any time thereafter.

▶ **To install DLC**

1. Click **Start**, point to **Settings**, and click **Control Panel**.
2. Double-click **Network**.
3. Click the **Protocols** tab, and then click **Add**.

You also can configure network bindings for DLC. Network bindings are connections between network cards, protocols, and services. The order of the bindings is significant to DLC because an adapter is specified at the DLC interface as a number—typically 0 or 1 (although Windows NT DLC can support up to 16 physical adapters). The number corresponds to the index of the adapter in the DLC bindings section.

If you have only one NIC installed, DLC applications use a value of 0 to refer to this adapter, and you need not make any changes to the bindings. If you have more than one adapter card, you might want to modify the bindings.

You can manually change DLC bindings by clicking **Network** in **Control Panel** and selecting the **Bindings** tab. The changes you can make are to:

- Enable a binding
- Disable a binding
- Move the order (priority) of the bindings up or down

▶ **To change a DLC binding**

1. Click **Start**, point to **Settings**, and then click **Control Panel**.
2. Double-click **Network**, and then click the **Bindings** tab.
3. In Show Bindings for, enter All Protocols.
4. Double-click **DLC Protocol**.
5. Select the binding you want to change and click the appropriate button.
6. Click **OK**.

DLC Driver Parameters in the Registry

Unlike other Windows NT protocol drivers, DLC does not bind to a medium access control (MAC) driver until an adapter **open** command is issued. When an adapter is opened for the first time, the DLC protocol driver writes some default values into the Registry for that adapter. These values control the various timers that DLC uses, whether DIX frames should be used over an Ethernet link, and whether bits in a destination address should be swapped (that is, used when going over a bridge that swaps destination addresses).

The timer entries in the Registry are supplied because program-supplied timer values might not be sufficient. There are three timers used by DLC link communication:

- T1—the response timer
- T2—the acknowledgment delay timer
- Ti—the inactivity timer

Each timer is split into two groups—**TxTickOne** and **TxTickTwo**, where x is 1, 2, or i.

Typically, these timer values are set when a program opens an adapter and/or creates a Service Access Point (SAP).

The Registry contains entries used to modify timer values. Registry entries for DLC are found in the following location:

```
HKEY_LOCAL_MACHINE\SYSTEM\CurrentControlSet\Services\DLC\Parameters
  \<Adapter Name>
```

When you edit a timer entry value, the change takes effect the next time the adapter is opened (for example, by rerunning the application).

Communicating with SNA Hosts Using DLC

One of the major uses of the DLC protocol is connecting personal computers to Systems Network Architecture (SNA) hosts—that is, IBM mainframe or midrange computers such as the AS/400.

SNA provides equivalent functionality to the OSI Network, Transport, Session, and Presentation levels (although functionality might differ at each level). Because the DLC layer and the OSI Data Link layer are almost identical in functionality, a programming interface was developed for the DLC layer and passed on to programmers wanting to use this level of interface. The interface is described in the IEEE 802.2 standard.

Note   DLC is not robust enough to handle multi-threaded programming.

Figure 14.1 compares the SNA and OSI models.

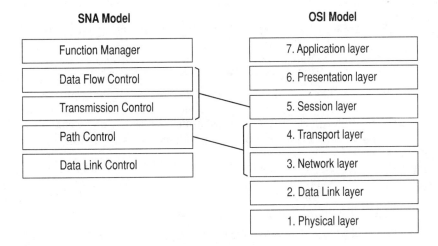

Figure 14.1   Comparison of SNA and OSI Models

With the Token Ring Interface Connection (TIC), any SNA host can communicate with a token ring network. With the LAN Interface Connection (LIC), an AS/400 computer can communicate with an Ethernet network.

Figure 14.2 illustrates a mainframe connectivity path using token ring.

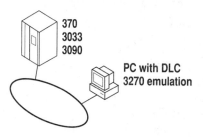

Figure 14.2 Mainframe Connectivity Path Using Token Ring

The Microsoft SNA Server uses the DLC protocol device driver when communicating to mainframes by using the token ring interface. Detailed configuration and installation information is provided in the *Microsoft SNA Server Installation Guide* and the *Microsoft SNA Server Administration Guide*.

Changing the Locally Administered Address

There might be times when you want to change or override the network address of the NIC when running the DLC protocol. You might want to do this, for example, when communicating directly to a mainframe. Certain configurations of mainframe software require the network address of the devices connecting to it to follow a set format, and so it might be necessary to change the card's network address. You can do this through the Registry Editor.

The following example is for an IBM Token Ring adapter. This parameter is supported on other NICs as well, but not necessarily on all.

▶ **To change the address of an adapter card**

1. Click **Start**, and then click **Run**.
2. Type **regedit**, and click **OK**.
3. When the Registry Editor starts, select the following key:

    HKEY_LOCAL_MACHINE\SYSTEM\CurrentControlSet\Services\ibmTOKMC01

4. On the **Edit** menu, click **Add Value**.
5. Type **NetworkAddress** in **Value,** select **REG_SZ** for data, and then click **OK**.
6. Type the 12-digit Locally Administered Address (LAA) that you need to communicate to the mainframe.

    If you don't know this address, see your network administrator or operations group.

7. Close the Registry Editor and restart your computer for the modification to take effect.

8. From the command prompt, run the following command to report the active MAC address:

```
net config rdr
```

If the MAC address is the same as the LAA you entered in the Registry Editor, the LAA has taken effect.

For information about running the Registry Editor, use online Help and the keyword Registry.

Using DLC to Connect to Print Devices

You can also use DLC to provide connectivity to Hewlett-Packard local area network print devices that are directly attached to the network, not to a specific computer. The DLC protocol must be installed on the Windows NT-based print server that is used to configure and administer the network-attached print device.

To connect to and configure the Hewlett-Packard print device, you must install the DLC protocol and the Hewlett-Packard Network Port monitor on the Windows NT-based print server. Install the DLC protocol before using the Add Printer Wizard. Use the Add Printer Wizard to install the Hewlett-Packard Network Port and configure the print device.

Before starting the Add Printer Wizard:

- Run self-test on the Hewlett-Packard print device to obtain the network adapter card address. The card address is a unique 12-byte number that is supplied by the card manufacturer.

- Choose a logical name for the printer. This logical name will be used to identify the printer and will be associated to the card address.

▶ **To configure a Hewlett-Packard print device that is directly connected to the network**

1. Click **Start**, point to **Settings**, and click **Printers**.

2. Double-click **Add Printer**.

3. Select **My Computer**, and click **Next**.

4. Click **Add Port**.

5. Select the Hewlett-Packard Network Port and click **OK**.

6. In **Name**, type the printer name.

7. If the print device is already attached to the network, select the appropriate card address in **Card Address**.

   If the Hewlett-Packard print device is already attached to the network, the number you obtained from the print device self-test appears in the **Address** list box. If it does not appear, make sure that the print device is correctly attached and is connected on the same subnet as the Windows NT-based print server. DLC cannot be used to connect to printers on the far side of a router.

8. If the print device is not attached, or you are working off-line, type the card address number in **Card Address**.

9. Click **OK**.

   The Add Printer Wizard will complete the configuration of the print device.

For more information about using the Print Wizard, see Help.

C H A P T E R   1 5

Remoteboot

The Remoteboot service is a Windows NT Server feature that starts MS-DOS, Microsoft Windows 3.1, and Microsoft Windows 95 clients over the network. You install and configure the Remoteboot service on the server and then customize it to be more effective for your particular network and for your users' needs.

For updated information about the Remoteboot service, see the *<systemroot>*\Rpl\Readme.txt file. The default location of the remoteboot directory is *<systemroot>*\Rpl. If you choose a different location to install the remoteboot directory, substitute that location for *<systemroot>*\Rpl throughout this chapter.

Understanding the Remoteboot Service

This section describes the architecture and operation of the Windows NT Server Remoteboot service.

For complete information about Windows NT file systems, security, and network planning issues, see Windows NT Server *Concepts and Planning*. This information will help you take best advantage of Windows NT Server at your site.

The Remoteboot Process

When you start, or boot, a computer, the operating system is loaded into its memory. The Windows NT Remoteboot service supports personal computers running MS-DOS, Windows 3.1, and Windows 95 (also called *clients* or *workstations*) that boot using software on the server's hard disk instead of the client's hard disk. Each of these clients has a network adapter, with a Remote Initial Program Load (RPL) ROM chip, that retrieves startup and configuration software from the server when the client starts. The client does not need a hard disk. This process is known as *booting remotely* or the *remoteboot process*.

Figure 15.1 shows a possible configuration of remoteboot clients and servers.

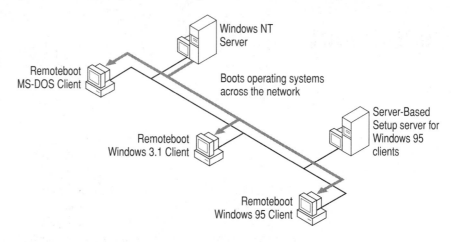

Figure 15.1   The remoteboot process

How Does Remoteboot Work?

The Remoteboot service works by providing two kinds of resources at the server:

- A *boot block*, which contains all the information needed to start the client when it boots
- The remoteboot *profile*, which defines the operating system environment of the client after it boots

The boot block and remoteboot profile are sent across the network in frames. A *frame* is a chunk of data, with some extra information. Sending a frame can be thought of as mailing a package of data, with the address and instructions for its use written on it.

When a remoteboot client is powered up, the network adapter is initialized and broadcasts a FIND frame (a boot request), as shown in Figure 15.2. The Remoteboot service receives the FIND frame, which contains the client's adapter ID.

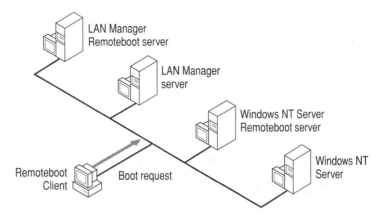

Figure 15.2   The remoteboot process: boot request

The Remoteboot service checks the remoteboot database on the server to see if a *workstation record* (a remoteboot database entry) already exists with this adapter ID. If it doesn't, the Remoteboot service records this adapter ID but does not boot the client. To boot the client, the administrator must convert this adapter ID record to a workstation record using Remoteboot Manager.

If a workstation record does exist with this adapter ID, the Remoteboot service sends a FOUND frame, containing the server's adapter ID, to the RPL ROM on the client. This is called a *boot acknowledgment* and is illustrated in Figure 15.3.

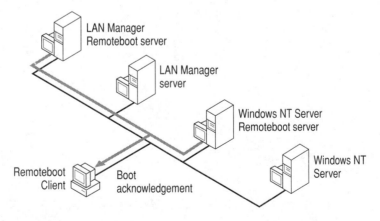

Figure 15.3   The remoteboot process: boot acknowledgment

The RPL ROM accepts the first FOUND frame it receives (it may receive more than one if several servers are running the Remoteboot service), and returns the SEND.FILE.REQUEST frame to the adapter ID of the server that sent the first FOUND frame. The following Figure shows the remoteboot client sending a boot block request.

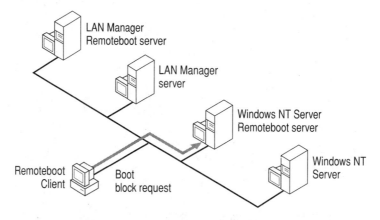

Figure 15.4   The remoteboot process: boot block request

When the Remoteboot service receives the SEND.FILE.REQUEST frame, it uses FILE.DATA.RESPONSE frames to send a boot block to the RPL ROM (as shown in Figure 15.5). The workstation record in the remoteboot database specifies which boot block to send (either MS-DOS or Windows 3.1). When the RPL ROM receives the last FILE.DATA.RESPONSE frame, it transfers execution to the entry point of the boot block.

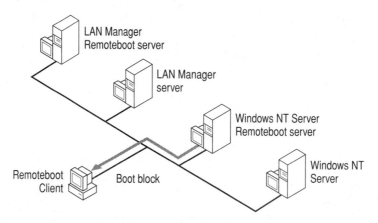

Figure 15.5   The remoteboot process: boot block transfer

The RPL ROM boots the operating system specified by the boot block as appropriate for the client. For a client running MS-DOS or Windows 3.1, this completes the basic boot process.

For a client intended to run Windows 95, the boot process continues. The client is now running Windows 95 real-mode (also identified as MS-DOS 7.0), using files on the remoteboot server. To complete the boot to Windows 95, the client does the following:

1. Creates a RAM disk. A *RAM disk* is an area of the computer's RAM memory set aside to operate as if it were a disk drive.

2. Copies Windows 95 real-mode files from the remoteboot server to the RAM disk.

3. Loads the Windows 95 real-mode network drivers and establishes a connection to a Server-Based Setup (SBS) server. The SBS server can be the same computer as the remoteboot server. An SBS server, described in the *Microsoft Windows 95 Resource Kit*, supports over-the-network installation of Windows 95 as well as shared installations (where some or all Windows 95 files reside on the server). For Windows NT remoteboot, the SBS server provides the Windows 95 files which the client uses to complete the Windows 95 boot process.

4. Connects to a server that has a machine directory with files specific to this client.

Why Use Remoteboot?

The Remoteboot service promotes the use of diskless clients by eliminating the need for a hard disk on each client. This has several advantages:

- Increased network security by using clients that do not have disk drives that can be used to illegally copy data and to introduce viruses

- Greater control over the distribution of information and software resources

- Ease of updating software centrally

- Reduced cost in buying and maintaining client computers

Using the Remoteboot service has advantages for clients with hard disks as well:

- Easy upgrading of software and operating systems on many clients

- Greater flexibility in standardizing clients while allowing custom configurations

In general, the Remoteboot service offers greater control to the network administrator.

Setting Up and Starting the Remoteboot Service

Before you can use the Remoteboot service, you must install a network adapter containing an RPL ROM chip on each client computer you plan to boot remotely. These adapters are available directly from network adapter manufacturers or from independent vendors. For more information about network adapters and RPL ROMs, contact your solution provider. A list of supported network adapters is provided in the next section of this chapter.

▶   **To set up the Remoteboot service (summary)**

1. Install Windows NT Server on a computer that will be the remoteboot server.

   There are three special considerations for the Remoteboot service:

   ▪   The server's computer name must not have spaces in it.

   ▪   It is strongly recommended that you install remoteboot files on a disk partition formatted with NT File System (NTFS) so that permissions are correctly set. Users will be able to read and write their own files in the remoteboot directory but not write to shared files or system configuration files. Also, the File Allocation Table (FAT) file system does not support more than approximately 100 remoteboot clients.

   ▪   Install the Data Link Control (DLC) and NetBIOS Extended User Interface (NetBEUI) protocols and ensure that clients can communicate with the server using these protocols (arrange proper routing, bridging, etc.).

2. Install the Remoteboot service on the remoteboot server.

   Or, convert an existing Microsoft LAN Manager for OS/2 remoteboot installation to run on Windows NT Server, and then install the Remoteboot service.

   Note   Windows NT Server does not support remote booting of OS/2 clients, Windows for Workgroups clients, Windows NT Workstation clients, or Windows NT Server clients.

   ---

3. Install MS-DOS and/or Windows 3.1 operating system files on the remoteboot server.

   If you are converting from LAN Manager remoteboot, this may not be necessary.

4. If you will have Windows 95 remoteboot clients, install Windows 95 real-mode (also identified as MS-DOS 7.0) files on the remoteboot server.

5. Start the Remoteboot service.

6. Check the installation for errors, including checking the Event Viewer log.

7. Create profiles (these define the working environment shared by one or more clients).

8. If you will have Windows 95 remoteboot clients, install a Server-Based Setup (SBS) server.

   This can be the same computer as the remoteboot server or it can be a separate server on the network. The SBS server must run the NetBEUI protocol.

9. If you will have Windows 95 remoteboot clients, create a location for machine directories.

   This can be on the same computer as the remoteboot server or SBS server, or it can be on a separate server on the network. The server containing machine directories must run the NetBEUI protocol.

This section provides step-by-step instructions for these actions. For instructions on managing remoteboot clients, see "Managing Remoteboot Clients" later in this chapter.

Disk Space Requirements

The first step in preparing to use the Remoteboot service is to ensure that the server has enough disk space for the files needed by the remote clients. Use the values in the following table as a guideline.

Table 15.1   Disk Space Requirements

Component	Disk space required
Microsoft Network Client version 2.2 for MS-DOS (LAN Manager version 2.2)— required for all client configurations	5.1 MB
MS-DOS 3.30	0.7 MB
MS-DOS 4.01	1.5 MB
MS-DOS 5.00	2.8 MB
MS-DOS 6.x	5.9 MB
Windows 3.1	12.4 MB
Windows 95	2.0 MB

Use this table to calculate the amount of disk space you need on the remoteboot server. For example, to install the Remoteboot service for a configuration of clients running MS-DOS 6.22, some with Windows 3.1, you need 23.4 MB of disk space, broken down as follows:

- 5.1 MB for the Network Client 2.2 for MS-DOS files
- 5.9 MB for the MS-DOS 6.22 files
- 12.4 MB for the Windows 3.1 files

In addition, you need room for personal copies of remoteboot profiles (if needed) and for directories for each client, where people store their own data. The amount of space to allot per client is up to you. You can also define a separate server (or servers) to contain machine directories for Windows 95 clients, to distribute the load of storing client-specific data. Each Windows 95 client needs its own machine directory with a minimum of 8 MB of disk space; more if users install additional software.

Windows 95 remoteboot clients require 8 MB of RAM and must be 386-based or higher. The server you use as a Server-Based Setup server requires 90 MB of disk space to store Windows 95 files.

Supported Network Adapters

These specific network adapters are supported by the Remoteboot service for Windows 95, Windows 3.1, and MS-DOS on the client (for the latest list see <*systemroot*>\Rpl\Readme.txt):

Note Only the ISA versions of these network adapter cards are supported for Windows 95 remoteboot clients. Note especially that the Remoteboot service does not support PCI, Token-Ring, or PNP adapters for Windows 95 remoteboot clients:

3Com EtherLink II	Novell NE2000
3Com EtherLink III	Western Digital/SMC EtherCard Plus (8000 series) (see Readme.txt for information about using the 8000 series with Windows 95)
AMD Series 2100 Ethernet	
Intel EtherExpress 16	
Intel EtherExpress PRO	

The following network adapters are supported by the Remoteboot service for Windows 3.1 and MS-DOS on the client (for the latest list see *<systemroot>*\Rpl\Readme.txt):

3Com EtherLink	Intel EtherExpress 16
3Com EtherLink Plus	Intel EtherExpress PRO
3Com EtherLink /MC	Madge Token-Ring
3Com EtherLink II	Nokia/ICL Ethernet IIe
3Com EtherLink III	Novell NE1000
3Com TokenLink	Novell NE2000
3Com TokenLink III	Racal Interlan NI 5210
3Com 3Station	Racal Interlan NI 6510
AMD Series 2100 Ethernet	Western Digital/SMC Ethernet
HP Ethertwist	Western Digital/SMC EtherCard Plus (8000 series)
IBM Token Ring	
IBM Ethernet	

Most network adapters work best with the Remoteboot service when using their default settings. However, if you need to modify these default settings in the Protocol.ini files, these files are located in *<systemroot>*\Rpl\Bblock\Netbeui*adapter*\Protocol.ini, where *adapter* is the name of the particular network adapter. For example, a Windows 95 client can have conflicts with interrupt 3 (IRQ3) for the network adapter.

Installing the Remoteboot Service on the Remoteboot Server

Have on hand the Windows NT Server compact disc. You will also need original product disks for any operating system that you want the remoteboot clients to run, such as MS-DOS or Windows 95 disks.

The installation procedure differs depending on whether you are installing a new remoteboot directory or converting an existing LAN Manager for OS/2 remoteboot directory. Use one of the two following procedures.

▶ **To install the Remoteboot service (with a new remoteboot directory)**

1. If they are not already installed, install the DLC and NetBEUI protocols on the server. The Remoteboot service requires DLC and NetBEUI.

2. Click **Start**, point to **Settings**, and click **Control Panel**.

3. Double-click **Network**.

4. In the **Network Settings** dialog box, click **Add Software**.

5. In the **Add Network Software** dialog box, select the **Remoteboot Service**.

6. In the **Remoteboot Setup** dialog box, type the full path and directory name where you want to install the remoteboot directory.

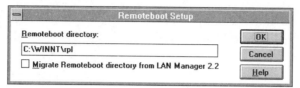

The default value is *<systemroot>*\Rpl. This is the directory shown in descriptions and examples.

7. Click **OK**.

8. Complete the dialog boxes that appear.

   For help with any dialog box, press F1.

See the post-installation information after the next procedure.

▶ **To install the Remoteboot service (converting a LAN Manager for OS/2 remoteboot directory)**

1. Use the Windows NT Server Upgrade for LAN Manager tools to convert the LAN Manager server's user accounts and file permissions. Then the remoteboot conversion can properly assign permissions and user account properties.

2. On the Windows NT Server computer, delete the RPLUSER global group (it is created by the Upgrade for LAN Manager tools). The **Fix Security** command of Remoteboot Manager will create an RPLUSER local group.

   Note that users who administer the Windows NT Remoteboot service must be members of the Administrators local group. The Upgrade for LAN Manager tools convert the LAN Manager RPLADMIN group to a Windows NT RPLADMIN global group, but it has no function under Windows NT.

3. Copy the entire remoteboot directory from the OS/2 server to the Windows NT Server computer.

   For example, if the LAN Manager remoteboot directory is \\SERVER3\C$\LANMAN\RPL and the Windows NT remoteboot directory is C:\Winnt\Rpl, type the following command at the Windows NT Server computer:

   xcopy /e \\server3\c$\lanman\rpl c:\winnt\rpl

   Keep a copy of the Rpl directory for later reference. Be especially sure to keep backup copies of any .ini, .cnf, and .fit files that were modified from their default state.

4. If they are not already installed, install the DLC and NetBEUI protocols on the server.

   The Remoteboot service requires DLC and NetBEUI.

5. In **Control Panel**, double-click **Network**.

6. In the **Network Settings** dialog box, click **Add Software**.

7. In the **Add Network Software** dialog box, click the **Remoteboot Service**.

8. In **Remoteboot Setup**, make the following choices:

   - In the **Remoteboot Directory** box, type the full path and directory name of the remoteboot directory on the Windows NT Server (for example, C:\Winnt\Rpl).

   - Select the **Migrate Remoteboot Directory From LAN Manager 2.2** check box.

9. Click **OK**.

10. Complete the dialog boxes that appear.

    For help with any dialog box, press F1.

11. Copy the new LAN Manager client software to locations in the Windows NT Server computer's Rpl directory, using the following commands:

    xcopy /e *d:***clients\rpl\bblock** **c:***systemroot***rpl\bblock**
    xcopy /e *d:***clients\rpl\fits** **c:***systemroot***rpl\fits**
    xcopy /e *d:***clients\rpl\rplfiles** **c:***systemroot***rpl\rplfiles**

    where *d:* is the computer's compact disc drive.

12. Run the **rplcnv** conversion program after remoteboot installation.

    The **rplcnv** program converts the RPL.MAP and RPLMGR.INI files used by the LAN Manager Remoteboot service into the System.mdb and Rplsvc.mdb files used by the Windows NT Remoteboot service database.

    This is the syntax for **rplcnv**:

    rplcnv *[path]*

    where *path* specifies an absolute path to the directory containing the RPL.MAP and RPLMGR.INI files. If this parameter is omitted, it is assumed that the files are in the current directory or in *<systemroot>*\Rpl.

13. Compare the new .ini, .cnf, and .fit files in the remoteboot directory to the backup copies you made before conversion.

    If you had modified the OS/2 versions of these files, you may want to transfer those modifications to the Windows NT versions. Do not simply copy the OS/2 versions over the Windows NT versions, because you might overwrite new data.

14. In Step 11 you installed new configurations. If you have profiles that you want to preserve from the LAN Manager installation, modify the profiles' Autoexec.bat and Config.sys files as follows:

   - Autoexec.bat: @Rpllink is no longer needed; this file has been replaced with Rpllnk.sys, which is loaded from Config.sys.

   - Config.sys: Add the following line as the first line in the file:

     ```
     DEVICE=C:\BINR\RPLLNK.SYS
     ```

Whether you install a new Rpl directory or migrate from OS/2, the installation process creates the following major directories:

- Rpl (at the location you specify during installation and with a different name if you want). This is the remoteboot directory.

- Rpl\Bblock. This directory contains boot blocks for each client configuration.

- Rpl\Fits. This directory contains *file index table* (FIT) files that translate references to a file on the client to a true path to the file on the server. For example, for a client using a profile shared with other clients, the FIT file would map C:\Config.sys to *server*\Rplfiles\Profiles*profile*\Config.sys, where *server* is the server's name and *profile* is the profile for this client.

- Rpl\Rplfiles. This directory contains files specific to each client as well as shared files such as profiles and operating system files. This directory is shared with the name Rplfiles.

- Rpl\Rplfiles\Binfiles\Dos*xxx*. These directories contain shared MS-DOS system files.

- Rpl\Rplfiles\Binfiles\Lanman.dos. This directory contains Microsoft Network Client version 2.2 for MS-DOS, the network software used by all remoteboot clients.

- Rpl\Rplfiles\Binfiles\Win95. This directory contains shared Windows 95 real-mode (also identified as MS-DOS 7.0) system files.

The first time you run Remoteboot Manager and choose the **Fix Security** command, it creates the RPLUSER local group and assigns permissions as appropriate throughout the Rpl directory.

For a complete explanation of the remoteboot directory structure, see "Directory, File Index, and Configuration File Details" later in this chapter.

Installing MS-DOS Files on the Remoteboot Server

When a client starts and requests an MS-DOS remoteboot, the remoteboot server gives it a boot block, which will load some version of the MS-DOS operating system. The server can also provide Windows 3.1 for the client. You must copy MS-DOS and Windows 3.1 files to the server; they are not shipped with Windows NT Server.

Note   You must have a separate, valid, software license for each client computer, including remoteboot clients, that runs MS-DOS, Microsoft Windows 3.1, or Microsoft Windows 95.

In the following procedure you install MS-DOS files on the server. For information about how to install Windows 3.1 files, see "Installing Windows 3.1 for MS-DOS Clients" later in this chapter. For information about how to install Windows 95 files, see "Installing Windows 95 for Windows 95 Clients" later in this chapter. You cannot install Windows 3.1 or Windows 95 until you have at least one MS-DOS remoteboot client running.

▶ **To copy MS-DOS 6.2*x* files to the server**

1. Check that the *<systemroot>*\Rpl\Rplfiles directory is being shared on the remoteboot server. It should have the share name Rplfiles.

2. From an MS-DOS client (running a version of MS-DOS 6.2*x* that you want to support on the remoteboot server), connect to the remoteboot server's Rplfiles share by typing:

   net use v: *server*\rplfiles

   where *server* is the name of the remoteboot server.

3. Copy all the MS-DOS files to the *<systemroot>*\Rpl\Rplfiles\Binfiles\Dos*xxx*
    directory, where *xxx* is the version number (for example, Dos622), by typing:

    copy c:\dos*.* v:\binfiles\dos622
    attrib -s -h c:\io.sys
    attrib -s -h c:\msdos.sys
    copy c:\io.sys v:\binfiles\dos622
    copy c:\msdos.sys v:\binfiles\dos622
    attrib +s +h c:\io.sys
    attrib +s +h c:\msdos.sys

    As shown, you may need to remove the hidden file attribute in order to copy
    these files and then reset the attribute after copying. You can do this with the
    MS-DOS **attrib** command.

    Note Do not set the hidden or system file attributes on the new copies of the
    files in the *<systemroot>*\Rpl\Rplfiles\Binfiles\Dos*xxx* directory.

    Copy files to an existing Dos*xxx* directory only; do not create a new directory.
    For example, any version of MS-DOS 6.2*x* must be copied to the existing
    Dos622 directory.

4. If you copied DOS files other than MS-DOS (such as PC-DOS), you must
    rename the following files. From the
    <systemroot>\Rpl\Rplfiles\Binfiles\Dos*xxx* directory on the remoteboot
    server, type:

    rename ibmdos.com msdos.sys
    rename ibmbio.com io.sys

Starting and Stopping the Remoteboot Service

The Remoteboot service is installed as a manual service, meaning that you
must start it intentionally each time you want it to run. If you want it to start
automatically each time the server starts, see the instructions in online Help for
the Services icon in Control Panel.

▶ **To start or stop the Remoteboot service**

1. Click **Start**, point to **Settings**, and then click **Control Panel**.

2. Double-click **Services**.

3. Click the **Remoteboot** service.

    You may need to scroll down the list of services to reach it.

4. Click **Start** or **Stop**.

   Pause and **Continue** have no effect on the Remoteboot service.

5. In the **Services** dialog box, click **Close**.

You can also use the **net start remoteboot** command to start the Remoteboot service and **net stop remoteboot** to stop it.

Starting Remoteboot Manager

Remoteboot Manager is an administrative tool for controlling the remoteboot process and managing remoteboot clients.

Remoteboot
Manager

▶ **To start Remoteboot Manager**

1. At the Windows NT Server computer, log on to a user account that belongs to the Administrators local group.

2. From the **Network Administration** program group, click the **Remoteboot Manager** icon.

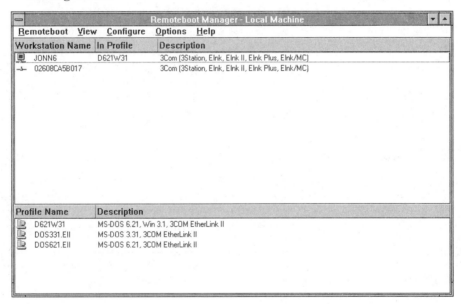

3. If you want to administer a remoteboot server other than the local computer, click **Set Focus** on the **Remoteboot** menu.

   Type the name of the remoteboot server, or choose the name from the **Select Computer** box.

   Or, from the command line, type **rplmgr** (or **rplmgr** *server*, where *server* is the name of a Windows NT Server computer).

Checking the Remoteboot Installation

After you start the Remoteboot service for the first time, check the server's event log for entries related to the Remoteboot service. Use Event Viewer in the Administrative Tools group.

You should also use Remoteboot Manager's configuration and security checking features after installation and after you add or remove support for an operating system.

▶   **To check the remoteboot configuration**

1. On the **Configure** menu, click **Check Configurations**.
2. Click **Yes**.

This checks which operating systems are available for remoteboot clients. Remoteboot Manager offers these as choices for profiles.

▶   **To check security settings in the remoteboot directory**

1. On the **Configure** menu, click **Fix Security**.
2. Click **Yes**.

This overwrites permissions throughout the *<systemroot>*\Rpl directory, creates accounts for remoteboot clients and the RPLUSER local account (if they don't already exist), and updates the **domain** entry in Lanman.ini files for remoteboot clients to match the server's own domain/workgroup.

Managing Profiles

When you use Remoteboot Manager for the first time, you must decide which profiles you need. A *profile* is the working environment shared by one or more clients. It consists of the operating system, the client computer and architecture type, the network adapter type, and all the other information needed to boot a client.

Note Remoteboot profiles are completely different from user profiles, which are used elsewhere in Windows NT Server.

To establish and name profiles, you choose from a list of configurations. A *configuration* is actually a template profile; a profile is created as a copy of one of the base configurations. Generally, you can find a configuration for any profile you want to create. Once the profiles are defined, it's easy to add clients.

Clients use profiles in either of two ways: sharing a profile or using a personal copy of a profile. The profile is the same in either case; the difference is in how the client uses it.

A profile can be shared by a group of similar client computers that use the same startup information. (All of the clients have the same Config.sys, Lanman.ini, and other configuration files, and those files are read-only.) For example, you may want to have a common profile that is shared by accounting, and another profile for sales and marketing. Or, you may want to create a profile shared by all Windows 3.1 users. Keep in mind, however, that the client computer architecture must be similar enough that the clients can share startup files. Clients that share profiles get their environment from a *<systemroot>*\Rpl\Rplfiles\Profiles*profile* directory (where *profile* is the name of the profile).

Sharing profiles is not practical in all cases. For example, a client may need customized system configuration files (like Config.sys). In this case, the client should use a personal copy of a profile. Changes to the startup information affect only the single client. Clients that have a personal copy of a profile get their environment from a *<systemroot>*\Rpl\Rplfiles\Machines*cname**profile*\Pro directory (where *cname* is the computer name and *profile* is the name of the profile). Users can edit any of the files in that directory, such as Config.sys.

When you upgrade operating systems and make software changes, you need to install them separately to each profile and copy of a profile.

▶ **To create a profile**

1. On the Remoteboot Manager **Remoteboot** menu, click **New Profile**.

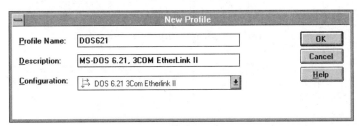

2. In **Profile Name**, type a name for this profile [no more than 16 characters, with no spaces or backslashes(\)].

3. In **Configuration**, enter a configuration.

   If the configuration you want is not present, you must install the appropriate operating system (see "Installing MS-DOS Files on the Remoteboot Server" earlier in this chapter) and check the configuration (on the **Configure** menu, click **Check Configurations**).

4. In **Description**, type a comment for the profile.

   The description should summarize the profile for easy recognition, such as **MS-DOS 6.22 VGA & 3Com 503 EtherLink II adapter**.

5. Click **OK**.

▶ **To change a profile**

1. Select an existing profile in **Remoteboot Manager**.

2. On the **Remoteboot** menu, click **Properties**.

3. Change the description of the profile, and then click **OK**.

   You can change only the description. To change any other settings, you must create a new profile.

▶ **To delete a profile**

1. Select an existing profile in Remoteboot Manager.

2. On the **Remoteboot** menu, click **Delete**.

3. If a message appears telling you that clients (workstation records) are still assigned to this profile, you can delete or reassign all of the clients at one time:

   ▪ In the error message dialog box, click **OK**.

   ▪ Select the profile.

   ▪ On the **View** menu, click **Workstations In Profile**.

   ▪ Select all of the workstation records (press CTRL and click all of the workstation records).

   ▪ On the **Remoteboot** menu, click **Delete**.

     Or, on the **Remoteboot** menu, click **Properties**. Choose a new profile for all of the clients, and then click **OK**.

4. In the **Confirmation** dialog box, click **OK**.

Once you have profiles set up, most remoteboot administration consists of managing the individual clients.

Managing Remoteboot Clients

When you have installed the Remoteboot service and the MS-DOS operating system files, and you have defined some profiles, you can use Remoteboot Manager to manage the remoteboot clients. You must boot at least one client on MS-DOS before you can install Windows 3.1 or Windows 95 remoteboot clients.

This section provides procedures for:

▪ Enabling and disabling the hard disk on a client.

▪ Adding a client to the Remoteboot service.

▪ Removing a client from the Remoteboot service.

▪ Installing Windows 95 for Windows 95 clients (includes setting up a Server-Based Setup server and, optionally, a server to hold machine directories).

▪ Installing Windows 3.1 for MS-DOS clients.

When a user starts a remoteboot client, what appears as the client's C drive is actually mapped to various locations on servers, such as a personal directory on a separate server. For an MS-DOS or Windows 3.1 client, the remoteboot server maps directories and files from various locations to the virtual C drive using a File Index Table (FIT) file; for more information, see "File Index Tables" later in this chapter. If the remoteboot client has a hard disk, the hard disk appears as drive D. Floppy disk drives keep their original drive letters.

Before you can use the Remoteboot service, each remoteboot client must have a network adapter with an RPL ROM chip installed. For a list of supported network adapters, see "Setting Up and Starting the Remoteboot Service" earlier in this chapter.

Enabling Remoteboot on a Client's Hard Disk

Before a client with a hard disk can be booted remotely, its hard disk must be properly configured for the Remoteboot service. This does not prevent users from accessing the hard disk after the client is booted.

Use the Microsoft Network Client version 2.2 **rplenabl** utility to prepare the client to use the Remoteboot service. Later, if you want to boot the client using its hard disk, run the **rpldsabl** utility to disable the remoteboot configuration.

Note Some RPL ROMs will take control of the client even though the hard drive is enabled, and so you may not need to run the **rplenabl** (or **rpldsabl**) utility on these clients. Try simply booting the computer, and then use **rplenabl** if needed.

▶ **To configure a client's hard disk for the Remoteboot service**

1. Insert a formatted MS-DOS floppy disk in the remoteboot server's floppy disk drive.

2. Copy the Rplenabl.exe and Rpldsabl.exe programs to the floppy disk by typing:

   copy c:*systemroot***\rpl\rplfiles\binfiles\binr\rpl??abl.exe** *a:*

   where *a:* is the floppy disk drive.

3. Start the remoteboot client, booting MS-DOS from the local hard disk.

4. Put the disk with the Rplenabl.exe program in the client's floppy disk drive and type:

   *a:***rplenabl**

   where *a:* is the client's floppy disk drive.

5. Remove the disk and press CTRL+ALT+DEL.

   The Remote Program Load Module information is displayed as the RPL ROM chip initializes the network adapter.

For instructions on using the **rpldsabl** utility, see "Deleting a Client" later in this chapter.

Adding a New Client

As described earlier in "Setting Up and Starting the Remoteboot Service," you created profiles for clients. You can add a new remoteboot client in two ways:

- Create a new remoteboot database record for the client and manually fill in the necessary data, including the client's network adapter ID number and the profile you want this client to use. This is only recommended when you know the network adapter ID number and you are copying an existing workstation record.

  When you copy an existing workstation record, you also copy the personal configuration information. For example, if the original workstation record uses a personal copy of a profile and has a customized installation of Windows 3.1, the profile and the Windows installation will be copied for the new client.

- Boot the client remotely with no special preparation on the server. This creates an *adapter* record on the server, which you can then convert to a workstation record by adding the client's name and profile. This is easier because you don't need to know the client's network adapter ID number.

▶ **To create a new workstation record manually**

1. Start Remoteboot Manager.

   Remember to log on to a user account that belongs to the Administrators local group.

2. On the **Remoteboot** menu, click **New Workstation**.

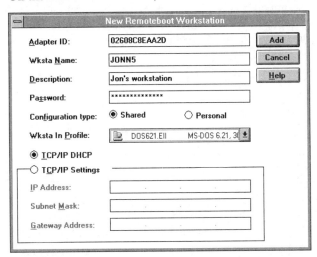

Or, select an existing workstation record. On the **Remoteboot** menu, click **Copy**.

3. In **Adapter ID**, type the client's network adapter ID number.

   This is a unique number supplied by the network adapter firmware. The adapter ID is 12 hexadecimal digits; the first six digits identify the adapter type. If you don't know the adapter ID, stop this procedure and go to the next procedure.

4. In **Wksta Name**, type a name for the client.

   The name can have no more than 15 characters [with no spaces or backslashes (\)]. The Remoteboot service will create a Windows NT user account with this name, not for the user but for the client computer itself.

   If the server's Rpl directory is on a FAT file system, use standard MS-DOS 8.3 format (eight characters, with an optional period and three more characters).

5. In **Description**, type a comment that describes the client.

6. In **Password**, type a password for the client computer's account (not for the user using the client computer).

7. Choose a configuration type:

   - Click **Shared** if this client can share its profile with other clients.

   - Click **Personal** if this client must use a personal copy of a profile so that you can customize the environment for the client.

8. In **Wksta In Profile**, enter a profile for this client.

    If none of the profiles are suitable, see "Setting Up and Starting the Remoteboot Service," earlier in this chapter, for instructions on creating profiles.

    If you see a profile in the list that appears to be appropriate, but it is marked as incompatible (or you see an error message about it being incompatible), then you may need to create a new configuration for this adapter type. See "Creating Remoteboot Configurations for New Adapters" later in this chapter.

9. In **TCP/IP Settings**, enter appropriate addresses only if the client will use TCP/IP and will not use DHCP for automatic address handling.

10. Click **Add**.

▶ **To create a new workstation record automatically**

1. Start Remoteboot Manager on the server.

    Remember to log on to a user account that belongs to the Administrators local group.

2. Start the remoteboot client.

    The client does not actually boot, but it does send a boot request to the server.

3. In Remoteboot Manager on the server, click **Refresh** on the **View** menu.

4. In Remoteboot Manager, select the adapter record that has appeared with the network adapter ID number in place of the client name.

5. On the Remoteboot menu, click **Convert Adapters**.

    Or, select more than one adapter record (hold down the CTRL key while clicking with the mouse). On the **Remoteboot** menu, click **Convert Adapters**. You will convert each of the selected records, one at a time.

    Or, do not select any adapter records. On the **Remoteboot** menu, click **Convert Adapters**. You will convert all of the adapter records to workstation records, one at a time.

6. In **Wksta Name**, type a name for the client.

    The name can have no more than 15 characters [with no spaces or backslashes (\)]. The Remoteboot service will create a Windows NT user account with this name, not for the user but for the client itself.

    If the server's Rpl directory is on a FAT file system, use standard MS-DOS 8.3 format (eight characters, with an optional period and three more characters).

7. In **Description**, type a comment that describes the client.

    The box already contains a comment provided by the network adapter itself.

8. Choose a configuration type:

- Click **Shared** if this client can share its profile with other clients.

- Click **Personal** if this client must use a personal copy of a profile so that you can customize the environment for the client.

9. In **Wksta In Profile**, click a profile for this client.

Profiles that are unsuitable for this type of adapter (determined by the first six digits of the network adapter ID number) are marked with a red X.

If none of the profiles are suitable, see "Setting Up and Starting the Remoteboot Service," earlier in this chapter, for instructions on creating profiles.

10. In **TCP/IP Configuration**, enter appropriate addresses only if the client will use TCP/IP and will not use DHCP for automatic address handling.

11. Click **Add**.

If you are converting more than one adapter ID record, the next record appears in the dialog box.

What You See on an MS-DOS or Windows 3.1 Client

When you boot the client, a remoteboot logon prompt appears:

```
Type Remoteboot username, or press enter if it is <workstation>:
```

This asks for the account name and password associated with the client itself, not for the user's own account name and password.

Once the boot is complete, the user should type a **net logon** command to log on with his or her own username and password.

When the client has completed a remote boot, the current directory is C:\, and the C drive is a virtual hard drive, parts of which are mapped to various places on the remoteboot server by the FIT file. For information about FIT files and translation pairs, see "Directory, File Index, and Configuration File Details" later in this chapter.

The C:\Wksta directory contains client-specific and profile-specific configuration files (such as Win.ini) and is different for each profile to which the client is joined. The C:\Data directory will always be the same, regardless of the profile used; the user can create files and directories there.

The C:\Dos and C:\Lanman.dos directories provide access to MS-DOS and network utilities. The C:\Binr directory provides access to shared real-mode utilities.

Local hard disks, if present, are assigned drive letters starting with D, unlike the local boot case, where the drive letters start with C.

Note If the server uses NTFS, a client assigned to a profile (rather than to a personal copy of a profile) can add or modify files only in certain directories on its virtual C drive. It cannot affect directories on the C drive that are shared with other clients (unless you explicitly grant permission to do so on the server).

A remoteboot client always runs the NetBEUI protocol. To run other protocols as well, see "Supporting Multiple Network Adapters and Protocols" later in this chapter.

Changing a Workstation Record

You can change any of the properties of a workstation record except the network adapter ID number.

▶ **To change a workstation record for a client**

1. Start Remoteboot Manager on the server.

   Remember to log on to a user account that belongs to the Administrators local group.

2. Select the workstation record.

   Or, select more than one record (hold down CTRL while clicking) to change properties for a group of clients at once.

3. On the **Remoteboot** menu, click **Properties**.

4. Update the information as needed.

5. Click **OK**.

Deleting a Client

When you no longer want to boot a workstation remotely, you can remove it from the list of workstations in the Remoteboot service.

▶ **To remove a client from the Remoteboot service**

1. Start Remoteboot Manager on the server.

   Remember to log on to a user account that belongs to the Administrators local group.

2. Select the workstation record for the client.

   Or, select more than one record (hold down CTRL while clicking) to delete a group of workstation records at once.

3. On the **Remoteboot** menu, click **Delete**.

4. Verify that you want to delete this workstation record.

If Remoteboot Manager originally created an account while creating a workstation record, removing the workstation record also removes the account associated with that client. If the account existed before the workstation record, then the account will remain after removing the workstation record.

If the client was a Windows 95 client, you may want to delete the client's machine directory.

If the client has a bootable hard drive, you need to disable the remoteboot process and allow the client to use the hard drive again.

▶ **To disable the Remoteboot process**

1. Start the client, booting MS-DOS remotely or from a floppy disk.

2. Put the disk with the Rpldsabl.exe program in the client's floppy disk drive and type:

    *a:***rpldsabl**

    where *a:* is the client's floppy disk drive.

    (If you don't have the disk anymore, see the section "Enabling Remoteboot on a Client's Hard Disk," earlier in this chapter, for instructions on making this disk.)

3. Remove the disk and press CTRL+ALT+DEL.

Installing Windows 95 for Windows 95 Clients

To support Windows 95 remoteboot clients, you must install Server-Based Setup (SBS) on a server, install the first Windows 95 client, and then install subsequent clients.

Installing SBS for Windows 95 Clients

For greater technical detail about SBS servers, see the *Microsoft Windows 95 Resource Kit*. When you set up an SBS server, you can use the server for remoteboot and for other purposes described in the *Microsoft Windows 95 Resource Kit*.

You will need a Windows 95 installation compact disc (not floppies) and a Windows 95 client computer.

▶   **To install an SBS server**

1. On the server that will contain SBS files, create a shared directory with 90 MB of space available. The shared directory can have any name.

   As you share the directory, assign read-only permission for regular users and full access for administrators. For example, use Server Manager to focus on the shared directory and set read-only permission for the Users group and full permission for the Administrators group. In **File Manager**, click **Share As** on the **Disk** menu, not **Permissions** on the **Security** menu.

2. Install one regular Windows 95 client on the network or use an existing one.

   You will use this client to configure the SBS server.

3. Log on to the Windows 95 client using an account that has write access to the shared directory on the SBS server.

4. Put the Windows 95 compact disc in the client's CD-ROM drive. In Windows Explorer, switch to the Admin\Nettools\Netsetup directory.

5. Double-click **Netsetup.exe**.

   Note that you must run Netsetup.exe at a Windows 95 client. It will encounter errors on a computer running Windows NT.

6. In the **Server-Based Setup** dialog box, click **Set Path**, and specify the path to the SBS server; then click **OK**.

   You can type a drive letter for a mapped drive, a network name for a server (for example, \\server1\sharedir), or a network path to a specific directory (for example, \\server1\sharedir\rpl\win95).

   The button name becomes **Change Path** if a server was defined previously.

7. Click **Install**.

   Server-Based Setup presents a series of dialog boxes so that you can complete these actions:

   - Specify an "install policy" for how users can install Windows 95 from the server. If you support only remoteboot clients, click **Server**. If you support other SBS functions as well, click **User's choice**. Do not click **Local hard drive**.

   - Set the source path for Windows 95 files.

     This is the path to the compact disc on the client.

   - If asked, specify that you do *not* want to create a default setup script.

     Setup scripts for Windows NT remoteboot installation require special settings.

   - Provide a CD Key number for product identification.

   Server-Based Setup copies Windows 95 files to the SBS shared directory.

8. At the remoteboot server, put the compact disc or floppy disk containing the Windows NT remoteboot for Windows 95 files into a drive. Change to the drive and then change to the Update\Win95 directory. Run **win95srv.bat** to update the Windows 95 files for remotebooting. For example:

```
d:
cd \update\win95
win95srv.bat <dest>
```

where *<dest>* is the shared directory on the SBS server.

9. If you are updating from version 3.51 or earlier of the Remoteboot service, start the Remoteboot service at the remoteboot server if it is not already started. Then, run the **rbootsrv.bat** program to update the remoteboot files and database for Windows 95 remotebooting. At the server's command prompt, type:

```
d:
cd \update\win95
rbootsrv.bat  <SBS_path>  <RPL_path>  [\\servername]
```

where:

- *<SBS_path>* is the path to the installed SBS server's Windows 95 files.
- *<RPL_path>* is the path to the remoteboot directory.
- *servername* is the name of the remoteboot server ; you can omit this if you are typing at the remoteboot server.

10. At the remoteboot server, start Remoteboot Manager.

11. On the **Configure** menu, click **Check Configurations** to activate the new configurations.

Installing the First Windows 95 Client

Installing the first Windows 95 client requires booting that client first to MS-DOS 6.2*x*, running Windows 95 Setup on the client, and then copying selected files from the client's machine directory to the remoteboot server. Once you have installed this first client, you can easily install subsequent clients by using SBS to make a modified copy of the original machine directory without having to run Windows 95 Setup again.

Each remoteboot client has a "machine directory," a directory on a server that contains client-specific configuration information and data. For example, the machine directory contains the following:

- Appropriate initialization and configuration files (including Win.ini and System.ini)
- System.dat and User.dat (the Registry)
- Files that define the Desktop, **Start** menu directories, and other programs
- The spool directory for printing
- The swap file and Temp directory

Machine directories can reside on the remoteboot server, on the SBS server, or on any designated server on the network. You may want to spread the load of machine directories across servers. The only qualifications for a machine directory server are sufficient disk space and running the NetBEUI protocol. To create a location for machine directories, simply make a shared directory on a server and share it with a name that does not contain spaces. For example, on a computer running Windows NT Server that will contain machine directories, type:

```
mkdir c:\rplmachines
net share machines=c:\rplmachines
```

Note The machine directories may not be subdirectories of the SBS directory.

Assign permissions to a machine directory so that only the users or administrators who will use the client have read and write permissions in the directory. If the machine directory is on an NTFS partition, assign permissions directly to the machine directories. If the machine directory is on a FAT partition, assign permissions to the shared directory containing the machine directories.

▶ **To install the first Windows 95 client**

1. Boot the new client to MS-DOS 6.2x, using procedures in "Adding a New Client" earlier in this chapter.

   You will need to run Windows 95 Setup while the client is booted from the Remoteboot service rather than when the client is booted from a floppy disk or hard drive.

2. Use the **net logon** command to log on using an account that has read access to the SBS server and write access to the shared directory that will contain this client's machine directory.

   A good example is the account of someone who will use this client because they will need this access anyway.

3. Synchronize the time and date settings of the client, the SBS server, and the remoteboot server. Differing settings can interfere with Windows 95 Setup.

4. Use the **net use** command to map drive letters to the SBS server and machine directory location, and then determine the highest drive letter in use on the computer.

   C: is a virtual hard drive mapped to parts of the remoteboot server. Each local hard drive partition (if any) takes another drive letter after C: (for example, D: and E: for two partitions). One more drive letter is reserved for use as a RAM drive during the Windows 95 boot process. Drive letters after that are available for use.

   For example, if you have a local hard drive with one partition, C: will be mapped to the remoteboot server, D: will be the local hard drive, E: is reserved for use as a RAM drive, and F: and higher are available for use. You would type:

   ```
   net use f: \\sbs_server\win95_share
   net use g: \\mach_server\mach_share
   ```

5. Change to the drive letter mapped to the SBS directory.

6. Run the Windows 95 Setup program by typing:

   ```
   setup  /t:temppath
   ```

   where **/t:** is required and *temppath* is a path to a directory in which to store temporary files during installation. For example, if G: is mapped to the shared directory containing the client's machine directory, you could type:

   ```
   setup  /t:g:\client1.tmp
   ```

   to store temporary files on that server.

   Do not delete the t:*temppath* directory until you have completed Step 12. Also, if you are installing two Window 95 clients simultaneously (for example, to support clients with different network adapters), choose separate temporary directories for each client.

   Make the following decisions during setup:

   - In the **Server-based Setup** dialog box, click **Set up Windows to run from a network server** if asked.

   - In the **Startup Method** dialog box, click **Start Windows from the network (remote boot server)**.

   - In the **Machine Directory** dialog box, when asked where to install Windows 95, type the path of the machine directory (using the drive letter specified in Step 4, for example, **g:\client1**).

   - In the **Setup Options** dialog box, click **Custom** setup.

   - In the **Analyzing Your Computer** dialog box, click **No, I want to modify the hardware list**.

Exclude as many hardware types and items from autodetection as possible. If autodetection crashes, run Setup again and exclude more items from autodetection. One problem could be that your network adapter is on IRQ2 or IRQ3; this conflicts with serial port detection with some network adapters.

- In the **Select Components** dialog box, click to clear the **Communications** check box (unless the client has a modem and you intend to use dial-up networking).

- In the **Network Configuration** dialog box, check that your network adapter and desired protocols are present and configured correctly.

  If there are no network adapters shown, you must add and configure your network adapter.

  If you add your network adapter, you must confirm the resource settings for the adapter. Select the adapter name in the **Network Configuration** dialog box, click **Properties**, and then click the **Resources** tab. Check that the settings displayed are correct (for example, the interrupt level). Then, click **OK** to force the Setup program to accept the settings; do not click **Cancel**.

  For details about protocols on Windows 95 remoteboot clients, see "Supporting Multiple Network Adapters and Protocols" later in this chapter.

- In the **Identification** dialog box, make sure that the workgroup for this client is the same as the workgroup or domain of the SBS server and machine directory server.

When the Windows 95 Setup program is done, reboot the client. The client will not yet boot to Windows 95; however, you must complete more steps first.

7. At the remoteboot server (or a client running Remoteboot Manager focused on the remoteboot server), start Remoteboot Manager.

8. Create a profile for the Windows 95 client. In **Configuration**, click the Windows 95 configuration corresponding to the client's network adapter type.

   If you are not sure which configuration to choose, check the profile that is currently associated with this client for booting MS-DOS and use the equivalent Windows 95 profile.

9. Edit the client's workstation record to assign the client to the Windows 95 profile.

10. At the remoteboot server (or a client with write access to the remoteboot server's Rpl directory), run the Rpl\Bin\Win95clt.bat program by typing:

```
cd <systemroot>\rpl\bin
win95clt  mach_directory  \\rpl_server  profile_name
```

where:

- *mach_directory* is the path to the client's machine directory.
- *\\rpl_server* is the name of the remoteboot server.
- *profile_name* is the name of the Windows 95 profile associated with the client.

For example, you could type:

```
cd \winnt\rpl\bin
win95clt  \\mach_server\mach_share\client1  \\rpl_server  win95elnk2
```

The Win95clt program copies client-specific Windows 95 real-mode (also identified as MS-DOS 7.0) boot files from the client's machine directory to the Rpl\Rplfiles\Profiles*<profile_name>* directory on the remoteboot server.

11. At the SBS server (or a client with write access to the SBS directory), edit the Machines.ini file in the SBS directory and add the following lines for the new client:

```
[adapter id]
SYSDATPATH=g:\machine_dir
g=\\mach_server\mach_share
```

where:

- *adapter id* is the network adapter ID, specified in the remoteboot workstation record for this client.
- *g:\machine_dir* is the location of the client's machine directory on a server; *g* is the drive letter assigned on the next line to the shared directory where the client's machine directory is located.
- *g=\\mach_server\mach_share* identifies the drive letter assigned to the shared directory where the machine directory resides. You must use the same drive letter and share name established in Step 4.

For example, you might add the following lines to Machines.ini:

```
[02608C8EAA2D]
SYSDATPATH=g:\client1
g=\\mach_server\mach_share
```

12. Reboot the Windows 95 client.

The client will now boot to Windows 95 and complete the Windows 95 Setup program.

Installing Subsequent Windows 95 Clients

Once you have installed a single client, subsequent clients of the same type will be much easier to install. These subsequent clients do not have to be exactly the same as the first, but they must use the same type of network adapter and the same adapter settings (IRQ, I/O address, etc.).

If you need to install a Windows 95 client that does have different configuration settings, you must treat the installation as a fresh installation; see "Installing the First Windows 95 Client" earlier in this section.

▶   **To install subsequent Windows 95 clients**

1. Boot the new client to MS-DOS 6.2*x*, using procedures in "Adding a New Client" earlier in this chapter.

2. Log on to a regular Windows 95 client (for example, the one you used to run **netsetup** when you established the SBS server).

    Use an account that has write access to the shared directory on the SBS server and to the shared directory containing machine directories.

3. Put the Windows 95 compact disc in the client's CD-ROM drive. In Windows Explorer, switch to the Admin\Nettools\Netsetup directory.

4. Double-click **Netsetup.exe**.

5. In the **Server-Based Setup** dialog box, click **Set Path**, and specify the path to the SBS server; then click **OK**.

    You can type a drive letter for a mapped drive, a network name for a server (for example, \\server1\sharedir), or a network path to a specific directory (for example, \\server1\sharedir\rpl\win95).

    The button name becomes **Change Path** if a server was defined previously.

6. Click **Add**.

7. In the **Set Up Machine** dialog box, click **Set Up One Machine** and then type the following information:

    - Computer name: type a computer name of the client (you must create a unique name).

    - Path to machine directory: type a network pathname for the machine directory you want to create for the client.

    - Existing machine directory: type the network pathname for an existing machine directory of a client similar to this one.

    For example, you might type the following values:

    - Computer name: client2

    - Path to machine directory: \\mach_server\mach_share\client2

    - Existing machine directory: \\mach_server\mach_share\client1

8. Click **OK**.

   You may see an error message about creating the machine directory. Check that the directory was created and that it contains several files; if so, then disregard the error message.

9. At the remoteboot server (or a client running Remoteboot Manager focused on the remoteboot server), start Remoteboot Manager.

10. Edit the client's workstation record to assign the client to the same Windows 95 profile as the first client.

11. Edit the Machines.ini file in the SBS directory. Add the following lines for the new client:

```
[adapter id]
SYSDATPATH=g:\machine_dir
g=\\mach_server\mach_share
```

   where:

   - *adapter id* is the network adapter ID, specified in the remoteboot workstation record for this client.

   - *g:\machine_dir* is the location of the client's machine directory on a server; *g* is the drive letter assigned on the next line to the shared directory where the machine directory is located.

   - *g=\\mach_server\mach_share* assigns a drive letter to the shared directory where the machine directory resides. Use the same drive letter used by the original Windows 95 remoteboot client.

   For example, you might add the following lines to Machines.ini:

```
[02608C8EAA2E]
SYSDATPATH=g:\client2
g=\\mach_server\mach_share
```

12. Reboot the Windows 95 client.

   The client will now boot to Windows 95 and complete the Windows 95 Setup program.

What You See on a Windows 95 Client

When you boot the client, a remoteboot logon prompt appears:

```
Type Remoteboot username, or press enter if it is <workstation>:
```

This asks for the account name and password associated with the client computer itself, not for your own user account name and password.

Windows 95 then prompts you twice for your username and password: once from a command prompt and again in a dialog box. At both of these prompts, enter your user account name and password.

Once Windows 95 has started, the C: drive is unassigned; it was assigned during the remoteboot process and is no longer needed. Each local hard drive partition takes another drive letter after C: (for example, D: and E: for two partitions). One more drive letter was used as a RAM drive during the Windows 95 boot process; you can now use it as a RAM drive for your own purposes. Two more drive letters, usually the next two drive letters in sequence, are mapped to the SBS server and to the shared directory containing the client's machine directory. When setting up the client, you choose exactly which two drive letters to map and they will always be the same for this client. Do not unmap or remap these drives elsewhere.

For example, if you have a local hard drive with one partition, C: is unmapped, D: is the local hard drive, E: is a RAM drive, F: is mapped to the SBS server, and G: is mapped to the shared directory containing the client's machine directory.

Installing Windows 3.1 for MS-DOS Clients

You can install Windows 3.1 in similar client environments simply by creating a profile for Windows 3.1 users and installing the Windows 3.1 environment in the profile. In this way, you can add as many new clients as you need without having to install the Windows 3.1 environment with each new addition. Keep in mind, however, that all the clients sharing the profile must be similar enough to share the same startup information.

If the clients are not similar, you create personal copies of profiles. If Windows 3.1 is already installed for a profile, and you create a new personal copy of that profile, the Windows 3.1 installation is part of the new copy, and you do not have to reinstall it. If you have established a personal copy of a profile and later want to add Windows 3.1, you must add it separately for that personal copy of the profile, or delete the personal copy of the profile and create a new one from a profile that does have Windows 3.1 installed.

To support Windows 3.1 for remoteboot clients:

- Install Windows 3.1 files on the remoteboot server. This makes the files easily available for client installations.

- Create a profile for Windows 3.1 users. Install Windows 3.1 once for all clients using the profile.

- Install Windows 3.1 separately for clients using a personal copy of a profile (if the profile did not support Windows 3.1 at the time you made the personal copy). Or, delete the client account and recreate it, making a personal copy of a profile that does support Windows 3.1.

Installing Windows 3.1 Files on the Server

Installing Windows 3.1 files on the server makes the files easily available for client installations.

▶ **To install Windows 3.1 files on the server**

1. Create an MS-DOS profile, if one does not exist. (For details, see "Setting Up and Starting the Remoteboot Service" earlier in this chapter.)

2. Boot a remoteboot client that will use Windows 3.1, and join it to the MS-DOS profile using Remoteboot Manager. (For details, see "Adding a New Client" earlier in this chapter.)

Note If you will use the shared Windows 3.1 profile method for similar clients, assign the client to use a profile, not a personal copy of a profile. If you will use the personal profile user method for different clients, assign the client to use a personal copy of a profile.

---

3. Reboot the client.

   At the remoteboot logon prompt (the prompt that first appears when you start the client), supply the name and password of an account that is a member of the Administrators group on the Windows NT Server computer.

4. If the client does not have a floppy disk drive, use the floppy disk drive of a server on the network:

   ▪ First, at the server (it doesn't have to be the remoteboot server), use File Manager or the **net share** command to share the server's floppy disk drive.

   ▪ Then, at the client, use File Manager or the **net use** command to connect to the shared floppy disk drive.

5. Put the Windows 3.1 Disk 1 in the floppy disk drive.

6. Run **setup /a** on the Windows 3.1 Disk 1 and install to C:\Win.

   Windows 3.1 files are expanded and put into the <*systemroot*>\Rpl\Rplfiles\Binfiles\Win directory on the remoteboot server.

Continue the installation. Depending on how you want to set up profiles, proceed to "Installing Windows 3.1 for a Profile" or to "Installing Windows 3.1 for a Personal Copy of a Profile."

Installing Windows 3.1 for a Profile

When you install Windows 3.1 for a profile, all clients that share that profile use Windows 3.1. Also, if you later assign a personal copy of the profile to a client, that client uses Windows 3.1.

▶ **To install Windows 3.1 for a profile**

1. Create a profile for Windows 3.1 users on the remoteboot server.

   Give the profile a specific name that suggests the Windows version and the operating system associated with it. For example, D62WIN31 tells you that this profile is for MS-DOS 6.2x with Windows version 3.1.

2. In Remoteboot Manager, assign a remoteboot client to the new profile (not using a personal copy of the profile).

3. Reboot the client.

   At the remoteboot logon prompt (the prompt that first appears when you start the client), supply the name and password of an account that is a member of the Administrators group on the Windows NT Server computer.

4. On the client, change to the Windows 3.1 directory by typing:

   cd \win

5. On the client, run **setup /n** to install Windows 3.1 in C:\Windows (do not choose to upgrade any existing Windows installations). Choose the express installation.

   If the client has memory trouble while running Setup, see "Configuring Memory for MS-DOS and Windows 3.1" later in this chapter.

6. Follow the instructions in the Setup program to modify the Autoexec.bat and Config.sys files.

   Note If Setup displays an error message saying that it cannot update your system files on drive C, choose **Cancel**. This creates Autoexec.win and Config.win files in the C:\Windows directory. Copy these files to C:\Autoexec.bat and C:\Config.sys, respectively.

7. Add the following lines to the end of the [386enh] section in the C:\Windows\System.ini file:

```
TimerCriticalSection=5000
UniqueDosPSP=True
PSPIncrement=2
```

8. Return to the MS-DOS prompt and copy all the files and directories in C:\Windows to C:\Wksta.pro\Win by typing:

xcopy /e c:\windows c:\wksta.pro\win

This makes the Windows 3.1 files available to all remoteboot clients that are joined to the profile.

If the **xcopy** command does not work on the client, you can copy the files from a command prompt on the server by typing the following command, all on one line:

xcopy /e c:*systemroot***\rpl\rplfiles\machines***client******profile***\wksta\win c:***systemroot***\rpl\rplfiles\profiles***profile***\wksta\win**

where *client* is the name of the client and *profile* is the name of the profile.

9. Reboot the remoteboot client and log on.

Installing Windows 3.1 for a Personal Copy of a Profile

If you assign a personal copy of a profile (without Windows 3.1) to a client, and then later decide that you want to install Windows 3.1 for that client, you can install Windows 3.1 separately for this client. Or, delete the client account and recreate it, making a personal copy of a profile that does support Windows 3.1.

You may want to install a separate copy of Windows 3.1 for a client if the client requires customized Windows 3.1 configuration files.

▶ **To install Windows 3.1 for a personal copy of a profile**

1. On the remoteboot server, assign the remoteboot client to an MS-DOS profile. Specify a personal copy of the profile.

2. Reboot the client.

   At the remoteboot logon prompt (the prompt that first appears when you start the client), supply the name and password of an account that is a member of the Administrators group on the Windows NT Server computer.

3. On the client, change to the Windows 3.1 directory by typing the following:

   cd \win

4. Run **setup /n** to install Windows 3.1 in C:\Windows (do not choose to upgrade any existing Windows installations). Choose the express installation.

   If the client has memory trouble while running Setup, see "Configuring Memory for MS-DOS and Windows 3.1" later in this chapter.

5. Follow the instructions in the Setup program to modify the Autoexec.bat and Config.sys files.

Note If Setup displays an error message saying that it cannot update your system files on drive C, choose **Cancel**. This creates Autoexec.win and Config.win files in the C:\Windows directory. Copy these files to C:\Autoexec.bat and C:\Config.sys, respectively.

---

6. Add the following lines to the end of the [386enh] section in the C:\Windows\System.ini file:

```
TimerCriticalSection=5000
UniqueDosPSP=True
PSPIncrement=2
```

7. When the Setup program is finished, reboot the client and log on.

Optimizing the Remoteboot Service

Once the Remoteboot service has been configured and customized for your network needs, Windows NT Server offers some additional ways to optimize the service. Most of the topics in this section deal with increasing performance. Other topics tell you how to further customize your configuration.

This section contains information on how to:

- Use the **rplcmd** utility to change the remoteboot database.
- Create remoteboot configurations for new adapters.
- Configure memory for MS-DOS and Windows 3.1.
- Configure memory for Windows 95.
- Set local swapping.
- Use a RAM drive on the client.
- Set hardware buffers.

Using the Remoteboot Command Utility (RPLCMD.EXE)

The **rplcmd** utility can be used to view and update records in the remoteboot database, including those that are inaccessible through Remoteboot Manager. This utility is for advanced administrators, not for casual use.

Before you use **rplcmd**, make sure that you have a backup copy of the remoteboot database. For details, see "Backing Up the Remoteboot Database" later in this chapter.

This is the syntax of **rplcmd**:

rplcmd *[\\computername]*

where *\\computername* specifies a remote computer where the Remoteboot service is running. If this parameter is omitted, **rplcmd** manages the Remoteboot service on the local computer.

The main **rplcmd** command prompt appears as:

```
Adapter Boot Config Profile Service Vendor Wksta [Quit]
```

Each command has the following effect:

- **Adapter** modifies adapter records (records of remoteboot clients that have been started but do not yet have a workstation record assigned).
- **Boot** modifies boot block records.
- **Config** modifies configuration records.
- **Profile** modifies profiles.
- **Service** controls the Remoteboot service.
- **Vendor** associates a vendor "name," or six-digit hexadecimal prefix, with a text comment describing the vendor.
- **Wksta** modifies workstation records.

To select a command, type the first letter in the command name and press ENTER. To return to the main menu, press CTRL+Z at any prompt and press ENTER.

Each of the main commands has further command prompts, including these common commands:

- **Add**—to add a new record.
- **Del**—to delete a record (or all records).
- **Enum**—to enumerate, or show information for, a record (or all records). You can enumerate information at different levels; level 0 gives you the least information per record.

Creating Remoteboot Configurations for New Adapters

The following section is for advanced administrators.

Note Before you use **rplcmd**, make sure that you have a backup copy of the remoteboot database. For details, see "Backing Up the Remoteboot Database" later in this chapter.

When the Remoteboot service receives a boot request, it looks up the workstation record associated with the client's network adapter ID (if there isn't one, then it creates an adapter record and does not attempt to boot the client). It then determines the profile associated with the workstation record and the configuration record that was used to create the profile. The configuration record contains a boot block record name, and more than one boot block record may have the same name. The Remoteboot service looks for a boot block record with this boot block record name and the vendor ID contained in the client's network adapter ID. The configuration record and the boot block record provide the information needed to boot the client.

Windows NT Server provides boot block and configuration records for the most popular network adapters.

Use the following procedure if Remoteboot Manager cannot assign a workstation record to the correct profile because the network adapter type is incompatible. This can happen when there is no existing boot block record mapping the network adapter vendor ID to the correct network adapter type. You must create a new boot block record specifying the vendor ID and the network adapter type. If any client with this network adapter type will boot to Windows 95, you must create an MS-DOS boot block record and a Windows 95 boot block record.

▶ **To create a new boot block record for a supported network adapter type**

● Use the **rplcmd** utility to add boot block records for the adapter and vendor ID. For details about the **rplcmd** utility, see the preceding section, "Using the Remoteboot Command Utility (RPLCMD.EXE)."

For **BootName**, use the name of an existing boot block record that boots clients with network adapters of this type (but with a different vendor ID).

For example, the following sequence of commands creates sample boot block records for MS-DOS and Windows 95:

```
C:\winnt\rpl> rplcmd
Adapter Boot Config Profile Service Vendor Wksta [Quit]: b
Add Del Enum: a
BootName=DOSX
VendorName=012345
BbcFile=BBLOCK\NETBEUI\dirname\DOSBB.CNF
        All other parameters are optional
BootComment=Name of this adapter
WindowSize=0
Adapter Boot Config Profile Service Vendor Wksta [Quit]: b
Add Del Enum: a
BootName=W95X
VendorName=012345
BbcFile=BBLOCK\NETBEUI\dirname\W95BB.CNF
        All other parameters are optional
BootComment=Name of this adapter
WindowSize=0
Adapter Boot Config Profile Service Vendor Wksta [Quit]: v
Add Del Enum: a
VendorName=012345
BootComment=Name of this adapter
```

Note In this example, and in those that follow, the value **012345** represents the "vendor name" or network adapter prefix. Replace this with the first six digits of the network adapter type's adapter identification number.

If the adapter prefix for the new adapter type matches that of an existing adapter type, modify the BootName field of the boot block and workstation record field to be unique among all boot block or workstation records corresponding to that adapter prefix. For example, use **DOS** for IBM Token Ring and **DOSI** for IBM Ethernet.

If you want to use a new remoteboot-compatible network adapter that is not already supported by Windows NT Server, you must manually create a new boot block, boot block record(s), and a configuration record corresponding to the new adapter. This allows the Remoteboot service and Remoteboot Manager to recognize the new adapter type.

Microsoft does not guarantee support for adapters that are not on the list of supported adapters (see "Supported Network Adapters" earlier in this chapter). Note especially that the Remoteboot service does not support PCI, Token-Ring, or PNP adapters for Windows 95 remoteboot clients.

To support Windows 95 clients with a particular network adapter type, you must create both an MS-DOS 6.2*x* configuration and a Windows 95 configuration.

▶ **To create an MS-DOS configuration for a new adapter**

1. Copy the MS-DOS device driver for the network adapter to the *<systemroot>*\Rpl\Bblock\Ndis directory.

2. Create the directory *<systemroot>*\Rpl\Bblock\Netbeui*adapter*, where *adapter* is the name of the adapter. Within this directory, create these files:

   - Dosbb.cnf

   - Protocol.ini

   Pattern these files after existing files in a corresponding directory, but substitute the new driver names in the Dosbb.cnf file, and the correct driver information in the Protocol.ini file.

3. Use the **rplcmd** utility to add a boot block record for the new adapter. For details about the **rplcmd** utility, see the preceding section, "Using the Remoteboot Command Utility (RPLCMD.EXE)."

   For example, the following sequence of commands creates a sample boot block record:

   ```
   C:\winnt\rpl> rplcmd
   Adapter Boot Config Profile Service Vendor Wksta [Quit]: b
   Add Del Enum: a
   BootName=DOSX
   VendorName=012345
   BbcFile=BBLOCK\NETBEUI\dirname\DOSBB.CNF
           All other parameters are optional
   BootComment=Name of this adapter
   WindowSize=0
   ```

4. Use the **rplcmd** utility to add the new configuration.

For example, the following sequence of commands creates a sample configuration:

```
C:\winnt\rpl> rplcmd
Adapter Boot Config Profile Service Vendor Wksta [Quit]: c
Add Del Enum: a
ConfigName=DOS622X
BootName=DOSX
DirName=DOS
DirName2=DOS622
FitShared=fits\dos622.FIT
FitPersonal=fits\dos622p.FIT
        All other parameters are optional
ConfigComment=DOS 6.22 <adapter name>
DirName3=
DirName4=
```

For **BootName**, enter the name of the boot block record you created in step 3.

▶ **To create a Windows 95 configuration for a new adapter**

1. Boot the client to MS-DOS 6.2*x* to confirm that the MS-DOS configuration is correct. For details, see "Adding a New Client" earlier in this chapter.

2. In the *<systemroot>*\Rpl\Bblock\Netbeui*adapter* directory, where *adapter* is the name of the adapter, copy the Dosbb.cnf file to W95bb.cnf.

3. Edit the new W95bb.cnf file to change the following line:

```
EXE BBLOCK\I13.COM ~ ~ ~
```

to read:

```
EXE BBLOCK\W95I13.COM ~ ~ ~
```

4. Use the **rplcmd** utility to add a boot block record for the new adapter. For details about the **rplcmd** utility, see the preceding section, "Using the Remoteboot Command Utility (RPLCMD.EXE)."

For example, the following sequence of commands creates a sample boot block record:

```
C:\winnt\rpl> rplcmd
Adapter Boot Config Profile Service Vendor Wksta [Quit]: b
Add Del Enum: a
BootName=W95X
VendorName=012345
BbcFile=BBLOCK\NETBEUI\dirname\W95BB.CNF
        All other parameters are optional
BootComment=Name of this adapter
WindowSize=0
```

5. If there is not already a Windows 95 configuration for this **BootName**, then use the **rplcmd** utility to add the new configuration.

For example, the following sequence of commands creates a sample configuration:

```
C:\winnt\rpl> rplcmd
Adapter Boot Config Profile Service Vendor Wksta [Quit]: c
Add Del Enum: a
ConfigName=W95X
BootName=W95X
DirName=DOS
DirName2=W95X
FitShared=fits\win95.FIT
FitPersonal=fits\win95p.FIT
        All other parameters are optional
ConfigComment=Windows 95 <adapter name>
DirName3=
DirName4=
```

For **BootName**, enter the name of the boot block record you created in step 4.

Configuring Memory for MS-DOS and Windows 3.1

Here are two tips for configuring the remoteboot client to use memory most efficiently while running MS-DOS version 5.0 or later, Windows 3.1 Setup, or Windows 3.1 itself.

Configuring EMM386.EXE

The Config.sys file contains a **device** line for Emm386.exe. This line is disabled (the line starts with REM) because you must calculate the parameters. This procedure is for a 386-based (or higher) client running MS-DOS 5.00 or later.

▶ **To configure Emm386 for more upper memory**

1. Find out how much conventional memory the client has (in decimal terms) by typing **mem** at the MS-DOS prompt.

2. Convert this number to hexadecimal format and drop the rightmost digit. To convert, you can use the **dectohex** command in the *<systemroot>*\Rpl\Rplfiles\Binfiles\Binr directory.

3. Edit the **device=Emm386.exe** line in the Config.sys file.

   ▪ Remove the **REM** designation at the beginning of the line. Check that the path specified for the file is the root (C:\) directory, not the C:\Dos directory.

   ▪ Use the remaining four digits of the hexadecimal value for the first **x=** value. (The second **x=** value is **9FFF** and should not be changed.)

   For example, if conventional memory is 598016, the hexadecimal value is 92000. In this case, use **x=9200-9FFF**.

Disabling SMARTDRV.SYS

Windows 3.1 installs a **device** command in the Config.sys file to use Smartdrv.sys. If your Windows 3.1 client seems to be operating slowly, experiment with disabling this line. Disabling Smartdrv.sys may speed the process up by giving Windows 3.1 memory on the client rather than on a disk cache.

▶ **To disable SMARTDRV.SYS**

• Disable the **device=SMARTDRV.SYS** line (precede it with **REM**) in the client's Config.sys file.

Configuring Memory for Windows 95

With Windows 95, you generally do not need to load Emm386 in the Config.sys file. When you need to exclude ranges of memory used by a network adapter card or other peripheral device, edit the System.ini file in the client's home directory. In the [386Enh] section, add a line like the following:

```
[386Enh]
EMMExclude=CC00-CFFF
```

Setting Up Local Swapping

You can increase performance on your Windows 95 and Windows 3.1 remoteboot clients by using the client's hard drive for swapping.

▶ **To set up local swapping on Windows 95 clients**

- Add a **pagingfile=***path* entry in the [386Enh] section of the System.ini file in the client's machine directory.

▶ **To set up local swapping on Windows 3.1 clients**

- Edit the **swapfile** line in the client's System.ini file to point to drive D.

Using a RAM Drive on the Client

You can optimize post-boot performance on your remoteboot clients by using a RAM drive. Use of a virtual disk, such as the Ramdrive.sys provided with most MS-DOS versions, can reduce network traffic by storing commonly used files and utilities locally. (If, however, the client does not have RAM to spare, using a virtual disk could increase swapping.)

The RAM drive should be placed first in the PATH environmental variable. Giving memory to file caches may also help performance, especially on the remoteboot server. For more information about memory management, see the documentation for the MS-DOS operating system and for the network client software.

Setting Hardware Buffers

To achieve maximum possible usage of upper memory blocks (UMBs) for MS-DOS 5.0 or later, set hardware buffers to be contiguous and as low as possible within the C000-F000 range.

By making sure that the address ranges (ROM and RAM) are as contiguous as possible, you will be able to create the largest single, free address range. This will provide more UMBs for MS-DOS than fragmenting the address ranges.

On PC/AT computers, refer to the hardware and software manuals that came with your adapters to determine the address ranges that can be set. Usually, this is done with jumpers on the adapter, but occasionally it must be changed with a setup program. Once you have determined the address ranges, arrange them to be as close together as possible without overlapping.

On PS/2 computers, you will need to run the reference disk and supply the ADF files (if they are not already on the disk) for all the adapters. Using the reference disk program, you can determine address ranges for each adapter, and then set them.

Directory, File Index, and Configuration File Details

The following sections describe the structure of the RPL directory and the formats of remoteboot configuration files.

The RPL Directory

The following illustration shows the subdirectories created in the *<systemroot>*\Rpl directory when you install the Remoteboot service.

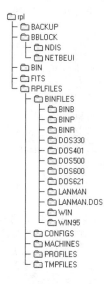

```
rpl
├── BACKUP
├── BBLOCK
│   ├── NDIS
│   └── NETBEUI
├── BIN
├── FITS
└── RPLFILES
    ├── BINFILES
    │   ├── BINB
    │   ├── BINP
    │   ├── BINR
    │   ├── DOS330
    │   ├── DOS401
    │   ├── DOS500
    │   ├── DOS600
    │   ├── DOS621
    │   ├── LANMAN
    │   ├── LANMAN.DOS
    │   ├── WIN
    │   └── WIN95
    ├── CONFIGS
    ├── MACHINES
    ├── PROFILES
    └── TMPFILES
```

Directories that are automatically installed should not be deleted (for example, do not delete C:\Tmp from a remoteboot client). If a directory is deleted, you must recreate it and set the permissions with the Remoteboot Manager **Fix Security** command, or you can use Remoteboot Manager to delete the affected workstation record and recreate it (after first saving any client-specific files).

In the *<systemroot>*\Rpl directory, the System.mdb and Rplsvc.mdb files contain the remoteboot database. The Jet.log file contains information used in recovery from power failures or other catastrophic interruptions.

File Index Tables

File index tables (or FIT files) are ASCII files containing filename lookup tables that enable file translation. Remoteboot client software translates a directory name or filename typed by the client user into the true directory name or filename on the server. In general, the client translates references of the form C:\... to *servername*\Rplfiles\... (that is, to locations in the *<systemroot>*\Rpl\Rplfiles directory on the server).

Windows 95 clients use a .fit file only in the early stages of their boot process. Once the client is running Windows 95, it uses storage defined by the SBS server and machine directory server.

File translation pairs consist of a prototype filename or prefix, followed by a space, and an actual filename or prefix, relative to the directory named on the first line [usually (Rplfiles)]. If the prototype matches a proper prefix of the name to be matched, the matched portion is replaced by the actual prefix. If there is an exact match (not just a prefix), the actual filename is substituted. If several prefixes match, the longest one is selected for substitution. A network path of the form *any_servername**sharename* may be included in the actual filename or prefix, in which case it overrides the directory listed on line one.

Examples:

- If the client requests access to C:\Win386.swp (for example, to open it for writing), the client software will use the .fit file to translate it into:

  `\\servername\RPLFILES\TMPFILES\(CNAME)\SWAPFILE.DAT`

  where (CNAME) is the client name.

- If C:\Config.sys is requested, the following will be used because it has the longest matching prefix (C:\):

  `\\servername\RPLFILES\PROFILES\(PROFILE)\CONFIG.SYS`

  where (PROFILE) is the profile name. The line near the top of each .fit file that starts with C:\ sends all C:\ references that aren't at least partially matched by other lines to the directory *servername*\Rplfiles\Profiles\(Profile).

Note that the "machine writeable files" section of each .fit file lists the files and directories to which the user has write access.

By convention there are usually two .fit files for each profile: one to be used when sharing the profile and one to be used with personal copies of the profile. For example, Dos622.fit is for clients that share the Dos622 profile, and Dos622p.fit is for personal copies of the Dos622 profile. The file format is the same, but the personal profile .fit translates most references to directories specific to the client rather than to directories shared with other clients. The .fit file used for Windows 95 clients has no differences between the shared and personal versions.

Fields in .fit files are separated with white space. The maximum line length is 512 characters. A comment line has a semicolon (;) as the first non-space character.

The following keywords have special meaning in a .fit file:

- **(PROFILE)** is the name of the profile assigned to this client.
- **(CNAME)** is the name of the client.
- **(RPLFILES)** is the *<systemroot>*\Rpl\Rplfiles directory, shared by the server with the sharename Rplfiiles.
- **(BINFILES)** is a directory for executable files. It is assumed to be relative to Rplfiles (\Rpl\Rplfiles\Binfiles).
- **(TMPFILES)** is a directory for temporary and swap files. It is assumed to be relative to Rplfiles (*<systemroot>*\Rpl\Rplfiles\Tmpfiles).

Boot Block Configuration Files

The boot block configuration file specifies the contents of the boot block sent to the client by the Remoteboot service and is designated by the .cnf extension. The boot block normally includes the Rplboot.sys, Rplstart.com, and Rpldisk.sys files and the real-mode network drivers. The boot block also contains some client-specific data (a copy of the workstation record from the remoteboot database) and some profile-specific data (the .fit file associated with the profile used).

A line in a .cnf file typically has three fields:

- Type
- Filename (path is relative to the *<systemroot>*\Rpl directory)
- Parameter(s)

All valid types are listed next, along with their expected filenames and parameters.

Fields in .cnf files are separated with white space. Spaces within a field are represented with a tilde (~). The maximum line length is 512 characters. A comment line has a semicolon (;) as the first non-space character.

Note The DRV and EXE types of boot block configuration files must be specified in the reverse order in which they would normally occur in a Config.sys file. For example, if ABC.DRV must appear before DEF.EXE in Config.sys, DEF.EXE must appear before ABC.DRV in the .cnf file.

RPL Type

The filename specified with the RPL type is the initialization program that runs on a client. There must be exactly one RPL type in a .cnf file. The initialization program is normally Rplboot.sys.

BASE Type

The value specified with the BASE type is a hexadecimal segment number that identifies the base address of the boot block. There can be only one BASE type in a .cnf file. If none is specified, **00C0h** is used as the default base address.

DAT Type

Files listed with the DAT type specify data files that should be stored on the boot block. The filename is relative to <*systemroot*>\Rpl.

LDR Type

The filename and parameters listed with the LDR type specify which loader to use on the client. The loader is the program that Rplboot.sys will pass control to; there can be only one LDR keyword. The loader is normally Rplstart.com.

DRV Type

The filename and parameters listed with the DRV type specify the device drivers used to form the boot block. The filename field specifies the name of the device driver. The DRV type has three parameter fields:

- The first field specifies parameters used by the device driver.
- The second field specifies any additional memory used by the device driver (in decimal kilobytes).
- The third field is **M** if the device driver can be moved in memory to reuse space that it doesn't need; it is ~ if the device driver cannot be moved.

   If the driver can be moved after initialization and its memory requirements are less than for the original driver image, Rplboot.sys moves the driver to reclaim some of the unused memory and adjusts all interrupt vectors that point into the driver's memory area. Some drivers cannot be moved because they record segment addresses that are correct during initialization but not after the driver has been moved.

EXE Type

Files listed with the EXE type specify executables (.exe and .com files) that are run during the boot process. The filename is the name of the executable, and the parameters field specifies arguments passed to the executable. EXE lines must be specified in reverse order—that is, the last one listed in the boot block configuration file will be the first one executed.

Supporting Multiple Network Adapters and Protocols

The method of supporting multiple network adapters or multiple protocols depends on whether the client runs Windows 95 or MS-DOS/Windows 3.1.

Using Multiple Network Adapters and Protocols with Windows 95

If the client has multiple network adapters, only one should have a RPL ROM. When you configure the client's workstation record in Remoteboot Manager, specify a profile corresponding to the network adapter with the RPL ROM.

You need NetBEUI and DLC connectivity to the remoteboot server in order to set up and boot a Windows 95 client. The network adapters and protocols defined in Windows 95 Setup become active once the Windows 95 real-mode client is booted. You no longer need NetBEUI or DLC at this phase, as long as you can access the SBS server and the shared directory containing your machine directory.

Using Multiple Network Adapters with MS-DOS and Windows 3.1

If a remoteboot MS-DOS or Windows 3.1 client computer has multiple network adapters, you will need to modify the boot block information for the adapter that has the RPL ROM chip.

▶ **To modify the boot block information**

1. Using Remoteboot Manager, create a new profile.

2. Add the network adapter driver to the *<systemroot>*\Rpl\Bblock\Netbeui*adapter*\Dosbb.cnf boot block configuration files, where *adapter* is the name of the adapter that has the RPL ROM chip on the client computer.

3. Update the *<systemroot>*\Rpl\Bblock\Netbeui*adapter*\Protocol.ini file with sections for the new network adapter driver.

Using Multiple Protocols with MS-DOS and Windows 3.1

A remoteboot MS-DOS or Windows 3.1 client always runs the NetBEUI protocol. This section describes how to install support for TCP/IP, DLC, and IPX protocols for use by remoteboot clients.

Installing TCP/IP Support

Before you set up clients to use TCP/IP, you must either enable DHCP to assign addresses automatically, or you must assign IP addresses and subnet masks for each client that will use TCP/IP. (See the *Windows NT Server TCP/IP* manual for more information about TCP/IP addresses.)

When you have arranged for addresses, you can then enable TCP/IP support.

▶ **To enable TCP/IP support**

1. Edit the *<systemroot>*\Rpl\Bblock\Netbeui*adapter*\Dosbb.cnf file, where *adapter* is the name of the network adapter. Remove the semicolon (;) in column one of this line:

   ```
   ;DRV    BBLOCK\TCPDRV.DOS /I:C:\LANMAN.DOS ~ ~
   ```

2. For each profile (or personal copy of a profile) that will support TCP/IP, edit the following files as described:

   - In *<systemroot>*\Rpl\Rplfiles\Profiles*profile*\Autoexec.bat, where *profile* is the name of the profile, enable **umb.com**, **nmstr**, and **load tcpip** by removing the **REM** designations at the beginnings of those lines.

   - In *<systemroot>*\Rpl\Rplfiles\Profiles*profile*\Config.sys, where *profile* is the name of the profile, enable **nemm.dos** by removing the **REM** designation at the beginning of that line.

3. Boot a client using one of the profiles altered in the last step.

Installing MS-DLC Support

▶ **To install MS-DLC support**

- At the client, type **load msdlc**.

  Or, add this command to the end of the client's Autoexec.bat file.

Installing IPX Support

When you install IPX support, you will need the Microsoft Network Client version 2.2 NetWare Connectivity disk and the Novell NetWare SHGEN-1 and SHGEN-2 disks (or the WSGEN disk).

Note IPX support is installed per adapter and is MS-DOS version specific. Follow the installation procedure for each adapter that will support IPX; define profiles for each version of MS-DOS that will support IPX.

▶ **To install IPX support**

1. On the server, edit the *<systemroot>*\Rpl\Bblock\Netbeui*adapter*\Dosbb.cnf file, where *adapter* is the name of the network adapter. Remove the semicolon (;) in column one of this line:

```
;DRV    BBLOCK\IPXNDIS.DOS ~ ~ ~
```

2. Create a new profile with a name that describes IPX support (for example, DOS62IPX).

Note IPX is MS-DOS version specific. You must create a separate profile for each version of MS-DOS that will support IPX.

---

3. Assign a client to the new profile.

4. Boot the client.

   At the remoteboot logon prompt (the prompt that first appears when you start the client), supply the name and password of an account that is a member of the Administrators group on the Windows NT Server computer.

5. If the client does not have a floppy disk drive, use the floppy disk drive of a server on the network:

   ▪ First, at the server (it doesn't have to be the remoteboot server), use File Manager or the **net share** command to share the server's floppy disk drive.

   ▪ Then, at the client, use File Manager or the **net use** command to connect to the shared floppy disk drive.

6. Put the Microsoft Network Client NetWare Connectivity disk in the floppy disk drive.

7. On the client, run the NetWare Connectivity Setup program by typing **a:nwsetup** (use a different drive letter if needed).

   When prompted, insert the Novell NetWare SHGEN-1 and SHGEN-2 disks (or the WSGEN disk).

8. Reboot the client.

   Supply the client password (if any).

9. Log on to the client with a normal user account.

10. To start using the IPX protocol, type **nwload**. Or, add this command to the end of the client's Autoexec/bat file.

    IPX is now installed on the client's profile and is available for use by other clients using this profile.

Backing Up the Remoteboot Database

The remoteboot database holds the configuration, workstation, and profile records and other data for the Remoteboot service. You should back up the database before and after you make significant changes and save the copies. The Remoteboot service automatically backs up the database every 24 hours (counting from when you start the service).

Because the Remoteboot service makes automatic backups (overwriting the current backup copies), and for good administrative procedure, you should occasionally archive copies of the backup files.

▶ **To back up the remoteboot database**

- On the **Configure** menu of Remoteboot Manager, click **Backup Database**.

The Jet.log, Rplsvc.mdb, and System.mdb files are backed up to the <*systemroot*>\Rpl\Backup directory.

▶ **To restore a backup copy of the remoteboot database**

- Copy the files from <*systemroot*>\Rpl\Backup (or other saved versions of the files) to the Rpl directory.

In the event of an emergency (such as a corrupted database), the Remoteboot service restores automatically from the <*systemroot*>\Rpl\Backup directory.

Troubleshooting Remoteboot

This section lists some common problems you may encounter using the Remoteboot service. For more troubleshooting information, see the \CLIENTS\RPL\README.TXT file on the Windows NT Server compact disc.

Remoteboot Service Won't Start

Check the server's event log, which can provide useful diagnostic information. In the **Administrative Tools** group, select **Event Viewer**.

Remoteboot Manager Won't Start

Be sure that you are logged on using an account that is a member of the Administrators local group.

Remoteboot Service Stops

Be sure that the server's own network configuration is correct, including hardware settings for the network adapter.

Remoteboot Client Won't Start

If a client won't boot remotely, or if you're having problems with the way the client is booting:

- Be sure that the server is running and that the Remoteboot service is running.

- The client must be on the same subnet as the server.

- Check Remoteboot Manager's list of adapters that have not yet been converted to workstation records. To update the list, choose **Refresh** from the **View** menu. If the client's adapter is on the list, convert the adapter record to a workstation record.

- Check the <systemroot>\Rpl\Fits directory. The server must have a .fit file for each profile that is to boot remotely.

- Each client must have an RPL ROM chip installed on or built into its network adapter. This ROM chip may need to be enabled via jumpers or a configuration program.

- Check the defaults for hardware settings in the <*systemroot*>\Rpl\Bblock\Netbeui*adapter*\Protocol.ini file.

- If the client has a hard disk, the hard disk may need to be prepared for the Remoteboot service using the **rplenabl** utility.

- If the remoteboot server is a backup domain controller, wait until the account you've added has been replicated (or force synchronization to the primary domain controller using Server Manager).

No Profiles Available

You have not yet created any profiles. See "Managing Profiles" earlier in this chapter.

No Configurations Available

On the Remoteboot Manager **Configure** menu, click **Check Configurations**. If there still are no configurations available, you have not yet copied MS-DOS files to the server. See "Installing MS-DOS Files on the Remoteboot Server" earlier in this chapter.

C H A P T E R   1 6

Microsoft Network Client Version 3.0 for MS-DOS

This chapter tells how to install and use Microsoft Network Client version 3.0 for MS-DOS. Network Client is software that you install on a computer running the MS-DOS operating system so that the computer can use resources on a network. For example, a computer with Network Client can use printers, programs, and data stored on a computer running Windows NT Server.

With Network Client, your computer can use resources on Microsoft networks, as well as other networks such as Microsoft LAN Manager networks.

In addition, if the computer had Novell NetWare installed before you install Network Client, you can still connect to NetWare resources (in addition to Microsoft network resources). For more information, see the Readme.txt file located in the directory that contains the Network Client files.

Making Installation Disks

A network administrator makes installation disks using the Network Client Administrator on a computer running Windows NT Server. For details, see Chapter 11, "Managing Client Administration," in the *Windows NT Server Concepts and Planning Guide*.

There are two kinds of Network Client installation disks:

- An *installation disk set* contains all of the Network Client software. For Network Client 3.0, this is just one disk. You install manually using only this disk.

- A *network installation startup disk* contains basic MS-DOS and Network Client software, just enough to start a client computer and then copy the full Network Client software over the network from the computer running Windows NT Server. This is usually faster than installing manually.

Setting Up and Configuring Network Client

The Setup program for Network Client identifies the computer's hardware and software, configures Network Client to run on the computer, and copies necessary files to the computer's hard disk.

Before you set up Network Client, you need to determine the following:

- The user name to be used

  The user name identifies a member of the workgroup or domain. Choose a unique name in the workgroup or domain.

- The name to be assigned to the computer

  This unique name identifies the computer within the network. Often this name is a variation of the user name.

- The name of the user's workgroup and/or domain

  This name determines how your computer fits in with other computers that are already organized into groups on the network. These are not names that you make up; they already exist on the network. Ask the network administrator if you don't know what names to use.

- Full redirector or basic redirector

  Full redirector means that you have all Network Client functions available, including logging on to domains and using advanced network applications. You can choose the basic redirector instead, which uses less memory and disk space, if you need only standard workgroup functions like connecting to shared files and printers.

  To use Microsoft Windows with Network Client, you must install the full redirector, and you must start it with the **net start full** command before starting Windows. Windows for Workgroups, Windows 95, and the Windows NT platform include their own network client capabilities, so you should not run Network Client with them.

  If you will also use the Remote Access Service (RAS) to connect to a network over a phone line, you must install the full redirector.

- The manufacturer and model of the network adapter

  The Setup program attempts to determine the model of network adapter in the computer. Some network adapters have additional configuration options; see the network administrator or the network adapter documentation if you need to change configuration options.

- The network protocol used on this network

  Your computer must use the same protocol as the computers to which it connects. If you don't know what protocol the computers on your network use, ask the network administrator.

There are other options that you can change with the Setup program, but these are the most important options.

▶ **To set up Network Client**

1. Depending on the type of installation disk you have:

   - For an installation disk set (all Network Client software is on the disk), put the disk in a floppy disk drive. If you put the disk in drive A, type **a:\setup** at the MS-DOS command prompt, and then press ENTER. If the floppy disk drive is a different letter, use that letter instead of **a**.

     If the computer displays an error message about lack of memory, you may need to stop other programs that take up memory, by stopping the programs or by altering the Autoexec.bat file and restarting the computer.

   - For a network installation startup disk, put the disk in drive A and restart the computer. When the computer restarts, it will automatically run the Network Client installation program.

     A prompt appears asking you for a username and password. Supply a username and password for an account with permission to connect to the directory on the computer running Windows NT Server where Network Client files are stored. When the computer displays a message about creating a password-list file, type **n** and then press ENTER.

     The client must make a connection to the shared directory on the computer running Windows NT Server. If the computer displays an error message saying that "the specified shared directory cannot be found," check that the computer running Windows NT Server is indeed sharing the directory.

     If the computer displays an error message about lack of memory, modify the Config.sys file on the network installation startup disk to use extended memory. For example, Emm386.exe and Himem.sys provide extended memory for MS-DOS 5.0 and later. If you do not have extended memory, use the NetBEUI or IPX protocols because they use less memory.

     The network installation startup disk was configured using default settings for the network adapter. Please verify that the default settings are correct for your network adapter and modify them if necessary. (The settings are in the A:\Net\protocol.ini file.)

2. Follow the instructions of the Setup program.

   If your network adapter does not appear in the list of supported network adapters, you may be able to use one of the following instead:

   - ArcNet-compatible for an ArcNet network adapter

   - NE1000-compatible for an 8-bit Ethernet network adapter that is not on the list

   - NE2000-compatible for a 16-bit Ethernet network adapter that is not on the list

   If this still doesn't work, contact the network adapter manufacturer to obtain a device driver disk compatible with Microsoft Network Client. When you receive the driver disk, run **Setup** and choose **Network Adapter Not Shown On List Below**, and then follow the instructions.

   If you need more information about any Setup dialog box, press F1 for Help.

The Network Client Setup program identifies the hardware on the computer, copies the Network Client files to the hard disk, and creates and modifies network configuration files. The Setup program creates System.ini and Protocol.ini files in the directory that contains the Network Client files. These files contain information about the computer's Network Client configuration.

Setup adds a **device** command to the Config.sys file to install the Ifshlp.sys device driver.

In the Autoexec.bat file, Setup adds to the **path** command the directory that contains the Network Client files. Also, if you specify that you want Network Client to start each time the computer is started, Setup adds the **net start** command. When **net start** runs, it examines the System.ini file, which contains information about the startup options you specified during Setup. Setup may add additional lines to the Autoexec.bat file to start programs needed for specific network protocols.

The changes Setup makes to the configuration files take effect when you restart the computer after the Setup program is finished.

If your startup information changes, you can update your configuration information by running Setup again. For example, you might change your workgroup name or network card.

▶ **To update a setting after you install Network Client**

1. Change to the directory that contains your installed Network Client files, and then type **setup** at the command prompt.

   Do not run the Setup.exe program that is on the installation disk.

   If the computer displays an error message about lack of memory, use the **net stop rdr** command to stop the Network Client software before running Setup. You may need to stop other programs that take up memory by stopping the programs or by altering the Autoexec.bat file and restarting the computer. After running Setup, either restart the computer or, if you didn't change any settings, restart Network Client by typing **net start rdr**.

2. Examine the list that the Network Client Setup program displays to find the entries that you want to change. If a setting needs to be updated, press the UP ARROW key until you select that setting, and then press ENTER.

3. Follow the instructions on your screen. If you need help at any time, press F1.

Using Network Client with the TCP/IP Protocol

The MS-DOS TCP/IP implementation for Microsoft Network Client version 3.0 for MS-DOS supports:

- An MS-DOS-based interface.
- Domain name resolver (DNR) to resolve hostname-to-IP address mappings if your network has a Domain Name System (DNS) server.
- The Dynamic Host Configuration Protocol (DHCP).
- Windows Internet Name Service (WINS) resolution.
- Windows Sockets.

MS-DOS-based clients do not support following features which are provided by TCP/IP-32 for Windows for Workgroups version 3.11, TCP/IP for Windows 95, and Windows NT Workstation and Windows NT Server versions 3.5, 3.51, and 4.0:

- Support for DNS resolution using WINS
- Support for WINS resolution using DNS
- Name registration with the WINS database. (MS-DOS-based computers are clients, not servers, and do not generally need registration.)
- Ability to act as a WINS proxy node
- Support for multiple network adapters

- Support for Internet Group Management Protocol (IGMP).
- DHCP command-line switches for Ipconfig.exe (use the DHCP Administration utility instead). Specifically, Ipconfig.exe does not support the following switches, which are available in the Ipconfig.exe utilities for Windows for Workgroups and the Windows NT platform:
  - IPCONFIG /release
  - IPCONFIG /renew
  - IPCONFIG /?
  - IPCONFIG /all

Getting Help

MS-DOS users can carry out Network Client commands in two ways: by using the pop-up interface or by typing commands at the MS-DOS command prompt. For information on using the pop-up interface, see the section "Using Network Client" later in this chapter. For both methods, Help is available for quick information about specific Network Client commands or features.

▶ **To get help for commands typed at the MS-DOS command prompt**

- Type the command name followed by **/?**, or type **net help** followed by the second word in the **net** command.

  For example, for information about the **net view** command, at the MS-DOS command prompt type **net view /?** or type **net help view**.

▶ **To get a summary of all Network Client commands**

- At the MS-DOS command prompt, type **net /? | more** and press ENTER.

▶ **To get help while using the pop-up interface**

- Press F1 or ALT+H.

Starting Network Client and Logging On

During Setup, you specify whether you want Network Client to start automatically every time the computer is started. You also specify whether a prompt appears to log on to the workgroup and/or to a domain at startup time. The default settings are to automatically start Network Client and prompt for logon each time the computer is started.

If you specify in Setup that Network Client should not start automatically, the user must start it.

▶   **To start Network Client and log on to the workgroup**

1. At the MS-DOS command prompt, type **net logon** and press ENTER.

2. If Network Client hasn't started, a prompt asks whether to start the workstation service. Type **y** and then press ENTER.

3. If the prompt displaying the user name is correct, press ENTER.

   If you are logging on at someone else's computer, type your user name, and then press ENTER.

4. At the prompt for a password, type your password, and then press ENTER.

   If you are logging on for the first time, you can specify any password up to 14 characters long. A prompt asks you to type your password again to confirm that it is correct. This is your workgroup password.

5. If you are logging on for the first time, and the computer is in a Windows NT Server domain, a prompt for the domain password appears. Type your domain password and press ENTER.

After you type your password(s), Network Client reestablishes your *persistent connections*, if you have any. These are connections that you made before and specified that you want to have reestablished every time you log on to your workgroup. For more information, see the Help for **net use**.

Your workgroup password authorizes access to your password list file, which is a list of the passwords for connections made that are password-protected. If you do maintain a password list file, and you do log on to a domain, the password list file will also hold your domain password. For more information about the password list file and how to change your password, see the Help for **net password**.

If you have trouble starting or using Network Client, see the "Troubleshooting" section later in this chapter.

Using Network Client

MS-DOS users can issue Network Client commands by using the pop-up interface or by typing commands at the MS-DOS command prompt.

If you use the pop-up interface, you don't have to remember the syntax for the equivalent Network Client command at the MS-DOS command prompt. The pop-up interface also allows you to view your current connections, browse for shared resources, and make new connections in an easy-to-use environment. It is a character-based utility; you must use the keyboard rather than a mouse.

Experienced MS-DOS users who are familiar with Network Client commands may prefer to type commands at the MS-DOS command prompt rather than using the pop-up interface.

Loading and Displaying the Pop-up Interface

You can load and display the pop-up interface simultaneously or as two separate operations. Loading and displaying the pop-up interface simultaneously is easier than performing the operations separately, and it makes more efficient use of memory. You load and display the interface by typing a single command. When you finish using the interface, Network Client unloads it from memory, freeing about 29K of memory for programs. The disadvantage is that you cannot use the interface while using another program.

▶ **To load and display the pop-up interface simultaneously**

1. At the MS-DOS command prompt, type **net** and press ENTER.

   The pop-up interface appears.

2. When you finish using the interface, press ESC. Network Client unloads the interface from memory.

The advantage of loading and displaying the pop-up interface separately is that you can display it at any time, either from the MS-DOS command prompt or while you are using another program. One disadvantage is that you need to use separate commands to load, display, and unload the interface. Also, the pop-up interface occupies about 29K of memory, whether you are using it or not, until you explicitly unload it from memory.

▶ **To load and display the pop-up interface separately**

1. At the MS-DOS command prompt, type **net start popup** and press ENTER.

   Note If the pop-up interface is loaded into memory automatically when you start the computer, skip this step.

   ---

2. When you want to display the pop-up interface, press CTRL+ALT+N.

   If, during Setup, you chose a key other than N to display the pop-up interface, press CTRL+ALT plus the key you specified.

When you finish using the pop-up interface, you can unload it from memory.

▶ **To unload the pop-up interface from memory**

- At the MS-DOS command prompt, type **net stop popup** and press ENTER.

Using Shared Directories

With Network Client, members of your workgroup can exchange information using shared directories. Shared directories are directories to which all users on a network have access. You use shared directories the same way you use the directories on your local hard disk, except that you have to connect to shared directories before you can use the files on them.

To use a file in a shared directory, you need to know the name of the computer that contains the shared directory and the name of the shared directory that contains the file you want. After you establish a connection, you treat the shared directory as if it were a disk drive on your computer.

You connect to a shared directory by assigning a drive letter to it.

▶ **To connect your computer to a shared directory**

1. Display the pop-up interface as described in the preceding section.
2. In the Path field of the Disk Connection pop-up, type two backslashes, the name of the computer, and the shared directory that you want to connect to.

   For example, to connect to a directory named Public on a computer named Rene, type **\\rene\public** in the Path field.

   If you're not sure of the name of the computer or directory you want to connect to, you can browse through a list by choosing the Browse button (press ALT+B, and then press F1 for help). Browsing will show you only the computers in your workgroup.
3. To assign a drive letter to the shared directory, choose the Drive field by pressing ALT+V, type the drive letter you want to use, and then press ENTER.

   If you do not specify a drive letter for the shared directory, Network Client assigns the first available drive letter.
4. If you want to connect your computer to the shared directory every time you log on, make sure an X appears in the Reconnect At Startup check box.

   To select or clear the Reconnect At Startup check box, press ALT+R.
5. To connect to the shared directory specified in the Path field, choose the Connect button by pressing ALT+C.

You can also connect to a shared directory by typing **net use** at the MS-DOS command prompt. For information on the **net use** command and its syntax, see the Help for **net use**.

For information about browsing for shared directories and disconnecting from a shared directory, press F1 in the pop-up interface, or see the Help for the **net view** and **net use** commands.

Note Your workgroup may include computers that share directories but do not appear in the **Browse** dialog box. You can try connecting to these computers, even though you cannot browse for their names.

Using Shared Printers

You can print files with Network Client by sending them from your computer to printers that are shared by members of your workgroup. Connecting to a shared printer allows you to use it as if it were physically connected to your computer. You connect your computer to a shared printer by assigning a parallel port (LPT) to it. You can use port LPT1, LPT2, or LPT3.

▶ **To connect your computer to a shared printer**

1. Display the pop-up interface, as described earlier in this chapter.

2. Choose the **Show Printers** button by pressing ALT+S.

3. In the Port field of the **Printer Connection** dialog box, type two backslashes and the number of the parallel port (LPT) that you want to assign to the shared printer, and then press TAB.

4. In the Path field, type the name of the computer and shared printer that you want to connect to. For example, to connect to a printer named Laser that is physically connected to a computer named Clive, type **\\clive\laser** in the Path field.

5. If you want to connect your computer to this printer every time you log on to your workgroup, make sure an X appears in the **Reconnect At Startup** check box.

   To select or clear the **Reconnect At Startup** check box, press ALT+R.

6. To connect to the shared printer specified in the Path field, choose the **Connect** button by pressing ALT+C.

You can also issue the **net use** command at the MS-DOS command prompt to connect to a shared printer. For information on the **net use** command and its syntax, see the Help for **net use**.

For information about browsing for shared printers and disconnecting from a shared printer, press F1 in the pop-up interface, or see the Help for the **net view** and **net use** commands.

Note Your workgroup may include computers that share printers but do not appear in the **Browse** dialog box. You can try connecting to these computers, even though you cannot browse for their names.

After you connect your computer to a shared printer, you can print formatted files from the application you used to create them. You can also print unformatted text files from MS-DOS with the **print** command. For more information, see the Help for the **print** command.

You can also display the pop-up interface to pause, resume, or delete a print job, and to view the print queue, which is the list of files that are waiting to print on a particular printer. For information, see the Help for the pop-up interface or for the **net print** command.

Using Network Client with Microsoft Windows

This section contains information about configuring Microsoft Windows so that it runs with Network Client.

Note Windows for Workgroups, Windows 95, and Windows NT include their own network client capabilities, so you should not run Network Client with them.

To use Microsoft Windows with Network Client, you must install the full redirector, and you must start it with the **net start full** command before starting Windows.

▶ **To configure Windows to run with Network Client**

1. Start Windows.

2. In the **Main** group, choose the **Windows Setup** icon.

   The **Windows Setup** window appears. It lists your current display, keyboard, mouse, and network settings.

3. From the **Options** menu, choose **Change System Settings**.

   The **Change System Settings** dialog box appears.

4. Open the list for the **Network** setting by clicking the arrow to the right of it. Or press TAB until you select the **Network** setting, and then press ALT+DOWN ARROW to open the list.

5. Click **Microsoft** Network (or 100% compatible), or select it by pressing the UP ARROW or DOWN ARROW key.

6. Click **OK**.

   Setup may prompt you to insert a Windows Setup disk in drive A. If it does, insert the disk. However, if the file for the Microsoft Network device driver is in a directory on your hard disk, you can type its path in the box instead.

7. Choose the OK button.

Troubleshooting

This section provides help if you encounter problems when using Network Client.

Network Client Will Not Start After a Successful Setup

If Network Client won't start after you complete Setup, try the following steps to solve the problem:

- Make sure that all cables and connectors are securely fastened and that the network adapter is securely in its slot.

- If the network adapter came with a diagnostics program, try running the program. For more information, see the documentation that came with the network adapter.

- Run the **net diag** command. You can use **net diag** to test a specific connection with another computer or you can use **net diag /status** to see the status of your own network adapter. For information, type **net help diag** at the MS-DOS command prompt.

- If you are using an external transceiver, specify the correct setting. For more information, see the following section, "Specifying an External Transceiver."

- Make sure the correct base memory address and interrupt request (IRQ) settings are specified for the network adapter. For more information, see "Checking and Changing Network-Adapter Settings," later in this chapter.

- Make sure the **device** command for EMM386 in your Config.sys file excludes the memory address used by your network adapter. For more information, see "Making Sure EMM386 Doesn't Conflict with the Network Adapter," later in this chapter.

- Make sure the network adapter is on the list provided in Setup. If your network adapter is not on this list, you might be able to get it to work by using a generic setting. For more information, see the Setup instructions earlier in this chapter.

- Make sure the network adapter is using a different interrupt (IRQ) than the mouse. For more information about determining what interrupt to assign to the network adapter, see the documentation that came with the network adapter.

- If you are using the NWLink (IPX/SPX-compatible) protocol, make sure the network adapter is set for the proper network topology type. NWLink supports Ethernet network adapters only on 802.2 topology and token ring and FDDI network adapters only on 802.3 topology.

- You might need to change the network adapter's configuration settings. If you have an ISA adapter that is configured by using jumpers and switches, you might need to change their positions or settings. If you have a software-configured adapter, use the configuration program that came with the network adapter to change your settings. For more information, see the documentation that came with the network adapter.

Specifying an External Transceiver

This section applies to you only if your network adapter is attached to an *external transceiver*. An external transceiver is a small box that connects the network cable to the cable that attaches to a network adapter. Only some Ethernet network adapters use external transceivers.

▶ **To specify that you are using an external transceiver**

1. Start the Network Client Setup program, as described in the section "Setting Up and Configuring Network Client" earlier in this chapter.

2. Select Change Network Configuration by pressing the UP ARROW key, and then press ENTER.

   A list of options for modifying network-adapter and protocol settings appears.

3. Select Change Settings by pressing the UP ARROW key, and then press ENTER.

   A list of network-adapter and protocol settings appears.

4. Press the UP ARROW key until you have selected the Transceiver setting, and then press ENTER.

   A list of values appears.

5. From the list of values, select External, Thick, or DIX (depending on what kind of transceiver you have) by pressing the UP ARROW or DOWN ARROW key. Then press ENTER.

   The new value appears on the Transceiver line in the list of network-adapter settings.

6. Press ENTER, and then follow the instructions on the screen to complete Setup.

7. When Setup is complete, restart the computer by pressing ENTER.

   If Network Client still does not start, proceed to the following section.

Checking and Changing Network-Adapter Settings

The Network Client Setup program examines your computer's configuration and attempts to determine the network adapter's base memory address and interrupt request (IRQ) setting. If Setup incorrectly identifies these, Network Client will not start.

For information about determining the correct settings yourself, see the documentation that came with the network adapter.

After you determine the correct base memory address and interrupt setting, you can specify them by running Setup again.

▶ **To change the base memory address or interrupt setting**

1. Start the Network Client Setup program, as described earlier in this chapter.

2. Select Change Network Configuration by pressing the UP ARROW key, and then press ENTER.

   A list of options for modifying network-adapter and protocol settings appears.

3. Select Change Settings by pressing the UP ARROW key, and then press ENTER.

   A list of network-adapter and protocol settings appears.

4. If you want to change the setting for the network adapter's interrupt, proceed to step 5. If you want to change the setting for the network adapter's base memory address, do the following:

    ▪ Select the setting for the base memory address by pressing the UP ARROW key, and then press ENTER. This setting is named Memory Window, RAM Address, or something similar. You might have to press the PAGE UP or PAGE DOWN key to find this setting.

       A list of values appears.

    ▪ Select the base memory address you want by pressing the UP ARROW or DOWN ARROW key, and then press ENTER.

       The new value appears on the base memory address line in the list of network-adapter settings.

5. If you do not want to change the network adapter's interrupt setting, proceed to step 6. If you want to change the setting, do the following:

    ▪ Select the interrupt setting by pressing the UP ARROW key, and then press ENTER. This setting is named IRQ_Level, Interrupt, or something similar. You might have to press the PAGE UP or PAGE DOWN key to find this setting.

       A list of values appears.

    ▪ Select the interrupt you want by pressing the UP ARROW or DOWN ARROW key, and then press ENTER.

       The new value appears on the interrupt line in the list of network-adapter settings.

6. Choose The Listed Options Are Correct by pressing ENTER. Then follow the instructions on the screen to complete Setup.

7. When Setup is complete, restart the computer by pressing ENTER.

If Network Client still does not start, proceed to the following section.

Making Sure EMM386 Doesn't Conflict with the Network Adapter

If you use the EMM386 memory manager, make sure that it does not use the same memory that the network adapter uses. If you are using a different memory manager, such as QEMM or 386MAX, see the documentation that came with that memory manager.

▶   **To ensure that EMM386 doesn't conflict with the network adapter**

1. Use any text editor to open the Config.sys file.

2. Look for the **device** command line for the EMM386 memory manager. It should look similar to the following:

   ```
   device=c:\dos\emm386.exe
   ```

   If the Config.sys file does not contain a **device** command for EMM386, you are not using EMM386.

3. If the Config.sys file contains a **device** command for EMM386, add the following to that command line:

   x=*mmmm-nnnn*

   For *mmmm*, specify the base memory address of your network adapter. For *nnnn*, specify a value that is 32K greater than *mmmm* by using the following method:

   If the second character in *mmmm* is 8, the last three characters you specify for *nnnn* should be FFF. For example, if the base memory address is D800, the **device** command line should look similar to the following:

   ```
   device=c:\dos\emm386.exe x=D800-DFFF
   ```

   If the second character in *mmmm* is 0, the last three characters you specify for *nnnn* should be 7FF. For example, if the base memory address is C000, the **device** command line should look similar to the following:

   ```
   device=c:\dos\emm386.exe x=C000-C7FF
   ```

Note This method for determining the value for *nnnn* is based on a network-adapter device driver that uses 32K of memory. The values for *mmmm* and *nnnn* are hexadecimal numbers. Check your network-adapter documentation to see if the network adapter uses more or less than 32K of memory. If it does, adjust the value for *nnnn* accordingly. For example, if the adapter uses only 16K of memory, the characters to specify for *nnnn* in the preceding two examples would be DBFF and C3FF, respectively.

---

4. Save the Config.sys file, and then quit the text editor.

5. Restart the computer.

Shared Resources Are Not Listed

If the names of shared resources do not appear when you use the **Browse** dialog box in the pop-up interface or when you type **net view** at the MS-DOS command prompt, try the following:

- Make sure the network-adapter settings are correct. For more information, see "Specifying an External Transceiver" and "Checking and Changing Network-Adapter Settings," earlier in this section.

- Sometimes, when a computer in your workgroup is turned off or restarted, you won't be able to see other computers on the network for a few minutes. Wait a few minutes, and then check again.

- If you know the name of the shared directory or printer you want to connect to, try connecting to it by typing the path of the shared directory or printer in the Path field of the **Disk Connections** or **Printer Connections** dialog boxes. Or specify the path by using the **net use** command at the MS-DOS command prompt.

The Computer You Want to Connect to Is Not Listed

If a computer on the network does not appear when you use the **Browse** dialog box in the pop-up interface or when you type **net view** at the MS-DOS command prompt, one of the following might be the cause:

- The computer might have been recently restarted. Wait a few minutes, and then try again.

- If a computer is part of another workgroup (not your own), you cannot use the **Browse** dialog box in the pop-up interface to display it. To see a list of computers in another workgroup, you must use the **net view** command with the **/workgroup** option at the MS-DOS command prompt. For more information, type **net help view** at the MS-DOS command prompt.

The Mouse Doesn't Work Correctly

If the mouse worked correctly before you set up Network Client, but doesn't work afterward, the mouse might be using the same interrupt setting as the network adapter. Try assigning a different interrupt to the network adapter.

For information about determining the correct interrupt setting for the network adapter, see the documentation that came with the network adapter. For information about how to change the interrupt setting, see "Checking and Changing Network-Adapter Settings," earlier in this section.

Error 234: Additional Data is Available

When you browse the network using the **net view** command from a computer running Network Client, the following error appears:

NET3513: More data is available than can be returned by LAN Manager.

This problem occurs when you browse a computer that has a share name longer than 12 characters.

The NET3778 Error Message Appears

When you log on to a domain across a router using the TCP/IP protocol from a LAN Manager 2.2c client computer or a Network Client 3.0 client computer configured as a WINS client, the NET3778 error message appears.

To work around this problem, add the following entry for a domain controller in the LMHOSTS file:

#DOM:<domain name>

Wrong Persistent Connection Is Removed

After you create several persistent network connections in Network Client 3.0 and attempt to remove a specific network connection, it is not removed. The most recent persistent network connection is removed. For example, if you have network connections assigned to drives E, G, and F (in this order), and you attempt to remove drive E, drive F is removed. This problem does not occur if you use the following command:

net use e: /d

Network Clients Are Unable to Change Their Passwords

If the account policy **User must log on in order to change password** is checked in Windows NT 3.5, 3.51, or 4.0, Network Client for MS-DOS 3.0 clients are unable to change their passwords. The policy is meant to keep users with expired accounts from being able to change their passwords. However, these clients receive Access Denied errors when they attempt to change their passwords, regardless of their account status.

This problem occurs because Network Client sets an inappropriate flag when it requests a password change on a Windows NT Server.

To work around this problem, turn off the **User must log on in order to change password** policy in User Manager on the computer running Windows NT Server.

Troubleshooting Network Client and DHCP

If you have problems using Network Client with the Dynamic Host Configuration Protocol (DHCP), use the following troubleshooting steps, utilities, and Resources to resolve the problem.

Troubleshooting Steps

1. Simplify your computer's boot configuration by removing terminate-and-stay-resident (TSR) programs, and third-party utilities from your Config.sys and Autoexec.bat files. Remove or minimize the use of memory managers. If you correct the problem, add back functionality until you discover the utility or combination of utilities that is creating the problem.

2. Verify that the Protocol.ini and System.ini files reflect your configuration. For more information:

   - See Section 16, "Network Settings in System.ini," of the Readme.txt file in the Microsoft Network Client directory.

   - Check the Help available in Setup.exe. Use the F1 key to get clarification on a specific option.

   - Query in the Microsoft Knowledge Base for the name of your specific network interface card (NIC).

Note The Windows NT Knowledge Base (KB) is available in Help files on the Windows NT Server Resource Kit CD.

---

3. Force Microsoft Network Client to recreate the hidden DHCP configuration file (Dhcp.prm). To do this:

   A. Use the **Attrib** command to remove the hidden and read-only file attributes.

   B. Delete the file.

   C. Quit and restart Microsoft Network Client to allow the file to be recreated.

      Network Client automatically creates the Dhcp.prm (a hidden binary file) in the installation directory.

4. Verify that the IP is functioning correctly by using the **ping**, **net view**, **net config**, and **net diag** commands on Network Client.

For more information see:

- The Help available for each command by typing **/?**. For example, **net view /?**. For **ping** help, type the command without any parameters.

- The Readme.txt file in the Microsoft Network Client directory. Check the table of contents for sections that pertain to your specific installation.

Troubleshooting Utilities

You can run **Ipconfig** on the client computer to check the client's IP configuration. For more information, see:

- Section 21, "Ipconfig.exe and Controlling DHCP Leases," in the Readme.txt file in the Microsoft Network Client directory.
- The following Knowledge Base articles:
  - Q94069: Microsoft TCP/IP Protocol Comparison and FAQ
  - Q123285: IPCONFIG Displays Invalid Results
  - Q130538: DHCP-Enabled MS-DOS Clients Do Not Resolve Host Names

You can run DHCP Manager on Windows NT Server to check the DHCP Server configuration. Use the **Scope Active Leases** option to verify that leasing is occurring. For more information, see:

- The Microsoft Windows NT Server *Networking Supplement*.
- Knowledge Base article Q120829 titled "DHCP (Dynamic Host Configuration Protocol) Basics."

Note The Windows NT Knowledge Base (KB) is available in Help files on the Windows NT Server Resource Kit compact disc.

Troubleshooting Resources

If the troubleshooting topics in this chapter don't help you resolve your Network Client problem, see the Readme.txt file in the Microsoft Network Client installation directory, or query the Microsoft Knowledge Base.

Note The Windows NT Knowledge Base is available in Help files on the Windows NT Server Resource Kit compact disc.

Appendixes

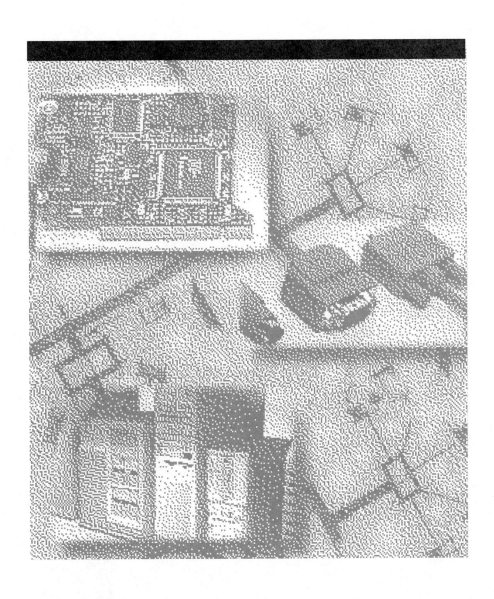

APPENDIX A

TCP/IP Utilities Reference

This appendix is a reference for using Microsoft TCP/IP utilities, which are diagnostic and connectivity utilities for network and connectivity administration. These client utilities are provided for file transfer, terminal emulation, and network diagnostics.

Diagnostic commands help you detect TCP/IP networking problems. *Connectivity commands* enable users to interact with and use resources on Microsoft hosts and non-Microsoft hosts such as UNIX workstations. The following commands are included:

- Diagnostic commands: **arp**, **hostname**, **ipconfig**, **lpq**, **nbtstat**, **netstat**, **ping**, **route**, and **tracert**
- Connectivity commands: **finger**, **ftp**, **lpr**, **rcp**, **rexec**, **rsh**, **telnet**, and **tftp**

Important All passwords used by Windows networking services are encrypted. However, the **ftp**, **ftpsvc**, **rexec**, and **telnet** connectivity utilities all rely on clear-text password authentication by the remote computer. Clear-text passwords are not encrypted before being sent over the network. This enables another user equipped with a network analyzer on the same network to steal a user's remote account password. For this reason, it is strongly recommended that users of these utilities choose different passwords than their Windows NT-based workgroup, workstation, or domain for the passwords used on non-Microsoft remote computers to which they connect by using the **ftp**, **ftpsvc**, **rexec**, and **telnet** utilities.

Note Switches used in the syntax for TCP/IP commands are case-sensitive. For example, for **nbtstat**, the switch **-R** has a different effect from the **-r** switch.

See also the topic "TCP/IP Procedures Help" in Control Panel Help.

arp

This diagnostic command displays and modifies the IP-to-Ethernet or Token Ring physical address translation tables used by the Address Resolution Protocol (ARP).

Syntax

arp -a [*inet_addr*] [**-N** [*if_addr*]]
arp -d *inet_addr* [*if_addr*]
arp -s *inet_addr ether_addr* [*if_addr*]

Parameters

-a

Displays current ARP entries by querying TCP/IP. If *inet_addr* is specified, only the IP and physical addresses for the specified host are displayed.

-d

Deletes the entry specified by *inet_addr*.

-g

Same as **-a**

-s

Adds an entry in the ARP cache to associate the IP address *inet_addr* with the physical address *ether_addr*. The physical address is given as 6 hexadecimal bytes separated by hyphens. The IP address is specified using dotted decimal notation. The entry is static. It will not be automatically removed from the cache after the timeout expires and will not exist after a reboot of your computer.

-N [*if_addr*]

Displays the ARP entries for the network interface specified by *if_addr*.

ether_addr

Specifies a physical address.

if_addr

Specifies, if present, the IP address of the interface whose address translation table should be modified. If not present, the first applicable interface will be used.

inet_addr

Specifies an IP address in dotted decimal notation.

finger

This connectivity command displays information about a user on a specified host running the Finger service. Output varies based on the configuration of the remote host.

Syntax

finger [**-l**] [*user*]@ *hostname* [...]

Parameters

-l

Displays information in long list format; not supported on all remote computers.

user

Specifies the user you want information about. Omit the *user* parameter to display information about all users on the specified host.

@*hostname*

Specifies the host name or IP address of the remote computer whose users you want information about.

ftp

This connectivity command transfers files to and from a host running an FTP server service, for example the Microsoft Internet Information Server. (A service is called a daemon in UNIX). **Ftp** is a complete session-oriented file transfer protocol. **Ftp** can be used interactively or by processing ASCII text files.

Syntax

ftp [**-v**] [**-n**] [**-i**] [**-d**] [**-g**] [**-s:** *filename*] [*hostname*]

Parameters

-v

Suppresses display of remote server responses.

-n

Suppresses autologon upon initial connection.

-i

Turns off interactive prompting during multiple file transfers.

-d

Enables debugging, displaying all **ftp** commands passed between the client and server.

-g

Disables filename globbing, which permits the use of wildcard characters in local file and path names. (See the **glob** command in the TCP/IP Procedure Help.)

-s: *filename*

Specifies a text file containing **ftp** commands; the commands automatically run after **ftp** starts. Use this switch instead of redirection (>).

hostname
Specifies the host name or IP address of the remote host to connect to. The host, if specified, must be the last parameter on the line.

The following table lists the **ftp** commands. For details about syntax of individual **ftp** commands, choose the **ftp commands** topic in the TCP/IP Procedure Help.

Table A.1   FTP Commands in Windows NT

Command	Purpose
!	Runs the specified command on the local computer.
?	Displays descriptions for **ftp** commands. **?** is identical to **help**.
append	Appends a local file to a file on the remote computer using the current file type setting.
ascii	Sets the file transfer type to ASCII, which is the default.
bell	Toggles a bell to ring after each file transfer command is completed. By default, the bell is off.
binary	Sets the file transfer type to binary.
bye	Ends the FTP session with the remote host and exits **ftp**.
cd	Changes the working directory on the remote host.
close	Ends the FTP session with the remote server and returns to the command interpreter.
debug	Toggles debugging. When debugging is on, each command sent to the remote host is printed, preceded by the string --->. By default, debugging is off.
delete	Deletes files on remote hosts.
dir	Displays a list of a remote directory's files and subdirectories.
disconnect	Disconnects from the remote host, retaining the **ftp** prompt.
get	Copies a remote file to the local host using the current file transfer type.
glob	Toggles filename globbing. Globbing permits use of wildcard characters in local file or path names. By default, globbing is on.
hash	Toggles hash-sign (#) printing for each data block transferred. The size of a data block is 2048 bytes. By default, hash-sign printing is off.
help	Displays descriptions for **ftp** commands.
lcd	Changes the working directory on the local host. By default, the current directory on the local host is used.
literal	Sends arguments, verbatim, to the remote FTP server. A single FTP reply code is expected in return.
ls	Displays an abbreviated list of a remote directory's files and subdirectories.

Table A.1   FTP Commands in Windows NT *(continued)*

Command	Purpose
mdelete	Deletes files on remote hosts.
mdir	Displays a list of a remote directory's files and subdirectories. **Mdir** enables you to specify multiple files.
mget	Copies remote files to the local host using the current file transfer type.
mkdir	Creates a remote directory.
mls	Displays an abbreviated list of a remote directory's files and subdirectories.
mput	Copies local files to the remote host using the current file transfer type.
open	Connects to the specified FTP server.
prompt	Toggles prompting. **Ftp** prompts during multiple file transfers to enable you to selectively retrieve or store files; **mget** and **mput** transfer all files if prompting is turned off. By default, prompting is on.
put	Copies a local file to the remote host using the current file transfer type.
pwd	Displays the current directory on the remote host.
quit	Ends the FTP session with the remote host and exits **ftp**.
quote	Sends arguments, verbatim, to the remote FTP server. A single FTP reply code is expected in return. **Quote** is identical to **literal**.
recv	Copies a remote file to the local host using the current file transfer type. **Recv** is identical to **get**.
remotehelp	Displays help for remote commands.
rename	Renames remote files.
rmdir	Deletes a remote directory.
send	Copies a local file to the remote host using the current file transfer type. **Send** is identical to **put**.
status	Displays the current status of FTP connections and toggles.
trace	Toggles packet tracing; **trace** displays the route of each packet when running an **ftp** command.
type	Sets or displays the file transfer type.
user	Specifies a user to the remote host.
verbose	Toggles verbose mode. If on, all **ftp** responses are displayed; when a file transfer completes, statistics regarding the efficiency of the transfer are also displayed. By default, verbose is on.

hostname

This diagnostic command prints the name of the host on which the command is issued.

Syntax

hostname

This command has no parameters.

ipconfig

This diagnostic command displays all current TCP/IP network configuration values. This command is useful on computers running DHCP because it enables users to determine which TCP/IP configuration values have been configured by DHCP. If you enter only **ipconfig** without parameters, the response is a display of all of the current TCP/IP configuration values, including IP address, subnet mask, and default gateway.

Syntax

ipconfig [/all | /renew [*adapter*] **| /release** [*adapter*]]

Parameters

all
Produces a full display. Without this switch, **ipconfig** displays only the IP address, subnet mask, and default gateway values for each network card.

renew [*adapter*]
Renews DHCP configuration parameters. This option is available only on computers running the DHCP Client service. To specify an adapter name, type the adapter name that appears when you use **ipconfig** without parameters.

release [*adapter*]
Releases the current DHCP configuration. This option disables TCP/IP on the local computer and is available only on DHCP clients. To specify an adapter name, type the adapter name that appears when you use **ipconfig** without parameters.

lpq

This diagnostic utility is used to obtain the status of a print queue on a host running the LPD server. To use the **lpq** command from the Windows NT command prompt, you must first install the Microsoft TCP/IP Printing service from the **Network** option in **Control Panel**.

Syntax

lpq -S*Server* **-P***Printer* [**-l**]

Parameters

-S*Server*
　Specifies the name of the host that has the printer attached to it.

-P*Printer*
　Specifies the name of the printer for the desired queue.

-l
　Specifies that a detailed status should be given.

lpr

This connectivity utility is used to print a file to a host running an LPD server. You use the **lpr** command from the Windows NT command prompt, you must first install the Microsoft TCP/IP Printing service from the **Network** option in Control Panel.

Syntax

lpr -S*Server* **-P***Printer* [**-o***Options*] [**-C***Class*] [**-J***Jobname*] [-o option] [-x] [-d] *filename*

Parameters

-S*Server*
　Specifies the name of the host that has the printer attached to it.

-P*Printer*
　Specifies the name of the printer for the desired queue.

-C*Class*
　Specifies the content of the banner page for the class.

-J*Jobname*
　Specifies the name of this job.

-o option
　Indicates the type of the file (by default assumes a text file). Use "-o l" for binary PostScript files.

-x
　Indicates compatibility with SunOS version 4.1.x and earlier.

-d
　Send data file first.

filename
>The name of the file to be printed.

Notes

To print a nontext file, such as a PostScript file, from a Windows NT-based computer to a printer controlled by a UNIX computer, use the **lpr** utility with the **-ol** switch. The **l** option specifies that the print file should be passed as is to the printer, with no processing by the Lpdsvc service.

To print a nontext file from a UNIX computer to a printer controlled by a Windows NT-based computer, use the **lpr** utility on the UNIX computer with the **-l** switch. For details on the UNIX **lpr** utility, see your UNIX documentation.

nbtstat

This diagnostic command displays protocol statistics and current TCP/IP connections using NetBIOS over TCP/IP (NetBT).

Syntax

nbtstat [**-a** *remotename*] [**-A** *IPaddress*] [**-c**] [**-n**] [**-R**] [**-r**] [**-S**] [**-s**] [*interval*]

Parameters

-a *remotename*
>Lists the remote computer's name table using the computer's name.

-A *IPaddress*
>Lists the remote computer's name table using the computer's IP address.

-c
>Lists the contents of the NetBIOS name cache, giving the IP address of each name.

-n
>Lists local NetBIOS names.

-R
>Reloads the LMHOSTS file after purging all names from the NetBIOS name cache. Can be used if LMHOSTS LOOKUP is enabled on the computer. (To enable LMHOSTS LOOKUP, check **Enable LMHOSTS LOOKUP** on the **WINS Address** tab on the **TCP/IP Properties** page.

-r
>Lists name resolution statistics for Windows networking. On a Windows NT-based computer configured to use WINS, this option returns the number of names resolved and registered via broadcast or via WINS.

-S
>Displays both workstation and server sessions, listing the remote computers by IP address only.

-s
>   Displays both workstation and server sessions. It attempts to resolve the remote computer IP address to a name by using the name resolution services (including, but not limited to, HOSTS FILE LOOKUP) which are configured on the computer.

interval
>   Redisplays selected statistics, pausing *interval* seconds between each display. Press CTRL+C to stop redisplaying statistics. If this parameter is omitted, **nbtstat** prints the current configuration information once.

Notes   The column headings generated by the **nbtstat** utility have the following meanings.

In
>   Number of bytes received.

Out
>   Number of bytes sent.

In/Out
>   Whether the connection is from the computer (outbound) or from another computer to the local computer (inbound).

Life
>   The remaining time that a name table cache entry will live before it is purged.

Local Name
>   The local NetBIOS name associated with the connection.

Remote Host
>   The name or IP address associated with the remote computer.

Type
>   This refers to the type of name. A name can either be a unique name or a group name.

<03>
>   Each NetBIOS name is 16 characters long. The last byte has special significance, and is used to indicate specific NetBIOS applications that each identify themselves by using the NetBIOS computer name. (The <> notation is the last byte converted to a hexadecimal value.)

State

The state of NetBIOS connections. The possible states are shown in the following list:

State	Meaning
Connected	The session has been established.
Associated	A connection endpoint has been created and associated with an IP address.
Listening	This endpoint is available for an inbound connection.
Idle	This endpoint has been opened but cannot receive connections.
Connecting	The session is in the connecting phase where the name-to-IP address mapping of the destination is being resolved.
Accepting	An inbound session is currently being accepted and will be connected shortly.
Reconnecting	A session is trying to reconnect if it failed to connect on the first attempt.
Outbound	A session is in the connecting phase where the TCP connection is currently being created.
Inbound	An inbound session is in the connecting phase.
Disconnecting	A session is in the process of disconnecting.
Disconnected	The local computer has issued a disconnect, and it is waiting for confirmation from the remote computer.

netstat

This diagnostic command displays protocol statistics and current TCP/IP network connections.

Syntax

netstat [-a] [-e][-n][-s] [-p *protocol*] [-r] [*interval*]

Parameters

-a

Displays all connections and listening ports; server connections are usually not shown.

-e

Displays Ethernet statistics. This can be combined with the -s option.

-n

Displays addresses and port numbers in numerical form (rather than attempting name lookups).

-s

Displays per-protocol statistics. By default, statistics are shown for TCP, UDP, ICMP, and IP; the -p option can be used to specify a subset of the default.

-p *protocol*

Shows connections for the protocol specified by *proto*; *proto* (See notes) can be **tcp** or **udp**. If used with the **-s** option to display per-protocol statistics, *protocol* can be **tcp**, **udp**, **icmp**, or **ip**.

-r

Displays the contents of the routing table.

interval

Redisplays selected statistics, pausing *interval* seconds between each display. Press CTRL+C to stop redisplaying statistics. If this parameter is omitted, **netstat** prints the current configuration information once.

Notes

The **netstat** utility provides statistics on the following network components.

Statistic	Purpose
Foreign Address	The IP address and port number of the remote computer to which the socket is connected. The name corresponding to the IP address is shown, instead of the number, if the HOSTS file contains an entry for the IP address. In cases where the port is not yet established, the port number is shown as an asterisk (*).
Local Address	The IP address of the local computer, as well as the port number the connection is using. The name corresponding to the IP address is shown, instead of the number, if the HOSTS file contains an entry for the IP address. In cases where the port is not yet established, the port number is shown as an asterisk (*).
Proto	The name of the protocol used by the connection.
(state)	Indicates the state of TCP connections only. The possible states are:

CLOSED	FIN_WAIT_1	SYN_RECEIVED
CLOSE_WAIT	FIN_WAIT_2	SYN_SEND
ESTABLISHED	LISTEN	TIMED_WAIT
LAST_ACK		

nslookup

This diagnostic tool displays information from Domain Name System (DNS) name servers. Before using this tool, you should be familiar with how DNS works. **Nslookup** is available only if the TCP/IP protocol has been installed.

Syntax

nslookup [-*option* ...] [*hostname* | - [*server*]]

Modes

Nslookup has two modes: interactive and non-interactive.

If you only need to look up a single piece of data, use non-interactive mode. For the first argument, type the name or IP address of the host to be looked up. For the second argument, type the name or IP address of a DNS name server. If you omit the second argument, the default DNS name server will be used.

If you need to look up more than one piece of data, you can use interactive mode. Type a hyphen (-) for the first argument and the name or IP address of a DNS name server for the second argument. Or, omit both arguments (the default DNS name server will be used).

Parameters

-option ...

Specifies one or more **nslookup** commands as a command-line option. For a list of these optional commands, see the following Table A.2, Nslookup Commands in Windows NT. Each option consists of a hyphen (-) followed immediately by the command name and, in some cases, an equal sign (=) and then a value. For example, to change the default query type to host information and the initial timeout to 10 seconds, you would type:

```
nslookup -querytype=hinfo -timeout=10
```

The command line length must be less than 256 characters.

hostname

Look up information for *hostname* using the current default server or using *server* if specified. If *computer-to-find* is an IP address and the query type is **A** or **PTR**, the name of the computer is returned. If *hostname* is a name and does not have a trailing period, the default DNS domain name is appended to the name. (You can change this behavior by using the **nslookup set** command. Refer to the following Table A.2, Nslookup Commands in Windows NT. To look up a computer not in the current DNS domain, append a period to the name.

If you type a hyphen (-) instead of *hostname*, the command prompt changes to **nslookup** interactive mode.

server

Host name of the DNS server to use. If you omit *server*, the default DNS name server is used.

Notes

Interactive Commands

- To interrupt interactive commands at any time, press CTRL+C.
- To exit, type **exit**.
- The command line length must be less than 256 characters.
- To treat a built-in command as a host name, precede it with the escape character (\).
- An unrecognized command is interpreted as a host name.

Diagnostics   If the **nslookup** command fails, an error message prints. Possible errors are:

- **Timed out**

  The server did not respond to a request after a certain amount of time (changed with **set timeout**=*value*) and a certain number of retries (changed with **set retry**=*value*).

- **No response from server**

  No DNS name server is running on the server.

- **No records**

  The DNS name server does not have resource records of the current query type for the host, although the host name is valid. The query type is specified with the **set querytype** command.

- **Non-existent domain**

  The host name or DNS domain name does not exist.

- **Connection refused**

  –Or–

- **Network is unreachable**

  The connection to the DNS name server or Finger server could not be made. This error commonly occurs with **ls** and **finger** requests.

- **Server failure**

  The DNS name server found an internal inconsistency in its database and could not return a valid answer.

- **Refused**

  The DNS name server refused to service the request.

- **Format error**

  The DNS name server found that the request packet was not in the proper format. It may indicate an error in **nslookup**.

The following table shows the **nslookup** commands. For details about syntax for individual **nslookup** commands, choose the **nslookup commands** topic in the TCP/IP Procedure Help.

Table A.2   Nslookup Commands in Windows NT

Command	Purpose
exit	Exits interactive nslookup.
finger	Connects with the Finger server on the *current* host. The *current* host is defined when a previous lookup for a host was successful and returned the address information.
help	Displays a brief summary of **nslookup** commands.
ls	Lists information for a DNS domain. The default output contains host names and their IP addresses. (When output is directed to a file, hash marks (###) are printed for every 50 records received from the server.)
lserver	Changes the default server to the specified DNS domain. **Lserver** uses the initial server to look up the information about the specified DNS domain. (This is in contrast to the **server** command, which uses the current default server.)
root	Changes the default server to the server for the root of the DNS domain name space. Currently, the host G.ROOT-SERVERS.NET. is used. (This command is a synonym for **lserver g.root-server.net.**) The name of the root server can be changed with the **set root** command.
server	Changes the default server to the specified DNS domain. **Server** uses the current default server to look up the information about the specified DNS domain. (This is in contrast to the **lserver** command, which uses the initial server.)
set	Changes configuration settings that affect the behavior of the **nslookup** commands.
set all	Prints the current values of the configuration settings. Also prints information about the default server and host..
set cl[ass]	Changes the query class. (The class specifies the protocol group of the information.)
set [no]d2	Turns exhaustive debugging mode on or off. Essentially all fields of every packet are printed.
set [no] deb[ug]	Turns debugging mode on or off. With debugging on, more information is printed about the packet sent to the server and the resulting answer.
set [no] def[name]	If set, appends the default DNS domain name to a single-component lookup request. (A single component is a component that contains no periods.)

Table A.2   Nslookup Commands in Windows NT (continued)

Command	Purpose
set do[main]	Changes the default DNS domain to the name specified. The default DNS domain name is appended to a lookup request depending on the state of the **defname** and **search** options. The DNS domain search list contains the parents of the default DNS domain if it has at least two components in its name. For example, if the default DNS domain is mydomain.mycompany.com, the search list is mydomain.mycompany.com and mycompany.com. Use the **set srchlist** command to specify a different list. Use the **set all** command to display the list.
Set [no] ig[nore]	If set, ignores packet truncation errors.
Set po[rt]	Changes the default TCP/UDP DNS name server port to the value specified.
Set q[uerytype]	Changes the type of information query. More information about types can be found in RFC 1035. (The **set type** command is a synonym for **set querytype**.)
set [no] rec[urse]	If set, tells the DNS name server to query other servers if it does not have the information.
Set ret[ry]	Sets the number of retries. When a reply to a request is not received within a certain amount of time (changed with **set timeout**), the timeout period is doubled and the request is resent. The retry value controls how many times a request is re-sent before giving up.
Set ro[ot]	Changes the name of the root server. This affects the root command.
Set [no] sea[rch]	If set and the lookup request contains at least one period but does not end with a trailing period, appends the DNS domain names in the DNS domain search list to the request until an answer is received.
Set srchl[ist]	Changes the default DNS domain name and search list. A maximum of six names separated by slashes (/) can be specified. This command overrides the default DNS domain name and search list of the **set domain** command. Use the **set all** command to display the list.
Set ti[meout]	Changes the initial number of seconds to wait for a reply to a request. When a reply to a request is not received within this time period, the timeout is doubled and the request is re-sent. (The number of retries is controlled with the **set retry** option.)

Table A.2   Nslookup Commands in Windows NT *(continued)*

Command	Purpose
set ty[pe]	Changes the type of information query. More information about types can be found in RFC 1035. (The **set type** command is a synonym fo**r set querytype**.)
set [no] v[c]	If set, always uses a virtual circuit when sending requests to the server.
view	Sorts and lists the output of previous **ls** command(s).

References

For in-depth coverage of **nslookup**, see *DNS and BIND* by Paul Albitz and Cricket Liu, published by O'Reilly and Associates.

ping

This diagnostic command verifies connections to one or more remote computers.

Syntax

ping [**-t**] [**-a**] [**-n** *count*] [**-l** *length*] [**-f**] [**-i** *ttl*] [**-v** *tos*] [**-r** *count*] [**-s** *count*] [[**-j** *host-list*] | [**-k** *host-list*]] [**-w** *timeout*] *destination-list*

Parameters

-t
Pings the specified host until interrupted.

-a
Resolves addresses to host names.

-n *count*
Sends the number of ECHO packets specified by *count*. The default is 4.

-l *length*
Sends ECHO packets containing the amount of data specified by *length*. The default is 64 bytes; the maximum is 8192.

-f
Sends a Do Not Fragment flag in the packet. The packet will not be fragmented by gateways on the route.

-i *ttl*
Sets the time to live field to the value specified by *ttl*.

-v *tos*
Sets the type of service field to the value specified by *tos*.

-r *count*
Records the route of the outgoing packet and the returning packet in the record route field. A minimum of 1 to a maximum of 9 hosts must be specified by *count*.

-s *count*
Specifies the timestamp for the number of hops specified by *count*.

-j *host-list*

    Routes packets via the list of hosts specified by *host-list*. Consecutive hosts can be separated by intermediate gateways (loose source routed). The maximum number allowed by IP is 9.

-k *host-list*

    Routes packets via the list of hosts specified by *host-list*. Consecutive hosts cannot be separated by intermediate gateways (strict source routed). The maximum number allowed by IP is 9.

-w *timeout*

    Specifies a timeout interval in milliseconds.

destination-list

    Specifies the remote hosts to ping.

Notes

The **ping** command verifies connections to remote hosts by sending ICMP echo packets to the host and listening for echo reply packets. **Ping** waits for up to 1 second for each packet sent and prints the number of packets transmitted and received. Each received packet is validated against the transmitted message. By default, four echo packets containing 64 bytes of data (a periodic sequence of uppercase alphabetic characters) are transmitted.

You can use the **ping** utility to test both the host name and the IP address of the host. If the IP address is verified but the host name is not, you might have a name resolution problem. In this case, be sure that the host name you are querying is in either the local HOSTS file or in the DNS database.

The following shows sample output for **ping**:

```
C:\>ping ds.internic.net

Pinging ds.internic.net [192.20.239.132] with 32 bytes of data:

Reply from 192.20.239.132: bytes=32 time=101ms TTL=243
Reply from 192.20.239.132: bytes=32 time=100ms TTL=243
Reply from 192.20.239.132: bytes=32 time=120ms TTL=243
Reply from 192.20.239.132: bytes=32 time=120ms TTL=243
```

rcp

This connectivity command copies files between a Window NT computer and a computer running **rshd**, the remote shell server service or daemon. (A service is called a daemon in UNIX.) The **rcp** command can also be used for third-party transfer to copy files between two computers running **rshd** when the command is issued from a Windows NT-based computer. The **rshd** server service (daemon) is available on UNIX computers, but not on a Windows NT-based computer. The Windows NT-based computer can only participate as the computer from which the commands are issued. The remote computers must also support the **rcp** utility in addition to running **rshd**.

Syntax

rcp [-a | -b] [-h] [-r] *source1 source2 ... sourceN destination*

Parameters

-a

Specifies ASCII transfer mode. This mode converts the carriage return/linefeed characters to carriage returns on outgoing files, and linefeed characters to carriage return/linefeeds for incoming files. This is the default transfer mode.

-b

Specifies binary image transfer mode. No carriage return/linefeed conversion is performed.

-h

Transfers source files marked with the hidden attribute on the Windows NT-based computer. Without this option, specifying a hidden file on the **rcp** command line has the same effect as if the file did not exist.

-r

Recursively copies the contents of all subdirectories of the source to the destination. Both the *source* and *destination* must be directories.

source and *destination*

Must be of the form [*host*[.*user*]:]*filename*. If the [*host*[.*user*]:] portion is omitted, the host is assumed to be the local computer. If the *user* portion is omitted, the currently logged-on Windows NT user name is used. If a fully qualified host name is used, which contains the period (.) separators, then the [.*user*] must be included. Otherwise, the last part of the host name is interpreted as the user name. If multiple source files are specified, the *destination* must be a directory.

If the filename does not begin with a forward slash (/) for UNIX computers or a backward slash (\) for Windows NT-based computers, it is assumed to be relative to the current working directory. Under Windows NT, this is the directory from which the command is issued. On the remote computer, it is the logon directory for the remote user. A period (.) means the current directory. Use the escape characters (\ , ", or ') in remote paths to use wildcard characters on the remote host.

Notes

Remote Privileges

The **rcp** command does not prompt for passwords; the current or specified user-name must exist on the remote host and enable remote command execution via **rcp**.

The .rhosts File

The .rhosts file specifies which remote computer or users can assess a local account using **rsh** or **rcp**. This file (or a HOSTS equivalent) is required on the remote computer for access to a remote computer using these commands. **Rsh** and **rcp** both transmit the local user name to the remote computer. The remote computer uses this name plus the IP address (usually resolved to a host name) or the requesting computer to determine whether access is granted. There is no provision for specifying a password to access an account using these commands.

If the user is logged on to a Windows NT Server domain, the domain controller must be available to resolve the currently logged-on name, because the logged-on name is not cached on the local computer. Because the user name is required as part of the **rsh** protocol, the command fails if the user name cannot be obtained.

The .rhosts file is a text file where each line is an entry. An entry consists of the local host name, the local user name, and any comments about the entry. Each entry is separated by a tab or space, and comments begin with a hash mark (#), for example:

```
computer5    marie    #This computer is in room 31A
```

The .rhosts file must be in the user's home directory on the remote computer. (Normally a DNS name server is used instead of the .rhosts file.)

Additionally, have your host name added to the remote computer's /Etc/Hosts file. This enables the remote computer to authenticate remote requests for your computer using the Microsoft TCP/IP utilities.

For more information about a remote computer's specific implementation of the .rhosts file, see the remote computer's documentation

Specifying Hosts

Use the *host.user* variables to use a user name other than the current user name. If *host.user* is specified with *source*, the .rhosts file on the remote host must contain an entry for *user*.

If a host name is supplied as a full domain name containing periods, a user name must be appended to the host name. This prevents the last element of the domain name from being interpreted as a user name. For example,

```
rcp domain-name1.user:johnm  domain-name2.user:richr
```

Remote Processing

Remote processing is performed by a command run from the user's logon shell on most UNIX computers. The user's .profile or .cshrc is executed before parsing filenames, and exported shell variables can be used (using the escape characters or quotation marks) in remote filenames.

Copying Files

If you attempt to copy a number of files to a file rather than a directory, only the last file is copied. Also, the **rcp** command cannot copy a file onto itself.

Examples

These examples show syntax for some common uses of **rcp**.

To copy a local file to the logon directory of a remote computer:

```
rcp filename remotecomputer:
```

To copy a local file to an existing directory and a new filename on a remote computer:

```
rcp filename remotecomputer:/directory/newfilename
```

To copy multiple local files to a subdirectory of a remote logon directory:

```
rcp file1 file2 file3 remotecomputer:subdirectory/filesdirectory
```

To copy from a remote source to the current directory of the local computer:

```
rcp remotecomputer:filename
```

To copy from multiple files from multiple remote sources to a remote destination with different user names:

```
rcp remote1.user1:file1 remote2.user2:file2
    remotedest.destuser:directory
```

To copy from a remote computer using an IP address to a local computer (where the user name is mandatory because a period is used in the remote host name):

```
rcp 11.101.12.1.user:filename filename
```

rexec

This connectivity command runs commands on remote hosts running the rexecd service. **Rexec** authenticates the user name on the remote host by using a password, before executing the specified command.

Syntax

rexec *host* [**-l** *username*] [**-n**] *command*

Parameters

host
Specifies the remote host on which to run *command*.

-l *username*
Specifies the user name on the remote host.

-n
Redirects the input of **rexec** to NUL.

command
Specifies the command to run.

Notes

Rexec prompts the user for a password and authenticates the password on the remote host. If the authentication succeeds, the command is executed.

Rexec copies standard input to the remote *command*, standard output of the remote *command* to its standard output, and standard error of the remote *command* to its standard error. Interrupt, quit, and terminate signals are propagated to the remote command. **Rexec** normally terminates when the remote command does.

Using Redirection Symbols

Use quotation marks around redirection symbols to redirect onto the remote host. If quotation marks are not used, redirection occurs on the local computer. For example, the following command appends the remote file *remotefile* to the local file *localfile*:

```
rexec otherhost cat remotefile >> localfile
```

The following command appends the remote file *remotefile* to the remote file *otherremotefile*:

```
rexec otherhost cat remotefile ">>" otherremotefile
```

Using Interactive Commands

You cannot run most interactive commands. For example, **vi** or **emacs** cannot be run using **rexec**. Use **telnet** to run interactive commands.

route

This diagnostic command manipulates network routing tables.

Syntax

route [**-f**] [*command* [*destination*] [**MASK** *netmask*] [*gateway*] [METRIC *metric*]]

Parameters

-f

Clears the routing tables of all gateway entries. If this parameter is used in conjunction with one of the commands, the tables are cleared prior to running the command.

-p

When used with the **route add** command, makes a route persistent across restarts of the computer. By default, routes are not preserved when the computer is restarted. When used with the **route print** command, displays the list of registered persistent routes. Ignored for all other commands.

command

Specifies one of four commands.

Command	Purpose
print	Prints a route
add	Adds a route
delete	Deletes a route
change	Modifies an existing route

destination

Specifies the host to send *command*.

MASK

Specifies, if present, that the next parameter be interpreted as the *netmask* parameter.

netmask

Specifies, if present, the subnet mask value to be associated with this route entry. If not present, this parameter defaults to 255.255.255.255.

gateway

Specifies the gateway.

METRIC

Specifies the route metric (cost) for the destination.

Notes

The **route** utility does not accept a subnet mask value of 255.255.255.255 on the command line. To specify a subnet mask with this value, you must accept the default.

On a multihomed computer on which a network is available from more than one adapter card, all network traffic is passed over the first gateway defined. If you add a second gateway to the same network, the entry is added to the route table, but it is never used.

The **route** utility uses the Networks file to convert *destination* names to addresses. For the **route** utility to work correctly, the network numbers in the Networks file must specify all four octets in dotted decimal notation. For example, a network number of 284.122.107 must be specified in the Networks file as 284.122.107.0, with trailing zeroes appended.

All symbolic names used for *destination* or *gateway* are looked up in the network and host name database files NETWORKS and HOSTS, respectively. If the command is **route print** or **route delete**, wildcards may be used for the *destination* and *gateway*, or the *gateway* argument may be omitted.

rsh

This connectivity command runs commands on remote hosts running the rsh service. For information about the .rhosts file, see the **Rcp** command.

Syntax

rsh *host*[**-l** *username*] [**-n**] *command*

Parameters

host
-l *username*
> Specifies the user name to use on the remote host. If omitted, the logged-on user name is used.

-n
> Redirects the input of **rsh** to NUL.

command
> Specifies the command to run.

Notes

Rsh copies standard input to the remote *command*, standard output of the remote *command* to its standard output, and the standard error of the remote *command* to its standard error. **Rsh** normally terminates when the remote command does.

Using Redirection Symbols

Use quotation marks around redirection symbols to redirect onto the remote host. If quotation marks are not used, redirection occurs on the local computer. For example, the following command appends the remote file *remotefile* to the local file *localfile*:

```
rsh otherhost cat remotefile >> localfile
```

The following command appends the remote file *remotefile* to the remote file *otherremotefile*:

```
rsh otherhost cat remotefile ">>" otherremotefile
```

Using Rsh on a Windows NT Server Domain

If the user is logged on to a Windows NT Server domain, the domain controller must be available to resolve the currently logged-on name, because the logged-on name is not cached on the local computer. Because the *username* is required as part of the **rsh** protocol, the command fails if the *username* cannot be obtained.

The .rhosts File

The .rhosts file generally permits network access rights on UNIX computers. The .rhosts file lists computer names and associated logon names that have access to remote computers. When issuing **rcp**, **rexec**, or **rsh** commands to a remote computer with a properly configured .rhosts file, you do not need to provide logon and password information for the remote computer.

The .rhosts file is a text file where each line is an entry. An entry consists of the local computer name, the local user name, and any comments about the entry. Each entry is separated by a tab or space, and comments begin with a hash mark (#), for example:

```
computer5   marie   #This computer is in room 31A
```

The .rhosts file must be in the user's home directory on the remote computer. For further information about a remote computer's specific implementation of the .rhosts file, see the remote computer's documentation. (Normally a DNS name server is used instead of the .rhosts file.)

telnet

This connectivity command starts terminal emulation with a remote host running a Telnet server service. Telnet provides DEC™ VT 100, DEC VT 52, or TTY emulation, using the connection-based services of TCP.

To provide terminal emulation from a Windows NT computer, the remote host must be running TCP/IP and a Telnet server service. The Windows NT-based Telnet client must also have a user account on the remote Telnet server.

The Telnet client can be started by selecting **Telnet** from the **Accessories** program group or by using the command prompt. The syntax and usage for starting the Telnet client from the command prompt is described next. For information about starting the Telnet client by selecting **Telnet** from the **Accessories** program group, see online Help.

Note Windows NT Server and Windows NT Workstation provide the **telnet** client utility but do not provide a Telnet server service (**telnetd**), also referred to as the Telnet daemon.

Syntax

telnet [host [*port*]]

Parameters

hostname
> Specifies the host name or IP address of the remote host with which you want to connect.

port
> Specifies the remote port you want to connect to. The default value is specified by the **telnet** entry in the Services file. If no entry exists in the Services file, the default connection port value is decimal 23.

tftp

This connectivity command transfers files to and from a remote computer running the Trivial File Transfer Protocol (TFTP) service. This utility is similar to **ftp**, but it does not provide user authentication, although the files require read and write UNIX permissions. **Tftp** can only be used for unidirectional transfer of files.

Syntax

tftp [**-i**] *host* [**get** | **put**] *source* [*destination*]

Parameters

-i
> Specifies binary image transfer mode (also called octet). In binary image mode, the file is moved literally byte by byte. Use this mode when transferring binary files.
>
> If **-i** is omitted, the file is transferred in ASCII mode. This is the default transfer mode. This mode converts the end-of-line (EOL) characters to a carriage return for UNIX and to a carriage return/linefeed for personal computers. Use this mode when transferring text files. If a file transfer is successful, the data transfer rate is displayed.

host
> Specifies the local or remote host.

get
> Transfers *destination* on the remote computer to *source* on the local computer.
>
> Because the TFTP protocol does not support user authentication, the user must be logged on, and the files must be writable on the remote computer.

put
> Transfers *source* on the local computer to *destination* on the remote computer.

source
> Specifies the file to transfer.

destination
> Specifies where to transfer the file.

tracert

This diagnostic utility determines the route taken to a destination by sending Internet Control Message Protocol (ICMP) echo packets with varying time-to-live (TTL) values to the destination. Each router along the path is required to decrement the TTL on a packet by at least 1 before forwarding it, so the TTL is effectively a hop count. When the TTL on a packet reaches 0, the router is supposed to send back an ICMP Time Exceeded message to the source computer. **Tracert** determines the route by sending the first echo packet with a TTL of 1 and incrementing the TTL by 1 on each subsequent transmission until the target responds or the maximum TTL is reached. The route is determined by examining the ICMP Time Exceeded messages sent back by intermediate routers. Notice that some routers silently drop packets with expired TTLs and will be invisible to **tracert**.

Syntax

tracert [**-d**] [**-h** *maximum_hops*] [**-j** *host-list*] [**-w** *timeout*] *target_name*

Parameters

-d
Specifies not to resolve addresses to host names.

-h *maximum_hops*
Specifies maximum number of hops to search for target.

-j *host-list*
Specifies loose source route along *host-list*.

-w *timeout*
Waits the number of milliseconds specified by *timeout* for each reply.

target_name
Name of the target host.

APPENDIX B

Port Reference for Microsoft TCP/IP

In TCP/IP, a *port* is the mechanism that allows a computer to simultaneously support multiple communication sessions with computers and programs on the network. A port is basically a refinement of an IP address; a computer that receives a packet from the network can further refine the destination of the packet by using a unique port number that is determined when the connection is established. A number of "well known" ports have reserved numbers that correspond to predetermined functions.

This appendix describes the Windows NT Server and Windows NT Workstation default port assignments for TCP/IP and UDP. The Services file controls port assignments used by Windows NT Server and Windows NT Workstation. The Services file is located in the \systemroot\Winnt\System32\Drivers\Etc\Services directory.

Port Assignments for Well Known Ports

Well known services are defined by RFC 1060. The relationship between the well known services and the well known ports is described in this excerpt from RFC 1340 (J. Reynolds and J. Postal, July 1992):

> The well known ports are controlled and assigned by the Internet Assigned Numbers Authority (IANA), and on most systems can only be used by system (or root) processes or by programs executed by privileged users.

> Ports are used in TCP to name the ends of logical connections that carry long term conversations. For the purpose of providing services to unknown callers, a service contact port is defined. This list specifies the port used by the server process as its contact port. The contact port is sometimes called the "well known port."

UDP ports are not the same as TCP ports, though to the extent possible, TCP and UDP may use the same port assignments. The UDP specification is defined in RFC 768.

The assigned ports use a small portion of the possible port numbers. For many years, the assigned ports were in the range 0 – 255. Recently, the range for assigned ports managed by the IANA has been expanded to the range 0–1023.

The following table describes both TCP and UDP port assignments for well known ports.

Table B.1   Port Assignments for Well Known Ports

Decimal	Keyword	Description
0/tcp, udp		Reserved
1/tcp, udp	tcpmux	TCP Port Service Multiplexer
2/tcp, udp	compressnet	Management Utility
3/tcp, udp	compressnet	Compression Process
4/tcp, udp		Unassigned
5/tcp, udp	rje	Remote Job Entry
6/tcp, udp		Unassigned
7/tcp, udp	echo	Echo
8/tcp, udp		Unassigned
9/tcp, udp	discard	Discard; alias=sink null
10/tcp, udp		Unassigned
11/udp	systat	Active Users; alias=users
12/tcp, udp		Unassigned
13/tcp, udp	daytime	Daytime
14/tcp, udp		Unassigned
15/tcp, udp		Unassigned [was netstat]
16/tcp, udp		Unassigned
17/tcp, udp	qotd	Quote of the Day; alias=quote
18/tcp, udp	msp	Message Send Protocol
19/tcp, udp	chargen	Character Generator; alias=ttytst source
20/tcp, udp	ftp-data	File Transfer [Default Data]
21/tcp, udp	ftp	File Transfer [Control], connection dialog
22/tcp, udp		Unassigned
23/tcp, udp	telnet	Telnet
24/tcp, udp		Any private mail system
25/tcp, udp	smtp	Simple Mail Transfer; alias=mail

Table B.1   Port Assignments for Well Known Ports *(continued)*

Decimal	Keyword	Description
26/tcp, udp		Unassigned
27/tcp, udp	nsw-fe	NSW User System FE
28/tcp, udp		Unassigned
29/tcp, udp	msg-icp	MSG ICP
30/tcp, udp		Unassigned
31/tcp, udp	msg-auth	MSG Authentication
32/tcp, udp		Unassigned
33/tcp, udp	dsp	Display Support Protocol
34/tcp, udp		Unassigned
35/tcp, udp		Any private printer server
36/tcp, udp		Unassigned
37/tcp, udp	time	Time; alias=timeserver
38/tcp, udp		Unassigned
39/tcp, udp	rlp	Resource Location Protocol; alias=resource
40/tcp, udp		Unassigned
41/tcp, udp	graphics	Graphics
42/tcp, udp	nameserver	Host Name Server; alias=nameserver
43/tcp, udp	nicname	Who Is; alias=nicname
44/tcp, udp	mpm-flags	MPM FLAGS Protocol
45/tcp, udp	mpm	Message Processing Module
46/tcp, udp	mpm-snd	MPM [default send]
47/tcp, udp	ni-ftp	NI FTP
48/tcp, udp		Unassigned
49/tcp, udp	login	Login Host Protocol
50/tcp, udp	re-mail-ck	Remote Mail Checking Protocol
51/tcp, udp	la-maint	IMP Logical Address Maintenance
52/tcp, udp	xns-time	XNS Time Protocol
53/tcp, udp	domain	Domain Name Server
54/tcp, udp	xns-ch	XNS Clearinghouse
55/tcp, udp	isi-gl	ISI Graphics Language
56/tcp, udp	xns-auth	XNS Authentication
57/tcp, udp		Any private terminal access
58/tcp, udp	xns-mail	XNS Mail
59/tcp, udp		Any private file service

Table B.1   Port Assignments for Well Known Ports *(continued)*

Decimal	Keyword	Description
60/tcp, udp		Unassigned
61/tcp, udp	ni-mail	NI MAIL
62/tcp, udp	acas	ACA Services
63/tcp, udp	via-ftp	VIA Systems - FTP
64/tcp, udp	covia	Communications Integrator (CI)
65/tcp, udp	tacacs-ds	TACACS-Database Service
66/tcp, udp	sql*net	Oracle SQL*NET
67/tcp, udp	bootpc	DHCP/BOOTP Protocol Server
68/tcp, udp	bootpc	DHCP/BOOTP Protocol Server
69/ udp	tftp	Trivial File Transfer
70/tcp, udp	gopher	Gopher
71/tcp, udp	netrjs-1	Remote Job Service
72/tcp, udp	netrjs-2	Remote Job Service
73/tcp, udp	netrjs-3	Remote Job Service
74/tcp, udp	netrjs-4	Remote Job Service
75/udp		Any private dial out service
76/tcp, udp		Unassigned
77/tcp, udp		Any private RJE service
78/tcp, udp	vettcp	Vettcp
79/tcp, udp	finger	Finger
80/tcp, udp	www	World Wide Web HTTP
81/tcp, udp	hosts2-ns	HOSTS2 Name Server
82/tcp, udp	xfer	XFER Utility
83/tcp, udp	mit-ml-dev	MIT ML Device
84/tcp, udp	ctf	Common Trace Facility
85/tcp, udp	mit-ml-dev	MIT ML Device
86/tcp, udp	mfcobol	Micro Focus Cobol
87/tcp, udp		Any private terminal link; alias=ttylink
88/tcp, udp	kerberos	Kerberos
89/tcp	su-mit-tg	SU/MIT Telnet Gateway
89/udp	su-mit-tg	SU/MIT Telnet Gateway
90/tcp, udp		DNSIX Security Attribute Token Map
91/tcp, udp	mit-dov	MIT Dover Spooler
92/tcp, udp	npp	Network Printing Protocol

Table B.1   Port Assignments for Well Known Ports *(continued)*

Decimal	Keyword	Description
93/tcp, udp	dcp	Device Control Protocol
94/tcp, udp	objcall	Tivoli Object Dispatcher
95/tcp, udp	supdup	SUPDUP
96/tcp, udp	dixie	DIXIE Protocol Specification
97/tcp, udp	swift-rvf	Swift Remote Virtual File Protocol
98/tcp, udp	tacnews	TAC News
99/tcp, udp	metagram	Metagram Relay
100/tcp	newacct	[unauthorized use]
101/tcp, udp	hostname	NIC Host Name Server; alias=hostname
102/tcp, udp	iso-tsap	ISO-TSAP
103/tcp, udp	gppitnp	Genesis Point-to-Point Trans Net; alias=webster
104/tcp, udp	acr-nema	ACR-NEMA Digital Imag. & Comm. 300
105/tcp, udp	csnet-ns	Mailbox Name Nameserver
106/tcp, udp	3com-tsmux	3COM-TSMUX
107/tcp, udp	rtelnet	Remote Telnet Service
108/tcp, udp	snagas	SNA Gateway Access Server
109/tcp, udp	pop2	Post Office Protocol - Version 2; alias=postoffice
110/tcp, udp	pop3	Post Office Protocol - Version 3; alias=postoffice
111/tcp, udp	sunrpc	SUN Remote Procedure Call
112/tcp, udp	mcidas	McIDAS Data Transmission Protocol
113/tcp, udp	auth	Authentication Service; alias=authentication
114/tcp, udp	audionews	Audio News Multicast
115/tcp, udp	sftp	Simple File Transfer Protocol
116/tcp, udp	ansanotify	ANSA REX Notify
117/tcp, udp	uucp-path	UUCP Path Service
118/tcp, udp	sqlserv	SQL Services
119/tcp, udp	nntp	Network News Transfer Protocol; alias=usenet
120/tcp, udp	cfdptkt	CFDPTKT
121/tcp, udp	erpc	Encore Expedited Remote Pro.Call
122/tcp, udp	smakynet	SMAKYNET
123/tcp, udp	ntp	Network Time Protocol; alias=ntpd ntp
124/tcp, udp	ansatrader	ANSA REX Trader
125/tcp, udp	locus-map	Locus PC-Interface Net Map Server
126/tcp, udp	unitary	Unisys Unitary Login

Table B.1   Port Assignments for Well Known Ports *(continued)*

Decimal	Keyword	Description
127/tcp, udp	locus-con	Locus PC-Interface Conn Server
128/tcp, udp	gss-xlicen	GSS X License Verification
129/tcp, udp	pwdgen	Password Generator Protocol
130/tcp, udp	cisco-fna	Cisco FNATIVE
131/tcp, udp	cisco-tna	Cisco TNATIVE
132/tcp, udp	cisco-sys	Cisco SYSMAINT
133/tcp, udp	statsrv	Statistics Service
134/tcp, udp	ingres-net	INGRES-NET Service
135/tcp, udp	loc-srv	Location Service
136/tcp, udp	profile	PROFILE Naming System
137/tcp, udp	netbios-ns	NetBIOS Name Service
138/tcp, udp	netbios-dgm	NetBIOS Datagram Service
139/tcp, udp	netbios-ssn	NetBIOS Session Service
140/tcp, udp	emfis-data	EMFIS Data Service
141/tcp, udp	emfis-cntl	EMFIS Control Service
142/tcp, udp	bl-idm	Britton-Lee IDM
143/tcp, udp	imap2	Interim Mail Access Protocol v2
144/tcp, udp	news	NewS; alias=news
145/tcp, udp	uaac	UAAC Protocol
146/tcp, udp	iso-ip0	ISO-IP0
147/tcp, udp	iso-ip	ISO-IP
148/tcp, udp	cronus	CRONUS-SUPPORT
149/tcp, udp	aed-512	AED 512 Emulation Service
150/tcp, udp	sql-net	SQL-NET
151/tcp, udp	hems	HEMS
152/tcp, udp	bftp	Background File Transfer Program
153/tcp, udp	sgmp	SGMP; alias=sgmp
154/tcp, udp	netsc-prod	Netscape
155/tcp, udp	netsc-dev	Netscape
156/tcp, udp	sqlsrv	SQL Service
157/tcp, udp	knet-cmp	KNET/VM Command/Message Protocol
158/tcp, udp	pcmail-srv	PCMail Server; alias=repository
159/tcp, udp	nss-routing	NSS-Routing
160/tcp, udp	sgmp-traps	SGMP-TRAPS

Table B.1   Port Assignments for Well Known Ports *(continued)*

Decimal	Keyword	Description
161/tcp, udp	snmp	SNMP; alias=snmp
162/tcp, udp	snmptrap	SNMPTRAP
163/tcp, udp	cmip-man	CMIP/TCP Manager
164/tcp, udp	cmip-agent	CMIP/TCP Agent
165/tcp, udp	xns-courier	Xerox
166/tcp, udp	s-net	Sirius Systems
167/tcp, udp	namp	NAMP
168/tcp, udp	rsvd	RSVD
169/tcp, udp	send	SEND
170/tcp, udp	print-srv	Network PostScript
171/tcp, udp	multiplex	Network Innovations Multiplex
172/tcp, udp	cl/1	Network Innovations CL/1
173/tcp, udp	xyplex-mux	Xyplex
174/tcp, udp	mailq	MAILQ
175/tcp, udp	vmnet	VMNET
176/tcp, udp	genrad-mux	GENRAD-MUX
177/tcp, udp	xdmcp	X Display Manager Control Protocol
178/tcp, udp	nextstep	NextStep Window Server
179/tcp, udp	bgp	Border Gateway Protocol
180/tcp, udp	ris	Intergraph
181/tcp, udp	unify	Unify
182/tcp, udp	audit	Unisys Audit SITP
183/tcp, udp	ocbinder	OCBinder
184/tcp, udp	ocserver	OCServer
185/tcp, udp	remote-kis	Remote-KIS
186/tcp, udp	kis	KIS Protocol
187/tcp, udp	aci	Application Communication Interface
188/tcp, udp	mumps	Plus Five's MUMPS
189/tcp, udp	qft	Queued File Transport
190/tcp, udp	gacp	Gateway Access Control Protocol
191/tcp, udp	prospero	Prospero
192/tcp, udp	osu-nms	OSU Network Monitoring System
193/tcp, udp	srmp	Spider Remote Monitoring Protocol
194/tcp, udp	irc	Internet Relay Chat Protocol

Table B.1   Port Assignments for Well Known Ports *(continued)*

Decimal	Keyword	Description
195/tcp, udp	dn6-nlm-aud	DNSIX Network Level Module Audit
196/tcp, udp	dn6-smm-red	DNSIX Session Mgt Module Audit Redir
197/tcp, udp	dls	Directory Location Service
198/tcp, udp	dls-mon	Directory Location Service Monitor
199/tcp, udp	smux	SMUX
200/tcp, udp	src	IBM System Resource Controller
201/tcp, udp	at-rtmp	AppleTalk Routing Maintenance
202/tcp, udp	at-nbp	AppleTalk Name Binding
203/tcp, udp	at-3	AppleTalk Unused
204/tcp, udp	at-echo	AppleTalk Echo
205/tcp, udp	at-5	AppleTalk Unused
206/tcp, udp	at-zis	AppleTalk Zone Information
207/tcp, udp	at-7	AppleTalk Unused
208/tcp, udp	at-8	AppleTalk Unused
209/tcp, udp	tam	Trivial Authenticated Mail Protocol
210/tcp, udp	z39.50	ANSI Z39.50
211/tcp, udp	914c/g	Texas Instruments 914C/G Terminal
212/tcp, udp	anet	ATEXSSTR
213/tcp, udp	ipx	IPX
214/tcp, udp	vmpwscs	VM PWSCS
215/tcp, udp	softpc	Insignia Solutions
216/tcp, udp	atls	Access Technology License Server
217/tcp, udp	dbase	dBASE UNIX
218/tcp, udp	mpp	Netix Message Posting Protocol
219/tcp, udp	uarps	Unisys ARPs
220/tcp, udp	imap3	Interactive Mail Access Protocol v3
221/tcp, udp	fln-spx	Berkeley rlogind with SPX auth
222/tcp, udp	fsh-spx	Berkeley rshd with SPX auth
223/tcp, udp	cdc	Certificate Distribution Center
224-241		Reserved
243/tcp, udp	sur-meas	Survey Measurement
245/tcp, udp	link	LINK
246/tcp, udp	dsp3270	Display Systems Protocol
247-255		Reserved

Table B.1   Port Assignments for Well Known Ports *(continued)*

Decimal	Keyword	Description
345/tcp, udp	pawserv	Perf Analysis Workbench
346/tcp, udp	zserv	Zebra server
347/tcp, udp	fatserv	Fatmen Server
371/tcp, udp	clearcase	Clearcase
372/tcp, udp	ulistserv	UNIX Listserv
373/tcp, udp	legent-1	Legent Corporation
374/tcp, udp	legent-2	Legent Corporation
512/tcp	print	Windows NT Server and Windows NT Workstation version 4.0 can send LPD client print jobs from any available reserved port between 512 and 1023. See also description for ports 721 to 731.
512/udp	biff	Used by mail system to notify users of new mail received; currently receives messages only from processes on the same computer; alias=comsat
513/tcp	login	Remote logon like telnet; automatic authentication performed, based on privileged port numbers and distributed databases that identify "authentication domains"
513/udp	who	Maintains databases showing who's logged on to the computers on a local net and the load average of the computer; alias=whod
514/tcp	cmd	Like exec, but automatic authentication is performed as for logon server
514/udp	syslog	
515/tcp, udp	printer	Spooler; alias=spooler. The print server LPD service will listen on tcp port 515 for incoming connections.
517/tcp, udp	talk	Like tenex link, but across computers; unfortunately, doesn't use link protocol (this is actually just a rendezvous port from which a TCP connection is established)
518/tcp, udp	ntalk	
519/tcp, udp	utime	Unixtime
520/tcp	efs	Extended file name server
520/udp	router	Local routing process (on site); uses variant of Xerox NS routing information protocol;alias=router routed
525/tcp, udp	timed	Timeserver
526/tcp, udp	tempo	Newdate
530/tcp, udp	courier	RPC

Table B.1   Port Assignments for Well Known Ports *(continued)*

Decimal	Keyword	Description
531/tcp	conference	Chat
531/udp	rvd-control	MIT disk
532/tcp, udp	netnews	Readnews
533/tcp, udp	netwall	For emergency broadcasts
540/tcp, udp	uucp	Uucpd
543/tcp, udp	klogin	
544/tcp, udp	kshell	Krcmd; alias=cmd
550/tcp, udp	new-rwho	New-who
555/tcp, udp	dsf	
556/tcp, udp	remotefs	Rfs server; alias=rfs_server rfs
560/tcp, udp	rmonitor	Rmonitord
561/tcp, udp	monitor	
562/tcp, udp	chshell	Chcmd
564/tcp, udp	9pfs	Plan 9 file service
565/tcp, udp	whoami	Whoami
570/tcp, udp	meter	Demon
571/tcp, udp	meter	Udemon
600/tcp, udp	ipcserver	Sun IPC server
607/tcp, udp	nqs	Nqs
666/tcp, udp	mdqs	
704/tcp, udp	elcsd	Errlog copy/server daemon
721-731/tcp	printer	Under Windows NT 3.5*x*, all TCP/IP print jobs *sent* from a Windows NT computer were sourced from TCP ports 721 through 731. This is changed for Windows NT Server and Windows NT Workstation version 4.0, which sources LPD client print jobs from any available reserved port between 512 and 1023.
740/tcp, udp	netcp	NETscout Control Protocol
741/tcp, udp	netgw	NetGW
742/tcp, udp	netrcs	Network based Rev. Cont. Sys.
744/tcp, udp	flexlm	Flexible License Manager
747/tcp, udp	fujitsu-dev	Fujitsu Device Control
748/tcp, udp	ris-cm	Russell Info Sci Calendar Manager
749/tcp, udp	kerberos-adm	Kerberos administration
750/tcp	rfile	Kerberos authentication; alias=kdc
750/udp	loadav	

Table B.1   Port Assignments for Well Known Ports *(continued)*

Decimal	Keyword	Description
751/tcp, udp	pump	Kerberos authentication
752/tcp, udp	qrh	Kerberos password server
753/tcp, udp	rrh	Kerberos userreg server
754/tcp, udp	tell	Send; Kerberos slave propagation
758/tcp, udp	nlogin	
759/tcp, udp	con	
760/tcp, udp	ns	
761/tcp, udp	rxe	
762/tcp, udp	quotad	
763/tcp, udp	cycleserv	
764/tcp, udp	omserv	
765/tcp, udp	webster	
767/tcp, udp	phonebook	Phone
769/tcp, udp	vid	
770/tcp, udp	cadlock	
771/tcp, udp	rtip	
772/tcp, udp	cycleserv2	
773/tcp	submit	
773/udp	notify	
774/tcp	rpasswd	
774/udp	acmaint_dbd	
775/tcp	entomb	
775/udp	acmaint_transd	
776/tcp, udp	wpages	
780/tcp, udp	wpgs	
781/tcp, udp	hp-collector	HP performance data collector
782/tcp, udp	hp-managed-node	HP performance data managed node
783/tcp, udp	hp-alarm-mgr	HP performance data alarm manager
800/tcp, udp	mdbs_daemon	
801/tcp, udp	device	
888/tcp	erlogin	Logon and environment passing
996/tcp, udp	xtreelic	XTREE License Server
997/tcp, udp	maitrd	

Table B.1   Port Assignments for Well Known Ports *(continued)*

Decimal	Keyword	Description
998/tcp	busboy	
998/udp	puparp	
999/tcp	garcon	
999/udp	applix	Applix ac
999/tcp, udp	puprouter	
1000/tcp	cadlock	
1000/udp	ock	

Port Assignments for Registered Ports

The registered ports are not controlled by the IANA and on most systems can be used by user processes or programs. Registered ports between 1024 and 5000 are also referred to as the *ephemeral* ports. Although the IANA cannot control uses of these ports, it does register or list uses of these ports as a convenience to the TCP/IP community. To the extent possible, these same port assignments are used with UDP. The registered ports are in the range 1024–65535.

This list specifies the port used by the Windows NT Server and Windows NT Workstation server process as its contact port for services and third-party software.

Note Programs that use Remote Procedure Call (RPC) to communicate can *randomly* select a registered port above 1024.

Table B.2   Port Assignments for Registered Ports

Decimal	Keyword	Description
1024		Reserved
1025/tcp, udp	blackjack	Network blackjack
1109/tcp	kpop	Pop with Kerberos
1167/udp	phone	
1248/tcp, udp	hermes	
1347/tcp, udp	bbn-mmc	Multimedia conferencing
1348/tcp, udp	bbn-mmx	Multimedia conferencing
1349/tcp, udp	sbook	Registration Network Protocol
1350/tcp, udp	editbench	Registration Network Protocol
1351/tcp, udp	equationbuilder	Digital Tool Works (MIT)

Table B.2   Port Assignments for Registered Ports *(continued)*

Decimal	Keyword	Description
1352/tcp, udp	lotusnote	Lotus Note
1512/tcp, udp	WINS	Reserved for future use for Microsoft Windows Internet Name Service
1524/tcp, udp	ingreslock	Ingres
1525/tcp, udp	orasrv	Oracle
1525/tcp, udp	prospero-np	Prospero nonprivileged
1527/tcp, udp	tlisrv	Oracle
1529/tcp, udp	coauthor	Oracle
1600/tcp, udp	issd	
1650/tcp, udp	nkd	
1666/udp	maze	
2000/tcp, udp	callbook	
2001/tcp	dc	
2001/udp	wizard	Curry
2002/tcp, udp	globe	
2004/tcp	mailbox	
2004/udp	emce	CCWS mm conf
2005/tcp	berknet	
2005/udp	oracle	
2006/tcp	invokator	
2006/udp	raid-cc	RAID
2007/tcp	dectalk	
2007/udp	raid-am	
2008/tcp	conf	
2008/udp	terminaldb	
2009/tcp	news	
2009/udp	whosockami	
2010/tcp	search	
2010/udp	pipe_server	
2011/tcp	raid-cc	RAID
2011/udp	servserv	
2012/tcp	ttyinfo	
2012/udp	raid-ac	
2013/tcp	raid-am	

Table B.2 Port Assignments for Registered Ports *(continued)*

Decimal	Keyword	Description
2013/udp	raid-cd	
2014/tcp	troff	
2014/udp	raid-sf	
2015/tcp	cypress	
2015/udp	raid-cs	
2016/tcp, udp	bootserver	
2017/tcp	cypress-stat	
2017/udp	bootclient	
2018/tcp	terminaldb	
2018/udp	rellpack	
2019/tcp	whosockami	
2019/udp	about	
2020/tcp, udp	xinupageserver	
2021/tcp	servexec	
2021/udp	xinuexpansion1	
2022/tcp	down	
2022/udp	xinuexpansion2	
2023/tcp, udp	xinuexpansion3	
2024/tcp, udp	xinuexpansion4	
2025/tcp	ellpack	
2025/udp	xribs	
2026/tcp, udp	scrabble	
2027/tcp, udp	shadowserver	
2028/tcp, udp	submitserver	
2030/tcp, udp	device2	
2032/tcp, udp	blackboard	
2033/tcp, udp	glogger	
2034/tcp, udp	scoremgr	
2035/tcp, udp	imsldoc	
2038/tcp, udp	objectmanager	
2040/tcp, udp	lam	
2041/tcp, udp	interbase	
2042/tcp, udp	isis	
2043/tcp, udp	isis-bcast	

Table B.2   Port Assignments for Registered Ports (*continued*)

Decimal	Keyword	Description
2044/tcp, udp	rimsl	
2045/tcp, udp	cdfunc	
2046/tcp, udp	sdfunc	
2047/tcp, udp	dls	
2048/tcp, udp	dls-monitor	
2049/tcp, udp	shilp	Sun NFS
2053/tcp	knetd	Kerberos de-multiplexer
2105/tcp	eklogin	Kerberos encrypted rlogon
2784/tcp, udp	www-dev	World Wide Web - development
3049/tcp, udp	NSWS	
4672/tcp, udp	rfa	Remote file access server
5000/tcp, udp	commplex-main	
5001/tcp, udp	commplex-link	
5002/tcp, udp	rfe	Radio Free Ethernet
5145/tcp, udp	rmonitor_secure	
5236/tcp, udp	padl2sim	
5555/tcp	rmt	Rmtd
5556/tcp	mtb	Mtbd (mtb backup)
6111/tcp, udp	sub-process	HP SoftBench Sub-Process Control
6558/tcp, udp	xdsxdm	
7000/tcp, udp	afs3-fileserver	File server itself
7001/tcp, udp	afs3-callback	Callbacks to cache managers
7002/tcp, udp	afs3-prserver	Users and groups database
7003/tcp, udp	afs3-vlserver	Volume location database
7004/tcp, udp	afs3-kaserver	AFS/Kerberos authentication service
7005/tcp, udp	afs3-volser	Volume management server
7006/tcp, udp	afs3-errors	Error interpretation service
7007/tcp, udp	afs3-bos	Basic overseer process
7008/tcp, udp	afs3-update	Server-to-server updater
7009/tcp, udp	afs3-rmtsys	Remote cache manager service
9535/tcp, udp	man	Remote man server
9536/tcp	w	
9537/tcp	mantst	Remote man server, testing
10000/tcp	bnews	

Table B.2   Port Assignments for Registered Ports *(continued)*

Decimal	Keyword	Description
10000/udp	rscs0	
10001/tcp	queue	
10001/udp	rscs1	
10002/tcp	poker	
10002/udp	rscs2	
10003/tcp	gateway	
10003/udp	rscs3	
10004/tcp	remp	
10004/udp	rscs4	
10005/udp	rscs5	
10006/udp	rscs6	
10007/udp	rscs7	
10008/udp	rscs8	
10009/udp	rscs9	
10010/udp	rscsa	
10011/udp	rscsb	
10012/tcp	qmaster	
10012/udp	qmaster	
17007/tcp, udp	isode-dua	

APPENDIX C

MIB Object Types for Windows NT

This appendix provides the managed-objects definitions contained in the following Windows NT-based MIBs:

- LAN Manager MIB-II for Windows NT
- Microsoft DHCP Server MIB
- Microsoft WINS Server MIB
- Microsoft Internet Information Server MIB
  - Microsoft FTP Server MIB
  - Microsoft Gopher Server MIB
  - Microsoft HTTP Server MIB

Note The Internet standards for Structure of Management Information (SMI) and MIB-II object types are defined in RFC 1155 and RFC 1213. Refer to those documents for definitions of the objects contained within SMI and MIB-II.

This appendix assumes that you are familiar with network management, TCP/IP, and SNMP. It also assumes that you are familiar with the concept of a *management information base* (MIB). If you are not familiar with TCP/IP or the Internet MIB-II, see *Internetworking with TCP/IP* by Douglas E. Comer (Prentice Hall, 1991) and *The Simple Book* by Marshall T. Rose (Prentice Hall, 1991).

LAN Manager MIB II for Windows NT

This MIB is documented in "LAN Manager 2.0 Management Information Base, LAN Manager MIB Working Group, Internet Draft: LanMgr-Mib-II" by Microsoft. The object definitions for this MIB are contained in the file named Lmmib2.mib.

The Windows NT implementation currently does not support the following objects:

- svSesNumConns
- svAuditLogSize
- wkstaErrorLogSize
- domLogonDomain

LanMgr-Mib-II-MIB DEFINITIONS ::= BEGIN

```
    IMPORTS
        enterprises, OBJECT-TYPE, Counter
            FROM RFC1155-SMI
        DisplayString
            FROM RFC1213-MIB;

    lanmanager  OBJECT IDENTIFIER ::= { enterprises 77 }
    lanmgr-2    OBJECT IDENTIFIER ::= { lanmanager 1 }
lanmgr-2 Tree

    common      OBJECT IDENTIFIER ::= { lanmgr-2 1 }
    server      OBJECT IDENTIFIER ::= { lanmgr-2 2 }
    workstation OBJECT IDENTIFIER ::= { lanmgr-2 3 }
    domain      OBJECT IDENTIFIER ::= { lanmgr-2 4 }


    Common Group

comVersionMaj OBJECT-TYPE
    SYNTAX  OCTET STRING
    ACCESS  read-only
    STATUS  mandatory
    DESCRIPTION
        "The major release version number of the software."
    ::= { common 1 }
```

comVersionMin OBJECT-TYPE
  SYNTAX OCTET STRING
  ACCESS read-only
  STATUS mandatory
  DESCRIPTION
      "The minor release version number of the software."
  ::= { common 2 }

comType OBJECT-TYPE
  SYNTAX OCTET STRING
  ACCESS read-only
  STATUS mandatory
  DESCRIPTION
      "The type of LAN Manager software this system is running.
      If no server is running, the node is a workstation. This
      object type is an octet string of length 4 treated as a bitmap
      (with the least significant bit being bit 0):

      OCTET 1   Software Type Bit
                - -
             workstation   0
             server   1
             sqlserver   2
             Primary DC   3
             Backup DC   4
             Time Source   5
             AFP Server   6
             Netware Server 7

      OCTET 2   undefined

      OCTET 3   undefined

      OCTET 4   undefined"
  ::= { common 3 }

comStatStart OBJECT-TYPE
  SYNTAX INTEGER
  ACCESS read-only
  STATUS mandatory
  DESCRIPTION
      "The time, represented as seconds since January 1, 1970, at
      which the statistics on this node were last cleared."
  ::= { common 4 }

comStatNumNetIOs OBJECT-TYPE
  SYNTAX Counter
  ACCESS read-only
  STATUS mandatory
  DESCRIPTION
    "The number of network I/O operations submitted on this node."
  ::= { common 5 }

comStatFiNetIOs OBJECT-TYPE
  SYNTAX Counter
  ACCESS read-only
  STATUS mandatory
  DESCRIPTION
    "The number of network I/O operations on this node that failed
    issue."
  ::= { common 6 }

comStatFcNetIOs OBJECT-TYPE
  SYNTAX Counter
  ACCESS read-only
  STATUS mandatory
  DESCRIPTION
    "The number of network I/O operations on this node that failed
    completion."
  ::= { common 7 }

The Server Group

svDescription OBJECT-TYPE
  SYNTAX DisplayString (SIZE (0..255))
  ACCESS read-write
  STATUS mandatory
  DESCRIPTION
    "A comment describing this server."
  ::= { server 1 }

svSvcNumber   OBJECT-TYPE
  SYNTAX INTEGER
  ACCESS read-only
  STATUS mandatory
  DESCRIPTION
    "The number of network services installed on this server."
  ::= { server 2 }

svSvcTable   OBJECT-TYPE
  SYNTAX SEQUENCE OF SvSvcEntry
  ACCESS not-accessible
  STATUS mandatory
  DESCRIPTION
        "A list of service entries describing network services installed
        on this server."
  ::= { server 3 }

svSvcEntry OBJECT-TYPE
  SYNTAX SvSvcEntry
  ACCESS not-accessible
  STATUS mandatory
  DESCRIPTION
        "The names of the network services installed on this server."
  INDEX   { svSvcName }
  ::= { svSvcTable 1 }
SvSvcEntry ::= SEQUENCE {
        svSvcName
            DisplayString,
        svSvcInstalledState
          INTEGER,
        svSvcOperatingState
          INTEGER,
        svSvcCanBeUninstalled
          INTEGER,
        svSvcCanBePaused
          INTEGER
        }

svSvcName OBJECT-TYPE
  SYNTAX DisplayString (SIZE (1..15))
  ACCESS read-only
  STATUS mandatory
  DESCRIPTION
        "The name of the network service described by this entry."

  ::= { svSvcEntry 1 }

svSvcInstalledState OBJECT-TYPE
    SYNTAX
        INTEGER {
            uninstalled(1),
            install-pending(2),
            uninstall-pending(3),
            installed(4)
        }
    ACCESS read-only
    STATUS mandatory
    DESCRIPTION
        "The installation status of the network service specified by
        this entry."
    ::= { svSvcEntry 2 }

svSvcOperatingState OBJECT-TYPE
    SYNTAX
        INTEGER {
            active(1),
            continue-pending(2),
            pause-pending(3),
            paused(4)
        }
    ACCESS read-only
    STATUS mandatory
    DESCRIPTION
        "The operating status of the network service specified by
        this entry."
    ::= { svSvcEntry 3 }

svSvcCanBeUninstalled OBJECT-TYPE
    SYNTAX
        INTEGER {
            cannot-be-uninstalled(1),
            can-be-uninstalled(2)
        }

    ACCESS read-only
    STATUS mandatory
    DESCRIPTION
        "Whether or not the network service specified by this entry
        can be uninstalled."
    ::= { svSvcEntry 4 }

svSvcCanBePaused OBJECT-TYPE
    SYNTAX
        INTEGER {
            cannot-be-paused(1),
            can-be-paused(2)
        }
    ACCESS read-only
    STATUS mandatory
    DESCRIPTION
        "Whether or not the network service specified by this entry
        can be paused."
    ::= { svSvcEntry 5 }

svStatOpens   OBJECT-TYPE
    SYNTAX Counter
    ACCESS read-only
    STATUS mandatory
    DESCRIPTION
        "The total number of files that have been opened on the server."
    ::= { server 4 }
svStatDevOpens OBJECT-TYPE
    SYNTAX Counter
    ACCESS read-only
    STATUS mandatory
    DESCRIPTION
        "The total number of communication devices opened on the server."
    ::= { server 5 }

svStatQueuedJobs   OBJECT-TYPE
    SYNTAX Counter
    ACCESS read-only
    STATUS mandatory
    DESCRIPTION
        "The total number of print jobs that have been spooled on the
        server."
    ::= { server 6 }

svStatSOpens   OBJECT-TYPE
    SYNTAX Counter
    ACCESS read-only
    STATUS mandatory
    DESCRIPTION
        "The number of sessions that have been started on the server."
    ::= { server 7 }

svStatErrorOuts OBJECT-TYPE
    SYNTAX Counter
    ACCESS read-only
    STATUS mandatory
    DESCRIPTION
        "The number of sessions disconnected due to an error on the
        server."
    ::= { server 8 }

svStatPwErrors OBJECT-TYPE
    SYNTAX Counter
    ACCESS read-only
    STATUS mandatory
    DESCRIPTION
        "The number of password violations encountered on the server."
    ::= { server 9 }
svStatPermErrors   OBJECT-TYPE
    SYNTAX Counter
    ACCESS read-only
    STATUS mandatory
    DESCRIPTION
        "The number of access permission violations encountered on this
        server."
    ::= { server 10 }

svStatSysErrors OBJECT-TYPE
    SYNTAX Counter
    ACCESS read-only
    STATUS mandatory
    DESCRIPTION
        "The number of system errors encountered on the server."
    ::= { server 11 }

svStatSentBytes OBJECT-TYPE
    SYNTAX Counter
    ACCESS read-only
    STATUS mandatory
    DESCRIPTION
        "The number of bytes sent by the server."
    ::= { server 12 }

svStatRcvdBytes OBJECT-TYPE
  SYNTAX Counter
  ACCESS read-only
  STATUS mandatory
  DESCRIPTION
      "The number of bytes received by this server."
  ::= { server 13 }

svStatAvResponse   OBJECT-TYPE
  SYNTAX INTEGER
  ACCESS read-only
  STATUS mandatory
  DESCRIPTION
      "The mean number of milliseconds it has taken this server
      to process a workstation I/O request."
  ::= { server 14 }

svSecurityMode OBJECT-TYPE
  SYNTAX
    INTEGER {
      share-level(1),
      user-level(2)
    }
  ACCESS read-only
  STATUS mandatory
  DESCRIPTION
      "The type of security being run at this server."
  ::= { server 15 }

svUsers OBJECT-TYPE
  SYNTAX INTEGER
  ACCESS read-only
  STATUS mandatory
  DESCRIPTION
      "The number of concurrent users this server is able to support."
  ::= { server 16 }

svStatReqBufsNeeded   OBJECT-TYPE
  SYNTAX Counter
  ACCESS read-only
  STATUS mandatory
  DESCRIPTION
      "The number of times the server has needed a request buffer in
      the process of handling a client request and could not allocate
      one."
  ::= { server 17 }

svStatBigBufsNeeded   OBJECT-TYPE
  SYNTAX Counter
  ACCESS read-only
  STATUS mandatory
  DESCRIPTION
    "The number of times the server has needed a big buffer in the
    process of handling a client request and could not allocate one."
  ::= { server 18 }

svSessionNumber OBJECT-TYPE
  SYNTAX INTEGER
  ACCESS read-only
  STATUS mandatory
  DESCRIPTION
    "The number of sessions clients have established to this server."
  ::= { server 19 }

svSessionTable OBJECT-TYPE
  SYNTAX SEQUENCE OF SvSessionEntry
  ACCESS not-accessible
  STATUS mandatory
  DESCRIPTION
    "A list of session entries corresponding to the current sessions
    clients have with this server."
  ::= { server 20 }

svSessionEntry OBJECT-TYPE
  SYNTAX SvSessionEntry
  ACCESS not-accessible
  STATUS mandatory
  DESCRIPTION
    "A session that is currently established to this server."
  INDEX   { svSesClientName, svSesUserName }
  ::= { svSessionTable 1 }

```
SvSessionEntry ::= SEQUENCE {
        svSesClientName
        DisplayString,
            svSesUserName
        DisplayString,
            svSesNumConns
                INTEGER,
            svSesNumOpens
                INTEGER,
            svSesTime
                Counter,
        svSesIdleTime
                Counter,
        svSesClientType
                INTEGER,
            svSesState
                INTEGER
                }

svSesClientName  OBJECT-TYPE
    SYNTAX  DisplayString (SIZE (1..15))
    ACCESS  read-only
    STATUS  mandatory
    DESCRIPTION
        "The name of the remote machine that has established the session."
    ::= { svSessionEntry 1 }

svSesUserName  OBJECT-TYPE
    SYNTAX  DisplayString (SIZE (1..20))
    ACCESS  read-only
    STATUS  mandatory
    DESCRIPTION
        "The name of the user at the remote machine that established the
        session."
    ::= { svSessionEntry 2 }

svSesNumConns  OBJECT-TYPE
    SYNTAX  INTEGER
    ACCESS  read-only
    STATUS  mandatory
    DESCRIPTION
        "The number of connections to server resources currently active
        across this session."
    ::= { svSessionEntry 3 }
```

svSesNumOpens OBJECT-TYPE
    SYNTAX INTEGER
    ACCESS read-only
    STATUS mandatory
    DESCRIPTION
        "The number of files, devices, and pipes that are open on this
        session."
    ::= { svSessionEntry 4 }

svSesTime OBJECT-TYPE
    SYNTAX Counter
    ACCESS read-only
    STATUS mandatory
    DESCRIPTION
        "The length of time in seconds this session has been established."
    ::= { svSessionEntry 5 }

svSesIdleTime OBJECT-TYPE
    SYNTAX Counter
    ACCESS read-only
    STATUS mandatory
    DESCRIPTION
        "The length of time in seconds this session has been idle."
    ::= { svSessionEntry 6 }
svSesClientType OBJECT-TYPE
    SYNTAX INTEGER {
        down-level(1),
        dos-lm(2),
        dos-lm-2(3),
        os2-lm-1(4),
        os2-lm-2(5),
        dos-lm-2-1(6),
        os2-lm-2-1(7),
        afp-1-1(8),
        afp-2-0(9),
        nt-3-1(10)
    }
    ACCESS read-only
    STATUS mandatory
    DESCRIPTION
        "The type of client that established the session."
    ::= { svSessionEntry 7 }

```
svSesState  OBJECT-TYPE
  SYNTAX  INTEGER {
        active(1),
        deleted(2)
     }
  ACCESS  read-write
  STATUS  mandatory
  DESCRIPTION
        "Used to indicate the state of this session.
        The deleted state will never be returned on a
        session but can be used in set requests to delete
        a session."
  ::= { svSessionEntry 8 }

svAutoDisconnects  OBJECT-TYPE
  SYNTAX  INTEGER
  ACCESS  read-only
  STATUS  mandatory
  DESCRIPTION
        "The number of sessions that the server has
        auto-disconnected due to timeout."
  ::= { server  21 }
svDisConTime  OBJECT-TYPE
  SYNTAX  INTEGER
  ACCESS  read-write
  STATUS  mandatory
  DESCRIPTION
        "The number of seconds the server waits before
        disconnecting an idle session.  A value of 0xffff
        indicates that idle sessions will never be disconnected."
  ::= { server  22 }

svAuditLogSize  OBJECT-TYPE
  SYNTAX  INTEGER
  ACCESS  read-write
  STATUS  mandatory
  DESCRIPTION
        "The maximum size in kilobytes that the server's audit
        log can attain."
  ::= { server  23 }
```

```
svUserNumber OBJECT-TYPE
  SYNTAX  INTEGER
  ACCESS  read-only
  STATUS  mandatory
  DESCRIPTION
      "The number of users that have accounts on this server."
  ::= { server 24 }

svUserTable OBJECT-TYPE
  SYNTAX  SEQUENCE OF SvUserEntry
  ACCESS  not-accessible
  STATUS  mandatory
  DESCRIPTION
      "The table of active user accounts on this server."
  ::= { server 25 }

svUserEntry OBJECT-TYPE
  SYNTAX  SvUserEntry
  ACCESS  not-accessible
  STATUS  mandatory
  DESCRIPTION
      "One of the user accounts on this server."
  INDEX  { svUserName }
  ::= { svUserTable 1 }
SvUserEntry ::= SEQUENCE {
    svUserName
    DisplayString
  }

svUserName OBJECT-TYPE
  SYNTAX  DisplayString (SIZE (1..20))
  ACCESS  read-only
  STATUS  mandatory
  DESCRIPTION
      "The name of the user account."
  ::= { svUserEntry 1 }

svShareNumber OBJECT-TYPE
  SYNTAX  INTEGER
  ACCESS  read-only
  STATUS  mandatory
  DESCRIPTION
      "The number of shared resources on this server."
  ::= { server 26 }
```

svShareTable OBJECT-TYPE
  SYNTAX SEQUENCE OF SvShareEntry
  ACCESS not-accessible
  STATUS mandatory
  DESCRIPTION
      "The table of shares on this server."
  ::= { server 27 }

svShareEntry OBJECT-TYPE
  SYNTAX SvShareEntry
  ACCESS not-accessible
  STATUS mandatory
  DESCRIPTION
      "A table entry corresponding to a single share on this server."
  INDEX { svShareName }
  ::= { svShareTable 1 }

SvShareEntry ::= SEQUENCE {
      svShareName
        DisplayString ,
      svSharePath
        DisplayString ,
      svShareComment
        DisplayString
    }
svShareName OBJECT-TYPE
  SYNTAX DisplayString (SIZE (1..12))
  ACCESS read-only
  STATUS mandatory
  DESCRIPTION
      "The name of the share."
  ::= { svShareEntry 1 }

svSharePath OBJECT-TYPE
  SYNTAX DisplayString (SIZE (1..255))
  ACCESS read-only
  STATUS mandatory
  DESCRIPTION
      "The local name of this shared resource."
  ::= { svShareEntry 2 }

svShareComment OBJECT-TYPE
  SYNTAX DisplayString (SIZE (0..255))
  ACCESS read-only
  STATUS mandatory
  DESCRIPTION
      "A comment associated with this share."
  ::= { svShareEntry 3 }

svPrintQNumber OBJECT-TYPE
  SYNTAX INTEGER
  ACCESS read-only
  STATUS mandatory
  DESCRIPTION
      "The number of print queues on this server."
  ::= { server 28 }

svPrintQTable OBJECT-TYPE
  SYNTAX SEQUENCE OF SvPrintQEntry
  ACCESS not-accessible
  STATUS mandatory
  DESCRIPTION
      "The table of print queues on this server."
  ::= { server 29 }
svPrintQEntry OBJECT-TYPE
  SYNTAX SvPrintQEntry
  ACCESS not-accessible
  STATUS mandatory
  DESCRIPTION
      "A table entry corresponding to a single print queue on this
      server."
  INDEX   { svPrintQName }
  ::= { svPrintQTable 1 }

SvPrintQEntry ::= SEQUENCE {
    svPrintQName
      DisplayString ,
    svPrintQNumJobs
      INTEGER
    }

svPrintQName OBJECT-TYPE
  SYNTAX DisplayString (SIZE (1..12))
  ACCESS read-only
  STATUS mandatory
  DESCRIPTION
      "The name of the print queue."
  ::= { svPrintQEntry 1 }

svPrintQNumJobs OBJECT-TYPE
  SYNTAX INTEGER
  ACCESS read-only
  STATUS mandatory
  DESCRIPTION
      "The number of jobs currently in this print queue."
  ::= { svPrintQEntry 2 }

  The Workstation Group

wkstaStatSessStarts OBJECT-TYPE
  SYNTAX Counter
  ACCESS read-only
  STATUS mandatory
  DESCRIPTION
      "The number of sessions that this workstation has initiated."
  ::= { workstation 1 }
wkstaStatSessFails OBJECT-TYPE
  SYNTAX Counter
  ACCESS read-only
  STATUS mandatory
  DESCRIPTION
      "The number of failed sessions that this workstation has
      experienced."
  ::= { workstation 2 }

wkstaStatUses OBJECT-TYPE
  SYNTAX Counter
  ACCESS read-only
  STATUS mandatory
  DESCRIPTION
      "The number of connections this workstation has initiated."
  ::= { workstation 3 }

wkstaStatUseFails OBJECT-TYPE
    SYNTAX Counter
    ACCESS read-only
    STATUS mandatory
    DESCRIPTION
        "The number of failed connections this workstation has
        experienced."
    ::= { workstation 4 }

wkstaStatAutoRecs OBJECT-TYPE
    SYNTAX Counter
    ACCESS read-only
    STATUS mandatory
    DESCRIPTION
        "The number of sessions broken and then automatically
        reestablished."
    ::= { workstation 5 }

wkstaErrorLogSize OBJECT-TYPE
    SYNTAX INTEGER
    ACCESS read-write
    STATUS mandatory
    DESCRIPTION
        "The size in kilobytes to which the workstation error log
        can grow."
    ::= { workstation 6 }

wkstaUseNumber OBJECT-TYPE
    SYNTAX INTEGER
    ACCESS read-only
    STATUS mandatory
    DESCRIPTION
        "The number of active uses the workstation is currently
        maintaining."
    ::= { workstation 7 }

wkstaUseTable OBJECT-TYPE
    SYNTAX SEQUENCE OF WkstaUseEntry
    ACCESS not-accessible
    STATUS mandatory
    DESCRIPTION
        "The table of active uses made by this workstation."
    ::= { workstation 8 }

```
wkstaUseEntry  OBJECT-TYPE
    SYNTAX  WkstaUseEntry
    ACCESS  not-accessible
    STATUS  mandatory
    DESCRIPTION
        "A use of a remote network resource."
    INDEX  { useLocalName, useRemote }
    ::= { wkstaUseTable 1 }

WkstaUseEntry ::= SEQUENCE {
        useLocalName
            DisplayString ,
        useRemote
            DisplayString ,
        useStatus
            INTEGER
    }

useLocalName  OBJECT-TYPE
    SYNTAX  DisplayString (SIZE (0..8))
    ACCESS  read-only
    STATUS  mandatory
    DESCRIPTION
        "The name of the local devicename (such as e: or lpt1:) that
        is redirected."
    ::= { wkstaUseEntry 1 }
useRemote  OBJECT-TYPE
    SYNTAX  DisplayString (SIZE (1..255))
    ACCESS  read-only
    STATUS  mandatory
    DESCRIPTION
        "The name of the remote shared resource to which the redirection
        has been made. (such as \\server\share)."
    ::= { wkstaUseEntry 2 }
```

```
useStatus  OBJECT-TYPE
  SYNTAX
    INTEGER {
      use-ok(1),
      use-paused(2),
      use-session-lost(3),
      use-network-error(4),
      use-connecting(5),
      use-reconnecting(6)
    }
  ACCESS  read-only
  STATUS  mandatory
  DESCRIPTION
      "The status of this connection."
  ::= { wkstaUseEntry 3 }
```

The Domain Group

```
domPrimaryDomain  OBJECT-TYPE
  SYNTAX  DisplayString (SIZE (1..15))
  ACCESS  read-only
  STATUS  mandatory
  DESCRIPTION
      "The name of the primary domain to which this machine belongs."
  ::= { domain  1 }
```

```
domLogonDomain  OBJECT-TYPE
  SYNTAX  DisplayString (SIZE (1..15))
  ACCESS  read-only
  STATUS  mandatory
  DESCRIPTION
      "The name of the domain to which this machine is logged on."
  ::= { domain  2 }
domOtherDomainNumber  OBJECT-TYPE
  SYNTAX  INTEGER
  ACCESS  read-only
  STATUS  mandatory
  DESCRIPTION
      "The number of entries in domOtherDomainTable."
  ::= { domain  3 }
```

domOtherDomainTable OBJECT-TYPE
   SYNTAX SEQUENCE OF DomOtherDomainEntry
   ACCESS not-accessible
   STATUS mandatory
   DESCRIPTION
        "The list of other domains which this machine is monitoring."
   ::= { domain 4 }

domOtherDomainEntry OBJECT-TYPE
   SYNTAX DomOtherDomainEntry
   ACCESS not-accessible
   STATUS mandatory
   DESCRIPTION
        "An entry in the table of other domains."
   INDEX { domOtherName }
   ::= { domOtherDomainTable 1 }

DomOtherDomainEntry ::= SEQUENCE {
      domOtherName
        DisplayString
      }

domOtherName OBJECT-TYPE
   SYNTAX DisplayString (SIZE (1..15))
   ACCESS read-write
   STATUS mandatory
   DESCRIPTION
        "The name of an additional domain which this machine is
        monitoring."
   ::= { domOtherDomainEntry 1 }

domServerNumber OBJECT-TYPE
   SYNTAX INTEGER
   ACCESS read-only
   STATUS mandatory
   DESCRIPTION
        "The number of entries in domServerTable."
   ::= { domain 5 }
domServerTable OBJECT-TYPE
   SYNTAX SEQUENCE OF DomServerEntry
   ACCESS not-accessible
   STATUS mandatory
   DESCRIPTION
        "The list of non-hidden servers that are on all of the
        domains this machine is monitoring."
   ::= { domain 6 }

```
domServerEntry OBJECT-TYPE
  SYNTAX DomServerEntry
  ACCESS not-accessible
  STATUS mandatory
  DESCRIPTION
      "An entry in the domain server table."
  INDEX  { domServerName }
  ::= { domServerTable 1 }

DomServerEntry ::= SEQUENCE {
    domServerName
      DisplayString
  }

domServerName OBJECT-TYPE
  SYNTAX  DisplayString (SIZE (1..15))
  ACCESS  read-only
  STATUS  mandatory
  DESCRIPTION
      "The name of a server on one of the domains which this
      machine is monitoring."
  ::= { domServerEntry 1 }

domLogonNumber OBJECT-TYPE
  SYNTAX  INTEGER
  ACCESS  read-only
  STATUS  mandatory
  DESCRIPTION
      "The number of entries in domLogonTable."
  ::= { domain 7 }
domLogonTable OBJECT-TYPE
  SYNTAX  SEQUENCE OF DomLogonEntry
  ACCESS  not-accessible
  STATUS  mandatory
  DESCRIPTION
      "The list of domain logons which this machine has processed.
      Available only on servers acting as primary or backup domain
      controllers.  To compile the complete table of all logons on
      a given domain, it is necessary to query all primary and backup
      domain controllers on the domain."
  ::= { domain 8 }
```

```
domLogonEntry OBJECT-TYPE
  SYNTAX  DomLogonEntry
  ACCESS  not-accessible
  STATUS  mandatory
  DESCRIPTION
      "An entry in the logon table."
  INDEX   { domLogonUser, domLogonMachine }
  ::= { domLogonTable 1 }

DomLogonEntry ::= SEQUENCE {
      domLogonUser
        DisplayString ,
      domLogonMachine
        DisplayString
    }

domLogonUser OBJECT-TYPE
  SYNTAX  DisplayString (SIZE (1..20))
  ACCESS  read-only
  STATUS  mandatory
  DESCRIPTION
      "The name of the user who is logged on to this domain."
  ::= { domLogonEntry 1 }

domLogonMachine OBJECT-TYPE
  SYNTAX  DisplayString (SIZE (1..15))
  ACCESS  read-only
  STATUS  mandatory
  DESCRIPTION
      "The name of the machine from which the user logged on."
  ::= { domLogonEntry 2 }

END
```

Microsoft DHCP Server MIB

The DHCP Server MIB contains object-types that are used to monitor the network traffic between remote hosts and the DHCP server.

DHCP-MIB DEFINITIONS ::= BEGIN

    IMPORTS
        enterprises,
        OBJECT-TYPE
            FROM RFC1155-SMI
        DisplayString
            FROM RFC1213-MIB
        microsoft,
        software
            FROM WINS-MIB;

-- microsoft OBJECT IDENTIFIER ::= { enterprises 311 }
-- software OBJECT IDENTIFIER ::= { microsoft 1 }

    dhcp   OBJECT IDENTIFIER ::= { software 3 }
    dhcpPar   OBJECT IDENTIFIER ::= { dhcp 1 }
    dhcpScope   OBJECT IDENTIFIER ::= { dhcp 2 }

    -- Dhcp MIB
  -- Parameters (Prefix Par)

    parDhcpStartTime OBJECT-TYPE
      SYNTAX DisplayString (SIZE (1..30))
      ACCESS read-only
      STATUS mandatory
      DESCRIPTION
        "Dhcp Server start time"
      ::= { dhcpPar 1 }

    parDhcpTotalNoOfDiscovers OBJECT-TYPE
      SYNTAX Counter
      ACCESS read-only
      STATUS mandatory
      DESCRIPTION
      "This variable indicates the number of
      discovery messages received"
      ::= { dhcpPar 2 }
parDhcpTotalNoOfRequests OBJECT-TYPE
      SYNTAX Counter
      ACCESS read-only

STATUS mandatory
DESCRIPTION
  "This variable indicates the number of
  requests received"
::= { dhcpPar 3 }

parDhcpTotalNoOfReleases OBJECT-TYPE
  SYNTAX Counter
  ACCESS read-only
  STATUS mandatory
  DESCRIPTION
    "This variable indicates the number of
    releases received"
  ::= { dhcpPar 4 }

parDhcpTotalNoOfOffers OBJECT-TYPE
  SYNTAX Counter
  ACCESS read-only
  STATUS mandatory
  DESCRIPTION
    "This variable indicates the number of
    offers sent"
  ::= { dhcpPar 5 }

parDhcpTotalNoOfAcks OBJECT-TYPE
  SYNTAX Counter
  ACCESS read-only
  STATUS mandatory
  DESCRIPTION
    "This variable indicates the number of
    acks received"
  ::= { dhcpPar 6 }

parDhcpTotalNoOfNacks OBJECT-TYPE
  SYNTAX Counter
  ACCESS read-only
  STATUS mandatory
  DESCRIPTION
    "This variable indicates the number of
    nacks received"
  ::= { dhcpPar 7 }
parDhcpTotalNoOfDeclines OBJECT-TYPE
  SYNTAX Counter
  ACCESS read-only
  STATUS mandatory
  DESCRIPTION

```
                    "This variable indicates the number of
                    declines"
                ::= { dhcpPar 8 }


    -- scope group (Prefix Scope)

            scopeTable OBJECT-TYPE
                SYNTAX  SEQUENCE OF ScopeTableEntry
                ACCESS  read-only
                STATUS  mandatory
                DESCRIPTION
                    "A list of subnets maintained by the server"
                ::= { dhcpScope 1 }


            scopeTableEntry  OBJECT-TYPE
                SYNTAX  ScopeTableEntry
                ACCESS  read-only
                STATUS  mandatory
                DESCRIPTION
                "This is the row corresponding to a subnet"
                INDEX   { subnetAdd }
                ::= { scopeTable 1 }


        ScopeTableEntry ::= SEQUENCE {
            subnetAdd
                IpAddress,

            noAddInUse
                Counter,

            noAddFree
                Counter,

            noPendingOffers
                Counter
            }
            subnetAdd  OBJECT-TYPE
                SYNTAX  IpAddress
                ACCESS  read-only
                STATUS  mandatory
                DESCRIPTION
                "This is the subnet address "
                ::= { scopeTableEntry 1 }
```

noAddInUse OBJECT-TYPE
SYNTAX Counter
ACCESS read-only
STATUS mandatory
  DESCRIPTION
    "This is the number of addresses in use"
  ::= { scopeTableEntry 2 }

noAddFree OBJECT-TYPE
SYNTAX Counter
ACCESS read-only
STATUS mandatory
  DESCRIPTION
    "This is the number of addresses that are free "
  ::= { scopeTableEntry 3 }

noPendingOffers OBJECT-TYPE
SYNTAX Counter
ACCESS read-only
STATUS mandatory
  DESCRIPTION
    "This is the number of addresses that are currently in the
      offer state"
  ::= { scopeTableEntry 4 }

END

Microsoft WINS Server MIB

The WINS server MIB contains object-types that are used to monitor the network traffic between remote hosts and the WINS server.

WINS-MIB DEFINITIONS ::= BEGIN

```
    IMPORTS
        enterprises,
        OBJECT-TYPE
            FROM RFC1155-SMI
        DisplayString
            FROM RFC1213-MIB;


microsoft    OBJECT IDENTIFIER ::= { enterprises 311 }
    software      OBJECT IDENTIFIER ::= { microsoft 1 }
    wins    OBJECT IDENTIFIER ::= { software 2 }
    par   OBJECT IDENTIFIER ::= { wins 1 }
    pull      OBJECT IDENTIFIER ::= { wins 2 }
    push      OBJECT IDENTIFIER ::= { wins 3 }
    datafiles     OBJECT IDENTIFIER ::= { wins 4 }
    cmd OBJECT IDENTIFIER ::= { wins 5 }


    -- WINS MIB
  -- Parameters (Prefix  Par)


    parWinsStartTime OBJECT-TYPE
        SYNTAX  DisplayString (SIZE (1..30))
        ACCESS  read-only
        STATUS  mandatory
        DESCRIPTION
            "WINS start time"
        ::= { par 1 }
    parLastPScvTime OBJECT-TYPE
        SYNTAX  DisplayString  (SIZE (1..30))
        ACCESS  read-only
        STATUS  mandatory
        DESCRIPTION
            "Most recent date and time at which planned scavenging
        took place.  Planned scavenging happens at intervals
        specified in the registry.  Scavenging involves
        changing owned non-refreshed entries to the released
        state. Further, replicas may be changed to tombstones,
        tombstones may be deleted, and revalidation of old
        replicas may take place"
        ::= { par 2 }
```

parLastATScvTime OBJECT-TYPE
    SYNTAX DisplayString (SIZE (1..30))
    ACCESS read-only
    STATUS mandatory
    DESCRIPTION
        "Most recent date and time at which scavenging as a
    result of administrative action took place"
    ::= { par 3 }

parLastTombScvTime OBJECT-TYPE
    SYNTAX DisplayString (SIZE (1..30))
    ACCESS read-only
    STATUS mandatory
    DESCRIPTION
        "Most recent date and time at which replica tombstone
    scavenging took place"
    ::= { par 4 }

parLastVerifyScvTime OBJECT-TYPE
    SYNTAX DisplayString (SIZE (1..30))
    ACCESS read-only
    STATUS mandatory
    DESCRIPTION
        "Most recent date and time at which revalidation of
    old active replicas took place"
    ::= { par 5 }
parLastPRplTime OBJECT-TYPE
    SYNTAX DisplayString (SIZE (1..30))
    ACCESS read-only
    STATUS mandatory
    DESCRIPTION
        "Most recent date and time at which planned replication
    took place. Planned replication happens at intervals
    specified in the registry"
    ::= { par 6 }

parLastATRplTime OBJECT-TYPE
    SYNTAX DisplayString (SIZE (1..30))
    ACCESS read-only
    STATUS mandatory
    DESCRIPTION
        "Most recent date and time at which administrator-
    triggered replication took place."
    ::= { par 7 }

parLastNTRplTime OBJECT-TYPE
  SYNTAX DisplayString (SIZE (1..30))
  ACCESS read-only
  STATUS mandatory
  DESCRIPTION
      "Most recent date and time at which network-triggered
  replication took place. Network-triggered replication
  happens as a result of an update notification message
  from a remote WINS"
  ::= { par 8 }

parLastACTRplTime OBJECT-TYPE
  SYNTAX DisplayString (SIZE (1..30))
  ACCESS read-only
  STATUS mandatory
  DESCRIPTION
      "Most recent date and time at which address change-
  triggered replication took place. Address change-
  triggered replication happens when the address of
  an owned name changes due to a new registration"
  ::= { par 9 }
parLastInitDbTime OBJECT-TYPE
  SYNTAX DisplayString (SIZE (1..30))
  ACCESS read-only
  STATUS mandatory
  DESCRIPTION
      "Most recent date and time at which the local database
  was populated statically from one or more data files"
  ::= { par 10 }

parLastCounterResetTime OBJECT-TYPE
  SYNTAX DisplayString (SIZE (1..30))
  ACCESS read-only
  STATUS mandatory
  DESCRIPTION
      "Most recent date and time at which the local counters
  were initialized to zero"
  ::= { par 11 }

parWinsTotalNoOfReg OBJECT-TYPE
    SYNTAX Counter
    ACCESS read-only
    STATUS mandatory
    DESCRIPTION
      "This variable indicates the number of
      registrations received"
    ::= { par 12 }

parWinsTotalNoOfQueries OBJECT-TYPE
    SYNTAX Counter
    ACCESS read-only
    STATUS mandatory
    DESCRIPTION
      "This variable indicates the number of
      queries received"
    ::= { par 13 }

parWinsTotalNoOfRel OBJECT-TYPE
    SYNTAX Counter
    ACCESS read-only
    STATUS mandatory
    DESCRIPTION
      "This variable indicates the number of
      releases received"
    ::= { par 14 }
parWinsTotalNoOfSuccRel OBJECT-TYPE
    SYNTAX Counter
    ACCESS read-only
    STATUS mandatory
    DESCRIPTION
      "This variable indicates the number of
      releases that succeeded"
    ::= { par 15 }

parWinsTotalNoOfFailRel OBJECT-TYPE
    SYNTAX Counter
    ACCESS read-only
    STATUS mandatory
    DESCRIPTION
      "This variable indicates the number of
      releases that failed"
    ::= { par 16 }

parWinsTotalNoOfSuccQueries OBJECT-TYPE
  SYNTAX Counter
  ACCESS read-only
  STATUS mandatory
  DESCRIPTION
    "This variable indicates the number of
    queries that succeeded"
  ::= { par 17 }

parWinsTotalNoOfFailQueries OBJECT-TYPE
  SYNTAX Counter
  ACCESS read-only
  STATUS mandatory
  DESCRIPTION
    "This variable indicates the number of
    queries that failed"
  ::= { par 18 }

parRefreshInterval OBJECT-TYPE
  SYNTAX INTEGER
  ACCESS read-write
  STATUS mandatory
  DESCRIPTION
    "This variable indicates the refresh interval.
    Unit is in milliseconds"
  ::= { par 19 }
parTombstoneInterval OBJECT-TYPE
  SYNTAX INTEGER
  ACCESS read-write
  STATUS mandatory
  DESCRIPTION
    "This variable indicates the tombstone interval.
    Unit is in milliseconds"
  ::= { par 20 }

parTombstoneTimeout OBJECT-TYPE
  SYNTAX INTEGER
  ACCESS read-write
  STATUS mandatory
  DESCRIPTION
    "This variable indicates the tombstone timeout.
    Unit is in milliseconds"
  ::= { par 21 }

parVerifyInterval OBJECT-TYPE
    SYNTAX INTEGER
    ACCESS read-write
    STATUS mandatory
    DESCRIPTION
        "This variable indicates the verify interval.
        Unit is in milliseconds."
    ::= { par 22 }

parVersCounterStartValLowWord OBJECT-TYPE
    SYNTAX Counter
    ACCESS read-write
    STATUS mandatory
    DESCRIPTION
        "This variable indicates the low word of the
        version counter that WINS should start with"
    ::= { par 23 }

parVersCounterStartValHighWord OBJECT-TYPE
    SYNTAX Counter
    ACCESS read-write
    STATUS mandatory
    DESCRIPTION
        "This variable indicates the high word of the
        version counter that WINS should start with"
    ::= { par 24 }
parRplOnlyWCnfPnrs OBJECT-TYPE
    SYNTAX INTEGER
    ACCESS read-write
    STATUS mandatory
    DESCRIPTION
        "This variable indicates whether or not
                replication should be done with non-configured   partners. If
            not set to zero, replication will be done only   with partners listed
            in the registry (except when an
        update notification comes in)"
    ::= { par 25 }

parStaticDataInit OBJECT-TYPE
    SYNTAX INTEGER
    ACCESS read-write
    STATUS mandatory
    DESCRIPTION
      "This variable indicates whether static data should
      be read in at initialization and reconfiguration time.
      Update of any MIB variable in the parameters   group
constitutes reconfiguration"
    ::= { par 26 }

parLogFlag OBJECT-TYPE
    SYNTAX INTEGER
    ACCESS read-write
    STATUS mandatory
    DESCRIPTION
      "This variable indicates whether logging should be
      done. Default behavior is to do logging"
    ::= { par 27 }

parLogFileName OBJECT-TYPE
    SYNTAX DisplayString
    ACCESS read-write
    STATUS mandatory
    DESCRIPTION
      "This variable gives the path to the log file"
    ::= { par 28 }
parBackupDirPath OBJECT-TYPE
    SYNTAX DisplayString
    ACCESS read-write
    STATUS mandatory
    DESCRIPTION
      "This variable gives the path to the backup directory"
    ::= { par 29 }

parDoBackupOnTerm OBJECT-TYPE
    SYNTAX INTEGER {
           no(0),
           yes(1)
           }
    ACCESS read-write
    STATUS mandatory
    DESCRIPTION
"This variable specifies whether WINS should do
        backup on termination. Setting it to 1 holds no
        meaning unless parBackupDirPath is set also"

```
                    ::= { par 30 }

            parMigrateOn  OBJECT-TYPE
               SYNTAX  INTEGER {
                       no(0),
                       yes(1)
                       }
               ACCESS  read-write
               STATUS  mandatory
               DESCRIPTION
            "This variable specifies whether static records
                       in the WINS database should be treated as
                       dynamic records during conflicts with new
                       dynamic registrations"
               ::= { par 31 }

-- datafiles group (Prefix  df)

            dfDatafilesTable OBJECT-TYPE
               SYNTAX  SEQUENCE OF DFDatafileEntry
               ACCESS  read-write
               STATUS  mandatory
               DESCRIPTION
                   "A list of datafiles specified under the Datafiles
               key in the registry.  These files are used for
               static initialization of the WINS database"
               ::= { datafiles 1 }
            dfDatafileEntry OBJECT-TYPE
               SYNTAX  DFDatafileEntry
               ACCESS  read-write
               STATUS  mandatory
               DESCRIPTION
                "data file name"
               INDEX   { dfDatafileIndex }
               ::= { dfDatafilesTable 1 }

            DFDatafileEntry ::= SEQUENCE {
                   dfDatafileIndex
                       INTEGER,
                   dfDatafileName
                       DisplayString
                       }

            dfDatafileIndex OBJECT-TYPE
               SYNTAX  INTEGER
               ACCESS  not-accessible
```

STATUS mandatory
DESCRIPTION
"Used for indexing entries in the datafiles table.
It has no other use"
::= { dfDatafileEntry 1 }

dfDatafileName OBJECT-TYPE
SYNTAX DisplayString
ACCESS read-write
STATUS mandatory
DESCRIPTION
"Name of the datafile to use for static initialization"
::= { dfDatafileEntry 2 }

-- pull group (Prefix pull)

pullInitTime OBJECT-TYPE
SYNTAX INTEGER
ACCESS read-write
STATUS mandatory
DESCRIPTION
"This variable indicates whether pull should be
done at WINS invocation and at reconfiguration.
If any pull group's MIB variable is set, that
constitutes reconfiguration"
::= { pull 1 }

pullCommRetryCount OBJECT-TYPE
SYNTAX INTEGER
ACCESS read-write
STATUS mandatory
DESCRIPTION
"This variable gives the retry count in
case of communication failure when doing pull replication.
This is the maximum number of retries that will be
done at the interval specified for the partner
before WINS will stop for a certain number (canned) of
replication time intervals before starting again."
::= { pull 2 }

pullPnrTable OBJECT-TYPE
SYNTAX SEQUENCE OF PullPnrEntry
ACCESS read-write
STATUS mandatory
DESCRIPTION
"A list of partners with which pull replication needs

to be done"
::= { pull 3 }

pPullPnrEntry OBJECT-TYPE
  SYNTAX PullPnrEntry
  ACCESS read-write
  STATUS mandatory
  DESCRIPTION
    "This is the row corresponding to a partner"
  INDEX { pullPnrAdd }
    ::= { pullPnrTable 1 }

PullPnrEntry ::= SEQUENCE {
  pullPnrAdd
    IpAddress,

  pullPnrSpTime
    DisplayString,

  pullPnrTimeInterval
    INTEGER,

  pullPnrMemberPrec
    Counter,
  pullPnrNoOfSuccRpls
    Counter,

  pullPnrNoOfCommFails
    Counter

  }
pullPnrAdd OBJECT-TYPE
  SYNTAX IpAddress
  ACCESS read-write
  STATUS mandatory
  DESCRIPTION
    "This is the address of the remote WINS partner"
  ::= { pPullPnrEntry 1 }

  pullPnrSpTime OBJECT-TYPE
  SYNTAX DisplayString
  ACCESS read-write
  STATUS mandatory
  DESCRIPTION
    "This variable gives the specific time at which
    pull replication should occur"

```
        ::= { pPullPnrEntry 2 }

    pullPnrTimeInterval  OBJECT-TYPE
      SYNTAX  INTEGER
      ACCESS  read-write
      STATUS  mandatory
      DESCRIPTION
        "This variable gives the time interval for
        pull replication"
      ::= { pPullPnrEntry 3 }
    pullPnrMemberPrec  OBJECT-TYPE
    SYNTAX INTEGER {
         low(0),
         high(1)
      }
    ACCESS  read-write
    STATUS  mandatory
     DESCRIPTION
        "This is the precedence to be given to members of
        the special group pulled from the WINS. Note:
        the precedence of locally registered members of a
        special group is more than any replicas pulled in"
      ::= { pPullPnrEntry 4 }

    pullPnrNoOfSuccRpls  OBJECT-TYPE
    SYNTAX  Counter
    ACCESS  read-only
    STATUS  mandatory
     DESCRIPTION
        "The number of times replication was successful with
        the WINS after invocation or reset of counters"
      ::= { pPullPnrEntry 5 }

    pullPnrNoOfCommFails  OBJECT-TYPE
    SYNTAX  Counter
    ACCESS  read-only
    STATUS  mandatory
     DESCRIPTION
        "The number of times replication was unsuccessful with
        the WINS due to communication. failure (after invocation or  reset of
counters)"
        ::= { pPullPnrEntry 6 }

    pullPnrVersNoLowWord  OBJECT-TYPE
      SYNTAX  Counter
    ACCESS  read-only
```

STATUS mandatory
DESCRIPTION
"The low word of the highest version number found in records owned by this WINS."
::= { pPullPnrEntry 7 }
pullPnrVersNoHighWord OBJECT-TYPE
SYNTAX Counter
ACCESS read-only
STATUS mandatory
DESCRIPTION
"The high word of the highest version number found in records owned by this WINS."
::= { pPullPnrEntry 8 }

-- push group (Prefix - push)
pushInitTime OBJECT-TYPE
SYNTAX INTEGER
ACCESS read-write
STATUS mandatory
DESCRIPTION
"This variable indicates whether a push (that is, a notification message) should be done at invocation."
::= { push 1 }

pushRplOnAddChg OBJECT-TYPE
SYNTAX INTEGER
ACCESS read-write
STATUS mandatory
DESCRIPTION
"This variable indicates whether a notification message should be sent when an address changes"
::= { push 2 }

pushPnrTable OBJECT-TYPE
SYNTAX SEQUENCE OF PushPnrEntry
ACCESS read-write
STATUS mandatory
DESCRIPTION
"A list of WINS partners with which push replication is to be initiated"
::= { push 3 }

pushPnrEntry OBJECT-TYPE
SYNTAX PushPnrEntry
ACCESS read-write
STATUS mandatory

```
                    DESCRIPTION
                    "This is the row corresponding to the WINS partner"
                 INDEX   { pushPnrAdd }
                 ::= { pushPnrTable 1 }
            PushPnrEntry ::= SEQUENCE {
              pushPnrAdd
                 INTEGER,

              pushPnrUpdateCount
                 INTEGER
                    }

              pushPnrAdd OBJECT-TYPE
                 SYNTAX  IpAddress
                 ACCESS  read-write
                 STATUS  mandatory
                 DESCRIPTION
                    "Address of the WINS partner"
                 ::= { pushPnrEntry 1 }

              pushPnrUpdateCount OBJECT-TYPE
                 SYNTAX  INTEGER
                 ACCESS  read-write
                 STATUS  mandatory
                 DESCRIPTION
                    "This variable indicates the number of updates that
                     should result in a push message"
                 ::= { pushPnrEntry 2 }

        -- cmd group (Prefix - cmd)

              cmdPullTrigger OBJECT-TYPE
                 SYNTAX  IpAddress
                 ACCESS  read-write
                 STATUS  mandatory
                 DESCRIPTION
                    "This variable, when set, will cause the WINS to
                     pull from the remote WINS identified by the IpAddress"
                 ::= { cmd 1 }
```

```
        cmdPushTrigger OBJECT-TYPE
            SYNTAX  IpAddress
            ACCESS  read-write
            STATUS  mandatory
            DESCRIPTION
                "This variable, when set, will cause the WINS to
                push a notification message to the remote WINS
                identified by the IpAddress"
            ::= { cmd 2 }
cmdDeleteWins OBJECT-TYPE
            SYNTAX  IpAddress
            ACCESS  read-write
            STATUS  mandatory
            DESCRIPTION
                "This variable, when set, will cause all information
                pertaining to a WINS (data records, context
                information) to be deleted from the local WINS.
                Use this only when owner-address mapping table is
                getting to near capacity. Note: Deletion of all
                information pertaining to the managed WINS is not
                permitted"
            ::= { cmd 3 }

        cmdDoScavenging OBJECT-TYPE
            SYNTAX  INTEGER {                    °
                no(0),
                yes(1)
                }
            ACCESS  read-write
            STATUS  mandatory
            DESCRIPTION
                "This variable, when set, will cause WINS to do
                scavenging."
            ::= { cmd 4 }

        cmdDoStaticInit OBJECT-TYPE
            SYNTAX  DisplayString
            ACCESS  read-write
            STATUS  mandatory
            DESCRIPTION
                "When this variable is set, WINS will do static
                initialization using the file specified as the value.  If  0 is specified,
WINS will do static  initialization using the files specified in the registry (can be
read-written using Datafile table"
            ::= { cmd 5 }
```

```
cmdNoOfWrkThds OBJECT-TYPE
  SYNTAX  INTEGER (1..4)
  ACCESS  read-write
  STATUS  mandatory
  DESCRIPTION
    "Sets the number of worker threads in WINS"
  ::= { cmd 6 }
cmdPriorityClass OBJECT-TYPE
  SYNTAX  INTEGER {
      normal(0),
      high(1)
      }
  ACCESS  read-write
  STATUS  mandatory
  DESCRIPTION
    "Sets the priority class of WINS to normal or high"
  ::= { cmd 7 }

cmdResetCounters OBJECT-TYPE
  SYNTAX  INTEGER
  ACCESS  read-write
  STATUS  mandatory
  DESCRIPTION
    "Resets the counters. Value is ignored"
  ::= { cmd 8 }

cmdDeleteDbRecs OBJECT-TYPE
  SYNTAX  IpAddress
  ACCESS  read-write
  STATUS  mandatory
  DESCRIPTION
    "This variable, when set, will cause all data records
    pertaining to a WINS to be deleted from the local WINS. Note: Only
data records are deleted."
  ::= { cmd 9 }

cmdDRPopulateTable OBJECT-TYPE
  SYNTAX  IpAddress
  ACCESS  read-write
  STATUS  mandatory
  DESCRIPTION
    "This variable can be set to retrieve records of
    a WINS whose Ip address is provided. When set,
    the table is populated immediately"
  ::= { cmd 10 }
cmdDRDataRecordsTable OBJECT-TYPE
```

SYNTAX SEQUENCE OF CmdDRRecordEntry
ACCESS read-only
STATUS mandatory
DESCRIPTION
  "This is the table that stores the data records.
  The records are sorted by name.
  Note: the table is cached (to save on overhead on WINS). To
repopulate the table, set cmdDRDataRecordsTable mib var"
  ::= { cmd 11 }

cmdDRRecordEntry OBJECT-TYPE
  SYNTAX CmdDRRecordEntry
  ACCESS read-write
  STATUS mandatory
  DESCRIPTION "Data record owned by WINS whose address
    was specified when CmdDRRecordsTable was
    set"
  INDEX { cmdDRRecordName }
  ::= { cmdDRDataRecordsTable 1 }

CmdDRRecordEntry ::= SEQUENCE {
    cmdDRRecordName
      DisplayString,
    cmdDRRecordAddress
      OCTET STRING,
    cmdDRRecordType
      INTEGER,
    cmdDRRecordPersistenceType
      INTEGER,
    cmdDRRecordState
      INTEGER
      }

cmdDRRecordName OBJECT-TYPE
  SYNTAX OCTET STRING (SIZE(1..255))
  ACCESS read-only
  STATUS mandatory
  DESCRIPTION
    "Name in the record"
  ::= { cmdDRRecordEntry 1 }
cmdDRRecordAddress OBJECT-TYPE
  SYNTAX OCTET STRING
  ACCESS read-only
  STATUS mandatory
  DESCRIPTION

"Address(es) of the record. If the record is
a multihomed record or a special group, the
addresses are returned sequentially in pairs.
Each pair is comprised of the address of the
owner WINS followed by the address of the
machine (multihomed)/member (special group).
Note: Following SNMP's convention, the records
are always returned in network byte order"
::= { cmdDRRecordEntry 2 }

cmdDRRecordType OBJECT-TYPE
SYNTAX INTEGER {
unique(0),
normalgroup(1),
specialgroup(2),
multihomed(3)
}
Note: The preceding order should not be disturbed. It is the same as-- in
winsintf.h (WINSINTF_RECTYPE_E)
ACCESS read-only
STATUS mandatory
DESCRIPTION
"Type of the record"
::= {cmdDRRecordEntry 3 }

cmdDRRecordPersistenceType OBJECT-TYPE
SYNTAX INTEGER {
static(0),
dynamic(1)
}
ACCESS read-only
STATUS mandatory
DESCRIPTION
"Persistence type of the record"
::= { cmdDRRecordEntry 4 }
cmdDRRecordState OBJECT-TYPE
SYNTAX INTEGER {
active(0),
released(1),
tombstone(2),
deleted(3)
}
-- Note: The preceding order should not be disturbed. It is the same as
-- in winsintf.h (WINSINTF_STATE_E)

```
-- for a SET operation only released and deleted values are
-- allowed
     ACCESS  read-only
     STATUS  mandatory
     DESCRIPTION
       "State of the record."
     ::= { cmdDRRecordEntry 5 }

 cmdWinsVersNoLowWord OBJECT-TYPE
     SYNTAX  INTEGER
     ACCESS  read-only
     STATUS  mandatory
     DESCRIPTION
       "The low word of the version number counter of the WINS"
     ::= { cmd 12 }

 cmdWinsVersNoHighWord OBJECT-TYPE
     SYNTAX  INTEGER
     ACCESS  read-only
     STATUS  mandatory
     DESCRIPTION
       "The high word of the version number counter of the WINS"
      ::= { cmd 13 }
 END
```

Microsoft Internet Information Server (IIS) MIB

The Microsoft Internet Information Server MIB contains objects that provide information about network communications and performance on the IIS Server. The base object for the InternetServer MIB is 1.3.6.1.4.1.311.1.7 and is currently composed of several MIBs that branch from this base object:

- FTP Server MIB
- Gopher Server MIB
- HTTP Server MIB

The InternetServer section of the OID name tree is organized as follows:

```
iso (1)
    org(3)
        dod(6)
            internet(1)
                private(4)
                    enterprises(1)
                        microsoft(311)
                            software(1)
                    InternetServer(7)
                        FtpServer(2)
                            FTPStatistics(1)
                        W3Server(3)
                            W3Statistics(1)
                        GopherServer(4)
                            GopherStatistics(1)
```

Microsoft FTP Server MIB

```
FtpServer-MIB DEFINITIONS ::= BEGIN


        IMPORTS
            enterprises,
            OBJECT-TYPE,
            Counter
                FROM RFC1155-SMI
            internetServer
                FROM InternetServer-MIB;
--    microsoft      OBJECT IDENTIFIER ::= { enterprises 311 }
--    software       OBJECT IDENTIFIER ::= { microsoft 1 }
--    internetServer OBJECT IDENTIFIER ::= { software 7 }
      ftpServer      OBJECT IDENTIFIER ::= { internetServer 2 }
      ftpStatistics  OBJECT IDENTIFIER ::= { ftpServer 1 }
```

-- FTP Server Statistics

```
totalBytesSentHighWord OBJECT-TYPE
    SYNTAX  Counter
    ACCESS  read-only
    STATUS  mandatory
    DESCRIPTION
        "This is the high 32-bits of the total number of
        of BYTEs sent by the FTP Server"
    ::= { ftpStatistics 1 }

totalBytesSentLowWord OBJECT-TYPE
    SYNTAX  Counter
    ACCESS  read-only
    STATUS  mandatory
    DESCRIPTION
        "This is the low 32-bits of the total number of
        of BYTEs sent by the FTP Server"
    ::= { ftpStatistics 2 }

totalBytesReceivedHighWord OBJECT-TYPE
    SYNTAX  Counter
    ACCESS  read-only
    STATUS  mandatory
    DESCRIPTION
        "This is the high 32-bits of the total number of
        of BYTEs received by the FTP Server"
    ::= { ftpStatistics 3 }

totalBytesReceivedLowWord OBJECT-TYPE
    SYNTAX  Counter
    ACCESS  read-only
    STATUS  mandatory
    DESCRIPTION
        "This is the low 32-bits of the total number of
        of BYTEs received by the FTP Server"
    ::= { ftpStatistics 4 }
totalFilesSent OBJECT-TYPE
    SYNTAX  Counter
    ACCESS  read-only
    STATUS  mandatory
    DESCRIPTION
        "This is the total number of files sent by this
        FTP Server"
    ::= { ftpStatistics 5 }
```

totalFilesReceived OBJECT-TYPE
    SYNTAX Counter
    ACCESS read-only
    STATUS mandatory
    DESCRIPTION
        "This is the total number of files received by this
        FTP Server"
    ::= { ftpStatistics 6 }

currentAnonymousUsers OBJECT-TYPE
    SYNTAX INTEGER
    ACCESS read-only
    STATUS mandatory
    DESCRIPTION
        "This is the number of anonymous users currently
        connected to the FTP Server"
    ::= { ftpStatistics 7 }

currentNonAnonymousUsers OBJECT-TYPE
    SYNTAX INTEGER
    ACCESS read-only
    STATUS mandatory
    DESCRIPTION
        "This is the number of nonanonymous users currently
        connected to the FTP Server"
    ::= { ftpStatistics 8 }

totalAnonymousUsers OBJECT-TYPE
    SYNTAX Counter
    ACCESS read-only
    STATUS mandatory
    DESCRIPTION
        "This is the total number of anonymous users that
        have ever connected to the FTP Server"
    ::= { ftpStatistics 9 }
totalNonAnonymousUsers OBJECT-TYPE
    SYNTAX Counter
    ACCESS read-only
    STATUS mandatory
    DESCRIPTION
        "This is the total number of nonanonymous users that
        have ever connected to the FTP Server"
    ::= { ftpStatistics 10 }

maxAnonymousUsers OBJECT-TYPE

SYNTAX Counter
ACCESS read-only
STATUS mandatory
DESCRIPTION
    "This is the maximum number of anonymous users
    simultaneously connected to the FTP Server"
::= { ftpStatistics 11 }

maxNonAnonymousUsers OBJECT-TYPE
    SYNTAX Counter
    ACCESS read-only
    STATUS mandatory
    DESCRIPTION
        "This is the maximum number of nonanonymous users
        simultaneously connected to the FTP Server"
    ::= { ftpStatistics 12 }

currentConnections OBJECT-TYPE
    SYNTAX INTEGER
    ACCESS read-only
    STATUS mandatory
    DESCRIPTION
        "This is the current number of connections to the
        FTP Server"
    ::= { ftpStatistics 13 }

maxConnections OBJECT-TYPE
    SYNTAX Counter
    ACCESS read-only
    STATUS mandatory
    DESCRIPTION
        "This is the maximum number of simultaneous
        connections to the FTP Server"
    ::= { ftpStatistics 14 }
connectionAttempts OBJECT-TYPE
    SYNTAX Counter
    ACCESS read-only
    STATUS mandatory
    DESCRIPTION
        "This is the number of connection attempts that
        have been made to the FTP Server"
    ::= { ftpStatistics 15 }

logonAttempts OBJECT-TYPE
    SYNTAX Counter
    ACCESS read-only

STATUS mandatory
DESCRIPTION
    "This is the number of logon attempts that have
    been made to the FTP Server"
::= { ftpStatistics 16 }

END

Microsoft Gopher Server MIB

GopherServer-MIB DEFINITIONS ::= BEGIN

IMPORTS
    enterprises,
    OBJECT-TYPE,
    Counter
        FROM RFC1155-SMI
    internetServer
        FROM InternetServer-MIB;

--   microsoft   OBJECT IDENTIFIER ::= { enterprises 311 }
--   software   OBJECT IDENTIFIER ::= { microsoft 1 }
--   internetServer OBJECT IDENTIFIER ::= { software 7 }
    gopherServer   OBJECT IDENTIFIER ::= { internetServer 4 }
    gopherStatistics OBJECT IDENTIFIER ::= { gopherServer 1 }
-- Gopher Server Statistics

    totalBytesSentHighWord OBJECT-TYPE
        SYNTAX Counter
        ACCESS read-only
        STATUS mandatory
        DESCRIPTION
            "This is the high 32-bits of the total number of
            of BYTEs sent by the Gopher Server"
        ::= { gopherStatistics 1 }

    totalBytesSentLowWord OBJECT-TYPE
        SYNTAX Counter
        ACCESS read-only
        STATUS mandatory
        DESCRIPTION
            "This is the low 32-bits of the total number of
            of BYTEs sent by the Gopher Server"
        ::= { gopherStatistics 2 }

    totalBytesReceivedHighWord OBJECT-TYPE

    SYNTAX Counter
    ACCESS read-only
    STATUS mandatory
    DESCRIPTION
        "This is the high 32-bits of the total number of
        of BYTEs received by the Gopher Server"
    ::= { gopherStatistics 3 }

totalBytesReceivedLowWord OBJECT-TYPE
    SYNTAX Counter
    ACCESS read-only
    STATUS mandatory
    DESCRIPTION
        "This is the low 32-bits of the total number of
        of BYTEs received by the Gopher Server"
    ::= { gopherStatistics 4 }

totalFilesSent OBJECT-TYPE
    SYNTAX Counter
    ACCESS read-only
    STATUS mandatory
    DESCRIPTION
        "This is the total number of files sent by this
        Gopher Server"
    ::= { gopherStatistics 5 }
totalDirectorySent OBJECT-TYPE
    SYNTAX Counter
    ACCESS read-only
    STATUS mandatory
    DESCRIPTION
        "This is the total number of directory listings sent
        by this Gopher Server"

    ::= { gopherStatistics 6 }

totalSearchesDone OBJECT-TYPE
    SYNTAX Counter
    ACCESS read-only
    STATUS mandatory
    DESCRIPTION
        "This is the total number of searches done by this
        Gopher Server"
    ::= { gopherStatistics 7 }

currentAnonymousUsers OBJECT-TYPE
    SYNTAX INTEGER

ACCESS read-only
STATUS mandatory
DESCRIPTION
    "This is the number of anonymous users currently
    connected to the Gopher Server"
::= { gopherStatistics 8 }

currentNonAnonymousUsers OBJECT-TYPE
    SYNTAX INTEGER
    ACCESS read-only
    STATUS mandatory
    DESCRIPTION
        "This is the number of nonanonymous users currently
        connected to the Gopher Server"
    ::= { gopherStatistics 9 }

totalAnonymousUsers OBJECT-TYPE
    SYNTAX Counter
    ACCESS read-only
    STATUS mandatory
    DESCRIPTION
        "This is the total number of anonymous users that
        have ever connected to the Gopher Server"
    ::= { gopherStatistics 10 }

totalNonAnonymousUsers OBJECT-TYPE
    SYNTAX Counter
    ACCESS read-only
    STATUS mandatory
    DESCRIPTION
        "This is the total number of nonanonymous users that
        have ever connected to the Gopher Server"
    ::= { gopherStatistics 11 }

maxAnonymousUsers OBJECT-TYPE
    SYNTAX Counter
    ACCESS read-only
    STATUS mandatory
    DESCRIPTION
        "This is the maximum number of anonymous users
        simultaneously connected to the Gopher Server"
    ::= { gopherStatistics 12 }

maxNonAnonymousUsers OBJECT-TYPE
    SYNTAX Counter
    ACCESS read-only

STATUS mandatory
DESCRIPTION
"This is the maximum number of nonanonymous users
simultaneously connected to the Gopher Server"
::= { gopherStatistics 13 }

currentConnections OBJECT-TYPE
SYNTAX INTEGER
ACCESS read-only
STATUS mandatory
DESCRIPTION
"This is the current number of connections to the
Gopher Server"
::= { gopherStatistics 14 }

maxConnections OBJECT-TYPE
SYNTAX Counter
ACCESS read-only
STATUS mandatory
DESCRIPTION
"This is the maximum number of simultaneous
connections to the Gopher Server"
::= { gopherStatistics 15 }
connectionAttempts OBJECT-TYPE
SYNTAX Counter
ACCESS read-only
STATUS mandatory
DESCRIPTION
"This is the number of connection attempts that
have been made to the Gopher Server"
::= { gopherStatistics 16 }

logonAttempts OBJECT-TYPE
SYNTAX Counter
ACCESS read-only
STATUS mandatory
DESCRIPTION
"This is the number of logon attempts that have
been made to this Gopher Server"
::= { gopherStatistics 17 }

abortedConnections OBJECT-TYPE
SYNTAX Counter
ACCESS read-only
STATUS mandatory
DESCRIPTION

"This is the number of aborted connections that have
been made to this Gopher Server"
::= { gopherStatistics 18 }
END

Microsoft HTTP Server MIB

HttpServer-MIB DEFINITIONS ::= BEGIN

IMPORTS
    enterprises,
    OBJECT-TYPE,
    Counter
        FROM RFC1155-SMI
    internetServer
        FROM InternetServer-MIB;

```
--    microsoft      OBJECT IDENTIFIER ::= { enterprises 311 }
--    software       OBJECT IDENTIFIER ::= { microsoft 1 }
--    internetServer OBJECT IDENTIFIER ::= { software 7 }
      httpServer     OBJECT IDENTIFIER ::= { internetServer 3 }
      httpStatistics OBJECT IDENTIFIER ::= { httpServer 1 }
```

-- Http Server Statistics

    totalBytesSentHighWord OBJECT-TYPE
        SYNTAX Counter
        ACCESS read-only
        STATUS mandatory
        DESCRIPTION
            "This is the high 32-bits of the total number of
            of BYTEs sent by the Http Server"
        ::= { httpStatistics 1 }

    totalBytesSentLowWord OBJECT-TYPE
        SYNTAX Counter
        ACCESS read-only
        STATUS mandatory
        DESCRIPTION
            "This is the low 32-bits of the total number of
            of BYTEs sent by the Http Server"
        ::= { httpStatistics 2 }

    totalBytesReceivedHighWord OBJECT-TYPE
        SYNTAX Counter
        ACCESS read-only

STATUS mandatory
DESCRIPTION
        "This is the high 32-bits of the total number of
        of BYTEs received by the Http Server"
::= { httpStatistics 3 }

totalBytesReceivedLowWord OBJECT-TYPE
    SYNTAX Counter
    ACCESS read-only
    STATUS mandatory
    DESCRIPTION
        "This is the low 32-bits of the total number of
        of BYTEs received by the Http Server"
    ::= { httpStatistics 4 }

totalFilesSent OBJECT-TYPE
    SYNTAX Counter
    ACCESS read-only
    STATUS mandatory
    DESCRIPTION
        "This is the total number of files sent by this
        Http Server"
    ::= { httpStatistics 5 }
currentAnonymousUsers OBJECT-TYPE
    SYNTAX INTEGER
    ACCESS read-only
    STATUS mandatory
    DESCRIPTION
        "This is the number of anonymous users currently
        connected to the Http Server"
    ::= { httpStatistics 6 }

currentNonAnonymousUsers OBJECT-TYPE
    SYNTAX INTEGER
    ACCESS read-only
    STATUS mandatory
    DESCRIPTION
        "This is the number of nonanonymous users currently
        connected to the Http Server"
    ::= { httpStatistics 7 }

totalAnonymousUsers OBJECT-TYPE
    SYNTAX Counter
    ACCESS read-only
    STATUS mandatory
    DESCRIPTION

"This is the total number of anonymous users that
have ever connected to the Http Server"
::= { httpStatistics 8 }

totalNonAnonymousUsers OBJECT-TYPE
    SYNTAX Counter
    ACCESS read-only
    STATUS mandatory
    DESCRIPTION
        "This is the total number of nonanonymous users that
        have ever connected to the Http Server"
    ::= { httpStatistics 9 }

maxAnonymousUsers OBJECT-TYPE
    SYNTAX Counter
    ACCESS read-only
    STATUS mandatory
    DESCRIPTION
        "This is the maximum number of anonymous users
        simultaneously connected to the Http Server"
    ::= { httpStatistics 10 }
maxNonAnonymousUsers OBJECT-TYPE
    SYNTAX Counter
    ACCESS read-only
    STATUS mandatory
    DESCRIPTION
        "This is the maximum number of nonanonymous users
        simultaneously connected to the Http Server"
    ::= { httpStatistics 11 }

currentConnections OBJECT-TYPE
    SYNTAX INTEGER
    ACCESS read-only
    STATUS mandatory
    DESCRIPTION
        "This is the current number of connections to the
        Http Server"
    ::= { httpStatistics 12 }

maxConnections OBJECT-TYPE
    SYNTAX Counter
    ACCESS read-only
    STATUS mandatory
    DESCRIPTION
        "This is the maximum number of simultaneous
        connections to the Http Server"

::= { httpStatistics 13 }

connectionAttempts OBJECT-TYPE
    SYNTAX Counter
    ACCESS read-only
    STATUS mandatory
    DESCRIPTION
        "This is the number of connection attempts that
        have been made to the Http Server"
    ::= { httpStatistics 14 }

logonAttempts OBJECT-TYPE
    SYNTAX Counter
    ACCESS read-only
    STATUS mandatory
    DESCRIPTION
        "This is the number of logon attempts that have
        been made to this Http Server"
    ::= { httpStatistics 15 }
totalGets OBJECT-TYPE
    SYNTAX Counter
    ACCESS read-only
    STATUS mandatory
    DESCRIPTION
        "This is the number of requests using the GET method
        that have been made to this Http Server"
    ::= { httpStatistics 16 }

totalPosts OBJECT-TYPE
    SYNTAX Counter
    ACCESS read-only
    STATUS mandatory
    DESCRIPTION
        "This is the number of requests using the POST method
        that have been made to this Http Server"
    ::= { httpStatistics 17 }

totalHeads OBJECT-TYPE
    SYNTAX Counter
    ACCESS read-only
    STATUS mandatory
    DESCRIPTION
        "This is the number of requests using the HEAD method
        that have been made to this Http Server"
    ::= { httpStatistics 18 }

totalOthers OBJECT-TYPE
    SYNTAX Counter
    ACCESS read-only
    STATUS mandatory
    DESCRIPTION
        "This is the number of requests not using the GET,
        POST, or HEAD method that have been made to this Http
        Server"
    ::= { httpStatistics 19 }

totalCGIRequests OBJECT-TYPE
    SYNTAX Counter
    ACCESS read-only
    STATUS mandatory
    DESCRIPTION
        "This is the number of Common Gateway Interface (CGI)
        requests that have been made to this Http Server"
    ::= { httpStatistics 20 }

totalBGIRequests OBJECT-TYPE
    SYNTAX Counter
    ACCESS read-only
    STATUS mandatory
    DESCRIPTION
        "This is the number of Binary Gateway Interface (BGI)
        requests that have been made to this Http Server"
    ::= { httpStatistics 21 }

totalNotFoundErrors OBJECT-TYPE
    SYNTAX Counter
    ACCESS read-only
    STATUS mandatory
    DESCRIPTION
        "This is the number of requests the Http server could
        not satisfy because the requested resource could not
        be found"
    ::= { httpStatistics 22 }

END

APPENDIX D

Windows Sockets

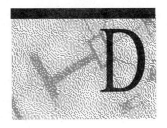

The Windows Sockets application programming interface (API) provides a standard Windows interface to many transports (protocols) with different addressing schemes such as TCP/IP and IPX. The Windows Sockets API is designed to provide a programming standard for all platforms.

Windows Sockets is a programming interface based on the familiar "socket" interface from the University of California at Berkeley. Windows Sockets is an industry standard used by software developers and is part of the public Windows Open Systems Architecture (WOSA).

This appendix provides the following information about Windows Sockets:

- An overview of Windows Sockets as implemented in Windows NT Server and Windows NT Workstation

- A description of Windows Sockets programs from third-party vendors that support cross-platform computing.

- A list of TCP/IP utilities compliant with Windows Sockets.

- Instructions for developers on how to obtain the latest information, specifications, and sample programs needed to develop Windows Sockets compliant programs for the Microsoft family of 32-bit and 16-bit Windows operating systems.

The information in this appendix supersedes information about TCP/IP and the Windows Sockets API in the following sources:

- Chapter 10, "Overview of Microsoft TCP/IP for Windows NT," and Appendix A, "TCP/IP Utilities Reference," of the *Windows NT Networking Guide, Volume 1*

- Chapter 1, "Overview of Microsoft TCP/IP," and Chapter 11 "Utilities Reference," of the *TCP/IP* book for Microsoft Windows NT Server

Overview of Windows Sockets

When referring to the seven layers of the OSI model for network communications, Windows Sockets functions at the session layer interface to the transport layer. In other words, Windows Sockets is an interface between applications and the transport protocol and works as a bi-directional pipe for incoming and outgoing application data. Windows Sockets is implemented as a dynamic-link library (DLL) that allows applications and the transport service to be dynamically bound together at run time.

Windows Sockets was originally designed for use with the TCP/IP transport protocol. However, extensions to Windows Sockets now allow use of non-TCP/IP transport protocols with Windows Sockets. Windows Sockets as implemented in Windows NT Server and Windows NT Workstation provides a true transport-independent interprocess communication service. Windows Sockets in Windows NT Server and Windows NT Workstation supports the following transport protocols:

- TCP/IP
- Novell IPX/SPX
- Digital DECnet
- Xerox Network Systems (XNS)

Note Windows NT Server and Windows NT Workstation version 4.0 implement 32-bit Windows Sockets version 2.0. Earlier versions of Windows NT implement 32-bit Windows Sockets version 1.1. The specifications for Windows Sockets are open, public specifications. See the section "Developing Programs Using Windows Sockets" at the end of this appendix for a list of Microsoft and other Internet sites from which you can receive information about Windows Sockets.

TCP/IP Utilities Compatible with Windows Sockets

As mentioned earlier, Windows Sockets was originally designed for use with TCP/IP. Many commonly used TCP/IP utilities are compatible with the Windows Sockets provided with Windows NT Server and Windows NT Workstation. These TCP/IP utilities are as follows:

- **arp**
- **finger**
- **ftp**
- **hostname**
- **ipconfig**
- **lpq**
- **lpr**
- **nbtstat**
- **netstat**
- **nslookup**
- **ping**
- **rcp**
- **rexec**
- **route**
- **rsh**
- **telnet**
- **tftp**
- **tracert**

For a complete description of each of these utilities, see online Help or refer to Appendix A, "TCP/IP Utilities Reference."

Third-party Software for TCP/IP and Windows Sockets

Most TCP/IP users either use programs that comply with the Windows Sockets standard, such as the TCP/IP utilities **ftp** or **telnet,** or third-party programs. TCP/IP-aware programs from vendors that comply with the Windows Sockets standard can run on virtually any TCP/IP implementation.

Other typical third-party programs include graphic connectivity utilities (for example, those that connect to the Internet), terminal emulation software, Simple Mail Transport Protocol (SMTP) and electronic mail clients, network printing utilities, SQL client programs, and corporate client-server programs.

> **Note** For information about Microsoft partners and solution providers who provide Windows Sockets-compliant software, contact Microsoft Sales and Services at 1-800-426-9400 and request the catalog "Microsoft InfoSource," part number #098-62986. This catalog provides information about Microsoft partners and solution providers who provide a wide range of third-party hardware, software, and services.

Third-party software can also be used to implement a seamless network environment between Windows NT Server and Windows NT Workstation computers and UNIX networks. To do this, additional third-party software is required for:

- Support for Network File System (NFS), the de facto standard for UNIX file sharing
- The ability to run the most common UNIX graphical user interface, X Window, on Windows NT Server and Windows NT Workstation computers.

Third-party programs provide Windows NT-based support for NFS. These third-party programs allow Windows NT-based computers and programs to connect to UNIX-based file directories and to access data, while the UNIX systems in the network can access the Windows NT Server and Windows NT Workstation file directories and file data.

The Windows Sockets standard ensures compatibility with third-party programs for X Window. Currently available third-party programs include X Window manager programs and client libraries. These programs and libraries allow development of X Window client programs for Windows NT Server and Windows NT Workstation computers.

> **Note** Windows NT Server and Windows NT Workstation documentation uses the standard terminology for the client and server relationship, where the client is the workstation and the server is the computer that provides shared resources to network users. There is a portion of the UNIX world in which this relationship is reversed. The client is the server, and the server is the client. In UNIX X window terminology, the client software resides on the computer that performs the processing, and the server software resides on the computer that displays the output.

Developing Programs Using Windows Sockets

The Windows Sockets API is an open, public specification based on the Berkeley (BSD) Sockets APIs that are a de facto standard for UNIX network programming. Because the Windows Sockets API is similar to the Berkeley Sockets API, UNIX applications can be easily ported to the Windows NT Server, Windows NT Workstation, and Windows 95 platforms.

Note Developers can also use the protocol-independent Windows Sockets API to develop programs for the AppleTalk stack, the underlying mechanism that allows Windows NT Servers using Services for Macintosh to share files and printers with Macintosh networks.

The Windows Sockets standard allows a developer to create a program with a single common interface and a single executable that can run over many types of TCP/IP implementations. The Windows Sockets API provides the following:

- A familiar networking API for programmers using Windows NT Server, Windows NT Workstation, Windows 95, Windows 3.11 or higher, and UNIX.

- Binary compatibility between vendors for heterogeneous Windows-based TCP/IP stacks and utilities.

- Support for both connection-oriented and connectionless protocols.

Windows Sockets version 2.0 provides a clean architecture for plugging in service providers. Specifications for the next generation of Windows Sockets version 2.0 and earlier versions are available from the Internet, and in the Microsoft Win32 Software Developers Kit.

▶   **To get current Windows Sockets information from the Microsoft Developers Network**

- Connect to: **//www.microsoft.com/intdev/inttech/winsock.htm**

▶   **To get a copy of the specification for the next generation of Windows Sockets, Windows Sockets version 2.0**

- Connect to: **//www.stardust.com/wsresource/winsock2**

  Or, connect to: **//www.intel.com/IAL/winsock2**

▶ **To get a copy of the Windows Sockets specifications by using anonymous FTP**

1. Make sure you have write permission in your current working directory.

2. At the command prompt, start **ftp**, and then connect to **ftp.microsoft.com** (or **198.105.232.1**).

3. Log on as **anonymous**.

4. Type your electronic mail address for the *password*.

5. Type **cd \bussys\winsock\spec11**, and then press ENTER.

6. Use the **dir** command to see the list of available file types.

   If you want binary data such as in the Microsoft Word version, type **bin**, and then press ENTER.

▶ **To subscribe to the Windows Sockets mailing list**

- Send electronic mail to **listserv@sunsite.unc.edu** with a message body that contains **subscribe winsock** *your email-address*.

  You can use the same procedure to subscribe to additional mailing lists called **winsock-hackers** and **winsock-users**.

APPENDIX E

RAS Reference

This appendix presents information on Remote Access Service (RAS), and Windows NT 4.0 RAS, in three sections. The first section gives an overview of the most important modem compatibility standards and how they work within RAS. The second section is a series of quick-reference charts to give you a high-level perspective of how RAS works during a call to a Windows NT RAS server. The last section contains reference tables for RAS server and client computers that detail the different versions of RAS and the features they support.

RAS and Modem Compatibility Standards

The following information is an overview of the most important modem standards, how they can be categorized into four compatibility levels, and how they pertain to RAS and RAS data compression. This information, along with the RAS online Help topic "Modifying MODEM.INF," also enables you to implement unsupported modems with RAS versions 1.x, RAS for Windows for Workgroups 3.11, and RAS for Windows NT versions 3.1, 3.5, and 3.51.

You can apply most of the information to RAS for Windows 95; however, RAS for Windows 95 does not use a Modem.inf file. Instead, it uses Telephone Application Programming Interface (TAPI), which relies on entries in the Windows 95 registry for modem initialization. To implement unsupported modems with RAS for Windows 95, it is recommended that you obtain a modem driver from the modem manufacturer.

Windows NT 4.0 RAS also includes support for TAPI as well as supporting new modems through the Universal Modem Driver (Unimodem). RAS continues to support modems for older legacy systems. To configure a previously installed unsupported modem to work with RAS, add an entry for that modem in the Modem.inf file.

Supported Media

Depending on the RAS version, RAS supports X.25, ISDN, Null Modem, and asynchronous modem communication. RAS does not support synchronous communication and therefore cannot communicate with a synchronous serial port. Synchronous communication synchronizes the transmission by controlling the timing and the duration of data signals.

Asynchronous communication means that each byte is framed with a start and stop bit. RAS sends data asynchronously to the serial port, and the serial port sends data asynchronously to the modem. The asynchronous modem then strips the start and stop bit from each byte (a byte is also referred to as character) and converts the characters into blocks that are then sent synchronously (not asynchronously) to the other modem by using an error control protocol. The other modem disassembles these synchronous blocks, and frames each character with a start and stop bit before sending it on to the serial port of the RAS server. The serial port then sends it to the RAS server service. This process occurs during a communication call similar to that shown in Figure E.1.

Leased line communication using asynchronous serial ports and either asynchronous or synchronous modems can be implemented under some circumstances, as long as RAS can treat the connection as an asynchronous null modem connection. Some modems support both synchronous and asynchronous communication.

Asynchronous Communication

To understand asynchronous modem communication using RAS, you need to understand the following four compatibility levels in relation to RAS:

- Modem Command Language
- Modem Modulation Standards
- Modem Error Control Standards
- Modem Data Compression Standards and RAS Data Compression

Figure E.1 shows these four compatibility levels being implemented during a WAN connection. The different levels are shown below the section of the asynchronous RAS link to which they apply:

- modem command language affects command compatibility between RAS and the local modem, modem modulation standards affect the telephone line speed;

- compatibility between two modems, modem error control standards affect the local and remote modem level of error control compatibility;

- modem compression standards affect the local and remote modem data compression compatibility; and

- RAS data compression affects data compression between the local and remote computer.

In the diagram, the RAS client is on the right side and the RAS server on the left side, and they are connected over external modems.

Notice that a RAS client or server acts as Data Terminal Equipment (DTE), and a modem acts as Data Communications Equipment (DCE).

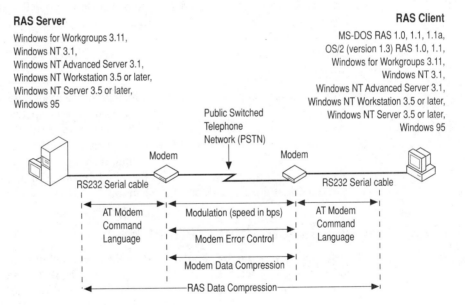

RAS Server

Windows for Workgroups 3.11,
Windows NT 3.1,
Windows NT Advanced Server 3.1,
Windows NT Workstation 3.5 or later,
Windows NT Server 3.5 or later,
Windows 95

RAS Client

MS-DOS RAS 1.0, 1.1, 1.1a,
OS/2 (version 1.3) RAS 1.0, 1.1,
Windows for Workgroups 3.11,
Windows NT 3.1,
Windows NT Advanced Server 3.1,
Windows NT Workstation 3.5 or later,
Windows NT Server 3.5 or later,
Windows 95

Public Switched
Telephone
Network (PSTN)

Modem

Modem

RS232 Serial cable

RS232 Serial cable

AT Modem
Command
Language

Modulation (speed in bps)

Modem Error Control

AT Modem
Command
Language

Modem Data Compression

RAS Data Compression

Figure E.1   Modem Compatibility Standards

RAS and the Modem Command Language

For a modem to be compatible with any communication software running on the local computer, the software must be compatible with the *modem command language*, also referred to as the *modem command set*. The command set configures the other three compatibility levels of the modem according to the needs of the local software (RAS), the supported modem standards of the modem being called, and the users' preferences. For certain modems, the modem command set works between the local and remote modems as well as between the local communications software and the local modem.

Command set compatibility between RAS modem drivers and the local modem is advantageous, but not a requirement. Many manufacturers advertise that their modem is 100 percent compatible with the popular Hayes AT command set, or that it is compatible with another popular modem's command set. This generally means that the modem uses the same commands as Hayes modems for basic operations such as dial, hang up, reset, and answer. It does not imply that the modem uses the same commands for configuration of modulation, error control, or data compression. However, if your modem is not compatible with any supported modem's command set, you can customize the RAS modem driver by modifying the Modem.inf file (or Modems.inf file in RAS versions 1.*x*) to make it compatible with virtually any modem's command set. For additional information on modifying the Modem.inf file, see the RAS Help topic "Modifying Modem.inf."

Command set compatibility between the local modem and the remote modem is not a requirement for RAS. Command set compatibility between the local and remote modem is only important if both modems are designed to be configurable by a command received from the other modem. For example, an administrator may call from home and issue a command to change the default settings during the next power up of the modem in the office; however, this specialized feature is not important during RAS communication.

RAS and Modem Modulation Standards

The modem modulation standards affect the telephone line speed compatibility between two modems, as shown in the following Table E.1. For two modems to communicate, their modulation standards must be compatible.

The modulation standard only defines the speed or permitted speed range between the modems. The speed between the computer and the modem can be different and depends on the serial hardware, the microprocessor speed in the computer, and whether or not hardware flow control or XON/XOFF software flow control is enabled.

Table E.1 shows the most popular modulation schemes in the left column and their corresponding speed range in bits per second (bps) in the right column.

Table E.1   Modulation Schemes and Modem Speeds

Popular modulation schemes	Modem-to-modem speed
V.22 (ITU-T (formerly CCITT) Standard)	1200 bps
V.22 *bis* (ITU-T (formerly CCITT) Standard)	2400 bps
V.32 (ITU-T (formerly CCITT) Standard)	4800 to 9600 bps
V.32 *bis* (ITU-T (formerly CCITT) Standard)	4800 to 14400 bps
V.fc and V.fast (Proprietary Modulation Schemes)	2400 to 28800 bps
V.34 (ITU-T (formerly CCITT) Standard)	2400 to 28800 bps

Figure E.2 shows that modulation standards take effect only on the modem-to-modem (DCE-to-DCE) link. Speeds between DTE and DCE are independent of modem modulation standards and often differ from the DCE-to-DCE speed. When speeds are different, *hardware flow control* or *software flow control* support is required so that data is not lost when transmission speed between the modems is less than transmission speed between the DTE and DCE, or when transmission between the modems is temporarily delayed due to retransmission of data that was corrupted during transmission. RAS versions 1.0 and 1.1 do not support hardware or software flow control. RAS versions 1.1a and later support hardware flow control.

Figure E.2 also displays the different modulation standards below the DCE-to-DCE link to which they apply. The column to the right of the center column displays the RAS clients' DCE-to-DTE speeds that occur in relation to the DCE-to-DCE speeds on the same row in the center column. Depending on your modem's capabilities, these speeds should be set in the corresponding RAS client versions that are displayed in the far right column. The highest supported DTE-to-DCE speeds that should be set on the RAS server (depending on its modem[s] capabilities) are displayed in the column to the left of the center column. The rightmost column lists the RAS client versions and the leftmost column lists the RAS server versions whose highest supported modulation rate corresponds to the modulation standard in the center column.

For example, in the "9600 bps, V.32" entry in the center column, the columns to the left and right show that the DTE-to-DCE speeds are also 9600 bps, and that this was the highest supported modulation mode of RAS versions 1.0 and 1.1.

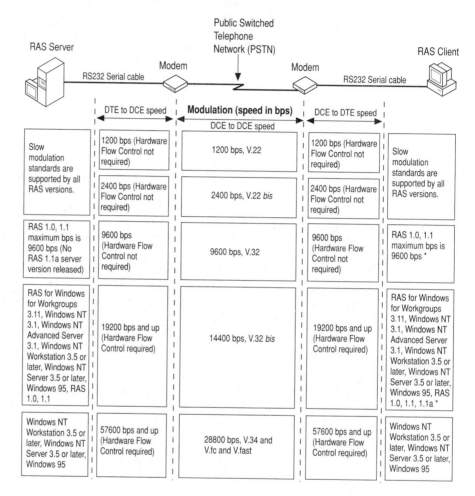

Figure E.2   Modulation Standards and RAS

*RAS 1.0 and 1.1 were tested only with US Robotics V.32 *bis* modems at 14400 bps line speed. The modems were configured for V.42, V.42 *bis*, and V.32 *bis*. The OS/2 1.3 LAN Manager RAS 1.0 or 1.1 server had an intelligent DigiBoard installed.

Modem Speed and Modulation Change During a Connection

When connecting, modems do not always negotiate their fastest built-in modulation rate. Depending on the quality of the phone line connection and the quality of the modem hardware, two modems may negotiate a certain modulation standard, but may not use the maximum speed defined in that standard. For example, two V.34 modems, made by the same or different manufacturers, may negotiate a modulation rate in 2400-bps increments somewhere between 2400 bps and 28800 bps. They may agree to use 2400 bps because of noise in the telephone line.

Even though the line speed may be only 2400 bps, these V.34 modems are still using the V.34 modulation scheme. V.34 modulation also enables the modems to change the line speed dynamically during a call, in response to changes in the phone line quality. Other modulation standards may also enable the modems to connect at slower speeds, but may not enable the modems to dynamically adjust the line speed during a connection.

To change to a different modulation scheme, as opposed to just changing the speed within a modulation scheme while the modems have a connection, the modems need to support an error control protocol that supports this functionality. The non-standard MNP10 error control protocol is an example. However, the MNP10 protocol is needed only if the modem is not a V.34 modem and only if the modem needs to downshift from 4800 bps V.32/V.32 *bis* to 2400 bps V.22 *bis* (or upshift, accordingly).

RAS is usually oblivious to the dynamic speed changes. However, MNP10 modulation does change, and very slow connections that may occur with cellular modems or with low quality telephone lines may cause time-out problems in the RAS network protocols. Only Windows 95 supports cellular modem connections.

Table E.2 displays the fastest possible modulation mode likely to be negotiated when modems configured with the same or different modulation modes attempt to make a connection. This table assumes that modems with different modulation configurations and capabilities are configured to enable them to negotiate up or down to the highest modulation standard that the other modem supports. If both modems are not configured to negotiate to a different modulation, and their modulation settings differ, they cannot establish a connection.

For example, if a V.22 *bis* (2400 bps) modem and a V.32 *bis* (14400 bps) modem try to establish a connection and the V.32 *bis* modem is not configured to negotiate down to V.22 *bis*, the modems are unable to establish a connection. If the V.22 *bis* modem is not configured to negotiate down, but the V.32 *bis* modem is configured to negotiate down, then the modems can connect at V.22 *bis* (but not at V.22).

Table E.2   Modulation Modes

Modulation selected on calling modem	V.34	V.fc/V.fast	V.32 *bis*	V.32	V.22 *bis*	V.22
V.22 (1200bps)	V.22	V.22	V.22	V.22	V.22	V.22
V.22 *bis* (2400 bps)	V.22 *bis*	V.22 *bis*	V.22 *bis*	V.32 *bis*	V.22 *bis*	V.22
V.32 (9600 bps)	V.32	V.32	V.32	V.32	V.22 *bis*	V.22
V.32 *bis* (14400 bps)	V.32 *bis*	V.32 *bis*	V.32 *bis*	V.32	V.22 *bis*	V.22
V.fc / V.fast (28800 bps)	V.fc/V.fast (V.32 *bis* if V.fc/V.fast is not supported by answering modem)	V.fc/V.fast	V.32 *bis*	V.32	V.22 *bis*	V.22
V.34 (28800 bps)	V.34	V.fc/V.fast (V.32 *bis* if V.fc/V.fast is not supported by calling modem)	V.32 *bis*	V.32	V.22 *bis*	V.22

Note   V.fc and V.fast are proprietary modulations that use modulation technology similar to V.34. Therefore, two V.fc or two V.fast modems from different manufacturers may not be able to connect at V.fc or V.fast, respectively, and may have to negotiate down to V.32 *bis*. Also, the use of the V.fc and V.fast names may be inconsistent between manufacturers, making it difficult for a buyer to determine compatibility between these modems. The V.34 standard does not include support for V.fc and V.fast. Therefore, some V.34 modems that do not support V.fc or V.fast fall back to V.32 *bis* when connecting with a V.fc or V.fast modem.

How to Make Unsupported Modems Work in pre-Windows NT 3.5 RAS Versions

You may be able to make RAS 1.1a, RAS for Windows for Workgroups 3.11, and RAS for Windows NT version 3.1 work with an unsupported modem (for example, a V.fc,V.fast, or V.34 modem, which is unsupported in these versions). If you want to use a V.fc, V.fast, or V.34 modem, it is recommended that you use a RAS client computer that has a 486 processor or later, and a serial port that has a 16550 UART chip or later. If problems occur, configure your modem to use V.32 *bis*.

The easiest way to get an unsupported modem supported under RAS for Windows for Workgroups 3.11 or RAS for Windows NT 3.1 is to obtain a modem that is supported in RAS for Windows NT 3.5 or 3.51. The following procedure assumes that you have a modem that is supported in Windows NT 3.5 or 3.51. If your modem is not supported in Windows NT 3.5 or 3.51 or you have RAS 1.1a, skip the following procedure, but read the rest of this chapter, and then follow the instructions in the Help topic "Modifying MODEM.INF."

▶ **To make an unsupported modem work**

1. From the RAS for Windows NT 3.5 or 3.51 MODEM.INF file, copy the section that applies to your modem.

2. Load MODEM.INF into a text editor and append the copied section to the RAS for Windows for Workgroups 3.11 or Windows NT 3.1 MODEM.INF file.

3. Remove the lines that start with the following words from the section you appended:

   DETECT_STRING=

   DETECT_RESPONSE=

   Note RAS modem autodetection is not supported in RAS for Windows for Workgroups 3.11 and RAS for Windows NT 3.1.

   ---

4. Save MODEM.INF, and then quit the text editor.

5. Restart your computer.

6. Depending on whether you have Windows NT 3.1 or Windows for Workgroups 3.11, continue with the following corresponding section.

▶ **To make an unsupported modem work in Windows for Workgroups 3.11**

1. Restart the RAS client software, and then choose **Configure** from the **Setup** menu.

2. Select your modem from the **Device** field, and then click **OK**.

   RAS is now ready to use your modem.

▶ **To make an unsupported modem work in Windows NT 3.1**

1. Start Control Panel, and then choose the **Network** icon.

2. Select **Remote Access Service** from the list of Installed Network Software, and then click **Configure**.

3. In the **Remote Access Setup** dialog box, click **Configure**.

4. In the **Attached Device** box, select the modem name that corresponds to the section you just copied to Modem.inf, and then click **OK**.

   RAS is now ready to use your modem.

RAS and Modem Error Control Standards, Modem Data Compression Standards, and RAS Data Compression

Error control and modem compression are optional features that are available with most modems made in the last few years. For reliable connections, the local and remote modem error control standards must be compatible; and for improved throughput, their modem data and RAS data compression standards must be compatible.

Table E.3 shows the error control and modem data compression standards available with most modems. If you use modem compression, use the error control standard in the cell above the compression value. For instance, if you want to enable error control and modem compression, MNP4 is used with MNP5 or V.42 is used with V.42 *bis*. MNP4 error control cannot be combined with V.42 *bis* compression, nor can V.42 error control be combined with MNP5 compression. MNP4 and MNP5 are older standards and are less efficient than V.42 and V.42 *bis*.

Table E.3   Modem Error Control and Compression Protocols

Modem Error Control Protocol	**MNP4**	**V.42 w/ LAPM**	**MNP10 for cellular and land modem connections**
Modem Compression Protocol	**MNP5 (up to 2:1 compression)**	**V.42 *bis* (up to 4:1 compression)**	V.42 *bis* or MNP5

(MNP = Microcom Networking Protocol)

Note MNP10 is a new, nonstandard, reliable connection protocol not available on most modems. It was designed to overcome cellular modem signal distortion; however, it also makes land connections more reliable. It is not compatible with the Motorola MC2 cellular protocol, nor the AT&T EC2 cellular protocol, as of July 1995. MNP10 is combined with V.42 *bis* compression.

Figure E.3 illustrates modem error control standards, modem compression standards, and RAS software data compression. The Figure has three horizontal sections whose titles you can find in the center column directly below the modem-to-modem link graphic at the top of the Figure. To read the information in this Figure, decide which of the following three sections you want to focus on: Modem Error Control, Modem Data Compression, or RAS Data Compression. Then find that section in the center column and read the entries to the left and right in the same horizontal row. This enables you to determine whether the standard or feature also applies to the modem-to-computer link, and which RAS client versions and server versions support the modem or RAS feature in this section.

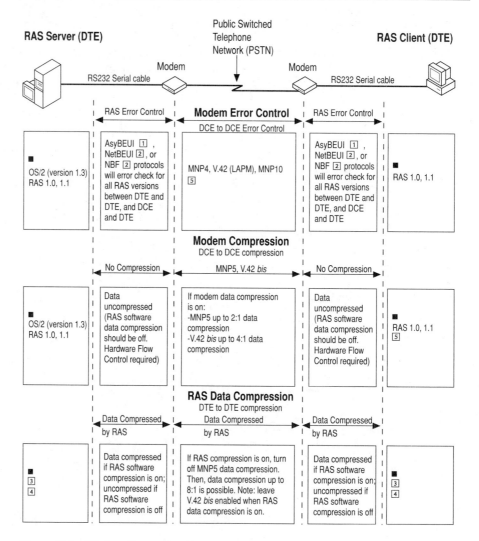

Figure E.3   Modem Error Control Standards, Modem Compression Standards, and RAS Software Data Compression

■RAS for Windows for Workgroups 3.11, Windows NT 3.1, Windows NT Advanced Server 3.1, Windows NT Workstation 3.5 or later, Windows NT Server 3.5 or later, Windows 95.

1̄ AsyBEUI applies to RAS versions 1.x only.

2̄ NetBEUI applies to RAS for Windows for Workgroups 3.11, and NBF applies to Windows NT versions 3.1, 3.5, and 3.51.

3. In case you have not disabled your RAS software compression on the **Options** menu of your RAS client, check the size of the RASMAC.386 files. If it has only 27193 bytes, it does not have RAS compression. If RASMAC.386 has 49209 bytes, then it has RAS compression support. The file with RAS compression support can be obtained on the Windows NT 3.5 U.S. Service Pack 2 CD in the SUPPORT\RAS directory.

4. In case you have not disabled your RAS software compression on the **Options** menu of your RAS client, check the size of the ASYNCMAC.SYS file. If it has only 33732 bytes, it does not have RAS compression. The releases of ASYNCMAC.SYS with 53188 bytes and 53716 bytes have RAS compression support. The files with RAS compression support can be obtained on the Windows NT 3.5 U.S. Service Pack 2 compact disc in the SUPPORT\RAS directory.

5. RAS 1.0 and 1.1 were tested only with US Robotics V.32 *bis* modems at 14400 bps line speed. The modems were configured for V.42, V.42 *bis*, and V.32 *bis*. The OS/2 1.3 LAN Manager RAS 1.0 or 1.1 server had an intelligent DigiBoard installed.

Modem Error Control

The first section of the preceding Figure E.3 shows that modem error control (MNP4, V.42 [LAPM], MNP10) standards take effect only between modems (DCE-to-DCE link). For RAS versions 1.0 and 1.1, these standards are not supported; however, in RAS version 1.1a and later these standards are activated.

MNP4 is the oldest and least efficient of the three error control standards; V.42 is newer and more efficient than MNP4; and MNP10 is the newest (nonstandard) protocol, although it is not available in many modems. MNP10 is designed to enable change of modulation modes during connections and to operate under extremely adverse environments where V.42 fails. Error control between computer and modem (DTE and DCE) is handled automatically by the RAS protocol by encompassing the entirety of the connection—not only the connection between DTE and DCE, but the connection between RAS client and RAS server (DTE-to-DTE).

Modem Data Compression

The second section of Figure E.3 shows that modem data compression (MNP5, V.42 *bis*) standards take effect only between modems (DCE-to-DCE link). For RAS versions 1.0 and 1.1, these standards are not supported. However, if you are using RAS version 1.1a or later, you should activate modem compression (along with hardware flow control) if you are calling a Windows for Workgroups 3.11 or Windows NT RAS server. You should not activate modem compression if you are calling a RAS 1.0 or 1.1 OS/2 version 1.3 server with LAN Manager 2.1 or later. For more information, see the footnote ⑤ following Figure E.3.

RAS Data Compression

The third section of Figure E.3 shows that RAS data compression and decompression happen between computers (DTE-to-DTE link) without involving modem compression. The modem receives RAS-compressed data and just passes it along to the other modem. Thus, modem compression is not involved in this part of the Figure. With RAS data compression, MNP5 modem compression must be turned off in order to prevent redundancy, because data that are already highly compressed by RAS might grow larger before transmission if MNP5 modem compression is enabled simultaneously.

RAS data compression can be four times as efficient as MNP5, and about twice as efficient as V.42 *bis* modem data compression, unless a previously compressed file is transmitted. V.42 *bis* can detect whether it is about to expand data that it is supposed to compress. V.42 *bis* can also automatically suspend itself until the data is once again compressible. It is advised that you leave V.42 *bis* enabled at all times, but not use MNP5 with RAS data compression.

To avoid data loss due to data buffer overflow, you must enable hardware flow control in the RAS client whenever you are using modem compression or RAS data compression. You may turn hardware flow control on in the RAS user interface of the following RAS versions: Windows for Workgroups 3.11, Windows 95, Windows NT versions 3.1, 3.5, and 3.51. RAS versions 1.0 and 1.1 do not support hardware flow control. RAS version 1.1a requires that a hardware flow control command be set in the Modems.inf file on the command.init line containing the modem initialization string for your modem.

Note RAS 1.1a ships with the Mcomp.inf file that issues hardware flow control and maximum baud rate commands for all modems supported by that file. To use hardware flow control with a supported modem, you must save the Modems.inf file (which contains modem commands that disable hardware flow control) and copy the Mcomp.inf file to the name Modems.inf.

RAS and Unsupported Modems

If you have an unsupported modem or want to customize the Modem.inf file and want to use compression, and you are using RAS versions later than 1.x on the RAS server and client, it is recommended that you turn on V.42 *bis* modem compression and RAS software data compression. If you want to use RAS data compression, leave the most efficient error control protocol that is available on your modem turned on. For additional information, see the RAS Help topic "Modifying Modem.inf."

To use modem compression with an unsupported modem on the RAS 1.1a client (that does not have the RAS data compression feature), append a custom modem section to the MODEMS.INF file and create an initialization string that enables hardware flow control, V.42 *bis* compression, and V.42 error control, if available. Be sure to check that your modem is not already supported in the RAS 1.1a MCOMP.INF file that ships with RAS 1.1a. To create your custom modem section, model your section after an existing section in MCOMP.INF.

Modem Standard Combinations Supported by the Different RAS Versions

Table E.4 is a historical view of the different RAS versions and the modem standard combinations they supported when they were released. Newer RAS versions support all down-level modem compression and error control combinations. The table shows only the most important standard combinations. If there is more than one column for a RAS version, the rightmost column displays the highest modem standards supported by that RAS version.

The leftmost column of that RAS version shows a combination of standards that may occur with less capable modems. For example, the highest modulation rate RAS 1.1a supported at the time of release is V.32 *bis*; this means it also supports V.32 and V.22 *bis* which were supported by RAS 1.1 and 1.0. Because this table is only a historical view, it does not reflect that an older RAS version can possibly support a newer modulation standard than is shown in the table. For example, the table shows RAS for Windows for Workgroups 3.11 as supporting only V.32 *bis* as the highest modulation scheme. This is because V.fc, V.fast, and V.34 modulation scheme modems did not exist yet and therefore were not available for testing. However, RAS for Windows for Workgroups 3.11 may work properly with a V.34 modem in the right configuration. To make it work properly, you may have to use a computer with one or more of the following components:

- 486 or later processor
- 4 MB of RAM
- An asychronous serial board that has a 16550 UART chip

Table E.4   History of RAS Versions and Supported Modem Standards

RAS versions/ modem standards	RAS 1.0	RAS 1.1a*	RAS 1.1a*	RAS for Windows for Workgroups version 3.11	RAS for Windows NT versions 3.1, 3.5, and 3.51	Remote Network Access for Windows 95 (RNA)
Modem command set	Hayes AT, etc.	Hayes AT, etc.	Hayes AT, etc.	Hayes AT, etc.	Hayes AT, etc.	Hayes AT, etc.
Modulation	V.22 *bis* (2400 bps) and V.32 (9600 bps)	V.32 (9600 bps)	V.32 *bis* (14400 bps)	V.32 *bis*	Windows NT 3.1: V.fc, V.fast (28800 bps); Windows NT 3.5 and 3.51: V.34 (28800 bps)	V.34 (28800 bps)
Error control	Not Supported	MNP4 (may also use V.42)	V.42 with LAPM (may also use MNP4)	V.42 with LAPM (may also use MNP4)	V.42 with LAPM (may also use MNP4)	V.42 with LAPM (may also use MNP4)
Modem compression	Not Supported	MNP5 (may also use V.42 *bis* if V.42 is enabled)	V.42 *bis* (may also use MNP5 if MNP4 is enabled)	Use RAS data compression along with V.42 *bis* ☐ (may also use MNP5 with MNP4 enabled and RAS data compression disabled)	Use RAS data compression along with V.42 *bis* ☐ (may also use MNP5 with MNP4 enabled and RAS data compression disabled)	RAS data compression is automatically used. Enable V.42 *bis* ☐ (may also use MNP5 with MNP4 enabled)

*RAS 1.0 and 1.1 were tested only with US Robotics V.32 *bis* modems at 14400 bps line speed. The modems were configured for V.42, V.42 *bis*, and V.32 *bis*. The OS/2 1.3 LAN Manager RAS 1.0 or 1.1 server had an intelligent DigiBoard installed.

☐ If an uncompressed file is transmitted between two Microsoft RAS computers, RAS software compression increases throughput significantly more than V.42 *bis* compression. Do not enable modem compression (MNP5) along with RAS software compression, because it may decrease throughput.

> **Note** RAS clients running version 1.0 or 1.1 on the MS-DOS platform should be upgraded to at least RAS version 1.1a, which can be obtained from Microsoft at no charge. RAS server version 1.0 and 1.1 on the OS/2 1.3 platforms were never updated. In general, for RAS 1.x versions on MS-DOS or OS/2 1.3, it is recommended that you upgrade to RAS for Windows for Workgroups 3.11, RAS for Windows 95, or Windows NT 4.0 because of improved performance, new features, and the new, easier-to-use interface.

RAS Communication Quick Reference

If you are a network administrator, consultant, or support engineer, you can use the following quick reference tables to gain a high-level perspective of how RAS works over a WAN connection. These quick reference tables are high-level diagrams that show you at what point which RAS client features (of any Microsoft RAS version to date) execute when you make a call to a Windows NT RAS server.

How to Read the Diagrams

Specifically, these diagrams show how a call flows from a RAS client over different media (telephone lines, an ISDN line, or an X.25 network) through third-party security (or other) devices into the RAS server's port (serial or ISDN) and through the RAS server's architectural software layers to the RAS server service and, eventually, the RAS server. For a specific RAS client, you can also see whether it supports modem pools and other third-party pre- or post-connect devices (via pre- and post-connect scripts in the Switch.inf file or RAS Terminal pop-up screens), whether it supports Pad.inf scripts for X.25 communication, and at what point during a call these scripts or Terminal screens execute.

The tables include the full path of all possible, but not necessary, events that can happen during a RAS call. To see the possible flow of events when a RAS client initiates a call to a Windows NT RAS server, first determine what type of communication medium you will be using: telephone lines, an ISDN line, an X.25 dial-up, or an X.25 with an Eicon card. Then, using the table specific to your situation, follow the path from the RAS client to the RAS server.

Information Not Included in the Diagrams

The diagrams do not show specific Windows NT RAS client security features for calling up third-party PPP or SLIP servers. To learn more about available Windows NT security features, see the Help topic "Configuring Security." Note that Windows NT RAS can function as a SLIP client, but not as a SLIP server.

The diagrams also do not show direct serial (null modem) connections. For additional information about null modem connections, see Appendix B, "RAS Cabling," in the *Microsoft Windows NT Networking Supplement*.

ISDN Notes

When you call from a RAS client by using ISDN, the Pre-connect script/Terminal and Post-connect script/Terminal options are not available. This is because there is no ISDN standard defined on how ASCII characters are to be transmitted. For a detailed explanation of ISDN, see the Microsoft Knowledge Base article "Integrated Services Digital Network (ISDN)" (Q99767).

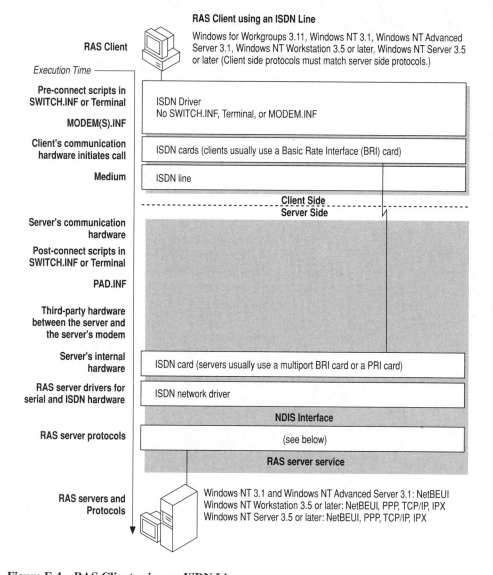

RAS Client using an ISDN Line

Windows for Workgroups 3.11, Windows NT 3.1, Windows NT Advanced Server 3.1, Windows NT Workstation 3.5 or later, Windows NT Server 3.5 or later (Client side protocols must match server side protocols.)

RAS Client

Execution Time

Pre-connect scripts in SWITCH.INF or Terminal

ISDN Driver
No SWITCH.INF, Terminal, or MODEM.INF

MODEM(S).INF

Client's communication hardware initiates call

ISDN cards (clients usually use a Basic Rate Interface (BRI) card)

Medium

ISDN line

Client Side
Server Side

Server's communication hardware

Post-connect scripts in SWITCH.INF or Terminal

PAD.INF

Third-party hardware between the server and the server's modem

Server's internal hardware

ISDN card (servers usually use a multiport BRI card or a PRI card)

RAS server drivers for serial and ISDN hardware

ISDN network driver

NDIS Interface

RAS server protocols

(see below)

RAS server service

RAS servers and Protocols

Windows NT 3.1 and Windows NT Advanced Server 3.1: NetBEUI
Windows NT Workstation 3.5 or later: NetBEUI, PPP, TCP/IP, IPX
Windows NT Server 3.5 or later: NetBEUI, PPP, TCP/IP, IPX

Figure E.4   RAS Client using an ISDN Line

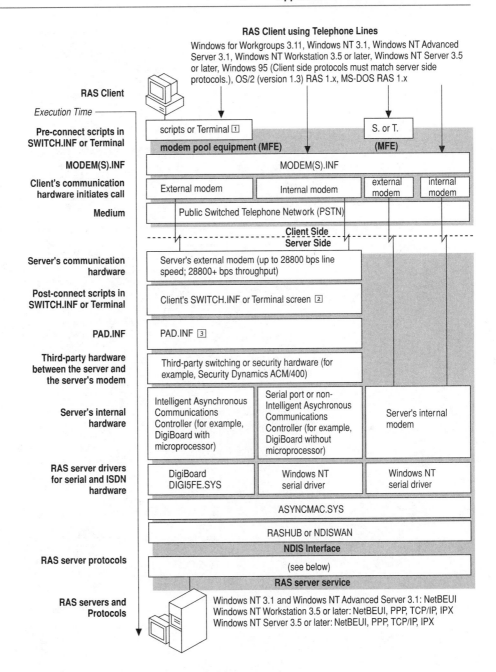

Figure E.5   RAS Client using Telephone Lines

[1] RAS 1.*x*: no scripts or Terminal; Windows 95: no scripts

[2] not in RAS 1.*x*

[3] not in RAS 1.0

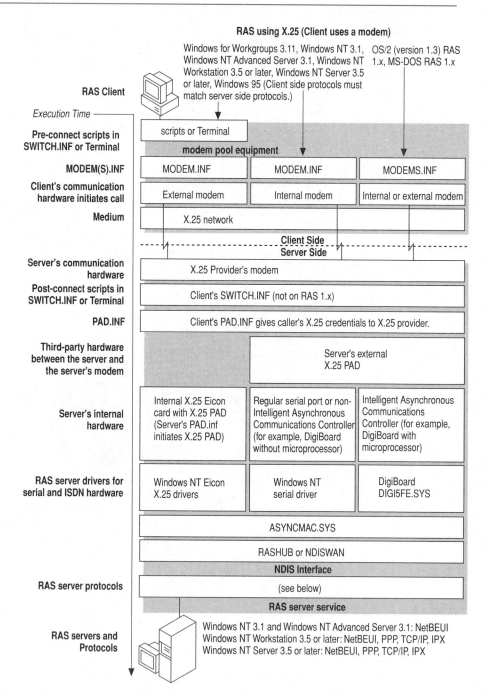

Figure E.6   RAS using X.25 (Client uses a modem)

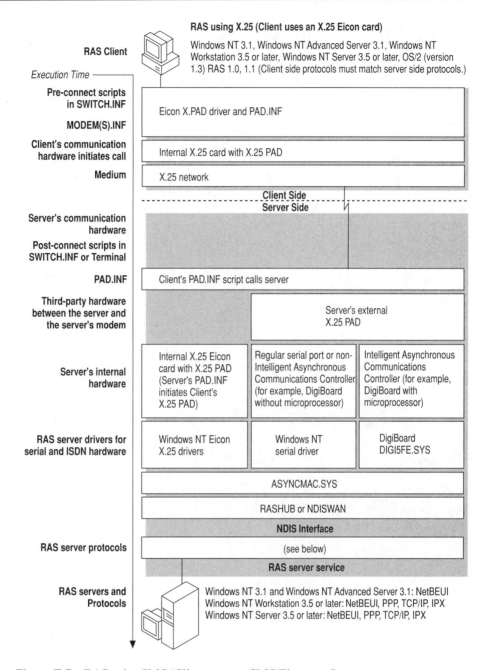

Figure E.7   RAS using X.25 (Client uses an X.25 Eicon card)

Microsoft Remote Access Version Features

The following tables list the most important features of all RAS server and client versions that were released before October 1995. The first table lists the features of RAS server versions; the second table lists the features of RAS client versions.

Table E.5   RAS Server Versions

Operating system	RAS version	Proprietary MS Protocol support	PPP support (protocols tunneled through PPP Protocol)	SLIP support (protocols tunneled through SLIP Protocol)	Medium
OS/2 1.31 (not OS/2 2.x) with LAN Manager 2.x	RAS 1.0	AsyBEUI [1]	No	No	Serial
OS/2 1.31 (not OS/2 2.x) with LAN Manager 2.x	RAS 1.1 (no 1.1a available)	AsyBEUI	No	No	Serial; X.25
Windows for Workgroups 3.11	Windows for Workgroups 3.11 "Point-to-Point Server"; Supports only access to its own resources	NetBEUI, which is backward compatible with AsyBEUI	No, but third-party PPP TCP/IP software is available	No	Serial; ISDN; No internal X.25 board support
Windows NT 3.1 (acting as a RAS server)	RAS for Windows NT 3.1	Uses NBF [2]	No	No	Serial; ISDN; X.25
Windows NT Advanced Server 3.1	RAS for Windows NT 3.1	Uses NBF	No	No	Serial; ISDN; X.25

RAS software compression	Flow control support	Highest tested bps rate for modems (not ISDN lines)	Number of simultaneous RAS ports (incoming calls) supported	Types of modems tested
No	No	9600 bps	16 ports	Analog; Null Modem
No	No	9600 bps (V.32) [3]	16 ports (13 with x.25 card)	Analog; Null Modem
A	Yes	19200 bps (using V.32 *bis*, V.42, and V.42 *bis*)	1 port only (RAS client may access only server's local drives. No network access)	Analog; Null Modem
A	Yes	57600 bps (using V.32 *bis*, V.42, and V.42 *bis*)	1 port only	Analog; Null Modem
A	Yes	57600 bps (using V.32 *bis*, V.42, and V.42 *bis*)	64 ports	Analog; Null Modem

Table E.5 RAS Server Versions *(continued)*

Operating system	RAS version	Proprietary MS Protocol support	PPP Support (protocols tunneled through PPP Protocol)	SLIP Support (protocols tunneled through SLIP Protocol)	Medium
Windows NT 3.5 Server and Windows NT 3.5 Workstation (Both can act as a RAS server)	RAS for Windows NT 3.5	Supports NBF	NBF, IPX, TCP/IP	No SLIP server functionality	Serial; ISDN; X.25
Windows NT 3.51 Server and Windows NT 3.51 Workstation (Both can act as a RAS server)	RAS for Windows NT 3.51	Supports NBF	NBF, IPX, TCP/IP	No SLIP server functionality	Serial; ISDN; X.25
Windows 95	Remote Network Access for Windows 95 (RNA)	Supports NBF	NBF, IPX	No SLIP server functionality	Serial; No internal X.25 board support

RAS software compression	Flow control support	Highest tested bps rate for modems (not ISDN lines)	Number of simultaneous RAS ports (incoming calls) supported	Types of modems tested
B	Yes	57600 bps (using V.34, V.fc/V.fast, V.42, and V.42 *bis*)	Windows NT 3.5 Server: 256 ports. Windows NT 3.5 Workstation: 1 port	Analog; Null Modem
Compatible with all RAS software compression methods	Yes	57600 bps (using V.34, V.fc/V.fast, V.42, and V.42 *bis*)	Windows NT 3.51 Server: 256 ports. Windows NT 3.51 Workstation: 1 port	Analog; Null Modem; certain PCMCIA modems [4]
B	Yes	57600 bps (using V.34, V.fc/V.fast, V.42, and V.42 *bis*)	1 port only (RAS client may access server's drive and network resources)	Analog; Null Modem; PCMCIA modems; certain cellular modems [5]

A: Compatible with Windows NT 3.1, Windows NT Advanced Server 3.1, and Windows for Workgroups 3.11 RAS compression. To achieve RAS software compression compatibility with Windows NT 3.5 Workstation or Server clients, you must install Windows NT 3.5 SP2 on the Windows NT 3.5 Workstation or Server computer that is acting as the RAS client.

B: Compatible with a Windows NT 3.5 Workstation or Server RAS client. To achieve RAS software compression compatibility with Windows NT 3.1, Windows NT Advanced Server 3.1, or Windows for Workgroups 3.11 RAS clients, you must install Windows NT 3.5 SP2 on your Windows NT 3.5 Workstation or Server computer that is acting as a RAS server.

[1] Used in RAS 1.*x*.

[2] NetBEUI Frame Protocol (NBF) which is backward compatible with AsyBEUI and NetBEUI (Windows for Workgroups 3.1)

[3] Modem error control (MNP4, V.42) and modem compression (MNP5, V.42 *bis*) are not supported, with the following exception: 19200 bps was tested with US Robotics V.32 *bis* modems and an intelligent DigiBoard on a server running OS/2 version 1.3 with LAN Manager 2.1 and RAS 1.1 using V.42 error checking and V.42 *bis* modem compression.

[4] Consult the Windows NT 3.51 Hardware Compatibility List (HCL) for a listing of supported PCMCIA modems. If your modem is not listed, you can check the Windows NT 3.51 Modem.inf file contents to see whether your PCMCIA modem was included after the HCL was printed.

[5] Consult the updated Windows 95 Hardware Compatibility List (HCL) on the Microsoft Internet Web server.

Table E.6   RAS Client Versions

Operating system	RAS version	Proprietary MS Protocol support	PPP Support (protocols tunneled through PPP Protocol)	SLIP Support (protocols tunneled through SLIP Protocol)	Medium
MS-DOS 5.0 and later	RAS 1.0	AsyBEUI [1]	No	No	Serial
MS-DOS 5.0 and later	RAS 1.1	AsyBEUI	No	No	Serial; X.25
MS-DOS 5.0 and later	RAS 1.1a	AsyBEUI	No	No	Serial; X.25
OS/2 1.31 (not OS/2 2.x) with LAN Manager 2.x	RAS 1.0	AsyBEUI	No	No	Serial
Windows for Workgroups 3.11	RAS for Windows for Workgroups 3.11	NetBEUI; compatible with AsyBEUI	No, but third-party PPP TCP/IP software is available	No	Serial; ISDN; X.25 dial-up only [3]
Windows NT 3.1	RAS for Windows NT 3.1	Uses NBF [2]	No	No	Serial; X.25; ISDN
Windows NT Advanced Server 3.1 (acting as a RAS client)	RAS for Windows NT Advanced Server 3.1	Uses NBF	No	No	Serial; X.25; ISDN
OS/2 1.31 (not OS/2 2.x) with LAN Manager 2.x	RAS 1.1	AsyBEUI	No	No	Serial; X.25

RAS software compression	Flow control support	Support for scripts to interact with third party devices (X.25 dial-up and security hosts)	Interactive Terminal screen [5]	Highest tested bps rate for modems (not for ISDN)	Types of modems tested
No	No	No	No	9600 bps	Analog; Null Modem
No	No	X.25 dial-up: Use PAD.INF	No	9600 bps (V.32) [4]	Analog; Null Modem
No; use modem compression	Yes	X.25 dial-up: Use PAD.INF	No	19200 bps (tested with V.32 *bis*, V.42, and V.42 *bis* enabled	Analog; Null Modem
No	No	No	No	9600 bps	Analog; Null Modem
No	No	X.25 dial-up: Use PAD.INF	No	9600 bps [4]	Analog; Null Modem
A	Yes	X.25 dial-up: Use PAD.INF; Third-party intermediary security devices: Use SWITCH.INF file	Yes	19200 bps	Analog; Null Modem
A	Yes	X.25 dial-up: Use PAD.INF; Third-party intermediary security devices: Use SWITCH.INF file	Yes	57600 bps (using V.32 *bis*, V.42, and V.42 *bis*)	Analog; Null Modem
A	Yes	X.25 dial-up: Use PAD.INF; Third-party intermediary security devices: Use SWITCH.INF file	Yes	57600 bps (using V.32 *bis*, V.42, and V.42 *bis*)	Analog; Null Modem

Table E.6   RAS Client Versions (*continued*)

Operating system	RAS version	Proprietary MS Protocol support	PPP Support (protocols tunneled through PPP Protocol)	SLIP Support (protocols tunneled through SLIP Protocol)	Medium
Windows NT 3.5 Server and Windows NT 3.5 Workstation (Both can act as a RAS client)	RAS for Windows NT 3.5	Supports NBF	NBF, IPX, TCP/IP	TCP/IP	Serial; X.25; ISDN
Windows NT 3.51 Server and Windows NT 3.51 Workstation (Both can act as a RAS client)	RAS for Windows NT 3.51	Supports NBF	NBF, IPX, TCP/IP	TCP/IP	Serial; X.25; ISDN
Windows 95	Remote Network Access for Windows 95 (RNA)	Supports NBF	NBF, IPX TCP/IP	TCP/IP	Serial; X.25 dial-up only [3]

[1] Used in RAS 1.*x*.

[2] NetBEUI Frame Protocol (NBF) which is compatible with AsyBEUI and NetBEUI (Windows for Workgroups 3.11)

[3] Internal X.25 card not supported on Windows for Workgroups 3.11

[4] Modem error control (MNP4, V.42) and modem compression (MNP5, V.42 *bis*) are not supported, with the following exception: 19200 bps was tested with US Robotics V.32 *bis* modems and an intelligent DigiBoard on a server running OS/2 version 1.3 with LAN Manager 2.1 and RAS 1.1 using V.42 error checking and V.42 *bis* modem compression.

[5] Interactive Terminal screen can be invoked to log on to third-party PPP hosts or intermediary security devices.

[6] Consult the Windows NT 3.51 Hardware Compatibility List (HCL) for a listing of supported PCMCIA modems. If your modem is not listed, you can check the Windows NT 3.51 Modem.inf file contents to see whether your PCMCIA modem was included after the HCL was printed.

RAS software compression	Flow control support	Support for scripts to interact with third party devices (X.25 dial-up and security hosts)	Interactive Terminal screen [5]	Highest tested bps rate for modems (not for ISDN)	Types of modems tested
B	Yes	X.25 dial-up: Use PAD.INF; Third-party intermediary security devices: Use SWITCH.INF file	Yes	57600 bps (using V.34, V.fc/V.42, and V.42 *bis)*	Analog; Null Modem
Compatible with all RAS software compression methods	Yes	X.25 dial-up: Use PAD.INF; Third-party intermediary security devices: Use SWITCH.INF file	Yes	57600 bps (using V.34, V.fc/V.42, and V.42 *bis*	Analog; Null Modem; certain PCMCIA modems [6]
B	Yes	Use SCRIPTER.EXE ▣ for scripting connections with:- X.25 dial-up providers; third-party intermediary security devices; SLIP dial-up servers; PPP dial-up servers	Yes	57600 bps	Analog; Null Modem; PCMCIA modems; certain cellular modems ▪

A: Compatible with Windows NT, Windows NT Advanced Server 3.1, and Windows for Workgroups 3.11 RAS compression. To achieve RAS software compression compatibility with Windows NT 3.5 Workstation and Server RAS servers, you must install the Windows NT 3.5 SP2 on the Windows NT 3.5 Workstation or Server that is acting as the RAS server.

B: Compatible when calling a Windows NT 3.5 Workstation or Server that is acting as a RAS server. To achieve RAS software compression compatibility with Windows NT 3.1, Windows NT Advanced Server 3.1, or Windows for Workgroups 3.11 RAS servers, you need to install Windows NT 3.5 SP2 on your Windows NT 3.5 Server or Workstation that is acting as a RAS client.

▣ Windows 95 ships with SCRIPTER.EXE in the \ADMIN\APPTOOLS\DSCRIPT directory. The Windows 95 PLUS! software package of tools contains an upgraded version of SCRIPTER.EXE. **Note** SCRIPTER.EXE does not support pre-connect scripts to communicate with modem pool equipment. Instead, check the **Bring Up Terminal Window Before Dialing** option in the **Option** dialog box of the **Properties** of your connection to communicate interactively with your modem pool or pre-connect device.

▪ Consult the updated Windows 95 Hardware Compatibility List (HCL) on the Microsoft Internet Web server*

APPENDIX F

Routers and Switches

As networks increase in size, powerful computers and sophisticated applications drive the need for greater network bandwidth, performance, and scalability. Users are concerned with sending and receiving data quickly and reliably.

This appendix first provides an overview of the routing and switching technologies. It then describes the routing and switching equipment selected and installed at Terra Flora, the fictitious case study described in Chapters 4 and 5 of this book, and gives the technical and business reasons for those choices.

Note Terra Flora is a totally fictitious corporation. The names of companies, products, people, characters, and data mentioned herein are fictitious and are in no way intended to represent any real individual, company, product, or event, unless otherwise noted.

Routing

The routing process allows messages (or *data packets)* to be delivered from a node on one network to a node on another network using the most appropriate, efficient path (or *route).* Routing environments employ routers, which function at the network layer of the OSI model (described in Chapter 1 of this book).

Routers direct data packets to the proper network and deliver them to the appropriate node on that network. The router uses *routing protocols*, a set of rules governing the exchange of information between nodes, to direct packets to their destination. The sending node (referred to as *source)* and receiving node (referred to as *destination)* must use either the same protocols or a protocol converter in order to communicate. Routers also allow data packets to be transmitted over dissimilar networks, such as Ethernet, Token Ring, and FDDI, without having to be translated.

Determining the most appropriate, efficient path is protocol-specific. Some protocols determine the path by *hop count*, which is the number of routers between the source and the destination; other protocols determine the path by analyzing the available bandwidth and calculating which route provides the best quality of service.

In a routing environment, each physical destination must be uniquely identified. Most routing protocols are based on an addressing scheme that uses a network, and a node number that identifies each node.

When a computer on an internetwork wants to communicate with a node on another network, the network layer software creates a packet. The packet contains the data to be sent, the address of the sender (source address), and the address of the destination (destination address).

The following diagram illustrates how packets break down information, such as the sender, sender address, destination address, and data.

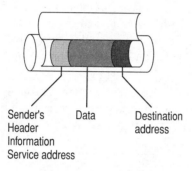

Sender's   Data   Destination
Header   address
Information
Service address

Figure F.1   Data Packet Structure

The packet is put inside the appropriate frame for transmission across the network.

The network layer software also determines whether the destination resides on the local network or another network. If the destination address is on another network, the data packet is sent to the router that is attached to the local network. When the router receives the data packet, it removes the *frame* encapsulating the data packet and examines the destination address of the network-layer packets to find on which network the node resides.

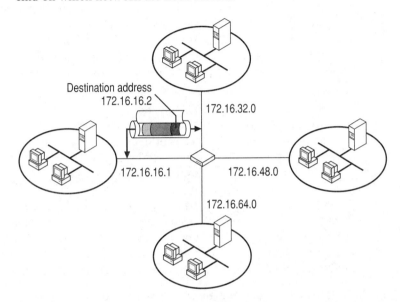

Figure F.2   Packet Routing Across Multiple Networks

The router then compares the network information to its routing table, which contains directions on how to get to various places on the internetwork. There can be a number of networks and routers between a source and destination. When the destination's network is found in the table, the router puts the network-layer packet into the appropriate frame for the next network over which the packet will be transmitted, and sends it to the next network in the direction of the destination node. Each router between the source and destination network functions in this manner.

When the router attached to the network containing the destination node receives the packet, it removes the frame encapsulating the network-layer packet and compares the destination network address to its routing table.

When the router determines that it is directly attached to the destination network, it examines the packet for the destination node number, which is compared to the router's Address Mapping Table. This table correlates the packet's network-layer address to the device's Media Access Control (MAC) address. When a match is found, the router puts the data from the packet into the appropriate frame and sends it to the destination node.

Switching

Switching uses temporary connections for routing information. This communications method is widely implemented in local area networks and provides better performance on the LAN than routers in two ways:

- First, switches provide a means of directing a frame to the appropriate output port, typically using the data-link layer addressing. The hardware itself forwards the frame to the output port. Routers use software programs on the network to route frames. Because the data-link layer does not use software to forward frames to the proper route, performance is improved.

- Second, switches improve performance by enabling communication between logical groupings of users. Only one communication at a time can take place in a routing environment. The computers must wait until the line is free to communicate. Switches act as bridges, allowing the messages to be routed from one port on the switch to another. There is no requirement to wait until the communication finishes before communicating.

Switching technology uses *switches*, which are multiport devices that create temporary paths to send frames directly to a device based on its MAC address. There are three basic switching technologies: Configuration, Frame, and Cell. Another technology, Frame-to-Cell translation, enables the migration to cell-based backbones without changes to the host network's interface.

Configuration switching, or *port switching,* allows individual ports to be assigned to individual segments within a multi-segmented network hub. This provides the equivalent of an intelligent patch panel for network centers and wiring closets. Port assignments are performed when devices are initially attached to networks. This type of switching offers the ability to segment networks quickly for better performance. Configuration switching operates at the physical level and is transparent to end systems and upper-layer protocols.

Frame switching is a connectionless technology that provides cost-effective bandwidth to the workgroup and to multiplexed, low-speed traffic from the wiring closet onto high-speed down links. Operating at the data-link layer, frame switches "learn" the destination MAC addresses of each attached computer. Through the MAC address of each received frame, the switch forwards the packet to the output port attached to the computer with the same MAC address. The output port can be directly attached to the computer, to a shared access segment with multiple users, or to another frame switch, which, in turn, is connected to the destination. Frame switching supports both Ethernet Frame switching and Token Ring switching. *Ethernet Frame switching* supports shared or dedicated 10-Mbps or 100-Mbps connections. A *Token Ring switch*, also referred to as a *segment switch*, is a high-capacity, high port-density frame-relaying engine that forwards data simultaneously, among all ports, at wire speed (4/16-Mbps).

Cell switching, also called *asynchronous transfer mode* (ATM), is a high-speed technology that switches fixed-length, 53-byte cells at speeds of 155-Mbps and higher. Designed to carry voice, video, and data traffic, cell switching supports asynchronous traffic. Cell switching also supports different classes of traffic: loss-sensitive, delay-sensitive, delay-variance sensitive, and various combinations of these.

Backbone Link Node

Backbone Link Node (BLN) is the Bay Networks multiprotocol router/bridge. The symmetric multiprocessor architecture of BLN satisfies the high-performance and availability requirements of backbone internetworks using, for example, 100BASE-T, FDDI, HSSI, ATM, and SNA. Its symmetric multiprocessor architecture uses multiple MC68060- and MC68040-based Fast Routing Engines (FRE), multiple dual PowerPC microprocessor-based ATM Routing Engine (ARE) processor modules, and Bay Networks 1-Gbps Parallel Packet Express (PPX). The BLN provides 300,000 pps forwarding performance when equipped with the MC68060-based FRE. The dual PowerPC-based ARE supports 155 Mbps full-duplex virtual network routing to provide connectivity between multiple virtual LANs over a single ATM interface.

The BLN supports 4 FRE/ARE processor modules, 16 LAN interfaces, and 32 serial interfaces. A BLN configured with symmetric multiprocessors, redundant LAN interfaces, processor interconnects, power supplies, and software image storage is completely fault resilient. A redundant router capability also provides another level of network fault tolerance.

28000 Series Ethernet/Fast Ethernet Switches

For bandwidth-intensive applications, the Bay Networks 28000 series of switches enhance existing Ethernet LANs and provide 2 gigabits per second (Gbps) of internal switching and scalable 10/100 megabits-per-second (Mbps) dedicated bandwidth to support high-demand networks. These features enable the switch to provide scalable, dedicated bandwidth to attached end users, shared-media segments, servers, and high-end workstations.

All 28000 series switches include two high-speed, front-panel expansion ports for supporting direct 200 Mbps, full-duplex connection to other switches. Up to seven 28000 switches can be linked in a single stack, providing a scalable solution. The 28000 switches support redundant links between devices, in which one link automatically assumes standby status to provide a backup data path in the event of a primary-link failure.

Optivity: Comprehensive SNMP-based Network Management

All Bay Networks routers, intelligent hubs, and high-speed switches are fully manageable through the industry's best and most sophisticated suite of integrated network management, Bay Networks Optivity Enterprise family of network management applications which includes:

- Optivity LAN provides comprehensive switching hubs and remote troubleshooting of client/server problems.
- Optivity ATM delivers management services for Bay Networks-based ATM networks.
- Optivity Design & Analysis focuses on enterprise network planning, analysis, and reporting.
- Optivity Internetwork performs real-time router performance monitoring and status reporting.

Routing and Switching on Terra Flora Networks

In Chapter 4 of this book, we proposed a plan for uniting the three independent and diverse networks of the fictitious company, Terra Flora. One of the company's main goals was to centralize all administration.

Note Terra Flora is a totally fictitious corporation. The names of companies, products, people, characters, and data mentioned herein are fictitious and are in no way intended to represent any real individual, company, product, or event, unless otherwise noted.

Terra Flora elected to use Bay Networks products, which combine a distributed management support foundation with SNMP-based tools for comprehensive router configuration, monitoring, and control. They will implement the Bay Networks Switched Internetworking Service (BaySIS) architecture. This extensible switched internetworking architecture is comprised of four basic services—transport, policy, operation, and design—which are implemented across the enterprise network. In this way, Terra Flora will integrate multiprotocol routing, switching, and shared-media and wide-area solutions into a cohesive, switched topology, all managed by a single network management system.

The Bay Networks Access Stack Note (ASN) router has a stackable architecture. Up to four ASN units are supported in one stack. An ASN stack supports up to 40 network interfaces and 200,000 pps forwarding performance, providing a superior path for growth. The MC68040 processor in the ASN's integrated design maintains high forwarding and filtering rates, regardless of the number of protocols and network interfaces used, even when processing Simple Network Management Protocol (SNMP) management inquiries.

The ASN meets the connectivity needs of the Terra Flora remote branch offices by offering modularity and flexibility for building configurations. The ASN provides network connectivity through a selection of net modules and adapter modules. An ASN can support up to four net modules, such as 100BASE-T, 10BASE-T Ethernet, 4/16 Mbps Token Ring, FDDI, Synchronous, and ISDN BRI, to meet a wide variety of connectivity requirements. Wide-area services, such as PPP, X.25, Frame Relay, SMDS, HDLC encapsulation, and ATM DXI, are supported by the ASN synchronous interface.

The method used to accomplish this consolidation of resources and information is described next.

The following diagram of the network shows the NENTS40B0FO1, NENTS40DIV01, NENTS40ENT01, EUNTS4ENT01, and EUNTS40DIV01 servers running multi-provider router (MPR) software. MPR passes requests to the various network providers configured in the system. These servers are connected to a Bay Networks Backbone Link Node (BLN) router through T1 links.

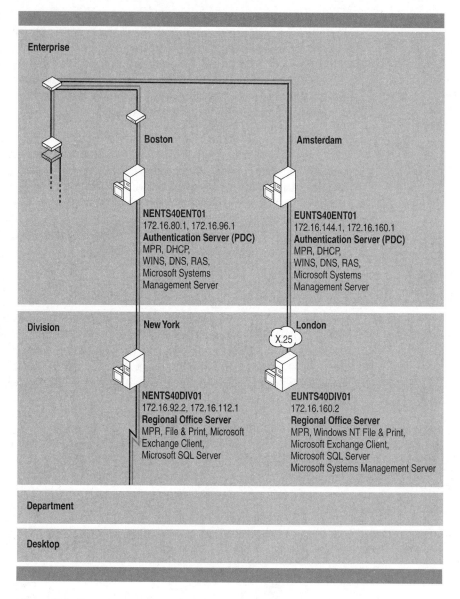

Figure F.3   Remote Enterprise Multi-provider Routing

The BLN creates a multi-protocol, collapsed, WAN backbone that provides a centralized wide-area infrastructure. The BLN is also connected to another BLN over a T3 link which is attached to two Bay Networks 28000 Series Fast Ethernet switches to form a multiprotocol LAN backbone. These two switches appear logically on the Terra Flora network diagram as three switches. One 28000 switch connects to the Terra Flora Enterprise level; the second 28000 switch connects to the Terra Flora Division, Department, and Desktop levels.

The ASN is connected to the first BLN by means of a dedicated leased line to provide access to branch servers and corporate systems. The Bay Networks router is configured to support a dial-on-demand feature, which is used when additional capacity is required between the corporate and remote regional offices. For example, during monthly end processing, transmission of data frequently exceeds the 128K capacity of the leased line. The Bay Network's dial-on-demand feature then establishes a second connection to provide additional bandwidth.

Recovery from leased line failure is provided through the ASN dial backup feature, which provides a two-point, fault-tolerance measure. Two lines are configured at Terra Flora. The second line is activated or used only when the first line goes down. This means that although two lines are available, usage charges apply only to the line that is being used. This reduces operational costs by delivering the connection only when needed and ensuring continued operation in the event of a network failure.

The entire network infrastructure is managed by the Bay Networks Optivity network management tools. These tools enable the network manager to configure the routers and switches, monitor and evaluate the network, and react to problems on the network from a central console.

The collapsed WAN backbone interconnects the Terra Flora LANs and computing devices across long distances by way of the T1 and T3 links. The LAN backbone ensures that traffic is directed to the destination over the best possible route and, when coupled with the switches' dedicated high-speed connections, ensures high data throughput. Because routing is employed on both the LAN and WAN backbones, all resources, such as nodes, servers, and computers, can interoperate, regardless of the type of network they are on and the distance between them.

Because of this connectivity, users at the New York retail store now have access to the applications and records contained in servers NENTS40B0FO1, NENTS40DIV01, NENTS40ENT01, EUNTS4ENT01, and EUNTS40DIV01, as well as to all information and applications at the Enterprise, Division, Department, and Desktop levels.

Security measures can be put in place in the router to block access to particular portions of the network. For example, filters can be configured in any of the BLNs to drop data destined for a network based on source address or destination address. The data packet information is examined and, if it is being sent to a specific server, the data will be discarded, thus limiting access to the network.

In the network diagram, the routers allow access from regional remote retail stores to corporate resources. Data is transmitted from these remote locations over WAN links, ensuring that individuals in the corporate and regional offices have needed information to satisfy current and future customer needs. This information is also passed to the appropriate corporate offices to maintain records, ensuring that all stores have adequate merchandise to sell to the consumer. Sales information from the retail stores can be sent in a timely fashion to the Enterprise and Division computers for processing inventory management, billing purposes, and so forth.

Stocking information, changes in products, sales incentive programs, advertising literature, and other information can be easily transmitted from corporate headquarters to the retail stores and all other remote Terra Flora sites over the internetwork.

The routers determine the best possible paths for sending data and avoiding breakdowns in communications. Through the router's lookup table, changes in the network are reported to the routers and the tables are updated with information about the new configuration. This enables IP traffic to be rerouted if, for example, a network change prevents the sent message from reaching its destination. This ensures continued communications.

Corporate data, such as employee lists, resource materials, and accounting facilities, are also accessible from anywhere no the internetwork through routing. Authorized users can access this information from their offices and interoperate with others around the corporation, using a variety of applications.

The Bay Networks Optivity console functions as a centralized point of administration for managing all network resources. Management servers offer a number of services including Logon Authentication, replicated User Account databases, centralized Network services, Name Resolution services, and Backup Services at the Enterprise level. These provide a consistent, master copy of common information and resources. A centralized architecture of file and print application servers is in place to provide heterogeneous file and print interfaces, integration services, backup services, and intranet services. All of these servers are accessible throughout the internetwork through the routers.

The configuration of the Bay Networks equipment is as follows:

BLN Base Unit with:

- Quad-port Ethernet Intelligent Link Module with 32 MB memory
- Single-port High-Speed Serial Interface (HSSI) Intelligent Link Module
- Quad-port Synchronous Intelligent Link Module with 32 MB memory
- Dual-port Multichannel T1 Intelligent Link Module
- Backbone Node Corporate Software Suite Version 10.0

BLN Base Unit with:

- Quad-port Ethernet Intelligent Link Module with 16 MB memory
- Single-port High-Speed Serial Interface (HSSI) Intelligent Link Module
- Quad-port Synchronous Intelligent Link Module with 16 MB memory
- Single-port Multichannel T1 Intelligent Link Module with 8 MB memory
- Backbone Node Corporate Software Suite Version 10.0

28000 Series Switch

- Model 28115 Fast Ethernet Switch
- 16-port 10/100 Ethernet Switch

ASN Base Unit

- Dual Ethernet Net Module
- Dual Synchronous Net Module
- Multimode FDDI Net Module
- 32 MB DRAM
- ASN Corporate Software Suite Version 10.0

Network Management Software

- Optivity for OpenView (MS-DOS-compatible version)

APPENDIX G

NetBIOS Names

Microsoft networking services running on a Windows NT-based computer are identified by using NetBIOS names. NetBIOS names can be used to identify a unique computer or a special group of computers. NetBIOS names are 16 characters in length and the 16th character is a special character used by most Microsoft networking services. Various networking service and group names are registered with a WINS server by direct name registration from WINS-enabled computers or by broadcast on the local subnet by non-WINS enabled computers.

The **nbtstat** command is a utility that you can use to obtain information about NetBIOS names. In the following example, the **nbtstat -n** command produced this list of registered NetBIOS names for user "Davemac" logged on to a computer configured as a primary domain controller and running under Windows NT Server with Internet Information Server.

Name	16TH	Type	Description
DAVEMAC1	<00>	UNIQUE	workstation service name
DAVEMAC1	<20>	UNIQUE	server service name
DAVEMACD	<00>	GROUP	domain name
DAVEMACD	<1C>	GROUP	domain controller name
DAVEMACD	<1B>	UNIQUE	master browser name
DAVEMAC1	<03>	UNIQUE	messenger name
INet~Services	<1C>	GROUP	Internet Information Server group name
IS~DAVEMAC1....<00>		UNIQUE	Internet Information Server unique name
DAVEMAC1+++++++<BF>		UNIQUE	network monitor name

NetBIOS Unique Names

The following table lists the default 16th byte value appended to unique NetBIOS computer names by various Microsoft networking services.

Table G.1   16th Byte Character for Unique Names

16th Byte	Identifies
<00>	Workstation service name. In general, this is the name that is referred to as the *NetBIOS computer name*.
<03>	Messenger service name used when receiving and sending messages. This is the name that is registered with the WINS server as the messenger service on the WINS client and is usually appended to the computer name and to the name of the user currently logged on to the computer.
<1B>	Domain master browser name. This name identifies the primary domain controller and indicates which clients and other browsers to use to contact the domain master browser.
<06>	RAS server service
<1F>	NetDDE service
<20>	Server service name used to provide sharepoints for file sharing.
<21>	RAS client
<BE>	Network Monitor agent
<BF>	Network Monitor utility

NetBIOS Group Names

The following table lists the default 16th byte character appended to commonly used NetBIOS group names.

Table G.2   Default 16th Byte Character for NetBIOS Group Names

16th Byte	Identifies
<1C>	A domain group name, which contains a list of the specific addresses of computers that have registered the domain name. The domain controller registers this name.
	WINS treats this as a domain group, where each member of the group must renew its name individually or be released. The domain group is limited to 25 names. When a static 1C name is replicated that clashes with a dynamic 1C name on another WINS server, a union of the members is added, and the record is marked as static. If the record is static, members of the group do not have to renew their IP addresses.
<1D>	The master browser name that is used by clients to access the master browser. There is one master browser on a subnet. WINS servers return a positive response to domain name registrations but do not store the domain name in their databases. If a computer sends a domain name query to the WINS server, the WINS server returns a negative response. If the computer that sent the domain name query is configured as h-node or m-node, it will then broadcast the name query to resolve the name.
<1E>	A Normal group name. Browsers can broadcast to this name and listen on it to elect a master browser. These broadcasts are for the local subnet and should not cross routers.
<20>	A special group name called the Internet group that is registered with WINS servers to identify groups of computers for administrative purposes. For example, "printersg" could be a registered group name used to identify an administrative group of print servers.
MSBRO WSE,	Instead of a single appended 16th character, "_MSBROWSE_," is appended to a domain name and broadcast on the local subnet to announce the domain to other master browsers.

Index

A

H

I

M

Make your presence **felt**
on the **Internet** or within
your own
intranet.

This book is not about developing Web site content (although it touches on it). BUILD YOUR OWN WEB SITE shows you how to publish your content on the Internet or your corporate intranet using Microsoft® Windows NT® Server and Microsoft Internet Information Server—even if you have little or no programming or networking experience. In this helpful guide, you will find everything you need to know about:

- How the Internet or an intranet works
- Why Windows NT Server is the platform to choose
- How to calculate choices of hardware, connections, security, bandwidth, and routing
- How to set up your system, maintain security, create content, and observe Internet etiquette
- How to configure your system, deal with maintenance issues, and plan for the future
- How to become an Internet service provider

BUILD YOUR OWN WEB SITE also familiarizes you with hot new technologies such as Java and ActiveX™.

If you're ready to establish your organization on the Internet or to set up your own intranet, BUILD YOUR OWN WEB SITE is the smart place to start.

U.S.A.	**$29.95**
U.K.	£27.99 [V.A.T. included]
Canada	$39.95

ISBN 1-57231-304-8

Get self-paced hands-on, training
for supporting local and wide area networks.

This kit is designed to provide you with a general understanding of the technical concepts and components of local (LAN) and wide area (WAN) network environments, and to prepare you to successfully complete the Networking Essentials Microsoft Certified Professionals Exam. Functioning as both a course and a reference, it provides explanations, details, and specifications that will answer your questions after the lessons are over. To make the material easy to find, general networking topics have been broken out into their own units. The companion compact disc contains networking simulation exercises and demonstrations that reinforce the information in the text.

U.S.A.	**$99.95**
Canada	$135.95

[*Recommended*]
ISBN 1-55615-806-8

Microsoft Press

Learn to use
Microsoft® Windows NT® Workstation
version 4.0
in fast, easy steps!

If you're a new user who needs to get up to speed quickly on Windows NT Workstation, this book-and-disk tutorial will teach you the fundamental concepts—from starting the operating system through securing your system and sharing information within a workgroup. The proven Step by Step self-paced training system, with integrated practice files on disk, begins with the features that are most important to you and presents them in a way that makes remembering them easy. In addition to mastering the basics of Windows NT Workstation 4.0, you'll quickly learn how to use Mail, Schedule+, and other Microsoft Windows NT–based applications.

U.S.A.	**$29.95**
U.K.	£27.99 [V.A.T. included]
Canada	$39.95
ISBN 1-57231-225-4	

Microsoft® Press